Artificial Intelligence Applications in Distance Education

Utku Kose
Usak University, Turkey

Durmus Koc
Usak University, Turkey

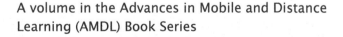

A volume in the Advances in Mobile and Distance
Learning (AMDL) Book Series

Information Science
REFERENCE
An Imprint of IGI Global

Managing Director:	Lindsay Johnston
Production Editor:	Jennifer Yoder
Development Editor:	Austin DeMarco
Acquisitions Editor:	Kayla Wolfe
Typesetter:	Thomas Creedon
Cover Design:	Jason Mull

Published in the United States of America by
Information Science Reference (an imprint of IGI Global)
701 E. Chocolate Avenue
Hershey PA, USA 17033
Tel: 717-533-8845
Fax: 717-533-8661
E-mail: cust@igi-global.com
Web site: http://www.igi-global.com

Library of Congress Cataloging-in-Publication Data

Artificial intelligence applications in distance education / Utku Kose and Durmus Koc, editors.
  pages cm
  ISBN 978-1-4666-6276-6 (hardcover) -- ISBN 978-1-4666-6277-3 (ebook) -- ISBN 978-1-4666-6279-7 (print & perpetual access) 1. Distance education--Computer-assisted instruction. I. Kose, Utku, 1985- II. Koc, Durmus, 1985-
  LC5803.C65.A78 2014
  371.35'8--dc23
                                        2014017275

This book is published in the IGI Global book series Advances in Mobile and Distance Learning (AMDL) (ISSN: 2327-1892; eISSN: 2327-1906)

British Cataloguing in Publication Data
A Cataloguing in Publication record for this book is available from the British Library.

For electronic access to this publication, please contact: eresources@igi-global.com.

Advances in Mobile and Distance Learning (AMDL) Book Series

Patricia Ordóñez de Pablos
Universidad de Oviedo, Spain

ISSN: 2327-1892
EISSN: 2327-1906

Mission

Private and public institutions have made great strides in the fields of mobile and distance learning in recent years, providing greater learning opportunities outside of a traditional classroom setting. While the online learning revolution has allowed for greater learning opportunities, it has also presented numerous challenges for students and educators alike. As research advances, online educational settings can continue to develop and advance the technologies available for learners of all ages.

The **Advances in Mobile and Distance Learning** (AMDL) Book Series publishes research encompassing a variety of topics related to all facets of mobile and distance learning. This series aims to be an essential resource for the timeliest research to help advance the development of new educational technologies and pedagogy for use in online classrooms.

Coverage

- Administration and Organization
- Economics of Distance and M-Learning
- Virtual Universities
- Online Class Management
- Student-Teacher Interaction
- Student-Student Interaction
- Managing Sustainable Learning
- Mobile Learning
- Accreditation
- Role of Faculty

IGI Global is currently accepting manuscripts for publication within this series. To submit a proposal for a volume in this series, please contact our Acquisition Editors at Acquisitions@igi-global.com or visit: http://www.igi-global.com/publish/.

Titles in this Series

For a list of additional titles in this series, please visit: www.igi-global.com

Handbook of Research on Emerging Priorities and Trends in Distance Education Communication, Pedagogy, and Technology
T. Volkan Yuzer (Anadolu University, Turkey) and Gulsun Eby (Anadolu University, Turkey)
Information Science Reference • copyright 2014 • 480pp • H/C (ISBN: 9781466651623) • US $315.00 (our price)

Practical Applications and Experiences in K-20 Blended Learning Environments
Lydia Kyei-Blankson (Illinois State University, USA) and Esther Ntuli (Idaho State University, USA)
Information Science Reference • copyright 2014 • 519pp • H/C (ISBN: 9781466649125) • US $175.00 (our price)

Cases on Professional Distance Education Degree Programs and Practices Successes, Challenges, and Issues
Kirk P.H. Sullivan (Umeå University, Sweden) Peter E. Czigler (Örebro University, Sweden) and Jenny M. Sullivan Hellgren (Umeå University, Sweden)
Information Science Reference • copyright 2014 • 315pp • H/C (ISBN: 9781466644861) • US $175.00 (our price)

Mobile Pedagogy and Perspectives on Teaching and Learning
Douglas McConatha (West Chester University, USA) Christian Penny (West Chester University of Pennsylvania, USA) Jordan Schugar (West Chester University, USA) and David Bolton (West Chester University, USA)
Information Science Reference • copyright 2014 • 335pp • H/C (ISBN: 9781466643338) • US $175.00 (our price)

DISSEMINATOR OF KNOWLEDGE

www.igi-global.com

701 E. Chocolate Ave., Hershey, PA 17033
Order online at www.igi-global.com or call 717-533-8845 x100
To place a standing order for titles released in this series, contact: cust@igi-global.com
Mon-Fri 8:00 am - 5:00 pm (est) or fax 24 hours a day 717-533-8661

Table of Contents

Detailed Table of Contents

Chapter 1
    Utku Kose, Usak University, Turkey

In today's world, intelligent systems play an important role in improving humankind's life standards and providing effective solutions for real-world-based problems. In this sense, such intelligent systems are the research outputs of the Artificial Intelligence field in Computer Science. Today, in many fields intelligent systems are widely used to obtain effective and accurate results for the problems encountered. At this point, education is one of the most remarkable fields in which lots of Artificial Intelligence-oriented research works are performed. When we consider the education field in terms of the latest technological developments, we can also see that the e-learning technique and more generally distance education approach are highly associated with the applications of Artificial Intelligence. Therefore, in this chapter the author explores the trends within the interaction between Artificial Intelligence and Distance Education. The chapter is a brief report on current trends of applications of "intelligent distance education" solutions. It also provides a short focus on the future possibilities of the relation of Artificial Intelligence and Distance Education.

Chapter 2
    Azadeh Heidari, Islamic Azad University, Iran
    Leila Nemati-Anaraki, Islamic Azad University, Iran

In Digital Libraries (DLs) as an innovative community environment, knowledge is nutrition, and the environment for knowledge sharing is the essential condition. As the knowledge is the heart of digital libraries, it is imperative for them to promote the innovation activities embodied by teaching and scientific research through an efficient knowledge-sharing environment. In digital environment, the role of knowledge has become even more significant. Moreover, DLs perform many knowledge-based activities, and by nature, the knowledge-sharing process is embedded in DL systems. These modern knowledge management environments need modern technologies in order to perform properly for end users and online researchers. Therefore, the aim of this chapter is to provide a model for global knowledge networking with utilizing digital libraries and artificial intelligence. The specific objectives are to describe a framework of digital libraries and concepts of Knowledge Management (KM). The chapter finds some significant overlaps between DLs and KM and integrates the knowledge-sharing process with DLs and artificial intelligence. The integration of KM and knowledge sharing can add value to develop a global knowledge networking process model so users around the globe can make use of this knowledge transmission.

Chapter 3

Increasing student numbers lead to new needs in the education sector. New systems are needed due to expert numbers that are insufficient in specialties, such as instructors, directors, and advisors. Type, goal, and specialty of intelligent systems programmed to satisfy this need are being developed with each passing day. The aim of this chapter is to develop an intelligent system that provides support with schedule, academic orientation, choice of profession, and career planning to students. To make a regular schedule for students would generally cause an inappropriate program, which is hardly followed by students in case they were indiscriminately prepared without any information about students' characteristics. Instead of this method, it is the point to be familiar with the academic success, study, resting, and even meal time of the student, and to know which lessons are studied on which days and to make an appropriate schedule for studying. According to the teachers, it is time-consuming and difficult to perform this method for all students. Within this scope, an intelligent system preparing a study schedule is developed considering the students' characteristics and study habits.

Chapter 4

Higher education in accounting has witnessed, in time, a massive development, a fact that has required the identification of the most efficient training methods based on competencies so as to meet the new professional challenges. Computer-based training represents a didactic method that improves accounting education. This chapter presents some elements regarding e-learning in accounting and how the educational software can include artificially intelligent elements that may humanize the dialogue of the teacher-computer, like pedagogical agents. The authors present the main ideas of how they designed and developed a multi-agent system that has been incorporated into an educational soft that was tested and validated within an experiment with the students from the specialization of Accounting and Management Information Systems of the Vasile Alecsandri University of Bacău, Romania.

Chapter 5

One of the most important functions of distance learning systems is determining the student knowledge level and performance clearly. In traditional education systems, students can be assessed in single-stage via tests and homework studies, which consist of multiple-choice questions. However, this method cannot provide accurate results since it is not able to evaluate student knowledge level and question difficulty level. In this chapter, a system and software structure that can determine student knowledge levels, topic difficulty level, and question difficulty levels according to instant student answers for the exam is introduced. In forming student knowledge levels, content monitoring and test data taken from distance education vocational school were used. In this way, more accurate results have been obtained. The fuzzy logic technique has been used to determine (classify) student knowledge levels and topic difficulty levels clearly. In order to determine next questions adaptively, the stored questions have been classified with division clustering methods, and the most suitable questions for the related student knowledge level have been found by using the nearest neighbor algorithm.

Information and communication technologies have led to new developments in education. Time and place independent education has emerged. Furthermore, different characteristics and huge numbers of individuals have made the use of new technological methods inevitable. In this context, distance education has become a popular education method to meet the emerging needs, increasing satisfaction, and learning performance of students. Mobile technology, intelligent systems, and Three Dimensional (3D) animations also provide enhancements in this field. In addition, distance education systems should be selected and developed properly for target students and environments. For this purpose, the assessment of prominent studies provides a road map for new research. In this sense, this chapter evaluates intelligent distance education studies in literature. Furthermore, it proposes a novel Artificial Neural Network (ANN)-based distance education system for Mehmet Akif Ersoy University. This ANN-based system can be implemented on Mehmet Akif Ersoy University infrastructure with agent. The proposed system consists of a learning management system, Web conferencing system, and an ANN agent. The agent's inputs that are already stored in Mehmet Akif Ersoy University's distance education databases can be easily retrieved. This agent provides reusability of course content and Web conferencing records.

In the context of Chaos Theory and its applications, forecasting time series of a chaotic system is an attractive work area for the current literature. Many different approaches and the related scientific studies have been introduced and done by researchers since the inception of this working area. Newer studies are also performed in order to provide more effective and efficient approaches and improve the related literature in this way. On the other hand, it is another important research point to ensure effective educational approaches for teaching Chaos Theory and chaotic systems within the associated courses. In this sense, this chapter introduces a Web-based, intelligent, educational laboratory system for forecasting chaotic time series. Briefly, the system aims to enable students to experience their own learning process over the Web by using a simple interface. The laboratory system employs an Artificial Intelligence-based approach including a Single Multiplicative Neuron System trained by Intelligent Water Drops Algorithm in order to forecast time series of chaotic systems. It is possible to adjust parameters of the related Artificial Intelligence techniques, so it may possible for students to have some knowledge about Artificial Intelligence and intelligent systems.

Computers have been used in educational environments to carry out applications that need expertise, such as compiling, storing, presentation, and evaluation of information. In some teaching environments that need expert knowledge, capturing and imitating the knowledge of the expert in an artificial environment and utilizing computer systems that have the ability to communicate with people using natural language might reduce the need for the expert and provide fast results. Expert systems are a study area of artificial intelligence and can be defined as computer systems that can approach a problem for which an answer is being sought like an expert and present solution recommendations. In this chapter, the definition of expert systems and their characteristics, information about the expert systems in teaching environments, and especially their utilization in distance education are given.

During a typical e-learning process, there are many different factors that should be taken into consideration to keep the stability of the process or improve the process to get more effective results. Nowadays, employing Artificial Intelligence-based approaches is one of the most popular ways to improve the process and obtain the desired objectives rapidly. In this sense, there are many different kinds of scientific works in order to improve the related literature. However, ensuring control among the performed Artificial Intelligence-based e-learning process is a critical point because there is sometimes a misunderstanding about employing intelligent e-learning process that running intelligent educational tools or materials does not always mean the related e-learning process will improve greatly. In order to ensure that there should be some managerial procedures focused on some aspects of the process, this chapter aims to introduce a managerial model that can be used for especially Artificial Intelligence-supported e-learning content flow in order to improve the educational process. The suggested model is usable for the educational institutions, which focus on especially Artificial Intelligence-oriented e-learning solutions, research works, and educational activities.

The chapter presents a case study of using data mining tools to solve the puzzle of inconsistency between students' in-class performance and the results of the final tests. Classical test theory cannot explain such inconsistency, while the classification tree generated by one of the well-known data mining algorithms has provided reasonable explanation, which was confirmed by course exit interviews. The experimental results could be used as a case study of implementing Artificial Intelligence-based methods to analyze course results. Such analyses equip educators with an additional tool that allows closing the loop between assessment results and course content and arrangements.

Chapter 11

Aslihan Tufekci, Gazi University, Turkey

In recent years, the amount of software developed to be used in the fields of computer-assisted teaching, e-learning, and distance education, and their quality levels have greatly varied. In order to meet the increasing demand for effective and suitable coursewares at an optimum level, the most convenient method is believed to be that these coursewares should be developed by teachers themselves, and a considerable number of quality studies focusing on these coursewares should be conducted to improve educational processes in general. At this point, the studies and projects benefitting from the advantages of artificial intelligence-based approaches are becoming frequently available in the related literature as an innovative trend. The current chapter deals with the design and development of an "expert system shell program" on the basis of certain specific goals and needs mentioned in the literature. The main objective of the study is to assist teachers in developing their own courseware by using this particular program. The shell program developed within the scope of this study was tested on a group of people that consists of teachers from different fields of teaching and education levels, and its effectiveness was evaluated through certain methods.

Chapter 12

Tuncay Yigit, Suleyman Demirel University, Turkey
Arif Koyun, Suleyman Demirel University, Turkey
Asim Sinan Yuksel, Suleyman Demirel University, Turkey
Ibrahim Arda Cankaya, Suleyman Demirel University, Turkey
Utku Kose, Usak University, Turkey

Blended Learning is a learning model that is enriched with traditional learning methods and online education materials. Integration of face-to-face and online learning with blending learning can enhance the learning experience and optimize seat time. In this chapter, the authors present the teaching of an Algorithm and Programming course in Computer Engineering Education via an artificial intelligence-supported blended learning approach. Since 2011, Computer Engineering education in Suleyman Demirel University Computer Engineering Department is taught with a blended learning method. Blended learning is achieved through a Learning Management System (LMS) by using distance education technology. The LMS is comprised of course materials supported with flash animations, student records, user roles, and evaluation systems such as surveys and quizzes that meet SCORM standards. In this chapter, the related education process has been supported with an intelligent program, which is based on teaching C programming language. In this way, it has been aimed to improve educational processes within the related course and the education approach in the department. The blended learning approach has been evaluated by the authors, and the obtained results show that the introduced artificial intelligence-supported blended learning education program enables both teachers and students to experience better educational processes.

Intelligent Tutoring Systems have proven their worth in multiple ways and in multiple domains in education. In this chapter, the proposed Agent-Based Distributed ITS using CBR for enhancing the intelligent learning environment is introduced. The general architecture of the ABDITS is formed by the three components that generally characterize an ITS: the Student Model, the Domain Model, and the Pedagogical Model. In addition, a Tutor Model has been added to the ITS, which provides the functionality that the teacher of the system needs. Pedagogical strategies are stored in cases, each dictating, given a specific situation, which tutoring action to make next. Reinforcement learning is used to improve various aspects of the CBR module: cases are learned and retrieval and adaptation are improved, thus modifying the pedagogical strategies based on empirical feedback on each tutoring session. The student modeling is a core component in the development of proposed ITS. In this chapter, the authors describe how a Multi-Agent Intelligent system can provide effective learning using Case-Based Student Modeling.

Clustering student data is a central task in the educational data mining and design of intelligent learning tools. The problem is that there are thousands of clustering algorithms but no general guidelines about which method to choose. The optimal choice is of course problem- and data-dependent and can seldom be found without trying several methods. Still, the purposes of clustering students and the typical features of educational data make certain clustering methods more suitable or attractive. In this chapter, the authors evaluate the main clustering methods from this perspective. Based on the analysis, the authors suggest the most promising clustering methods for different situations.

Most of the distance educational systems consider only little, or no, adaptivity. Personalization according to specific requirements of an individual student is one of the most important features in adaptive educational systems. Considering learning and how to improve a student's performance, these systems must know the way in which an individual student learns best. In this context, this chapter depicts an application of evolutionary algorithms to discover students' learning styles. The approach is mainly based on the non-deterministic and non-stationary aspects of learning styles, which may change during the learning process in an unexpected and unpredictable way. Because of the stochastic and dynamic aspects enclosed in learning process, it is important to gradually and constantly update the student model. In this way, the student model stochastically evolves towards the real student's learning style, considering its fine-tuned strengths. This approach has been tested through computer simulation of students, and promising results have been obtained. Some of them are presented in this chapter.

With the outstanding improvements in technology, the number of e-learning applications has increased greatly. This increment is associated with awareness levels of educational institutions on the related improvements and the power of communication and computer technologies to ensure effective and efficient teaching and learning experiences for teachers and students. Consequently, there is a technological flow that changes the standards of e-learning processes and provides better ways to obtain desired educational objectives. When we consider today's widely used technological factors, Web-based e-learning approaches have a special role in directing the educational standards. Improvements among m-learning applications and the popularity of the Artificial Intelligence usage for educational works have given great momentum to this orientation. In this sense, this chapter provides some ideas on the future of intelligent Web-based e-learning applications by thinking on the current status of the literature. As it is known, current trends in developing Artificial Intelligence-supported e-learning tools continue to shape the future of e-learning. Therefore, it is an important approach to focus on the future. The author thinks that the chapter will be a brief but effective enough reference for similar works, which focus on the future of Artificial Intelligence-supported distance education and e-learning.

Foreword

by Gerhard-Wilhelm Weber and Pandian Vasant

The purpose of this book *Artificial Intelligence Applications in Distance Education* is to deeply inquire, reflect, and comprehensively expose this current and emerging cutting edge technology in important fields of investigation and high-performance facilities for original, innovative, and novel real-world applications in the modern world and its area of Education. During the previous decades, the analytical tools and the methodological toolbox of computer science and applied mathematics, of informatics and statistics, in emerging analytics, algorithms and Information Technologies has gained the attention of numerous researchers and practitioners from all over the world, providing a strong impact also in natural sciences, engineering, economy finance, and information technologies.

The contributing authors of this book are experienced scientists from all over the globe; they utilize and further refine the deep model-based methods of mathematics and the less model-based so-called smart or intelligent algorithms with their roots in the engineering disciplines, in computer science, and informatics. The second ones are often named as heuristics and model-free; they are less rigorous mathematically, but released from the firmness of calculus, in order to integrate nature- and, especially, bio-inspired approaches to efficiently cope with hard problems. The rise of these algorithms from Artificial Intelligence which is, as we understood, rather natural and intuitive often happened in parallel to the powerful progress in mathematics that is model-based mainly. Nowadays, labeled by names like Statistical Learning and Machine Learning, Metaheuristics and Matheuristics, and by Operational Research, model-free and model-based streamlines of traditions and approaches meet and exchange in various centres of research, at important congresses, and in remarkable projects and agendas all around the world to overcome misunderstandings and wrong perceptions of different kinds between those two academic avenues, but to benefit from synergy effects, to jointly advance scientific progress and to provide a service to the solution of urgent real-life challenges. Such huge problems exist in every area of the modern world and academics, in engineering, the economy, social sciences, life and human sciences, and development and the improvement of living conditions and future perspectives.

Among the variety of these subjects and, in fact, including all of them, the distinguished editors selected the area of Education which may be regarded as a foundation for them all. At the same time, Education has the potential to be supported by all the other areas and subjects, especially, from the modern high-tech ones, from advances in social sciences, and social media and networks and, of course, as explained above, Artificial Intelligence. In this book, a special emphasis lies on Distance Education.

It is a remarkable achievement for this new book and its editors that they have strongly contributed to this important process in science and culture, for having opened the floor to scientists and practitioners in order to expose their recent experiences and insights, their core results and main techniques.

To all the authors of these valuable chapters, we extend our cordial appreciation and gratitude for having shared their devotion, excellence, and vision with the entire academic community and mankind. We are very thankful to the publishing house *IGI Global*, and to the editorial team, *Dr. Utku Köse,* and his colleagues, for having provided the chance and the floor for these experts to publish their outstanding achievements and contributions. We express our sincere thankfulness to them for having ensured a premium book of a high standard academic, applied, and social importance!

We wish all of you lots of joy in reading this exciting work, and we hope a great benefit is gained from it of personal and societal kind.

Sincerely yours,

Gerhard-Wilhelm Weber
Middle East Technical University, Turkey

Pandian Vasant
Universiti Teknologi Petronas, Malaysia
January 2014

Gerhard-Wilhelm Weber *is a Professor at IAM, METU, Ankara, Turkey. His research is on optimization and control (continuous and discrete), OR, financial mathematics, on life, bio and human sciences, dynamical systems, data mining, statistical learning, inverse problems, environment and development. He is involved in the organization of scientific life internationally. He received both his Diploma and Doctorate in mathematics and economics / business administration at Aachen University of Technology (RWTH Aachen),and his Habilitation (second doctorate) at Darmstadt University of Technology (TU Darmstadt). He held Professorships by proxy at the University of Cologne, Germany, and Chemnitz University of Technology, Germany, before he worked at Cologne Bioinformatics Center and then, in 2003, went to Ankara. At IAM, METU, he is in the Programs of Financial Mathematics, Actuarial Sciences, and Scientific Computing. He is the Assistant to the Director of IAM and a member of four further graduate schools, departments, and institutes of METU.*

Pandian Vasant *was born in Sungai Petani, Malaysia in 1961. Currently, he is a Senior Lecturer of Mathematics and Optimization in the Fundamental and Applied Sciences Department at Universiti Teknologi Petronas in Tronoh, Perak, Mlaysia. He graduated in 1986 from the University of Malaya (MY) in Kuala Lumpur, obtaining his BSc Degree with Honors (II Class Upper) in Mathematics and in 1988, he also obtained a Diploma in English for Business from Cambridge Tutorial College, Cambridge, England. In 2002, he obtained his MSc (By Research) in Engineering Mathematics from the School of Engineering and Information Technology from the University of Malaysia Sabah, Malaysia, and has a Doctoral Degree (Ph.D, 2004-2008) from University Putra Malaysia in Malaysia. His main research interests are in the areas of Optimization Methods and Applications to Decision Making and Industrial Engineering, Fuzzy Optimization, Computational Intelligence, and Hybrid Soft Computing.*

Foreword

by Gonca Telli Yamamoto

In the not too distant past, like 50 years ago, life was roughly foreseeable. There were a few choices one could make, and there were few options to choose from. However, the rapid development of technology increased our options excessively. This makes it harder and harder for us to make estimations for the future. We are all just trying to catch up with the new trends, while time is becoming more and more valuable each day. This being the case, adopting less time consuming practices seems more preferable; therefore, a need to emphasize distance education and e-learning applications has arisen.

The Information and Communication Technologies Revolution caused an upheaval in the social and educational texture. Most people would never have guessed twenty years ago that the educational applications would be where ICT is today. The Internet, Learning Management Systems (LMS), E-learning, m-learning, wireless technologies, and holograms are only a few of them. Who would have guessed that Artificial Intelligence would be a key part of our educational vocabulary a decade ago? It was just in the TV serials such as 'Star Trek.' Now we are witnessing science-fiction coming true.

Distance education has changed its shell within the century. The world's most prestigious universities have realized the importance of e-learning and began to use it in their courses. Not only the prestigious universities, but also all universities that want to thrive will be forced to use e-learning in the near future. We could say the distance learning component will increase its share in general learning over time, as technology takes its place among the basic needs and these instruments of training will be demanded by the wider masses (Yamamoto & Karaman, 2011).

Starting from correspondence teaching, distance education has come a long way in Artificial Intelligence. Artificial Intelligence (AI) can be defined as the operating systems that would do assessments and decision-making in various situations like human intelligence. According to Ranier and Cegielski (2013), AI is a subfield of computer science that studies the thought processes of humans and recreates the effects of those processes via machines, such as computers and robots.

Artificial intelligence applications, despite not being commonly used in distance education, require further dissemination. Artificial intelligence is one of the tools that have the potential to replace the old, accepted methods, ways, and means with continuous development. What is important here is to think outside the box: you cannot put new wine in old bottles.

This book covers some important Artificial Intelligence subjects. These are:

- Digital Library Proposition
- Educational Support Systems
- Intelligent Questioning Systems
- Intelligent Learning/Tutoring Systems
- Effective Courseware Design and Development

It is best to understand all these subjects and to create new bottles to put the new wine into. So, read on.

Gonca Telli Yamamoto
Okan University, Turkey
January 2014

Gonca Telli Yamamoto *received a BS degree in 1989 from the Business Administration of Marmara University, in Turkey. She received an MS degree in 1992 from Marmara University (Marketing and Production Management), Turkey and she completed a PhD degree in 1997 at Marmara University in the field of Marketing. She is currently a Professor at Okan University, in Turkey. She is also the Distance Education Center Director at Okan University, and her research interests include mobile marketing, e-marketing, strategic marketing management, marketing strategies, and high tech marketing.*

REFERENCES

Ranier, R. K., & Cegielski, C. G. (2013). *Introduction to Information Systems* (4th ed.). Singapore: John Wiley & Sons Singapore Pte Ltd.

Yamamoto, G. T., & Karaman, F. (2011). Education 2.0. *On the Horizon, 19*(2), 109–117.

Foreword

by Omer Deperlioglu

Nowadays, we are experiencing a new type of information era along rapid developments in many different technologies. When we take our daily life into consideration, we can see that mobile communication and computer technologies have an important role in making our life style better and more stable against the dynamic flow of the world. Additionally, almost every person is highly connected with computers and the related technologies in order to do their work, or just spending time. It is important that advanced communication and computer technology based devices are highly integrated into our life by shaping our daily lives and ensuring some practical aspects to form our activities in simpler modes rather than experiencing everything in a complex and confusing manner.

Changes among technologies are depended on academic - scientific developments and also improvements occurring in the related literatures. When we consider the used technologies from this perspective, we can see that many different scientific approaches are combined in a single technological object and take part under both theoretical and applied infrastructure under these technologies. For instance, intelligent applications running in our smart mobile phones or tablets are based on the usage of software related techniques from the Artificial Intelligence field of Computer Science.

Artificial Intelligence is one of today's the most important research areas, and it is very popular with its effectiveness on providing effective solutions for almost all fields in the life. Advanced, flexible, mathematical infrastructure and strong logical, algorithmic approaches designed under this area make it a wide-spread, long running scientific factor to support many other disciplines for newer developments. It seems that the future will also be formed thanks to Artificial Intelligence.

The book *Artificial Intelligence Applications in Distance Education* focuses on education, which is one of the most important application subjects of Artificial Intelligence. In more detail, it gives emphasis on a widely active educational approach: distance education. Because of the functions on removing distance and time limitations, the distance education approach and associated techniques should be highly supported by Artificial Intelligence. The future of education will be determined with the employment of intelligent systems within educational studies. So, the chapters provided in this book give us a chance to see the current potential of Artificial Intelligence in application along distance education activities and enables us to think about the future better.

I feel very thankful to the editor *Utku Kose*, and his colleague *Durmus Koc*, for providing their valuable effort and time to form such a valuable reference study for a wide-scope literature. Also, I wish all the readers to have an enjoyable reading experience.

Omer Deperlioglu
Afyon Kocatepe University, Turkey
January 2014

Omer Deperlioglu *received a BS degree in 1988 in electrical education from Gazi University in Turkey. He received an MS degree in 1996 from Afyon Kocatepe University, Turkey and he completed a PhD. degree in 2001 from Gazi University in the field of controlling switch-mode dc-dc converters with neuro-fuzzy systems. He is currently an Associate Professor in the Afyon Kocatepe University, in Turkey. His research interests include computer-based control systems, fuzzy logic control, neuro-fuzzy control, power electronics, distance education, and e-learning.*

Preface

As it is known, much has changed in the past five years. At this point, sensitive and dynamic aspects of the society make it very adaptive to any changes that may occur. Changes in standards of the daily life highly depend on many different factors and may be sociological, economical, or technological. Technological changes can be easily adapted to by society by enabling people to feeling the adaptation as "keeping the trend." If we focus on the details of our daily activities, we can easily see the effects of changes among technologies and become aware of some revolutionary developments and improvements that may be hidden for us. We are in a rapidly changing world and trying to keep ourselves adaptive to the changes, especially after the era of modern knowledge society.

When we think about functions of the modern knowledge society, it can be clearly expressed that the society always needs innovative and effective approaches to keep reaching to the desired information in a fast and efficient way to make it easier to share information with anyone. In time, all these needs have caused revolutionary changes in many fields. In this sense, education is one of the most remarkable fields, and it has a key role in enabling individuals and preparing them for the conditions of the knowledge society.

The education field has a natural feature, which takes it into a great interaction with the developments in both communication and computer technologies. Today, Internet has a big impact on educational activities, and many educational institutions employ this technology in order to perform their teaching-learning processes in more effective and efficient ways. Improvements in computer technology also make it possible to design advanced educational approaches and make it possible to experience educational processes in cases of time and zone limitations. From this perspective, Distance Education and its techniques like e-learning and m-learning are widely used by educational institutions in order to make it possible to receive education and instruction.

Distance Education has many advantages that make it a durable approach, but when we focus more on the complex and chaotic style of human behavior, it is always a vital need to make the related educational approaches/techniques adaptive. Because any behavior in Distance Education activities can affect the whole educational flow and cause negative outputs at the end, the related behaviors, which can be determined via advanced intelligent, mathematical-logical algorithms should be taken into consideration to change some conditions and adjust them according to the human factor. All of these explore an important academic and scientific interaction between the Artificial Intelligence and Distance Education.

The objective of this book is to introduce Artificial Intelligence-Based Distance Education works and applications that are employed to overcome the related problem expressed above and improve teaching-learning experiences during educational processes. By explaining and introducing the related works/applications, readers who are interested in the related fields (Artificial Intelligence, Distance Education, E-Learning, etc.) will be enabled to improve their knowledge about the literature and the developments in it. Furthermore, the book also aims to explore a research concept that we call "Intelligent Distance Education." This concept includes many different scientific studies associated with combining Distance Education and Artificial Intelligence. The development of Intelligent Distance Education applications or systems is a greatly improving interest area.

The prospective audience of the book, *Artificial Intelligence Applications in Distance Education*, will be scientists, engineers, researchers, and academicians, as well as anyone interested in both Artificial Intelligence and education (more specifically Distance Education).

This book includes 14 chapters about research works that have been performed based on both Artificial Intelligence and Distance Education. The content of the related chapters are overviewed briefly in the following paragraphs.

CHAPTER 1

In today's world, intelligent systems play an important role in improving humankind's life standards and providing effective solutions for real-world-based problems. In this sense, such intelligent systems are the research outputs of the Artificial Intelligence field in Computer Science. Today, in many fields intelligent systems are widely used to obtain effective and accurate results for the problems encountered. At this point, education is one of the most remarkable fields in which lots of Artificial Intelligence-oriented research works are performed. When we consider the education field in terms of the latest technological developments, we can also see that the e-learning technique and more generally distance education approach are highly associated with the applications of Artificial Intelligence. Therefore, in this chapter the author explores the trends within the interaction between Artificial Intelligence and Distance Education. The chapter is a brief report on current trends of applications of "intelligent distance education" solutions. It also provides a short focus on the future possibilities of the relation of Artificial Intelligence and Distance Education.

CHAPTER 2

In Digital Libraries (DLs) as an innovative community environment, knowledge is nutrition, and the environment for knowledge sharing is the essential condition. As the knowledge is the heart of digital libraries, it is imperative for them to promote the innovation activities embodied by teaching and scientific research through an efficient knowledge-sharing environment. In digital environment, the role of knowledge has become even more significant. Moreover, DLs perform many knowledge-based activities, and by nature, the knowledge-sharing process is embedded in DL systems. These modern knowledge management environments need modern technologies in order to perform properly for end users and online researchers. Therefore, the aim of this chapter is to provide a model for global knowledge networking with utilizing digital libraries and artificial intelligence. The specific objectives are to describe a framework of digital libraries and concepts of Knowledge Management (KM). The chapter finds some significant overlaps between DLs and KM and integrates the knowledge-sharing process with DLs and artificial intelligence. The integration of KM and knowledge sharing can add value to develop a global knowledge networking process model so users around the globe can make use of this knowledge transmission.

CHAPTER 3

Increasing student numbers lead to new needs in the education sector. New systems are needed due to expert numbers that are insufficient in specialties, such as instructors, directors, and advisors. Type, goal, and specialty of intelligent systems programmed to satisfy this need are being developed with each passing day. The aim of this chapter is to develop an intelligent system that provides support with schedule, academic orientation, choice of profession, and career planning to students. To make a regular schedule for students would generally cause an inappropriate program, which is hardly followed by students in case they were indiscriminately prepared without any information about students' characteristics. Instead of this method, it is the point to be familiar with the academic success, study, resting, and even meal time of the student, and to know which lessons are studied on which days and to make an appropriate schedule for studying. According to the teachers, it is time-consuming and difficult to perform this method for all students. Within this scope, an intelligent system preparing a study schedule is developed considering the students' characteristics and study habits.

CHAPTER 4

Higher education in accounting has witnessed, in time, a massive development, a fact that has required the identification of the most efficient training methods based on competencies so as to meet the new professional challenges. Computer-based training represents a didactic method that improves accounting education. This chapter presents some elements regarding e-learning in accounting and how the educational software can include artificially intelligent elements that may humanize the dialogue of the teacher-computer, like pedagogical agents. The authors present the main ideas of how they designed and developed a multi-agent system that has been incorporated into an educational soft that was tested and validated within an experiment with the students from the specialization of Accounting and Management Information Systems of the Vasile Alecsandri University of Bacău, Romania.

CHAPTER 5

One of the most important functions of distance learning systems is determining the student knowledge level and performance clearly. In traditional education systems, students can be assessed in single-stage via tests and homework studies, which consist of multiple-choice questions. However, this method cannot provide accurate results since it is not able to evaluate student knowledge level and question difficulty level. In this chapter, a system and software structure that can determine student knowledge levels, topic difficulty level, and question difficulty levels according to instant student answers for the exam is introduced. In forming student knowledge levels, content monitoring and test data taken from distance education vocational school were used. In this way, more accurate results have been obtained. The fuzzy logic technique has been used to determine (classify) student knowledge levels and topic difficulty levels clearly. In order to determine next questions adaptively, the stored questions have been classified with division clustering methods, and the most suitable questions for the related student knowledge level have been found by using the nearest neighbor algorithm.

CHAPTER 6

Information and communication technologies have led to new developments in education. Time and place independent education has emerged. Furthermore, different characteristics and huge numbers of individuals have made the use of new technological methods inevitable. In this context, distance education has become a popular education method to meet the emerging needs, increasing satisfaction, and learning performance of students. Mobile technology, intelligent systems, and Three Dimensional (3D) animations also provide enhancements in this field. In addition, distance education systems should be selected and developed properly for target students and environments. For this purpose, the assessment of prominent studies provides a road map for new research. In this sense, this chapter evaluates intelligent distance education studies in literature. Furthermore, it proposes a novel Artificial Neural Network (ANN)-based distance education system for Mehmet Akif Ersoy University. This ANN-based system can be implemented on Mehmet Akif Ersoy University infrastructure with agent. The proposed system consists of a learning management system, Web conferencing system, and an ANN agent. The agent's inputs that are already stored in Mehmet Akif Ersoy University's distance education databases can be easily retrieved. This agent provides reusability of course content and Web conferencing records.

CHAPTER 7

In the context of Chaos Theory and its applications, forecasting time series of a chaotic system is an attractive work area for the current literature. Many different approaches and the related scientific studies have been introduced and done by researchers since the inception of this working area. Newer studies are also performed in order to provide more effective and efficient approaches and improve the related literature in this way. On the other hand, it is another important research point to ensure effective educational approaches for teaching Chaos Theory and chaotic systems within the associated courses. In this sense, this chapter introduces a Web-based, intelligent, educational laboratory system for forecasting chaotic time series. Briefly, the system aims to enable students to experience their own learning process over the Web by using a simple interface. The laboratory system employs an Artificial Intelligence-based approach including a Single Multiplicative Neuron System trained by Intelligent Water Drops Algorithm in order to forecast time series of chaotic systems. It is possible to adjust parameters of the related Artificial Intelligence techniques, so it may possible for students to have some knowledge about Artificial Intelligence and intelligent systems.

CHAPTER 8

Computers have been used in educational environments to carry out applications that need expertise, such as compiling, storing, presentation, and evaluation of information. In some teaching environments that need expert knowledge, capturing and imitating the knowledge of the expert in an artificial environment and utilizing computer systems that have the ability to communicate with people using natural language might reduce the need for the expert and provide fast results. Expert systems are a study area of artificial intelligence and can be defined as computer systems that can approach a problem for which an answer is being sought like an expert and present solution recommendations. In this chapter, the definition of expert systems and their characteristics, information about the expert systems in teaching environments, and especially their utilization in distance education are given.

CHAPTER 9

During a typical e-learning process, there are many different factors that should be taken into consideration to keep the stability of the process or improve the process to get more effective results. Nowadays, employing Artificial Intelligence-based approaches is one of the most popular ways to improve the process and obtain the desired objectives rapidly. In this sense, there are many different kinds of scientific works in order to improve the related literature. However, ensuring control among the performed Artificial Intelligence-based e-learning process is a critical point because there is sometimes a misunderstanding about employing intelligent e-learning process that running intelligent educational tools or materials does not always mean the related e-learning process will improve greatly. In order to ensure that there should be some managerial procedures focused on some aspects of the process, this chapter aims to introduce a managerial model that can be used for especially Artificial Intelligence-supported e-learning content flow in order to improve the educational process. The suggested model is usable for the educational institutions, which focus on especially Artificial Intelligence-oriented e-learning solutions, research works, and educational activities.

CHAPTER 10

The chapter presents a case study of using data mining tools to solve the puzzle of inconsistency between students' in-class performance and the results of the final tests. Classical test theory cannot explain such inconsistency, while the classification tree generated by one of the well-known data mining algorithms has provided reasonable explanation, which was confirmed by course exit interviews. The experimental results could be used as a case study of implementing Artificial Intelligence-based methods to analyze course results. Such analyses equip educators with an additional tool that allows closing the loop between assessment results and course content and arrangements.

CHAPTER 11

In recent years, the amount of software developed to be used in the fields of computer-assisted teaching, e-learning, and distance education, and their quality levels have greatly varied. In order to meet the increasing demand for effective and suitable coursewares at an optimum level, the most convenient method is believed to be that these coursewares should be developed by teachers themselves, and a considerable number of quality studies focusing on these coursewares should be conducted to improve educational processes in general. At this point, the studies and projects benefitting from the advantages of artificial intelligence-based approaches are becoming frequently available in the related literature as an innovative trend. The current chapter deals with the design and development of an "expert system shell program" on the basis of certain specific goals and needs mentioned in the literature. The main objective of the study is to assist teachers in developing their own courseware by using this particular program. The shell program developed within the scope of this study was tested on a group of people that consists of teachers from different fields of teaching and education levels, and its effectiveness was evaluated through certain methods.

CHAPTER 12

Blended Learning is a learning model that is enriched with traditional learning methods and online education materials. Integration of face-to-face and online learning with blending learning can enhance the learning experience and optimize seat time. In this chapter, the authors present the teaching of an Algorithm and Programming course in Computer Engineering Education via an artificial intelligence-supported blended learning approach. Since 2011, Computer Engineering education in Suleyman Demirel University Computer Engineering Department is taught with a blended learning method. Blended learning is achieved through a Learning Management System (LMS) by using distance education technology. The LMS is comprised of course materials supported with flash animations, student records, user roles, and evaluation systems such as surveys and quizzes that meet SCORM standards. In this chapter, the related education process has been supported with an intelligent program, which is based on teaching C programming language. In this way, it has been aimed to improve educational processes within the related course and the education approach in the department. The blended learning approach has been evaluated by the authors, and the obtained results show that the introduced artificial intelligence-supported blended learning education program enables both teachers and students to experience better educational processes.

CHAPTER 13

Intelligent Tutoring Systems have proven their worth in multiple ways and in multiple domains in education. In this chapter, the proposed Agent-Based Distributed ITS using CBR for enhancing the intelligent learning environment is introduced. The general architecture of the ABDITS is formed by the three components that generally characterize an ITS: the Student Model, the Domain Model, and the Pedagogical Model. In addition, a Tutor Model has been added to the ITS, which provides the functionality that the teacher of the system needs. Pedagogical strategies are stored in cases, each dictating, given a specific situation, which tutoring action to make next. Reinforcement learning is used to improve various aspects of the CBR module: cases are learned and retrieval and adaptation are improved, thus modifying the pedagogical strategies based on empirical feedback on each tutoring session. The student modeling is a core component in the development of proposed ITS. In this chapter, the authors describe how a Multi-Agent Intelligent system can provide effective learning using Case-Based Student Modeling.

CHAPTER 14

Clustering student data is a central task in the educational data mining and design of intelligent learning tools. The problem is that there are thousands of clustering algorithms but no general guidelines about which method to choose. The optimal choice is of course problem- and data-dependent and can seldom be found without trying several methods. Still, the purposes of clustering students and the typical features of educational data make certain clustering methods more suitable or attractive. In this chapter, the authors evaluate the main clustering methods from this perspective. Based on the analysis, the authors suggest the most promising clustering methods for different situations.

CHAPTER 15

Most of the distance educational systems consider only little, or no, adaptivity. Personalization according to specific requirements of an individual student is one of the most important features in adaptive educational systems. Considering learning and how to improve a student's performance, these systems must know the way in which an individual student learns best. In this context, this chapter depicts an application of evolutionary algorithms to discover students' learning styles. The approach is mainly based on the non-deterministic and non-stationary aspects of learning styles, which may change during the learning process in an unexpected and unpredictable way. Because of the stochastic and dynamic aspects enclosed in learning process, it is important to gradually and constantly update the student model. In this way, the student model stochastically evolves towards the real student's learning style, considering its fine-tuned strengths. This approach has been tested through computer simulation of students, and promising results have been obtained. Some of them are presented in this chapter.

CHAPTER 16

With the outstanding improvements in technology, the number of e-learning applications has increased greatly. This increment is associated with awareness levels of educational institutions on the related improvements and the power of communication and computer technologies to ensure effective and efficient teaching and learning experiences for teachers and students. Consequently, there is a technological flow that changes the standards of e-learning processes and provides better ways to obtain desired educational objectives. When we consider today's widely used technological factors, Web-based e-learning approaches have a special role in directing the educational standards. Improvements among m-learning applications and the popularity of the Artificial Intelligence usage for educational works have given great momentum to this orientation. In this sense, this chapter provides some ideas on the future of intelligent Web-based e-learning applications by thinking on the current status of the literature. As it is known, current trends in developing Artificial Intelligence-supported e-learning tools continue to shape the future of e-learning. Therefore, it is an important approach to focus on the future. The author thinks that the chapter will be a brief but effective enough reference for similar works, which focus on the future of Artificial Intelligence-supported distance education and e-learning.

This book offers a great opportunity for the scientists and researchers in the field of Artificial Intelligence and Distance Education to disseminate their original, quality, novel, and innovative research work findings and obtained results to the global research scholars.

Utku Kose
Usak University, Turkey

Durmus Koc
Usak University, Turkey

Acknowledgment

We would like to take this great opportunity to sincerely thank the following friends and colleagues for their kind help and valuable support on the book content: Aslihan Tufekci, Bogdan Pătruţ, Gerhard-Wilhelm Weber, Gonca Telli Yamamoto, Omer Deperlioglu, Pandian Vasant, and Tuncay Yigit. Their fabulous ideas, suggestions, feedback, and also constructive comments for the improvement of the organization and quality of the book are gratefully acknowledged.

Furthermore, we sincerely thank the group at IGI Global in Hershey PA, USA, for their great help and excellent support on this project. In particular, special thanks to Mr. Austin DeMarco, Ms. Jan Travers, and Ms. Christine Smith of IGI Global for their great and valuable cooperation.

Utku Kose
Usak University, Turkey

Durmus Koc
Usak University, Turkey

Chapter 1
On the Intersection of Artificial Intelligence and Distance Education

Utku Kose
Usak University, Turkey

ABSTRACT

In today's world, intelligent systems play an important role in improving humankind's life standards and providing effective solutions for real-world-based problems. In this sense, such intelligent systems are the research outputs of the Artificial Intelligence field in Computer Science. Today, in many fields intelligent systems are widely used to obtain effective and accurate results for the problems encountered. At this point, education is one of the most remarkable fields in which lots of Artificial Intelligence-oriented research works are performed. When we consider the education field in terms of the latest technological developments, we can also see that the e-learning technique and more generally distance education approach are highly associated with the applications of Artificial Intelligence. Therefore, in this chapter the author explores the trends within the interaction between Artificial Intelligence and Distance Education. The chapter is a brief report on current trends of applications of "intelligent distance education" solutions. It also provides a short focus on the future possibilities of the relation of Artificial Intelligence and Distance Education.

INTRODUCTION

It is clear that the life standards, which form our living styles, determine our status in the context of communities, and shape viewpoints on the world are changed in a rapid manner, as a result of developments in different technologies. Newer technological developments enable humankind to take less active role on solving problems of daily life because there have been great efforts on designing and developing advanced systems to support and help people to overcome their problems in a fast and easy way. In this sense, mechanical systems have given their roles on improving the life to electronic devices appeared in time. We can now say that our life has been covered with electronic devices and especially advanced electronic devices, which support us in our daily activities, have taken an important part in our life; because of their intelligent mechanisms to overcome problems of needing fast, effective, and accurate solution approaches. At this point, such electronic devices include some essential features and functions employed from some specific scientific fields.

DOI: 10.4018/978-1-4666-6276-6.ch001

Because of their role on automatically deciding and providing solution ways, such devices are called as "intelligent systems".

In today's modern world, intelligent systems have an important role on improving humankind's life standards and providing effective solutions for real-world based problems. In this sense, such intelligent systems are the research outputs of the Artificial Intelligence field in Computer Science. With its effective approaches, methods, and techniques on many problems and so wide application scope, Artificial Intelligence field has become one of the most popular and long-term research areas for scientists. In time, different types of approaches, methods, techniques of Artificial Intelligence have been employed in problems of different fields and because of success among different research works, the scope of the Artificial Intelligence has improved. Today, we can express that in many fields, intelligent systems are widely used to obtain effective and accurate results for the problems encountered. At this point education is one of the most remarkable fields in which lots of Artificial Intelligence oriented research works are performed. When we consider the education field in terms of the latest technological developments, we can also see that the e-learning technique and more generally distance education approach are highly associated with the applications of Artificial Intelligence. So, it will be a remarkable approach to figure out the trends within the interaction occurred between Artificial Intelligence and Distance Education.

This chapter aims to provide a view on the intersection of Artificial Intelligence and Distance Education. As general, the chapter is a brief report on current trends on applications of "intelligent distance education" solutions. It is important that as a result of many research works performed on applying Artificial Intelligence over educational studies, some essential application titles indicating the intelligent mechanisms along educational processes have been expressed. Currently, these titles are one of key points to examine literature with a clear but deep enough view. In addition to

the focusing on the application orientations, the chapter also provides a short focus on the future possibilities on the relation of Artificial Intelligence and Distance Education. This chapter can also be accepted as an essential reference point to the start of our book: "Artificial Intelligence Applications in Distance Education".

In the sense of the related explanations, remaining content of the chapter is organized as follows: Next section is devoted to some brief explanations on the foundations of this chapter: Artificial Intelligence and Distance Education. Following that, the third section is focused on currently performed Artificial Intelligence based applications in the related Distance Education activities. After this section, there is a brief view on the future regarding to the applications of Artificial Intelligence in Distance Education and the last section ends with expressing some conclusions.

FOUNDATIONS

Briefly, this chapter has been written on the intersection of Artificial Intelligence and Distance Education. So, before discussing about essential Artificial Intelligence applications for Distance Education, it is a good way to have enough knowledge on the related subjects, which are main components of the chapter.

Artificial Intelligence

Artificial Intelligence is one of the most important application and research fields within the Computer Science. So, it is highly connected with most of sub-subjects examined under the Computer Science. It is possible to make two different definitions for the Artificial Intelligence. One definition can be made as Artificial Intelligence is a term that is used to describe the feature, function or characteristic of computer systems or machines that try to simulate human-thinking behavior or human intelligence. On the other hand; the other definition accepts the Artificial Intelligence as a field of Computer Science, which is based on research studies or developments on providing intelligent systems simulating the human-thinking behavior or human intelligence. When it is examined under the literature, we can also see some alternative definitions. According to McCarthy (2007), "it is the science and engineering of making intelligent machines, especially intelligent computer programs." Additionally, Berkeley (1997) defines the Artificial Intelligence as "the study of man-made computational devices and systems which can be made to act in a manner which we would be inclined to call intelligent."

Artificial Intelligence is a wide-scope field, which requires some technical pre-knowledge and good mathematical and algorithmic thinking abilities to perform the related research and application works well and properly. Generally, research works on this field include programming computer systems for certain traits like (Technopedia, 2014):

- Knowledge.
- Reasoning.
- Problem solving.
- Perception.
- Learning.
- Planning.

All of the mentioned traits figure out intelligent systems – mechanism in which certain algorithmic structures are run in order to ensure the related problem solving infrastructure. When the related literature examined in detail, it can be seen that there have been a remarkable research and application efforts to improve the related Artificial Intelligence field and provide effective solutions for especially real world based problems. In this way, many different Artificial Intelligence oriented approaches, methods, or techniques have been introduced by scientists – researchers.

Today, there are many different Artificial Intelligent based approaches, methods or techniques that are widely used in many different fields for providing effective and efficient solutions for

the problems within these fields. Some popular Artificial Intelligent based techniques can be expressed briefly as below:

Fuzzy Logic

It is an important Artificial Intelligence technique, which is especially used to design and develop intelligent, problem-solving control systems. As different from the crisp logic, the fuzzy logic is used to recognize more than simple true and false values. With the help of this technique, linguistic variables are evaluated with degrees of truthfulness and falsehood. Thus, an effective and strong approach, which tries to simulate the human thinking and behaviors, is obtained (Köse, & Deperlioğlu, 2010). This technique is based on the fuzzy set theory, which was first introduced by Lotfi Asker Zadeh (Zadeh, 1967).

Artificial Neural Networks

Artificial neural networks are parallel and distributed data processing systems, which were developed to be used for simulating features and functions of the human brain. In more detail, they are known as network structures consist of process elements, which are connected to each other via weighted connections. Artificial neural networks are capable of learning from their environments and improve the process performance through learning (Elmas, 2003; Uğur, & Kınacı, 2006).

Evolutionary Algorithms like Genetic Algorithms and Negative Selection Algorithm

Evolutionary algorithms are some kind of algorithm structures, which have been designed and developed based on features and functions of the evaluation theory. In this sense; within an evolutionary algorithm, a number of artificial objects – creatures search over the solutions space of the problem. During this process, they compete continually with each other to discover optimal areas of the solution space. At the end of the related process, the most successful of the objects – creatures will evolve to discover the optimal solution of the problem (Jones, 1998). According to different evolutionary-based systems, different kinds of algorithms have been introduced by researchers and scientists and they are widely used for finding effective and efficient solutions for real-world based problems.

Nature-Inspired Optimization Algorithms like Particle Swarm Optimization (PSO), Ant Colony Optimization (ACO), and Artificial Bee Colony (ABC)

Nature-inspired optimization algorithms (these algorithms can also be evaluated under the 'Swarm Intelligence' title) are some kind of algorithm structures, which are originally based on dynamics, which occur in the natural life. In this sense, the evolutionary algorithms are also known as nature-inspired algorithms, but because of their main function regarding to the evaluation theory, they are also categorized under a different title. On the other hand, the working mechanism and the related features and functions of a nature-inspired algorithm are based on mathematical calculations, which were formed to simulate original, natural dynamics. Mainly, nature-inspired optimization algorithms are based on the search mechanism of the algorithm objects for finding optimal solution(s) within the solution spaces of problems (Yang, 2011).

Other Remaining Techniques like Support Vector Machines (SVM)

There are also many other Artificial Intelligence techniques that have been introduced in order to provide alternative solutions for the problems regarding to the related field. For example; support vector machine is a remarkable and important technique, which is used for especially classification and regression. In this sense, support vector

machines are known as supervised learning models employing learning algorithms that analyze data and recognize patterns. In more detail, it can be expressed that a support vector machine is used for constructing a hyper-plane or set of hyper-planes in a high or infinite dimensional space used for classification, regression, or any other tasks (Cortes, & Vapnik, 1995; Wikipedia, 2013).

As it can be understood from the explanations, there are many different ways to categorize Artificial Intelligent techniques because of wide application and usage spectrums of each technique. Furthermore, there are also many ways to form different kind of systems (for example; "expert systems" or unnamed hybrid systems) including the related techniques and providing different approaches and methods to improve the literature and introduce alternative solutions for the problems. At this point, the term "intelligent systems" can be used within this chapter to indicate both single Artificial Intelligence technique and a typical hybrid system formed by two or more Artificial Intelligence technique. In this sense, especially the "hybrid system" approach is an important and popular way that is widely preferred by researchers and scientists within the Artificial Intelligence. When the literature regarding to the field is examined, readers can find many examples of hybrid systems formed by two or more Artificial Intelligence techniques.

Distance Education

Because of rapid developments within the technology, the education field has also improved in time; by employing more advanced and accurate ways to make both teaching and learning processes better. In this sense, especially improvements in communication and computer technologies have given a rise to better educational conditions provided via educational technologies. It can be expressed that by using information and communication technologies, a remarkable improvement has been succeeded in education. Distance education is one of the most important factors that take active part in this improvement and are widely used among educational studies today.

Generally, distance education can be defined as a planned education experience using a wide spectrum of technologies to reach learner in a distance place and is designed to encourage learning interaction and certification of learning with special techniques (Greenberg, 1998, Kaya, 2002; Keegan, 2004; Passerini, & Granger, 2000). Distance education consists of many methods and technologies that enable people to take education from anywhere, on anytime. Distance education activities have been done by using tools like television, CD-ROMs, video cassettes and letter. Nowadays, as a result of rapid improvements in technology, more advanced tools like computers, Internet and mobile devices have been included in distance education studies. Especially using combination of computer and Internet technologies in distance education has caused forming new techniques that can be examined under the distance education. Nowadays, different types of distance education based techniques like e-learning (electronic learning), web based learning, and m-learning (mobile learning) are widely used among educational studies and employed along the related research studies in the literature.

Additionally, some educational approaches like blended learning are also used widely in order to combine advantages of both face-to-face education and distance education related techniques.

As it was also mentioned before, the latest distance education oriented works are highly supported by Artificial Intelligence approaches, methods, and techniques. By employing intelligent mechanisms among educational tools or materials, educational experiences are improved by ensuring effectiveness and efficiencies for both teachers and students. Figure 1 provides a schema explaining the intersection between the Artificial Intelligence and the Distance Education. At this point, it will also be a good approach to briefly express current trends on applications of intelligent distance education solutions.

CURRENT TRENDS ON APPLICATIONS OF INTELLIGENT DISTANCE EDUCATION SOLUTIONS

Nowadays, there are many different trends on applications of Artificial Intelligence based distance education studies – solutions. It can be expressed that most of these studies are related to design of e-learning tools – materials, which can be used

Figure 1. A schema explaining the intersection between the Artificial Intelligence and the Distance Education

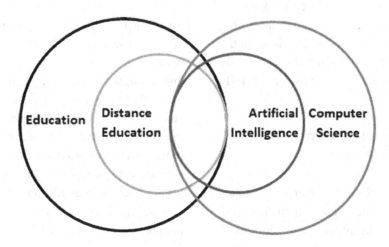

along the related teaching – learning activities. From more general perspective, distance education studies of educational institutions are also affected by "intelligent solutions"; in terms of especially managerial and organizational activities.

We can examine the related applications on employing Artificial Intelligence within Distance Education from different perspectives. These are:

- **Learners:** Students oriented solutions (like improving students' own-learning experiences, efficiencies along learning activities…etc.).
- **Educators:** Teachers oriented solutions (like supporting teachers along their teaching activities via expert systems, enabling teachers to plan their courses in an effective manner…etc.).
- General solutions focusing on activities performed by both teachers and students.
- General solutions aiming to improve distance education based processes (designing intelligent distance education models, strategies…etc.).
- Specific solutions, which focus on specific problems within Distance Education activities (like performing exams, evaluating student or / and teacher performances, grading, tracking educational activities… etc.).

The listed perspectives are some kind of ways along the trends in current conditions within distance education related activities. Some of the foremost trends in the sense of intelligent distance education applications can be explained briefly as follows:

Design and Development of Intelligent Software

One of the most remarkable trends among distance education related studies are based on designing and developing intelligent software solutions to be used along the courses provided by educational institutions. In this sense, such software can directly aim to support the default course structure or improve the course experience by changing its flow greatly. Especially e-learning oriented needs enable researchers to design Web-based software solutions, which can be accessed from anywhere, on anytime. Additionally, some certain Artificial Intelligence techniques may also be applied in development of specific intelligent software systems, which are some kind of simulators or applied environments used along certain technical and abstract courses.

Briefly, it is possible to list some typical forms of such software as follows:

- Software systems based on expert system approach.
- Intelligent tutoring systems.
- Intelligent examination systems.
- Intelligent environments combining more than one types of intelligent software – program.
- Intelligent software systems for preparing educational materials.
- Intelligent educational games.

Design and Development of Intelligent Decision Making Systems

Especially for educational institutions, it may be necessary to make an optimum decision along complex educational plans that have been made for a long period of educational process. Additionally, it may also necessary to direct the managerial operations automatically; according to sensitive, fast changing, dynamic environmental conditions. At this point, it is a good way to design and develop intelligent decision making systems. For this aim, expert systems are one of the most remarkable solutions that can be employed. Here, such expert systems are not used for learning or teaching activities as different from roles of expert system based software systems expressed under the previous sub-title.

Forming Intelligent Evaluation Systems

Evaluating both students' and teachers' performances is a vital approach in Distance Education oriented activities. Because of this, there should be more emphasis on forming effective evaluation mechanisms in order not to affect the educational flow and ensure a good way to evaluate the performed learning – teaching processes in terms of desired objectives. In order to meet with the related needs, Artificial Intelligent based evaluation systems are widely used among educational institutions. In this context, intelligent software systems to prepare exams, tests, or quizzes in an accurate manner are some of the most popular approach in today's Distance Education related activities. It is also important that such evaluation systems may be focused on not only students' performances among the courses but also on their learning styles, changing behaviors along the related learning activities. Finally, such evaluation systems are also based on evaluating teachers' performances during the performed Distance Education courses.

Ensuring Security and Stability in Distance Education Oriented Activities

When communication and computer technologies are employed in especially educational studies, it is an important aspect to ensure security for keeping the processes stable and at optimum level in order to evaluate the outputs of the educational processes accurately. Because there are many alternative works to use some limitations and disadvantages of the related technologies used along Distance Education activities, there will always be some ways to hack such organizational systems in order to have unfair gains. In this sense, not only the general structure of the formed Distance Education structure but also used intelligent software systems have critical potentials to be used maliciously.

Because of this, there have been remarkable efforts on designing and developing intelligent control mechanisms to diagnose such malicious activities, or any other bugs or disadvantages – limitations within especially software systems.

It is possible to examine security ensuring ways from some different perspectives. These are:

- Data security (ensuring security for data kept for Distance Education processes, ensuring encryption techniques to ensure secure data flow…etc.).
- Security for malicious activities (plagiarism detection, bug fixes in software systems…etc.).
- Security for potential dangerous environmental factors (ensuring security for software or hardware based resources, controlling the data flow…etc.)

When we consider the "stability" factor, it is also an important task to keep the Distance Education activity flow stable in order to have successful educational processes and obtain desired objectives easily. At this point, some intelligent management or control models can be designed and developed by researchers. In this sense, this task can also be associated with the trend of "Design and Development of Intelligent Decision Making Systems" (which was previously explained).

IDEAS ON FUTURE POSSIBILITIES

Previous titles have focused on giving some brief information on application trends that can be examined within the intersection of Artificial Intelligence and Distance Education. It is clear that these trends may give us some ideas about future possibilities and enable readers to have more idea about potentials of the intersection occurred between Artificial Intelligence and Distance Education.

We can express some ideas on future possibilities as follows:

- As a result of improvement in communication and computer technologies, both mobile technology and Internet technology have a great impact in today's life standards. It is also important that these technologies are well-structured platforms for performing Artificial Intelligence supported Distance Education activities effectively. It can be expressed that the influence of these technologies will continue in the future making intelligent Distance Education software solutions more popular and effective in terms of educational activities.
- Educational activities performed in especially Distance Education approach are connected with many different factors that should be taken into consideration in order to provide well-defined, effective educational experiences. In the future, more factors regarding to the Distance Education will be taken into consideration by the Artificial Intelligence field; in order to remove limitations of the related factors and making the educational processes more stable.
- As it is known, today's popular Distance Education technique: e-learning can be divided into many different sub-subjects like Web based learning, or m-learning; because of improvements in Internet and mobile technologies. In the future, developments of new and more advanced mobile devices will enable researchers to take using features and functions of such devices for deciding which Artificial Intelligence oriented approaches, methods, or techniques will be effective on ensuring the desired intelligent educational tools – materials – software systems.

- Like any other fields, Artificial Intelligence field has a dynamic and rapidly changing structure, which is highly sensitive against improvements and developments occurred in time. Because of this, there will always be a continuing effort on designing new Artificial Intelligence techniques in order to solve real world based problems, or provide more effective solutions for already solved ones. At this point, new techniques will be applied in also education field (and also in Distance Education) in order to provide effective solutions and improve the related literature.
- Importance of the education increases in time as a result of growing needs for reaching to the wanted information and sharing it rapidly. So, more resources for newer research works in education field are activated in order to ensure strong enough approaches. In this sense, there will be more need for employing Artificial Intelligence oriented things in future works within the education field. In the future, there may be some works to design specific Artificial Intelligence techniques that can be used for only educational aims. It is also possible to express that a special sub-research area regarding to educational researches may be formed under the Artificial Intelligence field.

CONCLUSION

In this chapter, intersection of Artificial Intelligence and Distance Education has been taken into consideration and a brief report on current trends and application orientations has provided. Additionally, some ideas on future possibilities have also been expressed in order to enable readers to have more idea about the related subject. As it was indicated under the first section, the chapter can be accepted as an essential reference point to the start of the book: "Artificial Intelligence Applications in Distance Education".

By taking the current conditions into consideration and strong aspects of both Artificial Intelligence and Distance Education, we can clearly express that the popularity of Artificial Intelligence applications within Distance Education processes will continue in a rapidly improving way. Because Distance Education employs the most remarkable and recent educational techniques associated with the communication and computer technologies, the application potentials of this approach will be constant. On the other hand, the Artificial Intelligence will also have an extremely important, constant role on changing the nature of the world with intelligent systems; by affecting almost every fields including the education field.

REFERENCES

Berkeley, I. S. N. (1997). *What is artificial intelligence?*. Retrieved from http://www.ucs.louisiana.edu/~isb9112/dept/phil341/wisai/WhatisAI.html

Cortes, C., & Vapnik, V. (1995). Support-vector network. *Machine Learning, 20*, 1–25. doi:10.1007/BF00994018

Elmas, Ç. (2003). *Artificial neural network – theory, architecture, training, implementation <> Yapay sinir ağları – teori, mimari, eğitim, uygulama*. Ankara, Turkey: Seçkin Press. (In Turkish)

Greenberg, G. (1998). Distance education technologies: Best practices for K-12 settings. *IEEE Technology and Society Magazine, 17*(4), 36–40. doi:10.1109/44.735862

Jones, G. (1998). Genetic and Evolutionary Algorithms. In Encyclopedia of Computational Chemistry, (pp. 1-10). Academic Press.

Kaya, Z. (2002). *Distance Education*. Ankara: PegemA.

Keegan, D. (2004). *Foundations of Distance Education*. New York: Routledge.

Köse, U., & Deperlioğlu, Ö. (2010). An educational, virtual laboratory system for fuzzy logic. In *Proceedings of International Symposium on Computing in Science and Engineering 2010* (pp. 1335-1342). Aydın, Turkey: Gediz University.

McCarthy, J. (2007). *What is artificial intelligence.* Retrieved from http://www-formal.stanford.edu/jmc/whatisai.html

Passerini, K., & Granger, M. J. (2000). A developmental model for distance learning using the internet. *Computers & Education, 34*(1), 1–15. doi:10.1016/S0360-1315(99)00024-X

Technopedia. (2014). *Artificial Intelligence (AI).* Retrieved from http://www.techopedia.com/definition/190/artificial-intelligence-ai

Uğur, A., & Kınacı, A. C. (2006). *Classification of web pages by using artificial intelligence techniques and artificial neural networks <> Yapay zeka teknikleri ve yapay sinir ağları kullanilarak web sayfalarinin siniflandirilmasi*. Ankara, Turkey: Inet-TR. (In Turkish)

Support Vector Machine. (2013). In *Wikipedia*. Retrieved from http://en.wikipedia.org/wiki/Support_vector_machine

Yang, C.-S. (2011). *Nature-inspired metaheuristic algorithms*. Frome, UK: Luniver Press.

Zadeh, L. A. (1965). Fuzzy sets. *Information and Control, 8*(3), 338–353. doi:10.1016/S0019-9958(65)90241-X

ADDITIONAL READING

Baker, M. J. (2000). The roles of models in Artificial Intelligence and Education research: a prospective view. *Journal of Artificial Intelligence in Education, 11*, 122–143.

Borkar, S., & Rajeswari, K. (2014). Attributes Selection for Predicting Students' Academic Performance using Education Data Mining and Artificial Neural Network. *International Journal of Computers and Applications*, 86.

Brusilovsky, P. (1999). Adaptive and intelligent technologies for web-based eduction. *KI, 13*(4), 19-25.

Brusilovsky, P., & Peylo, C. (2003). Adaptive and intelligent web-based educational systems. *International Journal of Artificial Intelligence in Education, 13*(2), 159–172.

Carbonell, J. R. (1970). AI in CAI: An artificial-intelligence approach to computer-assisted instruction. *Man-Machine Systems. IEEE Transactions on, 11*(4), 190–202.

Casey, D. M. (2008). A Journey to Legitimacy: The Historical Development of Distance Education through Technology. *TechTrends, 52*(2), 45–51. doi:10.1007/s11528-008-0135-z

Chakraborty, U. K., Konar, D., Roy, S., & Choudhury, S. (2014). Intelligent fuzzy spelling evaluator for e-Learning systems. *Education and Information Technologies*, 1–14.

Charniak, E., Riesbeck, C. K., McDermott, D. V., & Meehan, J. R. (2014). *Artificial intelligence programming*. Psychology Press.

Cheng, P., Zhao, K., Xu, W., & Li, Y. (2014, January). Research on Personalized Mathematics Intelligent Tutoring System. In *Proceedings of the 2012 International Conference on Cybernetics and Informatics* (pp. 615-622). Springer New York.

Dede, C. (1996). The evolution of distance education: Emerging technologies and distributed learning. *American Journal of Distance Education, 10*(2), 4–36. doi:10.1080/08923649609526919

Devedžić, V. (2004). Web intelligence and artificial intelligence in education. *Journal of Educational Technology & Society, 7*(4), 29–39.

Fadzil, M., & Munira, T. A. (2008, August). Applications of Artificial Intelligence in an Open and Distance Learning institution. In *Information Technology, 2008. ITSim 2008. International Symposium on* (Vol. 1, pp. 1-7). IEEE.

Feldman, J., Monteserin, A., & Amandi, A. (2014). Detecting students' perception style by using games. *Computers & Education, 71*, 14–22. doi:10.1016/j.compedu.2013.09.007

Garrett, B. M., & Roberts, G. (2004). Employing Intelligent and Adaptive Methods for Online Learning. In C. Ghaoui (Ed.), *E-Education Applications: Human Factors and Innovative Approaches* (pp. 208–219). Pennsylvania: Information Science Publishing. doi:10.4018/978-1-93177-792-6.ch012

Garrison, D. R. (1985). Three generations of technological innovations in distance education. *Distance Education, 6*(2), 235–241. doi:10.1080/0158791850060208

Gregg, D. G. (2007). E-learning agents. *The Learning Organization, 14*(4), 300–312. doi:10.1108/09696470710749245

Keegan, D. (1996). *Foundations of distance education*. Psychology Press.

Kerka, S. (1996). *Distance Learning, the Internet, and the World Wide Web*. ERIC Digest.

Kotsiantis, S., Pierrakeas, C., & Pintelas, P. (2004). Predicting students' performance in distance learning using machine learning techniques. *Applied Artificial Intelligence, 18*(5), 411–426. doi:10.1080/08839510490442058

Marković, M., Kostić Kovačević, I., Nikolić, O., & Nikolić, B. (2014). INSOS—educational system for teaching intelligent systems. *Computer Applications in Engineering Education*. doi:10.1002/cae.21595

Moore, M. G., & Kearsley, G. (2011). *Distance education: A systems view of online learning.* Cengage Learning.

Muggleton, S. (2014). Alan Turing and the development of Artificial Intelligence. *AI Communications*, 27(1), 3–10.

Pelton, J. N. (1990). Technology and Education: Friends or Foes?.

Qiao, Z. F., Guo, J. X., & Zhao, J. C. (2014). Research on Web Application Technology in Distance Education Personalized Recommendation System. *Advanced Materials Research*, 859, 416–421. doi:10.4028/www.scientific.net/AMR.859.416

Russell, S. J., Norvig, P., Canny, J. F., Malik, J. M., & Edwards, D. D. (1995). *Artificial intelligence: a modern approach* (Vol. 2). Englewood Cliffs: Prentice hall.

Schmidt, C. T., Cottier, P., & Choquet, C. (2004). Learning with the Artificial Sciences: A Paradigmatic Shift. *Proceedings of the 18th World Congress on Computing (WCC–2004 HCE).*

Shoham, Y. (1993). Agent-oriented programming. *Artificial Intelligence*, 60(1), 51–92. doi:10.1016/0004-3702(93)90034-9

Van Eck, R. (2007). Building artificially intelligent learning games. *Games and simulations in online learning: Research and development frameworks*, 271-307.

Verduin, J. R., & Clark, T. A. (1991). Distance education: The foundations of effective practice.

Xu, H. (2014, January). Studies on the Key Technologies of the Intelligent Database in the Distance Education System. In *Proceedings of the 2012 International Conference on Cybernetics and Informatics* (pp. 765-770). Springer New York.

Zhao, M., Ni, W., Zhang, H., Lin, Z., & Yang, Y. (2014). A Knowledge-Based Teaching Resources Recommend Model for Primary and Secondary School Oriented Distance-Education Teaching Platform. In *Frontier and Future Development of Information Technology in Medicine and Education* (pp. 511–521). Springer Netherlands. doi:10.1007/978-94-007-7618-0_50

KEY TERMS AND DEFINITIONS

Artificial Intelligence: (1) A term that is used to describe the feature, function or characteristic of computer systems or machines that try to simulate human-thinking behavior or human intelligence. (2) A field of Computer Science, which is based on research studies or developments on providing intelligent systems simulating the human-thinking behavior or human intelligence.

Distance Education: An educational approach, which allows individuals to experience educational processes via some communication and computer technology based materials; from anywhere, on anytime.

Intelligent Decision Making Systems: Artificial Intelligence based decision making system, which users can receive immediate feedback in the time of making critical – strategic decisions.

Intelligent Learning Environments: A form of computer software, which employs Artificial Intelligence based programs for different learning (e-learning) activities.

Intelligent System: A term that is used to define a system, which was designed and developed based on Artificial Intelligence approach(es), method(s) or technique(s).

Intelligent Tutoring System: An Artificial Intelligence based computer software, which provides immediate and customized feedbacks to students – learners.

Chapter 2
Global Knowledge Networking (GKN) with Utilizing of Digital Libraries:
A Proposed Model

Azadeh Heidari
Islamic Azad University, Iran

Leila Nemati-Anaraki
Islamic Azad University, Iran

ABSTRACT

In Digital Libraries (DLs) as an innovative community environment, knowledge is nutrition, and the environment for knowledge sharing is the essential condition. As the knowledge is the heart of digital libraries, it is imperative for them to promote the innovation activities embodied by teaching and scientific research through an efficient knowledge-sharing environment. In digital environment, the role of knowledge has become even more significant. Moreover, DLs perform many knowledge-based activities, and by nature, the knowledge-sharing process is embedded in DL systems. These modern knowledge management environments need modern technologies in order to perform properly for end users and online researchers. Therefore, the aim of this chapter is to provide a model for global knowledge networking with utilizing digital libraries and artificial intelligence. The specific objectives are to describe a framework of digital libraries and concepts of Knowledge Management (KM). The chapter finds some significant overlaps between DLs and KM and integrates the knowledge-sharing process with DLs and artificial intelligence. The integration of KM and knowledge sharing can add value to develop a global knowledge networking process model so users around the globe can make use of this knowledge transmission.

INTRODUCTION

The digital revolution of the past few decades has had a radical impact on library practices in collecting, organizing, storing, retrieving, and disseminating information globally. With the advent and widespread use of computers, expert systems, and new artificial intelligence, libraries are now transforming their information handling activities into digital format. Nowadays, different

DOI: 10.4018/978-1-4666-6276-6.ch002

phrases have appeared in the literature to describe the changing face of a library in the context of the adoption of technological innovations in library practices (Harter, 1997).

Developments in digital technologies and interoperability of systems enable cross-sectoral participation and harvesting of metadata, while the internet provides the delivery mechanism. Nowadays, organizations have encouraged creating digital material and converting existing material into digital format (Kumar, 2010).

On the other hand, digital library provides an excellent opportunity to widely disseminate our documentary heritage and greatly increase access to library collections as well as current research literature (Das, Sen, & Dutta, 2010). However, libraries provide knowledge to people, their role in the progress process is apparent. Libraries, especially digital libraries, plan to meet the information and knowledge needs of communities so; library managers and librarians increasingly accept the importance of knowledge for development. The role of knowledge and information on the day-to-day life of people is distinguished and digital libraries are more required.

The overwhelming growth of DLs has opened up new horizons in library and information science, addressing core requirements of the information age and the world of information technology, as well as new sub-areas like knowledge management. In digital environment, the role of knowledge has become even more significant. These modern knowledge management environments need modern technologies in order to perform properly for end- users and online researchers, so Knowledge sharing is seen as a central concept of KM, which focuses more attention on tacit knowledge. The tacit knowledge can be communicated through interaction, collaboration, and conversations in communities/networks of practice. Many approaches exist on which models of both DLs and KM have been built, but an integrated model of KM process and as a result, global knowledge networking with utilizing DLs and artificial intelligence can rarely be found in the literature. Some

works have focused on KM issues in DL, but they do not represent the central theme of the present work (e.g. Chen, 1999; Rydberg-Cox et al., 2000; Hicks and Tochtermann, 2001).

Digital libraries and knowledge management are innovations, the implementation of which is still nascent in developing countries. However, they hold the promise of becoming key technologies for knowledge creation and management in the future (Upadhyay & Moni, 2010).

Bhatt (2010) believes that: "when libraries turn out to be hub of development activities, they cease to be silent, serious reading/learning centers. Librarians alone cannot organize the wide range of extension activities and outreach services. The development of information activities cannot succeed unless people own them. On the other hand, librarians need to be multi skilled. Besides, knowledge sharing has to be promoted in the libraries by outreach activities".

DIGITAL LIBRARIES

Digital libraries can be studied from different point of views. These libraries may include as new forms of information centers, information retrieving systems, and information supporting systems. Digital libraries can also control new technologies in order to direct information resources, electronic emission, long distance education, and other activities.

From various definitions, we may conclude that the unique characteristics of digital libraries include: mass storage of information resources, information resources in diversified media, network transmission of information resources, distributed information resources management, highly shared information resources, intelligent retrieval technologies, and information services without space and time limitations (Zhou, 2005).

Digital libraries, as an organized collection of digital information are transferring information services into knowledge services in order to deliver better services to the knowledge society.

Therefore, despite knowledge sharing and knowledge management, they should make use of proper technologies.

In 1965, J.C.R. Licklider coined the phrase ''library of the future'' to refer to his vision of a fully computer-based library, and ten years later, F.W. Lancaster wrote of the soon-to-come "paperless library" (Harter, 1997). Nowadays, phrases like "virtual library", "electronic library", "library without walls", "internet library", "digital library" etc. have appeared in the literature to describe the changing face of a library in the context of the adoption of technological innovations in library practices. Although these terms are often used interchangeably, they are distinct from one another. Being emerged in the 1990s, the concept of digital libraries has become very popular among the disciplines of computer science, cognitive science, and library and information science (LIS).

Fox and Urs (2002) describe building blocks of DLs emphasizing which parts are "digital" vs. "library". Of the six parts, computing and networking belong to "digital" while collections, services and community are related to "library", and content shares the common aspects of both the terms. A conceptual framework for DL systems as described by Del Bimbo, Gradmann, & Ioannidis (2004) consists of three major layers: contents, management, and usage. As a core system, management is responsible for the management of the contents and for providing the necessary functionality. Being the user interaction component, usage deals with all aspects of the interface between the users and the systems.

use but not for sale". In effect, it is an institution oriented towards collections and custody, where people may make use of the facilities. Whereas a digital library is an assemblage of digital computing, storage, and communications machinery together with the content and software needed to reproduce, emulate and extend the services provided by conventional libraries. In other words, a digital library is a computer–based system for acquiring, storing, organizing, searching and distributing digital materials for end user access. It is not just a collection of material in electronic form; it includes a browser interface and perhaps a virtual space and society. It requires less space and the data can be made available through communication networks to anyone anywhere, while facilitating searches with speed. The digital is not a single entity and as such is linked to the resources of many such collections (Vasupongayya et al., 2011; Sun & Yuan, 2012).

Digital libraries will also include digital materials that exist outside the physical and administrative bounds of any one. Digital library, will serve particular communities or constituencies, as traditional libraries do now, though those communities may be widely dispersed throughout the network, and will require both the skills of librarians and well as those of computer scientists to be viable (Warr & Hangsing, 2009). Definition of digital library involves three key components, which constitute the theoretical framework underlying digital libraries, namely: (1) People, (2) Information resources, and (3) Technology (Sun & Yuan, 2012).

CHARACTERISTICS OF DIGITAL LIBRARIES

All conventional libraries basic functions focus on collection, organization, and dissemination of information resources. Traditionally a "library is a place in which books, manuscripts, musical scores, or other literary and artistic materials are kept for

FUNCTIONS OF DIGITAL LIBRARIES

The rapid development of the internet in the 1990s and its embrace by the library and information community enabled the concept of the digital libraries, whose function can be defined as the collection, storage, and processing of vast information and knowledge into a systemic project through digitalization and the internet, while providing convenient and highly efficient retrieval and inquiry services. To this effect, at a minimum, the core services expected of a digital library system includes a repository service for storing and managing digital objects; a search service to facilitate information discovery; and a user interface through which end-users interact with the digital objects. The introduction of the DL has raised library modernization to a new level with over time (Sun & Yuan, 2012).

Digital libraries promise new societal benefits, starting with the elimination of the time and space constraints of traditional bricks-and-mortar libraries. Unlike libraries that occupy buildings accessible only to those who walk through their doors, digital libraries reside on inter-networked data storage and computing systems that can be accessed by people located anywhere. At their full potential digital libraries will enable any citizen to access a considerable proportion of all human knowledge from any location. From an access vantage, the Internet provides a preview of the possibilities (Jadhav, 2011).

The role of a digital library is essential to collect, manage, preserve, and make accessible digital objects. The following are some of the functions of digital libraries:

1. To provide a friendly interface to users;
2. To avail network facilities;
3. To support library functions;
4. To enhance advanced search, access and retrieval of information;
5. To improve the library operations;
6. To enable one to perform searches that is not practical manually;
7. To protect owners of information;
8. To preserve a unique collection through digitization (Lee King, 2009).

THE WORKING CONTENT OF DIGITAL LIBRARIES

In the information age, the role of librarians is changing gradually. They will develop forward to be the information navigators and information experts in the society. Accordingly, compared with the traditional librarians, their work contents are very different. What digital librarians mainly do are as follows:

- Select, acquire, preserve, organize, and manage digital collections;
- Design the technical architecture of digital library;
- Describe the content and attributes of items (metadata);
- Plan, implement, and support digital services such as information navigation,
- Consultation and transmit services;
- Establish friendly user interface over the network;
- Set up relative standards and policies for the digital library;
- Design, maintain, and transmit added value information products;
- Protect digital intellectual property in network environment; and
- Insure information security (Zhou, 2005).

THE SERVICE MODE OF THE DIGITAL LIBRARIANS

No matter what the library will develop into, its target to meet the increasing information and knowledge requirements of humans will remain unchanged. In the digital libraries, digital librarians will provide readers with various, dynamic, and advanced services in the initiative and innovative pattern, including:

- Analyzing and processing different kind of information resources;
- Activating and finding potential value hid in any information;
- Providing added valued information products and services at the right time and right place; and
- Finding the right users for information and provide personalized and tailored services (Zhou, 2005).

DIGITAL LIBRARIAN'S INTERFACE FUNCTIONS AND ROLES IN THE MANAGEMENT OF DLs

A fundamental role of digital librarian in digital libraries is to act as an intermediary, who brings together users and information (Figure 1). Digital library access tools are the right set of tools used in novel ways to tackle a plethora of challenges and opportunities for information access technology and faster access. There is a variety of information retrieval techniques, including metadata searching, and full-text document searching. In knowing what

can or cannot be retrieved from the digital library information sources, the digital librarian acts as an expert in the acquisition of digital information (Figure 2).

The method used to store, find, and retrieve digital information from digital libraries is called the access method. The technology used to access information digitally provides "navigation paths or digital library access tools" through the digital information system (Sreenivasulu, 2000).

DLs provide high quality and well-organized information. Many of the powerful characteristics of DLs rely on metadata. Librarians describe the resources of catalogues and other collections through metadata in order to facilitate efficient delivery of information (Garcia- Crespo, 2011).

KNOWLEDGE MANAGEMENT

Different disciplines use the term "knowledge" to denote different things, and so defining it precisely and exactly is not so easy. According to Drucker (1999), knowledge is personal and intangible in nature, whereas information is tangible and avail-

Figure 1. Digital librarian`s interface functions, skills, roles in the management of DLs (Sreenivasulu, 2000)

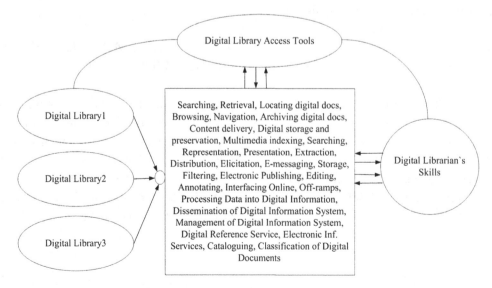

Figure 2. Digital information access and retrieval (Sreenivasulu, 2000)

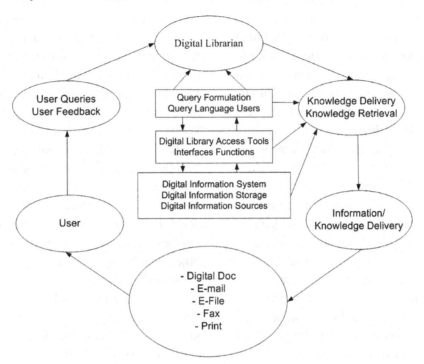

able to anyone who cares to seek it out. Davenport and Prusak (1998) define knowledge as a fluid mix of framed experience, values, contextual information, and expert insight that provides a framework for evaluating and incorporating new experiences and information. They further mention that in organizations, knowledge often becomes embedded not only in documents or repositories, but also in organizational routines, processes, practices, and norms. Within the field of KM, knowledge has broadly been categorized as explicit and tacit. Very simply, explicit knowledge is described as documented or codified knowledge while tacit knowledge is non-documented or non-codified one. According to Polanyi (1966), tacit knowledge is personal, context-specific, and therefore hard to formalize and communicate. Explicit knowledge, on the other hand, refers to knowledge that is transmittable in formal, systematic language. Nonaka (1991) also distinguishes between explicit and tacit knowledge as: "explicit knowledge is formal and systematic. For this reason, it can be easily communicated and shared, in product specifications, a scientific formula, or a computer program. Tacit knowledge is highly personal. It is hard to formalize and therefore difficult, if not impossible, to communicate".

Nonaka and Takeuchi (1995) define KM as the capability of an organization to create new knowledge, disseminate it throughout the organization, and embody it in products, services, and systems. A comprehensive idea about KM has been given by Davenport and prusak (1998) as ". . . is concerned with the exploitation and development of the knowledge assets of an organization with a view to furthering the organization's objectives. The knowledge to be managed includes both explicit, documented knowledge, and tacit, subjective knowledge. Management entails all of those processes associated with the identifying, sharing, and creating of knowledge. This requires systems for the creation and maintenance of knowledge repositories, and to cultivate and facilitate the sharing of knowledge and organizational learning".

As a business concept, KM emerged during the mid-1990s and received considerable attention from many scholars and practitioners. A number of fields associated with information systems, business and management, LIS, computer science, communications, have practiced KM etc. Wen (2005) describes its emergence first in the business sector, then in higher education, and now in library management. Although the emergence of KM can be traced to only last decade, Hawkins (2000) claims that for many in the academic world, KM is an old concept, a function historically performed by librarians. Broadbent (1998), on the other hand, mentions that KM is not about managing or organizing books or journals, searching the internet for clients or arranging for the circulation of materials, rather she considers these activities as parts of KM spectrum and processes in some way. KM in its simplest sense, can be described as the management of both explicit (recorded) and tacit knowledge.

The new knowledge management is a name for debates, models and actions that cause the spread of the knowledge management area in sharing, prevailing, knowledge recovering, and harmonizing organizational knowledge like creating or developing of knowledge (Beyadar & Gardali, 2011).

In the Libraries, especially digital ones, Knowledge Management is a process of creation, organization, diffusion (transition of knowledge), use and exploitation of knowledge (McInerney, 2002). Therefore, libraries as knowledge institutions are one of the important knowledge assets in our society. The core is knowledge sharing, which is the chief condition for innovation activities.

KNOWLEDGE MANAGEMENT AND DIGITAL LIBRARIES

Knowledge management as the need of nowadays organizations is indispensable, so our movement toward management must be predetermined and preplanned.

Whether inside of the organization or outside, the knowledge base in virtual organizations are more developed and spread out in comparison with the other organization (Beyadar & Gardali, 2011).

Digital libraries based on creation and use of knowledge, globalization, successful innovation, and share the best operation can perform a proper knowledge management process.

Knowledge Management has rapidly moved beyond the stage of a fad and established itself as a key part of many libraries' knowledge strategy. Knowledge management is not a technical project. It is driven by business objectives to create business value, and technology must meet these objectives (Gartner, 2002).

Knowledge management has emerged today as a multidisciplinary subject. The objective of knowledge management in libraries is to promote knowledge innovation. Nemati-Anaraki and Heidari (2011) offered that: "Digital libraries provide knowledge highways through the web so, their role toward a knowledge management is critical. Not only the digital library must be seen as merely a digitized collection of information objects, but also it must be seen as an environment bringing together collections, services, and people to support the full cycle of creation of data, information, and knowledge".

The purpose of knowledge management applications is to create, capture, organize, access, and use the intellectual assets of the organizations like digital libraries.

The new system integrated new components, such as a knowledge library, a forum for urgent requests, and platforms for knowledge sharing in order to gain not only explicit, but also especially tacit knowledge – which is the most important source of innovation – and to improve on the traditional knowledge repositories. The web-based knowledge library, composed of thousands of knowledge bids, is this knowledge system's central component. The bids are structured to categorize the experience gained from ongoing and completed projects. The "urgent request" platform is Share Net's second most important component. It allows a user to enter urgent questions that other users, who regularly scan through this forum to check if they are able to contribute their experience, will answer. Digital libraries could become knowledge repositories by effectively categorizing, analyzing, and organizing their contents. Some of the overlapping areas where DL and KM have opportunity to contribute to each other are: (Figure 3).

Objectives

The main objective of both DL and KM is as same as to provide users with access to knowledge resources. KM possesses information, technology, and management perspectives that can also be the basis for DL system.

Contents

Data, information, and knowledge are the main resources in DL as well as in KM. DL emphasizes on digitally coded articulated or explicit knowledge while KM focuses on both tacit and explicit knowledge either in digital or in physical form.

Figure 3. Significant overlaps between DL and KM

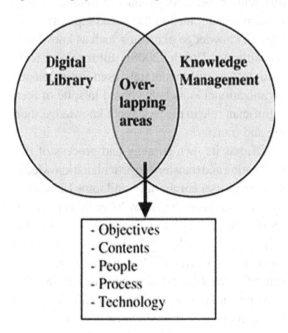

The tacit dimension of KM can contribute to DL in developing a mechanism for converting, storing, and sharing knowledge of internal staff of DL.

People

People (Users) are the key actors in the organizational processes and the main users of information and/or knowledge systems. People with the proper blend of technical, managerial, behavioral, cognitive, and interpersonal skills can play significant role in designing, operating, and maintaining a DL and a KM system. End users need to be trained and skilled in both the cases.

Process

KM encompasses a number of sub-processes like knowledge creation process, knowledge collection and storage process, content management process, knowledge update process etc. Both KM and DL can share almost same mechanism of life cycle process of information/knowledge. They follow the same procedure of acquisition, processing, organization, storage, retrieval and dissemination of information and/or knowledge for its proper utilization.

Technology

DL system integrates a wide range of computing and communication technologies including more advanced and fast processing digital technologies, digital repositories, information retrieval engines, document management systems, electronic publishing systems, web-based technologies like internet, intranets, extranets etc. These technologies are more or less concerned to KM system along with group wares, collaborative tools, knowledge portals, knowledge creation technologies etc. Some important tools and techniques like indexing, taxonomies, codification, metadata, data mining, database management, knowledge mapping techniques etc. are being used in DL and in KM for the management of contents and their retrieval (Roknuzzaman, Kanai, & Umemoto, 2009).

The concept of KM would be less powerful for organizations without knowledge-oriented technologies. Technology's most valuable role in KM is extending the reach and enhancing the speed of knowledge transfer. Knowledge engineering, digital networks, the internet and intranets are not KM but only enabling technologies for managing knowledge. KM technology enables users to simultaneously access internet sites, databases, intranets, and other internal/external resources as if the information existed in a single location. Improved collaborative technologies enhance person-to-person communication, thus helping in the development of knowledge across organizational and geographical boundaries (Ghosh & Jambekar, 2003).

KNOWLEDGE SHARING SYSTEMS AND DIGITAL LIBRARIES

Knowledge provides a template or guideline for decisions and actions. For the knowledge-based company, managing organizational knowledge is a way of establishing a competitive advantage. Knowledge sharing is central to this goal (Kimblea & Bourdonb, 2008). Knowledge sharing is not only the biggest challenge and obstacle in knowledge management, but also the most important factor in measuring the performance of the knowledge management or organizational learning. Within an organization, knowledge sharing can be done through informal, unsystematic, and non-daily routines (Zahra, Neubaum, & Larrañeta, 2007). Knowledge sharing is the process of being aware of knowledge needs and making knowledge available to others by constructing and providing technical and systematic infrastructure. Numerous studies have addressed issues related to knowledge sharing at various levels within organizations and between types of organizations (Kim & Ju, 2008). Lee (2001) defined knowledge sharing as activities

of transferring or disseminating knowledge from one person, group or organization to another. Bartol and Srivastava (2002) defined knowledge sharing as individuals sharing organizationally relevant information, skills, opinions, ideas, and suggestions with one another. Song (2001) noted that through efficient and effective knowledge sharing, organizations are able to increase innovating and creativity, increasing profit and reducing costs, and reducing risks due to uncertainty (yeh, et al., 2011).

Bou-Llusar and Segarra-Cipres (2006) discuss that firms like to achieve knowledge from external sources rather than internally because external knowledge seems to be rare and unique. Goh (2002) explores a conceptual framework to explain how effective knowledge transfer can be managed. Pérez-Nordtvedt, et al. (2008), suggest that the attractiveness of external knowledge is a key factor that contributes to the effectiveness for transferring of knowledge between organizations.

Knowledge sharing as a kind of networked activity is depends on technology and IT. They are important tools in Knowledge sharing, as information systems (IS) and ICTs can be used to synthesize and facilitate KS within or between different organizations (Alavi & Leidner, 2001). Employees can enter both tacit and explicit knowledge in knowledge platforms such as knowledge repositories (Busch, 2008). Information technologies are still moderately used for increasing organizational knowledge based in spite of their significant role in the process of knowledge sharing and transfer.

DL has its own strategy and process of disseminating and transferring articulated knowledge items to its user community, and some LIS people perceive this process as knowledge sharing. In this sense, knowledge sharing is not a new for DL, but it is much more than knowledge dissemination process of DL. Knowledge sharing is seen as a central concept of KM, which focuses more attention on tacit knowledge. The tacit knowledge can be communicated through interaction, collaboration, and conversations in communities/networks of practice. The introduction of KM provides DL an opportunity to promote a collaborative, innovative, and knowledge-sharing culture.

The term of Knowledge sharing aims to do something useful with knowledge and enhance knowledge sharing is made in two paradigms: one paradigm is to manage existing knowledge, which includes the development of knowledge repositories (memos, reports, articles, and reports), knowledge compilation, etc. Another paradigm is to manage knowledge-specific activities, that is, knowledge acquisitions, creation, distribution, communication, sharing, and application (SKyrme, 2000). Knowledge management consists of the administration of knowledge assets of an organization and sharing and enlargement of those assets.

Today, the aim of KM in digital era is connecting researchers in network communities to establish new relationship and gain experience. A full-fledged the knowledge-networked society implies that every researcher has an access to the network that is an essential infrastructural facility. A knowledge-networked society should pose no trans-border barriers and be able to communicate knowledge in any format. To enhance knowledge sharing, it is important to manage technology, which Artificial Intelligence (A.I) and Expert Systems (E.S) are as tools for building the systems.

Technology has taken a leading role in the course of library, development history, from automating, digitizing, and networking. Libraries, especially DLs should be made better use of technology to accelerate the system and then with the use of these technologies (A.I and E.S), we can find, create and package the knowledge as it is shown in the Figure 4:

As mentioned before, we implement the knowledge management techniques in order to manage our knowledge, so in digital environment, we need modern technologies to perform knowledge management. Artificial intelligence is one of these unique and effective tools for managing our knowledge.

For establishing an efficient digital library environment, many high technologies will be used including data warehousing, data mining, text mining, knowledge extracting, knowledge mapping[1], and information visualizing etc. Besides, in order to grasp extended contents or knowledge, resource description framework (RDF) should be prepared and markup language will be the choice for this aim, and semantic web pages will be useful for understanding of knowledge (Shuchun, 2002). AI system is one of the basic and modern tools for integrating technology and knowledge managing processes in digital environment, in order to deliver proper knowledge to proper user.

Figure 4. A part of knowledge management system perspective (Adopted from Meso & Smith, 2000), Quoted in Setiarso, 2009, p. 506

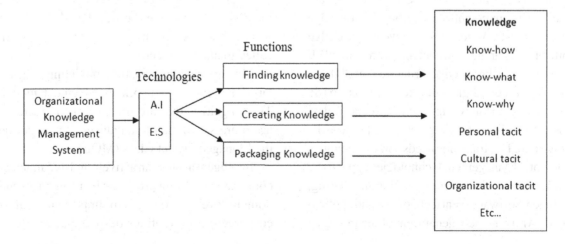

ARTIFICIAL INTELLIGENCE

Intelligent agents belong to artificial intelligence area that promises tremendous potential in all areas of life. Intelligent agents can be broadly defined as a software entity that carries out some set of operations on behalf of a user or another program with some degree of independence or autonomy (Lohani & Jeevan, 2007). In general, agents can be defined as programs that perform tasks such as retrieving and delivering information and automating repetitive tasks.

We can make use of knowledge technology to discover the tacit knowledge. Strong analysis and derivative capability are the main characteristics of knowledge services. One of these powerful services performs by AI systems.

To success of knowledge services depends on its use of knowledge technology, while the knowledge repository focuses on the gathering, creating, and storing of large volumes of knowledge, the on-line analytical processing (OALP) tools provide the means to manipulate and analyze the knowledge. On one hand, new approaches in artificial intelligence help to develop and refine new insights into collected knowledge. A web-based repository can lift knowledge content clearly into a web based knowledge unit database that can link with others and using intelligence tools can mine tacit knowledge from a lot of explicit information.

On the other hand, to meet user's needs, professional information services should focus on identifying, analyzing, and coordinating the needs of various potential user groups. Knowledge services must do their best to reveal knowledge from different angles and contents in order to fulfill every person`s knowledge structure (Ju, 2006).

In this respect, digital libraries need some basic tools in order to knowledge their contents. Today, DLs have truly become a gateway to the world's knowledge. This transition needs new technologies to operate. Management technologies expand the frontiers of knowledge representation and sharing, intelligent software agent technology, and application of AI, is the new generation of technology.

INTELLIGENT AGENT AND INTELLIGENT MANAGEMENT NETWORKS

Nowadays, distributing intelligent management networks is viewed as one of the fastest growing areas of research and new application development in network management. There are other researchers for these topics, but none in terms of normalization of the knowledge of the intelligent agents. Typical work in related fields includes intelligent agents such as Yang & Chang (2011), who present a system to collect information through the cooperation of intelligent agent software, in addition to provide warnings after analysis to monitor and predict some possible error indications among controlled objects in the network.

INTELLIGENT AGENT STRUCTURE

A managed object can be viewed as a mediator between the network management interface and the hardware. In other words, an intelligent agent is a managed object situated within and a part of an environment, which senses that environment and acts on it, over time, in pursuit of its own knowledge agenda and to execute autonomous management actions. Our essential idea behind network management is the possibility of the intelligent agent to exist in different heterogeneous networks. In fact, we may consider an intelligent agent as a category of managed objects. Then, intelligent agents may be developed as if they would be always on the same resource network called managed object.

Management information modeling plays a large part in this network management model. The languages that are the easiest to create an agent are specification languages, which define the Managed Object Class (MOC).

Intelligent agents can actively and dynamically cooperate in solving problems by using task- and domain-level protocols. An important goal is convergence on solutions despite incomplete or inconsistent knowledge or data. It stands on three essential properties:

- Autonomy or self-government independence: The intelligent agent decides when and under which condition he/she will perform what actions. The autonomy is explicitly required not only as property, but as also as reactive, proactive, and cooperative behavior.
- Communication, which is the ability to speak with a peer, with humans (through an interface agent), or with devices.
- Cooperating agents are collaborative when they are able to work together (Martin et al., 2012).

AI AND DIGITAL LIBRARIES

As mentioned before, DLs are one of the most active areas of research and development in modern library science to match the improvements in technology and never-ending demand for information in a form that is easily accessible by users. An automated classification and search programs are critical to digital libraries. Users need a way of filtering this data into a more manageable situation and will be at odds in identifying the useful references from the mass of documents available. However, having agents to perform tasks like searching and filtering can ultimately reduce the information overload to a degree. Based on a customized user profile (either input by the user or create by a program which has studied and learned about the user), intelligent agents can search on subjects of interests to a user and sort and present the resulting information. Further, intelligent agents can be used to provide in-context guidance and advice to searchers, to provide low-level reference assistance, and to instruct users in using library resources, services, and applications.

Acting as an effective mediator between the searcher and information, the intelligent agent can provide:

- Assistance with database selection;
- Automated searching and retrieval of information based on users queries;
- Assistance with query structuring (for example matching users terms to controlled vocabularies, subheadings, and thesaurus terms, suggesting similar concepts or terms);
- Assistance with strategy modification; and
- Assistance with the interpretation of sorting and search results.

Agents are also useful in identifying and selecting best databases that suits a particular search. The number of online databases has grown from several hundred to several thousand over the last ten years, which poses a problem to information specialists or end-users. Therefore, these intelligent agents can easily select the proper database and answer the query effectively (Lohani & Jeevan, 2007).

Knowledge management as disciplines draws from a broad spectrum of disciplines and technologies such as artificial intelligence, an expert system that help in automating the process of cognition. So global knowledge networking based on the digital libraries, knowledge management and artificial intelligence as a core of KM for better Knowledge Sharing is proposed.

PROPOSING THE MODEL FOR GLOBAL KNOWLEDGE NETWORKING BASED ON DLs AND AI

The vision of global knowledge networking (GNN) is to redefine the pattern, function, and responsibility of digital libraries, and to make warm, harmonious and cooperative knowledge sharing between them. It could promote communication, interaction, cooperation, learning, sharing, could transmit tacit knowledge to explicit one, and could be beneficial to knowledge depositing, storage, application, and innovation. The goal is to provide physical and virtual fields for communication and innovation to furnish abundant information resources, repository and knowledge navigation, to offer convenient internet and powerful computer equipment, to provide interactive virtual community and collaboration software, to furnish network digging and analyzing tools, to offer information and knowledge service interdisciplinary and cross-department, to provide training for information literacy, information fluency and special skills, and to promote culture of trust, collaboration and innovation, and so on. (Shuhuai et al., 2009).

Technology has revolutionized the concept of libraries. Networking and computing technologies have now become sufficiently advanced to allow the design and deployment of large digital libraries which are not only capable of supporting conventional end-user functions but also provide networked access to printed and non-printed materials, including images as well as audio and video files (ke & Hwang 2000).

Because of the digital nature, information resources can be shared over the powerful network. With the innovative use of information technology and the integration of many tools and techniques developed thus far in the near future, information provision can be more complete, faster and more broad-based. Information can be accessed anywhere, anytime by anyone who needs it. (Pandian & Karisiddappa, 2007). In addition, with the usage of knowledge management and knowledge sharing techniques and technology tools, like artificial intelligence and expert systems we can propose a global knowledge networking system.

In view of this perspective, the study develops an integrated framework of a DL system that can be evolved through the process of KM, KS and AI. As can be found from the study, the framework consists of three main separate layers (*Figure 5*): one is AI at the core of the model, the second layer is a digital library and the user, who make benefit from this GNN model, is located in the outer layer. KM and KS are transmitted around these three layers and this transmission makes benefit chain of knowledge and information. All

of the elements of a DL system have their own knowledge aspects, and as an integral part of DL, KM is embedded in DL system at any time and in any part. KM as a generic process refers to the acquisition, organization, storage, and retrieval, dissemination of knowledge and receiving relevant feed for further modification and adjustment. The KM process can suitably fit in DL environment, and hence, it is suggested to adopt this process for promoting DL a knowledge-enabled and knowledge-driven organization. On the other hand, for knowledge information, analyzing and delivering proper knowledge to proper online users, we need some technologies like AI. The model is expected to support innovation, sharing and socialization of knowledge and to enhance the effectiveness of global knowledge networking with proper utilization of both recorded knowledge and experience and expertise of the library. DLs thereby can be transformed into a more efficient knowledge sharing organization for its community establishing a knowledge link or knowledge networking within and outside the library. Thus, the study encourages DL practitioners to adopt KM process and AI techniques on which the entire DL system can be designed, operated, and maintained, and ultimately, values can be derived from the system.

CONCLUSION

In recent years, the network is composed of a massive data and information. This advancement brings many threats and opportunities. Preparing and diffusing of knowledge from various information resources and utilization of electronic knowledge sharing spheres is ideal. The constantly increasing number of knowledge resources is changing the forms of knowledge sharing channels especially on the internet so in this case digital libraries represent a new breed of software applications.

Figure 5. A global knowledge networking model based on DLs and AI (Inspired from Shuhuai et al., Conceptual model for Knowledge Commons (KC), 2009)

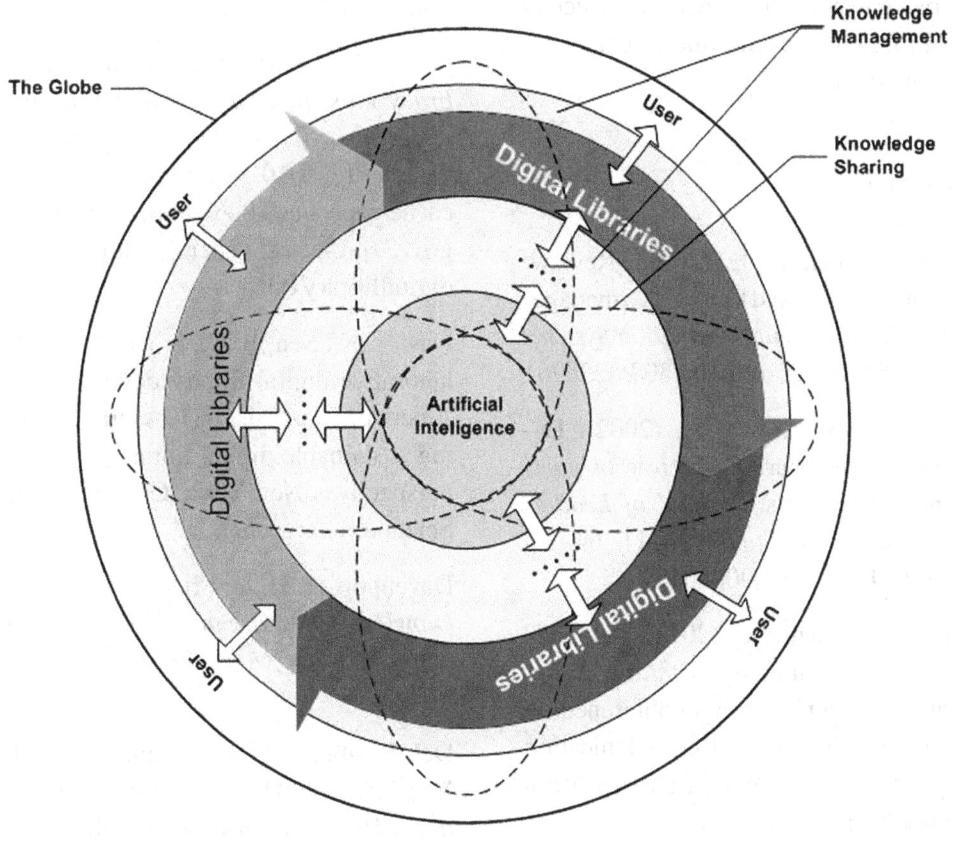

On the other hand, with the further growth of the artificial intelligence, and quicken the technological requirements, networks, and digital environments like digital libraries, users can easily make benefit from information services more efficient.

In order to promote efficient knowledge sharing activities in digital environment, the flow of data, information, and knowledge must be strengthened. Efficient knowledge management in digital space requires proper technological advancements with powerful infrastructure.

Digital libraries promise new societal benefits, starting with the elimination of the time and space. Digital libraries reside on inter-networked data storage and computing systems that can be accessed a considerable proportion of all human knowledge from any location (Sun & Yuan, 2012).

Knowledge management in digital libraries should be focused on effective research and development of knowledge, creation of knowledge bases and exchange and sharing of knowledge for online users. Knowledge has become important productive factor in the modern digital information systems, like digital libraries. Therefore, it is very essential to focus on knowledge management system in DLs by which the timely information services can be provided for online users.

Both KM and DL are closely allied in their objectives of satisfying users' needs, fundamental concepts of content management and the process of work. Utilizing from intelligent agents like artificial intelligence in these knowledge environments can promote DLs situation. DLs and KM are complemented to each other and with making use of information technologies like artificial intelligence; we can shape a global knowledge networking, where everybody from all over the globe, can make benefit of knowledge, which is transmitted in DLs, the environments which are equipped with AI technology.

REFERENCES

Alavi, M., & Leidner, D. E. (2001). Review: knowledge management and knowledge management systems. *Management Information Systems Quarterly, 25*(1), 107–136. doi:10.2307/3250961

Bartol, K. M., & Srivastava, A. (2002). Encouraging knowledge sharing: the role of organizational reward systems. *Journal of Leadership & Organizational Studies, 9*(1), 64–76. doi:10.1177/107179190200900105

Beyadar, H., & Gardali, K. (2011, October). *Knowledge management in organizations*. Paper presented at the 5th international conference on application of information and communication technologies. Baku, Azerbaijan. Retrieved from www.aict.info/2011/

Bhatt, M. I. (2010). Harnessing technology for providing knowledge for development: New role for libraries. In T. Ashraf (Ed.), Developing sustainable digital libraries: Socio-technical perspectives. New York: IGI-Global (Information Science References).

Bou-Llusar, J. C., & Segarra-Cipres, M. (2006). Strategic knowledge transfer and its implications for competitive advantage: an integrative conceptual framework. *Journal of Knowledge Management, 10*(4), 100–112. doi:10.1108/13673270610679390

Broadbent, M. (1998). The phenomenon of knowledge management: what does it mean to the information profession? *Information Outlook, 2*(5), 23–34.

Busch, P. (2008). *Tacit knowledge in organizational learning*. Hershey, PA: IGI Publishing. doi:10.4018/978-1-59904-501-6

Chen, H. (1999). *High-performance digital library classification systems: from information retrieval to knowledge management*. Retrieved October 13, 2010, from http://citeseer.ist.psu.edu/cache/papers/cs/18268/http:zSzzSzwww.dli2.nsf.govzSzprojectszSzchen.pdf/high-performance-digitallibrary.Pdf

Das, A. K., Sen, B. K., & Dutta, C. (2010). Collaborative digital library development in India: A network analysis. In T. Ashraf (Ed.), Developing sustainable digital libraries: Socio-technical perspectives. New York: IGI-Global (Information Science References).

Davenport, T. H., & Prusak, L. (1998). *Working knowledge: how organizations manage what they know*. Boston, MA: Harvard Business School Press.

Del Bimbo, A., Gradmann, S., & Ioannidis, Y. (Eds.). (2004, July). *Future research directions*. Retrieved from www.delos.info/files/pdf/events/2004_Jul_8_10/D8.pdf

Drucker, P. (1999). *Management Challenges for the 21st Century*. New York, NY: Harper Business.

Fox, E. A., & Urs, S. R. (2002). Digital libraries. *Annual Review of Information Science & Technology, 36*, 503–589.

Garcia-Crespo, A. et al. (2011). Digital libraries and Web 3.0. The Callimachus DL approach. *Computers in Human Behavior, 27*, 1424–1430. doi:10.1016/j.chb.2010.07.046

Gartner. (2002). *Knowledge management attracts Powerhouse vendors*. Retrieved November 8, 2009, from www.gartner.com

Ghosh, M., & Jambekar, A. (2003). Networks, digital libraries and knowledge management: trends & development. *DESIDOC Bulletin of Information Technology, 23*(5), 3–11.

Goh, S. C. (2002). Managing effective knowledge transfer: an integrative framework and some practice implications. *Journal of Knowledge Management, 6*(1), 23–30. doi:10.1108/13673270210417664

Harter, S. P. (1997). Scholarly communication and the digital library: problems and issues. *Journal of Digital Information, 1*(1). Retrieved April 12, 2009 from http://journals.tdl.org/jodi/article/view/jodi-3/4

Hawkins, B. (2000). Libraries, knowledge management, and higher education in an electronic environment. *ALIA 2000 Proceedings*. Retrieved June 25, 2005, from www.alia.org.au/conferences/alia2000/proceedings/brian.Hawkins.html

Hicks, D., & Tochtermann, K. (2001). Personal digital libraries and knowledge management. *Journal of Universal Computer Science, 7*(7), 550–565.

Jadhav, K. A. (2011). Digital library: Today's need- A review. *International Multidisciplinary Research Journal, 1*(11), 17–19.

Ju, Y. (2006). Leveraging levels of information services and developing knowledge services: The trend of information services in libraries. *Library Management, 27*(6/7). doi:10.1108/01435120610702341

Ke, H., & Hwang, M. (2000). The development of digital libraries in Taiwan. *The Electronic Library, 18*(5), Retrieved May 20, 2012, from http://www.emeraldinsight.com/10.1108/02640470010354590

Kim, S., & Ju, B. (2008). An analysis of faculty perceptions: Attitudes toward knowledge sharing and collaboration in an academic institution. *Library & Information Science Research, 30*, 282–290. doi:10.1016/j.lisr.2008.04.003

Kimblea, C., & Bourdonb, I. (2008). Some success factors for the communal management of knowledge. *International Journal of Information Management, 28*(6), 461–467. doi:10.1016/j.ijinfomgt.2008.08.007

Kumar, B. (2010). Digital library and repositories: An Indian initiative. In T. Ashraf (Ed.), Developing sustainable Digital Libraries: socio-technical perspectives. New York: IGI-Global (Information Science References).

Lee, J. N. (2001). The impact of knowledge sharing, organizational capability and partnership quality on is outsourcing success. *Information Management Journal, 38*(5), 323–335. doi:10.1016/S0378-7206(00)00074-4

Lee King, D. (2009). Building the Digital Branch: Guidelines for Transforming Your Library Website. *Library Technology Reports, 45*(6), 5–9.

Lohani, M., & Jeevan, V. K. J. (2007). Intelligent software agents for library applications. [from www.emeraldinsight.com..]. *Library Management, 28*(3), 139–151. Retrieved November 5, 2011 doi:10.1108/01435120710727983

Martin, A. et al. (2012). A framework for development of integrated intelligent knowledge for management of telecommunication networks. *Expert Systems with Applications, 39*, 9264–9274. doi:10.1016/j.eswa.2012.02.078

McInerney, C. (2002). Knowledge management and the dynamic nature of knowledge. *Journal of the American Society for Information Science and Technology, 53*(12), 1009–1018. doi:10.1002/asi.10109

Nemati-Anaraki, L., & Heidari, A. (2011, October). *Knowledge management process in digital age: proposing a model for implementing E-learning through digital libraries*. Paper presented at 5th international conference on application of information and communication technologies. Baku, Azerbaijan. Retrieved November 6, 2011, from www.aict.info/2011/

Nonaka, I. (1991). The knowledge creating company. *Harvard Business Review*, *69*(6), 96–104.

Nonaka, I., & Takeuchi, H. (1995). *The knowledge creating company: how Japanese companies create the dynamics of innovation.* New York, NY: Oxford University Press.

Pandian, M. P., & Karisiddappa, C. R. (2007). *Emerging technologies for knowledge resource management.* Oxford, UK: Chandos Publishing.

Perez-Nordtvedt, L. P., Kedia, B. L., Datta, D. K., & Rasheed, A. A. (2008). Effectiveness and efficiency of cross-border knowledge transfer: an empirical examination. *Journal of Management Studies*, *45*(4), 714–744. doi:10.1111/j.1467-6486.2008.00767.x

Polanyi, M. (1966). *The tacit dimension.* London: Routledge & Kegan Paul.

Roknuzzaman, M., Kanai, H., & Umemoto, K. (2009). Integration of knowledge management process into digital library system: a theoretical perspective. *Library Review*, *58*(5), 372-386. Retrieved July 26, 2011, from www.emeraldinsight.com/0024-2535.htm

Rydberg-Cox, J., et al. (2000). Knowledge management in the Perseus digital library. *Ariadne*, *25*. Retrieved March 13, 2012, from www.ariadne.ac.uk/issue25/rydberg-cox/intro.html

Setiarso, B. (2009). *Knowledge management and knowledge sharing in Indonesia Institute of Sciences: facing lot of changes to disseminate scientific knowledge for the society.* Paper presented at the Asia-Pacific Conference on Library & Information Education & Practice. New York, NY.

Shuchun, P (2002). *Digital libraries and knowledge management: Basis for agricultural scitech innovation.* Retrieved January 1, 2010, from http://zoushoku.narc.affrc.go.jp/ADR/AFITA/afita/afita-conf/2002/part7/p507.pdf

Shuhuai, R. et al. (2009). From information commons to knowledge commons: Building a collaborative knowledge sharing environment for innovative communities. *The Electronic Library*, *27*(2), 247–257. doi:10.1108/02640470910947593

Skyrme, D. J. (2000). *Knowledge networking: creating the collaborative enterprise.* Read Educational and Professional Publishing Ltd.

Song, S. (2001). An internet knowledge sharing system. *Journal of Computer Information Systems*, *42*(3), 25–30.

Sreenivasulu, V. (2000). The role of digital librarian in the management of digital information systems (DIS). *The Electronic Library*, *18*(1), 12–20. doi:10.1108/02640470010320380

Sun, J., & Yuan, B.-Z. (2012). Development and characteristic of digital library as a library branch. In *Proceedings of International Conference on Future Computer Supported Education.* Elsevier.

Upadhyay, P. K., & Moni, M. (2010). Digital library and E-governance: Moving towards sustainable rural livelihood. In T. Ashraf (Ed.), Developing sustainable Digital Libraries: Socio-technical perspectives. New York: IGI-Global (Information Science References).

Vasupongayya, S. et al. (2011). Open source library management system software: a review. *World Academy of Science Engineering and Technology*, *77*, 973–978.

Warr, H., & Hangsing, P. (2009, March). Open source digital library software: A literature review. In T. M. Devi & C. I. Singh (Eds.), *National Seminar on Preservation and Conservation of Information Resources in Knowledge Society: Issues, Challenges and Trends* (pp. 238-258). Canchipur: Manipur University.

Wen, S. (2005, March). *Implementing knowledge management in academic libraries: A pragmatic approach.* Paper presented at the third China-US Library Conference. Shanghai, China.

Yang, S., & Chang, Y. (2011). An active and intelligent network management system with ontology-based and multi-agent techniques. *Expert Systems with Applications, 38*(8), 10320–10342. doi:10.1016/j.eswa.2011.02.115

Zahra, S. A., Neubaum, D. O., & Larraneta, B. (2007). Knowledge sharing and technological capabilities: the moderating role of family involvement. *Journal of Business Research, 60*(10), 1070–1079. doi:10.1016/j.jbusres.2006.12.014

Zhou, Q. (2005). The development of digital libraries in China and the shaping of digital librarians. *The Electronic Library, 23*(4). doi:10.1108/02640470510611490

ADDITIONAL READING

Abdullah, A., & Zainab, A. N. (2008). The digital library as an enterprise: the Zachman approach. *The Electronic Library, 26*(4), 446–467. doi:10.1108/02640470810893729

Alavi, M., & Leidner, D. E. (2001). Review: knowledge management and knowledge management systems. *Management Information Systems Quarterly, 25*(1), 107–136. doi:10.2307/3250961

Alvesson, M. (2004). *Knowledge Work and Knowledge-intensive Firms*. Oxford: Oxford University Press.

Arms, W. Y. (2000). *Digital libraries*. Cambridge, MA: The MIT Press.

Ashraf, T., & Gulati, P. A. (2010). Digital libraries: A sustainable approach. Developing sustainable Digital Libraries: socio-technical perspectives. New York: IGI-Global (Information Science References).

Baker, D., & Evans, W. (2008). *Digital library economics: an academic perspective*. Oxford, UK: Chandos publishing.

Chantaraskul, S., & Cuthbert, L. (2008). An intelligent-agent approach for congestion management in 3G networks. *Engineering Applications of Artificial Intelligence, 21*(4), 619–632. doi:10.1016/j.engappai.2007.05.004

Chowdhury, G. G., & Chowdhury, S. (2003). *Introduction to digital libraries*. London: Facet publishing.

Clarke, T., & Clegg, S. R. (2000). *Changing paradigms: the transformation of management knowledge for the 21st Century*. London: HarperCollins Business.

Denford, J. S. (2013). Building knowledge: developing a knowledge-based dynamic capabilities typology. *Journal of Knowledge Management, 17*(2), 175–194. Retrieved July 3, 2013 doi:10.1108/13673271311315150

Diaz-Valenzuela, I. et al. (2013). An automatic system for identifying authorities in digital libraries, Elsevier. *Expert Systems with Applications, 40*, 3994–4002. doi:10.1016/j.eswa.2013.01.010

Donate, M. J., & Guadamillas, F. (2011). Organizational factors to support knowledge management and innovation. *Journal of Knowledge Management, 15*(6), 890–914. doi:10.1108/13673271111179271

Grant, K. (2011). Knowledge management, an enduring but confusing fashion. *Electronic Journal of Knowledge Management, 9*(2), 117–131.

Helgoson, M., & Kalhori, V. (2012). *A conceptual model for knowledge integration in process planning*. Paper presented at 45th CIRP Conference on Manufacturing Systems, Procedia CIRP 3, (pp. 573–578).

Hendriks, P. H.J. & Sousa, C. A.A. (2013). Practices of management knowing in university research management. *Journal of Organizational Change Management, 26*(3), 611-628. DOI 10.1108/09534811311328605.

Hislop, D. (2010). Knowledge management as an ephemeral management fashion. *Journal of Knowledge Management, 14*(6), 779–790. doi:10.1108/13673271011084853

Kimble, C. (2013). Knowledge management, codification and tacit knowledge. *Information Research, 18*(2), 577. Retrieved June 27, 2013

Kruk, S. R., & Decker, S. (2007). JeromeDL: The semantic digital library. *In Proceedings Semantic Technology Conference*, San José, California.

Lagzian, F., Abrizah, A., & Wee, M. C. (2013). An identification of a model for digital library critical success factors. *The Electronic Library, 31*(1), 5–23. doi:10.1108/02640471311299100

Liangxian, D., Junxia, Q., & Pengfei, G. (2012). *The Application of Semantics Web in Digital Library Knowledge Management.* Paper presented at the International Conference on Applied Physics and Industrial Engineering, ELSEVIER, Physics Procedia, 24, (pp. 2180–2186).

Loptin, L. (2006). Library digitization projects, issues and guidelines: a survey of literature. *Library Hi Tech, 24*(2).

Minati, G. (2012). Knowledge to manage the knowledge society. *The Learning Organization, 19*(4), 296–297. doi:10.1108/09696471211226707

Mingers, J. (2008). Management knowledge and knowledge management: realism and forms of truth. *Knowledge Management Research & Practice, 6*(1), 62–76. doi:10.1057/palgrave.kmrp.8500161

Morales López, V., Ortega Carrillo, M., & Poom Bustamente, T. (2013). *Technological knowledge framework towards organizational knowledge transfer in Mexico.* Paper presented at the 2nd International Conference on Integrated Information, Elsevier Procedia-Social and Behavioral Sciences, 73, (pp. 556 – 563).

Serenko, A., & Bontis, N. (2013). Global ranking of knowledge management and intellectual capital academic journals. *Journal of Knowledge Management, 17*(2), 307–326. Retrieved July 3, 2013 doi:10.1108/13673271311315231

Serenko, A., Bontis, N., & Moshonsky, M. (2012). Books as a knowledge translation mechanism: citation analysis and author survey. *Journal of Knowledge Management, 16*(3), 495–511. doi:10.1108/13673271211238797

Sloan, B. G. (1998). Service perspectives for the digital library remote reference services. *Library Trends, 47*(1), 117–143.

Tang, J., Fong, A. C. M., Wang, B., & Zhang, J. (2012). A unified probabilistic framework for name disambiguation in digital library. *IEEE Transactions on Knowledge and Data Engineering, 24*, 975–987. doi:10.1109/TKDE.2011.13

van den Berg, H. A. (2011). Vertical integration: applying an economic calculus to knowledge. *International Journal of Learning and Intellectual Capital, 8*(4), 399–417.

van den Berg, H. A. (2013). Three shapes of organizational knowledge. *Journal of Knowledge Management, 17*(2), 159–174. doi:10.1108/13673271311315141

Wallace, D. P., Fleet, C. V., & Downs, L. J. (2011). The research core of the knowledge management literature. *International Journal of Information Management, 31*(1), 14–20. doi:10.1016/j.ijinfomgt.2010.10.002

Wu, J. J., & Huang, R. H. (2008). Design and implementation of a personal digital library platform. *Proceedings of 2008 IEEE International Symposium on IT in Medicine and Education, IEEE*, Retrieved February 19, 2011, from http://ieeexplore.ieee.org/stamp/stamp.jsp?tp¼&arnumber¼44743893

KEY TERMS AND DEFINITIONS

Artificial Intelligence: (1) A term that is used to describe the feature, function, or characteristic of computer systems or machines that try to simulate human-thinking behavior or human intelligence. (2) A field of computer science, which is based on research studies or development on providing intelligent systems simulating.

Digital Librarian: In the information age, the role of librarians is changing gradually. They will develop forward to be the information navigators and information experts in the society. In the digital libraries, digital librarians will provide readers with various, dynamic and advanced services in the initiative and innovative pattern.

Digital Library: (1) Digital Library is a "Collection of digital objects (text, video and audio) along with methods for access and retrieval, [as far as users are concerned] and also for selection, organization, and maintenance. Delving into this definition, the library is an organized body that holds collections – digital objects - that have been grouped into categories, presumably for access purposes. Therefore, a digital Library is an informal collection of information, stored in digital formats and accessible over a network, together with associated services.

Global Knowledge Networking: Global Knowledge Networking in digital libraries is to redefine the pattern, function, and responsibility, and to make warm, harmonious and cooperative knowledge sharing between them. It could promote communication, interaction, cooperation, learning and sharing, and could transmit tacit knowledge to explicit knowledge, and could be beneficial to knowledge depositing, storage, application, and innovation.

Intelligent Agents: Intelligent agents belong to an artificial intelligence area that promises tremendous potential in all areas of life. Intelligent agents can be broadly defined as a software entity that carries out some set of operations on behalf of user or another program with some degree of independence or autonomy. An intelligent agent is a managed object situated within and a part of an environment, which senses that environment and acts on it, over time, in pursuit of its own knowledge agenda and to execute autonomous management actions.

Knowledge Management: As the need of nowadays organization is indispensable, so our movement toward management must be predetermined and preplanned. Knowledge management is a process of creation, organization, diffusion (transition of knowledge), use and exploitation of knowledge.

Knowledge Sharing: Knowledge sharing is the process of being aware of knowledge needs and making knowledge available to others by constructing and providing technical and systematic infrastructure. Knowledge sharing is set of activities for transferring or disseminating knowledge from one person, group or organization to another.

ENDNOTES

[1]   Mapping the knowledge is another basic tool for managing the knowledge. Mapping the knowledge can visually supplement connections and relations among pieces of data, information and knowledge. Mapping the knowledge repository can help in finding knowledge structure and relations. The maps show where the knowledge is located (Ju, 2006).

Chapter 3
Intelligent Educational Support System

Duygu Mutlu-Bayraktar
Istanbul University, Turkey

ABSTRACT

Increasing student numbers lead to new needs in the education sector. New systems are needed due to expert numbers that are insufficient in specialties, such as instructors, directors, and advisors. Type, goal, and specialty of intelligent systems programmed to satisfy this need are being developed with each passing day. The aim of this chapter is to develop an intelligent system that provides support with schedule, academic orientation, choice of profession, and career planning to students. To make a regular schedule for students would generally cause an inappropriate program, which is hardly followed by students in case they were indiscriminately prepared without any information about students' characteristics. Instead of this method, it is the point to be familiar with the academic success, study, resting, and even meal time of the student, and to know which lessons are studied on which days and to make an appropriate schedule for studying. According to the teachers, it is time-consuming and difficult to perform this method for all students. Within this scope, an intelligent system preparing a study schedule is developed considering the students' characteristics and study habits.

INTRODUCTION

Use of man power is relatively reduced while computer technology goes into human life and it starts to give way to intelligent systems that can be controlled by computer. Nowadays, computer technology is effectively used in many sectors such as health, banking, communication, transportation, electric-electronic, engineering and security. In addition, computer technology is used in the field of educational sciences in different and effective application ways.

One of the problems of educational sciences is high student numbers due to increase in global population. To solve the problem, educators try to prepare individual learning and study platforms by using technology.

Computer provides social, occupational and pedagogic reality to education and this enabled effective and efficient use of computer in education. The intelligent systems developed for this purpose is designed as the systems that can think, decide and adapt to itself to various situations (Akkoyunlu, 1995). The intelligent systems used for education are computer based educational software that can interact with student, contribute to learning and present content according to readiness of student. In addition, they can give feedback like a guide and

DOI: 10.4018/978-1-4666-6276-6.ch003

keep student personal information and data about the relationship with the system (Murray, 1998). Intelligent educational systems decide to present information according to pedagogical guidance, data from individuals and rules and it adapts itself according to personal information requirement. This distinguishes it from other computer based educational systems.

Most studies have showed that educational software applying different methods are effective when individual differences are considered in terms of learning period and outcome (Al-Hammadi and Milne, 2004; Altın, 2006). In addition to using as tutorial software, intelligent educational systems are used for different purposes such as guiding student, assessment and evaluation (Mark & Greer, 1993; Günel, 2010). In this study, an intelligent system suitable to individual characteristics of students was developed for guidance.

INTELLIGENT SYSTEMS

The stages of Knowledge Acquisition are present to take the conclusion by configuring information in the intelligent system. Within the context of this study, the system was programmed in line with these processes. They are: Acquisition, Representation, Validation, Inferencing, Explanation.

These stages in the system include revealing the rules and procedures used during problem solving and collaboration of knowledge engineer and leading expert to code. Knowledge Acquisition includes obtaining information from people, books, documents, sensors, and computer files. Representation is the stage that obtained information is organized. It includes formation of knowledge map and to code in knowledge base. Validation is to validate and confirm the information in knowledge base by using test conditions until the quality reaches acceptable level. Inferencing includes interpretation by using database by using database and then, it includes design of software that provide to present suggestion

about certain points. Explanation is the stage that includes explaining and presenting the inferences in line with information and rules (Jones, 2008).

Intelligent Systems contain two sub-systems (Lee & Kim, 1998). Knowledge Base and Inference Mechanism. Knowledge base can be organized according to one or more configurations (schemes) such as databases, associative, hierarchal, network etc. Created knowledge representative schemes have 2 basic features: They are recorded to computer memory by coding with current programming languages. The facts and contents of representative schemes are designed in such a way that other information can be reconsidered (Jones, 2008).

In intelligent systems, information should be represented properly for effective study of knowledge inference mechanism. For this purpose, some representative schemes were determined.

Representation in Logic: It is the oldest representative scheme. Knowledge entrance is done, premises or facts. These are the inputs of logical process. The logical process functions with these inputs. Outputs are produced: inferences and results.

- **Propositional Logic:** This suggestion includes expression that can be true or false. After what it is known, it becomes an input that is used to derive new suggestions or inferences. Rules are used to determine whether new suggestions are true (T) or false (F).

- **Lists:** Lists and trees are kind of representation of information found in hierarchical structure. They are the series that relevant materials are written. Ex: The name list of employees in company, the to do list, the list of products in catalogue etc. They are used when objects are grouped, categorized or graded according to relationship or line. Objects are grouped as similar materials. Relationship between groups are demonstrated with connections.

- **Decision Tree:** It is similar to semantic net that is connected with rules. Rule-based decision trees are obtained after period of information retrieval.

After knowledge representation, decision process is started to deduce. There are some methods used in this period (Magoulas, et al., 2001; Weiss, 2000; Jang, et al., 1997).

- **Case-Based Reasoning:** It estimates the period of solving new problems by using solutions of old similar problems as base. The presence of previous situations is necessary to solve a problem for formation of period of reconsidering.
- **Markov Decision Processes:** They model, plan and control the decision process periods within the mathematical frame under the partially controls of random or decision plan. The difficulties of modelling of complicated situations and the absence of memory are the disadvantages of this period.
- **Neuro-Fuzzy Processes:** They are the periods that are obtained by assimilating human neural network to learning and communication network. The disadvantage of this period is that numerous parameters should be determined. Therefore, interpretation part is complicated.
- **Blackboard System:** It is an artificial intelligence application and uses blackboard model as base. This system is based on interpretation as a result of brainstorming of agents. Blackboard system is used as workplace for cooperative studies.
- **Rule-Based Systems:** They are the models that a set of rules determines the period by giving decision within the frame of specific conditions. The difficulties of determination of proper rules for various situations and the absence of degree of accuracy are the disadvantages of these systems.

BACKGROUND

Nowadays, intelligence system studies obtained according to student characteristics are frequently used in educational platforms. These studies are important in terms of personalization of learning and effective learning.

In the system called NEFCLASS, Al-Hammadi and Milne (2004) used fuzzy neural network method to categorize students according to learning performance before their acceptance to college. The grades of high school students and the success status of students in college entrance exam were accepted as inputs of the system. The outputs aimed to determine the performances of accepted students after first period. The obtained results showed the requirement of use of the system.

In the study carried out by Aguilar et al., Fuzzy and Multiagent systems were developed to reinforce additional processes and activities in addition to lectures. It is aimed to provide effective learning periods to students in line with determined learning goals. The learning plan of this system was approved by collaborative studies of mathematics experts. The results of the application were obtained students of primary education.

This system is a platform including learning period, which is personalized according to student, predetermined features in line with goals. The system does not provide same platform for each student. It is based on characteristic of students.

In the study carried out by Altın (2006), subtraction carried out by second grade students was considered according to with and without need of use of ten's place in two-digit natural numbers. It was aimed that learning experiences connected to this issue were determined in terms of intelligent educational system's student model. Therefore, kinds of questions that will be asked to students were tried to be determined to find the source of mistakes in pre-learning in addition to pre-learning efficiency.

In one of the study, determination of student personality was the most important part. Stereotype Student Model was preferred for construction of student model. In this model, students are separated into different levels and contents and questions proper to the levels are given to students. The result of pre-test applied to student and the average of grades taken in this course were used to determine student level. Missing parts in determination of levels were tried to be overcome through this. Also, it has been thought that students have different knowledge for each topic and their needs are different according to that different placement tests have been applied for each sub-topic. The most ideal structure was tried to be constructed with two different level settings (Turan, 2007).

In the study carried out by Mitrovic, Ohhlson and Barrow (2013), Tutoring technologies for supporting learning from errors via negative feedback are quite improved and their significances in empirical evaluations have been verified. However, the significance of positive feedback in the practice of expert tutoring is emphasized via observations of empirical tutoring dialogs. They made an assumption about that to minify student uncertainty about doubtful but correct problem solving steps actuates positive feedback. Positive feedback should interact with three pieces of explanatory information: (a) those features of the condition that performed the correct action with both in general terms and reference to the particulars of the problem state; (b) the explanation of the action at a conceptual level and (c) the significant aspect of the change in the problem state which was originated by the action. We define how a positive feedback capability was applied in a mature, constraint-based tutoring system, SQLTutor that helps about teaching students via learning from their errors. Empirical evaluation demonstrates that learning speed of students interacting with the enhanced version of SQL-Tutor was twice as faster than the speed of the students interacting with classic version giving only error feedback.

In the study carried out by Günel (2010), a system design revealing educational terms in the training content presented to student was carried out by using, primarily, method of document indexation of search engines. Therefore, intelligent educational system gives meaning to training content as semantic and answers the question what should be taught to student. Also, suggested system constructs concept map about training content automatically by revealing the relationship between terms. Then, student model was constructed with concept map model. In addition, a differential equation model determining degrees of difficulty of questions dynamically which was inspired from population dynamics was presented.

In the study of Badaracco and Martinez (2013), The Computerized Adaptive Tests (CAT) is the tool commonly used for the diagnosis process in Intelligent Tutor System based on Competency education (ITS-C). The item selection process for formation of a CAT has an important role because the best item selection must be guaranteed for contribution to student evaluation at any time. The mechanisms of item selection recommended in the literature have some limitations which reduce the effectiveness of CAT and its adaptation to the student profile. This paper presents a new algorithm for item selection based on a multi-criteria decision model which incorporates knowledge of experts guided by blurry linguistic information that handles previous limitations and improves the preciseness of diagnosis and the adaptation of CAT to qualification level of student. At last, such an algorithm is served in a mobile tool for an ITS-C.

A general methodology and architecture to develop a new conversational intelligent tutoring system (CITS) named Oscar which guides a tutoring conversation and dynamically estimates and adapts to learning style of a student is suggested in the paper written by Latham et al. (2012). The aim of Oscar is to simulate a human tutor by indirectly modeling the learning style during tutoring and individualizing the tutorial to boost confidence and enhance the efficacy of the learning experience. the methodology and architecture of The Oscar CITS are free of the learning styles model and tutoring subject domain. Oscar CITS was applied via using the Index of Learning Styles (ILS) model for submitting an SQL tutorial. Sizes of ILS model are presented in Figure 1.

It is possible to construct an intelligent Web-based education system using the set of integrated tools described in Peredo et al. (2011)'s paper. Aim of the study is to build a web learning environment which can be modified depending on the Learner. The web learning environment consists of four parts: Authoring Tool, Evaluation System, Interactive Voice System and a Virtual Laboratory for programming in Java, all of which use Web Services and are easily adaptable to the management, authoring, delivery and monitoring of learning content. A multi-agent system was used for the decision-making process of the intelligent Web-based education system.

Aparicio et al. (2012) defines the details of the development of an Intelligent Information Access system which is used as the basis to generate and evaluate a constructivist learning methodology with undergraduate students. In a defined clinical case, the system automatically perceives important concepts and it enables an objective evaluation after an appropriate selection process of the case considered knowledge level of the students. The applied learning methodology is deeply related to case-based, concept-based and internet-based learning. In despite of increasing theoretical research about the use of information technology in higher education, implementations which evaluate learning and perceptions of students and compare objective results with a free internet search is rarely found.

Peixoto, Boarati and Forte (2012) have aimed at developing a system that will help people designing user interfaces and relating the knowledge of experts with an expert system named "GuideExpert". To this end, the system detects the cognitive style and attention deficiencies of users and help designers to design interfaces suitable for them.

Muñoz-Merino, et al., (2012) have modeled and applied a new and innovative intelligent tutoring system called Information System for Competition based on problem solving in Education (ISCARE). In a course, it enables the competition among students to enhance their learning process. The idea behind the system is that it gets ideas from Swiss-system commonly used in chess and adapts these ideas to the educational field. The competition contains different rounds and tournaments. In

Figure 1. Index of learning styles dimensions (Latham et al, 2012)

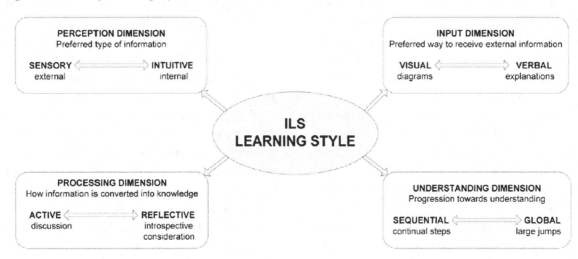

Figure 2. Architecture for development web based education systems (Peredo, et al., 2011)

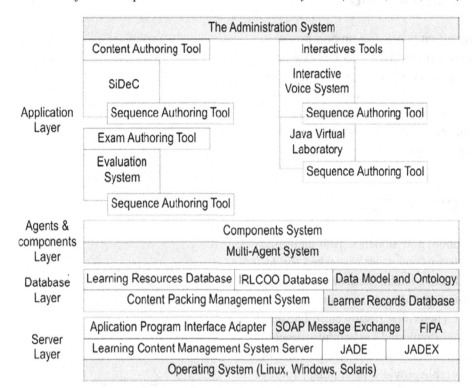

each round, students are divided into two groups that compete with each other and different questions that should be solved in a limited time are given to each group. At the end of each round, students are available to see their partial points and they can see their final points after a tournament. To model and implement the system, lots of knowledge from various disciplines was used. So, ISCARE contains various functionality such as registration of the student into the system, tournament formation, the registration and assignment of students to tournaments, tournament life cycle administration (started, in execution, finished, etc.), the supplementation of different exercises to tournaments, the calculation of groups for each round via different algorithms, the assignment of exercises per round and groups, the students' scores per round and tournament, the administration of the students' ratings or monitoring information. This paper submits the ISCARE intelligent tutoring system via defining its various options, menus or

functionality in addition to its architecture and the specific modeling to attain the desired properties (Muñoz-Merino, et al., 2012).

Waalkens, Aleven and Taatgen (2013) developed three versions of the same intelligent tutoring systems to solve linear algebraic equations which are different only in the amount of freedom given to students. One situation involved that students rigorously adhere to a standard strategy, the other two enabled minor and major variations, respectively. The study proposes that an Intelligent tutoring system should present at least a small amount of freedom, validating, in spite of a limited degree, one source of complexity in Intelligent tutoring systems architectures in the early levels of problem solving practice within a complex domain. More than allowing students to choose their own solution strategy within a defined problem is required to guide students for development of strategic flexibility.

THE PURPOSE OF STUDY

It is quite important to provide support proper to students' characteristics in counselor service given during education period. The goal of this study is to develop an intelligent system that provides support about schedules for daily study periods, which are convenient to learners' characteristics during education period.

INTELLIGENT SYSTEM

First, a table about how students spent their time after school during one week was asked for developed intelligent system. Students were asked to write what they did each hour interval (e.g. studying, social activities, resting etc.). The data obtained through this period was helpful to develop options to be presented to student during writing of software. This table provided preliminary survey about which data in student daily study habits was need to be used.

After this survey, the studies to determine purposeful rules were carried out. Rules are arranged to provide reasoning, for example, to understand whether student repeats the lectures given in the school or he/she studies the lecture that will be given next day.

Software development period started with determination of the rules. First, in the software, students should enter their grades in previous semester into the system. This will present the information to the system about for which lecture student should spare time. Then, a table was constructed that student entered the weekly schedule (See Figure 6). This will be used to decide the relationship between the lectures in the school and the lectures that student studies at home. After this step, a table was developed that student entered study time, the lecture studied and activities performed during 2 weeks (See Figure 3). This table forms a knowledge base for intelligent system according to the information of student study habits.

Figure 3. Students' data entry

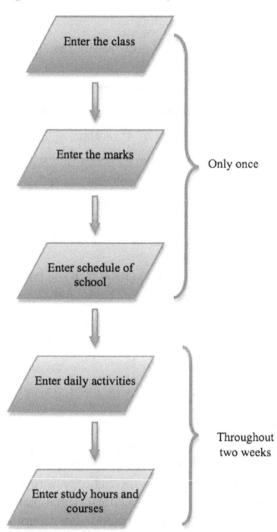

After all these information, the system provides a schedule for student to study regularly after 2 weeks. The system aims to personalize learning by providing a schedule parallel student's habits in line with information about which time and what kind of study or activities student performs (See Figure 7).

The system was developed according to rule-based model. This model is a method that rules determines the period by giving decision within the frame of specific conditions. In the study, rules were determined before programming the system. Some of the rules are:

- The dinnertime will be determined according to the time that student eats.
- It will be determined which lecture student prefers to study.
- The activities performed by student will be determined according to day and time.
- Time for bed and waking time of student will be determined.

Within the frame of these rules, the daily study habits of student, lectures studied, times and day for the lectures are determined. In addition, information about activities performed and their days are determined. All these information is used during decision process and a work schedule is developed. The system was programmed with Asp.Net after all necessary preliminary surveys. Software engineering supported the process during programming. The system, primarily, takes the educational level information of student (primary-high school). It displays lectures proper educational level according to the information. When student entered the grades of these lectures, it gave academic success information (See Fig. 3). The table can be filled by choosing day, time, activity categories to get information about the student study habits. It is aimed to get 2-week information of student. For this purpose, the day that student does not enter the information is send with a reminder message to cell phone. Therefore, the lack of information is tried to be prevented by this method. The information is taken from persons at Knowledge Acquisition stage of the system. Obtained information is organized at database at Representation stage. At Validation stage, warning messages are sent to student to provide entrance of information to relevant sites and to prevent the

Figure 4. Home page of the program

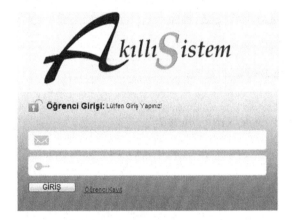

Figure 5. Student registration page

Figure 6. Weekly schedule screen

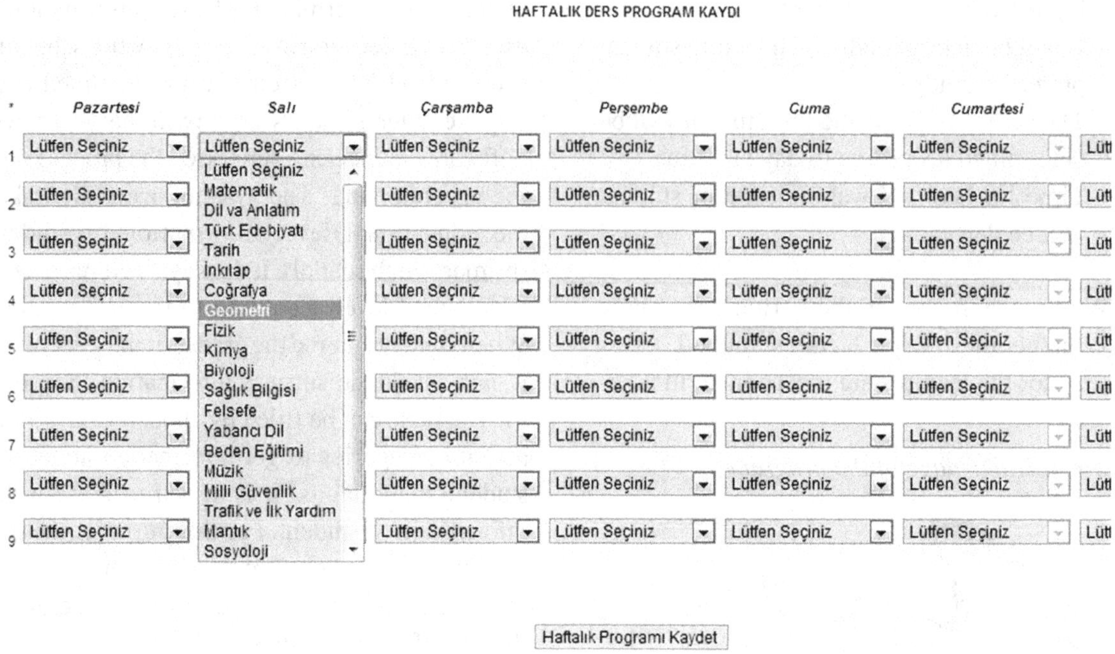

HAFTALIK DERS PROGRAM KAYDI

*	Pazartesi	Salı	Çarşamba	Perşembe	Cuma	Cumartesi	
1	Lütfen Seçiniz	Lütfen Seçiniz	Lütfen Seçiniz	Lütfen Seçiniz	Lütfen Seçiniz	Lütfen Seçiniz	Lütf
2	Lütfen Seçiniz	Matematik	Lütfen Seçiniz	Lütfen Seçiniz	Lütfen Seçiniz	Lütfen Seçiniz	Lütf
3	Lütfen Seçiniz	Türk Edebiyatı / Tarih	Lütfen Seçiniz	Lütfen Seçiniz	Lütfen Seçiniz	Lütfen Seçiniz	Lütf
4	Lütfen Seçiniz	Coğrafya / Geometri	Lütfen Seçiniz	Lütfen Seçiniz	Lütfen Seçiniz	Lütfen Seçiniz	Lütf
5	Lütfen Seçiniz	Fizik / Kimya	Lütfen Seçiniz	Lütfen Seçiniz	Lütfen Seçiniz	Lütfen Seçiniz	Lütf
6	Lütfen Seçiniz	Sağlık Bilgisi / Felsefe	Lütfen Seçiniz	Lütfen Seçiniz	Lütfen Seçiniz	Lütfen Seçiniz	Lütf
7	Lütfen Seçiniz	Beden Eğitimi	Lütfen Seçiniz	Lütfen Seçiniz	Lütfen Seçiniz	Lütfen Seçiniz	Lütf
8	Lütfen Seçiniz	Müzik / Milli Güvenlik	Lütfen Seçiniz	Lütfen Seçiniz	Lütfen Seçiniz	Lütfen Seçiniz	Lütf
9	Lütfen Seçiniz	Mantık / Sosyoloji	Lütfen Seçiniz	Lütfen Seçiniz	Lütfen Seçiniz	Lütfen Seçiniz	Lütf

Dropdown list options: Lütfen Seçiniz, Matematik, Dil va Anlatım, Türk Edebiyatı, Tarih, İnkılap, Coğrafya, Geometri, Fizik, Kimya, Biyoloji, Sağlık Bilgisi, Felsefe, Yabancı Dil, Beden Eğitimi, Müzik, Milli Güvenlik, Trafik ve İlk Yardım, Mantık, Sosyoloji

Haftalık Programı Kaydet

Figure 7. Page that activities done after school during two weeks are entered

Günlük Bilgiler

Kayıt Tarihi-(Dün)-DİKKAT !!! Sisteme dün giriş yapılmadığı için önce dün kı günlük bilgilerini girmelisin !!!2012-12-18 00:00:00

00:00	Lütfen Seçiniz	06:00	Lütfen Seçiniz	12:00	Lütfen Seçiniz	18:00	Lütfen Seçiniz
01:00	Lütfen Seçiniz	07:00	Lütfen Seçiniz	13:00	Lütfen Seçiniz	19:00	Lütfen Seçiniz
02:00	Lütfen Seçiniz	08:00	Lütfen Seçiniz	14:00	Lütfen Seçiniz	20:00	Lütfen Seçiniz
03:00	Lütfen Seçiniz	09:00	Lütfen Seçiniz	15:00	Lütfen Seçiniz	21:00	Lütfen Seçiniz
04:00	Lütfen Seçiniz	10:00	Lütfen Seçiniz	16:00	Lütfen Seçiniz	22:00	Lütfen Seçiniz
05:00	Lütfen Seçiniz	11:00	Lütfen Seçiniz	17:00	Lütfen Seçiniz	23:00	Lütfen Seçiniz

Günlük Bilgilerimi Kaydet

Figure 8. Schedule that intelligent system creates

DERS PROGRAMI TAKIP

Hoşgeldin Fatma Çakır ‖ ÇIKIŞ

				DERS PROGRAMI			
SAAT	PAZARTESİ	SALI	ÇARŞAMBA	PERŞEMBE	CUMA	CUMARTESİ	PAZAR
00:00	Uyku	Uyku	Uyku	Uyku	Uyku	Uyku	Uyku
01:00	Uyku	Uyku	Uyku	Uyku	Uyku	Uyku	Uyku
02:00	Uyku	Uyku	Uyku	Uyku	Uyku	Uyku	Uyku
03:00	Uyku	Uyku	Uyku	Uyku	Uyku	Uyku	Uyku
04:00	Uyku	Uyku	Uyku	Uyku	Uyku	Uyku	Uyku
05:00	Uyku	Uyku	Uyku	Uyku	Uyku	Uyku	Uyku
06:00	Uyku	Uyku	Uyku	Uyku	Uyku	Uyku	Uyku
07:00	Okul	Okul	Okul	Okul	Okul	Okul	Okul
08:00	Okul	Okul	Okul	Okul	Okul	Okul	Okul
09:00	Okul	Okul	Okul	Okul	Okul	Okul	Okul
10:00	Okul	Okul	Okul	Okul	Okul	Okul	Okul
11:00	Okul	Okul	Okul	Okul	Okul	Okul	Okul

lack of information. During inferencing stage, the system interprets from information according to the rules. During Explanation stage, the results obtained according to the information and the rules are presented to student as a table and opinions of student are taken. In addition, the system can add inputs such as activity, lecture etc. entered newly by student to its own system and then it can add them among available options.

FINDINGS

This intelligent system was applied to 5 high school students and their opinions about both contribution of the system to users and usage of it were taken. Students indicated that the system provided contribution to study period in terms of daily study tracking and order and individuality. In addition, they stated that some activities in their daily lives were absent in the system. As a result of this opinion, a module was programmed to add the activities that were not added before into the system among available activities when they are entered.

Besides students, the system was presented to psychological counselors and their opinions were taken. Teachers indicated that the system was effective in terms of reaching to students and forming new programs easily for changing semesters. In addition, they suggested that schedule should be prepared via taking information during one week instead of two weeks after formation of first study schedule by students. By taking this opinion into consideration, a new schedule is created if data are close to each other when old information is compared to new information taken during one week for each time after formation of first schedule by students. In the case of data having large changes according to old schedule, it is asked to student to enter information from two weeks.

CONCLUSION AND RECOMMENDATIONS

Nowadays, guidance and facilitative roles of educators become difficult or inefficient due to increase in student number. Technological supports such as web sites, educational software, tutorials are considered to overcome these problems. These supports cannot give convenient results for each student because they are presented according to general student profile. To prevent this, the programs that record student information and make reasoning and inferences in line with these information present suggestions focusing on individual learning.

Intelligent Systems being developed present convenient learning platforms, activities and guidance to student according to the results of interpretation of student's characteristics (Günel & Aşlıyan, 2010; El-Khoury, et al., 2005). To obtain meaningful information from individual characteristics of student is important for tracking, development and updating of the systems. In addition, it is important for providing information about learning levels, study styles and individual differences of students (Doğan & Çamurcu, 2008).

The software that students are included personally and that they can lead, interfere and learn something comes into prominence instead of the software that students are guided according to standard properties. The results of the studies about the intelligent systems prepared according to learner characteristics show also parallelism (Keleş, et al., 2009; McQuiggan & Lester, 2006; Nkambou, Gauthier & Frasson, 1996). Learning and guidance are more individualized in these systems that learner characteristics are used as knowledge base. This is one of the features of intelligent systems that distinguish them from other educational systems.

In this study, an intelligent educational system that can be used without a counsellor was designed by focusing on learner characteristics. There will be important contributions of this system to students in terms of preparation of more proper study schedule. It is thought that this kind of program can be effective for students having intense study periods to study efficiently before high school and university entrance exams carried out in some countries. This program prepared according to characteristics of both primary and high school students makes educators' works quite easy.

As a result of the study, it was tried to make the system more efficient and useful via updating it at intervals according to feedbacks obtained from counselor and students. Moreover, it is actively used by students who prepare for university entrance exam.

In addition to this study, developing an intelligent support system that makes tests about students' academic successes, professional interests and academic self-respect and makes suggestions to student via evaluating results and also suggests proper department and university by combining test results with practice test results of students followed from the system are aimed as a further study. In this way, developing expert and intelligent support systems by taking increasing student number into account in terms of remote and formal education for the future will start to be seen as new trends in educational process.

REFERENCES

Aguilar, R., Mu~noz, V., González, E.J., Noda, M., Bruno, A., & Moreno, L. (2011). *Fuzzy and Multiagent Instructional Planner for an Intelligent Tutorial System*. Paper presented at Appl. Soft Comput. New York, NY.

Akkoyunlu, B. (1995). Bilgisayarların Eğitimde Kullanılması ve Bilgisayar Okuryazarlığı. *Eğitim ve Bilim, 19*(96), 23-30, 33-35.

Altın, B. (2006). *İlköğretim 2. Sınıf Öğrencilerinin Matematik Dersindeki Öğrenme Yaşantılarının Bilgisayarda Hazırlanan Zeki Öğretim Sistemlerine Göre İncelenmesi.* (Unpublished master dissertation). Dokuz Eylül University, İzmir, Turkey.

Aparicio, F., De Buenaga, M., Rubio, M., & Hernando, A. (2012). An intelligent information access system assisting a case based learning methodology evaluated in higher education with medical students. *Computers & Education, 58,* 1282–1295. doi:10.1016/j.compedu.2011.12.021

Badaracco, M., & Martinez, L. (2013). A fuzzy linguistic algorithm for adaptive test in Intelligent Tutoring System based on competences. *Expert Systems with Applications, 40,* 3073–3086. doi:10.1016/j.eswa.2012.12.023

Bahçeci, F. & Gürol, M. (2010). A Model Proposal On Applications Of Intelligent Tutoring Systems In The Edecation. *e-Journal of New World Sciences Academy, 5*(2).

Doğan, B., & Çamurcu, A. (2008). Association Rule Mining from an Intelligent Tutor. *Journal of Educational Technology Systems, 36,* 433–447. doi:10.2190/ET.36.4.f

El-Khoury, S., Richard, P. R., Aimeur, E., & Fortuny, J. M. (2005). Development of an Intelligent Tutorial System to Enhance Students' Mathematical Competence in Problem Solving. In G. Richards (Ed.), *Proceedings of World Conference on E-Learning in Corporate, Government, Healthcare, and Higher Education 2005* (pp. 2042-2049). Chesapeake, VA: AACE.

Günel, K. (2010). *Zeki Öğretim Sistemlerinde Öğrenci Değerlendirme Modelleri Üzerine.* (Unpublished master dissertation). Ege University, İzmir, Turkey.

Günel, K., & Aşlıyan, R. (2010). Extracting Learning Concepts from Educational Texts in Intelligent Tutoring Systems Automatically. *Expert Systems with Applications, 37*(7), 5017–5022. doi:10.1016/j.eswa.2009.12.011

Jang, J. S. R., Sun, C. T., & Mizutani, E. (1997). *Neuro-fuzzy and Soft Computing, A Computational Approach to Learning and Machine Intelligence.* Upper Saddle River, NJ: Pearson Education.

Jones, T. M. (2008). *Artificial Intelligence: A Systems Approach.* Infinity Science Press LLC.

Keleş, A., Ocak, R., Keleş, A., & Gülcü, A. (2009). ZOSMAT: Web-based intelligent tutoring system for teaching–learning process. Expert Systems with Applications 36(2), 1229–1239.

Latham, A., Crockett, K., McLean, D., & Edmonds, B. (2012). A conversational intelligent tutoring system to automatically predict learning styles. *Computers & Education, 59,* 95–109. doi:10.1016/j.compedu.2011.11.001

Lee, K. C., & Kim, H. S. (1998). A Fuzzy Cognitive Map-based Bidirectional Inference Mechanism: An Application to Stock Investment Analysis. *Intelligent Systems in Accounting Finance & Management, 6*(1), 41–57. doi:10.1002/(SICI)1099-1174(199703)6:1<41::AID-ISAF119>3.0.CO;2-J

Magoulas, G. D., Papanikolaou, K. A., & Grigoriadou, M. (2001). Neuro-fuzzy synergism for planning the content in a web-based course. *Informatica, 25,* 39–48.

Mark, M. A., & Greer, J. E. (1993). Evaluation Methods for Intelligent Tutoring Systems. *Journal of Artificial Intelligence in Education, 4,* 129–153.

McQuiggan, S. W., & Lester, C. L. (2006). Diagnosing Self-efficacy in Intelligent Tutoring Systems: An Empirical Study. *Lecture Notes in Computer Science, 4053,* 565-574.

Mitrovic, A., Ohlsson, S., & Barrow, D. K. (2013). The effect of positive feedback in a constraint-based intelligent tutoring system. *Computers & Education, 60,* 264–272. doi:10.1016/j.compedu.2012.07.002

Muñoz-Merino, P. J., Molina, M. F., Muñoz-Organero, M., & Kloos, C. D. (2012). An adaptive and innovative question-driven competition-based intelligent tutoring system for learning. *Expert Systems with Applications*, *39*, 6932–6948. doi:10.1016/j.eswa.2012.01.020

Murray, T. (1998). Authoring Knowledge Based Tutors: Tools for Content, Instructional Strategy, Student Module and Interface Design. *Journal of the Learning Sciences*, *7*(1), 5–64. doi:10.1207/s15327809jls0701_2

Peixoto, C. S. A., Boarati, S. S., & Forte, C. E. (2012). Heuristics for User Interface Design in the Context of Cognitive Styles of Learning and Attention Deficit Disorder. In P. Vizureanu (Ed.), *Advances In Expert Systems* (pp. 85–100). Rijeka: InTech. doi:10.5772/51455

Peredo, R., Canales, A., Menchaca, A., & Peredo, I. (2011). Intelligent Web-based education system for adaptive learning. *Expert Systems with Applications*, *38*, 14690–14702. doi:10.1016/j.eswa.2011.05.013

Srinivasan, B., & Parthasarathi, R. (2013). An intelligent task analysis approach for special education based on MIRA. *Journal of Applied Logic*, *11*(1), 137–145. doi:10.1016/j.jal.2012.12.001

Şuşnea, E. (2013). Improving Decision Making Process in Universities: A Conceptual Model of Intelligent Decision Support System. *Procedia - Social and Behavioral Sciences*, *76*, 795-800.

Turan, F. (2007). *Stereotip Öğrenci Modeli Kullanılarak Zeki Öğretim Sistemi Tasarımı.* (Unpublished master dissertation). Marmara University, İstanbul, Turkey.

Waalkens, M., Aleven, V., & Taatgen, N. (2013). Does supporting multiple student strategies lead to greater learning and motivation? Investigating a source of complexity in the architecture of intelligent tutoring systems. *Computers & Education*, *60*, 159–171. doi:10.1016/j.compedu.2012.07.016

Weiss, G. (2000). *Multiagent Systems: A Modern Approach to Distributed Artificial Intelligence.* Cambridge, MA: MIT Press.

ADDITIONAL READING

Aguilar, R., Mu῀noz, V., González, E.J., Noda, M., Bruno, A., & Moreno, L. (2011). Fuzzy and MultiAgent Instructional Planner for an Intelligent Tutorial System. *Applied Soft Computing*, *11*, 2142–2150. doi:10.1016/j.asoc.2010.07.013

Aguilar, R. Mu῀noz, V., González, E.J., Noda, M., Bruno, A. & Moreno, L. (2011). *Fuzzy and Multiagent Instructional Planner for an Intelligent Tutorial System.* Paper presented at Appl. Soft Comput., 2011, pp.2142-2150.

Aparicio, F., De Buenaga, M., Rubio, M., & Hernando, A. (2012). An intelligent information access system assisting a case based learning methodology evaluated in higher education with medical students. *Computers & Education*, *58*, 1282–1295. doi:10.1016/j.compedu.2011.12.021

Arnau, D., Arevalillo-Herráez, M., Puig, L., & González-Calero, J. A. (2013).. . *Computers & Education*, *63*, 119–130.Fundamentals of the design and the operation of an intelligent tutoring system for the learning of the arithmetical and algebraic way of solving word problems doi:10.1016/j.compedu.2012.11.020

Bramer, M., & Devedzic, V. (2004). *Artificial Intelligence Applications and Innovations*, Kluwer Academic Publishers, Newyork, 2004

Doğan, B., & Çamurcu, A. (2008). Association Rule Mining from an Intelligent Tutor. *Journal of Educational Technology Systems, 36,* 433–447. doi:10.2190/ET.36.4.f

Duarte, M., & Butz, B., P., & Miller, S. M. (2008). An Intelligent Universal Virtual Laboratory (UVL). *IEEE Transactions on Education, 51,* 1, 2–9. doi:10.1109/TE.2006.888902

Duo, S., & Ying, Z. C. (2012). Personalized E- learning System Based on Intelligent Agent. *Physics Procedia, 24,* 1899–1902. doi:10.1016/j.phpro.2012.02.279

Granic, A., & Glavinic, V. (2005). *User Interface Aspects of a Web-based Educational System,* Proceedings of the International Conference on Computer as a Tool.

Hatzilygeroudis, I., Prentzas, J., & Garofalakis, J. (2005). *Personalized Learning in Web-Based Intelligent Educational Systems: Technologies and Techniques,* Proceedings of the 11th International Conference on Human-Computer Interaction.

Kay, J. (2000). *Stereotypes, Student Models and Scrutability,* In Gauthier, G., Frasson, C. and VanLehn, K. (eds.). Proc. of 5th International Conference on Intelligent Tutoring Systems, Montreal, Springer (2000).

Keleş, A., Ocak, R., Keleş, A., & Gülcü, A. (2009). ZOSMAT: Web-based intelligent tutoring system for teaching–learning process. Expert Systems with Applications Volume 36, Issue 2, Part 1, Pages 1229–1239.

Latham, A., Crockett, K., McLean, D., & Edmonds, B. (2012). A conversational intelligent tutoring system to automatically predict learning styles. *Computers & Education, 59,* 95–109. doi:10.1016/j.compedu.2011.11.001

Magoulas, G. D., Papanikolaou, K. A., & Grigoriadou, M. (2001). Neuro-fuzzy synergism for planning the content in a web-based course. *Informatica, 25,* 39–48.

McQuiggan, S. W. and Lester, C. L. (2006). Diagnosing Self-efficacy in Intelligent Tutoring Systems: An Empirical Study. *Lecture Notes in Computer Science,* Volume 4053, 565-574.

Minaei-Bigdoli, B., Kortemeyer, G., & Punch, W. F. (2004). *Enhancing Online Learning Performance: An Application of Data Mining Methods,* The 7th IASTED International Conference on Computers and Advanced Technology in Education (CATE 2004), Kauai, Hawaii, USA, (August 2004) 173-178.

Mitrovic, A., Ohlsson, S., & Barrow, D. K. (2013). The effect of positive feedback in a constraint-based intelligent tutoring system. *Computers & Education, 60,* 264–272. doi:10.1016/j.compedu.2012.07.002

Mitrovic, A., Ohlsson, S., & Barrow, D. K. (2013). The effect of positive feedback in a constraint-based intelligent tutoring system. *Computers & Education, 60,* 264–272. doi:10.1016/j.compedu.2012.07.002

Muñoz-Merino, P. J., Molina, M. F., Muñoz-Organero, M., & Kloos, C. D. (2012). An adaptive and innovative question-driven competition-based intelligent tutoring system for learning. *Expert Systems with Applications, 39,* 6932–6948. doi:10.1016/j.eswa.2012.01.020

Murray, T. (1998). Authoring Knowledge Based Tutors: Tools for Content, Instructional Strategy, Student Module and Interface Design. *Journal of the Learning Sciences, 7*(1), 5–64. doi:10.1207/s15327809jls0701_2

Noh, M. N., Ahmad, A., Halim, S. A., & Ali A. M. (2012).Intelligent Tutoring System using Rule-based And Case-based: A Comparison. Procedia - Social and Behavioral Sciences, Vol. 67, 454-463.

Özyurt, Ö., Özyurt, H., & Baki, A. (2013). Design and development of an innovative individualized adaptive and intelligent e-learning system for teaching–learning of probability unit: Details of UZWEBMAT. *Expert Systems with Applications*, *40*, 2914–2940. doi:10.1016/j.eswa.2012.12.008

Peixoto, C. S. A., Boarati, S. S., & Forte, C. E. (2012). Heuristics for User Interface Design in the Context of Cognitive Styles of Learning and Attention Deficit Disorder. In P. Vizureanu (Ed.), *Advances In Expert Systems* (pp. 85–100). Rijeka: InTech. doi:10.5772/51455

Shen, R., Han, P., & Yang, F. (2003, July-September). Data Mining and Case-based Reasoning for Distance Learning. *International Journal of Distance Education Technologies*, *1*(3), 46–58. doi:10.4018/jdet.2003070104

Tang, T. Y., & Chan, K. (2002). Feature Construction for Student Group Forming Based on Their Browsing Behaviors in an E-learning System, *Lecture Notes In Computer Science*; Vol. 2417 archive Proceedings of the 7th Pacific Rim International Conference on Artificial Intelligence: *Trends in Artificial Intelligence* (2002) 512-521.

Waalkens, M., Aleven, V., & Taatgen, N. (2013). Does supporting multiple student strategies lead to greater learning and motivation? Investigating a source of complexity in the architecture of intelligent tutoring systems. *Computers & Education*, *60*, 159–171. doi:10.1016/j.compedu.2012.07.016

Weiss, G. (2000). *Multiagent Systems: A Modern Approach to Distributed Artificial Intelligence*. Cambridge, Mass.: MIT Press.

Yu, P., Own, C., & Lin, L. (2001). *On learning behavior analysis of web based interactive environment*, International Conference ICCEE, Oslo.

KEY TERMS AND DEFINITIONS

Case-Based Reasoning: It estimates the period of solving new problems by using solutions of old similar problems as base. It means adapting old solutions to meet new demands. It uses old experiences to understand and solve new problems.

Decision Tree: It is used to determine the optimum course of action or show a statistical probability. It is the process which is similar to semantic net that is connected with rules.

Intelligent Educational Systems: The Intelligent Educational Systems are educational computer systems designed for support and improvement of education, learning, and teaching process in the domain knowledge. These systems involve mental capabilities such as the reasoning ability, planning, solving problems, thinking, and learning.

Intelligent Systems: These are computer systems that have mental capabilities, like adaptability, memory, reasoning, learning, and most importantly the ability to manage uncertain and imprecise information.

Knowledge Acquisition: Knowledge Acquisition is the extraction of knowledge from sources and its transfer to the knowledge base and then to the inference engine.

Knowledge Inferencing: Inferencing includes comment by using database and then, it includes design of software that provide to present suggestion about certain points.

Rule-Based Systems: These are used to store and manipulate knowledge to interpret information in a useful way. They are the models that a set of rules determines the period by giving decision within the frame of specific conditions.

Chapter 4
Designing a Multi-Agent System for Improving the Accounting E-Learning

Bogdan Pătruţ
Vasile Alecsandri University of Bacau, Romania & EduSoft, Romania

ABSTRACT

Higher education in accounting has witnessed, in time, a massive development, a fact that has required the identification of the most efficient training methods based on competencies so as to meet the new professional challenges. Computer-based training represents a didactic method that improves accounting education. This chapter presents some elements regarding e-learning in accounting and how the educational software can include artificially intelligent elements that may humanize the dialogue of the teacher-computer, like pedagogical agents. The authors present the main ideas of how they designed and developed a multi-agent system that has been incorporated into an educational soft that was tested and validated within an experiment with the students from the specialization of Accounting and Management Information Systems of the Vasile Alecsandri University of Bacău, Romania.

INTRODUCTION

This chapter has an interdisciplinary nature, finding itself on the crossroads of accounting, distributed artificial intelligence and the sciences of education. The chapter is based on (Patrut, 2010), (Patrut, 2013a) and (Patrut, 2013b).

The education in accounting should be formative and not informative; therefore there should be a transition from a type of education based on providing knowledge to one that is based on competencies development, from teacher-centered education to student-centered education. These things are successfully achieved in interactive distance education.

Higher education in accounting has witnessed great development in time contributing, on the one hand, to the training of many promotions of accounting professionals and, on the other hand, to the promotion of accounting both as practical activity and scientific theory. Expanding accounting education requires finding the most efficient methods of knowledge-based instruction so as to cope with the new professional challenges.

Whereas skills or competencies refer to the attributes required so that persons may profess as professionals, competence refers to actually demonstrating the professing of the profession.

In (Patrut, 2013a) we formulated the professional competencies acquired through the account-

DOI: 10.4018/978-1-4666-6276-6.ch004

ing higher education and we identified the learning units that the student needs in order to acquire them, within an interactive educational process.

For the subject of "Fundamentals of Accounting" the specific competencies are:

1. Knowledge and understanding competences;
2. Competences to explain/consult and interpret/demonstrate accounting principles, the procedures of the accounting method etc.;
3. **Instrumental:** Applicative competences;
4. **Attitudinal Competencies:** Obeying the financial-accounting legislation; assuming responsibility for the suggested economic solutions; developing logical accounting thinking; developing ethical conduct.

Legislators are constantly establishing new fiscal or accounting regulations that affect the content of the learning process in accounting. Legislative changes are natural in a dynamic society like Romania - a country that adjusts its economic and legal system to the one of the European Union and that tends towards a functional market economy.

Secondly, the Romanian society constantly feels the need of forming new accounting specialists, adapted to the market requirements. The number of companies has constantly increased; some of them disappear to give way to others that are more adjusted to the requirements of the European Union; there are mergers or divisions of companies and all the financial-accounting problems have to be dealt with by accounting professionals. Their number has increased in recent years and this fact shows both the interest of people in the accounting profession as well as the need for specialists in this field.

As well, the new information and communication technology have altered the role of the accountant a lot. According to the International Accountants Federation, the accounting professional is not only required to use information systems and practice computer operation skills, but he should also play a major role as part of a team involved in evaluating, designing and managing information systems.

Moreover, the role of the (Romanian) accountant has changed as he no longer has to be a mere "bookkeeper", but an advisor for the manager. The knowledge based society, the occurrence of adaptable and intelligent companies, of virtual organizations face accountants with other new challenges. Thus, the accounting profession experiences new dimensions, and accounting education should take this into account.

The computer comes to support accounting education. Accounting education keeps up with technology and teachers have to anticipate its impact upon the learning ways. Computer-based training represents a didactic method that improves education and facilitates the student's access to a greater amount of well-organized and structured information that may be viewed in different ways. This didactic method enjoys special pedagogic qualities given by the synthesis between programmed training and the technological availabilities of the computer.

What is it that makes a teacher irreplaceable in the training-educational process? Obviously, it is neither the amount of information that he may own nor the possibility that he may easily pass it on to his students but rather his human, social nature, the ability to select the appropriate information for the appropriate time, the ability to correctly assess students, to give them rewards or warnings, to meet the students' expectations and show empathy. A gifted teacher puts himself into the student's shoes and, based on the mistakes that the latter makes, is able to guess the gaps that he has in the knowledge of the field and is, therefore, able to better guide his training process. The tests chosen, the questions asked by the teacher are crucial in a student's training (Patrut, 2013b).

A teacher is good if he manages to identify the weak and strong points of a student, if he manages to stimulate him when he turns lazy or gets bored, or to accurately provide the information needed in a certain context. His didactic style, his gestures, the teacher's face expressions, tone of voice and even the way in which he comes across as a person in front of his students can be significant elements that may bring success in the didactic act.

Nevertheless, no matter how talented the teacher may be, he cannot address a certain student particularly as this would be undemocratic. The teacher belongs to all the students and so that he has to adjust his discourse to address the majority.

The educational soft is preferable for an individualization of education, but how can we make the educational soft to behave like a teacher? This is the problem that we have approached in our research. The solution that we have chosen was to design, implement and use a multi-agent system.

The first educational software products focused more on learning by checking knowledge, but today, interactive programs support in constructing knowledge actively or may contain artificially intelligent elements that may humanize the dialogue teacher – computer, as we have shown in our chapter.

To that effect, we approach the field of multi-agent systems and we try to find out to what extent this new technology lends itself to the creation of an educational soft for training in accounting.

The multi-agent system that we have designed has been incorporated into an educational soft (ContTest) that was tested and validated within an experiment with the students from the specialization of Accounting and Management Information Systems of the Vasile Alecsandri University of Bacău, Romania.

COMPUTER-BASED TRAINING IN ACCOUNTING

Computer-based training (CBT) improves education and diversifies didactic strategies, facilitating the student's access to more, well-organized and variedly structured information that can be viewed in various ways. Obviously, this way of training uses directly the new information and communication technologies, but the pedagogic effects are the result of using various interactive educational software products, not of computers themselves. These can be both online courses, multimedia dictionaries as well specialized educational software.

In classic training methods, the central role often belongs to the teacher. Computer-based training confers this central role upon the student and takes into account the inheritance, experience, perspectives, training, talents, skills and needs of each student. Students have greater freedom and flexibility, and are given the chance to instruct themselves individually, at their own pace (Patrut, 2010).

The focus passes from teaching to learning. However, the designers of educational software have to focus upon teaching, on the sharing of knowledge. They have to find the best information to provide and also to stimulate motivation. Thus, creating educational software products should normally involve at least one programmer, a psycho-pedagogue and a specialist in the respective field of learning.

In educational software, the information is well organized according to the curricula of the subjects, but is adjusted to the potential of each student. Thus, such e-learning systems may contain didactic sequences and questions that cognitively challenge the student, in order to find the possible flaws in knowing the domain or the errors that he frequently repeats. We developed a multi-agent system for accounting e-learning and it operates in this way, too. Our system can reactivate previous didactic tasks and can obtain information or explanations required by a certain topic.

The Pedagogic Consequences of Interactive Learning in Accounting

Computer-based training (CBT) raises issues with which schools and teachers are faced with. There is the problem of equipping schools (classrooms, laboratories and libraries) with computers and multimedia equipments, then that of training teachers in ICTs. Many of these problems can be avoid by using the distance education. Thus, students use at home their own computers and they can influence their intellectual formation in a good way[1].

On the other hand, the educational process faces the issue of adjusting curricula to the requirements of CBT. Thus, interactive learning imposes major restructurings in the area of the content of the didactic process. Not only school curricula should be changed to adequately meet the ICTs, but handbooks, too, should refer to the new sources of information and documentation (web pages, educational software etc.) or they should change their form (electronic, interactive textbooks). For example, an electronic textbook on the fundamentals of accounting may contain lessons about invoices, bills where students will have to fill in various forms or to enter the data from such a document into a demonstrative program.

By using e-learning in accounting, the forms of organizing the didactic activity will be reconsidered and centered upon the individualization of the training process.

The advantages of computer-based training are:

- Stimulating the interest towards the new;
- Stimulating imagination;
- **Self-Training:** The students explore the information on their own;
- Developing logical and algorithmic thinking;
- Simulation of phenomena and processes on the screen;
- Multiple illustrations;
- Learning at one's own pace with no stress or emotions;
- The assessment of results can be objective.

Cârstea (2005) wrote about how to make a better use of the unique qualities of computers: interactivity, the precision of the performed op-

erations, the ability to offer multiple and dynamic representations of the phenomena and particularly the fact that they can interact consistently and differentially with each student separately.

Early CBT focused more on learning by checking knowledge. Today there are interactive software products which help built knowledge actively. Such software provides significant context for learning, promote reflection. It frees the student from many routine activities and stimulates an intellectual activity that is similar to the one while working.

In (Barry, 2007) it is shown that particularly e-learning using the Internet may have such advantages: it may constitute a very efficient learning form in the English language for those for which this is a foreign language, the students may save a lot of money and time because they do not attend classes at scheduled hours, there is no restriction concerning the appointment of lessons, the courses are flexible and each student may learn by stages, according to one's personal skills, and one can learn and work at the same time[2]. Many students even work in the field of accounting and may use the Internet resources to train themselves.

Another important aspect is that teachers will have to reconsider the didactic process, passing from form activities to content activities since students will have to acquire the general competencies by means of which to be able to apply their knowledge in concrete work tasks.

The teacher's role is in a permanent change. The teacher of accounting will be gradually relieved by the routine activity, but his tasks will widen by the fact that he will have to create programs or to design projects of programs and to adjust them to the requirements of interactive e-learning. As Nagy (2005) stated, the educational process turns from a teacher-centered system into a student-centered one.

Taking from (Roşca & al, 2002) the advantages of using interactive training, we shall further compare traditional and interactive accounting training.

1. First of all, we have to emphasize the fact that using the computer and the associated equipments individualize learning.
2. Interactive training also determines an increase in the student's motivation, and the playful nature of using certain training programs increases motivation.
3. Unlike traditional education, in interactive learning in accounting the student plays an active part. Interactivity supports the processes of creative learning by discovery.
4. The course attendant may have control over the content and the ways of accessing it.
5. Interactive accounting education brings about many changes in the teacher's status, the assessment techniques and also in the organizational space for carrying out the training activity. Thus, the teacher organizes the training resources, being able to give advices about what should be done during the educational interaction. With the help of the computer, testing and training can be simultaneously performed, assessment being thus continuous.

An advanced educational soft may efficiently combine all these types of educational soft. Thus, the educational soft that we have created contains:

*   Modules for the interactive presentation of knowledge: they present the principles of accounting, the operation rules of accounts etc.;
*   Modules for computer-based training: problems of financial accounting are automatically generated and the student is required to solve them;

Besides this technical combination, the educational soft created by us is a *intelligent training system*. Intelligent training systems are an advanced type of educational soft. Not only do they present knowledge, but they can also generate and solve problems in the field training which may lead to

checking the student's knowledge. Therefore, the pedagogic benefits brought by this category of educational software are obvious.

Besides the general pedagogic reasons, there are some other for which we regard the use of educational software as proper for accounting e-learning.

Examples of Interactive e-Learning in Accounting

Internationally, there are several preoccupations concerning accounting training by the use of ICTs, no matter if they are performed in an institutionalized environment or not. Many of these preoccupations deal with long-distance learning through the Internet.

Thus, for example, the University of Ohio (2007) offers students and the wide public a number of accounting paid training courses: the fundamentals of accounting, filling in payrolls using QuickBooks 2007, introduction to QuickBooks 2007. The QuickBooks 2007 system is designed for the accounting of small and middle-sized companies, and can be used both as a working-tool in accounting and as didactic tool.

Sitchawat (2005) presents the interactive e-learning system from Thailand; here, e-learning training is an additional training method used to improve the training of accounting graduates. Sitchawat suggests that universities assess their openness to e-learning even before actually using it in accounting training. Thus, universities were divided into two groups, to test the openness to the use of interactive training. The conclusion has been that Thai universities that are members of the Collaborative Research Network of Thailand are more open to this technology than the others. The eventual obstacles spring from the lack of time and technical staff that may help to develop CBT systems.

Private companies provide accounting training, too, by using the new information and communication technologies.

The company Kesdee Inc. (2007) offers online accounting courses on the following topics: understanding the frame of accounting, understanding the accounting process, understanding the financial analysis, understanding the accounting of depreciation, general accounting techniques and financial statements. The courses address any accounting professional from the industry, no matter if he represents a supplier, a user or an intermediary. The course uses a dynamic and computer-based instruction system and recommends only a minimum familiarization with the economic and financial-accounting terms.

The company "Mind Your Own Business", with subsidiaries in United Kingdom and Ireland, offers online courses for accountants: business training, training in practical accounting etc. (MYOB, 2007). MYOB provides course attendants with several video sequences that accompany the accounting systems. The system is interactive with the video sequences organized in modules. Each module may be run by each student according to one's needs until he acquires various skills and knowledge. As advantages, MYOB mentions the flexibility of the learning program, the minimum costs, lack of traveling, the flexible modular structure, and the practice on a real financial-accounting information system, the practical applications provided by the system.

Interesting educational software is Financial Accounting Tutor, provided by the company Almaris (2007). Currently at version 9, the product enjoys the following advantages: it emphasizes the accounting concepts and techniques, it has a user-friendly interface, the examples that accompany the the theoretical explanations have been carefully selected, it uses cutting-edge computer technology.

Anohina (2007) presents the architecture of an intelligent training system that helps students solve practical problems on the basis of certain artificial intelligence algorithms. The system contains two important modules, a pedagogic and a diagnosis one. The pedagogic module teaches the content to the student, and the other module diagnoses the current stage of the skills acquired by the student. According to the results, the system provides, now and then, a clue that will help the student solve the problems that he is faced with. The soft is part of the category of training intelligent systems and, although it does not relate to accounting, it may be adjusted to this field, also.

Also in our country, there is an interest in using the new information and communication technologies in accounting training. Several universities and companies offer introductory courses in accounting and even doctoral theses (ASE Bucharest).

There are also accounting portals or discussion sites, such as http://www.conta.ro or http://contabilitate.ablog.ro/. Several books were also issued on computer-based training in the economic field, including that of accounting: (Apostol, 2000), (Zamfir, 2007), (Lăcurezeanu, 2000), (Roşca & al, 2002) etc.

In our opinion, the existence of some e-learning systems is not enough for an interactive e-learning in accounting. Developing an educational soft for training in accounting has far better pedagogic results and incorporating intelligent agents in such software products has many advantages, as we shall demonstrate in the following section.

The Motivation behind Using Multi-Agent Intelligent Systems in Accounting Computer-Based Training

We have shown how new information and communication technologies come to support this type of modern education by offering learners automated possibilities of documentation and information, such as the educational soft. Although this does not replace the teacher, it can constitute a very efficient didactic tool when used together with the traditional tools.

But what is it that makes the teacher an irreplaceable element in the training-educational process? Obviously, neither the amount of information that he may hold nor the possibility that he may pass it on easily to his students but rather other elements related to his human, social nature. Thus, a teacher is appreciated according to his ability to assess students correctly, to give them rewards or criticism (by grading them). Also, a teacher who explains again by using variations in his formulations is even more appreciated by his students.

The more efficiently the teacher can use the didactic principle of retroaction, the more appreciated he will prove to be by students or course attendants. A competent teacher shows empathy. He places himself in the student's position and, on the basis of the errors that the student makes, is able to anticipate the gaps in the student's knowledge and can guide his training process in a more efficient manner. The tests and questions selected and applied by the teacher are crucial in training the student.

A good teacher manages to identify the weak and strong points of a student, manages to involve the student when the latter has become lazy or bored, or to accurately provide the information that he needs in a certain context.

The teacher's didactic style, gestures, face expression and even the way in which he comes across as a person in front of students may also be significant elements that may contribute to his didactic success.

Nevertheless, no matter how talented he may be, the teacher cannot address particularly to a single student as this would be neither democratic nor didactic. The teacher belongs to all the students, therefore he should adjust his speech in order to address the majority. The educational soft is preferable in individualizing education, but the self-training process is usually conducted by the student himself. In this situation, there occurs the need for an adjustable, intelligent educational soft.

The creation of an intelligent training system requires the incorporation of certain software elements with initiative, a certain humanized intelligent agent. These elements are very important in humanizing the artificial process, leading thus to the idea of using pedagogic intelligent agents in educational soft products.

Pedagogic intelligent agents can express human-like feelings; they can learn the user's interests, habits and preferences. To that effect, Microsoft Agent provides the programmer with small animated characters that display human and social behavior, and can substitute some of the teacher's features that we have presented above.

In conclusion, we consider that the use of computer-based training systems in accounting is purposeful but these have to be turned into intelligent systems. This justifies the development and use of multi-agent intelligent system for training in accounting.

In our opinion, such a system should facilitate:

- Access to the basic notions of financial accounting;
- The use of video sequences or animations to explain basic notions of accounting;
- The interactive dialogue between student and computer, very similar to the one between student and teacher;
- The use of illustrative examples for the accounting recording of various economic operations;
- The explanation of the operation rules of accounts;
- The generation of accounting problems from various areas of financial accounting, in Romanian;
- The checking of the students' solutions to the generated problems;
- The classification of the types of errors found with students and their correction;
- The grading of students according to the accumulated knowledge and the acquired skills.

All these have constituted fundamental issues in our research that was concluded with the development of a multi-agent system for interactive training in accounting.

INTELLIGENT AGENTS, MULTI-AGENT SYSTEMS, AND PEDAGOGICAL AGENTS

Certain software applications need the use of some intelligent agents[3] that are autonomous and flexible programs designed to reach their goals without the further intervention of the programmer. S. Franklin and A. Graesser (1998) define the agent as a computer system placed in an environment and being part of it, which can perceive the environment and acts on it, over time, following its own agenda to modify something it will perceive in the future. According to S. Russel and P. Norvig (2002) the agent is an entity that can perceive its own environment via sensors and can act on the environment via effectors.

In some situations there is necessary to endow the intelligent agents with new characteristics, closer to those of a human agent. Thus, for humanizing a software agent, it is necessary to integrate an affective subsystem: Bartneck (2003), Ortony, Clore, & Collins (1988), Pfeifer (1988), Bates (1994), and the agent should be endowed with a "body" either in real or in the virtual space. In the virtual space it can be a conversational agent, which can behaves smartly if we will add to it some new elements: feelings, temperament, gestures and movements close to those of a human being.

Thiry, Khator & al (2000) started with a new approach for distance learning: the intelligent agent-based approach. Even though the intelligent agents have many advantages, some problems are distributed or they are very complex and they cannot be solved by a single agent. Thus consider the necessity of grouping the agents into multi-agent systems, which can be organized in different ways. We developed an original way of organizing the agents into groups, in a multi-agent

system with pedagogical purposes. The multi-agent consists of many s-agents, which are small multi-agents systems, each s-agent dealing with an educational competency in the discipline to be learned. The multi-agent system was embedded in the educational software ContTest, which has the pedagogical functions of teaching accounting and assessing the students.

Conversational and Pedagogical Agents

Unlike a standard software agent, a conversational agent is no longer an abstract entity, invisible to the user, but it receives a visible shape. A conversational agent appears as an animated character, be it the moving image of a man, or on animal or another type of living entity. The agent is called conversational as it can "speak" to the human user, by using a traditional, textual conversation bubble, or even by using synthesized voices in order to reproduce texts, or through the use of pre-recorded audio files.

One of the technologies that enjoy great success among the developers of conversational agents is Microsoft Agent, one that offers the programmer small animated characters, with a proper human and social behavior. These characters can talk, animate, move in different ways on the screen from one spot to another and even record audio sequences or accept vocal commands (Patrut, 2003).

However, these characters are not sufficient to achieve an intelligent agent proper. Therefore it is necessary to have other control methods and programmable objects in order to achieve an intelligent interface between computer and the human user. These objects should interact with the Ms. Agent characters, to coordinate each other so as to effectively implement the essential features of an intelligent software agent. (Patrut, 2003), (Patrut, 2004a), (Patrut, 2010).

Conversational agents may be called *pedagogical agents* if the purpose for which they are used is didactic. Their goals are to teach a user or group of users (students) in a virtual teaching environment (intranet or internet). Pedagogical agents focus on perceiving the behavior of the learner, by furnishing informational and educational content, according to his level of knowledge and acquired abilities; also they focus on accumulating new information and creating skills matching the study area.

The environment in which a pedagogical agent acts is created by the learning student and his concrete learning situations. The agent acts via answers and questions, clues or suggestions, reinforcements or penalties, evaluations and even emotions on this environment, which trigger some progress the teaching progress.

Research has been made by Bates, Loyall, & Reilly (1992), Bates (1994) and Bach (2002), regarding the integration of some emotional compounds inside intelligent agents (emotions, feelings and their verbal and even facial expression), the accent going from intellectual to emotional. A great deal of these has been included in pedagogical agents (Jaques & al, 2001), (Jondahl & Mørch, 2000).

The expressing of emotions by the agent which instructs a student in a certain area can have a positive effect on teaching, depending on whether the student solves a problem or not. The full pack of software services Microsoft Agents allows the insertion of characters that interact with the user during the learning process in the educational software.

The integration of intelligent agents in a multi-agent instructional system can lead to remarkable results in the automatic teaching process. This way, skills specific to a certain job may develop (e.g. an accountant), overcoming the level of only furnishing knowledge, thing that the student can do by himself by using books, the Internet, or a data base.

Generally, pedagogical agents realized in different research contracts from different universities all over the world either deal with private areas (such as the field of military instruction, or the medical field), or don't present ways of achieving skills required by certain jobs, minding only the more or less efficient ways of offering information, according to the profile of the learning user (Arafa, Charlton, & Mamdani, 1997), (Okonkwo, 2001), Botelho & Coelho (2004), (Middleton & al, 2005).

Y. Arafa, P. Charlton, A. Mamdani (1997) and Cristoph Bartneck (2003) dealt with the integration of emotional aspects in the characters, taking over the model OCC of Ortony, Clore & Collins (2008)). Other researchers (Moreno, Person, Adcock, Van Eck & al, 2002), deal with the role of the stereotypes in realizing and using these animated agents in the teaching process, depending on the social, biological and cultural profile of the student. Despite the critical voices (such as that of Okonkwo (2001)) that deny the existence of advantages of emotional pedagogical agents, most researchers groups (as the one lead by Julita Vassileva (1997) worked hard in order to realize pedagogical agents based on purpose.

Jondahl and Mørch (2000) proposed an experiment of simulation of a system of pedagogical agents in a virtual learning environment, in order to study the benefits brought to the didactic process. Thus, before making a multi-agent system, they used human subjects who behaved as expected from a software system with pedagogical agents, offering the education and feed-back suited to humans. The latter had no idea of the human origin of the agents, but the experiment outlined certain advantages of a potential system. As such, we believe that before starting work in the realizing of a multi-agent teaching system, it is recommended that its utility be known in advance, as the advantages it might bring compared to other teaching software systems.

In (Ayoola and Phelan, 2010) a personalised agent-oriented mobile e-learning platform for adaptive third level education is presented.

Other researchers may be quoted as bearing interest in the field of pedagogical agents: J. Vassileva (1997), W. Lewis Johnson, P. Jaques, A.

Andrade, J. Jung, R. Bordini, R. Vicari (2001) and last but not least Pattie Maes (see http://web.media.mit.edu/~pattie/).

Advantages and Disadvantages of Using Pedagogical Agents

A first advantage of the pedagogical agents is that they can offer personalized instruction, each student learning at his own pace and focusing on a certain unit. This leads to the creation of an unstressful teaching environment; the pedagogical agents try to balance the best aspects of a human teacher and the best aspects of the artificially intelligent teaching systems. A pedagogical agent can be designed to express feelings and to manifest joy or sadness, according to the results obtained by the student during the academic program.

Creating a close to reality pedagogical agent triggers four important educational benefits:

- A pedagogical agent that shows interest in the student's progress can send the student the idea that he is there for him and he can encourage him to care more about his own progress;
- An emotional pedagogical agent who is, to a certain point, sensitive to the student's progress may interfere when he gets frustrated and before he starts losing interest;
- An emotional pedagogical agent can pass enthusiasm onto his student;
- A pedagogical agent with a complex and interesting personality can make studying into something fun. A student that enjoys interacting with a pedagogical agent may have a positive perception of studying generally, and, as a consequence, may spend more time studying.

Pedagogic agents can act as familiar teachers or trainers that may teach anything, starting from, for example, the summary of a lesson on the operation of accounts, and eventually providing a full course in accounting. The agents may teach anything, nevertheless they are better suited to teach objective knowledge that require accurate answers (true or false) rather than content based on theories or discussion (Patrut, 2010).

Pedagogical agents are not fit when an expert user ties to complete a task and the agent gets in his way, or when the users want to have a global view of the information or want direct access to unfiltered data. Furthermore, when work is done with children, it must be taken into account the fact that there is a very thin line between "pedagogical agent" and "fun". Young users might be more interested in interacting with the character that focusing on the tasks they are given. Other disadvantages of pedagogical agents are the facts that they are hard to design and implement or that the use of robotic voices may appear disturbing for some students.

MULTI-AGENT SYSTEM FOR ACCOUNTING E-LEARNING

We developed a multi-agent system, incorporated into an educational soft, which fulfills the functions of teaching and checking the students' knowledge in the fundamentals of financial accounting,.

As we have already previously anticipated, the designed multi-agent system is formed of several subsystems of intelligent agents. Every such subsystem is a (small) multi-agent system as well. We called it s-agent. An s-agent deals with teaching a lesson or a learning unit. It is made up of several agents, each with a particular role in the didactic process (assessment, teaching, checking and grading).

The Architecture of the Multi-Agent ContTest System

We were saying that a subsystem deals with teaching one learning unit. For example, the algorithm of accounting analysis will be a subsystem of pedagogic intelligent agents.

Each subsystem is closely related to the other subsystems and all the subsystems communicate to reach the common objective: the interactive training of the student. For example, the subsystem of accounting analysis communicates directly with the other subsystems by drawing on the learning units that logically (pedagogically) precede or follow accounting analysis.

Thus, we will have a subsystem of intelligent agents for the student's acquisition of each o the skills to be acquired in financial accounting (Patrut, 2010). We can regard each of these subsystems as being, in their turn, some "larger agents" of the general multi-agent system. And in order not to take the (atomic, elementary) agents for the subsystems regarded as agents, we shall name the latter s-agents.

Therefore, our multi-agent system will be made up of several s-agents, one for each skill or even learning unit and each s-agent will be made up of (atomic, elementary) agents that will accomplish a specific didactic task: teaching, testing, assessment etc.

For the s-agents we will have to establish:

- Their goals;
- The environment in which they act by sensors and effectors;
- Their architecture;
- The communications that occur among them within the general multi-agent system.

Each s-agent of the system has sensors that perceive the environment in which it is located as well as effectors by which it acts upon the environment. The environment is given by the current skills (including abilities and knowledge) of the student and the stage of their acquisition. The sensors are mechanisms (questions, tests, assessments etc.) by means of which the agent responsible for acquiring a skill can establish the level of that skill, in other words, it can tell how much the student has learned up to that moment. The effectors are given by mechanisms (explanations, instructions etc.) for improving the level of acquisition of a skill.

Each s-agent is made up of seven atomic agents that communicate and cooperate among themselves in pedagogic purposes. If at the level of the entire multi-agent system the nature of cooperation among the s-agents is related to the content to be taught (for example, the fundamentals of accounting) at the level of each s-agent we have a didactic cooperation. In the global system, the s-agents interact by mutual call, according to the internal logic of the subject to be taught, and within each s-agent the seven atomic agents cooperate on a didactic level. For example, one may teach certain accounting notions and another one may generate exercises to check the acquisition of those notions by the student.

Six agents are responsible for one didactic aspect each, irrespective of the nature of the learning unit or the skill that has to be acquired by the learner; a coordinating agent will mediate among the six agents (Figure 1).

How an S-Agent Operates

The coordination agent determines the way of operating of the whole s-agent, as it follows:

1. An entry into the s-agent is made, by means of other agents' calling;
2. An initial evaluation is performed (by the corresponding agent);
3. If the initial evaluation is a successful one, we can proceed to teach the new content;

Figure 1. The architecture of an s-agent

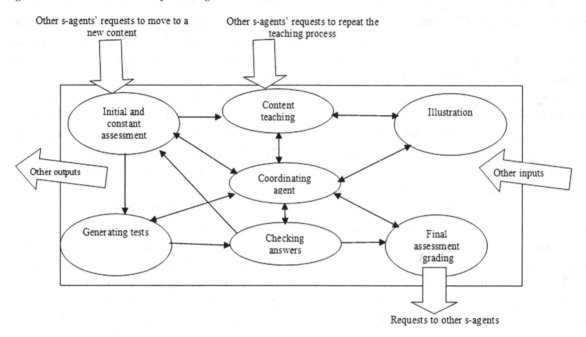

4. If the initial evaluation was not successful, a cycle of permanent evaluation is activated and the agents responsible for generating tests, checking answers and final evaluation and grading are called;

5. When leaving the cycle of permanent evaluation, the agent for teaching the content of the new lesson or learning unit is called in;

6. This agent can be called directly by other s-agents too in case of evaluations; they may find out that things are not working well and some notions need to be reviewed;

7. The teaching agent will call the exemplification agent in order to give suggestive examples for the theoretical notions already introduced to students;

8. Once the teaching is achieved, the coordination agent takes over and it can request a reevaluation in order to check out the learning stage or even the final evaluation so that the student can receive marks or grades;

9. If in need, other problems are treated (the occurrence of an unexpected error, the forced stop of the application, etc.).

The Assessment Agents

Initial and constant assessment is done according to the learning unit associated with the respective s-agent. For example, for the s-agent responsible with teaching accounting analysis, assessment may imply checking the following skills:

1. Identifying the patrimonial elements that suffer modifications;

2. Establishing the significance and size of these modifications;

3. Mentioning the corresponding accounts;

4. Applying the rules of operating the accounts to establish the part of the corresponding accounts – debit or credit – in which the operation analyzed is to be recorded.

Assessment implies generating certain questions and obtaining answers from the student. If the answers will be, eventually, correct for a large series of questions, we can say that the assessment was successful. In the contrary case, other s-agents are informed of the fat that they should work additionally because the student did not acquire the skills needed to move on to a new didactic content.

The assessment agent can be an agent with a layered architecture, each layer dealing with checking the acquisition of a certain skill (Patrut, 2010).

The Agents for Teaching and Illustrating the Content of the Current Learning Unit

Teaching a lesson, for example teaching the rules of operation for accounting accounts, can be done in various ways.

Usually, there will be a pedagogic agent because it is the most appropriate for such purposes. One may use the Microsoft Agent technology to animate a character as well as the multimedia technology, for example formerly shot videos with a person (an accounting teacher) that teaches a certain lesson.

We found the combined use of these technologies to be very useful. On the other hand, the Microsoft Agent character, although less human in aspect, can be more flexibly designed and can have a bidirectional message exchange with the learner. On the other hand, pre-made video sequences, although more rigid, will give the impression of a person's real presence that instructs the student in an interactive manner. Architecturally, the agent responsible with teaching a lesson will be a couple of two reactive agents.

One can easily see that Microsoft Agent 2.0 is an innovative technology that allows a new interactive type of communication between man and computer, complementing the graphic user interface which we are already used to. However, a character of the MS Agent type does not fully own the characteristics of an intelligent agent as it is defined in the field of artificial intelligence.

In (Patrut, 2010) we have shown that if we combine the facilities offered by the MS Agent type of objects with those of other controls, we can create new objects that can exhibit intelligent

behavior. These are intelligent pedagogic agents that can be used as teaching agents within any s-agent from the ContTest multi-agent system that we have developed.

The advantages of using a pre-made video sequences (Figure 2), in which real characters appear, are obvious. Teacher's moves and gestures cannot be replaced even by the most cutting-edge animated cartoon. The voice is no longer synthesized but real and does not raise any problems. The displaying of the previously filmed video sequences can be easily achieved either by the rest of software or by the user who learns. If video sequences occur spontaneously, they will create the impression of a real dialogue with a human, which will mean a personification of the agent responsible with content teaching.

The taught material can vary a lot in content and in the way of presentation. One may shoot from various angles, one may shoot a real teacher who gives real explanations using the chalk/marker on the blackboard or using a video-projector. Moreover, we can use even two teachers, eventually of different gender, who may occur by turns. Or we may suggest the user to choose one of the teachers at the beginning of the lesson.

There are three types of serious problems that occur when using video sequences:

- **Technical:** The size of the file, storing it, the size of the frame of the movie, graphic resolution, sound, brightness etc.;
- **Didactic:** The type of content that can be adjusted to the mould of video sequences and the type of content that cannot; the order in which it will be presented and the within which learning units;
- **Scenographic and Staging:** How much of the human body will be caught by the camera ? how should he gesticulate during the video? How should he talk, what voicing should he use?

Figure 2. Example of "teacher" in video sequence[4], explaining the accounting analysis

Technically speaking, it is obvious that the files will have to be relatively reduced in size so that they may fit into a classic storage unit (CD or DVD) together with the other the software components. Or they can be freely distributed on a Youtube channel. The use of several shorter files instead of a longer file would be preferable. The video clips should appear in a small frame (8 cm x 10 cm), so it may not distract the attention from other interface elements, simultaneously displayed on the screen.

The didactic content that will be taught must be selected from those learning units that do not require too elaborate explanations or solving exercises. Introductory theoretical elements, such as the object of accounting or the principles of accounting could be easily shot and presented by the pedagogic agents in the form of video sequences, that don't require special scenographic elements. On the other hand, explaining the way of realizing a financial balance sheet can constitute a special challenge in shooting a video. In this case the teacher will write with a black marker on a white board (Figure 2).

The teachers' outfit will be elegant, without excesses. The body posture will be straight, with mimics, gestures and intonation that will neither bore nor amuse the user. Even if the text will be read as if from a prompter (screen), the teacher has to be a good "actor" in order to avoid giving that impression, to look straight into the camera, seriously and persuasively, which will also mean authority in front of those who learn by using the software. The main disadvantage of using pre-made videos is that one cannot talk to the filmed teacher, even we can use some stereotype answers.

The illustration agent can be designed similarly to a teaching agent and the information for illustrations can be presented via three forms: pedagogic agent (character animated by the Microsoft Agent technology); video sequences (filmed real teachers); displayed formatted texts.

Illustrations can be briefly presented or elaborately presented, insisting upon the various aspects that may lead to a better understanding of the theory.

The Test-Generating and the Checking Answers Agents

The agent responsible with testing the student will generate questions, exercises or problems according the current learning unit. The easiest is to generate classic two-choice questions (for example, "yes / no" or "is debited / is credited"). Generating problems is always more complex, because it implies:

- Generating the text of a problem, in natural language (Romanian);
- Generating sums and assessing algebraic expressions;
- Generating correct answers.

We developed an original method to represent the accounting formulas by using regular expressions. The method was described in (Patrut, 2003) and (Patrut, 2004b).

We assume that the formal representation of the accounting formulas has three advantages:

- It helps to strictly define the rules for registration of the operations generating value movements in the financial accounting, the way they are stipulated by the corresponding regulations;
- It helps the persons that have no economic background to learn the rules;
- It allows computing programs to monitor the accounting learners.

As for example, in Figure 3, the text of an accounting problem is presented, with different amounts:

For such a problem, we have marked by [x], [y], etc. the variables that will receive random integral values, hundreds or thousands, and by [R], [S] and [T] the random values that are necessary to describe some algebraic expressions in accounting calculations are introduced. The algorithm described in (Patrut, 2004a) evaluates the following expressions: [x*R], [x*R*19/119] and [x*(1-R)], according to values that are generated for [x] and [R].

According to the Figure 4, the agent that checks if the given answer is correct will have a layered architecture. These layers will analyze al simple to complex ways a question has been answered, the question being provided by the agent in charge of generating tests. It is assumed that the answer was correct. Otherwise, it shall be considered that a minimal error occurred. If this is not the case either, more possible serious problems are considered, and so on. Depending on the error detected, correction measures are taken and the user receives guidance, but all errors of the same kind he made are counted.

We can see in the scheme presented in Figure 4 that the agent for generating tests (at the request of the agent in charge of generating content) will provide the user with questions, exercises and problems (step I). After generating tests, the agent responsible for checking the answers is appealed to (step II). Once the answer is checked, a new evaluation takes place (step III) and the cycle repeats. If, at some point in this cycle, after answers have been checked, they prove to be correct, the final evaluation and grading take place (step IV).

The agent responsible for these tasks will count all types of mistakes it has encountered until now (each layer it has met) and will give the student

Figure 3. A typical accounting problem where sums are randomly generated

The holder of an advance of [x] lei, amount received for a business related trip in another town it represent the deduction of expenses and the necessary document, justifying the amount of [x*R] lei[5], of which [x*R*19/119] represents the VAT, and returning the sum of [x*(1-R)] lei to the pay office.

Figure 4. The architecture of the checking answers agent

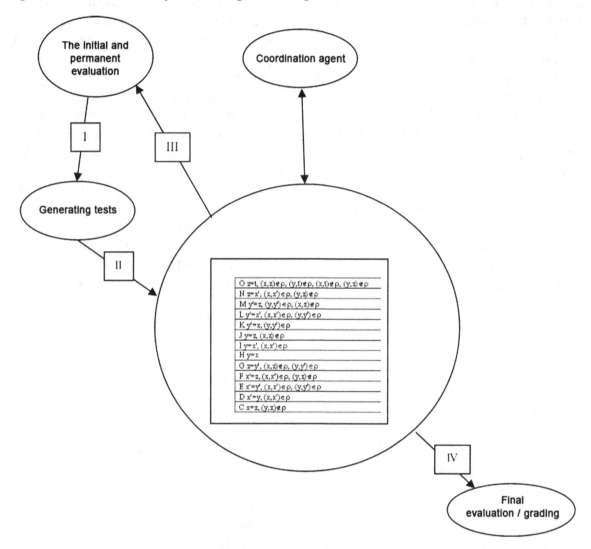

the corresponding grade. In addition, this agent may express emotions, depending on how well the student is prepared until that moment, the coordination agent may appeal to the grading agent during cycle 1-2-3 from Figure 4. Thus, the grading agent can express different feelings (of gratitude, discontentment) related to different moments from the student's testing.

As all types of accounting problems involve an accounting analysis, we will use the relationship of "confusion"/"confoundability" or "mixing-up" described in (Patrut, 2004b), (Patrut, 2010).

Therefore, we assume that a student may be wrong not only because he doesn't know the rules of the accounting analysis, but also because – for one or other reason – he makes confusion between two accounts. Certainly the accounts may be mistook, either because of the resembling names or because the wrong interpretation of some economic operations.

Therefore, marking by M the set of account from the general plan of accounts, a relationship of "confusion" between accounts can be defined (1)

$$\rho \subseteq MxM, \ (a,b) \in \rho \qquad (1)$$

meaning that, from one or other reason, account *a* can be mistaken for account *b*.

The relationship is symmetric, so (2), but not transitive too.

$$(a,b) \in \rho \rightarrow (b,a) \in \rho \qquad (2)$$

As the student gets examined and trained with the help of ContTest, the following problem arises: *is the system able to guide the student according to the confusions he makes (the current relationship ρ) or we must adapt the relationship ρ to the student's errors?*

Therefore, if the answer the systems waits for is $x = y$ and the student answers by $x = y'$, where $(y, y') \in \rho$, we can assume that that the student makes confusion between the *y* and *y'* accounts, but otherwise he would give the correct answer.

However, if the student responds by $x = z$, where $(y, z) \notin \rho$, we can assume either that knows very little about the right side of the accounting equivalence or he confuses the z account with the y one, and the relationship ρ is not defined properly. In this latter case, we can proceed as it follows (3)

$$\rho := \rho \cup \{(y, z),(z, y)\} \qquad (3)$$

In other words, we would add in the matrix the fact that *y* too can be confused with *z*. however, this adding should take place only if the students insists in responding with *z* instead of *y* and in other situations such as *u=y, y=u,* etc.

It is high possible that, in the case of a poorly trained student, if ρ is enriched like that, we will get to $(x, y) \in \rho, \ \forall \ x, \ y \in M$, which would lead to a very unpleasant situation. This is why it is better for the system to eliminate from ρ those pairs, corresponding to few situations encountered in the answers of the trained student.

Therefore, the ρ relationship evolves according to the wrong or correct answers of the student.

For an economic operation for which the correct answer is represented by the accounting formula x=y, we have considered 16 cases of possible answers. Each of them, except the first one (the correct answer) represents a certain type of error which denotes what the student does not know. Depending on the student's answer, we present you below the measures to be taken. They are described as implications or production rules, where we marked by:

- R = the rules according to which the accounts operate are presented (debiting the asset accounts, debiting the liability accounts, crediting the asset accounts, crediting the liability accounts).
- $P(x)$ = the detailed presentation of account x, where the accounts it gets contact with occur.
- $C (x,y)$ = making a comparison between x and y by presenting resemblances and differences between them.

The rules for correcting errors are presented in Figure 5 and have been presented in (Patrut 2004a) in a descriptive way.

The agent responsible for checking answers displays the result by using an animated character, a video sequence or a simple message or text box.

The Final Evaluation and Grading Agent

The agent responsible for the final evaluation and for grading the student (using grades, points or marks) makes a series of statistics on the student's answers (taken from the agent in charge of checking the answers). The final evaluation and grading agent will be appealed to in other moments of the application too by the coordination agent, if it considers that a partial evaluation or a feedback expressed by feeling is necessary, with a view to

Figure 5. Rules for correcting errors in accounting analysis

(1) $x=y \rightarrow \varnothing$ (correct answer)

(2) $x=y'$, $(y,y') \in \rho \rightarrow C(y,y') \wedge \rho := \rho - \{(y,y'),(y',y)\}$ if the number of confusions between y' and y decreases

(3) $x=z$, $(y,z) \notin \rho \rightarrow P(z) \wedge P(y) \wedge \rho := \rho \cup \{(y,z)\} \cup \{(z,y)\}$.

(4) $x'=y$, $(x,x') \in \rho \rightarrow C(x,x') \wedge \rho := \rho - \{(x,x'),(x',x)\}$ if the number of confusions between x' and x decreases

(5) $x'=y'$, $(x,x') \in \rho$, $(y,y') \in \rho \rightarrow C(x,x') \wedge C(y,y') \wedge \rho := \rho - \{(x,x'),(x',x),(y,y'),(y',y)\}$ if the x'=y' error occurs more often

(6) $x'=z$, $(x,x') \in \rho$, $(y,z) \notin \rho \rightarrow C(x,x') \wedge (3)$

(7) $z=y'$, $(x,z) \notin \rho$, $(y,y') \in \rho \rightarrow C(y,y') \wedge (3)$

(8) $y=x \rightarrow R(x,y)$

(9) $y=x'$, $(x,x') \in \rho \rightarrow R \wedge C(x, x')$

(10) $y=z$, $(x,z) \notin \rho \rightarrow P(z) \wedge P(x) \wedge R$

(11) $y'=x$, $(y,y') \in \rho \rightarrow R \wedge C(y, y')$

(12) $y'=x'$, $(x,x') \in \rho$, $(y,y') \in \rho \rightarrow C(x,x') \wedge C(y,y') \wedge R$

(13) $y'=z$, $(y,y') \in \rho$, $(x,z) \notin \rho \rightarrow C(y,y') \wedge R \wedge P(x) \wedge P(z)$

(14) $z=x'$, $(x,x') \in \rho$, $(y,z) \notin \rho \rightarrow C(x,x') \wedge R \wedge P(y) \wedge P(z)$

(15) $z=t$, $(x,z) \notin \rho$, $(y,t) \notin \rho$, $(x,t) \notin \rho$, $(y,z) \notin \rho \rightarrow P(x) \wedge P(y) \wedge P(z) \wedge P(t)$

determine the student to realize that he still has to learn or, on the contrary, that he has already acquired more skills and he is on the right path.

The tasks of this agent are to ensure the feedback to the student's answers, his training until that moment:

- Statistics regarding correct answers, wrong answers, partially correct answers, inversions, confusions, serious mistakes, calculation mistakes, delays, weaknesses, strengths, etc.;
- Giving the student grades, points, marks, penalties;
- Expressing feelings (contentment, discontentment, sadness, happiness, hope, fear, etc.).

Sometimes, displaying some statistical data is not the best form of feedback that can be offered to a person who learns something and solves some problems. It would be a waste of time and ink, probably, if for each correct or wrong answer of the student, the (real) teacher gave him a mark. Assessment during seminars, for example, can be also be done by verbal encouragements or warn-

ings. For simple questions, or after short testing periods, it is good for teachers to express verbally or even by mimics the attitude they have towards the student's current results.

If a student is at the beginning of an evaluation and makes few mistakes, the teacher can express his dissatisfaction. If the student persists in making mistakes, despite the teacher's effort to correct him, there may occurs the fear that the student will not acquire the respective skills. On the contrary, if right from the start the student answers correctly, there is feeling of hope, and if the student keeps answering correctly to all, or almost all, the question, the teacher will be satisfied.

The mimics of the teacher's face, as well as certain complimentary, encouraging or critical statements can be ways of partial grading and eventually there will be a mark from E to A, or a number of points or a certain general grade given to the student. Therefore, the final assessment and grading student should also exhibit human-like behavior similar to that of a real teacher. The agent should express feelings or emotions. The feelings can differ from one agent to another, as they differ from one teacher to another according to their temperament.

We developed architecture of intelligent agent, capable of "having" and expressing feelings or emotions, and even of exhibiting temperament. The architecture, that we called BeSGOTE, is an extension of the classic BDI architecture (Rao & Georgeff, 1991). The concepts upon which the BeSGOTE architecture relies were described in (Patrut, 2004b).

The BeSGOTE architecture consists of: Beliefs, States, Goals, Temperament, and Emotions/Feelings.

Experimental Data Using the ContTest System

ContTest can be operated both step by step by the student and automatically. If the multi-agent system is let to function automatically, then it will guide by itself the learning process and will monitor the student's activity. It will first select a certain lesson to test the student through exercises and questions. They will represent the initial evaluation. Depending on the student's success or failure, the system will pass the control to another agent so as to revise certain notions. At the beginning, the system tries to get an "image" of the student by knowing his knowledge stage.

It will then take the lessons one by one, calling an agent for each particular lesson, according to the order given by the accounting curriculum. It will generate automatically a question from the current lesson. The text of the question is randomly chosen from a list of predefined texts, and the sums are also randomly generated (for variables) or calculated (for expressions) by using an algebraic evaluator. The user will have to answer the question by filling some text boxes with the accounting formula he considers as appropriate. An article is represented by three text boxes: the first one is for the overdrawn account, the second – for the debit account, while the third is for the sum.

Also, explanations may be shown as video sequences that comprise lessons, explanations or stereotyped answers of real teachers (both sexes). They appear in three situations:

- At the explicit request of the student;
- When teaching some new notions;
- When the final evaluation agent wants to express certain feelings.

For example, the grading agent can expresses its hope about the student being on the right path, as he got good results so far.

The ContTest program has been used to train in accounting a group of students from Accounting and Management Information Systems. The chosen period for training using the ContTest system was when the professor was on the point of teaching the algorithm of the accounting analysis; the professor's assistant must practice it with students in seminars. Thus, the 100 students participating in the experiment were divided in two groups: the first one following the classical training phases – attending courses and seminars – and the other group entered the multimedia laboratory where they found the virtual teachers from the ContTest multi-agent system. After attending these classes, the 100 students met again to be examined by professors. A test comprising questions and exercises was given to them, with grades from 1 to 10 (maximum). The results of the test are shown in Figure 6. On the x axis there are the grades, and on the y axis the number of students obtaining those grades. In our case, ContTest led to better results than in the case of traditional learning methods. After the testing, the students trained using ContTest were given a questionnaire in order to check the utility of using a system of automatic training in this way.

Thus, most students consider this method of using an automatic system more than or at least as efficient as the traditional one. When asked "How do you generally appreciate the experiment

Figure 6. Grades obtained by subjects after applying the traditional and the ContTest training

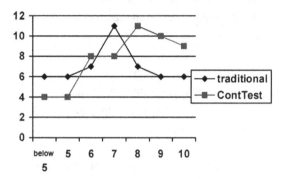

of using ContTest?" students gave the following favorable answers: interesting didactic experience, interesting experiment: 8; excellent check (better), less stressing: 7; better check, poor automatic teaching:6; less stress on evaluation: 5; the training-learning process in individualized, we work following our own pace: 4; ContTest can replace the teacher, it must be further developed: 3; better teaching: 1.

And the following unfavorable answers: entertainment: 5; waste of time: 5; dehumanizing the didactic process: 6.

Therefore, although opinions differ, if we divide all these answers in two categories, we will notice that we have more answers in favor of the ContTest system (73%) that against.

CONCLUSION AND DIRECTIONS FOR FUTURE RESEARCH

The accounting education must adjust itself to the new information and communication technologies, but also to the new challenges from the accounting professions, must keep up with the legislative modifications in the field and must meet the ever-increasing need of accountants. Computer-based training comes to support these ideas. Since classic educational software products do not have the qualities of a human teacher, we have considered the design of an intelligent educational soft for

interactive training in accounting as purposeful. The educational soft has been developed on the basis of a multi-agent system. The system has an original architecture based on an authentic organization of the agents into subsystems of intelligent agents called s-agents. Each s-agent deals with teaching a learning unit. Also, each s-agent has an internal structure of multi-agents system made up of six agents with a didactic role that are coordinated by one central agent. The six agents perform specific didactic tasks: initial assessment, teaching new knowledge, providing examples, generating questions, checking answers, evaluating the acquisition of competencies, grading the student. The pedagogic agents have been implemented by using a number of classic or novel technologies, or by combining these technologies. The grading agent has uses an original architecture of emotional agent to express feelings of satisfaction, dissatisfaction, fear or hope, to provide the student with an adequate feedback. The multi-agent system that we have designed has been incorporated into an educational soft (ContTest) that was tested and validated within an experiment with 100 students, which has shown that the ContTest soft has reached it objectives to a large extent: those of being an intelligent educational soft, a "virtual teacher".

There are several directions for improving the ContTest system and these are:

- Generalizing the test-generating agent so that it may be able to provide other types of problems according to various patterns, in Romanian; for generalization, it would be desirable that the words which contain the texts of the problems (and not only the sums) be chosen randomly.
- Generalizing the agent that checks the answer so as to adapt it to the new types of problems;
- Improving the illustration agent so as to generate more examples;

- Diversifying the methods of feedback in order to allow record vocal orders from the student;
- Adjusting the system to a distributed frame of work.

The ContTest system is a good start for any young researcher that wishes to improve the interactive training process in accounting, by using techniques of distributed artificial intelligence.

REFERENCES

Almaris. (2007). *Financial Accounting Tutor 9.0, Almaris.* Retrieved from http://www.almaris.com/fact/fact-overview.htm

Anohina, A. (2007). *Advances in Intelligent Tutoring Systems: Problem-solving Modes and Model of Hints.* Retrieved from http://www.riverland.edu/academics/AcademicPrograms.cfm

Apostol, C. (2000). *Instruirea asistată de calculator a managerilor în domeniul tehnologiei informaţiei.* Raport de cercetare la Contractul nr. 1253, 198/1996, Editura ASE, Bucureşti. Retrieved from http://www.biblioteca.ase.ro/catalog/rezultate.php?c=2&q=&st=s&tp1=1&tp2=1&tp3=1&tp4=1&tp5=1&tp6=1

Arafa, Y., Charlton, P., & Mamdani, A. (1997). *Modelling Personal Service Assistants with Personality: From Metaphor to Implementation.* Imperial College of Science, Technology & Medicine. Retrieved from http://citeseer.nj.nec.com/cs

Ayoola, O. L., & Phelan, E. M. (2010). Crafting a Personalised Agent-Oriented Mobile E-Learning Platform for Adaptive Third Level Education. In M. Beer, M. Fasli, & D. Richards (Eds.), *Multi-Agent Systems for Education and Interactive Entertainment: Design, Use and Experience.* Hershey, PA: IGI Global. doi:10.4018/978-1-60960-080-8.ch012

Bach, J. (2002). Enhancing Perception and Planning of Software Agents with Emotion and Acquired Hierarchical Categories. In *Proceedings of MASHO 02, German Conference on AI.* Karlsruhe, Germany: Academic Press.

Barry, J. (2007). *Advantages and Disadvantages of Online Courses.* Education Training Info. Retrieved from http://www.educationtraininginfo.com/articles/e001-advantages-and-disadvantages-of-online-courses.htm

Bartneck, C. (2003). *Integrating the OCC Model of Emotions in Embodied Characters.* University of Endhoven. Retrieved from http://citeseer.nj.nec.com/cs

Bates, J. (1994). *The Role of Emotion in Believable Agents. Communications of the ACM.*

Bates, J., Loyall, A. B., & Reilly, W. S. (1992). An Architecture for Action, Emotion, and Social Behavior. In *Proceedings of the Fourth Eurepean Workshop on Modeling Autonomous Agents in Multi-Agent World.* Academic Press.

Botelho, L. M., & Coelho, H. (n.d.). *Adaptive Agents: Emotion Learning.* University of Lisbon. Retrieved from http://citeseer.nj.nec.com/cs

Cârstea, M. (n.d.). *Instruirea Asistată de Calculator în Şcoala Românească.* Revista PC Report.

Franklin, S., & Graesser, A. (1998). It is an Agent, or just a Program? A Taxonomy for Autonomous Agents. In *Proceedings of Third International Workshop on Agent Theories, Architectures and Languages.* Springer-Verlag.

Jaques, P., Andrade, A., Jung, J., Bordini, R., & Vicari, R. (2001). *Using Pedagogical Agents to Support Collaborative Distance Learning.* Retrieved from http://citeseer.nj.nec.com/cs

Jondahl, S., & Mørch, A. (2000). *Simulating Pedagogical Agents in a Virtual Learning Environment.* University of Bergen, University of Oslo. Retrieved from http://citeseer.nj.nec.com/cs

Kesdee. (2007). *E-Learning Course - Financial Accounting*. KESDEE Inc. Retrieved from http://www.researchandmarkets.com/reports/310117

Lăcurezeanu, R. (2000). *Instruirea asistata de calculator în contabilitate si informatica*. (PhD thesis). Bucharest: ASE.

Lewis Johnson, W. (n.d.). *Pedagogical Agents in Virtual Learning Environments*. Retrieved from http://www.isi.edu/isd/johnson.html

Middleton, S., De Roure, D., & Shadbolt, N. (n.d.). *Capturing Knowledge of User Preferences: Ontologies in Recommender Systems*. University of Southampton, Marea Britanie. Retrieved from http://citeseer.nj.nec.com/cs

Moreno, K., Person, N., Adcock, A., & Van Eck, R. A. O. (2002). *Etiquette and Efficacy in Animated Pedagogical Agents: Rge Role of Stereotypes*. Retrieved from http://citeseer.nj.nec.com/cs

MYOB. (2007). *Mind Your Own Business*. Retrieved from http://www.myob.com

Nagy, A. (2005). The Impact of E-Learning. In E-Content: Technologies and Perspectives for the European Market. Berlin: Springer-Verlag.

Ohio University. (2007). *E-Learning: Accounting & Finance*. Retrieved from http://www.ohiou.edu/noncredit/Elearning/accounting.htm

Okonkwo, C. (2001). *Affective Pedagogical Agents and User Persuasion*. Department of CS, University of Saskatchewan, Canada. Retrieved from http://citeseer.nj.nec.com/cs

Ortony, A., Clore, G. L., & Collins, A. (1988). *The cognitive structure of emotions*. Cambridge, UK: Cambridge University Press. doi:10.1017/CBO9780511571299

Pătruţ, B. (2010). *Interactive Education in Accounting: A Multi-agent Solution*. Saarbrücken, Germany: LAP Lambert Academic Publishing.

Pătruţ, B. (2013a). Competences versus Competencies in Romanian Accounting Education. *International Journal of Academic Research in Business and Social Sciences*, *3*(1).

Pătruţ, B. (2013b). E-Teaching and E-Asessment in Accounting using Intelligent Pedagogical Agents. In *Proceedings of "Elearning and Software for Education"* (eLSE, Bucharest, 2013), (pp. 499-508). Retrieved from www.ceeol.com

Pătruţ, B. (2003). *Tehnologia Microsoft Agent pentru învăţarea regulilor de funcţionare a conturilor. Informatica Economica*, *4(28)*.

Pătruţ, B. (2004a). Agents for Learning Accounting Bases. In *Proceedings of CEECBIS04 (The Central and East European Conference in Business Information Systems)*. Academic Press.

Pătruţ, B. (2004b). Architecture for Intelligent Agents with Temperament. In *Proceedings of the International Conference on Computers and Communications*. Academic Press.

Pfeifer, R. (1988). Artificial intelligence models of emotion. In *Proceedings of the NATO Advanced Research Workshop*. Dordrecht, The Netherlands: Kluwer.

Rao, A. S., & Georgeff, M. P. (1991). Modeling Rational Agents within a BDI-Architecture. In *Proceedings of the 2nd International Conference on Principles of Knowledge Representation and Reasoning (KR'91)*. Retrieved from http://citeseer.ist.psu.edu/rao91modeling.html

Roşca, G., Apostol, C.-G., Zamfir, G., & Bodea, C.-N. (2002). Informatica instruirii. Bucharest: Editura Economică.

Russel, S., & Norvig, P. (2002). *Artificial Intelligence - A Modern Approach (2nd ed.)*. Prentice Hall.

Sitchawat, S. (2005). E-learning for Accounting Education in Thailand. In *Proceedings of World Conference on Educational Multimedia, Hypermedia and Telecommunications 2005* (pp. 110-115). Chesapeake, VA: AACE.

Thiry, M., Khator, S., Barcia, R. M., & Martins, A. (2000). *Intelligent Agent-Based Approach for Distance Learning.* Retrieved from http://citeseer.nj.nec.com/cs

Vassileva, J. (1997). *Goal-Based Pedagogical Agents.* Federal Armed Forces University. Retrieved from http://citeseer.nj.nec.com/cs

Weiss, G. (Ed.). (2000). *Multiagent Systems - A Modern Approach to Distributed Artificial Intelligence.* Cambridge, MA: The MIT Press.

Wooldridge, M. (2002). *Introduction to MultiAgent Systems.* Wiley & Sons.

Zamfir, G. (2000). Instruirea asistata de calculator in domeniul economic. Bucharest: Inforec. Retrieved from http://www.biblioteca.ase.ro/catalog/rezultate.php?c=2&q=&st=s&tp1=1&tp2=1&tp3=1&tp4=1&tp5=1&tp6=1

ADDITIONAL READING

Adachi, Y., Kawasumi, K., Ozaki, M., & Ishii, N. (2000). Development of accounting education CAI system. In *Proceedings of the Fourth International Conference on Knowledge-Based Intelligent Engineering Systems and Allied Technologies*, Volume 1, Issue, pp. 389 - 392.

Ainsworth, S. (2013). *Artificial Intelligence in Education*, Retrieved from http://www.psychology.nottingham.ac.uk/staff/com/c8clat/handout7.pdf

White, C. E., Jr. (1995). An analysis of the need for ES and AI in accounting education in Accounting Education. *International Journal (Toronto, Ont.)*, 4(3), 259–269.

Atrill, P., & McLaney, E. (2012). *Accounting and Finance for Non-Specialists* (8th ed.). Pearson.

d' Inverno, M., & Luck, M. (2004). *Formal Agent Decelopment: Framework to System*, http://citeseer.nj.nec.com/cs

Danubianu, M. Barala, A. (2013). Big Data - A Chance to Change the Academic Scene? in *Proceedings of the SMART 2013 International Conference*, "Social Media in Academia: Research and Teaching", Bacau, Romania, June 6-9, 2013.

Dastani, M., Hubner, J. F., & Logan, B. (Eds.). (2012). *Programming Multi-Agent Systems: 10th International Workshop*, ProMAS 2012, Valencia, Spain, June 5, 2012, Revised Selected Papers, Springer.

Demazeau, Y., Ishida, T., & Corchado Rodriguez, J. M. (Eds.). (2013). *Advances on Practical Applications of Agents and Multi-Agent Systems*, Proceedings of the 11th International Conference, PAAMS 2013, Salamanca, Spain, May 22-24, 2013.

Deperlioglu, O., & Köse, U. (2012). Design and Development of an E-Learning Environment for the Course of Electrical Circuit Analysis, in *Interdisciplinary Journal of E-Learning and Learning Objects,* Volume 8, 2012, http://www.academia.edu/2053337/Design_and_development_of_an_e-learning_environment_for_the_course_of_electrical_circuit_analysis

Elliot, C., Rickel, J., & Lester, J. C. (1997). Integrating Affective Computing into Animated Tutoring Agents. In *Proceedings of IJCAI Workshop of Animated Interface Agents*, Nagoya, Japan.

Feituri, M., & Funghi, F. (2010). Intelligent Agents in Education. In W. Ritke-Jones (Ed.), *Virtual Environments for Corporate Education: Employee Learning and Solutions* (pp. 321–341). IGI Global. doi:10.4018/978-1-61520-619-3.ch018

Georgeff, M., Pell, B., Pollack, M., Tambe, M., & Wooldridge, M. (2004). *The Belief-Desire-Intention Model of Agency*, http://citeseer.nj.nec.com/cs

Glaser, N. (2012). *Conceptual Modelling of Multi-Agent Systems: The Comomas Engineering Environment.* New York: Springer-Verlag.

Harrison, C. G., & Chess, D. M. Kershenbaum (2002). A *Mobile Agents: Are They a Good Ideea?* Research Report, Research Division, IBM, http://citeseer.nj.nec.com/cs

Heick, T. 10 Roles for Artificial Intelligence in Education, Retrieved from http://www.teach-thought.com/technology/10-roles-for-artificial-intelligence-in-education/ at 10/31/2012

Howden, N., Rönnquist, R., & Hodgson, A. Lucas, (2002). A *Jack Intelligent Agents^{TM} - Summary of an Agent Infrastructure*, http://www.agent-software.com

Jody, I. (Ed.). (2012). *Multi-agent System*. International Book Marketing Service Ltd.

Käser, T. Baschera. G.-M., Busetto, A.G., Klingler, S., Solenthaler, B., Buhmann, J. M., Gross, M. (2012), Towards a Framework for Modelling Engagement Dynamics in Multiple Learning Domains, in Susan Bull, Gautam Biswas (Eds.), Best of Artificial Intelligence in Education 2011.

Krupansky, J. (2003). *Issues and Thoughts on Software Agents*, http://www.agtivity.com/agthoughts.htm

Lanier, J. *Agents of Alienation*, http://www.cs.ucsd.edu/~goguen/courses/171sp02/lanier.agents.html

Manesh, H. F., & Schaefer, D. (2010). Virtual Learning Environments for Manufacturing in William Ritke-Jones (Ed.), Virtual Environments for Corporate Education: Employee Learning and Solutions, IGI Global, ISBN 9781615206193, Pages 89-109.

Mitkas, P. A., Kehagias, D., Symeonidis, A. L., & Athanasiadis, I. N. (2007). *A Framework for Constructing Multi-Agent Applications and Training Intelligent Agents*. Department of Electrical and Computer Engineering Aristotle University of Thessaloniki.

Nair, R., Tambe, M., & Marsella, S. (2003). *The Role of Emotions in Multiagent Teamwork: A Preliminary Investigation*, http://citeseer.nj.nec.com/cs

Pătruţ. B., Pătruţ, M., Cmeciu C. (Eds.) (2013). *Social Media and the New Academic Environment: Pedagogical Challenges*, IGI Global, Hershey, ISBN 978-1466628519

Pătruţ, M, Pătruţ, B. (Eds.) (2013). *Social Media in Higher Education: Teaching in Web 2.0*, IGI Global, Hershey, ISBN 978-1466629707

Pătruţ, V., Rotilă, A., Ciuraru-Andrica, C., Luca, M. (2009), *Accounting – A Semiotic Process*, in *Annals of Faculty of Economics*, University of Oradea, vol. 3, issue 1, pages 1105-1112.

Pătruţ, B. (2004), InterSchem – a Logical Scheme Interpreter, in Studii şi cercetări ştiinţifice. Seria matematică, Universitatea din Bacău.

Rickell, J. (2001). Intelligent Virtual Agents for Education and Training: Opportunities and Challenges. In A. de Antonio, R. Aylett, & D. Ballin (Eds.), *IVA 2001, LNAI 2190* (pp. 15–22). Springer-Verlag Berlin Heidelberg. doi:10.1007/3-540-44812-8_2

Schwartz, B. N. (2007). *Advances in Accounting Education Teaching and Curriculum Innovations*. IN, USA: Indiana University-South Bend.

Weiss, G. (2013). Multiagent Systems, MIT Press, 2013, 2nd edition, ISBN 978-0-262-01889-0

KEY TERMS AND DEFINITIONS

Accounting Analysis: A procedure used in accounting, having four steps: identifying the patrimonial elements that suffer modifications; establishing the significance and size of these modifications; identifying the corresponding accounts; applying the rules of operating the accounts to establish the part of the corresponding accounts – debit or credit – in which the operation analyzed is to be recorded.

Computer-Based Training (CBT): An interactive instructional approach in which the computer, taking the place of an instructor, provides the student with questions to be answered, choices or decisions to be made; the CBT then provides feedback based on the student's response.

Conversational Agent: An animated character, which can interact with the human user, by speaking, moving, gesturing etc.

Educational Software: Educational software is computer software, the primary purpose of which is teaching or self-learning.

E-Learning: All forms of electronically supported learning and teaching.

Intelligent Agent: An autonomous entity which observes through sensors and acts upon an environment using actuators and directs its activity towards achieving goals.

Interactive Learning: The learning process when a student puts together knowledge and skills by connecting with information and experiences provided by the teacher, that can be an artificial one, and the communication between the student and professor is bidirectional.

Multi-Agent System: A system composed of multiple interacting intelligent agents within an environment.

Pedagogical Agent: A conversational agent with a didactic purpose; pedagogical agents focus on perceiving the behavior of the learner, by furnishing informational and educational content, according to his level of knowledge and acquired abilities; also they focus on accumulating new information and creating skills matching the study area.

S-Agent: Small multi-agents system, each s-agent dealing with an educational competency in the discipline to be learned; each s-agent is made up of several agents, each with a particular role in the didactic process (assessment, teaching, checking and grading).

Software Agent: A complex software entity that is capable of acting with a certain degree of autonomy in order to accomplish tasks on behalf of its host.

ENDNOTES

[1] Obviously, the ICT used indiscriminately in, for example, violent video games may have negative consequences upon young people, but this phenomenon does not constitute the object of our discussion.

[2] Many students work and attend distance-learning courses by which they improve their training precisely in the field their are working.

[3] For detailed studies on the topic of software agents, intelligent agents, multi-agent systems etc. see (Weiss, 2010) and (Wooldridge, 2002).

[4] I would like to thank, in this way, my students, Andreea Schmidt, Claudia Ferenț, Andreea Miron, Simona Patrichi, and Mihai Corbu for the help they offered.

Chapter 5
Intelligent Questioning System Based on Fuzzy Logic

Omer Deperlioglu
Afyon Kocatepe Üniversitesi, Turkey

Guray Sonugur
Afyon Kocatepe Üniversitesi, Turkey

Kadir Suzme
Afyon Kocatepe Üniversitesi, Turkey

ABSTRACT

One of the most important functions of distance learning systems is determining the student knowledge level and performance clearly. In traditional education systems, students can be assessed in single-stage via tests and homework studies, which consist of multiple-choice questions. However, this method cannot provide accurate results since it is not able to evaluate student knowledge level and question difficulty level. In this chapter, a system and software structure that can determine student knowledge levels, topic difficulty level, and question difficulty levels according to instant student answers for the exam is introduced. In forming student knowledge levels, content monitoring and test data taken from distance education vocational school were used. In this way, more accurate results have been obtained. The fuzzy logic technique has been used to determine (classify) student knowledge levels and topic difficulty levels clearly. In order to determine next questions adaptively, the stored questions have been classified with division clustering methods, and the most suitable questions for the related student knowledge level have been found by using the nearest neighbor algorithm.

INTRODUCTION

As the Internet gains wide popularity around the world, e-learning is taken by the learners as an important study aid. In the past few years, designing useful learning diagnosis systems has become a hot research topic in the literature (Cheng, Lin, Chen, & Heh, 2005).With accelerated growth

of computer and communication technologies, researchers have attempted to adopt computer network technology for research on education. Notable examples include the development of computer-aided tutoring and testing systems (Hopper, 1992). According to a research result, contribution of e-learning to success is about 50%. So, e-learning can be much more effective than

DOI: 10.4018/978-1-4666-6276-6.ch005

other single direction, passive learning methods. There is a growing interest in online learning all over the world (Elango, Gudep, & Selvam, 2008) (Dadone, 2011).

In recent decades, the interactions of teachers and students are continually enriched and changed because of explosive growth in computer and internet technologies. There are more and more e-learning environments being developed for instructors and learners to take lessons or assessments (Chen, Huang, & Chu, 2005) (Huang, Chen, Huang, Jeng, & Kuo, 2008).

People interest in distance education systems has increased with developments in internet technologies. The main advance in distance education system has been comprised with passing from Web 1.0 to Web 2.0. Users were passive consumers of content with these tools as many of them have been called Web 1.0. To fulfill the shortages of Web 1.0 and to provide more effective interaction and collaboration, investigation for the ways of using blogs effectively, wikis, podcasts and social network in education has been started. The main characteristic of these tools called Web 2.0, is users' active participation in the content of creation process. In studies of learning and teaching, as well as efficacious evolution of technology, importance of active participation, critical thinking, social presence, collaborative learning and two way communications are also underlined for quality learning (Beldarrin, 2006) (Kocak, Usluel, & Mazman, 2009). With great support of Web 2.0 technologies, e-learning and distance education system's proportions increased rapidly in the teaching and learning sector. For this reason types of e-learning and distance education software has been increased in recent years.

E-learning systems, or Virtual Learning Environments (VLEs), are rapidly becoming an integral part of the teaching and learning process(Pituch & Lee, 2006). VLEs present a number of opportunities to business schools, including the potential to leverage a business school brand across geographical borders and the enhancement of face-to-face

teaching. Furthermore it enables improvements in communication efficiency, both between student and teacher, as well as among students(Martins & Kellermanns, 2004). A VLE is a web-based communications platform that allows students, without limitation of time and place, to access different learning tools, such as program information, course content, teacher assistance, discussion boards, document sharing systems, and learning resources (Martins & Kellermanns, 2004) (van Raaij & Schepers, 2008).

Despite the recent interest in online distance education in the higher education setting, there is scant literature concerning how to assess student performance in the online distance education environment. Since assessment is an important lens through which education is viewed (Bransford, Brown, & Cocking, 2000) (Kim, J.S., & Maeng, 2008). Because of the nature of the instruction of distance education courses, assessment and measurement become an even more critical part of the educational process. In the absence of the face-to-face interactions that enable teachers to use informal observations to gauge student response, online assessments become the singular means by which mastery over material is measured (Kerka & Wonacott, 2000).

In distance education assessment systems, students must be assessed with their current knowledge levels which is changing depend on different topics. A student may have different knowledge levels in different topics. System has to use this differences to increase student knowledge level each topic with preparing exams which is suitable to current student level.

The main goal of this study, developing a model and software about student assessment system which is depending on the student knowledge level to help instructors and trainers with producing useful feedback. This feedback information is used by instructors to assess their students fairly and accurately. In this way, the lecturers whom determined their students' knowledge level accurately, become more useful for their students to present them the most suitable learning environments. Finally, as a major aim, the system tries to increase the students' knowledge levels realizing all these processes in stages.

In the second section, background of this study has been explained. Intelligent question systems, web-based adaptive test systems, classifying students' knowledge level, questions and topics issues have been explained as well. Then, in the third section we mention about fuzzy logic model and data mining clustering methods which are the main part of the model. This is followed by a section in which we describe our models and present our application. In the last section, our results and future works are discussed.

BACKGROUND

Assessment is the most important part of education. Assessment is a general term that refers to all the ways lecturers gather feedback information. In general, assessment procedures serve different functions in the classroom, often being used for formative assessment, summative assessment, and self-assessment (Seng, Parsons, Hinson, & Sardo-Brown, 2003). Definition of formative assessment is to provide feedback during learning. Definition of summative assessment is to measure learning at the end of the process (Kim, Smith, & Maeng, 2000). Formative assessment provides interim information to both instructors and students (Crisp & Ward, 2008). In addition, lecturers also use summative assessment to realize how well they taught and how well students learned at the end of instruction (Black & William, 1998).

Assessment has always been a very significant step in the learning process. Its different forms are motivated by its different purposes: exams, so teachers can know if a student has reached the appropriate level of knowledge; *self-assessment*, for students to check how much they are learning; *questions*, so that teachers can provide the exact

type of feedback while teaching, etc. (Conejo, Guzmán, Millán, Trella, De-La-Cruz, & Ríos, 2004).

Performing examination is the best way to measure and evaluate student performance in distance education. These examinations must be assessed by considering each student's own special conditions. While assessing the results of the examination, question difficulty levels and student knowledge levels must be considered by the system. In distance education systems, the accurate evaluation of student's knowledge level is very important to increase student's knowledge level and support students with required contents.

Computer Adaptive Test

In recent years, exploring new educational tools has been triggered by great developments in computer and internet technologies. Computer Adaptive Tests (CAT) is one of the related educational tools. The CAT is a type of tests which is managed by software. Decision of choosing the next question and so determining the number of the question which will be asked, have been performed automatically by the software considering the student profile which is created and updated by the system depend on students interactions.

In this way, a CAT allows us to go back to a time when teachers could afford to evaluate each student orally by asking him/her a few well selected questions that were gradually more difficult for students with higher levels (to allow them to show how much they had learned), or easier for students with lower levels (so the lecturer could quickly diagnose that they had not learned enough). As the number of students in the classrooms grew larger and larger, lecturers were forced to evaluate their students using standard examinations almost exclusively. The problem with standard examinations is that, in order to be able to discriminate between all the different knowledge levels, they have to include questions at all levels of difficulty.

As a result, tests are longer and include questions that are not *informative* for some of the students taking them, either because they are too difficult or too easy (Klir & Yuan, 2000).

Difference between Traditional Education Systems and Web Based Distance Education Systems

E-learning environments offer some interesting benefits over traditional learning environments in terms of independence. Students' learning in an e-learning environment can be independent of distance, time, computing platform, and classroom size (Mahonen & Frantti, 2000).

Traditional learning environments emphasize fragmented knowledge and basic skills. The human instructor sets the criteria and controls the learning procedure. The instructor and the students interact directly. The whole procedure in the instructor's perspective is to prepare the content of the course, make slides or lecture notes to teach in class, hand out homework, design project assignments, and design quiz sand exams to evaluate the students. The students at different levels are in the same classroom under preaching of the same instructor and take the same pace to learn and review, which makes some more advanced students bored while making some other students who cannot follow up frustrated. E-learning refers to education that is enhanced by or delivered using digital media and information technology, typically over the internet. An e-learning environment has several advantages over the traditional learning environment in areas such as distance independence, time independence, computing platform independence, and classroom size independence (Shi, Liu, Shang, & Chen, 2005). Some important advantages of e-learning systems are listed as below.

- E-learning systems are able to present multimedia environments like videos, java applets, and animations etc. which are impossible to be presented within face-to-face learning.

- Testing times are decreased significantly.
- User's individual knowledge levels are able to be predicted more accurate.
- E-learning systems are able to prepare examinations depend on student's individual knowledge levels,
- E-learning systems are able to include built-in help links for students.
- Students' progress information can be monitored easily.

The major difference between CATs and traditional *Paper and Pencil Tests* is the *capability to adapt* to each individual student. That is the same difference which exists between traditional education systems and Intelligent Tutoring Systems.

This study has been developed to assist lecturers in their assessment process considering importance of the fairly and precisely assessing in online distance educations. Increasing students' level of success, primarily, knowledge level of the students must be determined accurately. Then suitable learning materials must be presented to students according to their determined knowledge level.

Student's knowledge level is not a unique value so a student may have different knowledge levels per each topic. In this study, student knowledge levels which are updated student's responds have been determined separately for each topic. Students' topic performance is updated by the system when the students respond questions which are belongs to related topic. Thus low-performing students are able to be supported by more useful learning environments in their low-performing topics.

The Fuzzy Logic Model has been used to determine student knowledge levels without any mistake. In this way it is allowed to determine system parameters like student success level (SSL), topic difficulty level and question difficulty level accurately.

The most suitable questions, which have been determined accurately according to student knowledge levels, are chosen by the adaptive questioning system via data mining clustering algorithms.

It is tried to improve student's knowledge level progressively by asking the related questions to the student.

RELATED MODELS

Fuzzy Logic Models

Fuzzy logic is a kind of logic that recognizes more than simple true and false values. Linguistic variables can be represented with degrees of truthfulness and falsehood with fuzzy logic. Fuzzy logic is an significant artificial intelligence technique because it is used to design and advance more accurate, advanced and intelligent technologies for understanding and controlling different systems that form humankind's actual life (Deperlioglu & Arslan, 2010).

Fuzzy set theory was first announced by Lotfi A. Zadeh (Zadeh, 1965) in a seminal paper at University of California at Berkeley, USA. After that, the theoretical ideas about the fuzzy logic have been expressed in many books written by Zimmerman (Zimmerman, 1996), Berkan and Trubatch (Berkan & Trubatch, 2000), Kartalopou-los (Kartalopoulos, 2000), Klir and Yuan (Klir & Yuan, 2000) and Bector and Chandra (Bector & Chandra, 2004). The Fuzzy logic was progressed from fuzzy set theory to reason with uncertain and vague information and to represent knowledge in an operationally powerful form. The main idea about progressing fuzzy logic from fuzzy set theory was to establish conceptual framework for linguistically represented knowledge (Mahonen & Frantti, 2000).

Defining membership functions in the fuzzy logic, after selecting fuzzy sets that will be used; a membership function for the sets should be assigned. A membership function is a typical curve that converts the numerical value of input within a range from 0 to 1, indicating the belongingness of the input to a fuzzy set (Deperlioglu & Kose, 2010) (Lee, 1990) (Majumdar & Ghosh, 2008).

Fuzzy sets in each input and output variable are defined by the assigned membership function. The membership functions for inputs and outputs have to be defined by expert experience (Kutuva, Reddy, Xiao, Gao, Hariharan, & Kulkarni, 2006). Because fuzzy systems are based on thinking of the person who has an expert experience about the subject the fuzzy logic used in.

Figure 1. Fuzzy logic membership functions

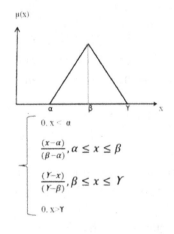

$$\begin{cases} 0, & x < \alpha \\ \dfrac{(x-\alpha)}{(\beta-\alpha)}, & \alpha \leq x \leq \beta \\ \dfrac{(\gamma-x)}{(\gamma-\beta)}, & \beta \leq x \leq \gamma \\ 0, & x > \gamma \end{cases}$$

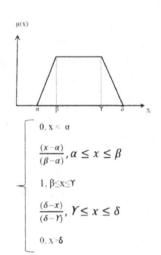

$$\begin{cases} 0, & x < \alpha \\ \dfrac{(x-\alpha)}{(\beta-\alpha)}, & \alpha \leq x \leq \beta \\ 1, & \beta \leq x \leq \gamma \\ \dfrac{(\delta-x)}{(\delta-\gamma)}, & \gamma \leq x \leq \delta \\ 0, & x > \delta \end{cases}$$

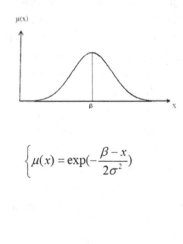

$$\left\{ \mu(x) = \exp(-\frac{\beta-x}{2\sigma^2}) \right.$$

The most used membership function types: triangle, trapezoid and Gaussian functions are described in Figure 1. Fuzzy Linguistic Rules transform the given input variables to the output variables. A fuzzy rule is created by writing a fuzzy if - then rule. For example in a fuzzy logic system that uses two inputs for one output, a simple rule may be written as follows:

IF (the soil IS VERY DRY) AND (the weather IS SUNNY) THEN (result IS MUCH WATER)

The fuzzy logic system produces the output from given input variables. This output is also a fuzzy set. Using the output value in real life, its fuzzy value should be translated into real values. This translation is named as defuzzification (Dadone, 2011). There are several deffuzification techniques which called as centroid, center of sums, mean of maxima and left-right maxima.

Data Mining

In e-learning systems, learners are in different age level, sex, and social role, their culture, education background, attention and interest are also exist a great difference. Giving corresponding learning content and tactics to realize teaching learners according to their needs is very difficult (Jun, Renhou, & Qinhua, 2004).

Data Mining can be used to extract knowledge from e-learning systems through the analysis of the information available in the form of data generated by their users. In this case, the main objective becomes finding the patterns of system usage by teachers and students and, perhaps most importantly, discovering the students' learning behavior patterns (Castro, Vellido, Nebot, & Mugica, 2007).

With the aid of data mining techniques we can analyze data to create patterns, data groups or profiles that cannot be seen easily with the naked eye. Received models can be successfully applied to make learning process more effective by additional functionalities of e-learning system, e.g. personalization of learning process (recommendation system), source of feedback for author of didactic contents or intrusion detection tools (Mantiuk, Aydin, & Myszkowski, 2008).

Yin and Lao (Tang, Lao, Li, Yin, Li, & Kilis, 2000) used data mining techniques (association rules) in an e-learning system to determine the relationship between learners' personality characteristics and learning behavior patterns.

THE DEVELOPED SYSTEM: IQS

In this study, several features of distance education systems have been determined from the database and used as input or output of the IQS. These features are explained under the section of Basic Features and Functions above.

Basic Features and Functions

Before explaining working mechanism of developed system, it is better to talk about basic features and functions. In this sense, important terms and approaches are introduced in the following sections.

Question Difficulty Level

All questions have a difficulty level which entered into the system. A question starts its life cycle with an initial difficulty level which is defined

Table 1. A part of database view which represents to current status of the student number 127

Question ID	QDL	DateTimeCode	IRC	TQC	IDL	Topic ID	FinalCode
127	0,5306	201103271758049	25	47	0,5	8	1

by the instructor. Then Question Difficulty Level (QDL) has been determined and updated in the database continuously according to the incorrect respond rates of the users. Table-1 below is one of example on how QDL is determined.

IRC represents the Incorrect Respond count of the user, TQC represents the Total Question Count responded by the user, IDL represents the Initial Difficulty Level defined by the instructors, FinalCode is the status if this record is current record or not.

$$QDL = \frac{\text{Incorrect respond count + Initial Difficulty Level}}{\text{Total respond count + Initial Difficulty Level}}$$

(1)

$$QDL = \frac{25+1}{47+2} = 0.5306$$

When the question 127 has been answered as incorrect again, the latest state of the table shown in Table 2.

$$QDL = \frac{26+1}{48+2} = 0.54$$

In the latest state as shown in the Table-2, QDL value increases a small amount and *QDL*, *DateTimeCode* and *FinalCode* values are updated in the database. During database updating QDL values have not been deleted completely. The values have been stored in the database with different date-time codes. In this way, progressing of the QDL values have been monitored by the instructors via report section of the software.

Classification of the Question Difficulty Levels

It is very important to classify difficulty level of questions in IQS. Generally, difficulty level, which is one of the main input parameter, has been classified as *easy* or *difficult*. However, making a classification only two categories will prevent arriving accurate results in the intelligent systems. There may be many of the students in one of distance education school and these students may have several knowledge level. For this reason, intelligent question systems must have more detailed question level categories.

In this chapter, Fuzzy Logic models have been used to classify question difficulty levels. As shown in Figure 2, question difficulty levels have been divided 5 main categories using triangle membership functions. QDL can take values ranging between [0-1]. 0 values represents easiest questions, 1 value represents most difficult questions. In this way questions able to be classified as %56,4 difficult and %23,7 very difficult e.g.

The categories used by the IQS are; Very Easy (VE), Easy (E), Medium (M), Difficult (D), Very Difficult (VD).

Boundary section value of the triangle membership function is 2/16 and support section value of the triangle membership function is 4/16.

Student Knowledge Level

In distance education systems, it is not said to all the students have a same knowledge level. Some of the students have high knowledge level but some of have not. Trainers have to determine each

Table 2. Latest state of the table after answering incorrectly for 127 numbered question

Question ID	QDL	DateTimeCode	IRC	TQC	IDL	Topic ID	FinalCode
127	0,5306	201103271758049	25	47	0,5	8	0
127	0,54	201103271804124	26	48	0,5	8	1

Figure 2. Classification of the QDL values

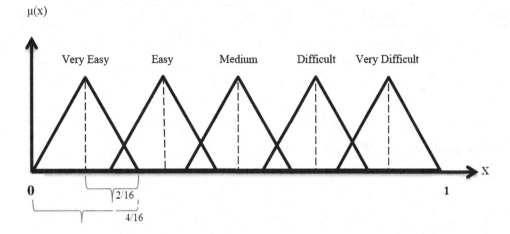

student's level accurately to decide how to increase his/her knowledge level. So, determining student knowledge level (SKL) accurately is one of the important issue in distance education systems. SKL values are changing between [0-1] range.

SKL values are not unique in the Intelligent Questioning System. All students have different knowledge levels in different topics. In IQS, all knowledge level values per each topic have been stored in the database tables. In this way, IQS is able to determine topics, which have not been succeeded by a student, and present useful feedbacks to instructors.

In IQS, a student's

$$SKL = \frac{\text{Correct responded question count}}{\text{Total responded question count}}$$

(2)

Determining a student's SKL value via database view which is obtained from Student table in the database system is shown in Table-3.

The current SKL value of the students which is numbered 111 in topic 7 is;

$$SKL(111)_7 = \frac{3}{5} = 0.6$$

In this way, SKL of the students are able to be determined per each topic continuously. Additionally, students' follow-up rates of the contents and time spent online values of the distance education system are used to determine SKL value.

SKL values are classified according to Fuzzy Logic Principals in a similar way with question difficulty levels. So there are five triangle membership functions which are categorized as Very Low (VL), Low (L), Medium (M), High (H) and Very High (VH) as shown in Figure 3.

Topic Difficulty Level

It can be said that if there are different student knowledge levels for each topic, there are different topic difficulty levels in the system. Therefore in IQS, topic difficulty levels (TDL) are used as one of input parameters of the system. TDLs have been classified with Fuzzy Logic model which consist of five triangle membership functions as shown in Fig-4. TDL values can be change between [0-1] ranges. 0 value represents the most easy topics and 1 value represents most difficult topics. TDL values are calculated as follows.

$$TDL = \frac{\text{Incorrect responded questions count in a specific topic}}{\text{Total responded questions count in a specific topic}}$$

(3)

Table 3. Determining student knowledge level

Student ID	Topic ID	Question ID	Question DL	Respond
111	7	41	0.3862	T
111	7	35	0.4157	T
111	7	87	0.2478	T
111	7	128	0.8127	F
111	7	108	0.5147	F

Figure 3. Classification of the SKL values

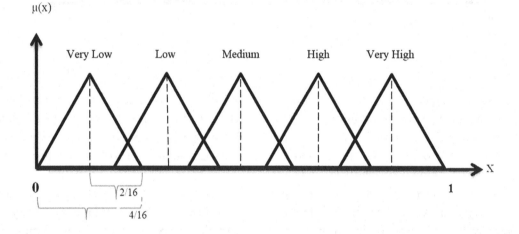

The example data of TDL values are shown in Table 4.

TDL value for topic numbered 7 is calculated as follows:

$$TDL_7 = \frac{25 + 39 + 14 + 20 + 11}{47 + 51 + 32 + 36 + 40} = 0.5291$$

Importance of the Timing

One of the main input parameter of the system is Question solving times. A student's correctly answering time contains useful information about his/her knowledge level. Determining knowledge level among two students which answer the same question correctly, depend on answering time. Question solving times have been used to produce new questions adaptively by the IQS.

The Question table in the database includes *Question Average Solving Time (QAST) and Maximum Solving Time* fields. Maximum solving time is defined by the instructor when the question is inputting into the IQS. Question Average Solving Time value is calculated by the system as follows:

$$QAST = \frac{\sum_1^n (\text{Solving Time})_n}{\sum_1^n (\text{Max Solving Time})_n} \quad (4)$$

n: Number of responses for a specific question

The example data of QAST values is shown in Table 5.

QAST value is calculated as follows:

$$QAST = \frac{32 + 29 + 40 + 40}{40 + 40 + 40 + 40} = 0.8812$$

Table 4. Calculating of the difficulty level of topic 8

Question ID	QDL	IRC	TQC	IDL	Topic ID	Final Code
127	0,5306	25	47	0,5	8	1
138	0,54	39	51	0,5	8	1
32	0,4411	14	32	0,5	8	1
102	0,5853	20	36	0,8	8	1

Figure 4. Classification of the TDL values

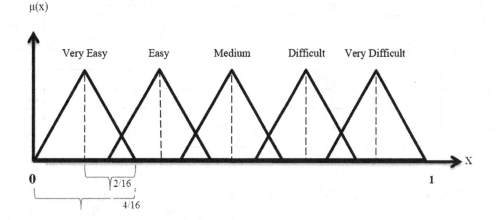

Average solving times are not only stored for questions but also stored students and topics.

Student Average Solving Time

Student average solving times (SAST) have been calculated per topic as well. It calculated as follows:

$$SAST = 1 - \frac{\sum_1^n (\text{Solving Time})_n}{\sum_1^n (\text{Max Solving Time})_n} \qquad (5)$$

n: Student's responses for a specific topic

The example data of SAST values are shown in Table 6.

Student numbered 54 SAST value in topic 8 calculated as follows:

$$SAST(54)_8 = 1 - \frac{32 + 60 + 19 + 40 + 40}{40 + 60 + 40 + 40 + 60} = 0.5042$$

Average Solving Time for the Topic Questions

This value is the average of topic questions' QAST values. Average solving time for the topic questions (ASTQ) calculated as follows:

$$ASTQ = \frac{\sum_1^n QAST_n}{n} \qquad (6)$$

The example data of the ASTQ values which obtained IQS database are shown in Table 7.

ASTQ value which own to topic 8 calculated as follows:

$$ASTQ = \frac{0,4879 + 0,3215 + 0,4199 + 0,4114 + 0,5147}{5}$$

$$ASTQ = 0.4301$$

Table 5. Solving times for 134 numbered question

Student ID	Question ID	Respond	Answer Time	Max Answer Time
54	134	T	32	40
101	134	T	29	40
78	134	F	40	40
63	134	F	40	40

Table 6. Average solving times for student 54 numbered

Student ID	Question ID	Topic ID	Respond	Answer Time	Max Answer Time
54	134	8	T	32	40
54	74	8	F	60	60
54	38	8	T	19	40
54	149	8	F	40	40
54	121	8	T	40	60

Classification of the Solving Times

Solving time values have been classified with Fuzzy Logic model which consist of five triangle membership functions as shown in Figure 5. The values can be change between [0-1] ranges. 0 value represents the slowest performance and 1 value represents most rapidly performance.

WORKING MECHANISM

As mentioned before, four important input data have been processed by the developed system with two groups. These input data groups are:

- **Student Knowledge Level (SKL):** Topic Difficulty Level (TDL).
- **Student Average Solving Time (SAST):** Average Solving Time for the Topic Questions (ASTQ).

Additionally, there are two output data which have been obtained from these inputs. These outputs are:

- Question Difficulty Level (QDL).
- Question Average Solving Time (QAST).

Processing schema of the obtaining Question difficulty level (QDL) is shown in Figure 6

The connection between outputs and inputs has been provided by rule base which is prepared by the experts. The output QDL value has been obtained from inference unit using Max-Min Theorem and defuzzificated by Sugeno Methods. In this way; QDL outputs are evaluated from SKL and TDL inputs, QAST outputs are evaluated from SAST and QAST inputs.

These output values; QDL and QAST, have been assigned to 1x2 question weight (QW) vector. In the IQS, all the questions have a weight vector which can be expressed as follows:

$$QW_{qid} = [\text{QDL QAST}] \qquad (7)$$

qid: Question Id

This vector's graphical expression in two-dimensional question space is shown in Figure 7.

Table 7. Solving time data from topic 8

Question ID	QAST	DateTimeCode	Topic ID
127	0,4879	201103271758049	8
101	0,3215	201103210954123	8
35	0,4199	201103242158049	8
87	0,4114	201103231435218	8
17	0,5147	201103221134125	8

Figure 5. Classification of the solving time values

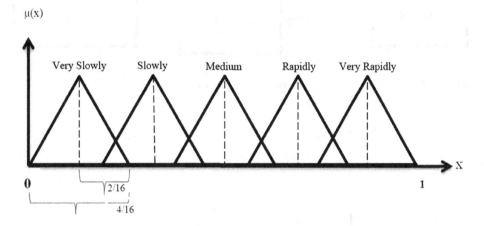

In fuzzy logic models, rule bases have been created by the experts' opinions. Fuzzy linguistic rules transform the given input variables to the output variables. A fuzzy rule is created by writing a fuzzy if - then rule (Yalcin & Köse, 2009). If – then rules, one of the important part of the IQS, has to be created attentively for getting proper results from the system. An example of a rule from the rule base is shown below:

If student knowledge level is low(l) and topic difficulty level is easy then question difficulty level is medium.

One of the rule base structures which have been used in IQS, is shown in Table 8.

Adaptive Question Selecting System

IQS database includes 1x2 dimensional question weight vectors for each question. These vectors represents to features of the questions. Graphical expression of the question weight vectors which are situated in a dispersed coordinates in the two-dimensional space, is shown in Figure 8.

Each point shown in the graphics, represent one of questions. These question weight vectors will be used to evaluate most appropriate question for the student, which is to be represented by the vector. In this sense, determining the nearest vector of the calculated question weight vector in the two dimensional space, clustering has to be used.

In this study, decreasing the fault rate in calculating the question weight vector value which is most appropriate to knowledge level of the selected student, data mining nearest neighbor algorithm is used. In this two-dimensional space, distance between two question weight vectors has been calculated by Euclidean Distance Method. According to this method:

Figure 6. Obtaining of the QDL value with processing SKL and TDL inputs

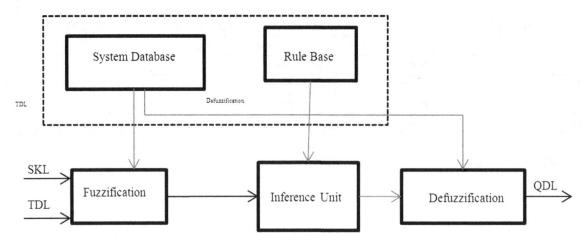

Figure 7. Graphical expression of the question weight vector

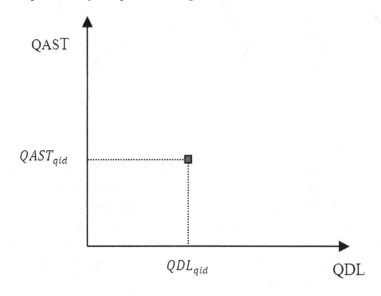

$$d(i,k) = \left(\sum_{j=1}^{d} \left| x_{ij} - x_{kj} \right|^2 \right)^{1/2} = \sqrt{(x_i - x_k)^T (x_i - x_k)}$$

(8)

All of the QW vectors in the space have been compared to calculated output vector according to Euclidean Distance methods, to determine nearest vector. Graphical expression is shown in Figure 9.

QDL and QAST values of the determined nearest neighbor vector are searching in the *Question* table in the database. When it is found, the question which will be asked next to the student, is determined.

Dataviews from the IQS database which are selected for example application are shown in Table 9. and Table 10.

According to the tables above; input vectors of student numbered 117 are:

Table 8. The example of the rule table

		STUDENT KL				
		VL	L	M	H	VH
TOPIC DL	VE	E	M	M	VD	VD
	E	E	M	M	D	VD
	M	E	E	E	M	D
	D	VE	VE	E	M	M
	VD	VE	VE	E	M	M

Figure 8. Question weight vectors positions in the two dimensional space

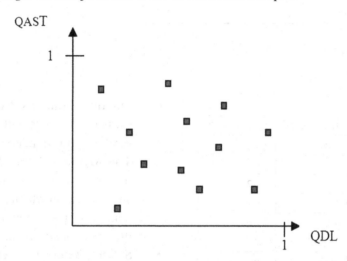

$$Input1_{117} = \begin{bmatrix} 0,527 & 0,874 \end{bmatrix}$$

$$Input2_{117} = \begin{bmatrix} 0,601 & 0,759 \end{bmatrix}$$

When these vectors have been applied assessing system as input, the obtained output question weight vector will be; $QW_{117} = \begin{bmatrix} 0,313 & 0,426 \end{bmatrix}$ as shown in Figure 10.

The obtained question weight vector: $QW_{117} = \begin{bmatrix} 0,313 & 0,426 \end{bmatrix}$ includes information about next question of the student numbered 117. For determining of the nearest question vector of the QW_{117}, an evaluating which based on nearest neighbor algorithm, have to be performed by the adaptive question selecting system as shown in Figure 11.

At the end of the processes, the most appropriate question has been calculated by the system for 117 numbered student as 45 numbered questions.

Usage of the System

In this section, developed software's properties will be explained.

Question Preparation System

Preparation of the question module is available for only instructors. In this module, prepared questions have been recorded in to the database by instructors. Firstly, question types, which are able to be selected (multiple choices, true/false, fill in the blanks, etc.), must be selected by the instructor. Input parameters of the questions are

Figure 9. Graphical expression of the determining nearest neighbor

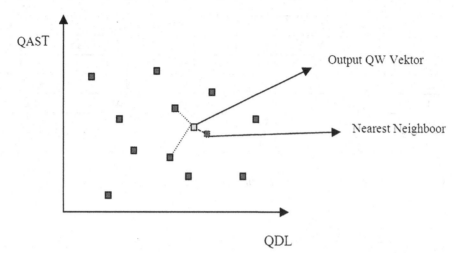

Table 9. Question dataview

Question ID	Topic ID	Question DL	Question AST
41	9	0.451	0.389
42	9	0.248	0.311
43	9	0.419	0.522
44	9	0.587	0.501
45	9	0.332	0.416
46	9	0.7714	0.6987
47	9	0.661	0.488
48	9	0.791	0.814
49	9	0.801	0.877
50	9	0.624	0.771

changing in a wide area with the type of questions. IQS Preparation of the Question module is presented in Figure 12. Each question type has specific parameters, besides there are some common parameters used preparing questions. These common parameters are:

Course and Topic Information

- **Question Activation Date:** This choice provides flexibility to instructors to activate questions in a later date.

- **Starting Difficulty Level:** Each question starts its life cycle with a starting difficulty level which is defined by the instructors.
- **The Message About Incorrect Answer:** In this section, instructors are able to write an explanation which includes useful information or links about question topic when the students give an incorrect answer.
- **Solving Time:** Instructors must be define maximum solving time in this section.

In this software, all of the courses and topics have been related to an instructor with database relations. So, when the instructor logs in to IQS, he/she is directly forwarded to his/her own section in the software. In this way, possible faults which will be made by the instructors are prevented by the system.

Exam Preparation System

In the exam preparing system, it is possible to prepare three kinds of exam. These are:

1. Static examinations composed by instructors.
2. Static examinations composed by students.
3. Examination includes follow-up questions.

Table 10. Student dataview

StudentID	TopicID	Student KL	Topic DL	Student AST	Topic AST
117	9	0.527	0.874	0.601	0.759

Figure 10. Assessment system

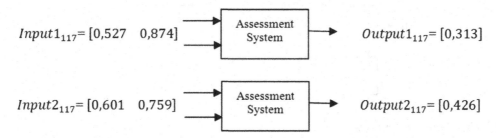

Figure 11. Adaptive question selecting system

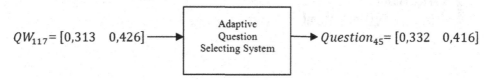

Instructors can compose only static examinations with preparing examination system and then they can introduce it to students using distance education software. They can also introduce it using IQS interface. The examination prepare menu in the software shown in Figure 13.

When the examination has been completed by the students, the answers have been transferred to IQS. After assessing, grades and result reports have been sent back to the distance education system or students can connect to IQS and monitor their own result reports. This process is shown in Figure 14.

In the static examinations users can choose minimum 5 and maximum 20 questions. Under these constraints, users can choose any number of questions with any difficulty level in the selected course and topics.

Unlike static examinations, in the follow-up examinations, exams can be composed by the students. During the preparation process; after courses and topics are selected by the students from the menu, decision about questions which posed to students, made by intelligent question

model, adaptively. Intelligent questioning model considers some parameters about distance education system such as student knowledge level, student average solving time, topic difficulty level, content monitoring rate etc. for choosing the most appropriate question for the student knowledge level. After the answering, system updates all the related data in the database and composed next question considering new levels of the student.

When the students give correct answers, their knowledge levels will be increased and difficulty levels of the questions will be increased in accordance with intelligent questioning model algorithm.

Evaluation

In distance education vocational school, 184 students were selected to test of the success of the IQS. Three kind of information about students were analyzed before applying IQS and after applying IQS. This information are:

Figure 12. Question preparation module

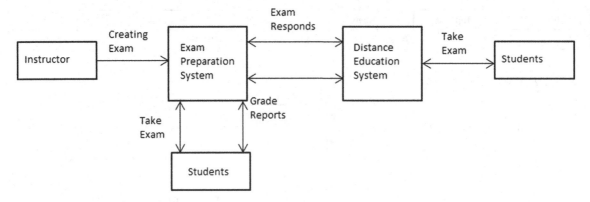

Figure 13. Exam preparation module

- Progressing of student knowledge level.
- Progressing of the students' course contents follow-up rates.
- Progressing of the students' connection rates.

Final exams and quizzes were used to calculate students' knowledge level before IQS starting. After IQS starting, SKL values were used. The contents follow-up rates and connection rates information were transferred from distance education local database. Progressing table is shown in Table 11.

According to the progressing table, there is an increase between after and before values of the information. It means that; this model is successful to increase students' knowledge level with asking questions in the examinations which are the most appropriate to student's knowledge level. Additionally, according to the follow up and connection information, when the students start to be able to solve the appropriate question, they feel good and their interests of the education increase linearly.

Figure 14. Common exam publishing between IQS and distance education system

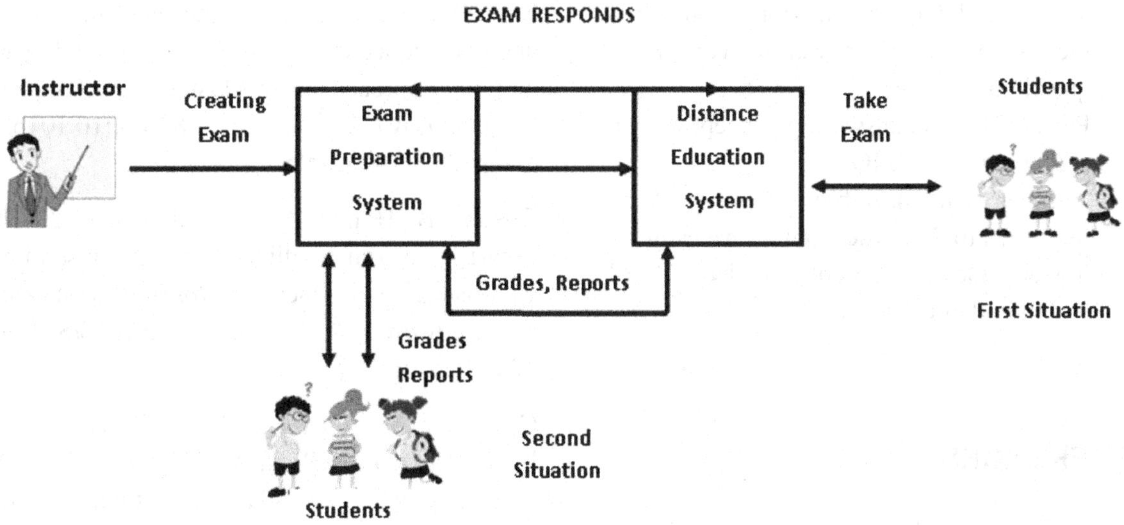

EXAM RESPONDS

Table 11. Progressing table

Analyzed Information	Number of Students	Average Values		Change
		Before	After	
Progressing of knowledge level	184	0,44	0,59	34,090909
Progressing of contents followed up rates	184	0,64	0,76	18,75
Progressing of total connected times of the students	184	0,66	0,81	22,727273

CONCLUSION

The IQS model has been developed to provide convenience to students and instructors of Afyon Kocatepe University

Distance Education Vocational School. The main objective of the related system is determining students' knowledge levels precisely and enabling instructors to present suitable e-learning materials in order to increase students' knowledge levels and also their interests in the school.

On every time a question is answered, question weight vectors, topic difficulty vectors, student knowledge level vectors and others are updated in the database. These processes continue constantly within the IQS. So, the system has a strong database structure. The built-in help mechanism,

which is a tool used for increasing student's knowledge level, allows students to notice their faults in incorrect answers for given questions. According to the table, which is shown in the evaluation section, the IQS system is successful in increasing students' knowledge levels and their interests in the school. For this reason, in order to obtain more useful results from the IQS system, the following improvements will also be realized as future works:

- In the IQS, all question values equals to 1 point normally. As a future work, when the student knowledge level is calculated, each question's value will be represented with its difficulty level. In this way, when *Low* level students give correct answer *to Very*

Difficult level question, his/her knowledge level will be increased more than when they give correct answer to *Very Easy* questions.

- Partially correct answering concept will be created within the IQS.
- Number of membership functions will be increased to 7 in order to improve estimating accuracy of student knowledge level and the other components.

REFERENCES

Bector, C., & Chandra, S. (2004). Fuzzy Mathematical Programming and Fuzzy Matrix Games. Springer.

Beldarrin, Y. (2006). Distance education trends: Integrating new technologies to foster student interaction and collaboration. *Distance Education*, 139–153. doi:10.1080/01587910600789498

Berkan, R. C. S. L. (2000). Fuzzy Systems Design Principles. New Delhi: Standard Publishers Distributors.

Black, P., D. W. (1998). Assessment and classroom learning. *Assessment in Education*, 7–74. doi:10.1080/0969595980050102

Bransford, J., Brown, A., & Cocking, R. (2000). *How People Learn, Brain, Mind, and Experience & School*. Washington, DC: National Academy Press.

Castro, F., Vellido, A., Nebot, A., & Mugica, F. (2007). Applying Data Mining Techniques to e-Learning. *Studies in Computational Intelligence*, 183-221.

Chen, J. N., Huang, Y. M., & Chu, W. C. (2005). Applying dynamic fuzzy petri net to web learning system. *Interactive Learning Environments*, 13.

Cheng, S.-Y., Lin, C.-S., Chen, H.-H., & Heh, J.-S. (2005). Learning and diagnosis of individual and class conceptual perspectives: an intelligent systems approach using clustering techniques. *Computers & Education*, 257–283. doi:10.1016/j.compedu.2004.02.005

Cheung, B., Hui, L., Zhang, J., & Yiu, S. (2003). Smart Tutor: an intelligent tutoring system in web-based adult education. *Journal of Systems and Software*, *68*, 11–68. doi:10.1016/S0164-1212(02)00133-4

Conejo, R., Guzmán, E., Millán, E., Trella, M., De-La-Cruz, J., & Ríos, A. (2004). SIETTE: A Web–Based Tool for Adaptive Testing. *International Journal of Artificial Intelligence in Education*, *14*, 1–33.

Crisp, V., & Ward, C. (2008). The development of a formative scenario-based computer assisted assessment tool in psychology for teachers. *Computers & Education*, *50*, 1509–1526. doi:10.1016/j.compedu.2007.02.004

Dadone, P. (2011). *Design Optimization of Fuzzy Logic Systems*. (Doctoral Dissertation Thesis). Virginia Polytechnic Institute and State University, Electrical Engineering.

Deperlioglu, O., & Arslan, Y. (2010). Design principles of web-based distance education system and sample application in Afyon Kocatepe University. *IET Software*, *50*, 283–293. doi:10.1049/iet-sen.2009.0061

Deperlioglu, O., & Kose, U. (2010). An Educational Virtual Laboratory System for Fuzzy Logic. In *Proceedings of 1st International Symposium on Computing in Science* (pp. 1335-1342). Kuşadası, Türkiye: Academic Press.

Depradine, C. (2003). Expert system for extracting syntactic information from Java code. *Expert Systems with Applications*, *25*, 187–198. doi:10.1016/S0957-4174(03)00046-0

Elango, R., Gudep, V., & Selvam, M. (2008). Quality of e-learning: an analysis based on e-learners perception of e-learning. *Electronic Journal of e-Learning, 6*, 1-44.

Hopper, S. (1992). Cooperative learning and computer-based instruction. *Educational Technology Research and Development*, 21–38. doi:10.1007/BF02296840

Huang, Y., Chen, J., Huang, T., Jeng, Y., & Kuo, Y. (2008). Standardized course generation process using dynamic fuzzy petri nets. *Expert Systems with Applications, 34*, 72–86. doi:10.1016/j.eswa.2006.08.030

Jun, L., Renhou, L., & Qinhua, Z. (2004). Study on the Personality Mining Method for Learners in Network Learning. *Journal of Xian Jiaotong University*, 575-576.

Kartalopoulos, S. (2000). *Understanding Neural Networks and Fuzzy Logic, Basic Concepts and Applications.* New Delhi: Prentice-Hall of India Pvt. Ltd.

Kerka, S., & Wonacott, M. (2000). *Assessing learners online, Practitioner file.* Retrieved from ERIC database, ED 448285.

Kim, N., & Maeng, Y. (2008). Online Student Performance Assessment: The Essentials. *Distance Education Report, 12*, 4–8.

Kim, Y., Smith, M., & Maeng, K. (2000). *Assessment in Online Distance Education: A Comparison of Three Online Programs at a University. Online Journal of Distance.*

Klir, G., & Yuan, B. (2000). *Fuzzy sets and Fuzzy logic: Theory and Applications.* New Delhi: Prentice-Hall of India Pvt. Ltd.

Kocak, Y., Usluel, S., & Mazman, G. (2009). Adoption of Web 2.0 tools in distance education. *International Journal of Human Sciences, 6*.

Kutuva, S., Reddy, N., Xiao, Y., Gao, X., Hariharan, S., & Kulkarni, S. (2006). A novel and fast virtual surgical system using fuzzy logic. In *Proceedings of the IADIS Virtual Multi Conference on Computer Science and Information Systems.* IADIS.

Lee, C. (1990). Fuzzy logic in control systems: Fuzzy logic controller-Part I/Part II. *IEEE Transactions on Systems, Man, and Cybernetics*, 404–435. doi:10.1109/21.52551

Lo, J., Wang, H., & Yeh, S. (2004). Effects of confidence scores and remedial instruction on prepositions learning in adaptive hypermedia. *Computers & Education, 20*, 45–63. doi:10.1016/S0360-1315(03)00064-2

Mahonen, P., & Frantti, T. (2000). Fuzzy Classifier for Star-Galaxy Separation. *The Astrophysical Journal*, 261–263. doi:10.1086/309424

Majumdar, A., & Ghosh, A. (2008). Yarn strength modeling using fuzzy expert system. *Journal of Engineered Fibers and Fabrics, 3*, 61–68.

Mantiuk, R., Aydin, T., & Myszkowski, K. (2008). Dynamic range independent image quality assessment. *ACM Transactions on Graphics.*

Martins, L., & Kellermanns, F. (2004). A model of business school students' acceptance of a web-based course management system. *Academy of Management Learning & Education, 3*, 7–26. doi:10.5465/AMLE.2004.12436815

Pituch, K., & Lee, Y. (2006). The Influence of System Characteristics on E-learning use. *Computers & Education, 47*, 222–244. doi:10.1016/j.compedu.2004.10.007

Seng, T., Parsons, R., Hinson, S., & Sardo-Brown, D. (2003). *Educational psychology, A practitioner–researcher approach.* Singapore: Thomson Learning Cengage Learning Asia.

Shi, H., Liu, H., Shang, Y., & Chen, S. (2005). Student Modeling in E-Learning Environments. *International Journal of Education and Information Technologies*, 2, 1–20.

Tang, C., Lau, R., Li, Q., Yin, H., Li, T., & Kilis, D. (2000). Personalized Courseware Construction Based on Web Data Mining. In *Proceedings of the First international Conf. on Web information Systems Engineering*, (pp. 204-211). Washington, DC: IEEE.

Tsaganou, G., Grigoriadou, M., Cavoura, T., & Koutra, D. (2003). Evaluating an intelligent diagnosis system of historical text comprehension. *Expert Systems with Applications*, 493–502. doi:10.1016/S0957-4174(03)00090-3

van Raaij, E., & Schepers, J. (2008). The acceptance and use of a virtual learning environment in China. *Computers & Education*, 50, 838–852. doi:10.1016/j.compedu.2006.09.001

Wang, T., Wang, K., & Huang, Y. (2008). Using a style-based ant colony system for adaptive learning. *Expert Systems with Applications*, 34, 2449–2464. doi:10.1016/j.eswa.2007.04.014

Yalcin, N., & Köse, U. (2009). *A Web Based Education System for Teaching and Learning Fuzzy Logic. ICITS'09 III* (pp. 378–385). Trabzon, Turkey: Uluslararası Bilgisayar ve Öğretim Teknolojileri Eğitimi Sempozyumu.

Zadeh, L. (1965). Fuzzy Sets. *Information and Control*, 8, 338–353. doi:10.1016/S0019-9958(65)90241-X

Zhang, J., Cheung, B., & Hui, L. (2001). An intelligent tutoring system, Smart Tutor. In *Proceedings of 2001 world conference on educational multimedia, hypermedia and telecommunications* (pp. 2130–2131). Academic Press.

Zimmerman, H. (1996). *Fuzzy Set Theory and Its Applications* (2nd ed.). New Delhi: Allied Publishers Limited. doi:10.1007/978-94-015-8702-0

ADDITIONAL READING

Cahng, F. (2002). Intelligent Assessment of Distance Learning. *Information Sciences*, 105–125.

Curran, C., & Saunders, R. (1992). The use of computer-based systems in the resource management of a developing national distance education programme. *Education and Computing*, 33–39. doi:10.1016/0167-9287(92)80008-Y

Dyehouse, J. (2007). A politics for interactivity: Progressivism and its limits in federal congressional deliberations of distance education policy. *Computers and Composition*, 404–420. doi:10.1016/j.compcom.2007.08.001

Exter, M., Harlin, N., & Bichelmeyer, B. (2008). Story of a conference: Distance education students' experiences in a departmental conference. *The Internet and Higher Education*, 11, 42–52. doi:10.1016/j.iheduc.2007.12.003

Fender, D. (2002). Student and faculty issues in distance education occupational safety and health graduate programs. *Journal of Safety Research*, 175–193. doi:10.1016/S0022-4375(02)00024-5 PMID:12216445

Fong, A., Siew, H., Yee, P., & Sun, L. (2006). Intelligent Question Bank and Examination System. *Proceedings of the 5th WSEAS International Conference on E-ACTIVITIES*. Venice,Italy.

Gal-Ezer, J., & Lupo, D. (2002). ntegrating internet tools into traditional CS distance education: students' attitudes. *Computers & Education*, 319–329. doi:10.1016/S0360-1315(01)00065-3

Guthrie, K., & McCracken, H. (2010). Making a difference online: Facilitating service-learning through distance education. *The Internet and Higher Education*, 153–157. doi:10.1016/j.iheduc.2010.02.006

Hossain, S., & Brooks, L. (2008). Fuzzy cognitive map modelling educational software adoption. *Computers & Education, 51,* 1569–1588. doi:10.1016/j.compedu.2008.03.002

Howell, S., Saba, F., Lindsay, N., & Williams, P. (2004). Seven strategies for enabling faculty success in distance education. *The Internet and Higher Education, 7,* 33–49. doi:10.1016/j.iheduc.2003.11.005

Huang, C., Chu, S., & Guan, C. (2007). Implementation and performance evaluation of parameter improvement mechanisms for intelligent e-learning systems. *Computers & Education, 49*(3). doi:10.1016/j.compedu.2005.11.008

Huang, C., Liu, M., Chu, S., & Cheng, C. (2007). An intelligent learning diagnosis system for Web-based thematic learning platform. *Computers & Education, 48,* 658–679. doi:10.1016/j.compedu.2005.04.016

Huang, M., Huang, H., & Chen, M. (2007). Constructing a personalized e-learning system based on genetic algorithm and case-based reasoning approach. *Expert Systems with Applications, 33,* 551–564. doi:10.1016/j.eswa.2006.05.019

Huang, Y., Lin, Y., & Cheng, S. (2009). An adaptive testing system for supporting versatile educational assessment. *Computers & Education, 52,* 53–67. doi:10.1016/j.compedu.2008.06.007

Hwang, G. (2002). A conceptual map model for developing intelligent. *Computers & Education, 40,* 217–235. doi:10.1016/S0360-1315(02)00121-5

Hwang, G., Lin, B., & Lin, T. (2006). An effective approach for test-sheet composition with. *Computers & Education, 46,* 122–139. doi:10.1016/j.compedu.2003.11.004

Kaburlasos, V., Marinagi, C., & Tsoukalas, V. (2008). Personalized multi-student improvement based on Bayesian cybernetics. *Computers & Education, 51,* 1430–1449. doi:10.1016/j.compedu.2008.01.004

Kanwar, A., & Daniel, J. (2010). Distance Education and Open Universities. International Encyclopedia of Education, 404-410.

Liao, Y. K. (2007).. . *Computers & Education, 48,* 216–233. doi:10.1016/j.compedu.2004.12.005

Lykourentzou, I., Giannoukos, I., Nikolopoulos, V., Mpardis, G., & Loumos, V. (2009). Dropout prediction in e-learning courses through the combination of machine learning techniques. *Computers & Education, 53,* 950–965. doi:10.1016/j.compedu.2009.05.010

Mason, R. (2000). From distance education to online education. *The Internet and Higher Education,* 63–74. doi:10.1016/S1096-7516(00)00033-6

Pavlekovic, M., Zekic-Susac, M., & Djurdjevic, I. (2009). Comparison of intelligent systems in detecting a child's mathematical gift. *Computers & Education, 53,* 142–154. doi:10.1016/j.compedu.2009.01.007

Rovai, A. (2003). A practical framework for evaluating online distance education programs. *The Internet and Higher Education,* 109–124. doi:10.1016/S1096-7516(03)00019-8

Sen, B., & Ucar, E. (2012). Evaluating the achievements of computer engineering department of distance education students with data mining methods. *Procedia Technology,* 262-267.

Sheremetov, L., & Arenas, A. (2002). EVA: an interactive Web-based collaborative. *Computers & Education, 39,* 161–182. doi:10.1016/S0360-1315(02)00030-1

Shi, H., Rodriguez, O., Shang, Y., & Chen, S. (2003). Integrating adaptive and intelligent techniques into a Web-based environment for active learning. In *Leondes. In Intelligent Systems: Technology and Applications* (Vol. 4, pp. 229–260). Boca Raton: CRC Press.

Tsolakidis, C., & Kostalias, C. (2007). *A Dynamic Web Site for the Distant Self-Assessment of Students. Conference ICL2007.* Austria: Villach.

Xenos, M. (2004). Prediction and assessment of student behaviour in open and distance education in computers using Bayesian networks. *Computers & Education*, *43*, 345–359. doi:10.1016/j.compedu.2003.09.005

Yeh, S. W., & Lo, J. J. (2005). Assessing meta-cognitive knowledge in web-based CALL. *Computers & Education*, 97–113. doi:10.1016/j.compedu.2003.12.019

Yengin, I., Karahoca, A., Karahoca, D., & Uzunboylu, H. (2011). Deciding which technology is the best for distance education: Issues in media/technology comparisons studies. *Procedia Computer Science*, *3*, 1388–1395. doi:10.1016/j.procs.2011.01.020

Young, A., & Lewis, C. (2008). Teacher education programmes delivered at a distance: An examination of distance student perceptions. *Teaching and Teacher Education*, *24*, 601–609. doi:10.1016/j.tate.2007.03.003

KEY TERMS AND DEFINITION

Computer Adaptive Testing (CAT): Cat is a form of computer-based test that selecting next question according to student's knowledge level.

Data Mining: Data Mining is an analytic process designed to explore data (usually large amounts of data - typically business or market related - also known as "big data") in search of consistent patterns and/or systematic relationships between variables, and then to validate the findings by applying the detected patterns to new subsets of data.

Distance Education: Distance education is education designed for learners who live at a distance from the teaching institution or education provider.

E-Learning: E-Learning is electronic learning, in which the learner uses a computer to learn a task, skill, or process. It is also referred to as computer-based training, web-based training, and online learning.

Euclidean Distance Method: Is a method that calculates the distance between two points or two vectors.

Fuzzy Logic: Type of reasoning based on the recognition that logical statements are not only true or false (white or black areas of probability) but can also range from 'almost certain' to 'very unlikely' (gray areas of probability). Software based on application of fuzzy-logic (as compared with that based on Formal Logic) allows computers to mimic human reasoning more closely, so that decisions can be made with incomplete or uncertain data.

Intelligent Questioning System: Is a system arranging the questions with different algorythms in order to determine the exact level of knowledge of the student.

Chapter 6
Review and Proposal for Intelligent Distance Education

Ali Hakan Işik
Mehmet Akif Ersoy University, Turkey

Göksel Aslan
Mehmet Akif Ersoy University, Turkey

ABSTRACT

Information and communication technologies have led to new developments in education. Time and place independent education has emerged. Furthermore, different characteristics and huge numbers of individuals have made the use of new technological methods inevitable. In this context, distance education has become a popular education method to meet the emerging needs, increasing satisfaction, and learning performance of students. Mobile technology, intelligent systems, and Three Dimensional (3D) animations also provide enhancements in this field. In addition, distance education systems should be selected and developed properly for target students and environments. For this purpose, the assessment of prominent studies provides a road map for new research. In this sense, this chapter evaluates intelligent distance education studies in literature. Furthermore, it proposes a novel Artificial Neural Network (ANN)-based distance education system for Mehmet Akif Ersoy University. This ANN-based system can be implemented on Mehmet Akif Ersoy University infrastructure with agent. The proposed system consists of a learning management system, Web conferencing system, and an ANN agent. The agent's inputs that are already stored in Mehmet Akif Ersoy University's distance education databases can be easily retrieved. This agent provides reusability of course content and Web conferencing records.

INTRODUCTION

Distance education has become the most popular way to enhance learning performance, to increase satisfaction and independence of students. It also diverts and changes education methodology. Moreover, it pays attention to the students'

requirements. Due to the great variety of user requirements in distance education, numerous methods and technologies have emerged to meet these requirements. In addition, differentiations between users, low success rate also force instructional designers to find new ways. In this basis, innovative ways should be used. For instance, three

DOI: 10.4018/978-1-4666-6276-6.ch006

dimensional (3D) animations provide interactivity and mobile technology, and ensure ease of use, time and place independence. Besides, adaptive agents modify distance education systems, in other words, making adjustments in accordance with the students' profile. Thus, adaptation and personalization of distance education systems are provided with these innovative ways.

Three dimensional materials are used in traditional and web based distance education. These contents are generally use virtual and augmented reality. These contents allow enhancements in distance education. Furthermore, they provide effective learning through interactivity and visualization of multimedia content (Liarokapis et al., 2004). It assists teaching of students. For instance, remote physics experiments (Ozvoldova et al., 2006), simulation control testing (Su et al., 2006), simulation of surgery (Perez et al., 2008), and virtual laboratories (Safigianni, et al., 2008; Bell, & Fogler, 2004). Okutsu and colleagues' study shows that 3D virtual environments are feasible platform to teach engineering students (Okutsu et al., 2013). In this context, 3DWebEPL Project is accomplished. 3D models of intensive care unit equipments are used to the train the biomedical technicians in this project. This project provides easy learning environment (Cetin, 2010). The 3D model also allows the visual simulation of the different types of study (Sampaio et al., 2010).

Mobile learning meets learners' needs such as flexibility, easy data accession to enable independent from time and place (Korucu, & Alkan, 2011; Cavus, & Al-Momani, 2010). In Cavus's study, students express their enjoyment with mobile devices and its LMS integration (Cavus, 2010a). Motiwalla claims that mobile learning will soon be an important component of distance education in a short time. However, this transition will not come into exist in one night (Motiwalla, 2007). As in all fields, there is a transition to mobile learning. It transforms from traditional to intelligent based structure. The intelligent mobile distance education system is able to fulfill the different individuals' requirements. It provides effective educational environment with variety of services. It contributes the learners to learn effectively (Chen et al., 2010). Simkova and colleagues' study also engage in the use of mobile technologies for supporting the education. It is concluded that using mobile device in teaching is effective. It also realizes new possibilities for education (Simkova et al., 2012).

Instead of fuzzy logic, artificial neural network is used as an intelligent algorithm in the proposed system. Moreover, input and output parameters of artificial neural network are innovative parameters which distinguish the system. There is not any distance education system in the literature and in our country that uses the same input and output parameters. The lack of literature in the field has been effective in the preparation of the system. Using statistical methods, performance values of developed system can be measured through the sensitivity, accuracy, and the regression parameters. Developed synchronous distance education system retrieves values such as duration of course content monitoring, the number of correctly answered questions in mid-term by the user. Afterwards, it provides re-monitoring of course content or virtual classroom session. By this way, students are guided in distance education through the artificial neural network algorithm. Instead of a one-way, bi-directional running system will be achieved. By this way, it is tried to increase the success and satisfaction of student.

Synchronous and Asynchronous Distance Education

Synchronous (simultaneous) and asynchronous (asynchronous) education alternatives are available in distance education. Asynchronous educational software is designed for the students and instructors to initiate and finish the training within desired time. This feature makes a fundamental change in the role of instructor. Asynchronous distance learning includes only the learning management system. It requires minimum infrastructure such as limited internet speed or bandwidth in education. Synchronous education uses information and communication technologies. It consists of virtual classroom and learning management system. In this education, simultaneous educational environment is formed through the video and audio sharing. In this case, the student has the feeling of presence in a real classroom.

Virtual Classroom Software

One of the most discussed issues arise on distance education is to ensure interaction like traditional education. Today, virtual classroom software, in other words web based conferencing system, is used for the provision of interaction between instructor and student. In this classroom, instructor and student situate in different places. However, they come together in virtual classroom. Online audio, video, and content sharing have been allowed in this software. Commercial and non-commercial virtual classroom software are available in the market. Adobe connect pro and open source Bigbluebutton are the most preferred ones. High license fees of commercial virtual classroom software and operational problems of the non-commercial software are the most important issues in this field.

Big Blue Button

BigBlueButton is open source virtual classroom software. It has a lot of open source components to create an integrated solution. Presentation sharing, integration with the learning management systems such as Sakai, Wordpress, Moodle, Joomla, Redmine, Drupal was added in 2010. With *BigBlueButton*,; sharing of audio, video, and desktop, instant messaging, white board, presenting of office files are offered. Listener, speaker and administrator roles are presented in the *BigBlueButton*. Listeners can send message

to other participants, watch the presentation, participate in conversation, and share the image. Speakers can manage the voice of the listeners and also make a presentation. Administrator manages all process in the *BigBlueButton*.

Adobe Connect Pro

With Adobe Connect Pro, the instructor and consultant are come together in virtual classroom through information and communication technology for better understanding of the course. This software also provide instant sharing of presentation, voice and video, office applications, web address in web based environment.

The subject of the system is to integration of neural network with synchronous distance education system. Main aims of the system are to provide a more effective use of distance education for the students and to increase the learning level, success rate and satisfaction of the students.

This chapter is organized as follows; firstly, emerging distance education systems and innovative papers in literature are summarized. Then, artificial neural network based distance education architecture is proposed and explained in detail. Finally, conclusion and future works related to the intelligent distance education are presented.

EVALUATION OF INTELLIGENT DISTANCE EDUCATION STUDIES IN LITERATURE

There has been little number of studies related to the intelligent distance education in literature. These studies can be divided into two main categories. These main categories are about the LMS and student. In LMS category, selection and improvement of intelligent distance education systems are done. In student category, success rate, intentions, performance, and knowledge evaluation of students are accomplished. Studies related to the student provide statistical results and feedback. In addition, it is important to evaluate intelligent distance education studies to provide road map for new studies. Prominent studies related to these fields are summarized below.

Oprea developed an artificial intelligence based expert system for students' performance evaluation. This system provides feedback about teaching and learning activity at a specific discipline (Oprea et al., 2010). Proposed system is shown in Figure 1. In Amandi and colleagues' study, the capture of student intentions can be supported by agents and used for specifying their intervention (Amandi et al., 2003). Chang proposes an intelligent solution to the automatic evaluation of students' performance (Chia-I Chang, 2002). In Stathacopoulou and colleagues' study, a neuro-fuzzy method is used to evaluate the students' knowledge and behavior (Stathacopoulou et al., 1999). Kalles and colleague analyze students' academic performance; describe success or failure in the exams by using defined rules (Kalles, & Pierrakeas, 2006). Shen and colleagues investigate the significance of the intelligent evaluation system in e-learning and propose an evaluation model (Shen et al., 2001).

However, LMS studies in literature are mainly focused on the improvement of LMS with adaptive agents, task-technology, and semantic web ontology. By this way, intelligence of LMS is provided. Generally, user profile is used as an input. In Rey-Lopez and colleagues' study, current SCORM standard is extended to permit adaptivity according to users' characteristics. Using inference rules, the adaptation parameters are retrieved from the user profile (Rey-López et al., 2009). Cuéllar and colleagues developed ontology based on procedure to achieve the integration of different e-learning database. In this study, relations of databases and entities are interpreted with semantic way. This interpretation allows to find precise information quickly (Cuéllar et al., 2011). In Yaghmaie and colleagues' study, an adaptive learning management system (LMS) is proposed. Proposed system is based upon multi-agent systems and uses both Sharable Content Object Reference Model (SCORM) 2004 and semantic Web ontology for learning content storage, sequencing and adaptation (Yaghmaie, & Bahreininejad, 2011). As it is seen in Figure 2, McGill and colleagues' study

Figure 1. Block Schema of evaluation system (Oprea, 2010)

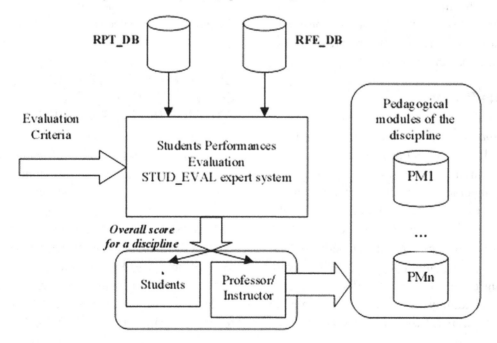

Figure 2. Task–technology fit architecture (McGill, & Klobas, 2009)

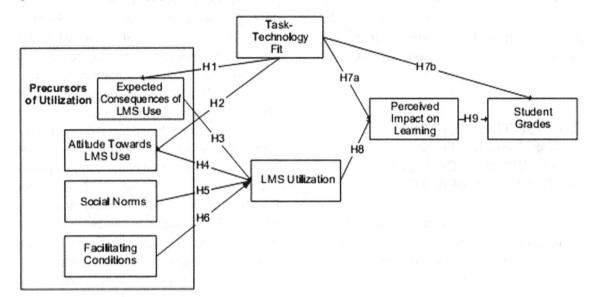

examines the usability of task–technology fit for LMSs. The importance of task–technology convenience is found in this work. Instructor norms have a notable effect in the performance of LMS but simplifying of conditions and common social norms do not play a role on learning via LMS (McGill, & Klobas, 2009).

Tsolis and colleagues suggest open source distance education system. It introduces profiling and customization services for the instructor and student. This system also adapts the educational content and tools in the basis of the obtained profile of user (Tsolis et al., 2010). Graf and colleague evaluate open source e-learning platforms with adaptation aspect (Graf, & List, 2005). Main aim of Chisanu and colleagues' study is to combine theoretical framework and to design framework for constructivist learning environment on learning management system (Chisanu et al., 2012). In Valderrama and colleagues' study, multi-agent architecture for web-based education is developed. In this architecture, sequencing and delivery of education materials with reusability are achieved (Peredo et al., 2005). Cuéllar and colleagues develop ontology based system to gather information from different learning management systems

(Cuéllar et al., 2011). Seridi and colleagues investigate the use of computational intelligence for adaptive course sequencing in distance education platform. Several experiments have shown the effectiveness of the proposed method (Seridi et al., 2006). Hedayati and colleagues propose two artificial intelligence methods (Artificial Neural Network and Support Vector Machine) for the multiple choice question classification in distance education (Hedayati et al., 2012). Amandi and colleagues introduce a solution for designing the connection between an educational application for distance learning and an assistant agent. In this solution, student's intentions can be supported by agents and used for specifying their intervention (Amandi et al., 2003). In Seridi and colleagues' another study, artificial neural network is used for generating adaptive lessons. The outcomes of study demonstrate that the approach is promising for constructing of dynamic adaptive learning for distance education (Seridi et al., 2006).

Moreover, analytic hierarchy process algorithm and artificial intelligent are used to select the LMS. In Cetin and colleagues' study, the analytic hierarchy process algorithm is used to choose the most appropriate LMS with defined priorities and criteria (Çetin et al., 2010). Cavus evaluates LMSs and chooses the best one that satisfies the requirements. In this process, artificial intelligent concepts with fuzzy logic values are used (Cavus, 2010b).

PROPOSED INTELLIGENT DISTANCE EDUCATION ARCHITECTURE FOR MEHMET AKIF ERSOY UNIVERSITY

Distance education is an educational method that uses information and communication technology to offer education. The main difference of the distance education from traditional education is it's using multimedia tools. There are many studies in the field of distance education. However, there are limited numbers of intelligent distance education system in the selection of teaching management system, adapting course content, evaluating the success rate of students. By this system, integrated distance education system that has unique artificial neural network inputs and outputs can be developed. The proposed system consists of training management system, virtual class software and artificial neural network agent software. In this system, artificial neural network based agent software will be integrated into synchronous distance education system.

The student will be able to display the contents and documents, participate in online midterm exams and follow the curriculum from securely logged on to the learning management system in the system. With the virtual class software, he will be able to re-monitor the courses that the supervisor of the course will teach as sharing image and voice online. The artificial neural network (ANN) based agent software in the system will provide management of the course contents in the learning management system and records in the virtual class. With the stated intelligent system, it will be determined whether the contents and

records will be re-used. The entries of the ANN based agent software will be obtained from the learning management system and the virtual class software. The entries of the stated system are time to display course content, the number of correctly and incorrectly answered questions from end-of-chapter evaluation questions in course content, the number of correctly and incorrectly answered questions in online midterm exams, the number of participating in virtual class session, duration of stay in virtual class session. With the outputs of ANN, the student will be directed in distance education. The guidance of students will be carried out by analyzing the course content or/and re-monitoring virtual classroom's records. Depend on the ANN; output of no need to analyze and re-monitoring can be found.

One of the fundamental aims of the intelligent distance education is to adapt instruction's opinion and learning environment to the learner's aim and capability (Oppermann, & Kinshuk, 1997). In addition, intelligent individualized learning platform is tried to be obtained (Ozyurt et al., 2013a; Ozyurt et al., 2013b; Ozyurt et al., 2012). To achieve these goals, a number of researches have been done. In literature, artificial neural network (ANN) and support vector machine (SVM) are commonly used as an intelligent algorithm. In this chapter, artificial neural network is employed as an intelligent algorithm in proposed agent architecture. As it is seen in Figure 3, this architecture which is in progress is based on reusing of course content and web conferencing records. It can be implemented to the distance education system by agent. All inputs of agent can be retrieved from databases. These inputs are already stored in these databases. With these data, artificial neural network (ANN) can be trained. In this training process, ANN computes students' data and understands the mechanics between students' profile and course materials. In addition, average values of students' profile can be obtained from Mehmet Akif Ersoy University's databases. These values can be used

Figure 3. The artificial neural network based architecture

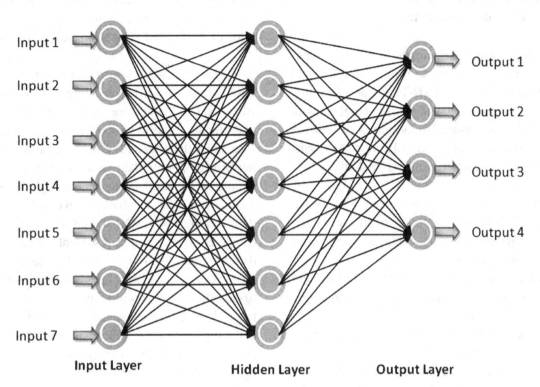

as a normalization parameter for artificial neural network inputs. Back propagation is used as training algorithm. In the training process, students' profiles are used as inputs.

MATLAB, which is mostly preferred for engineering applications, will be used for training and testing of artificial neural network. For implementation and testing of the proposed system on the students, a VPS (Virtual Private Server) with high bandwidth will be hired. Thus, it will be possible to perform any number of experiments with a high number of concurrent users. Then, application data can be obtained data from the students. By this way, training and testing of ANN over servers by using retrieved data can be achieved. In this system, it is aimed to increase learning success and satisfaction of students in distance education. By this system, learning management system, virtual classroom software, artificial neural network-based agent software are developed. SQL Server 2012 Express is planned to use for storing and querying the data.

Learning Management System

C # programming language will be used to develop learning management system modules. These modules are user adding module, the role and authorizations module, curriculum module, content insertion module, question identification module, exam module, assignments module, survey module, frequently asked questions module, comments and suggestions module, academic calendar module.

Virtual Classroom Software

C # programming language based modules will be developed within the scope of the virtual classroom software. These modules are user adding module, the role and authorizations Module, Course Schedule Module, Sound Sharing Module, Video Sharing Module, Recording Module, and Chat Module.

Artificial Neural Network-Based Agent Software

The feed-forward back propagation (Back Propagation) neural network based agent software will be developed by using MATLAB programming language. Training and testing of neural network based distance education system is carried out through the data that is obtained from student trials.

Proposed architecture inputs are shown below:

Input 1: Duration of course content monitoring.
Input 2: The number of correctly answered questions in section evaluation part of the course content.
Input 3: The number of incorrectly answered questions in section evaluation part of the course content.
Input 4: The number of correctly answered questions in mid-term.
Input 5: The number of incorrectly answered questions in mid-term.
Input 6: The number of attendance in web based conferencing system.
Input 7: The duration of attendance in web based conferencing system.

Outputs of proposed architecture are shown below:

Output 1: Course content must be revised again.
Output 2: Web conferencing records must be monitored again.

Output 3: Course content and web conferencing records must be monitored again.
Output 4: No need to revision and monitoring.

Figure 4 shows how artificial neural network based agent works. Proposed agent consists of adobe and LMS database, neural network based classification algorithm, and test side. In heuristic side, normalization and training of network are performed. As for data sources, two different databases are used in agents. Firstly, data are taken from these databases in which students' data stored. The result of mid-term questions can be given an example of students' data. Then, data are transferred to the new database. Based on these data, neural network algorithm is started to classification. For validating the agent, neural network should be evaluated with test data. Accuracy and regression values can be used to assess performance of the neural network. In every term, agent repeated the same process.

CONCLUSION AND FUTURE WORKS

Evolving of information and communication based distance education system is began with learning management system (LMS). Then, web conferencing software is added to the LMS, so synchronous system is obtained. After that, distance education is evolving from static to adaptive system. This adaptive system should be taken into account according to the students' needs,

Figure 4. Flow chart of artificial neural network based agent

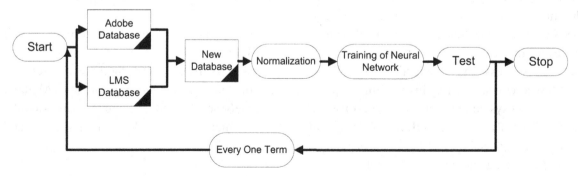

preference, abilities and background. This can be accomplished by students' profile and data. By this way, performance and effectiveness of educational process can be developed.

Although some developed learning management systems in literature are called as intelligent. However, they work as rule-based (If...Then... Else) method. Moreover, these rule-based systems are considered as intelligent. In addition, Commercial Corporation is focused on the development of the learning management system. This system communicates with virtual classroom software through web services. There are limited numbers of synchronous distance education system that handle high number of concurrently users in real time. With this chapter, innovative and integrated synchronous distance education system that use artificial neural network is developed. It will meet emerging requirements.

Fuzzy logic and artificial neural network are one of the main intelligent methods that are used in distance education systems. These methods are used to design course content and to assess the educational outcomes and student success in the literature. Abroad, there are few numbers of intelligent systems that include learning management system and virtual classroom software. In Turkey, intelligent methods in the field of distance education are used to develop asynchronous learning management system, to select instructional management system and to evaluate outcomes of these systems. Within the scope of the proposed system, synchronous distance education system based on artificial neural network that has unique input and output attributes are designed according to the priorities of our country's student data. Input and output parameters of the intelligent system, artificial neural network, and Turkish language supported interfaces are one of the distinguished features of the system. There is not any intelligent distance education system in the literature and in our country that has the same input and output parameters. The lack of literature in the field has been effective in the preparation of the proposal. With these features, system works in a bidirectional way.

Main objectives of intelligent distance education are to enhance user satisfaction, success rate and knowledge construction. It also facilitates the learning rate of the course. For this purpose, studies concerning the intelligent distance education in literature must be assessed carefully. In addition, there are few studies in evaluation of intelligent distance education studies. Due to this reason, this chapter has focused on the evaluation of these studies.

Intelligent agents have great important role in the web based distance education. Agents are used as an intelligent processing unit in distance education. In this context, this chapter proposes an artificial neural network based agent for Mehmet Akif Ersoy University. It is known that there is an implementation issue of proposed architecture in Mehmet Akif Ersoy University. However, six - year experience in distance education and adequate students' data to train the artificial neural network will solve this difficulty. Consequently, it is expected that the proposed architecture will provide significant developments in increasing learning level and success rate of the students. Another aim of the chapter is to highlight the importance of 3D model, mobile technology in distance education. With the outcomes of the chapter, intelligent distance education features may suit student's needs.

It is revealed in this chapter that main limitation of the intelligent distance education system is its user such as educator. It is well known that innovative and intelligent distance education system can be developed. However, if educator and student cannot properly use this system, it is not possible to obtain efficiency and performance. In this sense, system has to be developed according to user behavior and controlled by educator. For instance, intelligence system has to be modular for different students and environment.

Innovative ways such as 3D model, mobile technology, and intelligent algorithm enable new perspective to the education methodology. Today, 3D model and mobile technology are used as a complement to distance education. Furthermore, intelligent agents especially assess the performance of distance education and students. However, these enhancements should be presented in appropriate concept. Besides, they should be convenient to the specified environment and student. Therefore, enormous students' data to train the intelligent agent, people earning levels to determine the possibility of mobile learning should be collected. These requirements can be increased.

There is no doubt that intelligent agents are useful for distance education. However, there aren't commonly accepted methodology and sufficient studies in literature related to the issues. In this situation, it is not easy to transfer the intelligent based distance education completely. On the other hand, studies encourage us to future progress.

As a future study, students' behaviors, backgrounds and needs regarding the distance education can be added to the proposed intelligent distance education architecture. Different university data can be used to train the neural network. By this way, intelligent agent can be obtained for Turkey environment. In addition, different machine algorithms such as support vector machine can be used in proposed architecture for Mehmet Akif Ersoy University.

The results of the system, the original architecture of the neural network input and output attributes will provide roadmap for future works in the same field.

REFERENCES

Amandi, A., Campo, M., Armentano, M., & Berdún, L. (2003). Intelligent Agents for Distance Learning. *Journal of Informatics in Education*, 2(2), 161–180.

Amandi, A., Campo, M., Armentano, M., & Berdun, L. (2003). Intelligent Agents for Distance Learning. *Informatics in Education*, 2(2), 161–180.

Bell, J. T., & Fogler, H. S. (2004). *The application of virtual reality to (chemical engineering) education*. IEEE. doi:10.1109/VR.2004.1310077

Cavus, N. (2010) Investigating mobile devices and LMS integration in higher education: Student perspectives. In *Proceedings of World Conference on Information Technology*, (pp. 1469-1474). Academic Press.

Cavus, N. (2010). The evaluation of Learning Management Systems using an artificial intelligence fuzzy logic algorithm. *Advances in Engineering Software*, 41(2), 248–254. doi:10.1016/j.advengsoft.2009.07.009

Cavus, N., & Al-Momani, M. M. (2010). Mobile system for flexible education. In Proceedings of World Conference on Information Technology. Academic Press.

Cetin, A. (2010). 3D Web Based Learning of Medical Equipments Employed in Intensive Care Units. *Journal of Medical Systems*, 36(1), 167–174. doi:10.1007/s10916-010-9456-5 PMID:20703738

Çetin, A., Işık, A. H., & Güler, İ. (2010). Learning Management System Selection with Analytic Hierarchy Process. In *Proceedings of 13th International Conference on Interactive Computer Aided Learning,* (pp. 921-926). Academic Press.

Chen, J., Lu, H., Mo, W., & Wang, Z. (2010). The research and design of intelligence wireless Mobile Learning platform based on 3G. In *Proceedings of International Conference on e-Business and Information System Security (EBISS)*, (pp. 1 – 4). EBISS.

Chia-I Chang, F. (2002). Intelligent assessment of distance learning. *International Journal of information Sciences—Informatics and Computer Science, 140*(1), 105 – 125.

Chisanu, J., Sumalee, C., Issara, K., & Charuni, S. (2012). Design and develop of constructivist learning environment on learning management system. In Proceedings of WCES 2012, (pp. 3426 – 3430). WCES.

Cuéllar, M. P., Delgado, M., & Pegalajar, M. C. (2011). A common framework for information sharing in e-learning management systems. *Expert Systems with Applications, 38*(3), 2260–2270. doi:10.1016/j.eswa.2010.08.014

Cuéllar, M. P., Delgado, M., & Pegalajar, M. C. (2011). Improving learning management through semantic web and social networks in e-learning environments. *Expert Systems with Applications, 38*(4), 4181–4189. doi:10.1016/j. eswa.2010.09.080

Graf, S., & List, B. (2005). An Evaluation of Open Source E-Learning Platforms Stressing Adaptation Issues. In *Proceedings of Fifth IEEE International Conference on Advanced Learning Technologies,* (pp. 163-165). IEEE.

Hedayati, M., Kamali, S. H., & Shakerian, R. (2012). Comparison and Evaluation of Intelligence Methods for Distance Education Platform. *International Journal of Modern Education and Computer Science, 4*(3), 21–27. doi:10.5815/ijmecs.2012.04.03

Kalles, D., & Pierrakeas, C. (2006). *Using Genetic Algorithms and Decision Trees for a posteriori Analysis and Evaluation of Tutoring Practices based on Student Failure Models.* Springer.

Korucu, A. T., & Alkan, A. (2011). Differences between m-learning (mobile learning) and e-learning, basic terminology and usage of m-learning in education. In *Proceedings of World Conference on Educational Sciences*, (pp. 1925–1930). Academic Press.

Liarokapis, F., Mourkoussis, N., White, M., Darcy, J., Sifniotis, M., & Petridis, P. et al. (2004). Web3D and augmented reality to support engineering education. *World Transactions on Engineering and Technology Education, 3*(1), 11–14.

McGill, T. J., & Klobas, J. E. (2009). A task–technology fit view of learning management system impact. *Computers & Education, 52*(2), 496–508. doi:10.1016/j.compedu.2008.10.002

Motiwalla, L. F. (2007). Mobile learning: A framework and evaluation. *Computers & Education, 49*(3), 581–596. doi:10.1016/j.compedu.2005.10.011

Okutsu, M., DeLaurentis, D., Brophy, S., & Lambert, J. (2013). Teaching an aerospace engineering design course via virtual worlds: A comparative assessment of learning outcomes. *Computers & Education, 60*(1), 288–298. doi:10.1016/j.compedu.2012.07.012

Oppermann, R., & Kinshuk, R. R. (1997). *Adaptability and adaptivity in learning systems.* London: Knowledge Transfer.

Oprea, M. (2010). Artificial Intelligence Applied in Computer-Assisted Students Evaluation. In *Proceedings of International Conference on Virtual Learning,* (pp. 361-366). Academic Press.

Ozvoldova, M., Cernansky, P., Schuer, F., & Lustig, F. (2006). Internet remote physics experiments in a student laboratory. In Proceedings of iNEER, (pp. 297–304). iNEER.

Ozyurt, O., Ozyurt, H., & Baki, A. (2013). Design and development of an innovative individualized adaptive and intelligent e-learning system for teaching–learning of probability unit Details of UZWEBMAT. *Expert Systems with Applications, 40*, 2914–2940. doi:10.1016/j.eswa.2012.12.008

Ozyurt, O., Ozyurt, H., Baki, A., & Guven, B. (2012). Integrating computerized adaptive testing into UZWEBMAT Implementation of individualized assessment module in an e-learning system. *Expert Systems with Applications, 39*, 9837–9847. doi:10.1016/j.eswa.2012.02.168

Ozyurt, O., Ozyurt, H., Baki, A., & Guven, B. (2013). Integration into mathematics classrooms of an adaptive and intelligent individualized e-learning environment Implementation and evaluation of UZWEBMAT. *Computers in Human Behavior, 29*, 726–738. doi:10.1016/j.chb.2012.11.013

Peredo, R., Leandro, V., Ocan, B., & Sheremetov, L. B. (2005). Development of intelligent reusable learning objects for web-based education systems. *Expert Systems with Applications, 28*(2), 273–283. doi:10.1016/j.eswa.2004.09.003

Perez, J. F., Barea, R., Boquete, L., Hidalgo, M. A., & Dapena, M. (2008). Cataract surgery simulator for medical education & finite element/3D human eye model. In Proceedings of 3ª Conferencia Ibérica de Sistemas y Tecnologias de Información, (pp. 90–98). Academic Press.

Rey-López, M., Díaz-Redondo, R. P., & Fernández-Vilas, A., Pazos-Arias, J. J., García-Duque, J., Gil-Solla, A., & Ramos-Cabrer, M. (2009). An extension to the ADL SCORM standard to support adaptivity: The t-learning case-study. *Computer Standards & Interfaces Journal, 31*(2), 309–318. doi:10.1016/j.csi.2008.02.006

Safigianni, A. S., & Pournaras, S. K. (2008) Virtual laboratory arrangement for measuring characteristic power system quantities. In Proceedings of iNEER, (pp. 379–391). iNEER.

Sampaio, A. Z., Ferreira, M. M., Rosário, D. P., & Martins, O. P. (2010). 3D and VR models in Civil Engineering education: Construction, rehabilitation and maintenance. *Automation in Construction, 19*, 819–828.

Seridi, H., Sari, T., Khadir, T., & Sellami, M. (2006). Adaptive Instructional Planning in Intelligent Learning Systems. In *Proceedings of IEEE International Conference on Advanced Learning Technologies*, (pp. 133-135). IEEE.

Seridi, H., Sari, T., & Sellami, M. (2006). Adaptive Instructional Planning Using Neural. Networks in Intelligent Learning Systems. *The International Arab Journal of Information Technology, 3*(3), 183–192.

Shen, R., Tang, Y., & Zhang, T. (2001). The intelligent assessment system in Web-based distance learning education. In *Proceedings of IEEE Annual Frontiers in Education Conference,* (pp TF 7-11). IEEE.

Simkova, M., Tomaskova, H., & Nemcova, Z. (2012). Mobile education in tools. In *Proceedings of International Conference on Educational Research,* (pp. 10 – 13). Academic Press.

Stathacopoulou, R., Magoulas, G. D., & Grigoriadou, M. (1999). Neural Network-based Fuzzy Modeling of the Student in Intelligent Tutoring Systems. In *Proceedings of International Joint Conference on Neural Networks,* (pp. 3517–3521). Academic Press.

Su, J., Hu, J., & Ciou, Y. (2006). Low-cost simulated control experimentation conducted in Electrical Engineering Department of National Yulin University of Science and Technology. In Proceedings of iNEER, (pp. 397–408). iNEER.

Tsolis, D., Stamoub, S., Christiaa, P., Kampanaa, S., Rapakouliaa, T., Skoutaa, M., & Tsakalidisa, A. (2010). An adaptive and personalized open source e-learning platform. In *Proceedings of World Conference on Learning, Teaching and Administration,* (pp. 38–43). Academic Press.

Yaghmaie, M., & Bahreininejad, A. (2011). A context-aware adaptive learning system using agents. *Expert Systems with Applications, 38*(4), 3280–3286. doi:10.1016/j.eswa.2010.08.113

ADDITIONAL READING

Antal, M., & Koncz, S. (2011). Student modeling for a web-based self-assessment system. *Expert Systems with Applications*, *38*, 6492–6497. doi:10.1016/j.eswa.2010.11.096

Arriaga, F., Arriaga, A., Alami, M. E., Laureano, A. L., & Ramírez, J. (2003). *Fuzzy logic applications to students' evaluation in intelligent learning systems* (pp. 161–166). Zacatecas: Internacional de Informática y Computación de la ANIEI.

Baylari, A., & Montazer, G. A. (2009). Design a personalized e-learning system based on item response theory and artificial neural network approach. *Expert Systems with Applications*, *36*, 8013–8021. doi:10.1016/j.eswa.2008.10.080

Brusilovsky, P. (1999). Adaptive and intelligent technologies for web-based eduction. KI, 13(4), 19-25.

Brusilovsky, P., & Peylo, C. (2003). Adaptive and intelligent web-based educational systems. *International Journal of Artificial Intelligence in Education*, *13*(2), 159–172.

Brusilovsky, P., Santic, T., & De Bra, P. (2003). A flexible layout model for a web-based adaptive hypermedia architecture. In Proceedings of the AH2003 Workshop, TU/e CSN (Vol. 3, No. 04, pp. 77-86).

Cha, H. J., Kim, Y. S., Park, S. H., Yoon, T. B., Jung, Y. M., & Lee, J. H. (2006, January). Learning styles diagnosis based on user interface behaviors for the customization of learning interfaces in an intelligent tutoring system. InIntelligent tutoring systems (pp. 513-524). Springer Berlin Heidelberg.

Cheng, W. Y., Xiang, C. C., Hua, Z. C., & Ming, W. S. (2012, May). Based on the agent students comprehensive quality fuzzy assessment expert system. InControl and Decision Conference (CCDC), 2012 24th Chinese (pp. 3132-3135). IEEE.

Douce, C., & Porch, W. (2009). Evaluating accessible adaptable e-learning. In: Towards User Modeling and Adaptive Systems for All (TUMAS-A 2009): Modeling and Evaluation of Accessible Intelligent Learning Systems, Open Research Online, Volume 495, 1-9.

Essalmi, F., Ayed, L. J. B., Jemni, M., & Graf, S. (2010). A fully personalization strategy of E-learning scenarios. *Computers in Human Behavior*, *26*(4), 581–591. doi:10.1016/j.chb.2009.12.010

García, P., Amandi, A., Schiaffino, S., & Campo, M. (2007). Evaluating Bayesian networks' precision for detecting students' learning styles. *Computers & Education*, *49*(3), 794–808. doi:10.1016/j.compedu.2005.11.017

Henze, N., & Nejdl, W. (2003, May). Logically characterizing adaptive educational hypermedia systems. In International Workshop on Adaptive Hypermedia and Adaptive Web-based Systems (AH 2003).

Henze, N., & Nejdl, W. (2004). A logical characterization of adaptive educational hypermedia. *New Review of Hypermedia and Multimedia*, *10*(1), 77–113. doi:10.1080/13614560410001728128

Hu, Y., & Lian, Y. (2007, December). An adaptive E-learning portal for DSP learning. In Information, Communications & Signal Processing, 2007 6th International Conference on (pp. 1-5). IEEE.

Huang, C. J., Liu, M. C., Chu, S. S., & Cheng, C. L. (2004). Application of machine learning techniques to Web-based intelligent learning diagnosis system, Proceedings of the Fourth International Conference on Hybrid Intelligent Systems (HIS'04), Japan, (pp. 242 – 247).

Hui, C. L. P., & Paletta, M. (2011). *Artificial neural network for cooperative distributed environments* (pp. 189–212). Croatia.

Ishak, Z., Arshad, M. R. M., & Sumari, P. (2003, December). Adaptive hypermedia system in education: review of available technologies. InInformation, Communications and Signal Processing, 2003 and Fourth Pacific Rim Conference on Multimedia. Proceedings of the 2003 Joint Conference of the Fourth International Conference on (Vol. 3, pp. 1767-1771). IEEE.

Karahan, M. (2009). Architecture and Distributed Artificial Intelligence Techniques. *International Online Journal of Educational Sciences*, *1*(1), 1–28.

Klasnja-Milicevic, A., Vesin, B., Ivanovic, M., & Budimac, Z. (2011). E-Learning personalization based on hybrid recommendation strategy and learning style identification. *Computers & Education*, *56*, 885–899. doi:10.1016/j.compedu.2010.11.001

Leung, E. W. C., & Li, Q. (2001). Agent-based approach to e-learning: An architectural framework. In *The Human Society and the Internet Internet-Related Socio-Economic Issues* (pp. 341–353). Springer Berlin Heidelberg. doi:10.1007/3-540-47749-7_28

Li, K., & Chen, P. (2002). Design of Web-based Adaptive Learning System. InWorld Conference on Educational Multimedia, Hypermedia and Telecommunications (Vol. 2002, No. 1, pp. 287-292).

Mitrovic, A. (2003). An intelligent SQL tutor on the web. *International Journal of Artificial Intelligence in Education*, *13*(2), 173–197.

Negnevitsky, M. (2004). *Artificial intelligence: A guide to intelligent systems*. Boston, MA: Addison Wesley.

Nijhavan, H., & Brusilovsky, P. (2002). A framework for adaptive e-learning based on distributed re-usable learning activities. In World Conference on E-Learning in Corporate, Government, Healthcare, and Higher Education (Vol. 2002, No. 1, pp. 154-161).

Ozyurt, O., Ozyurt, H., Baki, A., & Guven, B. (2012). *An application of individualized assessment in educational hypermedia design of computerized adaptive testing system and its integration into UZWEBMAT* (Vol. 46, pp. 3191–3196). Procedia - Social and Behavioral Sciences.

Ozyurt, O., Ozyurt, H., Baki, A., Guven, B., & Karal, H. (2012). Evaluation of an adaptive and intelligent educational hypermedia for enhanced individual learning of mathematics A qualitative study. *Expert Systems with Applications*, *39*, 12092–12104. doi:10.1016/j.eswa.2012.04.018

Papanikolaou, K. A., Grigoriadou, M., Kornilakis, H., & Magoulas, G. D. (2003). Personalizing the Interaction in a Web-based Educational Hypermedia System: the case of INSPIRE. *User Modeling and User-Adapted Interaction*, *13*(3), 213–267. doi:10.1023/A:1024746731130

Russell, S. (2009). *Artificial intelligence: A modern approach*. Upper Saddle River, NJ: Prentice Hall.

Santamaria, P. G. (2006). CA-OLE: A Collaborative and Adaptive Online Learning Environment (Doctoral dissertation, University of Texas at Arlington).

Tsolis, D., Christia, P., Kampana, S., Polychronopoulos, E., Liopa, A., & Tsakalidis, A. (2012). OWLearn: An open source e-learning platform supporting adaptivity and personalization. *Intelligent Decision Technologies*, *6*(2), 97–104.

Vasilyeva, E., & Kozlov, D. (2005). Semantic Web and Agent-Based Technologies in Adaptation of e-Learning Systems.

Wang, H. C., Li, T. Y., & Chang, C. Y. (2006). A Web-based Tutoring System with Styles-matching Strategy for Learning Spatial Geometry, International Computer Symposium, Taipei-Taiwan, (pp. 331-355).

Weber, G., & Brusilovsky, P. (2001). ELM-ART: An adaptive versatile system for Web-based instruction. *International Journal of Artificial Intelligence in Education*, *12*, 351–384.

KEY TERMS AND DEFINITIONS

Agent: Software that controls the system.

Artificial Neural Network: A learning model originated from real neural network.

Asynchronous System: System that has only learning management system.

E-Learning: All forms of electronically supported learning and teaching.

Intelligent Distance Education: Innovative types of distance education that use intelligent methods such as artificial intelligence.

Interactive learning: The learning process when the student puts together knowledge and skills by connecting with information and experiences provided by the teacher, that can be an artificial one, and the communication between the student and professor is bidirectional.

Multi-Agent Systems: System consists of multiple interacting intelligent agents.

Synchronous System: System that has learning management system and web based conferencing system.

Chapter 7
A Web–Based Intelligent Educational Laboratory System for Forecasting Chaotic Time Series

Utku Kose
Usak University, Turkey

Ahmet Arslan
Selcuk University, Turkey

ABSTRACT

In the context of Chaos Theory and its applications, forecasting time series of a chaotic system is an attractive work area for the current literature. Many different approaches and the related scientific studies have been introduced and done by researchers since the inception of this working area. Newer studies are also performed in order to provide more effective and efficient approaches and improve the related literature in this way. On the other hand, it is another important research point to ensure effective educational approaches for teaching Chaos Theory and chaotic systems within the associated courses. In this sense, this chapter introduces a Web-based, intelligent, educational laboratory system for forecasting chaotic time series. Briefly, the system aims to enable students to experience their own learning process over the Web by using a simple interface. The laboratory system employs an Artificial Intelligence-based approach including a Single Multiplicative Neuron System trained by Intelligent Water Drops Algorithm in order to forecast time series of chaotic systems. It is possible to adjust parameters of the related Artificial Intelligence techniques, so it may possible for students to have some knowledge about Artificial Intelligence and intelligent systems.

INTRODUCTION

Chaos Theory is an important research field in Mathematics employing many applications in different disciplines like Physics, Engineering, Economics, Biology…etc. Its scope is based on scientific studies associated with the search on behavior of nonlinear dynamical systems, which are highly sensitive to their initial conditions (chaotic systems). In time several kinds of sub-working fields have also been introduced within the context of research studies on the Chaos Theory.

DOI: 10.4018/978-1-4666-6276-6.ch007

Control of Chaos, Chaos Synchronization and Chaotification (Anti-control of Chaos) are some sub-working fields that can be examined within the mentioned content. Additionally, there are also some other research orientations supporting these fields. At this point, forecasting (prediction – estimation of) time series of a chaotic system is an attractive work area for the current literature.

In time, many different approaches have been introduced to provide effective solutions for the related problem on forecasting time series of chaotic systems. Actually, this problem on forecasting time series of chaotic systems comes from the failure of forecasting methods, which are mainly used on stationary time series before (Gromov & Shulga, 2012). In this sense, the related methods were unable to provide effective solutions to forecast time series of chaotic systems and so, a remarkable effort on searching for a solution for this problem has been provided by researchers. Regards to the introduced approaches – methods, Artificial Intelligence based approaches, methods and techniques have an important role on providing solutions for the 'forecasting problem'.

On the other hand, it is also another important research point to ensure effective educational approaches for teaching Chaos Theory, chaotic systems within the associated courses given at universities or private institutes. Especially teaching the related sub-working fields (which were expressed in the first paragraph) of the Chaos Theory may direct anyone, who is interested in the related scientific field, to improve his / her knowledge for performing research works in the context of the associated literature. In time, technological developments have given a rise to employing more effective and efficient approaches to improve educational view and make something more possible to reach to the desired objectives of the "science". At this point, the latest improvements in educational technologies enable researchers to perform more effective works for improving individuals' experiences during teaching – learning processes. For example, designing and developing software systems to be used along computer-based educational processes is one of the most popular works in the literature.

This chapter introduces a Web-based, intelligent, educational laboratory system for forecasting chaotic time series. Briefly, the system aims to enable students to experience their own learning process over the Web; by using a simple interface. The laboratory system employs an Artificial Intelligence-based approach including a Single Multiplicative Neuron System trained by Intelligent Water Drops Algorithm in order to forecast time series of chaotic systems. Here, it has been aimed to provide an intelligent, effective enough approach to perform better forecasting operations while studying on the related subject over the Web-based system. It is possible to adjust parameters of the employed Artificial Intelligence techniques; so it may possible for students to have some knowledge about also Artificial Intelligence and intelligent systems. In this work, the effectiveness of the laboratory system was tested on time series provided by Lorenz System, Rössler System, Chen System, and an EEG time series.

The rest of the paper is structured as follows: The next section provides a brief literature review indicating the related "Background" on forecasting problem. Next, the Section 3 and 4 are devoted to the Artificial Intelligence approach employed in the Web-based laboratory system and in these sections, basics of the Single Multiplicative Neuron System, and the "training approach": Intelligent Water Drops Algorithm are explained briefly. Following that, the Section 5 is devoted to the brief explanation of the forecasting approach that was achieved by using the related Artificial Intelligence techniques. After that, the Section 6 introduces the Web-Based Intelligent Educational Laboratory System briefly and the Section 7 focuses on the evaluation process performed for evaluating effectiveness of the laboratory system. Finally, Section 8 outlines the conclusions that have been reached with this study and explains some future works.

BACKGROUND

Before discussing about the Web-based laboratory system, it is also important to discuss about forecasting approach running under the system. In this way, the technical advantages of the system can also be introduced. Furthermore, the forecasting approach used by the authors is also an alternative one for any other forecasting approaches, which take place in the related works from the literature. So, it will also be a good approach to discuss some about background regarding to the "forecasting" problem; before focusing on the approach provided by the authors. Some remarkable studies that have been performed (via Artificial Intelligence approaches, methods or techniques) in recent years are explained as below:

- There are many studies that have been performed based on the Ant Colony Optimization (ACO) in order to forecast different types of chaotic systems (Weng & Liu, 2006; Toskari, 2009; Hong, 2010; Niu, et al., 2010; Hong et al., 2011; Gromov & Shulga, 2012).
- Another Artificial Intelligence-based optimization algorithm: Particle Swarm Optimization (PSO) has been used by Ünler (2008) and Zhao & Yang (2009) in order to achieve an optimization based approach.
- There are some studies that have been performed via Artificial Neural Networks technique (Gan et al., 2010; Wong et al., 2010).
- Mirzaee (2009) has used the Genetic Algorithm in order to provide an alternative solution for the related problem.
- Hu and Zhang (2012) have introduced a forecasting approach based on both Chaotic Simulated Annealing Algorithm (CSAA) and Support Vector Machines (SVM).

- Liu and Yao (2009) have used an approach formed by PSO and Least Square SVM.
- There are also some more studies based on the usage of SVM approaches to forecast time series of chaotic systems (Quian et al., 2006; Farooq et al., 2007; Shi & Han, 2007; Zang et al., 2007; Li & Zhang, 2009; Yang et al., 2009).
- As being parallel with this study, Yadav et al. (2007) have performed a time series forecasting study based on Single Multiplicative Neuron (SMN). Additionally, Zhao and Yang (2009) have also used both PSO and SMN in order to forecast time series.

After providing a brief review of the literature, basics of both Single Multiplicative Neuron System and Intelligent Water Drops Algorithm must be explained before talking more about the problem-solving approach employed in the laboratory system. It is important for readers to know features and functions of the Single Multiplicative Neuron System and Intelligent Water Drops Algorithm in order to understand the technical advantages better.

SINGLE MULTIPLICATIVE NEURON SYSTEM

Single Multiplicative Neuron (SMN) System, which was firstly introduced by Yadav et al. (2007), is some kind of Artificial Intelligence - "learning" approach-system used for solving several problems like function approximation (Zhao and Yang, 2009). At this point, its features have been investigated via statistical learning theory introduced by Vapnik (1998). Briefly, the mathematical structure of the SMN system is explained as follows:

Mathematical Structure of the SMN System

A typical SMN system is formed with a single, specific artificial neural cell supported with a learning algorithm – approach. In this sense, it's a general scheme explaining its structure is represented in Figure 1.

As in the context of also Figure 1, $x = \{x_1, x_2, x_3, ..., x_n\}$ is the input vector with diagonal weight matrix w (its member is expressed as w_1, w_2, ... etc. in the figure) and bias vector $b = \{b_1, b_2, b_3, ..., b_n\}$ defining the Equation 3.1. A resulting vector (r) is then taken into the multiplication cell, whose operation is expressed in the Equation 3.2.

$$r = w_i . x_i + b_i \qquad (3.1)$$

$$\Psi = \prod_{i=1}^{n} r_i \qquad (3.2)$$

After the operation, the output of the SMN is determined via *logsis* function defined in the Equation 3.3:

$$y = \frac{1}{1 + e^{-u}} \qquad (3.3)$$

In the context of the desired output: y_d, the error value is then determined via Equation 3.4:

$$e = y_d - y \qquad (3.4)$$

At this point, it is aimed to minimize the error (e) value. In this sense, weight (w) and bias (b) parameters of the SMN system are adjusted with a learning algorithm – approach, in the context of a feedback mechanism.

There are many different kinds of approaches or algorithms that can be used for the learning process. As it was mentioned before, the Intelligent Water Drops Algorithm has been used for this aim, within the approach associated with this study. So, it is better to explain basics and general algorithm structure of the related algorithm.

INTELLIGENT WATER DROPS (IWDS) ALGORITHM

In the nature, it can be seen that natural rivers have many different turns and twists along their paths and at this point, it can be thought that why these turns and twists are created and is there any logic or some kind of intelligence behind them? Furthermore, it can also be thought that

Figure 1. A general scheme explaining the structure of SMN system

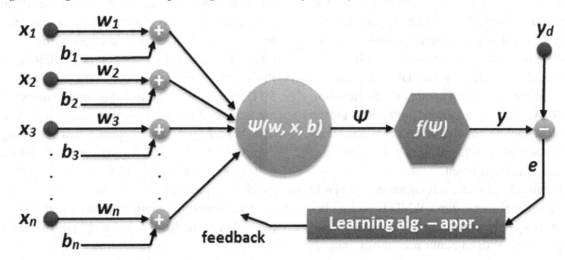

is it possible to design and develop intelligent algorithms according to the related mechanisms within natural rivers? All of these thought have been starting point for Shah-Hosseini to design and develop IWDs Algorithm. In general terms, Intelligent Water Drops (IWDs) Algorithm is a nature-inspired algorithm, which is based on the observation of the behavior of water drops. It is an algorithm, which was developed on the dynamic of a natural river system, reactions and actions that happen among water drops in a natural river (Shah-Hosseini, 2007; Shah-Hosseini, 2008; Shah-Hosseini, 2009).

Basics of the IWDs Algorithm

In a typical IWD Algorithm, some Intelligent Water Drops (IWDs) are created first and the related IWDs are based on two main properties: velocity and soil during the problem solving process. Velocity and soil properties are changed during the lifetime of a typical IWD. Within the algorithm steps, an IWD flows from a source to a destination.

While travelling from one point to another one, the related IWD removes some soil and consequently, it can gain some speed. At this point, the amount of the removed soil is added to the related IWD and this soil is non-linearly proportional to the inverse of the time needed for the IWD to flow from its current point to the next point. The related time interval is calculated by using some simple laws of physics (linear motion). Thus, the time taken is proportional to the velocity of the IWD and inversely proportional to the distance between the related two points (Shah-Hosseini, 2009). As it can be understood, both IWDs and the problem solving environment (for instance each path between two different points) have memories to track soil information.

During the problem solving process, an IWD has discrete flowing steps. While travelling between two different points, the IWD velocity value is increased by the amount nonlinearly propor-

tional to the inverse of the soil between the two points (As a result, a path with less soil let an IWD to become faster than a path having more soil). At this point, the IWD prefers the paths having low soils to the paths having high soils (In other words, paths with lower soils have more chance to be selected by an IWD). This path selection behavior is implemented by imposing a uniform random distribution on the soils of the available paths. Then, the probability of the next path to select is inversely proportional to the soils of the available paths (Shah-Hosseini, 2009).

General Algorithm Structure of the IWDs Algorithm

Within IWDs Algorithm, a typical problem is shown as the form of a graph (*N:* node set and *E:* edge set). After starting to problem solving steps, each created IWD begins constructing its solution by navigating on the nodes of the graph along the edges. This navigation continues until the related IWD completes its own solution. At this point, each IWD tries to find an optimal solution for the current iteration. When all IWDs in the solution space have completed their solutions, the current iteration of the algorithm is ended. At the end of each iteration, the best solution of the related iteration: T^{LB} (local best) is used to update the global best solution T^{GB}. This global best solution is stored until the end of the whole problem solving process. On the other hand, the amount of soil on the related edges of the T^{LB} is reduced according to quality of the solution. Following that, the next iteration is started with new IWDs (However, last remaining soils on the paths are kept) and the mentioned steps are repeated. The IWDs Algorithm is stopped when a stopping criteria is ensured. The stopping criterion can be a "maximum number of iterations value" or "a specific, expected solution value".

The mentioned algorithm steps can be explained in more detail as below (Shah-Hosseini, 2009):

Step 1: Initialization of static parameters:

- The graph (N, E) of the chosen problem is given to the algorithm. The quality of the global best solution T^{GB} is initially set to the worst value: $q(T^{GB}) = -\infty$.

- The stopping criterion (for instance; the maximum number of iterations) is determined by the user.

- The number of water drops N_{IWD} is set to a positive integer value, which is usually set to the number of nodes N_c of the graph.

- For velocity updating, the parameters are $a_v = 1$, $b_v = .01$ and $c_v = 1$.

- For soil updating, the parameters are $a_s = 1$, $b_s = .01$ and $c_s = 1$.

- The local soil updating parameter ρ_n, which is a small positive number less than one, is set as 0.9. On the other hand, the global soil updating parameter ρ_{IWD}, which is chosen from [0, 1], is set as $\rho_{IWD} = 0.9$.

- The initial soil on each path (edge) is determined with the constant: *InitSoil* such that the soil of the path between every two nodes i and j is set by $soil(i, j) = InitSoil$.

- The initial velocity of each IWD is determined with the constant: *InitVel*.

Step 2: Initialization of dynamic parameters:

- Every IWD has a visited node list $vc(IWD)$, which is initially empty: $vc(IWD) = \{ \}$.

- Each IWD's velocity is set to *InitVel*.

- All IWDs are set to have zero amount of soil.

Step 3: Spread the IWDs randomly on the nodes of the graph as their first visited nodes.

Step 4: Update the visited node list of each IWD, so they can include the nodes just visited.

Step 5: Repeat the calculations below for those IWDs with partial solutions:

- For the IWD residing in node i, choose the next node j, which does not violate any constraints of the problem and is not in the visited node list the related IWD, using the following probability equation:

$$p_i^{IWD}(j) = \frac{f(soil(i, j))}{\sum\limits_{k \notin vc(IWD)} f(soil(i, k))} \qquad (4.1)$$

such that

$$f(soil(i, j)) = \frac{1}{\varepsilon_s + g(soil(i, j))} \quad and$$

$$g(soil(i, j)) = \begin{cases} soil(i, j) & if \quad \min\limits_{l \notin vc(IWD)} (soil(i, l)) \geq 0 \\ soil(i, j) \;-\; \min\limits_{l \notin vc(IWD)} (soil(i, l)) & else \end{cases}$$

- Following that, add the newly visited node j to the list $vc(IWD)$.

- For each IWD flowing from node i to node j, update its velocity $vel^{IWD}(t)$ with the following equation:

$$vel^{IWD}(t + 1) = vel^{IWD}(t) + \frac{a_v}{b_v + c_v . soil^2(i, j)} \qquad (4.2)$$

($vel^{IWD}(t + 1)$ is the updated velocity of the IWD)

- For the IWD flowing on the path from node i to j, compute the soil value $\Delta soil(i, j)$ that the IWD loads from the path by using the following equation:

$$\Delta soil(i, j) = \frac{a_s}{b_s + c_s . time^2(i, j; vel^{IWD}(t + 1))} \qquad (4.3)$$

such that

$$time(i, j; vel^{IWD}(t+1)) = \frac{HUD(j)}{vel^{IWD}(t+1)}$$

(The heuristic undesirability: $HUD(j)$ is defined appropriately for the chosen problem).

- Update the soil $soil(i, j)$ of the path from node i to j traversed by the related IWD and also update the soil that the IWD carries $soil^{IWD}$ by using the following equations:

$$soil(i, j) = (1 - \rho_n) \cdot soil(i, j) - \rho_n \cdot \Delta soil(i, j) \tag{4.4}$$

$$soil^{IWD} = soil^{IWD} + \Delta soil(i, j) \tag{4.5}$$

Step 6: Find the local (iteration) best solution T^{LB} from all the solutions T^{IWD} found by the IWDs by using the following equation:

$$T^{LB} = \arg\max_{\forall T^{IWD}} q(T^{IWD}) \tag{4.6}$$

($q()$ is used to get quality of the obtained solution)

Step 7: Update the soils on the paths that form the current local best solution T^{LB} with the following equation:

$$soil(i, j) = (1 + \rho_{IWD}) \cdot soil(i, j)$$
$$-\rho_{IWD} \cdot \frac{1}{(N_{LB} - 1)} \cdot soil_{LB}^{IWD} \tag{4.7}$$
$$\forall (i, j) \in T^{LB}$$

(N_{LB} is used for the number of nodes in the solution: T^{LB}).

Step 8: Update the global best solution T^{GB} by the (current iteration) local best solution T^{LB} with the following equation:

$$T^{GB} = \begin{cases} T^{GB} & if\ q(T^{GB}) \geq q(T^{LB}) \\ T^{LB} & otherwise \end{cases} \tag{4.8}$$

Step 9: Control the stopping criterion. If it has not been reached yet, go to the Step 2.

Step 10: The IWDs algorithm is ended here with the global best solution: T^{GB}.

The general IWDs algorithm working mechanism is formed with the explained algorithm steps. At this point; after introducing the related Artificial Intelligence approaches, it is better to take emphasis on details of the forecasting approach, which is handled in the Web-based laboratory system.

FORECASTING APPROACH VIA SINGLE MULTIPLICATIVE NEURON (SMN) SYSTEM TRAINED BY INTELLIGENT WATER DROPS (IWDS) ALGORITHM

As it can be understood, forecasting process used in the laboratory system is formed with two different sessions, which are used for training the SMN system and forecasting a time series with the prepared – trained SMN system respectively. These sessions can be named as "training" and "forecasting" sessions. Figure 2 represents a schema explaining the forecasting approach in this work.

Binary Transformation for IWDs

In order to optimize problem notation – formulation and make it easier to obtain accurate results, a binary transformation approach has been used for IWDs taken place within the IWDs Algorithm. This transformation approach has been adapted from the "binary encoding strategy", which was introduced by Kennedy and Eberhart (1997) to be used in Particle Swarm Optimization (PSO) to

Figure 2. A schema explaining the forecasting approach

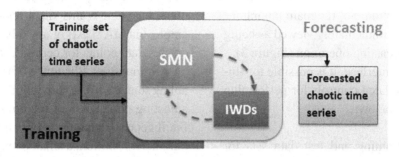

search the discrete space for special optimization processes. As similar to particles in the PSO, values of IWDs are transformed (encoded) into string bits formed by 1 and 0 values. During the related processes of the forecasting approach, necessary transformation – retransformation (encoding – decoding) operations are done in the context of weight (w) and bias (b) parameters of the SMN system. In order to get more information about the PSO – binary encoding strategy and so adapted approach in this study, readers are referred to the study done by Kennedy and Eberhart (1997).

Steps to Forecast Time Series of Chaotic Systems

By taking into consideration explained details, the related steps of the approach for solving the forecasting problem on time series of chaotic systems can be expressed as follows:

Step 1: Necessary parameters of the SMN system and IWDs Algorithm are determined before starting to a new forecasting session.

Step 2: The forecasting system is fed with the training set prepared specially for chaotic time series.

Step 3: The "training" session is performed to train the SMN system in the context of determined parameters and efforts of IWDs Algorithm.

Step 4: After the "training", session, current (trained) forecasting system is then used to forecast chaotic time series.

Generally, the system introduced within this study aims to forecast a chaotic time series according to its "three past values". In more detail, it can be said that the system structure aims to forecast $x(t+4)$, according to the four past values, which are $x(t)$, $x(t-4)$, and $x(t-8)$ respectively.

A WEB-BASED INTELLIGENT EDUCATIONAL LABORATORY SYSTEM FOR FORECASTING CHAOTIC TIME SERIES

The developed Web-based laboratory system has a simple interface, on which users - students can perform the related forecasting operations easily; by using the provided controls. The whole system has been designed and developed via ASP.Net technology; over the Microsoft Visual Studio 2012 development environment. The software system has been supported with also some additional components, which can be used for creating some visual objects like graphics. Some using features and functions of the system can be explained as follows:

Using Features and Functions of the Web-Based Laboratory System

Students can access to the Web environment of the system by typing the related Web address over any Web browser. At this point; in order to ensure a fast, and simple using experience, no authentication methods have been used at the first step in connection. So, the main laboratory system interface is immediately viewed as being active for any forecasting operation (Figure 3).

Over the main interface, it is possible for students to use the related controls for performing the tasks listed as below:

- Importing training and test data sets for forecasting process.
- Starting a training or test process.
- Adjusting parameters of the Artificial Intelligence techniques.
- Viewing graphic results of the processes.

All of the mentioned tasks can be done easily by using the buttons over the "Control Box" located on right side of the interface. Figure 4 shows the Control Box and functions of the provided buttons.

It is important that the system accepts training or/and test data sets as prepared in .csv file formats (form of the data in these files are explained briefly under the next section). These files can be provided by teachers to the students or students can prepare their own files if they have gained enough knowledge about chaotic time series and obtaining value points via different ways (for example; via MATLAB or any other algorithm that creates data points for certain chaotic systems).

An important advantage of the system is enabling students to use some additional controls for adjusting parameters of the employed Artificial Intelligence techniques. After clicking on the "AI Parameters" button, a small panel showing some additional controls associated with the parameters is viewed. It is important that the students may be directed to use these parameters to see what happens if they change some values; and in this way, they can be enabled to have some knowledge about the related techniques; Single Multiplicative Neuron System, and the Intelligent Water Drops Algorithm. Figure 5 shows the related panel for adjusting parameters.

EVALUATION

In order to evaluate its effectiveness of the Web-based laboratory system, it has been used for forecasting time series of Lorenz System, Rössler

Figure 3. Main interface of the web-based laboratory system

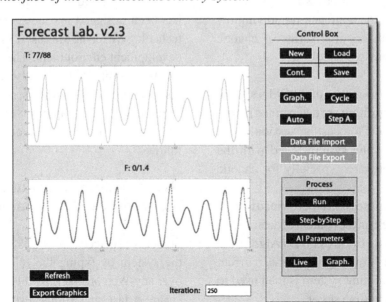

Figure 4. Control box and the buttons

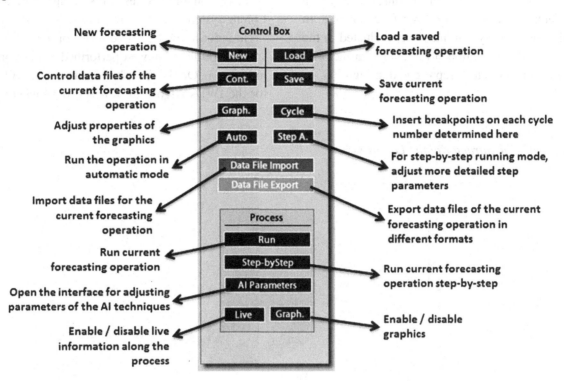

Figure 5. The panel for adjusting parameters of the SMN and the IWDs algorithm

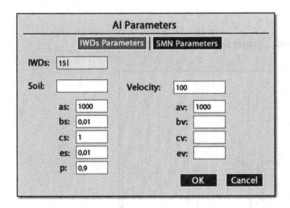

System, Chen System, and an EEG time series. For Lorenz, Rössler, and Chen System, data files containing 3000 rows in the form of "x(t+4): x(t), x(t-4), x(t-8)" values (as separately in one row for three time series; x, y, z). have been created via MATLAB solution – tool provided by Petras in a book study (2011). At this point, 1500 data rows were used for training session whereas other 1500 ones were employed for the forecasting session. On the other hand; for the EEG time series, the authors have formed a data file as similar to the ones introduced Petras and similar procedure has been done within the related sessions. In this sense, forecasting operation processes and obtained results for each process are explained as below:

Forecasting Time Series of Lorenz System

Briefly, the Lorenz System can be expressed as follows (Lorenz, 1963):

$$dx \ / \ dt = \sigma \ . \ (y - x)$$

$$dy \ / \ dt = r \ . \ x - y - x \ . \ z \qquad (6.2)$$

$$dz \ / \ dt = x \ . \ y - b \ . \ z$$

Default – standard values of the Lorenz system is determined as $\sigma = 10$, $b = 8/3$ and $r = 28$. In this study, the system has been evaluated in the context of the mentioned values. The attractor of the Lorenz system is represented in Figure 6.

A typical time series for x, y and z of the Lorenz system is also shown in Figure 7 below:

In order to forecast time series of the Lorenz system, 500 iterations were performed for the training session. On the other hand, number of IWDs for the IWDs Algorithm was set to 50 whereas

Figure 6. The attractor of the Lorenz system.

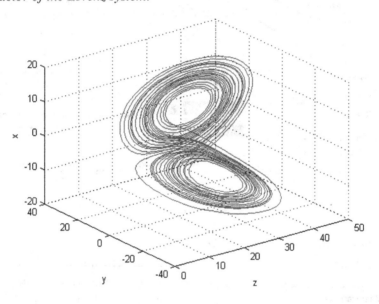

Figure 7. A typical time series for x (blue), y (green) and z (red) of the Lorenz system

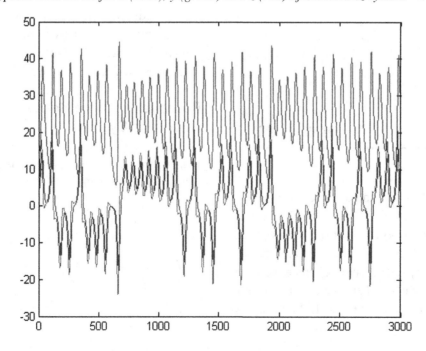

other parameters were set to their defaults. Figure 8, Figure 9, and Figure 10 represent general forecasting performance of the approach (as taken program the graphics produced over the interface):

Forecasting Time Series of Rössler System

Briefly, the Rössler System can be expressed as follows (Rössler, 1976):

$$dx / dt = -z - y$$

$$dy / dt = x + a \cdot y \qquad (6.3)$$

$$dz / dt = b + z \cdot (x - c)$$

Default – standard values of the Rössler system is determined as $a = 0.15$, $b = 0.20$ and $c = 10$. In this study, the system has been evaluated in the context of the mentioned values. The attractor of the Lorenz system is represented in Figure 11.

A typical time series for x, y and z of the Rössler system is also shown in Figure 12.

In order to forecast time series of the Rössler system, 500 iterations were performed for the training session. On the other hand, number of IWDs for the IWDs Algorithm was set to 50 whereas other parameters were set to their defaults. Figure 13, Figure 14, and Figure 15 represent general forecasting performance of the approach (as taken program the graphics produced over the interface):

Forecasting Time Series of Chen System

Briefly, the Chen System can be expressed as follows (Chen and Ueta, 1999):

$$dx / dt = a \cdot (y - x)$$

$$dy / dt = d \cdot x - x \cdot z + c \cdot y \qquad (6.4)$$

$$dz / dt = x \cdot y - b \cdot z$$

Figure 8. Forecasting performance for x time series of the Lorenz system; (a) original time series (b) forecasted time series

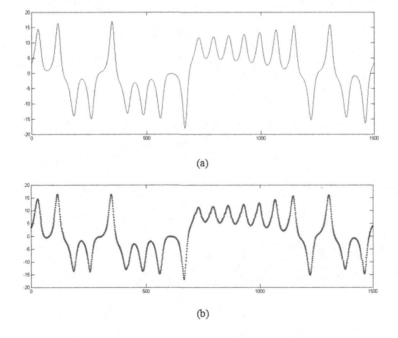

(a)

(b)

Figure 9. Forecasting performance for y time series of the Lorenz system; (a) original time series (b) forecasted time series

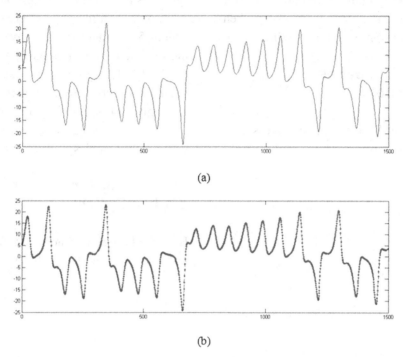

(a)

(b)

Figure 10. Forecasting performance for z time series of the Lorenz system; (a) original time series (b) forecasted time series

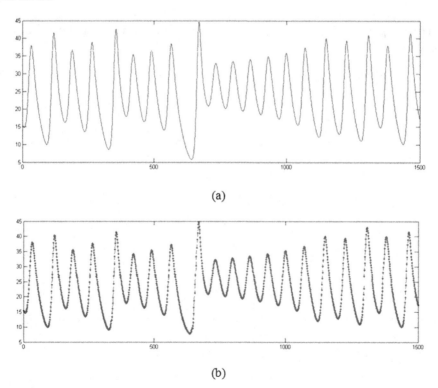

(a)

(b)

Figure 11. The attractor of the Rössler system

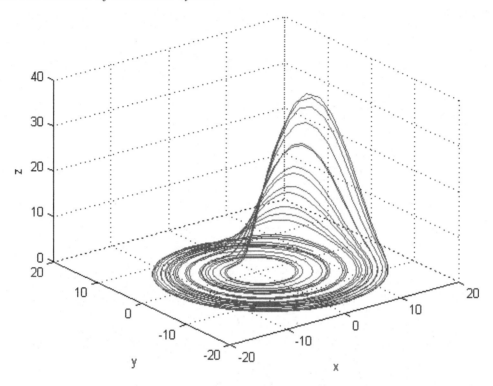

Figure 12. A typical time series for x (blue), y (green) and z (red) of the Rössler system

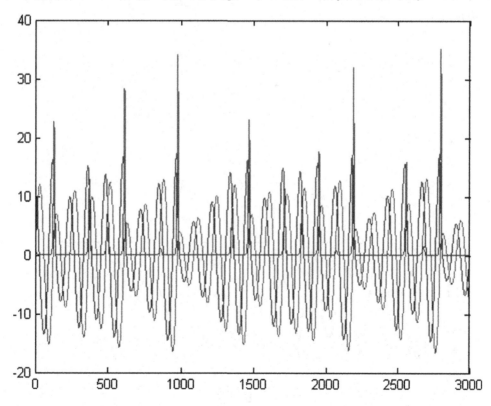

Figure 13. Forecasting performance for x time series of the Rössler system; (a) original time series (b) forecasted time series

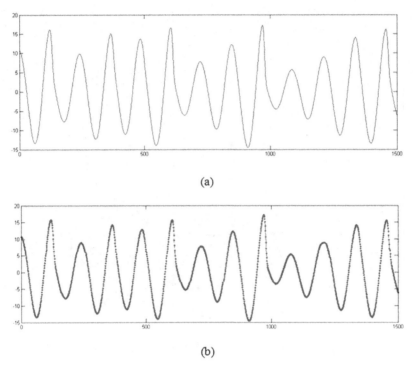

(a)

(b)

Figure 14. Forecasting performance for y time series of the Rössler system; (a) original time series (b) forecasted time series

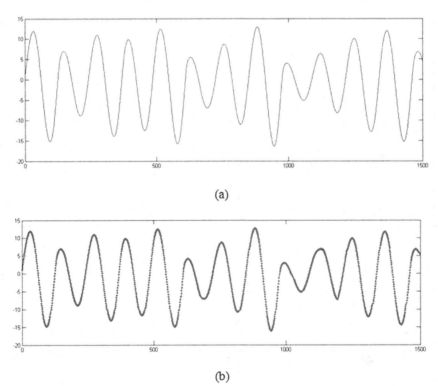

(a)

(b)

Figure 15. Forecasting performance for z time series of the Rössler system; (a) original time series (b) forecasted time series

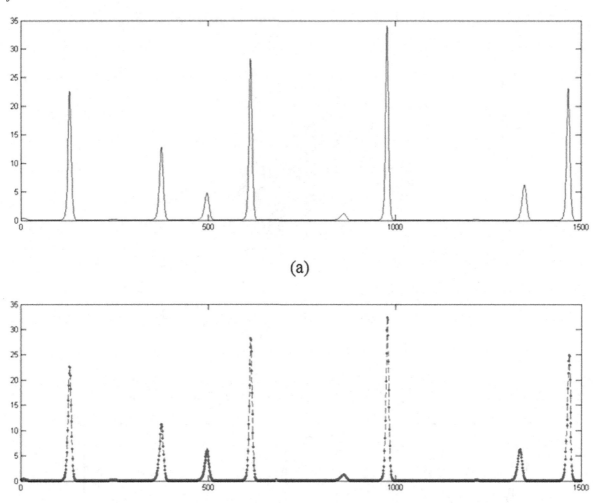

(a)

(b)

Default – standard values of the Chen system is determined as $a = 35$, $b = 3$, $c = 28$, and $d = -7$. In this study, the system has been evaluated in the context of the mentioned values. The attractor of the Chen system is represented in Figure 16.

A typical time series for x, y and z of the Chen system is also shown in Figure 17 below:

In order to forecast time series of the Chen system, 500 iterations were performed for the training session. On the other hand, number of IWDs for the IWDs Algorithm was set to 50 whereas

other parameters were set to their defaults. Figure 18, Figure 19, and Figure 20 represent general forecasting performance of the approach (as taken program the graphics produced over the interface):

Forecasting an EEG Time Series

As the fourth time series for the evaluation approach, a typical EEG time series has taken into consideration by the authors. In this sense, a sample EEG time series has been created by

Figure 16. The attractor of the Chen system

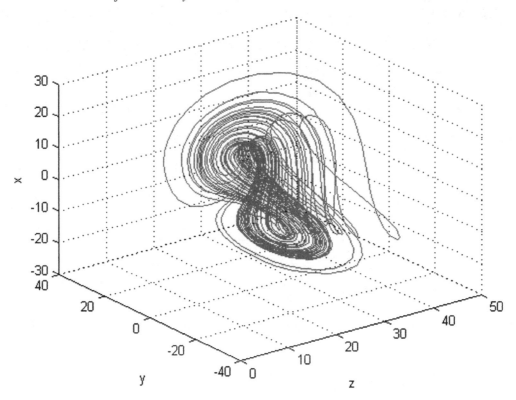

Figure 17. A typical time series for x (blue), y (green) and z (red) of the Chen system

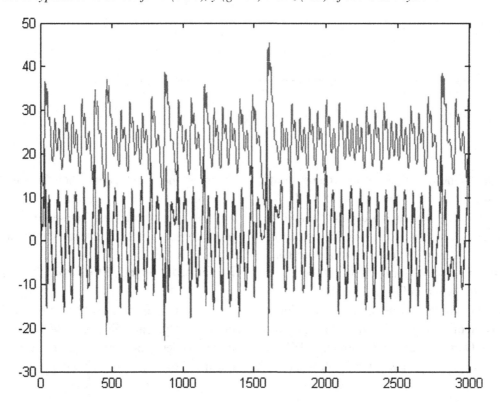

Figure 18. Forecasting performance for x time series of the Chen system; (a) original time series (b) forecasted time series

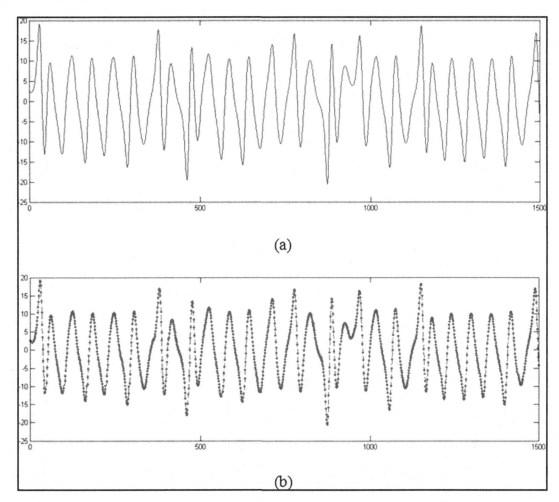

(a)

(b)

using the MATLAB – EEGLAB system, which was developed by Yeung et al. (2006) in order to generate simulated EEG data.

In order to forecast the EEG time series, 500 iterations were performed for the training session. On the other hand, number of IWDs for the IWDs Algorithm was set to 50 whereas other parameters were set to their defaults. Figure 21 represents general forecasting performance of the approach (as taken program the graphics produced over the interface):

As it can be understood from the forecasting efforts, the Web-based laboratory system is successful and accurate at forecasting chaotic time series; so, it can be used along educational processes for teaching - learning forecasting chaotic time series in the context of sub-working areas of the Chaos Theory.

CONCLUSION AND FUTURE WORK

The Web-based, intelligent, educational laboratory system, which was introduced in this chapter, provides a successful approach on forecasting chaotic time series, and so to be used for such educational processes for teaching - learning forecasting time series. In addition to the intelligent forecasting

Figure 19. Forecasting performance for y time series of the Chen system; (a) original time series (b) forecasted time series

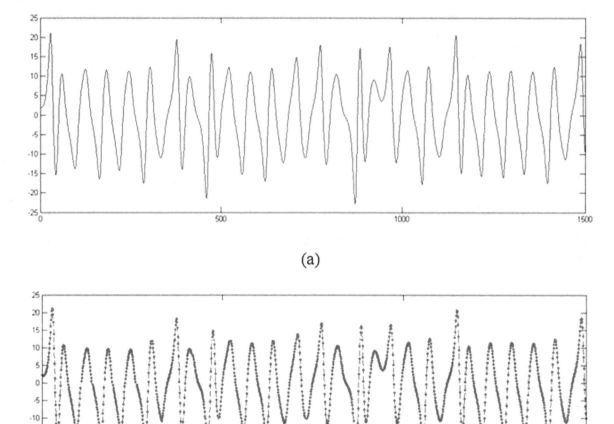

(a)

(b)

function of the system, it employs simple controls to provide a fast using experience for especially students. Because the system has no additional interface for some other Web-based mechanisms like authentication, adjusting system options... etc., it ensures an easy-to-use environment for using effectively for educational purposes. From the teacher perspective, the system is a simple tool for using along teaching processes on subjects of chaotic systems, chaotic time series, and any other associated subjects in this context.

When the technical infrastructure of the introduced system is taken into consideration, it can be expressed that the SMN system and IWDs Algorithm-based forecasting approach provides an effective problem-solving way to forecast time series of chaotic systems. General algorithmic structure of the newly developed nature-inspired algorithm (IWDs Algorithm) allows training the designed SMN system accurately and afterwards, the trained SMN system is used for forecasting the necessary time series flow. As it can be un-

Figure 20. Forecasting performance for z time series of the Chen system; (a) original time series (b) forecasted time series

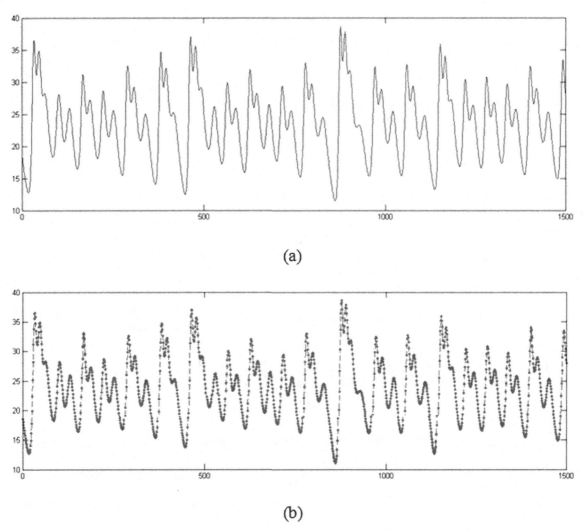

(a)

(b)

derstood, the approach has an easy-to-implement structure for the related problem. SMN system ensures a simple, easy-to-understand mathematical model and system structure and discrete binary encoding strategy used for the IWDs Algorithm also allows feeding the SMN system easily for preparing – training it to the forecasting task. All of simple mathematical structure has enabled the authors to develop the system in a well-organized structure causing fast viewing over the Web even bad Internet connections.

The performed evaluation process has been a key point for evaluating both educational and problem-solving potentials of the introduced system. During the evaluation process, the employed Artificial Intelligence approach has been used for performing forecasting operations on three different (time series of) chaotic systems (Lorenz System, Rössler System, Chen System, and an EEG time series) and according to the obtained results, the approach has acted as a successful forecaster. Briefly, it can be expressed that the SMN system and IWDs Algorithm-based approach is able to

Figure 21. Forecasting performance for the EEG time series; (a) original time series (b) forecasted time series

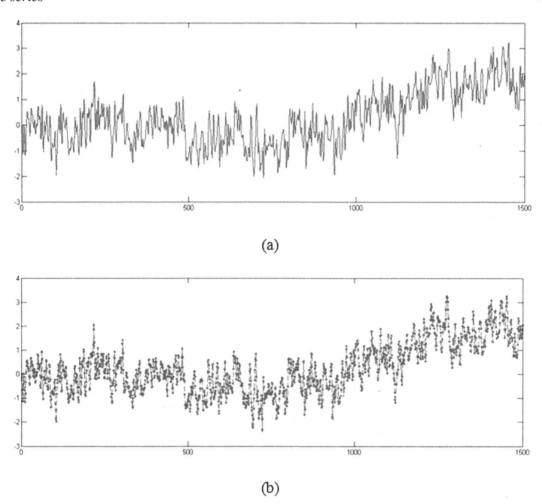

(a)

(b)

forecast time series of chaotic systems effectively. Eventually, this study provides an alternative way for solving the forecasting problem of chaotic system - time series and enables both teachers and students to have an effective and accurate tool that can be used along educational process with peace of mind.

In addition to the current form of the system, authors also think on some future developments in the sense of newer versions. It has been planned to improve the interface for enabling both teachers and students to adjust their own views and making it more effective to use the related controls over the system. Additionally, there will be some other works for providing more educational supportive objects over the system (for example; ready simulators for certain chaotic time series, interactive lecture notes...etc.). In addition to the introduced future works, there will also be some other works for the Artificial Intelligence-based infrastructure of system. In this sense, there will be also additional works to adjust mathematical model of the employed approach in order to improve its abilities to provide more accurate and faster forecasting processes. This works may include adjusting features and functions of both SMN system and the IWDs Algorithm.

REFERENCES

Chen, G., & Ueta, T. (1999). Yet another chaotic attractor. *International Journal of Bifurcation and Chaos in Applied Sciences and Engineering, 9,* 1465–1466. doi:10.1142/S0218127499001024

Farooq, T., Guergachi, A., & Krishnan, S. (2007). Chaotic time series prediction using knowledge based Green's kernel and least-squares support vector machines. In *Proceedings of the IEEE International Conference on Systems, Man and Cybernetics* (pp. 2669–2674). IEEE.

Gan, M., Peng, H., Peng, X., Chen, X., & Inoussa, G. (2010). A locally linear RBF network-based state-dependent AR model for nonlinear time series modeling. *Information Sciences, 180,* 4370–4383. doi:10.1016/j.ins.2010.07.012

Gromov, G. A., & Shulga, A. N. (2012). Chaotic time series prediction with employment of ant colony optimization. *Expert Systems with Applications, 39,* 8474–8478. doi:10.1016/j.eswa.2012.01.171

Hong, W. C. (2010). Application of chaotic ant swarm optimization in electric load forecasting. *Energy Policy, 38,* 5830–5839. doi:10.1016/j.enpol.2010.05.033

Hu, Y. X., & Zhang, H. T. (2012). Prediction of the chaotic time series based on chaotic simulated annealing and support vector machine. In *Proceedings of the International Conference on Solid State Devices and Materials Science* (pp. 506–512). Macao, China: Academic Press.

Kennedy, J., & Eberhart, R. C. (1997). A discrete binary version of the particle swarm algorithm. In *Proceedings of the World Multi-Conference on Systems, Cybernetics and Informatics* (pp. 4104–4109). Piscataway, NJ: Academic Press.

Li, H. T., & Zhang, X. F. (2009). Precipitation time series predicting of the chaotic characters using support vector machines. In *Proceedings of the International Conference on Information Management, Innovation Management and Industrial Engineering* (pp. 407–410). Xian, China: Academic Press.

Liu, P., & Yao, J. A. (2009). Application of least square support vector machine based on particle swarm optimization to chaotic time series prediction. In *Proceedings of the IEEE International Conference on Intelligent Computing and Intelligent Systems* (pp. 458–462). Shanghai, China: IEEE.

Lorenz, E. N. (1963). Deterministic non-periodic flows. *Journal of the Atmospheric Sciences, 20,* 130–141. doi:10.1175/1520-0469(1963)020<0130:DNF>2.0.CO;2

Mirzaee, H. (2009). Linear combination rule in genetic algorithm for optimization of finite impulse response neural network to predict natural chaotic time series. *Chaos, Solitons, and Fractals, 41,* 2681–2689. doi:10.1016/j.chaos.2008.09.057

Niu, D., Wang, Y., & Wu, D. D. (2010). Power load forecasting using support vector machine and ant colony optimization. *Expert Systems with Applications, 37,* 2531–2539. doi:10.1016/j.eswa.2009.08.019

Petras, I. (2011). *Fractional-order nonlinear systems: Modeling, analysis and simulation.* Berlin, Germany: Springer. doi:10.1007/978-3-642-18101-6

Quian, J. S., Cheng, J., & Guo, Y. N. (2006). A novel multiple support vector machines architecture for chaotic time series prediction. *Lecture Notes in Computer Science, 4221,* 147–156. doi:10.1007/11881070_25

Rössler, O. E. (1976). An equation for continuous chaos. *Physics Letters [Part A]*, *57*, 397–398. doi:10.1016/0375-9601(76)90101-8

Shah-Hosseini, H. (2007). Problem solving by intelligent water drops. In *Proceedings of the 2007 IEEE Congress on Evolutionary Computation* (pp. 3226-3231). Singapore: IEEE.

Shah-Hosseini, H. (2008). Intelligent water drops algorithm: A new optimization method for solving the multiple knapsack problem. *International Journal of Intelligent Computing and Cybernetics*, *1*, 193–212. doi:10.1108/17563780810874717

Shah-Hosseini, H. (2009). The intelligent water drops algorithm: A nature-inspired swarm-based optimization algorithm. *International Journal of Bio-Inspired Computation*, *1*, 71–79. doi:10.1504/IJBIC.2009.022775

Shi, Z. W., & Han, M. (2007). Support vector echo-state machine for chaotic time-series prediction. *IEEE Transactions on Neural Networks*, *18*, 359–372. doi:10.1109/TNN.2006.885113 PMID:17385625

Toskari, M. D. (2009). Estimating the net electricity energy generation and demand using the ant colony optimization approach. *Energy Policy*, *37*, 1181–1187. doi:10.1016/j.enpol.2008.11.017

Ünler, A. (2008). Improvement of energy demand forecasts using swarm intelligence: The case of Turkey with projections to 2025. *Energy Policy*, *36*, 1937–1944. doi:10.1016/j.enpol.2008.02.018

Vapnik, V. (1998). *Statistical learning theory*. New York: John Wiley and Sons, Inc.

Weng, S. S., & Liu, Y. H. (2006). Mining time series data for segmentation by using ant colony optimization. *European Journal of Operational Research*, *173*, 921–937. doi:10.1016/j.ejor.2005.09.001

Wong, W. K., Xia, M., & Chu, W. C. (2010). Adaptive neural network model for time-series forecasting. *European Journal of Operational Research*, *207*, 807–816. doi:10.1016/j.ejor.2010.05.022

Yadav, R. N., Kalra, P. K., & John, J. (2007). Time series prediction with single multiplicative neuron model. *Applied Soft Computing*, *7*, 1157–1163. doi:10.1016/j.asoc.2006.01.003

Yang, Z. H. O., Wang, Y. S., Li, D. D., & Wang, C. J. (2009). Predict the time series of the parameter-varying chaotic system based on reduced recursive lease square support vector machine. In *Proceedings of the IEEE International Conference on Artificial Intelligence and Computational Intelligence* (pp. 29–34). Shanghai, China: IEEE.

Yeung, E. N., Bogacz, R., Holroyd, C. B., Nieuwenhuis, S., & Cohen, J. D. (2006). *Generation of simulated EEG data*. Retrieved from http://www.cs.bris.ac.uk/~rafal/phasereset/

Zhang, J. S., Dang, J. L., & Li, H. C. (2007). Local support vector machine prediction of spatiotemporal chaotic time series. *Acta Physica Sinica*, *56*, 67–77.

Zhao, L., & Yang, Y. (2009). PSO-based single multiplicative neuron model for time series prediction. *Expert Systems with Applications*, *36*, 2805–2812. doi:10.1016/j.eswa.2008.01.061

ADDITIONAL READING

Ahmed, S. U., Shahjahan, M., & Murase, K. (2011). Injecting chaos in feedforward neural networks. *Neural Processing Letters*, *34*(1), 87–100. doi:10.1007/s11063-011-9185-x

Alligood, K. T., Sauer, T. D., & Yorke, J. A. (1996). *Chaos: An introduction to dynamical systems*. Berlin Heidelberg, Germany: Springer-Verlag.

Brighton, H., & Selina, H. (2007). *Introducing artificial intelligence*. Cambridge, United Kingdom: Icon Books Ltd.

Cheesman, M. J., Chen, S., Manchadi, M. L., Jacob, T., Minchin, R. F., & Tregloan, P. A. (2014). Implementation of a Virtual Laboratory Practical Class (VLPC) module in pharmacology education. *Pharmacognosy Communications*, *4*(1), 2–10. doi:10.5530/pc.2014.1.2

Chien, S., DeCoste, D., Doyle, R., & Stolorz, P. (1997). Making an impact: Artificial intelligence at the jet propulsion laboratory. *AI Magazine*, *18*(1), 103.

Clemente, J., Ramírez, J., & De Antonio, A. (2014). Applying a student modeling with non-monotonic diagnosis to Intelligent Virtual Environment for Training/Instruction. *Expert Systems with Applications*, *41*(2), 508–520. doi:10.1016/j. eswa.2013.07.077

D'Souza, A., Rickel, J., Herreros, B., & Johnson, W. L. (2001). An automated lab instructor for simulated science experiments. *Artificial Intelligence in Education: AI-ED in the Wired and Wireless Future*, 65-76.

Dobrzañski, L. A., & Honysz, R. (2010). Artificial intelligence and virtual environment application for materials design methodology. *Archives of Materials Science*, *70*, 70.

Dostál, P. (2013). The use of soft computing for optimization in business, economics, and finance. In P. Vasant (Ed.), *Meta-Heuristics Optimization Algorithms in Engineering, Business, Economics, and Finance* (pp. 41–86). Hershey, PA: Information Science Reference.

Egrioglu, E., Yolcu, U., Aladag, C. H., & Bas, E. (2014). Recurrent Multiplicative Neuron Model Artificial Neural Network for Non-linear Time Series Forecasting. *Procedia-Social and Behavioral Sciences*, *109*, 1094–1100. doi:10.1016/j. sbspro.2013.12.593

Elmas, Ç. (2003). *Artificial neural network – theory, architecture, training, implementation <> Yapay sinir ağları – teori, mimari, eğitim, uygulama*. Ankara, Turkey: Seçkin Press. (In Turkish)

Gershenson, C., Gonzalez, P. P., & Negrete, J. (2002). Thinking adaptive: Towards a behaviours virtual laboratory. *arXiv preprint cs/0211028*.

Gleick, J. (2008). *Chaos: Making a new science*. New York, NY: Penguin Books.

Gustavsson, I. (2002). Remote laboratory experiments in electrical engineering education. In *Devices, Circuits and Systems, 2002. Proceedings of the Fourth IEEE International Caracas Conference on* (pp. I025-1). IEEE.

Hartness, K. (2004). Robocode: using games to teach artificial intelligence. *Journal of Computing Sciences in Colleges*, *19*(4), 287–291.

Köse, U., & Deperlioğlu, Ö. (2010). An educational, virtual laboratory system for fuzzy logic. *International Symposium on Computing in Science and Engineering 2010* (pp. 1335-1342). Aydın / Turkey: Gediz University.

Liang, W. Y. (2014). Research and Development of Flash-Based Online Virtual Laboratory. *Applied Mechanics and Materials*, *509*, 198–201. doi:10.4028/www.scientific.net/AMM.509.198

López, I., & Iglesias, G. (2014). Efficiency of OWC wave energy converters: A virtual laboratory. *Applied Ocean Research*, *44*, 63–70. doi:10.1016/j.apor.2013.11.001

Lucci, S., & Kopec, D. (2012). [st century, Dulles, VA: Mercury Learning and Information.]. *Artificial Intelligence*, 21.

Luck, M., & Aylett, R. (2000). Applying artificial intelligence to virtual reality: Intelligent virtual environments. *Applied Artificial Intelligence*, *14*(1), 3–32. doi:10.1080/088395100117142

Mahajan, V., Agarwal, P., & Gupta, H. O. (2014). An artificial intelligence based controller for multilevel harmonic filter. *International Journal of Electrical Power & Energy Systems*, *58*, 170–180. doi:10.1016/j.ijepes.2014.01.020

Mosterman, P. J., Dorlandt, M. A., Campbell, J. O., Burow, C., Bouw, R., Brodersen, A. J., & Bourne, J. R. (1994). Virtual engineering laboratories: Design and experiments. *Journal of engineering. Education*, *83*(3), 279–285.

Niu, X., Wen, F., & Sun, Y. (2014). Research and Design on Virtual Experiment System Integration Based on WebService. *Open Journal of Social Sciences*, *2*, 74. doi:10.4236/jss.2014.22011

Noguez, J., & Sucar, L. E. (2005). A semi-open learning environment for virtual laboratories. In MICAI 2005: Advances in Artificial Intelligence (pp. 1185-1194). Springer Berlin Heidelberg.

Norman, T. J., & Jennings, N. R. (2002). Constructing a virtual training laboratory using intelligent agents. *International Journal of Continuing Engineering Education and Lifelong Learning*, *12*(1), 201–213. doi:10.1504/IJCEELL.2002.000429

Quesnel, G., Duboz, R., & Ramat, É. (2009). The Virtual Laboratory Environment–An operational framework for multi-modelling, simulation and analysis of complex dynamical systems. *Simulation Modelling Practice and Theory*, *17*(4), 641–653. doi:10.1016/j.simpat.2008.11.003

Sensarma, D., & Majumder, K. (2014, January). IWDRA: An Intelligent Water Drop Based QoS-Aware Routing Algorithm for MANETs. In *Proceedings of the International Conference on Frontiers of Intelligent Computing: Theory and Applications (FICTA) 2013* (pp. 329-336). Springer International Publishing.

Sheremetov, L., & Arenas, A. G. (2002). EVA: an interactive Web-based collaborative learning environment. *Computers & Education*, *39*(2), 161–182. doi:10.1016/S0360-1315(02)00030-1

Sivakumar, S. C., Robertson, W., Artimy, M., & Aslam, N. (2005). A web-based remote interactive laboratory for Internetworking education. *Education. IEEE Transactions on*, *48*(4), 586–598.

Tang, X.-L., Ren, J.-H., Zhuang, L., & Ca, C.-X. (2008). Application of neural network trained by chaos particle swarm optimization to prediction of silicon content in hot metal. *7th World Congress on Intelligent Control and Automation – Vol. 1-23* (pp. 2446-2449). New York, NY: IEEE.

Uğur, A., & Kınacı, A. C. (2006). *Classification of web pages by using artificial intelligence techniques and artificial neural networks <> Yapay zeka teknikleri ve yapay sinir ağlari kullanilarak web sayfalarinin siniflandirilmasi*. Ankara, Turkey: Inet-TR. (In Turkish)

Warwick, K. (2011). *Artificial intelligence: The basics*. London, United Kingdom: Routledge.

Winston, P. H. (1992). *Artificial intelligence*. Boston, MA: Addison Wesley.

Xing, B., & Gao, W. J. (2014). Intelligent Water Drops Algorithm. In Innovative Computational Intelligence: A Rough Guide to 134 Clever Algorithms (pp. 365-373). Springer International Publishing.

Yadav, R. N., Kalra, P. K., & John, J. (2007). Time series prediction with single multiplicative neuron model. *Applied Soft Computing*, *7*(4), 1157–1163. doi:10.1016/j.asoc.2006.01.003

Zhang, G., Lu, D., & Liu, H. (2014). A Visualization Method in Virtual Educational System. In *Frontier and Future Development of Information Technology in Medicine and Education* (pp. 421–429). Springer Netherlands. doi:10.1007/978-94-007-7618-0_41

Zhang, L., Liu, M., Shi, Z., & Ma, X. (2014, January). Research on Virtual Basic Laboratory and Experimental Teaching Resources Platform Based on Cloud Computing. In *Proceedings of the 9th International Symposium on Linear Drives for Industry Applications, Volume 2* (pp. 549-554). Springer Berlin Heidelberg.

Zhang, Y., & Wang, X.-Y. (2012). Fuzzy neural network based on a Sigmoid chaotic neuron. *Chinese Physics B*, *21*(2), 020507/1–020507/6. doi:10.1088/1674-1056/21/2/020507

Zhao, L., & Yang, Y. (2009). PSO-based single multiplicative neuron model for time series prediction. *Expert Systems with Applications*, *36*(2), 2805–2812. doi:10.1016/j.eswa.2008.01.061

KEY TERMS AND DEFINITIONS

Artificial Intelligence: (1) A term that is used to describe the feature, function or characteristic of computer systems or machines that try to simulate human-thinking behavior or human intelligence. (2) A field of Computer Science, which is based on research studies or developments on providing intelligent systems simulating the human-thinking behavior or human intelligence.

Chaos: A term used for defining the random – nonlinear and unpredictable behavior of something.

Chaos Theory: A scientific approach – research effort which is based on examining behaviors of nonlinear dynamical systems, which are highly sensitive to their initial conditions.

Chaotic Time Series: A time series, which employs chaotic actions - behaviors along the time period.

Chaotic: An adjective used for defining something which shows random – nonlinear and unpredictable behavior.

Time Series: A term defining the whole values which are obtained by a variable in course of time.

Web-Based Laboratory: An interactive, online software system, which generally aims to simulate a virtual laboratory environment on which users can perform some operations on specific applications or problems.

Chapter 8
Expert Systems in Distance Education

Duygu Mutlu-Bayraktar
Istanbul University, Turkey

Esad Esgin
Marmara University, Turkey

ABSTRACT

Computers have been used in educational environments to carry out applications that need expertise, such as compiling, storing, presentation, and evaluation of information. In some teaching environments that need expert knowledge, capturing and imitating the knowledge of the expert in an artificial environment and utilizing computer systems that have the ability to communicate with people using natural language might reduce the need for the expert and provide fast results. Expert systems are a study area of artificial intelligence and can be defined as computer systems that can approach a problem for which an answer is being sought like an expert and present solution recommendations. In this chapter, the definition of expert systems and their characteristics, information about the expert systems in teaching environments, and especially their utilization in distance education are given.

INTRODUCTION

One of the most discussed problems of distance education is whether the learning outputs taken without being in the same place with many students are better than the traditional methods (Miller, 2001). While it is seen in some studies that the results are equivalent, it is true that sometimes limitations occur due to lack of time, place, experts and abundance of students (LaBay & Comm, 2003; Mehlenbacher, et al., 2000; Chatpakkarattana & Khlaisang, 2012). The teachers, who are to get to know students and determine the appropriate type of instruction for them, have a very important role as experts in the success of distance education (Lin,

et al., 2005; Wiesner, 2000). As a solution for the lack of experts, systems which can simulate what an expert is doing, which are run to use human knowledge in the solution of problems that can usually be solved with high level capabilities, can be used to lead students in distance education and can be used as assisting systems in compiling data (Russell & Norvig, 2010).

The expert systems as an application of artificial intelligence are interactive decision tools that are created on the basis of knowledge gathered from the expert and which utilize information of events and experience to solve complex problems (Baykal & Beyan, 2004). In addition, they are defined as software that models reasoning and

DOI: 10.4018/978-1-4666-6276-6.ch008

decision processes of the one who is an expert on a subject (Nabiyev, 2005). Expert systems, designed to make the logic of a human expert available to others, preserve and transmit individual and collective experiences in specialized domains. They receive, keep and incorporate the experience which certain skilled ones in an organization have accumulated over the span of their professional lifetimes (Wachter & Gupta, 1997).

The first expert system known is the writings on Luxor papyrus dated around 3000 BC, found in Egypt, about the application of symptom-treatment-process situations according to "if-then" rules. The expert systems in the real sense of the meaning have been developed by the communities of artificial intelligence in the middle of 1960s with the idea that the combination of some reasoning rules and powerful computers, performance of expert, even superhuman, could be revealed. The first application examples of this period could be expressed as the development of DENDRAL by E.Feigenbaum and afterwards the appearance of MYCIN (Russel & Norvig, 2010; Turban et al., 2007).

The goal of the expert system is not to replace any expert; it is to facilitate common use of the expert knowledge by leading it into as many channels as possible. The expert improves himself in problem solving in areas which need special knowledge and becomes an expert on that subject. The expert systems gather all the knowledge about a subject which needs expertise from experts, printed and online sources such as journals, books, articles and store them in the database of the system. When needed, the expert system can deliver this knowledge to any person who wants to use it. Thus, the knowledge of the expert is put into more common use (Erkoç, 2008).

In traditional programming methods, the data in the database is effectively processed in the system according to the algorithm created by the programmer and a predetermined result is reached. But during knowledge processing, knowledge bases created by defined rules and facts are effectively processed in the system based on experience/

heuristic or similar methods independent of any algorithm. Expert systems are especially used in cases where quantitative data and mathematical modeling of traditional programming techniques are inadequate and judgmental knowledge based on expertise is needed. Result refining mechanisms are used in expert systems instead of algorithms (Russell & Norvig, 2010; Biondo, 1990; Sasikumar et. al., 2007; Turban et. al., 2007).

Expert systems are systems that also learn from new inputs. For example, when your car breaks down, you enter possible error symptoms and the computer stores them in the workplace. As a result, a hypothesis is developed in the workplace, the computer suggests you some checks, the results are saved in the workplace and thus it also learns this problem and its solution (Russell & Norvig, 2010; Turban et al., 2007).

Harmon and King (1985) contend that, as a greater volume of information is collected, merged and shaped into meaningful patterns more rapidly than ever, expert systems will play a major role in the reforming of conventional concepts of what composes an organization and how it is managed. Furthermore, traditional educational organizations are transformed into web-based learning environments including expert systems.

FEATURES AND STRUCTURE OF EXPERT SYSTEMS

The prominent characteristics of expert systems when compared with traditional systems are shown in Table 1 (Siler & Buckley, 2005; Biondo, 1990; Sasikumar et al., 2007; Turban et al., 2007).

Along with these characteristics, expert systems use inference methods instead of precise and clear algorithms. That's why the design of an expert system is a complicated and time consuming process.

Expert systems are comprised of two main sections: development environment and consulting environment. The development environment is used to structure the components of expert

Table 1. *Traditional and expert systems comparisons*

Traditional Systems	Expert Systems
Information and its processing takes place in the same program.	The knowledge base and processing mechanism are separate from each other.
The program doesn't make a mistake.	The program can make a mistake.
It doesn't explain how the results are obtained.	Explanation is a part of it.
It requires inputs completely. It doesn't operate otherwise.	Result can be obtained with lacking input.
It is tiring to make a change in the program.	It is easy to change the rules.
The system can only work when it is complete.	It can even work with a few rules (as a prototype).
It works algorithmically.	It works heuristically and logically.
Large databases can be managed effectively.	Large knowledge bases can be managed effectively.
Uses and presents data.	Leads to decision and knowledge.
The main goal is efficiency.	The main goal is effectiveness.
Coped with quantitative data easily.	Coped with qualitative data easily.
Representations of numerical data are used.	Symbolic and numeric representations of knowledge are used.
Numerical data or information is delivered.	Decision and knowledge is delivered.

systems and to introduce knowledge. The consulting environment is used by non-experts to access expert knowledge and receive suggestions. These two environments are generally composed of the following components (Biondo, 1990; Sasikumar et al., 2007; Turban et al., 2007):

- **Knowledge Base:** It consists of rules that contain the known facts and logical references about the domain.
- **Inference Engine:** It is interacting with all the other components and carries out reasoning according to the inputs it receives from them.
- **Blackboard/Workplace:** It is the short-term memory assigned for the explanation of a problem and for storing interim results.
- **User Interface:** It provides interaction with the user.
- **Explanation Subsystem/Justifier:** It explains the inferences of the system and justifies its results.
- **Knowledge Refining System:** It analyses system performance, provides self-learning and development.

It is required that the components and determinants of the expert's decision making procedure must be learned as much as possible to construct an expert system. This exposure must contain the logic process and the information which is operated. The goal is to simulate as closely as possible the process of the expert's decision making (Wachter & Gupta, 1997). There are a few methods to model the rationale of the decision making procedure such as fact tables, attribute hierarchies and decision trees (Awad, 1996). After modeling the process, it is converted into the language that is used by an expert system shell, or the model is programmed from the rough by an artificial intelligence language such as PROLOG or LISP.

Luconi et al. (1986) dispute types of expert systems in terms of the structure of the problem being addressed and to the level of involvement of the user. These types consist of the scale from well-structured problems, namely pure expert systems, and unstructured problems, namely expert support system. The user may alter data, procedures, objectives or strategies at any point in the decision making process in expert support systems which are scarce with this quality.

EXPERT SYSTEM APPLICATIONS IN EDUCATION

Web based WALLIS, was developed by Edinburgh University Mathematics School to determine the difficulties which the students face when they first start graduate education. Another goal of the system is to get students to study the content of the subject by having them apply theories and giving examples. The students can also receive information on different subjects by using related microworlds. A tree map of the scope is provided for the students to check the material. The feedback mechanism for the interactive activities of the system is based on Computer Algebra System. This mechanism is basically inspired from gaining cognitive skills and cognitive structure. In parallel to this mechanism, there is also a separate section for revealing the concept misunderstandings of the students and help them in their improvement. The students are led to a teaching aid about a problem which they cannot solve. If their answers are correct they can move on to the other step or see the solution. The students are led by verifying feedback (if concept misunderstandings are detected) or negative feedback that suggests that they try again. In addition to these, help is also provided according to the interaction history of the student. Help or application is presented to the students about the pages that they didn't study. This way, when the student cannot follow which sections he studied, the system provides help. This help is provided in case of the request of students, too (Mavrikis, Maciocia & Lee, 2007).

To improve students' exercises, an Intelligent Tutoring System should be able to respond the type of problems that students confronted with. It should also include the related knowledge components which will allow the expert system to compare the correct solution with the student's answer. On the other hand, exponential complexity time is one of the disadvantages, that weakens the correct real-time response. In the study of Jaques et al. (2013), PAT2Math, the expert system module of an Algebra Intelligent Tutoring System,

is introduced. This system aims to correct the student steps and model their knowledge components when solving equations. In addition, it also provides demonstration of problem solving. The researchers dispute mainly on the implementation of this module as a rule-based expert system. They describe how to decrease the complexity of this module from $O(nd)$ to $O(d)$, where n is the number of rules in the knowledge base, by applying some meta-rules. These meta-rules aim at inferring the students' treatment to generate a step. They tested this approach through a user study with forty-three seventh grade students. The students who interacted with this tool showed statistically higher scores on equation solving tests, after solving algebra exercises with PAT2Math during an approximately two-hour session, than students who solved the same exercises using only paper and pencil (Jaques, et al., 2013).

Peixoto, Boarati and Forte (2012) have aimed at developing a system which will help people designing user interfaces and relating the knowledge of experts with an expert system named "GuideExpert". To this end, the system detects the cognitive style and attention deficiencies of users and help designers to design interfaces suitable for them.

It is possible to construct an intelligent Web-based education system using the set of integrated tools described in Peredo et al. (2011)'s paper. Aim of the study is to build a web learning environment which can be modified depending on the Learner. The web learning environment consists of four parts: Authoring Tool, Evaluation System, Interactive Voice System and a Virtual Laboratory for programming in Java, all of which use Web Services and are easily adaptable to the management, authoring, delivery and monitoring of learning content. A multi-agent system was used for the decision-making process of the intelligent Web-based education system.

Despite the benefits of applying the Internet facilities to the learning process, previous research has determined difficulties in the use of this method. The main difficulty is that there is no

Figure 1. Architecture for development web based education systems (Peredo, et al., 2011)

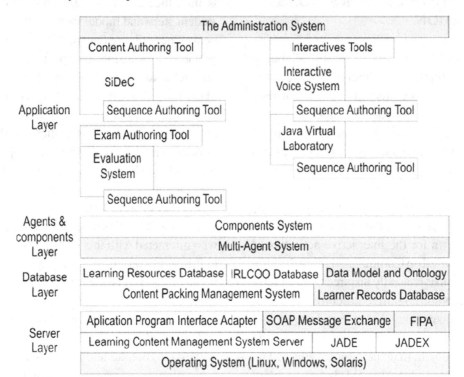

online instructional environment guiding students to use the Internet facilities in problem-solving. In the study of Hwang et al. (2011), the way how teachers solve problems online is analyzed and its results are used as the knowledge base of an expert system, which then helps students to improve their ability to use internet facilities to solve problems. In order to show the innovative approach, two experts are requested to make a performance evaluation for the system. It has been shown by the experimental results that this innovative approach can offer students accurate and constructive ideas which improve their problem-solving ability (Hwang, et al., 2011).

EXPERT SYSTEM APPLICATIONS IN DISTANCE EDUCATION

The modules that are used as the structure of the expert system, provides students with personalized feedback and problems. Besides, the error library expands according to the wrong answers and different student types can be determined. More personalization possibilities are provided in this way. These modules are:

The decision mechanism, it is the main program; it forms the decision mechanism of the program and decides according to the information it receives.

The knowledge base, it consists of the knowledge which the student has to learn. This knowledge can be presented with rule-based, semantic networks, frames and similar elements. However it is made, it will be an effective tool for the student to understand the provided information. An important aspect of this element is its skill in explaining the student why it has answered questions.

The student module, it stores the subjects students learn in the lesson and the development of them. This dynamic presentation is updated by using the diagnostic capacity of the system. Thus, a given knowledge and student knowledge can be compared.

Student-computer interface; it provides an easy way for the students to access knowledge and control the program. Graphics, symbols and visual languages are simpler and more effective ways in communication then writings. The interactive environment controls should be developed in order to improve judging skills of the students on what they have learned (Beck, 2007).

The pedagogic module, it arranges the educational communication between the student and the computer. In this way, it follows the development of the student and decides on when and what type of requirement he/she needs. It suggests clues for solving dilemmas, presents new materials or presents teacher support (Önder, 2001; Önder, 2002). The expert systems developed for use in the field of education are programmed with different modeling under similar modules. The rule based system shown in Figure 2 consists of those modules which are developed based on problem solving approach (Panjaburee, et al., 2010).

The modules of knowledge based expert system which are developed in a similar manner and modeled based on problem solving approach is shown in Figure 3. In the study by Hwang et al. (2011), an innovative approach is proposed, and it develops the knowledge base of an expert system by analyzing the online problem-solving behaviors of the teachers. Consequently, the expert system works as an instructor to assist the students in improving their web-based problem-solving ability. To demonstrate the innovative approach, two experts are asked to evaluate the performance of the expert system. Experimental results show that, the novel approach is able to provide accurate and constructive suggestions to students in improving their problem-solving ability.

According to the results of the study that Beck (2007) carried out, it is seen that students who study in environments where scenarios can be chosen have 25% higher learning performance than students who don't have the opportunity to choose.

Figure 2. Structure of the testing and diagnostic system (Panjaburee, et al., 2010)

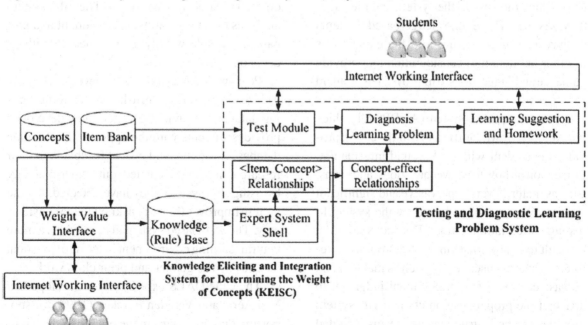

Figure 3. Model for developing web-based problem-solving advisor (Hwang, et al., 2011)

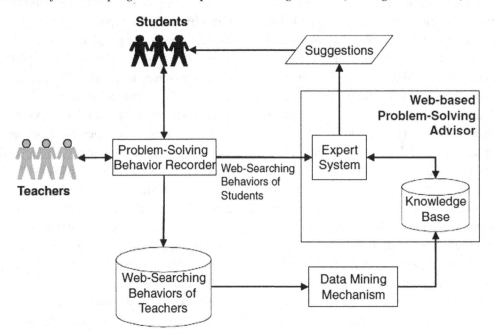

Song and Salvendy (2003) emphasize that the personal experience of experienced learners help novice users in e-learning systems a lot. It provides the arrangement of the system according to web experiences of the learners including the tools which they use in the system and the pages they visited. These knowledge-based systems analyze new users taking into the experiences of other learners into consideration and provide guidance and suggestions to improve their problem solving skills.

The audit reporting system (AUDPORT) which is developed by McDuffie and Smith (2006), provides the student with background information, instruction on how to answer questions, and terms, such as material versus pervasive and significant versus severe, which are used by the system to distinguish certain situations. Decisions would be difficult to approximate in the classroom. Therefore, the authors used terms, such as material and pervasive, to serve as professional judgment to arrive at the proper opinion choice. The system provides all the instructions and terms included in AUDPORT.

The intelligent system developed by Mutlu Bayraktar (2012) is a support system which provides the students with a personal study schedule after they enter their own studying habits. It is requested from the student to enter what they do after school for two weeks. Then the system analyzes the study habits of the student and prepares a suitable weekly study schedule with its decision base.

Post and Whisenand (2005) have developed a web-based expert system to help students in learning database design. The system they developed provides students with the opportunity of online database designing and instant feedback. In their research they have carried out experimentally by using this system, they have detected that the system improves the student knowledge considerably. The web based system also provides a more neutral learning environment in terms of personal factors such as gender and prior class work.

The CONDALS expert system developed by Van Aerle and Van den Bercken (1999) for supporting diagnosticians in the diagnosis decisions of beginner level reading and syllabification problems methodologically helps the detection process. The diagnosticians who participated in the research have reached a consensus that the system reached high levels of success.

Recently, the usage of expert systems in the game-based learning environments gained popularity as a research interest. The purpose of the study of Petit dit Dariel et al(2013) about game and expert systems, which is a three phased project, is to create and test a Serious Game to enhance nurses' clinical reasoning and determination skill in home-care and the settings of community. In the first phase of the project, which is the focal point of the paper, the development of a scenario, the graphic design and the game machine is included. Projects' second and third phases will test the Serious Game as an educational intervention (See Figure 4).

CONCLUSION AND RECOMMENDATIONS

While the traditional computer supported instruction is a method of including the computer among the tools in the teaching process, with instruction programs that are prepared by utilizing expert systems, the computer can be a support element to the teacher and even partially replace the tutor in case the tutor is not present. The best application of this standpoint is only revealed by adequately developing expert systems (Önder, 2003).

The educational software and distance education environments that are used nowadays lack the skill of perceiving the learning habits of the student and leading the instruction according to that. As a study area of artificial intelligence, intelligent systems and expert systems provide solutions in this area by both arranging the process and utilization as support systems in education. Expert systems provide more people with personalized education by taking the knowledge of the student and their learning characteristics into consideration.

In distance education, there are many advantages of using expert systems. They provide personalized learning environments and support. They increase the quality in education with correcting errors and giving recommendations on the errors. With learning capability, they can improve limited expertise. They provide flexibility for the learner. They improve information and help accessibility. They improve security. They don't get tired, they are not distracted. They increase problem solving and decision making skills (Russel & Norvig, 2010; Turban et al., 2007). They can be effective in the learning process more than most of the experts themselves by working better than them.

Figure 4. Serious game architecture (Petit dit Dariel, et al. 2013)

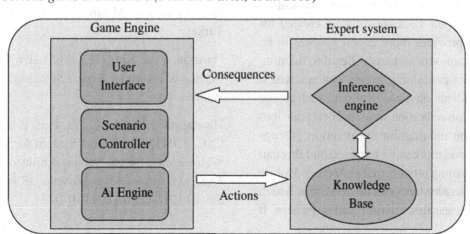

143

There are limitations as well as the advantages of the utilization of expert systems in education. It is difficult to find experts among people and the information that is received form the expert can be rare or costly. Besides, every expert might have a different evaluation on the situation. They can produce incorrect results/suggestions. The students and teachers might have a lack of trust as it is a computer instead of a real expert and this might prove to be a barrier in using expert systems (Russell & Norvig, 2010; Turban et al., 2007).

The learning environments created by analyzing the learning habits and characteristics of students are very important for the learners to adopt the system and for ease of access to the expert in distance education along with all its advantages and limitations. An expert system designed so that distance education environments get closer to students by making them more personalized and user friendly and simulate teacher-student interaction, will play a serious role in knowledge management and acquisition process with the artificial intelligence it has. It will outpace the traditional teaching environments especially by explaining its reaction to the student actions and by improving itself according to the feedback it receives from the teacher. What stands in the path of this is the fact that expert systems are still not developed easily and they are not common.

It is recommended that expert system preparation software for teachers who aim to develop expert systems to be used in distance education can be developed. Package software created for this reason provides more expert systems to be produced in amount and areas. Besides, learning environments containing expert systems which take the students physiological data such as eye tracking, brain activation areas and heart rate into consideration and examine the attention, perception of the students can be prepared and this can make the learning process more effective. Mobile expert learning systems can be developed which will provide learning anytime and anywhere. It might be easier to create knowledge bases which the expert systems will manage with the technologies and applications in smart mobile devices.

REFERENCES

Awad, W. (1996). *Building Expert Systems: Principles, Procedures, and Applications.* St. Paul, MN: West.

Baykal, N., & Beyan, T. (2004). *Bulanık Mantık Uzman Sistemler ve Denetleyiciler.* Ankara: Bıçaklar Kitabevi.

Beck, J. E. (2007). Does Learner Control Affect Learning?. In *Proceedings of the 13th International Conference on Artificial Intelligence in Education* (pp. 135-142). Los Angeles, CA: IOS Press.

Biondo, S. J. (1990). *Fundamentals of Expert Systems Technology: Principles and Concept.* Intellect Books.

Chatpakkarattana, T., & Khlaisang, J. (2012). The Learner Support System for Distance Education. *Creative Education, 3*(Supplement), 47–51. doi:10.4236/ce.2012.38B011

Erkoç, M. F. (2008). Yapay Zeka Perspektifinde Eğitime Yönelik Uzman Sistem Modellemesi [Expert System Modeling For Education By The Artifical Intelligence Perspective]. (Unpublished master's thesis). Marmara University, İstanbul, Turkey.

Harmon, P., & King, D. (1985). *Artificial Intelligence in Business: Expert Systems.* New York: Wiley.

Hwang, G. J., Chen, C. Y., Tsai, P. S., & Tsai, C. C. (2011). An Expert System for Improving Web-Based Problem-Solving Ability of Students. *Expert Systems with Applications, 38,* 8664–8672. doi:10.1016/j.eswa.2011.01.072

Jaques, P. A., Seffrin, H., Rubi, G., Morais, F., Ghilardi, C., Bittencourt, I. I., & Isotani, S. (2013). Rule-based expert systems to support step-by-step guidance in algebraic problem solving: The case of the tutor PAT2Math. *Expert Systems with Applications, 40*, 5456–5465. doi:10.1016/j.eswa.2013.04.004

LaBay, D. G., & Comm, C. L. (2003). A Case Study Using Gap Analysis to Assess Distance Learning Versus Traditional Course Delivery. *International Journal of Educational Management, 17*(6/7), 312–317. doi:10.1108/09513540310501003

Lin, C. B., Young, S. S. C., Chan, T. W., & Chen, Y. H. (2005). Teacher-Oriented Adaptive Web-Based Environment for Supporting Practical Teaching Models: A Case Study of "School for All". *Computers & Education, 44*, 155–172. doi:10.1016/j.compedu.2003.11.003

Luconi, F. L., Malone, T. W., & Scott Morton, M. S. (1986, Summer). Expert Systems: The Next Challenge for Managers. *Sloan Management Review*, 3–14.

Mavrikis, M. (2007). Towards Predictive Modeling of Student Affect from Web-Based Interactions. In R. Luckin, K. R. Koedinger, & J. Greer (Eds.), *Artificial Intelligence In Education* (pp. 169–176). Amsterdam: IOS Press.

McDuffie, R. S., & Smith, M. (2006). Impact of an Audit Reporting Expert System on Learning Performance: A Teaching Note. *Accounting Education (UK), 15*(1), 89–101. doi:10.1080/06939280600551585

Mehlenbacher, B., Miller, C. R., Covington, D., & Larsen, J. S. (2000). Active and Interactive Learning Online: A Comparison of Web-Based and Conventional Writing Classes. *IEEE Transactions on Professional Communication, 43*(2), 166–184. doi:10.1109/47.843644

Miller, S. (2001). How Near and Yet How Far? Theorizing Distance Teaching. *Computers and Composition, 18*, 321–328. doi:10.1016/S8755-4615(01)00065-2

Mutlu Bayraktar, D. (2012). *Intelligent System Preparing Study Program For Students*. Paper presented at the 6th International Technology, Education and Development Conference. Valencia, Spain.

Nabiyev, V. V. (2005). *Yapay Zeka: Problemler-Yöntemler-Algoritma* [Artificial Intelligence: Problems-Methodologies-Algorithm]. Ankara: Seçkin Yayıncılık.

Önder, H. H. (2001). *Yapay Zeka Programlama Teknikleri Ve Bilgisayar Destekli Eğitim* [Artificial Intelligence Programming Techniques and Computer Supported Education]. Paper presented at the International Educational Technologies Symposium. Sakarya, Turkey.

Önder, H. H. (2002). *Uzaktan Eğitimde ICAI ve Yapay Zeka Programlama Teknikleri* [ICAI In Distance Education and Artificial Intelligence Programming Techniques]. Paper presented at the Open and Distance Education Symposium. Eskişehir, Turkey.

Önder, H. H. (2003). Uzaktan Eğitimde Bilgisayar Kullanımı ve Uzman Sistemler [Computer Usage and Expert Systems In Distance Education]. *The Turkish Online Journal of Educational Technology, 2*(3), 142–146.

Panjaburee, P., Hwang, G. J., Triampo, W., & Shih, B. Y. (2010). A multi-expert approach for developing testing and diagnostic systems based on the concept-effect model. *Computers & Education, 55*, 527–540. doi:10.1016/j.compedu.2010.02.015

Peixoto, C. S. A., Boarati, S. S., & Forte, C. E. (2012). Heuristics for User Interface Design in the Context of Cognitive Styles of Learning and Attention Deficit Disorder. In P. Vizureanu (Ed.), *Advances In Expert Systems* (pp. 85–100). Rijeka: InTech. doi:10.5772/51455

Peredo, R., Canales, A., Menchaca, A., & Peredo, I. (2011). Intelligent Web-based education system for adaptive learning. *Expert Systems with Applications*, *38*, 14690–14702. doi:10.1016/j.eswa.2011.05.013

Petit dit Dariel, O.J., Raby, T., Ravaut, F., & Rothan-Tondeuret, M. (2013). Developing the Serious Games potential in nursing education. *Nurse Education Today*. doi: doi:10.1016/j.nedt.2012.12.014

Post, G. V., & Whisenand, T. G. (2005). An Expert System Helps Students Learn Database Design. *Decision Sciences Journal of Innovative Education*, *3*(2), 273–293. doi:10.1111/j.1540-4609.2005.00070.x

Russell, S. J., & Norvig, P. (2010). Artificial Intelligence - A Modern Approach (3rd ed.). Prentice Hall.

Sasikumar, M., Ramani, S., Raman, S. M., Anjaneyulu, K. S. R., & Chandrasekar, R. (2007). *A Practical Introduction to Rule Based Expert Systems*. New Delhi: Narosa Publishing House.

Siler, W., & Buckley, J. J. (2005). *Fuzzy Expert Systems And Fuzzy Reasoning*. John Wiley & Sons, Inc.

Song, G., & Salvendy, G. (2003). A Framework for Reuse of User Experience in Web Browsing. *Behaviour & Information Technology*, *22*(2), 79–90. doi:10.1080/0144929031000092231

Turban, E., Aronson, J. E., Liang, T., & Sharda, R. (2007). *Decision Support and Business Intelligence Systems* (8th ed.). Pearson Education.

Van Aerle, E. J. M., & Van den Bercken, J. H. L. (1999). The Development of A Knowledge-Based System Supporting the Diagnosis of Reading and Spelling Problems (II). *Computers in Human Behavior*, *15*, 693–712. doi:10.1016/S0747-5632(99)00041-2

Wachter, R. M., & Gupta, J. N. D. (1997). Distance Education and The Use of Computers as Instructional Tools for Systems Development Projects: A Case Study of The Construction of Expert Systems. *Computers & Education*, *29*(1), 13–23. doi:10.1016/S0360-1315(97)00027-4

Wiesner, P. (2000). Distance Education: Rebottling or A New Brew? *Proceedings of the IEEE*, *88*(7), 1124–1130. doi:10.1109/5.871313

ADDITIONAL READING

Amel Grissa Touzi and Mohamed Amine Selmi. (2012). ES-DM: An Expert System for an Intelligent Exploitation of the Large Data Set. Proceedings of the 4th International Conference on Intelligent Decision Technologies (IDT´2012), 16, 291-301.

Asabere, N. Y., & Enguah, S. E. (2012). Integration of Expert Systems in Mobile Learning. *International Journal of Information and Communication Technology Research*, *2*(1), 55–61.

Awad, W. (1996). *Building Expert Systems: Principles, Procedures, and Applications*. St. Paul: West.

Bing-ru, Y., Li, H., & Wen-bin, Q. (2012). The Cognitive-Base Knowledge Acquisition in Expert System. *Advances in Intelligent Systems and Computing*, *136*, 73–80. doi:10.1007/978-3-642-27711-5_11

Biondo, S. J. (1990). *Fundamentals of Expert Systems Technology: Principles and Concepts*. Norwood, New Jersey: Ablex Pub.

Darlington, K. (2000). *The Essence of Expert Systems*. Essex, England: Prentice Hall.

Fernando, A. Mikic Fonte, Juan C. Burguillo, Martín and Llamas Nistal. (2012). An intelligent tutoring module controlled by BDI agents for an e-learning platform. *Expert Systems with Applications*, *39*, 7546–7554. doi:10.1016/j.eswa.2012.01.161

Giarratano, J. C., & Riley, G. (2005). *Expert Systems, Principles and Programming* (4th ed.). Boston: PWS Publishing.

Grove, R. F. (2000). Internet-based Expert Systems. *Expert Systems: International Journal of Knowledge Engineering and Neural Networks*, *17*(3), 129–136. doi:10.1111/1468-0394.00135

Harmon, P., & King, D. (1985). *Artificial Intelligence in Business: Expert Systems*. New York: Wiley.

Hayashida, Y., Tanaka, R., & Giguruwa, N. (2009). "Web-Based Expert Learning System for Student Industrial Internship". Proceedings of the 4th International Conference on e-Learning.

Holsapple, C. W., & Winston, W. B. (1987). *Business Expert Systems*. New York: Irwin.

Hwang, G. J., Chen, C. Y., Tsai, P. S., & Tsai, C. C. (2011). An Expert System for Improving Web-Based Problem-Solving Ability of Students. *Expert Systems with Applications*, *38*, 8664–8672. doi:10.1016/j.eswa.2011.01.072

Hwang, G. J., Chen, C. Y., Tsai, P. S., & Tsai, C. C. (2011). An Expert System for Improving Web-Based Problem-Solving Ability of Students. *Expert Systems with Applications*, *38*, 8664–8672. doi:10.1016/j.eswa.2011.01.072

Ignizio, J. (1991). *Introduction to Expert Systems*. New York: McGraw-Hill.

Jackson, P. (1998). *Introduction To Expert Systems* (3rd ed.). Rochester, New York: Addison-Wesley.

Jaques, P. A., Seffrin, H., Rubi, G., Morais, F., Ghilardi, C., Bittencourt, I. I., & Isotani, S. (2013). Rule-based expert systems to support step-by-step guidance in algebraic problem solving: The case of the tutor PAT2Math. *Expert Systems with Applications*, *40*, 5456–5465. doi:10.1016/j.eswa.2013.04.004

McDuffie, R. S., & Smith, M. (2006). Impact of an Audit Reporting Expert System on Learning Performance: A Teaching Note. *Accounting Education (UK)*, *15*(1), 89–101. doi:10.1080/06939280600551585

Peixoto, C. S. A., Boarati, S. S., & Forte, C. E. (2012). Heuristics for User Interface Design in the Context of Cognitive Styles of Learning and Attention Deficit Disorder. In P. Vizureanu (Ed.), *Advances In Expert Systems* (pp. 85–100). Rijeka: InTech. doi:10.5772/51455

(2013). Petit dit Dariel, O.J., Raby, T. Ravaut, F., Rothan-Tondeuret, M. (2013). Developing the Serious Games potential in nursing education. *Nurse Education Today*. doi: doi:10.1016/j.nedt.2012.12.014

Post, G. V., & Whisenand, T. G. (2005). An Expert System Helps Students Learn Database Design. *Decision Sciences Journal of Innovative Education*, *3*(2), 273–293. doi:10.1111/j.1540-4609.2005.00070.x

Post, G. V., & Whisenand, T. G. (2005). An Expert System Helps Students Learn Database Design. *Decision Sciences Journal of Innovative Education*, *3*(2), 273–293. doi:10.1111/j.1540-4609.2005.00070.x

Romem, Y. (2008). Expert Systems: the Promise, the Disappointment, the Comeback. Bar-Ilan Univ. Israel, Unpublished Ph.D. dissertation.

Rosic, M., Stankov, S., & Glavinic, V. (2000). "Intelligent Tutoring Systems for Asynchronous Distance Education". 10th Mediterranean Electrotechnical Conference, MEleCon 2000, Vol. I.

Russell, S. J., & Norvig, P. (2010). "Artificial Intelligence - A Modern Approach (3. internat. ed.)". New Jersey: Prentice Hall.

Sakala, L. C., Muzurura, O., & Zivanai, L. (2010). The Use of Expert Systems has Improved Students Learning in Zimbabwe. *Journal of Sustainable Development in Africa*, *12*(3), 1–13.

Sasikumar, M., Ramani, S., Raman, S. M., Anjaneyulu, K. S. R., & Chandrasekar, R. (2007). *A Practical Introduction to Rule Based Expert Systems*. New Delhi: Narosa Publishing House.

Scott Grabinger, R., & David, H. Jonassen and Brent W. Wilson. (1990). "Building Expert Systems in Training and Education". New York: Praeger.

Turban, E., Aronson, J. E., Liang, T., & Sharda, R. (2007). *Decision Support and Business Intelligence Systems* (8th ed.). New Jersey: Pearson Education.

Wachter, R. M., & Gupta, J. N. D. (1997). Distance Education and The Use of Computers as Instructional Tools For Systems Development Projects: A Case Study of The Construction of Expert Systems. *Computers & Education*, *29*(1), 13–23. doi:10.1016/S0360-1315(97)00027-4

William Siler and James J. Buckley. (2005). *Fuzzy Expert Systems And Fuzzy Reasoning*. New Jersey: John Wiley & Sons, Inc.

Wong, B. K., & Monaco, J. A. (1995). Expert System Applications in Business: A Review and Analysis of The Literature (1977-1993). *Information & Management*, *29*(3), 141–152. doi:10.1016/0378-7206(95)00023-P

KEY TERMS AND DEFINITIONS

Expert: A person with a high level of knowledge or skill relating to a particular subject or activity.

Expert System: A computer system that asks questions and gives answers that have been thought of by a human expert.

Expert Systems in Distance Education: An adaptive distance education system which has the ability to self-learn on the basis of knowledge base that consists of rules received from experts.

Explanation Subsystem/Justifier: A module that explains the inferences of the system and justifies its results.

Heuristic Method: A process for solving the specific problems by creating some answers, may not be accurate, against the problems on the basis of experiences.

Inference Engine: A module that carries out reasoning according to the inputs it receives from other components of the system.

Knowledge Base: Rules that contain the known facts and logical references about the domain.

Knowledge Refining System: A module that analyses system performance, provides self-learning and development.

Chapter 9
For an Intelligent E-Learning:
A Managerial Model Suggestion for Artificial Intelligence Supported E-Learning Content Flow

Utku Kose
Usak University, Turkey

ABSTRACT

During a typical e-learning process, there are many different factors that should be taken into consideration to keep the stability of the process or improve the process to get more effective results. Nowadays, employing Artificial Intelligence-based approaches is one of the most popular ways to improve the process and obtain the desired objectives rapidly. In this sense, there are many different kinds of scientific works in order to improve the related literature. However, ensuring control among the performed Artificial Intelligence-based e-learning process is a critical point because there is sometimes a misunderstanding about employing intelligent e-learning process that running intelligent educational tools or materials does not always mean the related e-learning process will improve greatly. In order to ensure that there should be some managerial procedures focused on some aspects of the process, this chapter aims to introduce a managerial model that can be used for especially Artificial Intelligence-supported e-learning content flow in order to improve the educational process. The suggested model is usable for the educational institutions, which focus on especially Artificial Intelligence-oriented e-learning solutions, research works, and educational activities.

INTRODUCTION

In the context of educational developments; e-learning has an active role to improve both teaching and learning process, by combining basics of distance education approach with advanced information and communication technologies. Especially information and communication technologies give a rise to the e-learning technique as an effective and comprehensive learning way (Zhang, & Nunamaker, 2003). In time, appearance of innovative information and communication technologies has enabled researchers to design better e-learning models, which allow both teachers and learners to improve their abilities on taking active and effective roles within educational processes. Because of unstoppable improvements along the related scientific literatures, the e-learning

DOI: 10.4018/978-1-4666-6276-6.ch009

technique has been a key element for reaching to desired educational objectives in a fast and effective manner. Thus, there has always been a rapid growth in e-learning based educational environments – systems, or additional tools to support teaching and learning activities (Conole, & Dyke, 2004). It is also notable that the related growth has been proportional with the one that is seen in demand for such e-learning systems, or tools (Krishnamurthy, & O'Connor, 2013).

Nowadays, employing Artificial Intelligence based approaches is one of the most popular ways to improve the e-learning process and obtain the desired objectives rapidly. In this sense, there are many different kinds of scientific works in order to improve the related literature. However, ensuring control among the performed Artificial Intelligence based e-learning process is a critical point because there is sometimes a misunderstanding about employing intelligent e-learning process that running intelligent educational tools or materials does not always mean the related e-learning process will improve greatly. In order to ensure that there should be some managerial procedures focused on some aspects of the process.

Like any other educational techniques, or approaches; the e-learning technique also includes some factors, which determine its stability, quality, or effectiveness along a teaching – learning process (Alexander, 2001; Capece, & Campisi, 2013; Lim et al., 2007; Ong et al., 2004; Selim, 2007; Sun et al., 2008). These factors are vital ones among e-learning processes; even Artificial Intelligence oriented solutions are employed. Because of this, ensuring a desired intelligent e-learning process is depended on controlling the related factors carefully. Taking these factors into consideration enables us not only to keep the stability of the process but also improve it to get more effective results at the end. At this point, some people, who are especially Artificial Intelligence experts, or computer programmers have an important role to ensure effective educational processes in the light of intelligent approaches. According to this perspective, organization of e-

learning course contents or any task that is included in this concept can be evaluated as a vital point directly affecting the intelligent e-learning process. If intelligent e-learning course contents are directly produced by the educational institution, it is also an important issue to control the whole mechanism including some tasks like planning the Artificial Intelligence related approach with the support of a wide scope of experts, producing the contents, providing the contents to the learners, and evaluating data obtained from learners. It is clear that such control approach will give a rise to a careful, and more accurate Artificial Intelligence supported e-learning content flow causing a better intelligent e-learning process.

In the sense of the explanations above, this chapter aims to introduce a managerial model that can be used for especially Artificial Intelligence supported e-learning content flow, in order to improve the educational process. The suggested model is usable for the educational institutions, which focus on especially Artificial Intelligence oriented e-learning solutions, research works, and educational activities. With its theoretical aspects, the model can be defined as a detailed approach, which is directly based on tasks associated with only intelligent e-learning course contents. Because of this, it can also be integrated into a higher management strategy or model, which is used in an educational institution.

According to the research subject, the remaining content of this chapter is organized as follows: The next section briefly explains a general perspective, in which the introduced Artificial Intelligence supported e-learning content flow model is taken place. By considering the general perspective, it is aimed to give more ideas for readers to enable them to understand the role of the model better. Following to that, the third section is devoted to the details of the introduced model. In this section, groups included in the model and tasks of these groups are expressed briefly in order to unveil the definition of the concept: "managerial model for Artificial Intelligence supported e-learning content flow", which is associated with the mechanism provided by the model. Next, an example timetable, which explains a typical application of the suggested model, is provided under the fourth section. Finally, the chapter ends with conclusions and some explanations regarding to the future work.

GENERAL PERSPECTIVE

In an educational institution, which employs e-learning oriented research and educational activities, there are some essential tasks – objectives that should be taken into consideration to keep the stability within e-learning based works. Such educational institutions include some differences from other educational – academic units. Because their work area needs more concentration on the latest information and communication technologies, and also requires being flexible against improvement in these technologies. Furthermore, target audience of such educational institutions keeps a dynamic structure because of the adaptive feature of the applied educational approach. In the other words, educational programs or courses provided by e-learning based educational institutions differs from the ones given via traditional approaches; because of the "learning whenever, wherever" function of e-learning (or more generally, distance education). Additionally, these educational institutions should also have good education experts, academicians, or researchers because e-learning technique requires more efforts to focus on learners at distance place and give them desired awareness. When such e-learning approach is supported with Artificial Intelligence approaches, methods, or techniques, the situation becomes a more remarkable one because the related educational institutions should also employ Artificial Intelligence experts, or expert computer programmers to design and develop advanced educational tools or materials, which have "intelligent algorithmic mechanisms" within their infrastructure. Briefly, being stable at e-learning and also especially "intelligent e-learning" de-

pends on having some necessary requirements, or performing some essential tasks. At this point, success of the model, which is introduced in this chapter, also depends on the stability ensured at the educational institution. The most remarkable requirements and essential tasks regarding to "being stable" are listed briefly as follows:

- Having a well-structured organization structure and work flow.
- Having adequate, flexible infrastructure in the sense of information and communication technologies.
- Having well-equipped information technologies staff to keep infrastructure stable and perform essential works, which are related to the general work flow along the institution.
- Having well educated staff in the sense of using information and communication technologies.
- Having expert people, whose expertise is especially related to preparing educational programs, evaluation, and e-learning oriented research works.
- Having expert people, whose expertise is related to Artificial Intelligence based approaches, methods, or techniques.
- Having expert people, who can design and develop not only standard computer software but also advanced ones, which employ intelligent algorithmic mechanisms in order to ensure the desired intelligent educational solutions among teaching - learning activities.
- Being able to track rapid developments in information and communication technologies and being responsible for applying necessary updates and adapting new developments in a rapid manner.

As it can be understood from the list, a good management approach, and adequate relations with Computer Science, Artificial Intelligence field and especially information and communication technologies are remarkable criterions to ensure success along intelligent e-learning. It is also supposed that the model for Artificial Intelligence supported e-learning content flow takes place in an educational institution, which is capable of having the mentioned requirements and performing the related activities. In the other words, most of the mentioned points are typical preconditions, which directly or indirectly affect the suggested model in this chapter.

As another general perspective, it is also possible to locate the suggested model in a certain educational institution structure. It can be said that the managerial model for Artificial Intelligence supported e-learning content flow is an integrated part within the institution and employs communication channels with other managerial departments in the educational institution. In this way, it is aimed to enable upper level managerial departments to control the model working mechanism and apply any new organization strategies, or updates directly to the model. This approach is already necessary to keep a general perspective on management of the educational institution.

When the model is considered in the sense of general working mechanism of the institution, it can be said that the model takes place along planning and organizing Artificial Intelligence oriented educational solutions, preparation – production of Artificial Intelligence supported e-learning contents, determining any strategy for providing the contents effectively to the learners, receiving learner data, evaluating the data, and providing reports to the upper level managerial departments of the institution. General flow of these activities can be affected by different factors like general management strategy of the institution, structures of the courses, or features of the target learners…etc.

Explanations provided within previous paragraphs have drawn a general perspective, which defines stability, and success elements for an intelligent e-learning oriented educational institution, and points the applicability of the suggested model in terms these expressed elements. Further,

role of the model along working mechanism of the institution can also been figured out from the explanations. But it is also necessary to talk more about application aspects. For this aim, the next title is devoted to the details of the suggested model.

A MANAGERIAL MODEL FOR ARTIFICIAL INTELLIGENCE SUPPORTED E-LEARNING CONTENT FLOW

First of all, it is better to explain the meaning of the "Artificial Intelligence supported e-learning content flow" concept, in order to understand the main approach of the model. It is possible to express that e-learning contents are passed through some processes during e-learning. These processes can be evaluated as typical "life cycles" for the related contents. Some works like producing the contents, including them under specific courses, providing them to the learners are essential parts of this life cycle. Additionally, the cycle should also include an update action, which includes receiving learners' data related to the contents, and evaluating the received data to revise the contents for better future learning experiences. We can then combine all of these works under "a flow pointing a general time period", and define the whole time period as an "e-learning content flow". Additionally, employing Artificial Intelligence approaches, methods, or techniques within the related e-learning content enable us to evaluate the related flow as a "Artificial Intelligence supported flow", so making the term "Artificial Intelligence supported e-learning content flow" at the final. On the other hand, the term: "managerial model", which is used by the author in this chapter, indicates a total management approach for controlling the Artificial Intelligence supported e-learning content flow. It is aimed to improve e-learning process by obtaining benefits – positive effects from intelligent (e-learning – course) content aspects.

Default Structure of the Model

As default, the model consists of seven different groups. Five of them are related to different processes of general e-learning content flow whereas one group has the managerial role on other groups and the other one has a critical role to ensure the related scientific aspects of the Artificial Intelligence field. In this chapter, the related groups will be called as "Artificial Intelligence Group", "Management Group", "Educational Knowledge Group", "Production / Revision Group", "Presentation Group", "Data Group", and "Evaluation Group", respectively.

In the default structure, the Artificial Intelligence Group has the most remarkable role because of its scientific and academic roots. Briefly, this group has the key role to ensure an "intelligent e-learning experience"; otherwise, the related processes performed are just some kind of plain e-learning approaches. Additionally, the Management Group has also a special location because of its authority to manage other groups and ensure connection between these groups and the institution. On the other hand, remaining groups are included under a common, abstract environment. At this point, the educational institution may be using special software sets, or programs to perform the whole e-learning process. Because of this, "Production / Revision Group", "Presentation Group", and "Data Group" can be in touch with the IT department (or any equivalent department) of the institution, along the works. Figure 1 represents a schema showing the default structure of the model.

More details regarding to the groups are expressed under the following sub-sections:

Figure 1. Default structure of the model

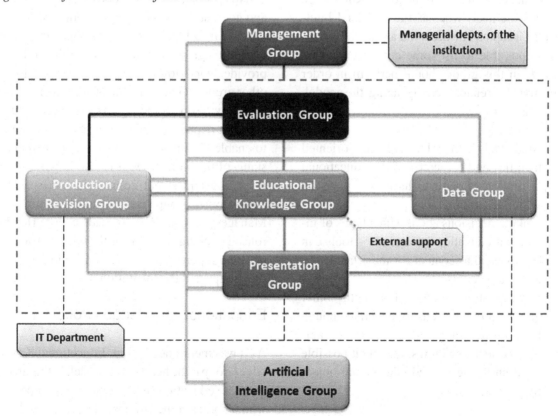

Artificial Intelligence Group

The Artificial Intelligence Group has the role of performing many critical activities and making decisions about "intelligent" – "Artificial Intelligence oriented" educational solutions, which are associated with the e-learning contents that will be provided along the educational processes. In this sense, there are Computer Science oriented people, who are also Artificial Intelligence experts. At this point, the group should employ also expert computer programmers, who can interact successfully with the Artificial Intelligence experts and design advanced computer programs, which will be directly used as e-learning content or will be integrated into some prepared ones. In this group, some critical decisions for analyzing needs for specific intelligent computer programs (like intelligent tutoring systems, or just intelligent mechanisms that will be integrated into plain programs...etc.) are made by the related staff. In the introduced model, the Educational Knowledge Group is the heart whereas the Artificial Intelligence Group can be accepted as the "brain".

It is possible to list some certain tasks that the staff in this group should perform in order to ensure the related activity along the model. These tasks are:

- Analyzing Artificial Intelligence oriented facilities and resources of the educational institution in order to have well plans on designing solutions.
- Making decisions about which types of intelligent educational materials – tools can be designed as content for the related subjects in the courses.
- Having strong interaction with other groups in order to ensure effective enough ideas on designing and creating the intelligent e-learning things, making it possible to reach to the desired educational objectives better.

- Designing algorithmic structures of the Artificial Intelligence based computer software or additional programs, systems.
- Designing logical or mathematical aspects of the related algorithmic structures that will be used along Artificial Intelligence based computer software or additional programs, systems.
- Designing supportive materials (like database, knowledge-base) and ensuring interaction with the related experts of the educational subjects (with interaction also Educational Knowledge Group).

Management Group

The Management Group informs other groups about new jobs given by the institution, tracks work flow along other groups, and give reports about the work-flow to the upper level departments of the educational institution. This group should employ people, who have good management skills and good abilities on communication with other people. In addition to the management based tasks, this group should also keep the ability to provide work-flow oriented suggestions to the other groups. Generally, the Management Group also provides periodic reports to the upper management departments of the institution, in order to enable the institution to keep informed about status of the work-flow. It is also important that if a good and fluent communication structure among other groups can be built with time, the Management Group can provide a more flexible role on tracking, or just runs the task of providing periodic reports and ensure connection between the groups and the institution.

Educational Knowledge Group

As it was mentioned before; Educational Knowledge Group is the heart of the model. In this group, there are education field oriented, expert people, who support all other groups (except from the Management Group) in the model. As it is known, planning e-learning contents, and producing them with appropriate approaches are key factors to ensure effective contents, which will enable learners to take part in an efficient learning process. Because of this, this group should employ lots of expert people, whose expertise are on educational program preparing, evaluation, and also e-learning. At this point, the term "expert people" is used to indicate academicians, researchers, scientists, or experts, who has the adequate level of expertise in especially education, distance education, and e-learning. According to the target learners, it is also possible to employ multidisciplinary staff to improve the effectiveness of the group. As it can be seen from the Figure 2, this group can also be supported via external sources including course lecturers, or any other people, who are interested in the related activities and can support the group. It is also important that this group is highly connected with the Artificial Intelligence Group, because designing and developing an effective, Artificial Intelligence supported e-learning content depends on a high synergy between the educators and the Computer Science, or Artificial Intelligence experts.

Production/Revision Group

Production/Revision Group employs the staff for performing all works regarding to producing an e-learning content. The related producing steps include high interaction with both Artificial Intelligence Group and the Educational Knowledge Group. Like the Artificial Intelligence Group, this group also employs expert computer programmers; but rather than just designing, computer programmers of this group directly codes – develops the related "intelligent" materials – additions – contents. In addition, there are also good computer graphic designers in this group in order to provide interactive and attractive enough intelligent contents.

Another important task of this group is also revising the e-learning contents, which require updates. Updates may be result of error reports, or data received from learners, Artificial Intelligence Group, and also Educational Knowledge Group. Because of this, there should be good interaction among the Production / Revision Group, the Artificial Intelligence Group, and the Evaluation Group.

It is important that especially computer graphic designers of this group should have a creative mind for producing interactive and attractive enough e-learning contents. The term: "content", which is used in this chapter, indicates not only text-based or visually supported course pages but also animation based applications, intelligent learning tools, and any other software – based applications on evaluation. The Artificial Intelligence oriented infrastructure examined and activated in the Artificial Intelligence Group is just for ensuring a strong enough code – algorithm structure and it

Figure 2. An example timetable on application of the model for one e-learning content

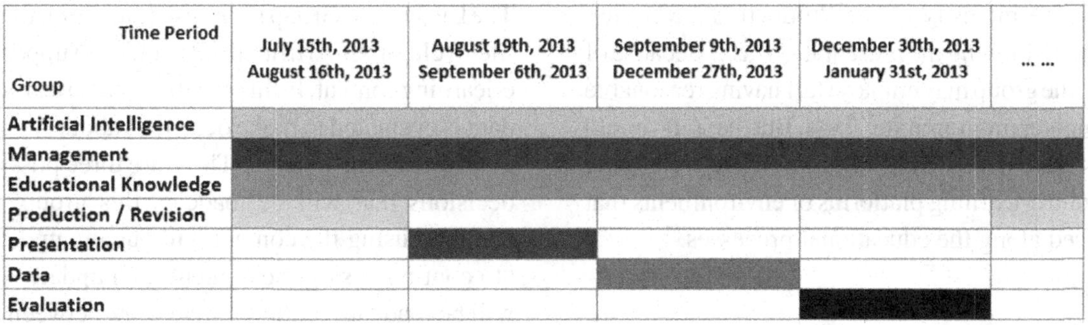

Time Period / Group	July 15th, 2013 August 16th, 2013	August 19th, 2013 September 6th, 2013	September 9th, 2013 December 27th, 2013	December 30th, 2013 January 31st, 2013	... ...
Artificial Intelligence					
Management					
Educational Knowledge					
Production / Revision					
Presentation					
Data					
Evaluation					

is limited when the content is evaluated in terms of its graphical design. Because of this, creative ideas should be taken into consideration while producing even an Artificial Intelligence based e-learning content of the course. In order to produce e-learning contents, which are compatible with the used e-learning platform(s) or environment(s), it is also important to have staff having knowledge on certain e-learning platforms or environments. For development of advanced e-learning applications, which include "intelligent working mechanisms" or any other advanced computing approaches, the group is already in touch with the Artificial Intelligence Group; but if it is needed to have support from some people having knowledge on other remarkable fields like Mathematics, or Statistics, this group has the first row to employ them or enable such people to work for both Artificial Intelligence and Production / Revision Group.

Presentation Group

The general task of the Presentation Group is to provide prepared Artificial Intelligence supported e-learning contents to the target learners. At this point, the group determines effective ways of presentation for the contents received from the Production / Revision Group. Presentation methods may differ according to the used e-learning platforms (like learning management systems) and need accurate decisions usually. But Presentation Group is supported by both Artificial Intelligence Group and the Educational Knowledge Group to analyze conditions and determine the best way of presentation. Actually, this group is organized to decrease intensity of the Production / Revision Group by taking the presentation task. Because of this, the group may employ staff having reasonable computer programming skills. But the staff should also have adequate level of knowledge on using certain e-learning platforms or environments that is used along the educational processes.

Data Group

After the presentation of an Artificial Intelligence supported e-learning content, the Data Group starts to obtain data from the learners. The task of obtaining data may include enabling learners to fill surveys, collecting ideas – feedbacks from learners, and tracking learners to get some statistical data. The function of this group is too important for the model; because obtained data are directly send to the Evaluation Group, which will determine the success level of an e-learning content, or make any decision on updates to fix problems or keep the content up-to-date. In order to achieve the desired work-flow, this group should employ people having knowledge on fields like Statistics, and Mathematics. It is also important for this people to use specific software or programs for Statistics, or computing approaches, and have reasonable computer programming skills (for writing specific programs). On the other hand, it is also required to have staff, who can apply Data Mining based operations on learners' data to get more different types of data sets that can be analyzed by the Evaluation Group. The Data Group is also connected with both Artificial Intelligence Group and the Educational Knowledge Group to discuss about data obtaining approaches (like preparing surveys, or writing specific programs to track learners' activities), or receiving suggestions on which types of data that can be received will be usable for the evaluation approaches.

Evaluation Group

The Evaluation Group is the last destination for the life cycle of an Artificial Intelligence supported e-learning content. In this group, received learners' data is evaluated to make decisions about success of an e-learning content. There are three possible decisions that will be made in this group: "to continue using the content without any update", "to continue using the content with updates that will be made in a collaborative work between the

Artificial Intelligence Group and the Production / Revision Group", or "to remove the content from the active e-learning process". Because decisions are critical to determine life cycles of the contents, this group should employ education field oriented, expert people. In addition to the support given by the Educational Knowledge Group, the staff employed in this group then will be able to make accurate decisions about used e-learning contents. Furthermore, it is also possible to use "intelligent decision support systems" to receive additional support from computers to think effectively about decisions. So, this group has also strong connections with the Artificial Intelligence Group.

The whole mechanism provided within the explained groups of the model indicates an active managerial work-flow, which continues along intelligent e-learning processes. Flexible amount of e-learning contents may affect work-flow of each group differently. Because of this, the Management Group has a critical task on tracking the whole work-flow. It is possible for the Management Group to enable some staff whose task is to ensure stable timing among works of the related groups.

AN EXAMPLE TIMETABLE ON APPLICATION OF THE MODEL

In order to make the application approach more clear, we can also illustrate the work-flow on an example timetable. In this way, work share among model groups and their tasks during a typical intelligent e-learning process can also be understood better. As it was also mentioned in the last paragraph of the previous section, the model employs an active managerial work-flow, which continues along intelligent e-learning processes. Therefore, it is difficult to provide a clear timetable pointing a work-flow for large amounts of e-learning contents at the same time. Because of this, the example timetable has been designed by taking one e-learning content into account. The related timetable is shown under the Figure 2.

As it can be seen from the Figure 2, the Management Group is active along the whole process because of its managerial approach on other groups. On the other hand, both Artificial Intelligence Group and the Educational Knowledge Group also show active approaches along the whole process because they are connected to all other groups to give support and ensure a collaborative work-flow.

CONCLUSION AND FUTURE WORK

In this chapter, a managerial model for the Artificial Intelligence supported e-learning content flow has been introduced. With this model, it is possible to have a more controlled approach on directing life cycles of the intelligent e-learning contents and ensuring a more advanced "flow" within a typical e-learning process. Additionally, the effectiveness of Artificial Intelligence oriented factors are also controlled to be in an optimum balance along the educational processes. By ensuring a good work-flow via this model, it is aimed to improve effectiveness of the active intelligent e-learning process. Because intelligent e-learning contents are important with their roles on enabling and directing learners to gain necessary knowledge, and awareness to continue their educational process in a distance education related technique. At this point, both model and the educational institution should also have some requirements and be running some vital tasks to reach to the complete success. These requirements and the related tasks have also been expressed in the chapter.

Following to the first introduction of the model, there will also be some future works on the model. In this sense, it is aimed to perform some works regarding to adapting the model to different kinds of educational institutions. In this way, some certain adapting approaches will be determined and it will also give a chance to think about designing a total management model for the whole educational institution. Additionally, there will also be both theoretical and applied studies to see if there will be need for any update on the default model. Finally, the Artificial Intelligence Group will be analyzed in more detail for testing potentials on including certain education related approaches of the Artificial Intelligence field.

REFERENCES

Alexander, S. (2001). E-learning developments and experiences. *Education + Training, 43*(4-5), 240-248.

Capece, G., & Campisi, D. (2013). User satisfaction affecting the acceptance of an e-learning platform as a mean for the development of the human capital. *Behaviour & Information Technology, 32*(4), 335–343. doi:10.1080/014492 9X.2011.630417

Conole, G., & Dyke, M. (2004). What are the affordances of information and communication technologies? *Association for Learning Technology Journal, 12*(2), 113–124. doi:10.1080/0968776042000216183

Krishnamurthy, A., & O'Connor, R. V. (2013). An analysis of the software development processes of open source e-learning systems. *Systems, Software and Services Process Improvement – Communications in Computer and Information Science, 364*, 60-71.

Lim, H., Lee, S.-G., & Nam, K. (2007). Validating e-learning factors affecting training effectiveness. *International Journal of Information Management, 27*(1), 22–35. doi:10.1016/j.ijinfomgt.2006.08.002

Ong, C.-S., Lai, J.-Y., & Wang, Y.-S. (2004). Factors affecting engineers' acceptance of asynchronous e-learning systems in high-tech companies. *Information & Management, 41*(6), 795–804. doi:10.1016/j.im.2003.08.012

Selim, H. M. (2007). Critical success factors for e-learning acceptance: Confirmatory factor models. *Computers & Education, 49*(2), 396–413. doi:10.1016/j.compedu.2005.09.004

Sun, P.-C., Tsai, R. J., Finger, G., Chen, Y.-Y., & Yeh, D. (2008). What drives a successful e-Learning? An empirical investigation of the critical factors influencing learner satisfaction. *Computers & Education, 50*(4), 1183–1202. doi:10.1016/j.compedu.2006.11.007

Zhang, D., & Nunamaker, J. F. (2003). Powering e-learning in the new millennium: An overview of e-learning and enabling technology. *Information Systems Frontiers, 5*(2), 207–218. doi:10.1023/A:1022609809036

ADDITIONAL READING

Ahmad, A. R., Basir, O. A., & Hassanein, K. (2004, December). Adaptive User Interfaces for Intelligent E-Learning: Issues and Trends. In ICEB (pp. 925-934).

Anderson, T. (Ed.). (2008). *The theory and practice of online learning*. Athabasca University Press.

Aroyo, L., & Dicheva, D. (2004). The New Challenges for E-learning: The Educational Semantic Web. *Journal of Educational Technology & Society, 7*(4), 59–69.

Au Yeung, H. H., Merchant, T., Chan, C. K. Y., Tsoi, K. H., Lam, J. C. K., Lo, H. Y. H., & Lei, M. (2014). *The New Era of e-Learning* (Vol. II). Interactive Learning and Assessment for Learning.

Babu, S. R., Kulkarni, K. G., & Sekaran, K. C. (2014, January). A Generic Agent Based Cloud Computing Architecture for E-Learning. In *ICT and Critical Infrastructure: Proceedings of the 48th Annual Convention of Computer Society of India-Vol I* (pp. 523-533). Springer International Publishing.

Brusilovsky, P. (2004, May). KnowledgeTree: A distributed architecture for adaptive e-learning. In *Proceedings of the 13th international World Wide Web conference on Alternate track papers & posters* (pp. 104-113). ACM.

Chakraborty, U. K., Konar, D., Roy, S., & Choudhury, S. (2014). Intelligent fuzzy spelling evaluator for e-Learning systems. *Education and Information Technologies*, 1–14.

Chao, C. H., Chen, Y. C., Yang, T. J., & Yu, P. L. (2014, January). Intelligent Classroom with Motion Sensor and 3D Vision for Virtual Reality e-Learning. In *The 2nd International Workshop on Learning Technology for Education in Cloud* (pp. 27-33). Springer Netherlands.

Clark, R. C., & Mayer, R. E. (2011). *E-learning and the science of instruction: Proven guidelines for consumers and designers of multimedia learning*. John Wiley & Sons. doi:10.1002/9781118255971

Dascalu, M. I., Bodea, C. N., Lytras, M., De Pablos, P. O., & Burlacu, A. (2014). Improving e-learning communities through optimal composition of multidisciplinary learning groups. *Computers in Human Behavior*, 30, 362–371. doi:10.1016/j.chb.2013.01.022

Garrison, D. R. (2011). *E-learning in the 21st century: A framework for research and practice*. Taylor & Francis.

Govindasamy, T. (2001). Successful implementation of e-learning: Pedagogical considerations. *The Internet and Higher Education*, 4(3), 287–299. doi:10.1016/S1096-7516(01)00071-9

Huang, C. J., Chu, S. S., & Guan, C. T. (2007). Implementation and performance evaluation of parameter improvement mechanisms for intelligent e-learning systems. *Computers & Education*, 49(3), 597–614. doi:10.1016/j.compedu.2005.11.008

Ismail, J. (2001). The design of an e-learning system: Beyond the hype. *The Internet and Higher Education*, 4(3), 329–336. doi:10.1016/S1096-7516(01)00069-0

Jochems, W., Koper, R., & Van Merrienboer, J. (Eds.). (2013). *Integrated e-learning: Implications for pedagogy, technology and organization*. Routledge.

Kuk, K., Milentijević, I., Rančić, D., & Spalević, P. (2014). Designing Intelligent Agent in Multilevel Game-Based Modules for E-Learning Computer Science Course. In *E-Learning Paradigms and Applications* (pp. 39–63). Springer Berlin Heidelberg. doi:10.1007/978-3-642-41965-2_2

Kurilovas, E., Kubilinskiene, S., & Dagiene, V. (2014). Web 3.0–Based personalisation of learning objects in virtual learning environments. *Computers in Human Behavior*, 30, 654–662. doi:10.1016/j.chb.2013.07.039

Liu, X., Saddik, A. E., & Georganas, N. D. (2003, May). An implementable architecture of an e-learning system. In *Electrical and Computer Engineering, 2003. IEEE CCECE 2003. Canadian Conference on* (Vol. 2, pp. 717-720). IEEE.

Nijhavan, H., & Brusilovsky, P. (2002). A framework for adaptive e-learning based on distributed re-usable learning activities. In *World Conference on E-Learning in Corporate, Government, Healthcare, and Higher Education* (Vol. 2002, No. 1, pp. 154-161).

Rosenberg, M. J. (2001). *E-learning: Strategies for delivering knowledge in the digital age* (Vol. 3). New York: McGraw-Hill.

Shih, T. K., Lin, N. H., & Chang, H. P. (2003, March). An intelligent e-learning system with authoring and assessment mechanism. In *Advanced Information Networking and Applications, 2003. AINA 2003. 17th International Conference on* (pp. 782-787). IEEE.

Welsh, E. T., Wanberg, C. R., Brown, K. G., & Simmering, M. J. (2003). E-learning: emerging uses, empirical results and future directions. *International Journal of Training and Development*, 7(4), 245–258. doi:10.1046/j.1360-3736.2003.00184.x

Woolf, B. P. (2010). *Building intelligent interactive tutors: Student-centered strategies for revolutionizing e-learning*. Morgan Kaufmann.

KEY TERMS AND DEFINITIONS

Artificial Intelligence Supported E-Learning Content Flow: The E-Learning Content Flow in which the related contents include Artificial Intelligence oriented approaches, methods, or techniques.

E-Learning Content Flow: The term that can be used for defining the life cycle of an e-learning content in which works like producing it, including it under specific courses, providing it to the learners, or updating it are performed.

E-Learning Content: Any tool, or material that belongs to e-learning activities.

Intelligent E-Learning: E-Learning supported with Artificial Intelligence oriented approaches, methods, or techniques.

Managerial Model: A model – architecture, which explains or figures out a management flow – organization of a system.

Chapter 10
Resolving the Paradox of Overconfident Students with Intelligent Methods

Denis Smolin
American University in Bosnia and Herzegovina, Bosnia

Sergey Butakov
Concordia University, Canada

ABSTRACT

The chapter presents a case study of using data mining tools to solve the puzzle of inconsistency between students' in-class performance and the results of the final tests. Classical test theory cannot explain such inconsistency, while the classification tree generated by one of the well-known data mining algorithms has provided reasonable explanation, which was confirmed by course exit interviews. The experimental results could be used as a case study of implementing Artificial Intelligence-based methods to analyze course results. Such analyses equip educators with an additional tool that allows closing the loop between assessment results and course content and arrangements.

INTRODUCTION

Introduction briefs the reader into the problem of the objective course material assessment, flaws in the standard statistical solutions to this problem, and the potential areas where some approaches from Artificial Intelligence (AI) domain could be useful.

Problem of student knowledge and skills assessment is as old as the education itself. All educators need a tool to check efficiency and effectiveness of their teaching materials and approach used in the classroom. Various test styles has been around for centuries but they always

raise questions if they are appropriate for checking student comprehension of the subject matter.

The area of student testing is much wider than one can assume. A test, as a measurement tool, and a testing algorithm, as a method to interpret test results, are very generic models of any measurement. It is applicable not only for measurement of student skills and knowledge, but also for almost any other activity. Testing consists of two major steps - data collection and interpretation. Interpretation implies some decision making, which is a large domain where methods of AI play important role. On one hand, classical testing is based on mathematical statistics and AI uses many statisti-

DOI: 10.4018/978-1-4666-6276-6.ch010

cal methods. On the other hand, modern tests for knowledge and skills are much more complex, as compared with their classical ancestors. AI equips the interpretation phase of testing with appropriate processing methods. These methods give fruitful results that are impossible to get with classical algorithms. This paper demonstrates an example of such an AI method.

Interpretation phase of the testing process is covered by two main theories in the field:

- **Classical Testing Theory (CTT):** Which is closely related to mathematical statistics. For example, Spearman correlation was initially developed for psychological testing (Traub, 1997).
- **Item Response Theory (IRT):** A latest theory that expands CTT and is claimed to be more precise for the case of computer-based testing process (Thissen & Mislevy, 2000).

Currently, classical testing theory, which is over 100 years old, is the most popular one. The question of comparative efficiency of these theories is ambiguous and requires detailed examination. Instead of attempting to invalidate the entire theory, the more productive approach is to investigate possible theory inconsistencies - so-called paradoxes, which consist of the cases the theory cannot explain. While applying CTT to student knowledge and skills one can simply find two paradoxes: a student with bad knowledge getting higher exam score and a student with presumably good knowledge of subject matter failing a major test.

CTT answers these questions with the concept of quality, defined with the statistical evidence. A test is of high quality, when it has high validity and reliability. There are different methods for validity and reliability evaluation. The majority of these methods are based on correlation coefficients, which obviously require a representative sample. In practice, it could be difficult to get enough data

to prepare such a sample. A test with proved statistical characteristics is called standardized and considered an unbiased measurement instrument. This test is correct for almost all students. All other tests assumed to be tests with indefinite quality. In some cases, it can also be considered a paradox, because the quality of tests can be proved with some other methods. Additionally the paradox may occur, when a student with presumably good knowledge fails high quality tests. It rarely happens and CTT has eliminated these cases from its scope by arguing that there is not enough information to evaluate them. For example, we may be unaware of all the personal circumstances that happened to the student during the exam time.

Standards provided by the American Educational Research Association (AERA) recommend certain number of implementations to be performed to verify quality of a test or a question (AERA, 1999). In many cases, educators do not have enough data to perform such a comprehensive statistical analysis. The underlying reasons for that could vary from cases where the number of students in a class is limited to very dynamic subject matters where noticeable changes in course elements must be implemented in every teaching cycle. Lack of statistics makes it difficult for educators to setup a proper verification process for course elements. As a solution they often use "hand-made" tests of undefined quality (Miller, 2009). In such cases, teachers cannot improve course elements because they have no adequate tools to perform verification. Without such a verification process, any of participants of the educational process may raise questions about the quality and relevance of the course and its elements.

The approach and tool outlined in this chapter paper provide an alternative approach to the test quality problem. This approach employs decision trees to tackle the problem of test quality assessment and to overcome the above mentioned paradoxes.

PROBLEM BACKGROUND: WEAKNESS OF STATISTICAL QUALITY ASSESSMENT

In teaching practice, basic assessment techniques usually include the following: interviews, tests, practical assignments, essays, etc. (Brown, 1997). Results are generally represented in percentage, while the importance of each element is specified by the weight in linear formula. Of course linear formula can be curved to a letter grade but the basic calculation is the same. For example:

Final grade = homework×25%+classwork×25%+midterm examination×25%+final examination×25% (1)

This grading approach leaves some open questions including the one actual abilities of the student to solve real world problems: (Higgins, 2010): "What does the final grade characterize: one's ability to solve problems within the data domain or the ability to follow class rules?"

The concept of validity could be useful to answer this question. This concept itself is multidimensional: it includes "construct validity", "predictive validity", etc. (Anastasi & Urbina, 1997). If one assumes the final grade as a measure of a student ability to solve problems, it has to be concluded that linear formula is non-valid (Smoline, 2008). Imagine a student who started a course with low grades, but finished it having excellent knowledge – see uphill grade curve on figure 1. In this case linear formula deprives the student from the maximum score. Even though it is possible to assign greater weights to the last weeks of the course, but it will obviously affect an A+ student who lets say lost motivation before the final exam.

To solve this kind of the problem educators usually use comprehensive high-quality final tests. But according to the axioms of the Classical Test Theory (CTT), it is possible to guess some answers and get a higher score by chance (Anastasi & Urbina, 1997). This situation looks like a dead lock where tests may not perform their role as they supposed to. Numerous works, for example (Brookhart & DeVoge, 2000 or O'Connor, 2009) discuss two common mistakes in test arrangements:

- Giving a low final grade to a gifted (but lazy) student and suppressing the student's motivation;
- Giving a high final grade to a student who cannot complete practical assignments but is capable of passing the final test.

Most of the educators deal with these problems on the daily basis. There is no dilemma for an educator if student's current performance correlates with the final test result, but what should be done if it does not? Figure 2 shows such a case. Some research groups called this case as problem of "overconfident" students (Moore & Healy, 2008; Dunning et. al., 2003).

The concept of quality can address the issue of grade inconsistency. The CTT states that any test in general and its assignments in particular should be standardized, i.e. to have statistically

Figure 1. (a) A strong student who lost motivation before the final examination and (b) a weak student with high motivation. The curves are indistinguishable with the formula 1.

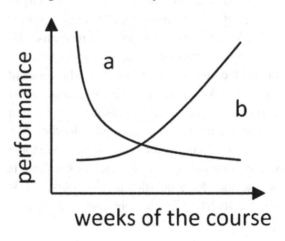

Figure 2. The problem of overconfidence: two students (curves 1 and 2), their in-class performance (curves marked as 1,2), and unexpected results for the final test

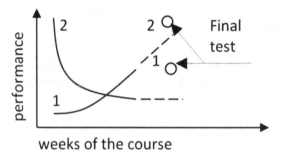

proven validity and reliability. In brief, the former is related to the distribution of testing results and the latter is related to the dispersion of this distribution in the series of experiments. Two examples: (a) question is non-valid if no one can answer it correctly or if everyone answers it; (b) question is non- reliable if it is easy for any student to guess the correct answer. Thus, true-and-false questions have low reliability, while open-answer questions have the higher reliability but low validity. It is also important to note that question quality depends not only on the form of the question, but also on the current context, e.g. on the previous questions. Finally, the overall test quality measured by validity and reliability is a function derived from the quality of all its questions, its structure and other factors (Messick, 1995).

AERA standard recommends test reliability to be kept at 0.75 or above for the simplest re-test case (AERA, 1999). Despite this recommendation implementations of the testing subsystems in most commonly used Course Management Systems (CMS) do not provide educators with the possibility to evaluate the validity of a question in multiple courses. For example, Moodle CMS (www.moodle.org) allows an educator to see some statistics on the question in one test but there is no statistics for a question across courses. Test score calculation in different CMS varies from

simple weighted sum to more advanced models that include penalties such as point reduction for incorrect attempts. Example of such weighted sum is provided below:

$$\text{Test result} = w_1 q_1 + \& . + w_n q_n \qquad (1.1)$$

where wi represents the weights of the questions and qn the question scores. This formula does not take into account order of questions and therefore test structure. Moreover, order in which questions are presented to the student can vary from one experiment to another because testing system may randomly shuffle questions. Technically if we assume some relations between questions that such a reshuffling makes it nearly impossible to obtain proper statistical evaluation of the test reliability as it is required by CTT.

PROPOSED DECISION

Non Statistical Methods

Issues mentioned above are the main drivers for the research projects aimed at the development of non-statistical mechanisms for quality assessment of the course elements. Romero et.al. have noted that statistical methods do not actually close the loop for educational process. Statistical evaluation of the teaching results does not equip an educator with proper recommendations on how to improve such course elements as quizzes (Romero et.al. 2012). In this project they suggested using Association Rule Mining (ARM) techniques to improve interpretation of quiz results by placing them on the matrix of the expected course knowledge. Such an approach allows seeing how the quizzes cover the required topics and analyze gaps in them (Romero et.al. 2012). Chen and Weng did similar attempt aimed at: (a) mining student opinions from lass structured answers and (b) linking them to course elements that caused less positive feedback. They also used ARM to evaluate large course structures such as teaching methodology or overall content of the course (Chen & Weng, 2009).

This paper is also attempting to provide non-statistical evaluation of course elements. It differs from the previous works in two ways. First it proposes to use decision tree mechanism to locate potentially problematic elements of the course. Second it focuses on the specific problem of inconsistency in course outcomes described above as a paradox of overconfident student. The rest of the paper describes the proposed methodology, outlines experimental results and discusses the potential benefits and limitations of implementation. Analysis of test data with iterative dichotomy algorithm

Table 1 represents more formal description of the paradox of overconfident students.

The table represents a situation when the final test score differs from the in-class performance. This raises a number of questions:

- Are current performance indicators incorrect? If yes, which ones provide the incorrect evaluations?
- Is the test non-valid?
- Are there some major changes happened in student attitude? Example of such changes may include the following: (a) weak, but motivated students; (b)strong, but not motivated students; (c) weak, but very lucky students, or students who cheat; (d) some other unknown reasons.

Simplified graph on Figure 3 shows that just one linear formula (e.g. formula 1.1) doesn't allow breaking the initial dataset into more than two subsets. This situation is well known since the beginning of the AI era and was originally introduced by Rosenblatt (Rosenblatt, 1962).

For the case represented in Fig. 3 it is necessary to use two linear formulas:

$$\text{overconfident if } \begin{cases} q_1 w_1 + q_2 w_2 < c_1 \\ q_1 w_1 + q_2 w_2 > c_2 \end{cases}$$

Or a non-linear one:

$$\text{overconfident if } a q_1^2 + b q_2^2 < c_1$$

Or a logical one:

$$\text{overconfident} = (q_1 w_1 + q_2 w_2 < c_1) \text{ and } (q_1 w_1 + q_2 w_2 > c_2)$$

Obviously, it would be helpful to have a tool that retrieves this formula from the sample data automatically as typical educators will not be ready to invest their time in manual data analysis. Ideally such a mechanism should be a part of data analysis toolset in CMS. Deep analysis of inconsistency would allow locating elements of the course that require extra attention from course developer or manager. From the formalization point of view such a task falls into a category of non-linear dichotomy. In this paper we selected C4.5 algorithm as one of the most well-known tools for this category of problems. Essential steps

Table 1. Testing data with non-linear dependencies

Question 1	Question …	Question N	Final Test Score	In-Course Performance
0	1	0	Low	High
1	1	0	High	Medium
1	1	1	High	High

Figure 3. The paradox of "overconfident" students (represented in Fig. 2) viewed as the problem of linear inseparability. To grade the result of the simplest test (with just two questions: q1 and q2) we might need more than one linear formula or a non-linear one. For example: 2◊3=5 is true (q1=true), question 2◊3=6 is false (q2=false) and vs. (marked with the stars). But never q1=q2=true or q1=q2=false. Here sign "◊" denotes addition or multiplication. There are two reasons to select answers as q1=q2 (marked with the circles): bad student knowledge or bad (non-valid) questions.

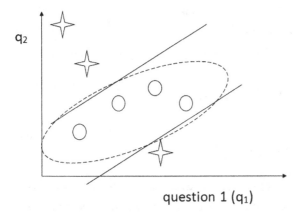

question 1 (q_1)

of the algorithm are outlined below according to Quinlan (Quinlan, 1993). The goal is to provide the educator with the tree of questions that differentiates the classes of "high" and "low" student performance.

The algorithm balances computational complexity of the tree building procedure with over-fitting problem. Over-fitted rules do not show real dependencies in the initial data, but they show occasional dependencies caused by random errors. To avoid these problems the algorithm uses a heuristic: for each logical division it selects a parameter with minimal entropy (and maximal information gain as a result). The entropy E of data set S (that contains n different classes) is defined as the function of fj. The latter is the proportion of value j in set S:

$$E(S) = -\sum_{j=1}^{n} f_j log_2 f_j$$

Here, E(S) is in [0..1] and 1 means chaos, while 0 coincides with a totally classified set. It uses log2, assuming two possible outcomes of an event: yes or no. The next step of the algorithm selects an attribute for the dichotomy. This idea is formalized as the information gain:

$$G(S, A) = E(S) - \sum_{i=1}^{m} f(A_i) E(S_{A_i})$$

Here, E(S) is the entropy of the set to be divided (it reduces after each division), f(Ai) is the proportion of cases (in S) where attribute A has value Ai. SA is the subset of S that contains only cases with the Ai value. Variable m is the number of different Ai values. As it can be seen from the description C4.5 algorithm allows iterative classification on the lass structured data which makes in ideal tool to tackle the complex task of quiz validity evaluation.

SOLUTIONS AND RECOMMENDATIONS

The experiment was done on one course that introduces computer science students to a new programming language. Although when students reach this senior level course they already have solid programming background but since the course was new to the program it was assumed that validity could be evaluated as "unknown". Prior to final test each students has been evaluated for in-class performance during semester. The evaluation was based on practical programming assignments. Sample of test protocols for the final exam along with in-class evaluations (low/high score in the rightmost column) is represented in Table 2.

Table 2. Example of final test protocols: 18 students answered 32 questions

No	1,2,3,4,5,6,7,8,9,10,11,12,13,14,15,16,17,18,19,20,21,22,23,24,25,26,27,28,29,30,31,32,Score,Class
37.	38. 1,0,0,0,1,0,1,1,1,1,0.5,1,0,1,0,0.5,0.5,1,1,1,1,0,1,0,0.5,0.5,1,1,0,0,0,0,17.5,low
39.	40. 1,1,1,0,0,0.5,0.5,1,1,1,1,0,1,0,1,1,0.5,1,1,1,0,1,1,1,1,0.5,1,1,0,0,0,0,21,low
41.	42. 1,1,1,0,1,0,1,1,1,1,1,0,0,1,1,1,1,1,1,1,0,1,1,1,1,0.5,1,1,0,0,0,0,22.5, high
43.	44. 1,0,1,0,1,0,1,1,1,1,1,1,1,1,1,1,1,1,1,1,0,0,1,1,1,1,1,0,1,1,1,26,low
45.	46. 1,0,1,1,0,0,1,0,1,1,1,1,0,1,1,1,1,1,1,0,1,1,1,0,0.5,1,1,0,0,1,1,22.5, high
47.	48. 1,0,0.5,1,1,1,1,1,1,1,0.5,0,1,1,1,1,1,1,1,1,0,1,1,1,0,1,1,1,0,1,0,0,24,low
49.	50. 1,1,1,1,1,1,1,1,0,1,0.5,0,0,1,0,0,1,0,1,1,1,1,1,1,1,1,1,0,1,0,0,0,0,20.5,low
51.	52. 1,0,1,1,0,0,0,0,1,0.5,0,0,1,0,0,0,0,1,0.5,0,0,1,1,0,1,0,1,0,1,0,0,0,0,11,low
53.	54. 1,0,1,1,1,1,1,1,1,1,0.5,0,0,1,1,0,1,0,0,1,0,0,1,1,0.5,0,1,0,0,0,0,18,low
55.	56. 1,0,1,1,1,1,1,1,1,1,0,0.5,0,0,1,0,1,1,1,1,0,1,1,1,0.5,0.5,1,1,0,1,1,1,23.5,low
57.	58. 1,0,0,0,1,0,1,1,0,1,0.5,0.5,0,1,0,0,1,1,1,1,0,1,1,1,1,0.5,0,1,0,0,0,0,16.5,low
59.	60. 1,1,1,0,1,0,1,0,1,0,0,1,0,1,1,0,0.5,1,1,1,0,1,1,1,0.5,0.5,0.5,0,0,0,0,0,17,low
61.	62. 0,1,1,0,0,0,1,0,1,1,0,1,1,0,1,1,0,0.5,1,1,1,0,1,1,0,1,0.5,1,1,0,0,1,1,20,high
63.	64. 1,0,1,0,1,1,1,1,1,1,0.5,0,0,0,1,1,1,1,1,1,1,1,1,1,0,0.5,1,0,0,1,1,1,23,high
65.	66. 1,0,1,0,1,0,1,1,1,1,0.5,0,0,1,0,0.5,1,1,1,1,0,1,1,1,0.5,1,1,1,0,1,1,1,22.5,low
67.	68. 1,1,1,0,1,0,1,1,1,1,1,0,0,0,0,1,1,1,1,1,1,0,1,1,1,0.5,1,0.5,0,0,0.5,0.5,21,low
69.	70. 1,0,1,1,1,1,1,1,1,1,0.5,0,0,0,1,0,0.5,1,1,0.5,0,1,1,1,1,1,1,1,0,0,1,1,22.5,low
71.	72. 1,0,0,1,0,0,1,1,0,1,0.5,0,0,1,0,0.5,1,1,1,1,0,1,1,1,1,0,0.5,1,0,0,0,0,16.5,low

The test questions were based on the questions from a standardized test on the topic provided by the industry leader in this particular programming language (http://www.embarcadero.com). The goal of such test was to evaluate the course and observe how student skills and knowledge of the subject matter match labor market expectations. Obviously, the expectations were "high" test grades from the students with "high" in-class performance and "low" test grades from the students with "low" in-class performance. However, a bit unexpected practical results came out.

In the table numbers 1, 2, ... 32 are question numbers, "Score" is the sum of these values and "Class" identifies student in-class performance. 0 in any position means that the student failed the question, 1 means that the student answered the question properly and 0.5 means that the student answered properly, but made some minor mistakes.

Contradictions are as follows: "high" student No.13 has 20 points, while many "low" students have higher scores (see line 2). "low" student No.4 has 26 points, this score is higher than any score of "high" students. Such a result may be caused by one of the following reasons:

- The test is non-valid.
- The course material is non-valid and it does not support the final test.
- The students cheated.

According to CTT to analyze the impact of different questions on the overall result it is required to exclude non-valid questions from the analysis. In this sample every student provided correct answer to the following questions: 1,7,10, 17,19,20,23, 26, and 29. These questions are eliminated from further analysis in Table 3.

As it can be seen from Table 3 there is still no linear boundary between "high" (score 15) and "low" (scores 14.5 and 17) students. Obviously, the classes are linearly inseparable. To clear the situation we interviewed our students and implemented the same course 3 times more. The sample of more than 100 cases shows that from the point of view of CTT the test is reliable (re-test correlation >0.8). CTT doesn't explain the paradox.

Finally, we turned back to the initial section of 18 students (see Table 2) and tried to explain the paradox logically. We have 4 students with "high" in-class performance. Their final test results are in the range [20..23] and the average is 22. We also have 14 students with relatively "low" in-class performance and their testing results are in the range [11..26], the average is 19.82. Among

the students with relatively "low" in-class performance we have 7 cases with a test score of more than 20, and 5 cases with a test result of more than 22 and even 3 cases with a result of more than 23. If case 22 assumed to be the "best case" and the boundary between "low" and "high" classes then this test works properly in 75% of cases for the "high" class and only in 65% cases for the "low" class. It could be explained by the fact that there are two basic groups among the students with relatively "low" in-class performance: (a) test results in the range [11 .. 21] and the average is 17.67; (b) test results in the range [22.5 .. 26] with the average 23.7

The last case illustrates the situation when the students with relatively "low" in-class performance unexpectedly demonstrate high final

Table 3. Students No.3, 4 and 13 evaluated with the help of valid questions

No.	2,3,4,5,6,8,9,11,12,13,14,15,16,18,21,22,24,25,27,28,30,31,32,score,class,
3	1,1,0,0,0.5,1,1,1,0,1,0,1,1,1,0,1,1,1,1,1,0,0,0,14.5,LOW
4	0,1,0,1,0,1,1,1,1,1,1,1,1,1,0,0,1,1,1,1,0,1,1,17,LOW
13	1,1,0,0,0,0,1,0,1,1,0,1,1,1,0,1,0,1,1,1,1,1,1,15,HIGH

Figure 4. Decision tree for explanation of the paradox of overconfident students

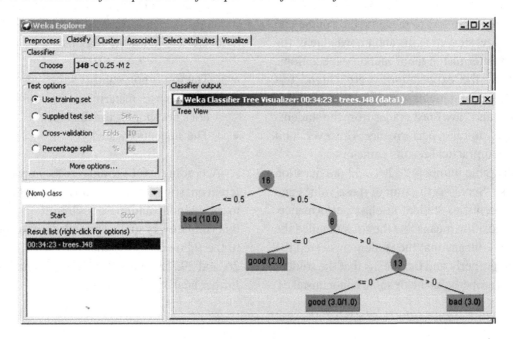

test results (see Figure 2, line 2). If the last group would be eliminated from the analysis the overall results would be ideal – 100% of "low" and "high" classes would be classified properly. Unfortunately that would force us to ignore 35% of test protocols. This situation illustrates the cases described in the Introduction when statistics does not differentiate students with (a) low performance and very high test results; and (b) high performance and high test results.

To solve this separation test C4.5 implementation from WEKA data mining tool has been used for advanced analysis of the case (Witten, 2011).

The tree shows that almost all students with low in-class performance did not answer question 16 correctly, but they did answer questions 8 and 13. In contrast, "high" students have problems with questions 8 and 13. Question 8 was on specific data entry components, question 13 on databases, and question 16 on multimedia procedures. Data entry components and databases are obviously related, while multimedia programming is a quite different field. We discussed this in detail in one of the classes, however students with low in class performance usually did not participate in discussions. That is why students from high in-class performance category answered the question correctly while their peers from the second category failed. But why did high performers fail questions on the databases? The topic was covered in class, but detailed practical coding examples were not provided while the final test questions were oriented towards practical programming. Having little experience with databases it was no wonder high performers failed these questions. But how did "low" students pass? Course exit interview gave possible answer. Many of the students with "low" in class performance were taking class on Oracle databases in the save semester. That class equipped them with the enough knowledge to answer these questions, while ones from high performing category did not take database course.

The separation of the cases provided by advanced algorithm points out the problem in course but does not provide straight forward solution to it. It is not clear what should be adjusted in the course: is it the test or is it the course content? Even more relevant question would be: what is more important to be well-prepared for practical work or to follow the course outline? The educators, managers and other stakeholders should take further steps to address this issue while the described approach helps to identify the problem on the very granular level.

FUTURE RESEARCH DIRECTIONS: AI FOR SYLLABUS DEVELOPMENT

The new intelligent instrument introduced in sections above opens a line of promising possibilities both in test and syllabus development. According to (AERA, 1999) test development process includes several steps and starts from the following items:

- Specifying the purpose of the test.
- Developing frameworks describing the knowledge and skills to be tested.

Both stages are strongly related to the course syllabus and program curriculum in total. Creating the list of skills and knowledge to be included in the test an educator should clarify the strategic goal: to measure student's level of proficiency or to measure student's knowledge of instructional materials.

For a good syllabus, these strategies are highly correlated. Better knowledge teaching materials guarantees better student proficiency in the field. In contrast, a mediocre syllabus adds nothing to useful knowledge. The main problem is in differentiating these "useful" and "useless" elements for the definite syllabus. It is comparatively simple for the list of practical skills, but much more difficult for theoretical topics. The boundaries of these theoretical topics are often uncertain and they are often intersected.

As a result, we have duplicates in some syllabi or missed topics in the curriculum in total. The second issue can be mitigated with the help of high quality curriculum templates, developed by the recognized institutions, such as Association for Computer Machinery (ACM, 2007). The first case is more complex – it depends not on the document quality itself, but on the student background. Good students often know much more, than a teacher can assume. As a result, some elements of the syllabus (see Figure 5) are known to them before the course starts and shall be deleted from this version of the syllabus. Some new topics should be also included to the course. Apparently, such operations (delete or include) to be supported with solid evidence.

Traditional test (tests of achievements or diagnostics tests) are not very useful for the case. Achievements tests evaluate student knowledge in general. The result is usually shown as the percentage of correct answers, but it is not always enough. Diagnostics tests report an educator on gaps in student education, but they cannot explain

the reasons of this situation. Artificial intelligence introduces a new look at the old task. Appling automated classification algorithms to the protocols of traditional tests an educator gets a set of advanced opportunities.

A computer test, adjusted to the course strategy in conjunction with AI methods allows optimizing the course syllabus and provides clear and unambiguous evidence for each change in the list of topics. This is a very promising idea for the on-going testing and learning software systems.

CONCLUSION

Project outlined in this paper have been aimed on resolving essence of the paradox of overconfident students. Results of the study show how the iterative dichotomy algorithm can help educators in locating potentially problematic elements in their courses. Evaluation of the proposed approach has been performed by detailed study of the paradox in a course where student in-class performance did not properly match results of course exit tests. While CTT analysis conducted for a bigger sample did not provide reasonable explanation of inconsistency, implementation of C4.5 iterative dichotomy

Figure 5. Course syllabi as decision trees. Both the syllabi include the same topic i.e. they are intersected.

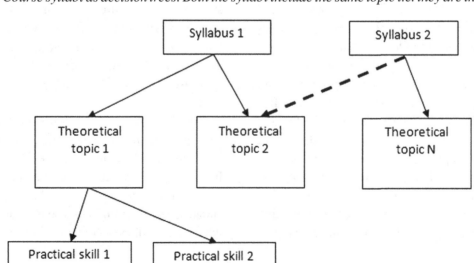

algorithm allowed locating course elements that caused such inconsistency. If compared with CTT the proposed approach has following advantages:

- It allows the validity and reliability analysis for the course questions, but does not imply strict size requirements on the test sample. While AERA recommends significant (≥ 100 cases) sample data (AERA, 1999) which may not be available, C4.5 allows performing quality analysis on a smaller samples.
- It allows automatic retrieval of non-linear scoring formulas from the test results which may help educators to evaluate relevance of course elements.
- It provides an objective mechanism for matching course outcome to its outline.

Very granular analysis that starts from course outcomes and digs down to individual course elements allows educators to focus attention on the personalized approach to each student and provides objective way to select elements for a the particular class. Resolving the specific paradox of overconfident student allows better adjustment for course expectations and outcomes. Generally speaking the proposed approach makes a step towards embedding routine quality assurance mechanism in CMS for interview-like and adaptive tests (Smoline, 2008). The ultimate goal for such mechanism embedded into learning management systems is to provide "uniformly precise scores for most test-takers in contrast to standard fixed tests" (Thissen & Mislevy, 2000). Experiment on limited dataset outlined in this paper requires more careful study on the larger data sets. The proposed architecture is already implemented in a small-scale learning and testing system called Chopin. Currently the system is being used for a number of courses and authors expect more field tests of the proposed approach to be performed in the nearest future.

REFERENCES

ACM CR. (2007). *ACM Curricula Recommendations*. Retrieved from http://www.acm.org/education/curricula-recommendations

AERA. (1999). *Standards for educational and psychological testing*. Amer Educational Research Assn.

Anastasi, A. (1997). Psychological Testing. Upper Saddle River, NJ: Prentice Hall

Brown, G. (1997). *Assessing student learning in higher education*. London: Routledge.

Chen, Y., & Weng, C. (2009). Mining fuzzy association rules from questionnaire data. *Knowledge-Based Systems Journal, 22*, 46–56. doi:10.1016/j.knosys.2008.06.003

Dunning, D., Johnson, K., Ehrlinger, J., & Kruger, J. (2003). Why people fail to recognize their own incompetence. *Current Directions in Psychological Science, 12*, 83–87. doi:10.1111/1467-8721.01235

Higgins, M., Grant, F., Thompson, P., & Montarzino, A. (2010). *Effective and efficient methods of formative assessment*. Cardiff, UK: Centre for Education in the Built Environment.

Messick, S. (1995). Validity of psychological assessment: Validation of inferences from persons' responses and performances as scientific inquiry into score meaning. *The American Psychologist, 50*, 741–749. doi:10.1037/0003-066X.50.9.741

Miller, D., Linn, R., & Gronlund, N. (2009). *Measurement and Assessment in Teaching*. Pearson.

Moore, D. A., & Healy, P. J. (2008). The trouble with overconfidence. *Psychological Review, 115*, 502–517. doi:10.1037/0033-295X.115.2.502 PMID:18426301

O'Connor, D. (2009). *How to grade for Learning, K-12*. Corwin Press.

Quinlan, J. R. (1993). *C4.5: Programs for Machine Learning*. Morgan Kaufmann Publishers.

Romero, C., Zafra, A., Luna, J. M., & Ventura, S. (2012). Association rule mining using genetic programming to provide feedback to instructors from multiple-choice quiz data. *Expert Systems: International Journal of Knowledge Engineering and Neural Networks*. doi: doi:10.1111/j.1468-0394.2012.00627

Rosenblatt, F. (1962). *Principles of Neurodynamics*. Washington, DC: Spartan Books.

Smolin, D. (2011). Testing with the Computer: State of the Art, Needs and Perspective. In *Advances in Psychology Research*, (pp. 71–76). New York: Nova Science Publishers.

Smoline, D. (2008). Some problems of computer-aided testing and interview-like tests. *Computers & Education*, *51*(2), 743–756. doi:10.1016/j.compedu.2007.07.008

Thissen, D., & Mislevy, R. J. (2000). Testing Algorithms. In H. Wainer (Ed.), *Computerized Adaptive Testing: A Primer*. Mahwah, NJ: Lawrence Erlbaum Associates.

Traub, R. (1997). Educational Measurement: Issues and Practice. *Classical Test Theory in Historical Perspective*, *16*(4), 8–14.

Witten, I. (2011). *Data Mining Practical Machine Learning Tools and Techniques*. Morgan Kaufmann.

ADDITIONAL READING

Agresti, A. (2002). *Categorical Data Analysis*. Hoboken, NJ: John Wiley and Sons. doi:10.1002/0471249688

Anderson, J. R. (2005). *Cognitive Psychology and its implications*. New York: Worth Publishers.

Angus, S McDonald. (2002). The impact of individual differences on the equivalence of computer-based and paper-and-pencil educational assessments. *Computers & Education*, *39*(3), 299–312. doi:10.1016/S0360-1315(02)00032-5

Chittaro, L., & Ranon, R. (2007). Web3D Technologies in Learning, Education and Training: Motivations, Issues, Opportunities. *Computers & Education*, *49*(1), 3–18. doi:10.1016/j.compedu.2005.06.002

Clarke, D. (1991). The Negotiated Syllabus: What Is It And How Is It Likely To Work? *Applied Linguistics*, *12*, 13–28. doi:10.1093/applin/12.1.13

Danielson, C., & McGreal, T. (2000). *Teacher Evaluation to Enhance Professional Practice*. Alexandria: ASCD.

Devroye, L., Györfi, L., & Lugosi, G. (1996). *A Probabilistic Theory of Pattern Recognition*. New York: Springer-Verlag. doi:10.1007/978-1-4612-0711-5

Diamond, R. (1998). *Designing & assessing courses & curricula: A practical guide*. San Francisco: Jossey-Bass Publishers.

Domingos, P., & Pazzani, M. (1997). On the optimality of the simple Bayesian classifier under zero-one loss. *Machine Learning*, *29*, 103–137. doi:10.1023/A:1007413511361

Duda, R. O., Hart, P. E., & Stork, D. G. (2001). *Pattern Classification*. Wiley.

Freund, Y., & Schapire, R. E. (1999). Large margin classification using the perceptron algorithm. *Machine Learning*, *37*(3), 277–296. doi:10.1023/A:1007662407062

Greenwald, A. (1997). Validity concerns and usefulness of student ratings of instruction. *The American Psychologist*, *52*(11), 1182–1186. doi:10.1037/0003-066X.52.11.1182 PMID:9357332

Grzymala-Busse, J. W. (1993). Selected Algorithms of Machine Learning from Examples. *Fundamenta Informaticae*, *18*, 193–207.

Hancock, T. R., Jiang, T., Li, M., & Tromp, J. (1996). Lower Bounds on Learning Decision Lists and Trees. *Information and Computation*, *126*(2), 114–122. doi:10.1006/inco.1996.0040

Herbrich, R. (2001). *Learning Kernel Classifiers: Theory and Algorithms*. MIT Press.

Hol, A. M., Vorst, H., & Mellenbergh, G. J. (2008). Computerized Adaptive Testing of Personality Traits. *Zeitschrift fur Psychologie mit Zeitschrift fur Angewandte Psychologie*, *216*(1), 12–21.

Květon, P., Jelínek, M., Vobořil, D., & Klimusová, H. (2007). Computer-based tests: the impact of test design and problem of equivalency. *Computers in Human Behavior*, *23*(1), 32–51. doi:10.1016/j.chb.2004.03.034

Lei, J., & Zhao, Y. (2007). Technology uses and student achievement: A longitudinal study. *Computers & Education*, *49*(2), 284–296. doi:10.1016/j.compedu.2005.06.013

Lilley, M., Barker, T., & Britton, C. (2004). The development and evaluation of a software prototype for computer-adaptive testing. *Computers & Education*, *43*(1–2), 109–123. doi:10.1016/j.compedu.2003.12.008

Lin, Y.-C., Lin, Y.-T., & Huang, Y.-M. (2011). Development of a diagnostic system using a testing-based approach for strengthening student prior knowledge. *Computers & Education*, *57*(2), 1557–1570. doi:10.1016/j.compedu.2011.03.004

llim H., (1996.) An Efficient Algorithm for Optimal Pruning of Decision Trees. *Artificial Intelligence,* *83*(2), 347-362.

Minsky, M., & Papert, S. (1972). *Perceptrons: An Introduction to Computational Geometry*. Cambridge, MA: The MIT Press.

Mitchell, T. M. (1997). *Machine Learning*. McGraw-Hill.

Murthy, S. K. (1998). Automatic Construction of Decision Trees from Data: A MultiDisciplinary Survey. *Data Mining and Knowledge Discovery*, *2*(4), 345–389. doi:10.1023/A:1009744630224

Naglieri, J. A., Drasgow, F., Schmit, M., Handler, L., Prifitera, A., Margolis, A., & Velasquez, R. (2004). Psychological testing on the Internet: new problems, old issues. *The American Psychologist*, *59*(3), 150–162. doi:10.1037/0003-066X.59.3.150 PMID:15222858

Nello Cristianini and John Shawe-Taylor. (2000). *An Introduction to Support Vector Machines and other kernel-based learning methods*. Cambridge University Press.

Nilsson, N. (2010). *The Quest for Artificial Intelligence: A History of Ideas and Achievements*. New York: Cambridge University Press.

Osgood, C., Sussy, C. J., & Tannenbaum, P. H. (1957). *The measurement of meaning. Urhana*. Chicago: University of Illinois Press.

Rokach, Lior; Maimon, O. (2008). *Data mining with decision trees: theory and applications*. World Scientific Pub Co Inc.

Rovai, A. P. (2003). A practical framework for evaluating online distance education programs. *The Internet and Higher Education*, *6*, 109–124. doi:10.1016/S1096-7516(03)00019-8

Russell S., Norvig P. (2003). *Artificial Intelligence: A modern approach*. University of California, Berkeley

Simpson, R. (1995). Uses and misuses of student evaluations of teaching effectiveness. *Innovative Higher Education*, *20*(1), 3–5. doi:10.1007/BF01228323

Siozos, P., Palaigeorgiou, G., Triantafyllakos, G., & Despotakis, T. (2009). Computer based testing using "digital ink": Participatory design of a Tablet PC based assessment application for secondary education. *Computers & Education*, *52*(4), 811–819. doi:10.1016/j.compedu.2008.12.006

Torresani, L. (2007). Advances in Neural Information Processing Systems: Vol. 19. *Lee K* (pp. 13850–1392). Large Margin Component Analysis.

Triantafillou, E. et al. (n.d.). The design and evaluation of a computerized adaptive test on mobile devices. *Computers & Education*, *50*(4), 1319–1330. doi:10.1016/j.compedu.2006.12.005

Triantafillou, E., Georgiadou, E., & Economides, A. A. (2008). The design and evaluation of a computerized adaptive test on mobile devices. *Computers & Education*, *50*(4), 1319–1330. doi:10.1016/j.compedu.2006.12.005

Underwood, J., & Szabo, A. (2003). Academic offences and e-learning: individual propensities in cheating Source. *British Journal of Educational Technology*, *34*(4), 467–477. doi:10.1111/1467-8535.00343

Wolf, P., Hill, A., & Evers, F. (2006). *Handbook for curriculum assessment*. University of Guelf.

Zadeh, L. (1975). The concept of a linguistic variable and its application to approximate reasoning. *Information Sciences*, *8*, 199–249. doi:10.1016/0020-0255(75)90036-5

Zadeh, L. A. (1965). Fuzzy sets. *Information and Control*, *8*(3), 338–353. doi:10.1016/S0019-9958(65)90241-X

KEY TERMS AND DEFINITIONS

Adaptive Syllabus/Test: A syllabus that can change its structure, while been implemented.

Linear Inseparability: Impossibility to solve a problem with the help of one straight line.

Overconfident Student: A student whose current performance does not correlates with the final test result.

Standardized Test: A test with statistically proved validity and reliability.

Test Quality: Its validity, reliability and economy.

Test Reliability: Refers to the consistency of measurements when the testing procedure is repeated on a population of individuals or groups.

Test Validity: Is the degree to which evidence and theory support the interpretations of test scores entailed by proposed uses of tests.

Testing Theory: There are two basic statistical theories in the field: Classical TT and IRT.

Chapter 11
Design and Development of an Expert System Shell Program and Evaluation of Its Effectiveness

Aslihan Tufekci
Gazi University, Turkey

ABSTRACT

In recent years, the amount of software developed to be used in the fields of computer-assisted teaching, e-learning, and distance education, and their quality levels have greatly varied. In order to meet the increasing demand for effective and suitable coursewares at an optimum level, the most convenient method is believed to be that these coursewares should be developed by teachers themselves, and a considerable number of quality studies focusing on these coursewares should be conducted to improve educational processes in general. At this point, the studies and projects benefitting from the advantages of artificial intelligence-based approaches are becoming frequently available in the related literature as an innovative trend. The current chapter deals with the design and development of an "expert system shell program" on the basis of certain specific goals and needs mentioned in the literature. The main objective of the study is to assist teachers in developing their own courseware by using this particular program. The shell program developed within the scope of this study was tested on a group of people that consists of teachers from different fields of teaching and education levels, and its effectiveness was evaluated through certain methods.

INTRODUCTION

Educational technology is a discipline focusing on the techniques and methods used to achieve the educational objectives and values determined by educational philosophies. After answering the questions "what" and "why", the concept particularly deals with "how" this particular situation can be realized. In other words, educational technology conceptualizes learning and teaching processes in a functional way by using related knowledge and skills in order to manage these processes effectively (Alkan, 1995).

DOI: 10.4018/978-1-4666-6276-6.ch011

Speaking in modern terms, educational technology develops, applies, evaluates and manages various designs by making use of all available factors (human power, knowledge, methods and techniques, tools and equipment and necessary arrangements) in order to analyze human learning systematically and scientifically in detail and to find appropriate solutions accordingly. In other words, educational technology is a specific discipline dealing with learning-teaching processes (Alkan *et al.*, 1995).

In today's world, the detailed examination of technological advances and innovations in terms of the solutions they might offer to solve the current problems encountered in the field of education and making use of these innovations as effectively as possible in the related processes are highly likely to increase the quality of the education provided. Therefore, it is necessary to initiate certain attempts to improve the processes provided within the framework of computer-assisted teaching and distance education and e-learning approaches. Thanks to these attempts, the related literature can be enriched by supporting these processes through more innovative and facilitating approaches. At this point, it is crucial to evaluate the recent common trends and techniques mentioned in the related literature. When considered from this point of view, it is possible to see that artificial intelligence-based approaches are among the most popular ones covered in the related literature. Providing valuable opportunities to conduct studies focusing on imitating human thinking process, artificial intelligence techniques are considered significant supplementary tools in educational processes, in which human factor plays a considerably important role.

The current study deals with the design and development processes of an "expert system shell program" on the basis of the needs and goals mentioned in the related literature. The main aim is to enable teachers to develop their own courseware by using this program. Developed within the scope of the study, the shell program was applied to a group of teachers from different fields of teaching and different levels of education, and its effectiveness was evaluated. At the end of this process, it was found that the shell program was suitable for the determined purposes.

The next section mainly deals with "artificial intelligence technique-approach", which forms the basis for the application, and aims at providing the readers with basic information about expert systems. The following section provides information about the design criteria and working principles of the shell program developed for the purposes of the current study. The evaluation process, which focuses on the effectiveness of the program and its suitability for the predetermined goals, is available under the next section and finally, the last section of the study is devoted to the results and the further studies planned within the framework of this process.

EXPERT SYSTEMS

This section specifically deals with the definition and working principles as well as the components of expert systems.

Definition of Expert System

In a broader sense, "expert system" is one of the most common applications of artificial intelligence technology, and it is a way of enabling a machine to perform a task that is normally expected to be performed by a human being. The related literature presents a lot of definitions that complement each other. For instance, Turban (1982) defines expert systems as follows: "It is a system using human knowledge stored in a computer to solve the problems that require a certain level of expertise. These systems might either be used by non-experts to solve such problems, or as intelligent assistants by experts". Similarly, according to Bonnet (1988), expert system is "computer software that stores and processes a wide range of information about a certain field. It is often developed by one or several human experts, and is able to achieve the success level of real human expert performances".

Human experts are the individuals equipped with specific skills, knowledge and experience in solving the problems encountered in certain fields. Expert systems, however, obtain this expert knowledge in some ways and store it in a computer. This knowledge is later available to anyone who wishes to access it. The real purpose here is not to replace human experts but to spread their knowledge to large masses and to provide opportunities enabling people to benefit from this knowledge as much as possible.

Among the main principles and objectives taken into consideration by expert system designers during the development process are as follows: substituting a human expert during his absence; collecting the knowledge and experience of as many experts as possible; being used in the training of candidate experts; and providing expertise services for certain projects that are expensive and are not rated as enjoyable by the experts.

It is difficult to bring the knowledge and experiences of experts together, especially of those who have expertise in more than one subject. Expert systems make it possible to store more knowledge and case knowledge than a human expert is able to. This conclusion implies that expert systems will be able to handle inference making easily tasks, which are very difficult to do with human experts. The information - knowledge to be stored in expert systems can be related to one single subject or several subjects that are related to each other. However, in both cases, the information - knowledge provided for the system will be more comprehensive than that of the experts who contribute to this information - knowledge provision process.

Recent studies show that expert systems increase the rate of production as well as the quality at company level while decreasing the cost considerably.

Structure of Expert System

Generally speaking, the components of an expert system are expert system, human expert(s), knowledge engineer, expert system development tools and the user. As defined earlier in this paper, expert system is "high performance computer software" used in finding solutions to the problems by using expert knowledge. "Expert" is an individual who has already acquired necessary skills and knowledge to solve the problems encountered in a particular field and gained working experience in the field for many years. By using his knowledge and unique personal methods, he is able to make comments about the problems and give valuable advice accordingly. Experts continuously collaborate and interact with the knowledge engineer during expert system development process. "Knowledge engineer" is knowledgeable about "artificial intelligence" and computer technology and knows how to design expert systems. "Expert system development tools" include programming languages used in the field of artificial intelligence as well as shell programs developed to establish an expert system (Yapicioglu, 1991). Finally, "user" is the individual who will use the system according to the instructions to be provided by the expert. The user is mostly a non-expert customer or a student who needs direct counseling. It is not necessary for the users to have detailed knowledge about computers and the possible problems. Most people prefer to use experts systems in order to make quicker and low-cost decisions (Yavuzer, 1996).

Arici (2001) suggests that the most important components of expert systems are "knowledge base" and "inference engine". The basic components of experts systems are shown in Figure 1 below.

Under the light of the information provided by Frenzel (1987), Babalik (2000) and Arici (2001), the basic components of expert systems can be explained as follows:

Figure 1. The structure of an expert system

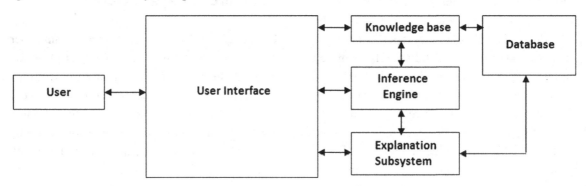

"Knowledge base" is the most central component of expert systems and stores the information - knowledge related to the field of application. The possible resources of knowledge to be obtained by this component are experts, books or empirical studies. "Knowledge" refers to the rules defining the phenomena and relationships (cases) related to the field of expertise. As for the representation of the knowledge demanded by an expert system in a computer environment, the most commonly used approach is "If-Then Rule", in which knowledge is organized in blocks of "if-then". Therefore, knowledge base is also sometimes called "rule-base". The aim of this base is to establish necessary connections between ideas and to ensure that the decision making mechanism functions properly in order to reach an accurate analysis of the problem.

"Inference engine" is the core component of an expert system. It is used to analyze the data and the rules available in the knowledge base. It gives the system the ability to reason, which is presented to the user in a logical way, and the solution is reached accordingly.

Inference engine has two main functions; namely inference and control. "Inference unit" carries out the search in knowledge base in order to determine whether there is any information - knowledge appropriate for the searched model or not. The most common approach to make an inference is to form a chain according to "if-then" rule. The rules are activated through fixed patterns available on "if-then" side of the knowledge base. Since the application of the rule leads to certain changes in the system, knowledge base keeps some of the rules valid and makes others invalid. Accepted as the brain of an expert system, inference engine uses a control strategy to find the rules in use and to decide which one to use. In fact, inference engine is computer software providing a method to formulate logical reasoning and possible results with the help of the available knowledge in knowledge base. In other words, inference mechanism checks the steps followed to solve a specific problem, makes necessary arrangements and decisions regarding how to use the information - knowledge in the system to realize the further processes as effectively as possible.

User interface provides the interaction between the user and the expert system. The system tries to produce a solution by interacting with the user who communicates the problem to the system. The system finds the solution by using the data provided by the user.

User interface is a significant factor affecting the performance of the user. Therefore, a considerable amount of time is spent on the design and the development of user interfaces. Menu and graphics interfaces are the most common environments to strengthen the interaction. In advanced expert systems, certain explanation and help modules are installed into the system in order to simplify the use of expert systems and to provide the users with the answers to the potential problems.

Information: Knowledge Processing in Expert Systems

There are three main steps in processing the information - knowledge in expert systems:

- Obtaining the information - Knowledge
- Formation in knowledge base
- Information - knowledge inference

Obtaining the Information: Knowledge

"Information - knowledge obtaining", a very difficult phase of any expert system development process, involves the acquisition of expert knowledge related to certain subjects from books, experts and experiments and the conversion of this knowledge into computer codes.

Formation in Knowledge Base

Thanks to artificial intelligence methods, computers have become smart machines that are capable of producing meaningful results. In order to create artificial intelligence programs, various methods have been developed with regards to "information - knowledge formation". The followings are among the most commonly used ones:

- Rule-Based.
- Framework-Based.
- Semantic Networks (Babalik, 2000; Arici, 2001).

Information: Knowledge Inference

Information - knowledge inference inference refers to examining all the structures and information available in the expert system quickly and systematically. The structure of "inference engine" depends on the characteristics of the problem field and the ways by which information is organized and viewed. Generally, there is not a single and explicit method to find a solution

in problem-solution processes that are based on "knowledge base". Therefore, it is necessary to search for several solutions to find the ideal one at each phase. Similarly, the control structure of problem solution systems also requires performing a search for several solutions. This particular structure defines a general plan for the selection of solution methods. In the inference engine of rule-based systems, there are two separate inference logarithms depending on the method followed to reach the solution, which are

- **Forwards Chaining:** This technique works upwards; from the available information - knowledge towards the results. The important thing here is whether the conditions in "if" part of any rules match with the available information. If it matches, the condition(s) in "then" section is applied. After each inference, the rules are applied again and again until certain results are found for the new inferences (Arici, 2001).
- **Backward Chaining:** In this technique, the engine starts from "then" part of the "if-then" rule during this search process and searches whether there is a rule supporting this result. The system looks at how the rules move. When there is a "then" part, which is suitable for the solution at hand, it deals with the conditions in "if" section of this rule. This process continues until all the rules supporting the results and interim results are found or no rule is left to be applied (Arici, 2001).

As mentioned above, expert systems are being widely used in our daily life. When they are examined within the scope of this study, we can see that a great variety of expert systems is used for educational purposes (Hartschuh, 1990). A detailed analysis of the related literature lists a lot of applications of expert systems in the field of education (Blaine *et al.,* 1977; Brown *et al.,* 1975 Burton, & Brown, 1976; Carnobell, 1970;

Ferrera *et al.*, 1987; Hartschuh, 1990; Haynes *et al.*, 1987; Kearsley, 1985; Lewis *et al.*, 1987; Nichol, 1985; Ozdemir, & Alpaslan, 2000; Roberts, & Park, 1983; Stevens *et al.*, 1982; Thorkildsen *et al.*, 1985-1986; Wertheimer, 1990). What is outstanding with these studies is that they are conducted for a long time period. This situation clearly shows how expert systems and artificial intelligence are used effectively for educational purposes.

Following the provision of basic knowledge about expert systems, the next section deals with the design process of the shell program and its working principles.

DESIGN AND WORKING PRINCIPLES OF SHELL PROGRAM

In this section, the design and working principles of the shell program developed within the scope of this study are explained in detail. In addition, technical and methodological information used during the design process and how courseware is prepared by using this program are among the information presented in this section.

Design of Shell Program

The design phase of the shell program requires the use of a certain number of computer software. Accordingly, Visual Basic programming language was used during code writing stage and SQL Server database management system was used to create the database structure, which is the knowledge base side of the program.

Hierarchical Structure of the Program

Before courseware preparation phase, it is necessary to understand the hierarchical structure of the shell program. The courseware to be prepared consists of pages / screens. These pages will form the topic, topics the section and sections the course, respectively (Figure 2).

While preparing the courseware, each teacher has to enter the necessary information into the given areas in the following order: course, section, topic and page. As the first step to prepare a courseware, when a teacher chooses "New" and "New Course" from the "File" menu, a new page appears on which the definitions regarding the courseware are required to be entered. The teacher is asked to enter the necessary definitions into the blank areas regarding the course such as "Name", "Content", "Goal", "Prequisties" and "References".

At this phase, a "course code" is automatically given by the system to store the information about the course in the database. After the teacher completes the phase by clicking "OK" icon, he is required to enter necessary information into the "Section" unit. The areas to be filled here are "Name", "Content", and "Goal". Next, the system gives a "section code" for further reference. The same procedures are followed for the "Topic" as well. The areas to be filled here are also "Name", "Content", and "Goal". Next, the system gives a `topic code` for this specific topic.

In this hierarchical structure, a "course code" is assigned by the system for each course to store all the information about this particular course. These codes are viewed in the database tables used to develop the program and the information in these database tables is associated via these codes.

Figure 2. The hierarchical structure of courses

Inference Engine

At every phase of a courseware design process by using a shell program, the tool bars change depending on the phase teachers are working on to avoid a potential chaos that might occur due to redundant icons and menus. The way to realize this change is to activate and deactivate these tool bars by using the principles of "forward chaining method" explained in detail in Section II.

Working Principles of Shell Program

By using the main menu in the program, it is quite easy to access already existing courses via "Course List" icon and even to work on these courses. It is also possible to create new course by using the shell program.

While preparing a courseware with this program, the hierarchical structure should be followed strictly, namely, "Courses", "Sections", "Topics", and "Pages" respectively. In other words, the course should be designed according to the following hierarchy: pages will form topics, topics sections and sections courses.

After clicking on "Course List", the tool bar changes and the already existing coursewares are viewed on the left side of the screen (Figure 3).

When one of these existing courses is clicked on, the user accesses the information about the course such as the name of the teacher and other details, that is the information entered while creating this particular course. The "plus" icon next to the course name or section name implies that there are existing courses or sections under the menu.

When a user wishes to create a new course, he must either click on "New Course" icon on the tool bar or choose "New" and "New Course" respectively from "File" menu. When it is necessary to create a new section or new topic under a course, the first thing to do is to click on this particular course or section. Later, "New Section" or "New Topic" option should be clicked on either from the tool bar or "File" menu.

After entering the necessary information about the course, section or topic is entered, it is possible to proceed to the next phase; which is the preparation of the courseware.

Figure 3. A course view on the program

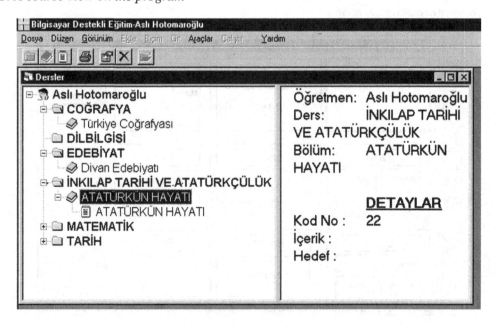

Course Formation

After entering the details about the course, section and topics by accessing to "Course List", it is possible to access courseware design page by clicking on "Open the Topic" icons on either "File" menu or tool bar. If there are previously prepared designs, they are viewed on the screen. If there are no previous designs, a blank page as well as a variety of templates is viewed to assist the user in creating a good design.

The page viewing the templates assists the user in designing the courseware when he wishes to add a new page to the course. The user is asked to double click on the chosen template or click on "OK" icon after the template is chosen. If the user wishes to create the design himself, he can use the blank page by clicking on that template. The general view of this screen is shown in Figure 4.

The tool bar on the left margin of "courseware design page" is called "Object Gallery" and includes a number of icons that will assist the user during the design process. The user works on his design by clicking on the control icons he wishes to use. The Object Gallery and the icons on it as well as their functions are shown in Figure 5.

Each icon available on Object Gallery helps the user to add a new control icon to the design (text, sound and picture etc). Placing the controls on the screen is realized by dragging the icon into the desired area after double clicking on the icon or placing the control icon by using the mouse after clicking once and arranging its size.

When sound, picture of video icon controls are placed on the design, the files can be uploaded from mobile disks or other file storage devices to these control areas.

Formation of the Tests

The shell program developed was also designed to assist teachers to prepare tests. The teacher may either add the tests to the end of each section / topic or tests might be prepared independently.

The first step in preparing a test is to choose "New" and "New Test" options successively from "File" menu. Under this heading there are two options: "Test Wizard" and "Create a Test Manually". In both options, the same screen is accessed, which views general information about the test to be prepared. Here, users are required enter certain information such as "Test Name",

Figure 4. Courseware design screen

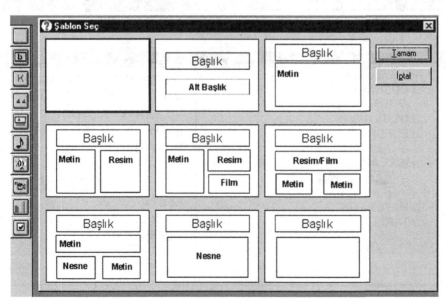

Figure 5. Object Gallery and functions of the icons

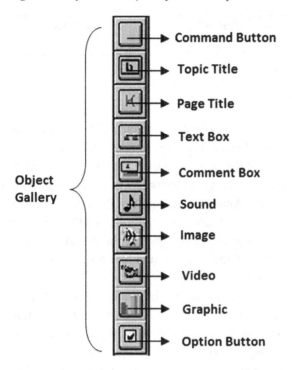

EVALUATION OF THE EFFECTIVENESS OF SHELL PROGRAM

This section presents detailed information about the following: the precautions taken to achieve valid and reliable results in the study; research model, data resources, data collection tools and development of these tools; and data collection and analysis.

"Content", "Goal" and "Prequisties", if applicable. Test preparation module also includes a Object Gallery similar to those in the previous modules. Called "Test Gallery", the gallery includes some templates prepared beforehand according to the question types such as multiple-choice, true/false, and fill-in-the-blanks.

Research Model

This study is based on general investigation and one group pre-test post-test models. The reason for combining these two models is to benefit from the advantages of both models as much as possible.

In the first phase of the study within the framework of investigation model, teachers' opinions about the shell program were obtained. This program was applied to the teachers and the success of the program was evaluated in the second phase by using one group pre-test post-test model, which is presented in Table 2.

Study Group

Before the actual application of the "courseware preparation shell program", a group of experts in the field, who are assumed to have enough knowledge and experience to evaluate such a program, were asked to state their opinions about the program. The study group of the current study consists of education programmers, educational technologists, measurement and evaluation experts, computer programmers, academicians and teachers from various fields of teaching and educational levels.

The criteria used in the selection of those in the working group are as follows:

- Having an adequate level of computer literacy.
- Having academic knowledge, at least at master's degree level, in the field of educational technologies.
- Having knowledge about distance education (e-learning), computer-assisted teaching and coursewares.

Of these criteria, "being knowledgable about distance education (e-learning), computer-assisted teaching and coursewares" and "having academic

Table 1. Research model

Group	Pre-Test	Emprical Investigation	Post-Test
G	T1	Program	T1

knowledge at least at master's degree level in the field of educational technologies" are predetermined to ensure that the experts are competent in the field. Similarly, "having adequate level of computer literacy" is a criterion to guarantee the comprehension of the process.

Subjects of the Study

In the second phase of the study within the framework of "empirical model", the data was collected from a total of 36 computer literate teachers and school administrators from different fields of teaching.

Data Collection Tools

In order to form a sound basis for the study and to achieve the predetermined goals, three types of data collection instruments were used in the current study; which are information form, evaluation survey and achievement test.

Information Form

Information form was developed to obtain information from the subjects of the study including their personal characteriscs and experience with regards to computer technology.

Evaluation Survey

This survey was developed to determine the opinions of the subjects regarding the "expert system shell program", and it consists of Likert type questions.

In order to ensure content validity of the survey, expert opinions were taken. In addition, the survey was piloted to measure construct validity and reliability, and factor analysis (Principal Component Analysis) was applied. Revised according to expert opinions and factors analysis results, the survey was finalized before the actual use. The total variance explanation rate for a single item is 49.790%.

It is necessary to test "internal consistency" in Likert type scales. The best method for this process is to calculate Crombach Alpha Reliability Coefficient, which should be closer to 1 as much as possible to achieve optimum reliability (Yapicioglu, 1991).

The Crombach Alpha Reliability was calculated as .95 for this survey.

Achievement Test

Used for the purpose of determining the knowledge level of the participants about the program before and after the application, this data collection instrument consists of multiple choice questions. The survey was prepared according to the contributions provided by the experts and students. Later, it was piloted with a teacher who has never used the program beforehand. In order to ensure the construct validity, factor analysis was applied on the results obtained from the piloting process. Later, the results of the piloting were examined together with the experts and the survey was revised and finalized accordingly. The data obtained were also used in the analysis of reliability tests and in the determination of the durations of the test. The total variance explanation rate of the survey for a single goal is 54.019%. As for the

Table 2. The results of the survey about the teachers' opinion regarding shell program

Item No	Item	1		2		3		4		5		n	x	ss
		f	%	f	%	f	%	f	%	f	%			
1	It is difficult to use the shell program.	-	-	4	11.1	4	11.1	19	58.2	8	22,2	35	3,88	,90
2	It is confusing to use the shell program.	1	2.8	3	8.3	3	8.3	23	63.9	5	13,9	35	3,80	,90
3	It is intuitional to use the shell program.	1	2.8	2	5.6	8	22.2	20	55.6	3	8,3	34	3,64	,85
4	It is enjoyable to use the shell program.	-	-	-	-	7	19.9	16	44.4	12	33,3	35	4,11	,73
5	It is difficult to learn how to use the shell program.	-	-	2	5.6	10	27.8	16	44.4	8	22,2	36	3,83	,85
6	It is confusing to learn how to use the shell program.	1	2.8	-	-	7	19.4	19	52.8	9	25,0	36	3,97	,84
7	It is intuitional to learn how use the shell program.	1	2.8	2	5.6	10	27.8	18	50.0	4	11,1	35	3,63	,88
8	It is enjoyable to learn how to use the shell program.	-	-	3	8.3	5	13.9	14	38.9	14	38,9	36	4,17	,85
9	I was able to prepare courseware by using the shell program.	-	-	3	8.3	14	38.9	14	38.9	5	13,9	36	3,58	,84
10	I was able to prepare courseware in a very short time by using the shell program.	-	-	3	8.3	15	41.7	12	33.3	6	16,7	36	3,58	,87
11	I save time in class by using the shell program.	-	-	2	5.6	9	25.0	17	47.2	8	22,2	36	3,86	,83
12	It is difficult to organize the course content by using the shell program.	-	-	1	2.8	12	33.3	20	55.6	3	8,3	36	3,69	,67
13	It is confusing to organize the course content by using the shell program.	-	-	1	2.8	11	30.6	19	52.8	5	13,9	36	3,78	,72
14	It is intuitional to organize the course content by using the shell program.	-	-	-	-	11	31.4	22	62.9	2	5,7	35	3,74	,56
15	It is enjoyable to organize the course content by using the shell program.	-	-	-	-	6	16.7	14	38.9	16	44,4	36	4,28	,74
16	It is difficult to correct the mistakes with this program.	1	2.8	-	-	7	19.4	23	63.9	5	13,9	36	3,86	,76
17	It is confusing to correct the mistakes with this program.	-	-	1	2.8	6	16.7	24	66.7	5	13,9	36	3,92	,65
18	It is intuitional to correct the mistakes with this program.	-	-	1	2.8	10	27.8	21	58.3	4	11,1	36	3,78	,68
19	It is enjoyable to correct the mistakes with this program.	-	-	1	2.8	7	19.4	12	33.3	16	44,4	36	4,19	,86
20	I am generally content with this program.	-	-	1	2.8	7	19.4	19	52.8	9	25,0	36	4,00	,76

calculation of reliability, split-half method was used. Alpha reliability coefficient for the first half of the survey was found to be .9246 and for the second half .9743.

Data Collection

The shell program developed was evaluated by a group of experts, and necessary revisions and additions were made accordingly. After this process, the revised version was given back to this expert group for approval and this version was approved by the experts for the application.

Following this approval, other data collection instruments were prepared, namely information form, evaluation survey and achievement test. When the shell program and the data collection instruments were finalized, they are organized as a traning program for the participants. Information form, which aims at determining the participants' personal characteristics and their experiences with computer technologies, was administered to them at the beginning of the training. In addition, they were given the achievement test as the pre-test to measure their background knowledge about the shell program. In the next phase, the subjects were provided with a full-day theoretical training about educational technologies, distance education (e-learning), computer-assisted teaching and coursewares. Later, the researcher gave half-day training on the shell program and its use by considering the data obtained from the pre-test. In this training, the participants were also asked to design sample coursewares they might use in their courses. Finally, an achievement test was administered to the teacher participants to measure their knowledge about the shell program before and after the training. After the administration of the achievement test, which is developed to furnish the users with the target behaviors regarding the use of shell program and used as pre and post-test, shell program evaluation survey was administered.

In order not to affect the flow of this section, the details related to certain evaluation approaches such as information form and achievement test were omitted in this paper. In this respect, the results obtained about teachers' opinions and the basic data regarding the achievement test are presented under the subtitles of the further sections.

Teachers' Opinions Regarding Shell Program

As for the purposes of the second subgoals of the study, the following question was asked: What are the opinions of the teachers about the expert system shell program developed? The "teachers' opinions" obtained were analyzed in terms of the following categories: "easiness to use", "easiness to learn how to use", "the organization of the information related to the subject" and "easiness to correct the mistakes". The results obtained from 5-point Likert-type survey (1-totally disagree, 2- disagree, 3- undecided, 4- agree and 5- totally agree) are presented in Table 2 below:

The results obtained show that expert system shell program used offers a successful approach.

Effectiveness of Shell Program in Terms of Use

The third sub goal of the current study focuses on the "effectiveness of the program with regards to preparing courseware". In order to test this objective, it was calculated whether there is a difference between the pre-test and post-test scores of the teachers using this shell program. For the purposes of this study, the participant teachers were administered a 38-item achievement test about the use of this particular program before and after in-service training program they were provided. The results of the test for pre-test and post-test scores of the teachers in the achievement test are provided in Table 3.

As we can clearly see from the data shown in Table 3 above, the mean score for the achievement test given as the pre-test is x= 16.235. This mean score increased to x=28.117 when the

Table 3. The t-test results for the pre-test post test scores of the teachers

Groups	n	x	ss	X1-X2	t	Significance
Pre-Test	34	16.235	12.434	-11.882	-5.592	.000
Post-Test	34	28.117	6.1829			

same test was administered as the post test to the same participants. In other words, the increase is approximately 12 points. In order to test whether this difference is meaningful or not, a paired t-test was applied to the data and it was found that the difference between pre and post test scores is significant (t=5.592) at α=0.05.

According to this finding, it can be concluded that the program was successful in practice and the teachers who had somewhat little or no previous experience with computers were considerably more successful after they started to use this program. This conclusion also implies that the teachers might be able to prepare courseware in practice by using this program. The relatively high scores obtained in the pre-test might be due to the fact that some of the teachers have already had certain amount of knowledge about computers before the actual study. However, it was found that the teachers who had no previous experience with computers were also able to prepare courseware successfully after the application of the training. This finding is also consistent with the data obtained from the teachers with regards to second subgoal of the study. According to this data, the teachers stated that it is possible to prepare courseware successfully and easily by using this shell program. The results of the actual application can also be said to support this finding as well.

CONCLUSION AND FUTURE WORK

The shell program developed within the scope of the current study mainly aims at meeting the demand for suitable coursewares for educational activities. The development process is based on the data obtained from detailed literature review. It is firmly believed that this study will make valuable contributions to the following issues: to assist teachers in coping with the problems faced while accessing coursewares; to apply and sustain certain approaches such as distance learning (e-learning) and computer-assisted teaching effectively and efficiently; to design coursewares on the basis of teachers' needs and facilities; and to increase the quality of educational processes.

Following the development process of the shell program, the evaluation process was initiated by testing the program on teachers from different fields of teaching and with different levels of experience in computer technology. According to the results obtained, the teachers stated that they were able to prepare courseware in a short time by using the shell program. In addition, they pointed out that they saved time by using this program and they were content with the program.

The results regarding the effectiveness of the shell in terms of use program showed that the program was successful in practice and the teachers with little experience with computers were successful after they used this program. This situation clearly implies that teachers will able to prepare courseware themselves by using this program. The high scores of some participants in the pre-test are due to the fact that they have already had a certain amount of knowledge about computers and two of the teachers are "computer course" teachers. The success rate can be increased by more practices through practice application technique. More importantly, it was found that the teachers with no previous computer experience were also able to prepare course software after the application of the program.

Depending on the expert system shell program used, the possible future works can also be listed as follows:

- The current shell program will be tested on larger groups and necessary improvements and updates will be made on the basis of the findings obtained.
- Detailed studies will be conducted on the limitations and the advantages of the teacher-prepared coursewares through shell program in terms of traditional educational process.
- Considering that teachers are likely to need a great amount of audio-visual materials, videos, photographs and animations while preparing courseware, there will be studies to increase the quality and quantity of such materials.
- Further studies will be carried out to determine how the program elements should be used during courseware preparation process to increase the efficiency of teaching and to what extent each element is effective in realizing this efficiency.
- It is also projected that various artificial intelligence techniques should be integrated into the program in order to improve certain processes of the program such as assessment.
- Finally, a number of studies will be conducted to test the program in different countries and educational institutions, and the results will be evaluated accordingly.

REFERENCES

Alkan, C. (1995). *Eğitim Teknolojisi*. Ankara: Atilla Publishing. (In Turkish)

Alkan, C., Deryakulu, D., & Şimşek, N. (1995). *Eğitim Teknolojisine Giriş: Disiplin, Süreç, Ürün*. Ankara: Onder Publishing. (In Turkish)

Arici, N. (2001). *Tarımsal İstatistik Analizlerinde Uzman Sistemlerin Kullanımı* [Usage of Expert Systems in Agricultural Statistical Analyzes]. (PhD Thesis). Ankara University, Institute of Natural Sciences, Ankara, Turkey.

Babalik, A. (2000). *Uzman Sistemlerin Teşhis Amaçlı Kullanımı* [Usage of Expert Systems for Diagnosis]. (Master's Thesis). Gazi University, Institute of Natural Sciences, Ankara, Turkey.

Blaine, L., & Smith, R. L. (1977). Intelligent CAI: The Role of the Curriculum in Suggesting Computational Models of Reasoning. In *Proceedings of the 1977 AC Annual Conference*, (pp. 241-246). Seattle, WA: AC.

Bonnet, A. (1988). *Expert Systems: Principles and Practise*. New York: Prentice Hall.

Brown, J. S., Burton, R. R., & Bell, A. G. (1975). SOPHIE: A step toward creating a reactive Learning environment. *International Journal of Man-Machine Studies*, 7, 675–696. doi:10.1016/S0020-7373(75)80026-5

Burton, R., & Brown, J. S. (1976). A tutoring and student modelling paragigm for gaming environments. *Computer Science Education*, 8(19), 236–246.

Carnobell, J. R. (1970). AI in CAI: An Artificial Intelligence approach to Computer assisted Instruction. *IEEE Transactions on Man-Machine Systems*, MMS11(4).

Ferrera, J. M., Prater, M. A., & Baer, R. (1987). Using an expert system for complex conceptual training. *Educational Technology*, 27(5), 43–49.

Frenzel, J. F. (1987). *Understanding Expert Systems*. Howard W. Sams & Company.

Hartschuh, W. (1990). Expert Systems in Education. Educational Resources Information Center (ERIC), ED329224.

Haynes, J. A., Pilato, V., & Malouf, D. B. (1987). Expert system for educational decision-making. *Educational Technology*, 27(5), 37–42.

Kearsley, G. (1985). The CBT advisor: An expert system program for making decisions about CBT. *Performance and Education*, 24(9), 15–17.

Lewis, M. W., Milson, R., & Anderson, J. (1987). The teacher's apprentice: Designing an Intelligent Authoring System for High School Mathematics. In Artificial Intelligence & Instruction Applications and Methods (pp. 269-301). Addison-Wesley Publishing Company.

Nichol, J. (1985). Classroom-based curriculum development, artificial intelligence and history teaching. *Journal of Curriculum Studies*, 17(2), 211–214. doi:10.1080/0022027850170210

Ozdemir, B., & Alpaslan, F. N. (2000). Web-Tabanlı Derslerde Öğrenciye Kılavuzluk Eden Akıllı Bir Ajan [An Intelligent Agent Guiding Students in Web-Based Courses]. In *Proceedings of Conference on Education in the Light of Informatics Technology*, (pp. 71-81). Ankara, Turkey: Academic Press.

Roberts, F. C., & Park, O. (1983). Intelligent computer-assisted instruction: An explanation and overview. *Educational Technology*, 23(12), 7–11.

Stevens, A. L., Collins, A., & Coldin, S. E. (1982). *Misconceptions in Student's Understanding*. New York: Intelligent Tutoring Systems.

Thorkildsen, R. J., Lubke, M. M., Myette, B. M., Beverly, M., & Parry, J. D. (1985-1986). Artificial intelligence: Applications in education. *Educational Research Quarterly*, 10(1), 2–9.

Turban, E. (1992). *Artificial Intelligence*. California State University at Long Beach.

Wertheimer, R. (1990). The geometry proof tutor: An "intelligent" computer-based tutor in the classroom. *Mathematics Teacher*, 84(4), 308–317.

Yapicioglu, N. (1991). *Uzman Sistemler ve Uygulamaları* [Expert Systems and Their Applications]. (Master's Thesis). Istanbul Technical University, Institute of Natural Sciences, Istanbul, Turkey.

Yavuzer, Y. (1996). *Uzman Sistemler ve Yapay Zeka*. Istanbul: War Academy Publishing. (In Turkish)

ADDITIONAL READING

Akerkar, R., & Sajja, P. (2010). *Knowledge-Based Systems*. USA: Jones & Bartlett Learning.

Asabere, N. Y., & Enguah, S. E. (2012). Integration of Expert Systems in Mobile Learning 1.

Biondo, S. J. (1990). *Fundamentals of Expert Systems Technology: Principles and Concept*. New Jersey: Intellect Books.

Brighton, H., & Selina, H. (2007). *Introducing artificial intelligence*. Cambridge, United Kingdom: Icon Books Ltd.

Cawsey, A. (1997). *The essence of artificial intelligence*. Upper Saddle River, NJ: Prentice Hall.

Ekbia, H. R. (2008). *Artificial dreams: The quest for non-biological intelligence*. New York, NY: Cambridge University Press. doi:10.1017/CBO9780511802126

Giarratano, J. C., & Riley, G. D. (2004). *Expert Systems: Principles and Programming*. Course Technology.

Hwang, G. J., Chen, C. Y., Tsai, P. S., & Tsai, C. C. (2011). An Expert System for Improving Web-Based Problem-Solving Ability of Students. *Expert Systems with Applications*, 38, 8664–8672. doi:10.1016/j.eswa.2011.01.072

Jackson, P. (1998). *Introduction to Expert Systems*. England: Addison-Wesley.

Jaques, P. A., Seffrin, H., Rubi, G., Morais, F., Ghilardi, C., Bittencourt, I. I., & Isotani, S. (2013). Rule-based expert systems to support step-by-step guidance in algebraic problem solving: The case of the tutor PAT2Math. *Expert Systems with Applications*, *40*, 5456–5465. doi:10.1016/j.eswa.2013.04.004

Jones, M. T. (2008). *Artificial intelligence: A systems approach (Computer science)*. Hingham, MA: Infinity Science Press.

Kou, G., Ergu, D., & Shi, Y. (2014). An integrated expert system for fast disaster assessment. *Computers & Operations Research*, *42*, 95–107. doi:10.1016/j.cor.2012.10.003

Lucci, S., & Kopec, D. (2012). [*st* century, Dulles, USA: Mercury Learning and Information.]. *Artificial Intelligence*, 21.

Luger, G. F. (2008). *Artificial intelligence: Structures and strategies for complex problem solving*. Boston, MA: Addison Wesley.

Magoulas, G. D., Papanikolaou, K. A., & Grigoriadou, M. (2001). Neuro-fuzzy synergism for planning the content in a web-based course. *Informatica*, *25*, 39–48.

Mark, M. A., & Greer, J. E. (1993). Evaluation Methods for Intelligent Tutoring Systems. *Journal of Artificial Intelligence in Education*, *4*, 129–153.

Mitrovic, A., Ohlsson, S., & Barrow, D. K. (2013). The effect of positive feedback in a constraint-based intelligent tutoring system. *Computers & Education*, *60*, 264–272. doi:10.1016/j.compedu.2012.07.002

Mourlas, C., & Germanakos, P. (2008). *Intelligent user interfaces: Adaptation and personalization systems and technologies*. Hershey, PA: Information Science Reference. doi:10.4018/978-1-60566-032-5

Murray, T. (1998). Authoring Knowledge Based Tutors: Tools for Content, Instructional Strategy, Student Module and Interface Design. *Journal of the Learning Sciences*, *7*(1), 5–64. doi:10.1207/s15327809jls0701_2

Neapolitan, R. E. (2012). *Probabilistic reasoning in expert systems: theory and algorithms*. CreateSpace Independent Publishing Platform.

Negnevitsky, M. (2004). *Artificial intelligence: A guide to intelligent systems*. Boston, MA: Addison Wesley.

Nilsson, N. J. (2009). *The quest for artificial intelligence*. New York, NY: Cambridge University Press. doi:10.1017/CBO9780511819346

O'Neil Jr, H. F., Ni, Y., Jacoby, A., & Swigger, K. M. (2013). Human benchmarking for the evaluation of expert systems. *Echnology Assessment in Software Applications*, 13.

Oentaryo, R. J., Er, M. J., Linn, S., & Li, X. (2014). Online Probabilistic Learning for Fuzzy Inference System. *Expert Systems with Applications*. doi:10.1016/j.eswa.2014.01.034

Peredo, R., Canales, A., Menchaca, A., & Peredo, I. (2011). Intelligent Web-based education system for adaptive learning. *Expert Systems with Applications*, *38*, 14690–14702. doi:10.1016/j.eswa.2011.05.013

Post, G. V., & Whisenand, T. G. (2005). An Expert System Helps Students Learn Database Design. *Decision Sciences Journal of Innovative Education*, *3*(2), 273–293. doi:10.1111/j.1540-4609.2005.00070.x

Russell, S. (2009). *Artificial intelligence: A modern approach*. Upper Saddle River, NJ: Prentice Hall.

Schalkoff, R. J. (2011). *Intelligent Systems: Principles, Paradigms and Pragmatics*. USA: Jones & Bartlett Learning.

Subramanian, M. R. (2014). Implementation of Combat Simulation Through Expert Support Systems. *Defence Science Journal*, *37*(4), 443–456.

Warwick, K. (2011). *Artificial Intelligence: The Basics*. London, UK: Routledge.

Winston, P. H. (1992). *Artificial intelligence*. Boston, MA: Addison Wesley.

Yasnoff, W. A., & Miller, P. L. (2014). Decision support and expert systems in public health. In *Public health informatics and information systems* (pp. 449–467). Springer London. doi:10.1007/978-1-4471-4237-9_23

Zhang, X. (2014, January). Research of Modern Physical Education Technology Based on Artificial Intelligence. In *Proceedings of the 2012 International Conference on Cybernetics and Informatics* (pp. 435-442). Springer New York.

KEY TERMS AND DEFINITIONS

Artificial: An an object, which is not natural but trying to simulate the related natural dynamics.

Artificial Intelligence: (1) A field of Computer Science, which is based on research studies or developments on providing intelligent systems simulating the human-thinking behavior or human intelligence.

Artificial Intelligence: (2) A term that is used to describe the feature, function or characteristic of computer systems or machines that try to simulate human-thinking behavior or human intelligence.

Educational Technology: The field in which technology oriented, supportive education materials are researched, analyzed, and applied.

Expert: Anyone, who has well-knowledge and well-structured experience on a particular field.

Expert System: An Artificial Intelligence system - technique, which is based on a software system using expert knowledge to evaluate a problem - diagnosis situation and give responses - feedback to the computer user.

Inference Engine: An algorithmic, logical and mathematical processing object, which is used to obtain results from some cases expressed in certain linguistic structures.

Inference: The action of obtaining logical conclusions from some premises.

Knowledge Base: A type of information - data base, which is derived from a human related experience or information.

Shell Program: A program - software structure, which is plain, simple and only focuses on the problem - objective scope.

Chapter 12

An Example Application of an Artificial Intelligence-Supported Blended Learning Education Program in Computer Engineering

Tuncay Yigit
Suleyman Demirel University, Turkey

Asim Sinan Yuksel
Suleyman Demirel University, Turkey

Arif Koyun
Suleyman Demirel University, Turkey

Ibrahim Arda Cankaya
Suleyman Demirel University, Turkey

Utku Kose
Usak University, Turkey

ABSTRACT

Blended Learning is a learning model that is enriched with traditional learning methods and online education materials. Integration of face-to-face and online learning with blending learning can enhance the learning experience and optimize seat time. In this chapter, the authors present the teaching of an Algorithm and Programming course in Computer Engineering Education via an artificial intelligence-supported blended learning approach. Since 2011, Computer Engineering education in Suleyman Demirel University Computer Engineering Department is taught with a blended learning method. Blended learning is achieved through a Learning Management System (LMS) by using distance education technology. The LMS is comprised of course materials supported with flash animations, student records, user roles, and evaluation systems such as surveys and quizzes that meet SCORM standards. In this chapter, the related education process has been supported with an intelligent program, which is based on teaching C programming language. In this way, it has been aimed to improve educational processes within the related course and the education approach in the department. The blended learning approach has been evaluated by the authors, and the obtained results show that the introduced artificial intelligence-supported blended learning education program enables both teachers and students to experience better educational processes.

DOI: 10.4018/978-1-4666-6276-6.ch012

INTRODUCTION

Blended learning has various definitions in litera-ture. In a study by Finn *et al.* (2004), C. Procter *et al.* (2003), it is defined as the combination of best features of traditional learning and online learning. However, the definition has evolved to encompass combinations of various learning strategies such as blending offline and online learning, blending structured and unstructured learning etc. Singh *et al.* (2003), Lotrecchiano *et al.* (2013). The goal is to combine the best parts of face-to-face edu-cation and online education. Students engage in interactive experiences. Additionally, the online courses provide students with rich multimedia content at anytime, anywhere with Internet ac-cess from university or home. This increases the scheduling flexibility of students. There are many ways of applying blended learning. There-fore there are no certain rules to define what the ideal blend might be. The term "blended" has a broad meaning and it includes the integration of e-learning and traditional face-to-face learning. The blend of these learning models depends on the online materials, the needs of the students, and the instructor requirements.

In our study, we define the blended learning as the coherent integration of face-to-face and e-learning to address our educational goals. When blended learning is understood and applied care-fully, it will offer great advantage for students and teachers, Geraldine *et al.* (2012). Some of these advantages are as follows:

- Blended learning supports effective and strong socializing environment through face-to-face learning.
- Students' academic performance can be improved through blended learning.
- It allows reaping a profit by minimizing the cost of education, travel, and classroom.
- Blended learning can diagnose a student's learning level.

- It provides an environment for students to work in a relaxed environment, instead of moving through school.
- It gives students full control of their education.

In our approach, face-to-face and e-learning models are combined. Main courses such as programming and hardware-based courses are taught face-to-face and the other courses are taught online. Online courses part into two sections as synchronized and asynchronized. Asynchronous courses are applied through Learning Manage-ment System (LMS). Students can access the past courses; submit their homework and projects through this system. Additionally, they are allowed to choose how they will access the necessary learning materials. In synchronized section of the online courses, students join the class in specific time determined by the department. Through this education model, the courses are followed interactively and independent of location in the same time zone. Owing to developing technology, students now have the opportunity to participate in education remotely and communicate online without meeting face-to-face as it is in traditional learning model. It is important that the related e-learning process has been supported with also an intelligent program, which is based on teaching C programming language. In this way, it has been aimed to improve educational processes within the related course and the education approach in the department. The blended learning approach has been evaluated by the authors and obtained results show that the introduced artificial intelligence supported blended learning education program enables both teachers and students to experience better educational processes.

The rest of the paper is organized as follows: In Section 2, we define the blended learning and its components, explain internet based, computer based and mobile learning that comprise the online learning section of blended learning. Section 3 presents the application of blended learning on Algorithm and Programming course that is taken by junior students in fall semester in Computer Engineering Department. In Section 4, we discuss about the Artificial Intelligence based program, which has been used along the e-learning side of the blended learning. Next, in Section 5, we discuss about the evaluation results of the performed educational application and finally, in Section 6, we provide conclusions of our study.

BLENDED LEARNING AND ITS COMPONENTS

In traditional learning, the classes are always physically located in specific places and the courses are thought at specific times. On the other hand, in blended learning, the learning process can take place at anytime, anywhere by benefiting from technology. Table 1 shows the main differences between the traditional learning model and the blended learning model Asif *et al.* (2012).

Blended learning is an educational model that is the combination of traditional (face-to-face) and online learning (e-learning) models Asif *et al.* (2012). It provides easily accessible and motivating learning environment by combining the motivation and inspiration of traditional learning approach with the convenience and flexibility of e-learning, Demirer et al. (2009). Online portion of blending learning model has two sub-parts that are network based and non-network based learning. While network based learning comprises of Internet and web based learning, the other part

comprises of computer based and mobile learning. Figure 1 shows the components of Blending learning model Hadjerrouit *et al.* (2008).

Online Learning (E-Learning)

Rapid evolution of technology has a positive effect on education system and changes the education environment. With the widespread use of the personal computers and Internet, computer based learning has been popular and the education environment has moved to Internet. In 21st Century, this technology has been indispensable part of our lives and the name is changed to e-Learning.

e-Learning is a learning and teaching model that is designed to be carried out by using electronic media, Bourne et al. (1996). It is less expensive than the traditional learning approach, not limited to a specific geographic location and more flexible in terms of time. It replaces the traditional learning where it cannot operate. While the computers make the learning easier, Internet technology acts as a communication bridge interconnecting other computers and people making the learning process interactive, Bell et al. (2013). Online learning or e-learning has two sub-parts that are Internet and web based learning Hadjerrouit *et al.* (2008).

Internet Based Learning

The formal use of Internet Based Learning began with the establishment of moderated newsgroups in 1960s, Georgiev et al. (2004). However, it is a new type of distance learning model that uses the Internet technology to deliver the course materials

Table 1. Differences between traditional learning and blended learning model

Main Features of Education	Traditional Learning	Blended Learning
Location	In Physical Classes (Not Flexible)	Anywhere (Flexible)
Learning Method	Face-to-Face	Face-to-Face and Online
Learning Time	At Specific Time (Not Flexible)	Any time (Flexible)
Technology Usage	No obligation for using the technology	It is a necessity to use the technology

Figure 1. Blended learning and its components

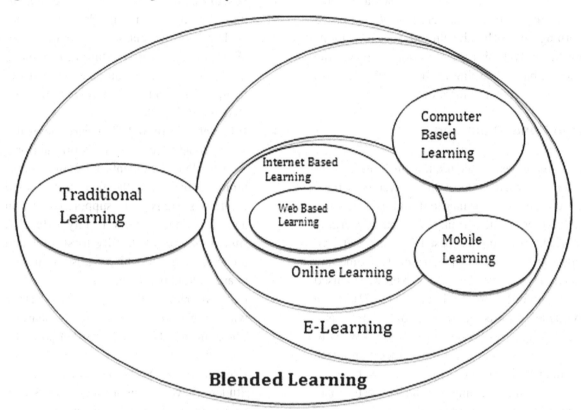

to students Torkul et al. (2005). In this model, a virtual communication way is established between the students and teacher. On one end, teacher lectures and on the other end students join the class and take courses from different cities, countries. The learner does not only takes information, she or he also contributes, interacts, constructs the knowledge that enable the learning process, Hill et al. (2004).

Universities, colleges, schools, training facilities have seen the power of the Internet and this power removed the time and place barriers for the delivery of education:

- Many companies have begun to develop computer-based training software and continuing to develop software modules that are accessible via an Internet browser.

- HTML editors, web-publishing tools are being used by many educators to prepare assignments, presentations, post announcements, videos, animations. to support course activities.

- Corporate organizations are now focused on rich multimedia systems to share knowledge within the company and train their employees by teaching them the new technology.

- Virtual universities are being established that offer online courses and degrees using Internet technologies.

- Software development companies such as Google, Microsoft, Adobe have been developing sophisticated learning platforms that include interactive collaboration tools such as email, interactive discussion, shared spaces, video conferencing.

Although there have been many advancements in technology that empowers the Internet based learning, current bandwidth and speed limitations are the only limiting factors that prevents the Internet based learning from being the de facto technology standard for education.

Web Based Learning

We use the web to acquire information. In computer engineering education, the web is increasingly used as a learning tool and as a delivery method for online learning. Web based learning is similar to computer based learning that provides an environment independent of time and location, yet differs because web browser is used for communication, Khalifa *et al.* (2002). It is a hypermedia based teaching program that uses the resources on World Wide Web (WWW) to promote and support learning process in a rich learning environment. In this model, web is used as learning and teaching tool and it is not the main goal, Boisvert et al. (2000).

Current research on web-based learning shows that one of the effective ways of learning and teaching is using the technology. Teachers, trainers can create interactive course materials that include online activities, animations, and presentations via programming or plug-ins. These affect the learning process in a positive way, and learning is meaningful and enjoyable.

In these types of systems, students login with a user name and password assigned to them. It is possible to generate student reports containing the exact time a student connected to the system, duration of connection, information regarding the lectures he/she studied, quizzes, exams he/she took. In addition, students' course performance can be evaluated, students and the teacher can meet online and realize interactive learning activities.

There are several types of teaching strategies for Web Based Learning. By applying some of these strategies, computer-engineering education can be more effective. Some of these strategies are:

- **Discussions:** This involves establishing relations, discussing ideas with other students in the classroom environment. Teachers can assign reading tasks, start a discussion; students can gain access to e-mail, discussion boards, or chat with other students and teacher.
- **Interactive Support:** Teachers can evaluate students based on their work and provide feedback. Students have the opportunity to partner with other students and create a synergy. The support can be in any direction such as faculty-to-faculty, student-to-student, faculty to student and it can make use of whiteboards, discussion boards, cloud based sharing.
- **Data Sharing:** This involves data sharing with others locally or remotely sharing. The collected data can be further analyzed to conduct a research, produce results.
- **Collaborative Software Development:** Students have the opportunity to work on a project with others independent of location and time, code together to develop a software product, share resources such as databases, exchanging ideas and documents and work on the same document simultaneously. Teachers can comment on the work, identify the weaknesses and improve students' ability to code.
- **Simulations:** Online simulations can help students better understand how stuff works by seeing them in action.
- **Data Exploration:** Students can see real world cases, use Web data to make decisions, develop and test software based on the data that has been gathered from the web.
- **Online Practice:** This involves accessing and preparing online materials; practicing and applying acquired knowledge, create exercises; code software using popular programming languages such as Java, Flash and distribute them online.

Computer Based Learning

This type of learning model contains computer-aided education. Learning materials and activities are delivered via computers without connecting to a network, Inga *et al.* (2013). Computers are used as an environment where the learning takes place. They are not the purpose, yet a learning tool that provides information to learners Pea *et al.* (1990). The underlying principles of this learning model are stimulation, response and strengthen elements. Along the learning process, students strengthen themselves by answering the questions directed at them and interact with the courses loaded to their computers that establish the learning.

There are many advantages of computer based learning in comparison to traditional face-to-face learning. Some of the advantages are:

- Location independency.
- Time and cost reduction.
- Ability to choose learning materials freely according to knowledge level and learning skills.
- Self-paced learning.
- Flexibility.
- Interactive learning.
- Applicability of different learning styles and facilitates the learning process.
- Develops computer and Internet skills.
- Building self-confidence, self-knowledge and encouragement through computer-based courses.

Although there are many advantages, there are some disadvantages. Some of these are:

- Causes falling behind if the students have low motivation or wrong studying habits.
- If students have weak computer skills, they may be confused or loose focus about course activities.
- Physical isolation from other students and the teacher.

- Unavailability of instructor when help is needed.
- Slow Internet connections or computers may have bad influence on learning.

Mobil Learning (M-Learning)

Mobile Learning (M-Learning) is the newest type of learning model where the learning process takes place in mobile phones or tablets, Georgiev et al. (2004). The term "Mobile" is also percepted as portability. Owing to this perception, the number of various devices and approaches that are to be used in this model has increased. M-Learning provides a new environment for the learning model that does not follow a formal and specific plan, Peters *et al.* (2010).

There are differences that separate this model from other learning activities. Most distinctive difference is that the learners are always on the move. This makes the learning process independent from time and location. The learner can start and interfere the learning process anytime, anywhere. Furthermore, people are to communicate with the rest of the world without needing big personal computers and cables.

According to the statistical data that International Telecommunication Union (ITU) published in 2013, currently, there are 6.8 billion mobile phones in the world, ITU *et al.* (2013). The results of this data shows that it is possible to reach these many people via M-Learning and how powerful this model can be. In the near future, integrating the flash animations, Web 2.0 tools and virtual reality applications to all mobile systems will make these platforms more attractive. Considering the advances in mobile technologies, fast Internet connection that the 4G technology provides and increasing number of mobile users, it is feasible to say that M-Learning will become more attractive, effective and it will be applied extensively in near future, Keskin *et al.* (2010).

THE APPLICATION OF BLENDED LEARNING IN COMPUTER ENGINEERING

This study analyzes the Algorithm and Programming course in an artificial intelligence supported blended learning program in 2012 and 2013 fall semesters. Before discussing about the artificial intelligence side of the work - approach, it is also better to talk about the general application of the blended learning approach in our study.

Algorithm and Programming course is given to the students who are enrolled in computer engineering program in Engineering Faculty in the first year of their education semester. The main purpose of this course is to help students gain programming abilities through participating in C programming applications. This course is taught for duration of 15 weeks with 3 hours theory, 1-hour lab. Subjects are divided into 8 main units as shown in Table 2.

Conceptualizing Phase: Programming Concept

Algorithm and Programming course is designed to support conceptualizing phase in blended learning model. The aim in this phase is to establish a connection between students past knowledge and course structure. The most important mission of the teacher is to eliminate the students' prejudgments about programming. Thus, the teacher needs to demonstrate that the students' past knowledge will help them to understand the new subjects about programming. For example, if the teacher is teaching while-loop structure and student has past knowledge of if condition, integers, students must be able to learn the new subjects by using their past knowledge. Teacher should prove that students' past knowledge is not the exact solution. If a student wants to create a set that includes ten numbers, they should use an array instead of defining ten variables. Therefore, the new learning concept is combined with stu-

Table 2. Weekly schedule of algorithm and programming course

Schedule	Units	Course Subject
Week 1	Unit 1	Description of Algorithm, Using flowchart, Mathematical expressions
Week 2		
Week 3		Using conditional expressions in algorithms
Week 4		Loop algorithm
Week 5	Unit 2	Basic input/output libraries
Week 6		Basic input/output transactions
Week 7	Unit 3	While loop, Do-While loop
Week 8	Midterm Exam	Midterm exam that includes first three units
Week 9	Unit 4	For loop, infinite and dead loops
Week 10	Unit 5	Arrays, Powers of array: loops, character arrays and multi-dimensional arrays.
Week 11	Unit 6	Structures in C Pointer with Structures Nested structures in C
Week 12	Unit 7	Definition of pointers Usage of pointers Pointers with functions
Week 13	Unit 8	Description of Function Function prototypes Local and global variables Some most frequently used functions in C
Week 14	Repetition Units	Course Summary
Week 15	Final Exam	Final exam that includes all units

dents' past knowledge. According to Hadjerrouit et al. (2008), some pedagogical methods can be applied to algorithm and programming concept:

- **Multiple Presentations:** Multiple presentations should be used when teaching programming. The presentation can be linguistic, verbal, symbolic and pictorial. All programming concepts must include many kinds of presentations.
- **Comparison and Opposition:** Programming concept should include comparison and opposition.

- **Forward and Backward Samples:** Samples should be referenced according to previous programming knowledge and the new programming concepts.
- **Investigation:** Applicability conditions of programming concepts should be investigated.
- **Classification and Categorization:** Concepts should be classified and categorized according to the specifications of concepts.

Structural Phase: Programming Action

Algorithm and Programming course is redesigned to support structural phase in blended learning model. This model is a process that computer programs are created with task-based activities [In our study, we have supported these activities with also artificial intelligence based C programming program, which enables students to solve problems via intelligent feedbacks (the program will be introduced in the Section 4)]. During the process, students are directed to produce C programs. This process should be continuous and always renew itself. Students must be able to build application with the knowledge they have already learned. Difficulty level of application should be made incremental such as spiral model. Assigning tasks that are feasible in real life motivates the students during structural phase. According to Hadjerrouit *et al.* (2008), programming requires analytical and critical thinking abilities, which are as follows:

- **Analysis and Design:** Having the ability to analyze and design is crucial since the students always tend to code without analyzing and designing. Students should learn to analyze programming problems by gaining the ability to analyze and design. In analysis phase, they should solve the programming problem and design a suit-

able algorithm before coding. It is required for a student to develop these skills before coding.
- **Improvement:** This strategy is highly important. Some problems are resolved through prior encountered and solved problems. Students should be able to renew their knowledge and improve themselves to solve similar problems.
- **Comparison and Opposition:** Comparison and opposition are alternative methods for finding the most effective solution.
- **Estimation of Program Behavior:** Estimation of Program behavior is an important subject. Thus, students should be able to estimate the situations about program behavior.
- **Producing Alternative Solutions:** Students usually have only one way to reach the solution during coding. When they find a solution, they directly start coding, and never stop. However, this approach is not effective since they may be alternative solutions that are more effective.

Face-to-Face Conversation Phase: Interactions, Collaborations, and Discussions

Algorithms and Programming course is designed to support the face-to-face conversation techniques of blended learning model. In other words, it is evaluating the programming techniques and activities of students through dialogs. This approach can be applied parallel to the first and second education models or separately. According to Hadjerrouit *et al.* (2008), some pedagogical strategies may be applied to this approach:

- **Illustration (Summarizing, Defining, Discussing):** This strategy facilitates student learning by allowing them to explain the programming process, produce solutions for new conditions and applying ideas.

- **Meta-Communication:** Students generally think that a solution is only valid for a specific program. However, the program must be readable and understandable by others, thus facilitating fixing the program specific errors. Establishing a clear meta-communication is important for successful programming. Teachers should explain and emphasize the importance of meta-communication to the students.

Online Resources

Most important criteria for online resources that are designed for conceptualization are preparing accurate presentations, accessibility, and effective illustrations. These criteria have direct influences upon students. Strategies for online resource strategies that are designed for conceptualization are as follows:

- Explaining the programming techniques according to pedagogical principles.
- Designing user-friendly interfaces and providing accurate links for study materials.
- Explaining the programming concepts in a clear and understandable manner.

In the next phase, online resources are re-designed to support structural methods. Most important online resources for structural methods are as follows:

- Preparing well-designed online programming examples for students to work with.
- Providing interactive online support for students to solve programming problems.
- Providing program codes that are easy to use and modify.

- Preparing online presentations that contain multiple components such as text, graphics, pictures and symbols.
- Providing links to past online exams and programming exercises.

Finally, this course is re-designed to support face-to-face conversation phase of blended education model, discussing students' solutions for programming exercise, sharing solutions with students and teachers via e-mail and Internet.

Thus, online resources should contain the followings:

- Synchronized communication for students to communicate in real time.
- Asynchronous communication for accessing forums, e-mails at anytime, anywhere.
- Programming questions that are to be solved by students individually or with a group and graded, commented on by teachers.

In addition to the related online resources, the intelligent side of our blended learning model approach can also be evaluated in the context of online resources (actually, the artificial intelligence program could be analyzed in every phase - application side of our model). The program is some kind of online material and can be used by students along the learning activities. It can be expressed here that the program is the most important educational component of our model; among other online resources.

Applied Artificial Intelligence Supported Blended Learning Model

Application of our blended learning model involves three methods in learning cycle. First, the teacher determines the concepts and the programming activities to be taught every week through 15 weeks. The teacher identifies the insufficiencies of the applied methods by examining the activities and establishes links between previously known concepts with the new concepts to be taught. Along these activities, an artificial intelligence based C programming teaching program takes active role in order to improve the process.

The main purpose of the course is to teach programming and provide algorithmic reasoning skills to students. Teacher cultivates the students' abilities to understand the programming concepts. Subsequently, students endeavor to produce solutions for programming problems. For instance, if the programming concepts that are to be taught are related to "while loop", students perform activities related to "while loop" structure. Students work individually or by joining to small groups. The task of the teacher is to direct the students to think more deeply, creatively. Learning how to program is an iterative and continuous process that lasts for 15 weeks and comprises of renewal, improvement and change. Students spend their most important time on programming activities. Through this time, students provide solutions and present their ideas. Along these activities, they are also directed with the artificial intelligence based program as a supportive component. Briefly, it can be said that students are free to spend their time on the program; but in our study the teacher is more encouraged to decide when the program will be used by the students along the educational process. So, it has given a flexible, intelligent blended learning flow along the work. As another flexible aspect of the model, teachers also have had the opportunity to improve themselves, renew course materials, and change the way they teach by meeting students face to face or creating online surveys, polls.

Blended Learning Studio Environment

Computer engineering department has a studio that includes synchronous and asynchronous education that is a part of blended learning. The studio is built in a 15 m² area that has a high level sound insulation. The studio has a fully equipped computer, a high definition camera and a microphone to create an interactive course environment. In addition, there is a smart board, which provides a large screen for teaching, and a projector that reflects computer screen to smart board (Figure 2).

Blended Learning Course Delivery Method

In computer engineering blended learning program, 30% of courses is taught face-to-face, and 70% is taught online. To protect the education quality, same teachers teach the courses in traditional

Figure 2. Some photos from the studio environment

education program and the distance education program. Additionally, students in traditional education program and blended learning program take the same exams at the same place. Teachers decide carefully when choosing face-to-face courses. Face-to-face courses must be suitable for online delivery and must enable interaction.

ARTIFICIAL INTELLIGENCE PROGRAM FOR TEACHING C PROGRAMMING

As it was mentioned before, the related e-learning process of the blended learning model of this study has been supported with also an artificial intelligence based program, which aims supporting the activities of teaching C programming language. The program has been designed and developed by Kose, and Deperlioglu (2012) along with some other Artificial Intelligence based programs, which were introduced in the context of their research work. Because the related programs have been applied successfully along different courses and caused positive results, programs have also been employed for some other experimental research works performed in different time and environment conditions (Tufekci, & Kose, 2013). From their work, the main features and functions of the program can be expressed briefly as follows (2012):

"The artificial intelligence based program for teaching C programming language is some kind of an intelligent learning environment in which students can take some exercises by using an easy to use interface and teachers can define new C programming exercises with the provided tools. The program allows teachers to create new exercises by using a management interface provided in the system. For each exercise, the teacher can define the problem text and develop what would be the correct solution to that problem in the same way as a student would do. Moreover, domain expert knowledge of the program can also be adjusted for specific exercises by using the management interface of the system. All of these operations can

be done easily by using the interface supported with drag and drop feature and simple system controls.

From students' perspective, the program interface is some kind of tool, which assembles different system controls to get the representation of solutions and deliver exercises, feedbacks and information. Over this program, students must apply their knowledge on C programming to develop solutions for given exercises. Related solutions must be given in a special form, which can be parsed and understood easily by the system of the program. To achieve this, some specific using features and functions were included in the system. For instance, the system interface allows solution C programs to be built by means of a drag and drop feature, which limits the actions that can be done in the program and focuses students' ideas on solving processes instead of writing C source codes. Eventually, this function permits the program to trace all actions performed by students and facilitates the adaptation, which can be provided by the system."

Figure 3 represent a screenshot from the interface viewed by students (Kose, & Deperlioglu, 2012).

"The interface, which can be viewed by students, consists of three different parts. These parts provide all necessary elements, which enable students to understand problem of the given exercise, develop a possible solution for this exercise and view obtained results. The first part is located on top of the interface and used to show 'problem text' of the given exercise. Under this part, the 'workspace', where students can develop a solution C code for the given exercise, is located. By using this part, the student can start to create a solution C code or edit the developed one according to the received feedbacks. It is easy to edit any written code (block) by double-clicking on it. The workspace includes two buttons named as 'Compile' and 'Runtime Screen' respectively. The 'Compile' button is used to execute developed solution programs. On the other hand, the 'Runtime Screen' button is used to open a new window, where students can view the "runtime" of

Figure 3. A screenshot from the interface viewed by students

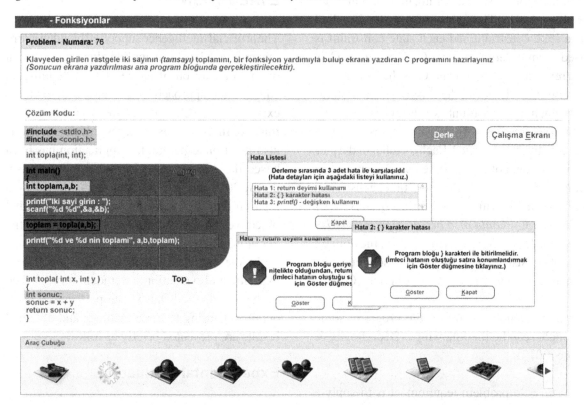

the solution program after the compiling process. After a successful compiling process, this window is also opened automatically by the program. The last part of the interface, which is also named as 'Tool Bar', is located under the workspace. The Tool Bar includes many different elements that can be used to develop a solution C program on the workspace. Students can use the provided elements to define different program parts like declarations, preprocessors, if statements, iteration (loops), functions…etc. Each element can be added to the workspace by dragging the element icon and dropping it into the workspace. When adding an element to the workspace, some additional information such as names, parameters, types… etc. is also requested by the system. The program also views different code types in separate 'layer' elements. This feature allows teachers and students to understand code structure easily and enables system to evaluate developed programs faster.

After developing a solution for the given exercise, the student can start the evaluation process by clicking on the Compile button. After the evaluation process, the program gives feedbacks about errors that were made within the solution program. Evaluation mechanism of the program is based on a domain prepared according to the expert knowledge. At this point, the domain of C programming is very complex. There is no fixed sequence of actions that will enable users to get the solution, nor is there only one solution for a given exercise. Indeed, there are an infinite number of C code combinations which will lead the user to a valid solution.

The program over here employs a student modeling called 'Constraint Based Modeling' for providing wide space of solutions. Constraint Based Modeling is based on Ohlsson's theory of learning from errors (Ohlsson, 1994). A formal notation has been introduced by Ohlsson and Rees to be used for constraints within models (Ohlsson, & Rees, 1991). The unit of knowledge is called as a state constraint and each state constraint is used as an ordered pair of $<C_r, C_s>$, where C_r is the relevance condition and C_s is the satisfaction condition. C_r identifies the class of problem states for which the constraint is relevant whereas C_s identifies the class of (relevant) states in which the constraint is satisfied. Each member of the pair can be thought of as a set of features or properties of a problem state. At the same time, constraints are encoded by rules of the form: *If C_r is satisfied, then C_s should also be satisfied; otherwise a principle is being violated*. Briefly, the domain model consists of a set of rules, which represent general principles that must not be broken (Corbett *et al.*, 1995)".

In the domain model of the program, some examples can be the followings (Deperlioglu, & Kose, 2012):

- C_r = 'a problem requirement is to apply a function to a range of numbers' and C_s = 'it must be the case that the solution program contains a loop'
- C_r = 'exist an assignation element' and C_s = 'it must be the case that there is a valid expression on the right-hand side of the element'
- C_r = 'exist an assignation element' and C_s = 'data types associated on both sides of the assignation must be equal'

In our study, we have also added some more examples - rules to the related domain model; according to our experiences along past educational processes at the Suleyman Demirel University Computer Engineering Department. In this way, we have also aimed to improve the standard model of the program employed here.

EVALUATION

The artificial intelligence supported blended learning approach has been applied along one term, in order to figure out if usage of such "intelligent educational approach" can enable students to experience effective educational processes and improve their academic success levels. As it was also mentioned before, the application has been based the Algorithm and Programming course; during 2012 and 2013 fall semesters. More details regarding to the course content and educational objectives have been expressed briefly under the Section 3.

In the context of the evaluation processes, experimental evaluation and student survey based evaluation methods have been performed. More details regarding to these methods and obtained results are presented briefly as follows:

Experimental Evaluation

In the experimental evaluation, a total of 200 students (from Computer Engineering Department of the Suleyman Demirel University, Turkey) have taken active part. 100 of the related students have formed the experimental group which will experience the artificial intelligence supported blended learning approach. Then remaining 100 students have formed the control group which will experience the traditional - default lectures. It is important that the groups were formed as balanced, according to the chosen students' academic success levels. The related experimental evaluation has been based on the percentage of students who have passed the Algorithm and Programming course, and also on mean grades of the groups. Passing the related course needs having a success grade, which is equal to or bigger than 60 [The success grade has been calculated via (0,4 * visa exam grade) + (0,6 * final exam grade)].

Table 3 presents the obtained experimental evaluation results at the end of the term; for the Algorithm and Programming course.

As seen from the results, it can be said that using Artificial Intelligence supported blended learning approach has enabled students to improve their grades and success levels for the Algorithm and Programming course.

Student Survey

In addition to the experimental evaluation method, a student survey based work has also been performed at the end the term – course. At this point; students, who have taken part in the experimental group, have filled a survey to give feedback about their opinions on 10 different statements regarding to the performed educational process and also employed intelligent C programming teaching program. Students have expressed their opinions on the Likert scale.

Statements provided in the performed student survey and the received responses for these statements are presented in Table 4.

According to the feedback - responses received via the Student Survey, we can express that the students had enjoyed the performed artificial intelligence supported blended learning process, liked using the intelligent C programming teaching program and had positive experiences along

Table 3. Obtained experimental evaluation results at the end of the term; for the algorithm and programming course

Group	Number of Students	Number of Students Who has Passed the Course	Mean Success Grade
Control	100	63 (63%)	64,88
Experimental	100	82 (82%)	76,30

Table 4. Student survey statements and the received responses

S. No	Statement	Responses for:*				
		1	2	3	4	5
1	"Thanks to the intelligent C programming program, I felt more self-confident about learning course subjects."	0	2	3	9	86
2	"I think it is better to take part in such intelligent blended learning processes rather than other approaches."	1	1	4	16	78
3	"I don't want to take part again in such learning - education process."	87	5	7	1	0
4	"I enjoyed the educational process performed along the term."	0	0	7	8	85
5	"By using the intelligent C programming teaching program, it is more effective to learn C."	0	4	8	14	74
6	"I felt that it was easier to learn difficult algorithm and programming subjects, thanks to the intelligent C programming program."	0	2	5	11	82
7	"It was difficult to use the intelligent C programming program."	79	11	9	1	0
8	"My academic success level has been improved after this learning - education process."	0	0	0	23	77
9	"I felt bored while studying on the intelligent C programming program."	80	11	8	1	0
10	"I think this learning - education process should be applied also in other technical courses."	0	4	6	8	82
* Likert Scale: 1: "I strongly disagree" 2: "I disagree" 3: "I have no opinion" 4: "I agree" 5: "I strongly agree"						

the application. It is also remarkable that they think their academic success levels have been improved and they also think positive on applying the related educational approach - process in other technical courses.

CONCLUSION

This study introduced the application of an artificial intelligence supported blended learning approach in Computer Engineering education. It is remarkable that the blended learning is one of the most appropriate educational solutions that can be applied in order to combine advantages of different educational aspects. Because of this, application side of our study has benefited from advantages provided by the blended learning. In this sense; in addition to the advantages of the blended learning, we have also employed an intelligent C programming teaching program in order to improve effectiveness of the educational process. Briefly, the employed program is based on using intelligent feedback mechanisms for directing students to solve C programing programs by thinking about their mistakes in the code structures. As an intelligent learning environment, the program is effective at enabling students to perform their own-learning process in an efficient way.

The introduced educational approach has been employed at the Algorithm and Programming course of Computer Engineering program given at the Suleyman Demirel University. For the application, resources of the university have been activated greatly along the term: 2012 and 2013 fall semesters. In the context of the evaluation, results of the performed experimental and student survey related evaluation processes show that the introduced "intelligent learning solution" is effective at enabling students to gain necessary theoretical and applied knowledge, and abilities on C programming. In terms of the applied learning model, students were satisfied with the educational

activities, which caused positive experiences during the process. More generally, obtained results encourage the authors to apply the related approach in different kinds of technical courses given at the Computer Engineering Department.

REFERENCES

Bell, B., & Federman, J. E. (2013). *E-Learning Works--Exactly How Well Depends on Its Unique Features and Barriers: CAHRS ResearchLink No. 1*. Center for Advanced Human Resource Studies, Cornell University.

Boisvert, L. (2000). Web-based learning. *Information Systems Management, 17*(1), 35–41. doi:10.1201/1078/43190.17.1.20000101/31212.5

Bourne, J. R., Brodersen, A. J., Ccampbell, J. O., Dawant, M. M., & Shiavi, R. G. (1996). A Model for On-Line Learning Networks in Engineering Education. *The Journal of Engineering Education, 85*(3), 253–262. doi:10.1002/j.2168-9830.1996.tb00241.x

Corbett, A. T., Anderson, J. R., & O'Brien, A. T. (1995). In P. Nichols, S. Chipman, & B. Brennan (Eds.), *Student modeling in the ACT programming tutor* (pp. 19–41). Erlbaum.

Demirer, V., & Sahin, I. (2013). Effect of blended learning environment on transfer of learning: An experimental study. *Journal of Computer Assisted Learning, 29*(6), 518–529. doi:10.1111/jcal.12009

Finn, A., & Bucceri, M. (2004). *A case study approach to blended learning*. Los Angeles, CA: Centra Software.

Georgiev, T., Georgieva, E., & Smrikarov, A. (2004, June). M-learning-a New Stage of E-Learning. In *Proceedings of International Conference on Computer Systems and Technologies-CompSysTech*. Academic Press.

Glogger, I., Holzäpfel, L., Kappich, J., Schwonke, R., & Nückles, M. (2013). *Development and Evaluation of a Computer-Based Learning Environment for Teachers: "Assessment of Learning Strategies in Learning Journals".* International Telecommunication Union (ITU).

Hadjerrouit, S. (2008). Towards a blended learning model for teaching and learning computer programming: A case study. *Informatics in Education-An International Journal, 7*(2), 181-210.

Hill, J. R., Wiley, D., Nelson, L. M., & Han, S. (2004). Exploring research on Internet-based learning: From infrastructure to interactions. In Handbook of research on educational communications and technology, (vol. 2, pp. 433-460). Academic Press.

Keskin, N. Ö. (2010). Mobil Öğrenme Teknolojileri ve Araçları. *Akademik Bilişim, 10,* 490.

Khalifa, M., & Lam, R. (2002). Web-based learning: effects on learning process and outcome. *IEEE Transactions on* Education, *45*(4), 350–356.

Khan, A. I., Shaik, M. S., Ali, A. M., & Bebi, C. V. (2012). Study of Blended Learning Process in Education Context. *International Journal of Modern Education and Computer Science, 4*(9), 23–29. doi:10.5815/ijmecs.2012.09.03

Köse, U., & Deperlioğlu, O. (2012). Intelligent learning environments within blended learning for ensuring effective c programming course. *International Journal of Artificial Intelligence and Applications, 3*(1), 105–124. doi:10.5121/ijaia.2012.3109

Lotrecchiano, G. R., McDonald, P. L., Lyons, L., Long, T., & Zajicek-Farber, M. (2013). Blended Learning: Strengths, Challenges, and Lessons Learned in an Interprofessional Training Program. *Maternal and Child Health Journal,* 1–10. PMID:23291875

Ohlsson, S. (1994). Constraint-based student modeling. In J. E. Greer, & G. I. McCalla (Eds.), *Student Modeling: The Key to Individualized Knowledge-based Instruction* (pp. 167–189). Berlin: Springer-Verlag.

Ohlsson, S., & Rees, E. (1991). The function of conceptual understanding in the learning of arithmetic procedures. *Cognition and Instruction, 8*(2), 103–179. doi:10.1207/s1532690xci0802_1

Pea, R. D. (1990). Augmenting the discourse of learning with computer-based learning environments. In *Proceedings of the NATO Advanced Research Workshop on Computer-Based Learning Environments and Problem Solving* (pp. 313-343). NATO.

Peters, K. (2009). m-Learning: Positioning educators for a mobile, connected future. *Mobile Learning, 113.*

Singh, H. (2003). Building effective blended learning programs. *Educational Technology, 43*(6), 51–54.

Torkul, O., Sezer, C., Över, T., & Över, A. G. T. (2002). İnternet destekli öğretim sistemlerinde bilişim gereksinimlerinin belirlenmesi. *Turkish Online, 122.*

Torrisi-Steele, G., & Drew, S. (2013). The literature landscape of blended learning in higher education: the need for better understanding of academic blended practice. In *Proceedings of International Journal for Academic Development.* Academic Press.

Tufekci, A., & Kose, U. (2013). Development of an artificial intelligence based software system on teaching computer programming and evaluation of the system. *Hacettepe Üniversitesi Eğitim Fakültesi Dergisi, 28*(2), 469–481.

ADDITIONAL READING

Allen, I. E., & Seaman, J. (2010). *Class Differences: Online Education in the United States, 2010*. Sloan Consortium.

Altıparmak. M., Kurt. I. D., & Kapıdere. M. (2011). Open-Source learning management systems in e-learning and distance education <> E-öğrenme ve uzaktan eğitimde açık kaynak kodlu öğrenme yönetim sistemleri (In Turkish). Akademik Bilişim'11 - XIII. Akademik Bilişim Konferansı Bildirileri 2 - 4 Şubat 2011 İnönü Üniversitesi, Malatya

Aydın, C. H. (2012). Assesment of blended in-service education in accordance with instructor opinions <> *Harmanlanmış hizmet-içi eğitimin öğretmen görüşleri doğrultusunda değerlendirilmesi* [In Turkish]. *Atılım Sosyal Bilimler Dergisi, 2*(1), 33–56.

Baker, M. J. (2000). The roles of models in Artificial Intelligence and Education research: a prospective view. *Journal of Artificial Intelligence in Education, 11*, 122–143.

Barbour, M. K., & Plough, C. (2012). Odyssey of the mind: Social networking in a cyberschool. *International Review of Research in Open and Distance Learning, 13*(3), 1–18.

Beldarrain, Y. (2006). Distance education trends: Integrating new technologies to foster student interaction and collaboration. *Distance Education, 27*(2), 139–153. doi:10.1080/01587910600789498

Bell, B. S., & Federman, J. E. (2013). E-learning in Postsecondary Education. *The Future of Children, 23*(1), 165–185. doi:10.1353/foc.2013.0007

Bliuc, A. M., Goodyear, P., & Ellis, R. A. (2007). Research focus and methodological choices in studies into students' experiences of blended learning in higher education. *The Internet and Higher Education, 10*(4), 231–244. doi:10.1016/j.iheduc.2007.08.001

Cooner, T. S. (2010). Creating opportunities for students in large cohorts to reflect in and on practice: Lessons learnt from a formative evaluation of students' experiences of a technology-enhanced blended learning design. *British Journal of Educational Technology, 41*(2), 271–286. doi:10.1111/j.1467-8535.2009.00933.x

Deepwell, F., & Malik, S. (2008). On campus, but out of class: an investigation into students' experiences of learning technologies in their self-directed study. *Research in Learning Technology, 16*(1).

Devedzic, V. (2004). Education and the semantic web. *International Journal of Artificial Intelligence in Education, 14*(2), 165–191.

El-Deghaidy, H., & Nouby, A. (2008). Effectiveness of a blended e-learning cooperative approach in an Egyptian teacher education programme. *Computers & Education, 51*(3), 988–1006. doi:10.1016/j.compedu.2007.10.001

Halverson, L. R., Graham, C. R., Spring, K. J., & Drysdale, J. S. (2012). An analysis of high impact scholarship and publication trends in blended learning. *Distance Education, 33*(3), 381–413. doi:10.1080/01587919.2012.723166

Huang, E. Y., Lin, S. W., & Huang, T. K. (2012). What type of learning style leads to online participation in the mixed-mode e-learning environment? A study of software usage instruction. *Computers & Education, 58*(1), 338–349. doi:10.1016/j.compedu.2011.08.003

Karaman. S., Ozen. U., Yildirim. S., & Kaban. A. (2009). Web-based education experience over open source education management system <> *Açık Kaynak Kodlu Öğretim Yönetim Sistemi Üzerinden İnternet Destekli (Harmanlanmış) Öğretim Deneyimi (In Turkish)*. Akademik Bilişim'09 - XI. Akademik Bilişim Konferansı Bildirileri 11-13 Şubat 2009 Harran Üniversitesi, Şanlıurfa.

Kaya, İ., & Engin, O. (2011). Using artificial intelligence techniques in process of quality improvement <> Kalite İyileştirme Sürecinde Yapay Zeka Tekniklerinin Kullanımı (In Turkish). *Pamukkale University Journal of Engineering Sciences, 11*(1).

Lilje, O., & Peat, M. (2012, October). Use of traditional and elearning components in a blended learning environment. In *Proceedings of The Australian Conference on Science and Mathematics Education (formerly UniServe Science Conference).*

Maritim, E. K. (2009). The distance learning mode of training teachers in Kenya: Challenges, prospects, and suggested policy framework. *Open Learning, 24*(3), 241–254. doi:10.1080/02680510903202100

Marshall, S. (2012). Determination of New Zealand tertiary institution e-learning capability: An application of an e-learning maturity model. *Journal of Open. Flexible and Distance Learning, 9*(1), 58–63.

Marshall, S., & Mitchell, G. (2004, January). Applying SPICE to e-learning: an e-learning maturity model? In *Proceedings of the Sixth Australasian Conference on Computing Education-Volume 30* (pp. 185-191). Australian Computer Society, Inc.

Mclaren, B. M., Scheuer, O., & Mikšátko, J. (2010). Supporting collaborative learning and e-Discussions using artificial intelligence techniques. *International Journal of Artificial Intelligence in Education, 20*(1), 1–46.

Ossiannilsson, E., & Landgren, L. (2012). Quality in e-learning–a conceptual framework based on experiences from three international benchmarking projects. *Journal of Computer Assisted Learning, 28*(1), 42–51. doi:10.1111/j.1365-2729.2011.00439.x

Pereira, J. A., Pleguezuelos, E., Meri, A., Molina-Ros, A., Molina-Tomás, M. C., & Masdeu, C. (2007). Effectiveness of using blended learning strategies for teaching and learning human anatomy. *Medical Education, 41*(2), 189–195. doi:10.1111/j.1365-2929.2006.02672.x PMID:17269953

Picciano, A. G., Seaman, J., Shea, P., & Swan, K.Sloan Foundation. (2012). Examining the extent and nature of online learning in American K-12 Education: The research initiatives of the Alfred P. Sloan Foundation. *The Internet and Higher Education, 15*(2), 127–135. doi:10.1016/j.iheduc.2011.07.004

Buckley S., Coleman, J. J., Davison, I., Morley, D., & Torgerson, J. (2013). *Effective Education.* Routledge, Taylor and Francis Group.

Sedig, K., & Parsons, P. (2012). Interactivity of Information Representations in e-Learning Environments. *Interactivity in E-Learning: Case Studies and Frameworks, 29.*

Smith, J., Groves, M., Bowd, B., & Barber, A. (2012). Facilitating the Development of Study Skills through a Blended Learning Approach. *International Journal of Higher Education, 1*(2), 108. doi:10.5430/ijhe.v1n2p108

Voogt, J., Almekinders, M., van den Akker, J., & Moonen, B. (2005). A 'blended' in-service arrangement for classroom technology integration: Impacts on teachers and students. *Computers in Human Behavior, 21*(3), 523–539. doi:10.1016/j.chb.2004.10.003

Yamamoto, Y., Nishimura, S., & Nojima, E. (2012, March). A Case Study on the Improvement of the Organization's issues on e-learning Higher Education in Japan, Part II: Focus on the Academic Coaches' and Graduates' Data. In *Society for Information Technology & Teacher Education International Conference* (Vol. 2012, No. 1, pp. 2178-2182).

Yapıcı. U., & Akbayın H. (2012). *High school students' views on blended learning <> üniversite öğrencilerinin karma eğitime bakışları (In Turkish).* Turkish Online Journal of Distance Education-TOJDE October 2012 ISSN 1302-6488 Volume: 13 Number: 4 Article

KEY TERMS AND DEFINITIONS

Artificial Intelligence: Study and development of intelligent machines and software that to perform the tasks requiring human intelligence.

Asynchronous: Not coordinated, not occurring at the same time.

Blended Learning: A learning model that is enriched with traditional learning method and online education materials.

Distance Education: Education in which students receive instruction over the Internet instead of going to school.

E-Learning: Internet based learning model that provides access to information independent of time and location.

Mobile: Being portable, the ability to move or to be moved.

Studio: Sound isolated workroom.

Synchronized: Being simultaneous, occurring at the same time.

Chapter 13
Agent–Based Distributed Intelligent Tutoring System Using Case–Based Reasoning

Shweta
Banasthali University, India

Praveen Dhyani
Banasthali University, India

O. P. Rishi
University of Kota, India

ABSTRACT

Intelligent Tutoring Systems have proven their worth in multiple ways and in multiple domains in education. In this chapter, the proposed Agent-Based Distributed ITS using CBR for enhancing the intelligent learning environment is introduced. The general architecture of the ABDITS is formed by the three components that generally characterize an ITS: the Student Model, the Domain Model, and the Pedagogical Model. In addition, a Tutor Model has been added to the ITS, which provides the functionality that the teacher of the system needs. Pedagogical strategies are stored in cases, each dictating, given a specific situation, which tutoring action to make next. Reinforcement learning is used to improve various aspects of the CBR module: cases are learned and retrieval and adaptation are improved, thus modifying the pedagogical strategies based on empirical feedback on each tutoring session. The student modeling is a core component in the development of proposed ITS. In this chapter, the authors describe how a Multi-Agent Intelligent system can provide effective learning using Case-Based Student Modeling.

INTRODUCTION

A major challenge in computer science education is to improve both instructional productivity and learning quality for a large and diverse population of students under real world constraints such as limited financial resources and in sufficient

qualified instructors. The literature in education suggests that students who are actively engaged in the learning process will be more likely to achieve success.

Intelligent Tutoring Systems are programs that possess a wide knowledge on certain matter, and their intention is to transmit this knowledge to the

DOI: 10.4018/978-1-4666-6276-6.ch013

students by means of an interactive individualized process, trying to emulate the form in which a tutor or human teacher would guide the student in his/her learning process. They are growing in acceptance and popularity for several reasons, including: (i) an increased student performance, (ii) a deepened cognitive development, and, (iii) a reduced time for the student to acquire skills and knowledge. Basically, an ITS is characterized for incorporating three models corresponding to three knowledge levels. Firstly, there is a domain model where the domain knowledge is gathered, that is to say the knowledge of what has to be taught. A student model represents the knowledge of the student, that is to say knowledge of what the student knows. Finally, there is a pedagogical model where the knowledge of the instructing strategies, that is to say how to teach the domain knowledge, is described. The goal for every ITS is to communicate its embedded knowledge in an effective manner.

One of the main problems in Intelligent Tutoring Systems (ITS) consists in adapting to the needs of the student who interacts at each moment. A way to provide user adaptation is by means of the so called pedagogical strategies, which specify how to sequence the contents, what kind of feedback has to be given during education, when and how the tutor's contents (problems, definitions, examples, and so on) have to be shown or explained. There has been a great research effort in learning strategies to be incorporated into ITS. As an example, Meyer has used the analogy to teach a less known domain from a more familiar one. The case based reasoning paradigm has also been an inspiration to help in obtaining new incrementing knowledge. When various strategies are implemented together in an ITS, as for instance in, the system selects the most appropriate one for the activity that the student is performing.

On the other hand, agent technology has been suggested by experts to be a promising approach to address the challenges of the modern computer based education. "An autonomous agent is a system situated within and a part of an environment that senses that environment and acts on it, over time, in pursuit of its own agenda and so as to effect what it senses in the future". Any agent, in accordance with this definition, satisfies four properties: autonomy, social ability, reactivity and pro-activeness. By using intelligent agents in an ITS architecture it is possible to obtain an individual tutoring system adapted to the needs and characteristics of every student.

In this chapter, we present an intelligent agent assisted system to support student-centered, self-paced, and highly interactive learning, a first step in building an effective active learning environment. The system provides a rich set of on-line contents and around the clock information access, maximizes the interactivity between the intelligent learning system and the students, and customizes the learning process to the needs of individual students. In the system, student's learning-related profiles, such as learning styles and back-ground knowledge, are used for selecting, organizing, and presenting the learning materials to individual students and in supporting active learning. It supports personalized and more pleasant interaction between the users and the learning systems, enables adaptive delivery of IT education content, facilitates automatic evaluation of learning outcomes, and provides easy-to-use authoring tools.

This chapter is structured as follows. Firstly, a general introduction is provided. Afterwards, the state of the art of agent-based ITS in education is offered. Next, we explain the objectives of our ITS and the elements that form its architecture. Afterwards, the pedagogic strategy as implemented in the Pedagogic Module and a detailed description of the agents that monitor the progress of the students and that propose new tasks is described. Lastly, we describe how a Multi-agent Intelligent Learning Environment can provide adaptive tutoring based in Case-Based Student Modeling (CBSM).

Agent Based Distributed ITS Using CBR

Agent based Distributed ITS is a Web-based, distributed, multi-agent learning system. The system ties the Web clients (for students) and the underlying information servers (for courseware and student profiles) together with the multi-agent resource management. The information and agents are supported by a distributed system consisting of workstations and storage devices connected via high-bandwidth networks. ABDITS is implemented using the prevalent technologies of the Internet, WWW and software agents (Figure 1).

Several characteristics specific to asynchronous learning make multi-agent systems attractive. First, the students of a virtual class on the Internet are widely distributed, and the number of potential participants is large. This renders static and centralized systems inadequate. A distributed multi-agent system with personalized agents for each student is very attractive. Secondly, the classes are dynamic in nature. The background, knowledge, and skill of active students will change over time. The learning materials and teaching methodologies of the courses will change too. Thirdly, students have different background and personality.

Figure 1. Framework of ABDITS

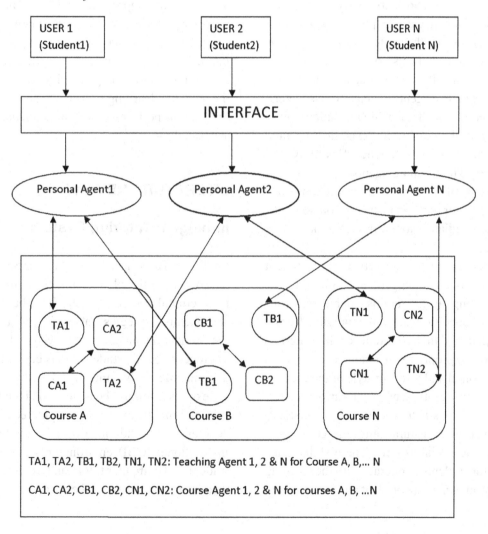

Teaching methodology should be tailored toward each student's interest and knowledge to make teaching and learning more effective. Furthermore, students often enroll in several courses at the same time. Coordination of learning on different topics for each student will enrich the learning experience. Finally, students tend to get together to discuss study topics and share common interests. Smooth communications, including visualizing and sharing common contexts, need to be supported. Hence, multi-agent systems have become a promising paradigm in education .

ABDITS consists of a number of specialized agents with different expertise. In ABDITS, each student is assigned a unique personal agent that manages the student's personal profile including knowledge background, learning styles, interests, courses enrolled in, etc. The personal agent talks to other agents in the system through various communication channels. An online course is supported by a collection of teaching and course agents. The course agents manage course materials and course-specific teaching techniques for a course. Multiple course agents exist on distributed sites to provide better efficiency, flexibility, and availability. The teaching agents can talk to any course agent of a course and often choose one nearby for better performance. The course agents also act as mediators for communication among students.

A teaching agent interacts with a student and serves as an intelligent tutor of a course. Each teaching agent obtains course materials and course-specific teaching techniques from a course agent and then tries to teach the materials in the most appropriate form and pace based on the background and learning style of the student. The teaching agents may adopt various cognitive skills such as natural language understanding, conversation, natural language generation, learning, and social aspects. These skills make it easier for students to interact with the teaching agents through natural forms of conversation and

expression. Multimedia presentations such as graphics and animation make difficult concepts and operations easier to understand.

The basic components of a teaching agent are a tutor module, a pedagogical module, and a student modeler. The tutor module creates exercises and questions according to the student's background and learning status, provides solutions, and explains the concepts and solutions to remedy student's misconceptions. It contains a problem generator, a problem solver, an explanation generator, and a domain knowledge base. The pedagogical module determines the timing, style, and content of the teaching agent's interventions. It is a case-based production system that uses the student model and pedagogical knowledge to determine the appropriate actions. The student modeler provides a model of a student based on her learning style, knowledge background, and interests. It may also incorporate the information gathered through dialogues with the student and the student's learning profile such as the actions the student performed and the explanations he/she asked for.

LITERATURE REVIEW

Intelligent Tutoring System

Intelligent Tutoring Systems (ITSs) are computer-based instructional systems with models of instructional content that specify what to teach, and teaching strategies that specify how to instruct the student in an intelligent way. They make inferences about a student's mastery of topics or tasks in order to dynamically adapt the content or style of instruction. The goal of an ITS is to apply artificial intelligence methods and techniques to develop highly individualized Computer-Based Instructional (CBI) environments in which the student and computer tutor can have a flexibility that is similar to the actual classroom. Such flexibility is important because without it, the system cannot be fully adaptive to the individual student's on-going learning needs during instruction.

The ITS was originated in the late 1950's and early 1960's (Urban-Lurain, 1996). Programmed Instruction (PI) was educationally fashionable during that period. According to Bunderson (Shute, 1994), PI expected the program designer to specify input and output in terms of entering skills and terminal behaviors of the learner. Sometimes PI was embedded in a computer program, known as Computer Assisted Instruction (CAI). Having well-defined curriculum and branching routines are the similarities between PI and CAI (Shute & Psotka, 1995). Shute and Psotka (1995) also pointed out that the continuum of CAI tutoring ranges from linear CAI to more complex branching CAI, to elementary intelligent computer-assisted instruction (ICAI), and to autonomous (or stand-alone) ICAI. Actually there is no explicit demarcation between CAI and ICAI (Wenger, 1987). In order to introduce intelligence into the programmed computer system, another research field, Artificial Intelligence (AI) is involved. AI provides a technical platform on which knowledge representation can be dealt with. It also supplies techniques such as inductive and deductive reasoning to support intelligent tutoring.

With the limitation of computer hardware, the ITS development was also limited. Shute and Psotka (1995) have listed dominant research issues of the 1970's. They are real-time problem generation, simple student modeling, knowledge representation, Socratic tutoring, skills and strategic knowledge, reactive learning environments, buggy library, expert systems and tutors, and overlay models/genetic graphing.

In the 1980's, ITSs were characterized by enormous growth. The dominant research issues were: model tracing, more buggy-based systems, case-based reasoning, discovery worlds, progression of mental models, simulations, natural language processing and authoring systems.

During the 1990's, "hot" ITS topics were characterized as follows (YI Sang et. al., 2001):

- How much learner control is necessary in the system?
- Should learners individually or collaboratively interact with ITS?
- Is learning situated and ongoing, or does it follow an information processing model?
- Has virtual reality (VR) uniquely contributed to learning beyond CAI, ITS, or even multimedia?

Different researchers have different perspectives about ITSs. Vasandani et. al., (1989) stated that the combination of simulator and tutor system constitutes an ITS because simulators coupled with an intelligent tutor can improve the weakness of the simulator, which is unable to provide appropriate help since it does not have the ability to evaluate a student's misconception from observed actions.

Schulmeister (1996) expressed the functional composition of the ITS consisting of modeling of a knowledge domain (domain model), which defines an expert's knowledge (also called expert model); a model of the student (student model), which defines the learner's current knowledge at any time in the course of the program (also called diagnosis model since the reproduction of the learners is meant to serve a diagnosis of the learning process); modeled educational strategies (tutor model, also called educational model); and an interface through which students or learners can communicate with ITS. Burns & Capps (1988) abstracted the ITS architecture as shown in Figure 2

Case Based Reasoning in ITS

Case-Based Reasoning (CBR) is a recent approach to problem solving and learning that has grown from a rather specific and isolated research area to a field of widespread interest (Bergmann, et al, 2003).

Figure 2. Components of an ITS (Burns & Capps, 1988)

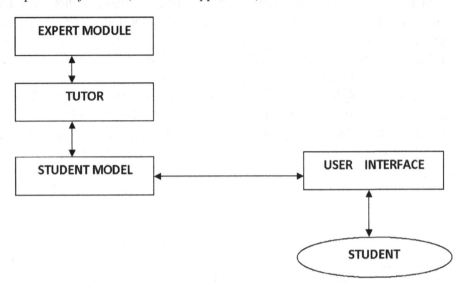

Case Based Reasoning is a method of developing knowledge based expert system that draws on examples of past experience in the expert domain that can be applied to new problem (Buta et. al., 1994). It is defined as a "computerized method that attempt to study solutions that were used to solve problem in the past to solve current problem by analogy or associations"(Leake,1996). CBR has been proposed as a more psychologically plausible model of the reasoning of an expert than rule based system and is claimed to be the essence of human reasoning (Riesback and Schank, 1989). CBR is an experience based, reasoning technology and therefore performs well in domains with documented or available expertise. CBR can also be beneficial, however, when a reasoner must solve problems that are quite different from prior experiences. As a case based reasoner applies cases to increasingly novel problems, the CBR process changes from simple reuse to more creative problem solving. Computer models of case-based reasoning (CBR) generally guide case adaptation using a fixed set of adaptation rules.

Case-based reasoning is a problem-solving paradigm that in many respects is fundamentally different from other major AI approaches. In-

stead of relying solely on general knowledge of a problem domain, or making associations along generalized relationships between problem descriptors and conclusions, CBR is able to utilize the specific knowledge of previously experienced, concrete problem situations (cases). A new problem is solved by finding a similar past case, and reusing it in the new problem situation. A second important difference is that CBR also is an approach to incremental, sustained learning, since a new experience is retained each time a problem has been solved, making it immediately available for future problems.

The study of CBR is driven by two primary motivations. The first, from cognitive science, is the desire to model human behavior. The second, from artificial intelligence, is the pragmatic desire to develop technology to make AI systems more effective. But consequently, it is natural to ask how CBR can advance AI technology. Discussions of this question have identified five main problems that can be ameliorated by case based reasoning:

1. **Knowledge Acquisition:** In CBR, case-based reasoner's reason from complete specific episodes, CBR makes it unnecessary

to decompose experiences and generalize their parts into rules. Some task domains are especially natural for CBR, with cases that are suitable for CBR already collected as part of standard problem-solving procedures. The cost of knowledge acquisition for CBR is very low. Of course, not all domains are natural CBR domains; cases may be unavailable, or may be available but in a hard-to-use form (e.g., cases described with natural language text). In these situations, applying CBR may depend on a significant ``case engineering'' effort to delimit the information that cases must contain, to define the representation for that information and to extract that information from available data. Likewise, applying CBR requires developing criteria for indexing and reapplying prior cases. (Mark et. al., 1996; Voss, 1995). However, even if this initial process requires considerable effort, CBR can still provide overall benefits for knowledge acquisition. First, experts who are resistant to attempt to distill a set of domain rules are often eager to tell their ``war stories''--the cases they have encountered. This facilitates gathering the needed data for CBR. Second, as discussed in the following point, after the initial case engineering effort it is often simple to augment and maintain the knowledge a CBR system needs.

2. **Knowledge Maintenance:** CBR offers a significant benefit for knowledge maintenance: a user may be able to add missing cases to the case library without expert intervention. Also, because CBR systems do incremental learning, they can be deployed with only a limited set of ``seed cases,'' to be augmented with new cases if (and only if) the initial case library turns out to be insufficient in practice. A CBR system needs only to handle the types of problems that actually occur in practice, while generative systems must account for all problems that are possible in principle.

3. **Increasing Problem-Solving Efficiency:** CBR reuse the prior solutions or cases. Reuse of prior solutions helps increase problem-solving efficiency by building on prior reasoning rather than repeating prior effort.

4. **Increasing Quality of Solutions:** When the principles of a domain are not well understood, rules will be imperfect. In that situation, the solutions suggested by cases may be more accurate than those suggested by chains of rules, because cases reflect what really happens (or fails to happen) in a given set of circumstances.

5. **User Acceptance:** A key problem in deploying successful AI systems is user acceptance: no system is useful unless its users accept its results. To trust the system's conclusions, a user may need to be convinced that they are derived in a reasonable way. This is a problem for other approaches but CBR systems· are based on actual prior cases that can be presented to the user to provide compelling support for the system's conclusions.

6. Successful use of CBR depends on addressing issues in how to acquire, represent, index, and adapt existing cases.

The basic tasks in CBR are: "input a problem, find a relevant solution, and adopt it"(Riesback & Schank, 1989). Its major processes involve remembering and adaptation (Chi & Kiang, 1992). Remembering is the process of retrieving a case or a set of cases from memory, and adaptation is a process of fixing an old solution to a new situation (Kolodner, 1994). Figure1.2 (a) shows the general flow chart of a case base reasoning system redrawn from Aamodt & Plaza, 1994.

General CBR cycle may be described by the following four Rs:

*   RETRIEVE the most similar case or cases
*   REUSE the information and knowledge in that case to solve the problem

- REVISE the proposed solution
- RETAIN the parts of this experience likely to be useful for future problem solving

A new problem is solved by retrieving one or more previously experienced cases, reusing the case in one way or another, revising the solution based on reusing a previous case, and retaining the new experience by incorporating it into the existing knowledge-base (case-base). The four processes each involve a number of more specific steps, which will be described in the task model.

Distributed Case Based Intelligent Tutoring System

Brusilovsky (1996) suggested that the Internet and Web-based distributed teaching through ITS can potentially deliver personalized course materials and services, and therefore, are potentially able to accommodate a larger variety of learners than what can be accommodated otherwise. A distributed ITS base of learning environment can be implemented practically by using a set of Web services. These Web services offer a set of software artifacts and technologies that service providers or users can modularize and encapsulate with well-defined standard interfaces, host on their platforms of choice, manage and either locally or remotely, transport over the Internet or an intranet by using standard protocols over and above TCP/IP, locate from central registry nodes .

With the rapid development of broad band-based communication networks such as wireless networks and optical networks, the agent based system, an effective and feasible infrastructure for distributed teaching and learning environments has been widely used to facilitate advanced leaning environments and solve many current problems of existing education systems(Andreas et.al., 2001). Over the past few years, many universities and colleges have made substantial progress in using agent based distributed teaching and systems such as Web-based learning tools and system, designed

for teaching and learning, and distributed ITS based teaching and learning applications (Brusilovsky et al., 1997, Stern, 1997).

Contreras, Caballero et.al., (2006) suggested that today, it is desirable for agent based distributed teaching & learning environments to provide smarter intelligent learning functions that offer personalized services with capabilities to learn, reason, have autonomy, and be totally dynamic. With intelligent learning environment, students can study their chosen subjects at any time, from anywhere and their teachers can instruct them from any location at any time. Further, with intelligent learning environments, different educational Institutions can collaborate to share education resources and manage them effectively (Brusilovsky, 1999). To this end, it is critical to embed intelligence in Agent based distributed teaching and learning environments in other words, to develop human-like intelligent agents by applying artificial intelligence (AI) techniques such as case-based reasoning, symbolic machine teaming, rule-based reasoning, and so on (Silveira & Vicari, 1997).

The case base intelligent tutoring systems can conduct learner analysis based on initial interaction with the learner; adapt the instruction to meet the student learning style; monitor the learner's progress, providing declarative knowledge when required; decide on the best way to present the next problem or instructional sequence diagnose problems and provide corrective feedback; and oversee the successful completion of the learning process (Heffeman et. al., 2006).

Most of distributed teaching & learning innovations have focused on course development and delivery, with little or no consideration to privacy and security as required elements. However, it is clear from the above trends that there will be a growing need for high levels of confidentiality, privacy, and trust in distributed teaching & learning applications, and that security technologies must be put in place to meet these needs.

Role of Agents in CBR based Intelligent Tutoring System

Santos and Rodriguez (2002) discussed an agent architecture that provides knowledge-based facilities for Distributed teaching & education. Their approach is to take advantage of recent standardization activities to integrate information from different sources (in standardized formats) in order to improve the learning process, both detecting learners problems and recommending new contents that can be more suitable for the learner's skills and abilities. Agent based distributed teaching & learning environments provides smarter intelligent learning functions that offer personalized services with capabilities to learn reason, have autonomy, and be totally dynamic. With intelligent learning environment, students can study their chosen subjects at any time and from anywhere and their teachers can instruct them from any location at any time, further, with intelligent learning environments, different educational Institutions can collaborate to share education resources and manage them effectively. To this end, it is critical to embed intelligence in Agent based distributed teaching and learning environments in other words, to develop human-like intelligent agents by applying artificial intelligence (AI) techniques such as case-based reasoning, symbolic machine teaming, rule-based reasoning, and so on(Weiss, 1999).

To provide such learning environments, a number of issues have to be solved:

- How to collaborate among different agents?
- How to secure the communication between agents?
- How to protect the privacy of student information?
- How to collect data students' behaviors and preferences for modeling their behaviors and background knowledge or their domain knowledge (which may involve a legal issue)?

- How to personalize the agent behavior?
- How to make the agent adaptation to dynamic leaning requirements?
- How to negotiate the resources in the heterogeneous agent based system?
- How to make a decision for choosing the suitable learning objects for the students, such as a course or subject?

An Intelligent agent performs teaching, learning, or administration tasks on behalf of teachers, learners, or administrators as a set of independent software tools or applications that communicates with other applications or agents within one or several computer environment(Vivacqua, 1999) (Thibodeau et al., 2000) (Ogata et al., 1999). Like human agents, the intelligent agents can be given the autonomy to make decisions and perform certain tasks for human beings. Fortunately, such demands can be satisfied with mature and prosperous research results from the AI society.

We believe that the use of intelligent agents applied to online learning environment can enable the design of "enhanced learning environment" (Fuhua Oscar Lin, 2005) that allow for the development and the assessment of social competences as well as the common professional competences. Examples of social competences include presenting ideas in a workgroup, providing and receiving criticism and, cooperating with others.

One could argue that online environments can hardly reproduce the richness of real face-to-face interaction. This argument is true if we associate the use of such environments with reproducing traditional human learning scenarios (e.g. classrooms, libraries, lectures). However, these environments can easily create learning scenarios with new roles and rules for human interaction. In order to stimulate interaction among students, such environments should adopt an exploratory rather than a directive approach to content. Thus, case based learning seems to be a better learning strategy to consider than the traditional strategies. Traditionally, case base learning is considered difficult to implement and manage in groups of more than 10 students. Also, the subjective component in how students are evaluated in case base learning is a sensitive point of discussion. Both arguments are based on the fact that traditional data describing student's contributions (frequency, exams, and grades) are insufficient when assessing the extent of students' performances.

We consider the use of intelligent agents as being a good approach for building collaborative online learning environments based on case base learning, because these agents can collect huge amount of data regarding students' interactions and present these data in a way that allows students and teachers to visualize what is going on and plan what to do. Students can plan their contributions for the projects in which they are participating, and educators can plan how to conduct the learning processes (Fuhua Oscar Lin, 2005).

"Agents" can be perceived as computing services that humans, or even other agents, can request in order lo accomplish their tasks. Some services may be simple and others rather complex. A way to determine the best agents (services) to be implemented is to identify who the actors are in the object of study, which roles they play, and (if possible) what kind of knowledge they use. Thus, while designing such an environment the developers should consider the agents as integrating three kinds of services:

1. Helping people to perform innovative activities (i.e. educators need to create groups, projects, assessment portfolios; students have to relate the solutions they create to the problems proposed, to negotiate with other students, to collaborate with them, and to criticize or judge their peers' work)
2. Stimulating social behavior within student's (i.e. if the system determines that two students are working on similar issues, ii can inform the students and give them information about how to contact each other)

3. Offering the educators clear and objective information about the students' performances (i.e., which students art more creative, who effectively products what, which students cannot collaborate, which students have to improve their reasoning skills etc.).

In the literature, very few authors have written on the use of agents for distributed teaching & learning (Fuhua Oscar Lin, 2005).

OBJECTIVES AND ARCHITECTURE OF THE AGENT-BASED DISTRIBUTED ITS USING CBR

In order to obtain good results, we propose to decompose the matter into theory, exercises and test questionnaires (Figure 1). The students study each topic of the matter reading theory first, then making exercises and finally answering to a test. The system will provide help to the students whenever it is necessary.

The first goal of the proposed ITS is that the student learn more and better. One characteristic to take into account in learning is the rhythm of the student (recognize the type of student i.e. beginner, intermediate or expert) is able to learn. Thus, the ITS has to adapt rhythm, it introduces the concepts to the learning rhythm of each student (for instance, to show more or less exercises, to show more or less tests, etc.). Another aspect widely considered in learning theory is reinforcement by rewarding a correct answer and penalizing the errors (by means of messages, sounds, etc.).

Another goal in our environment is to enhance teaching as well as learning. One of the main problems a professor faces when teaching is that he does not know the skills of his student. Our proposal leads to conclusions that "teach how to teach". Within this objective there is the need to make the matter more comprehensive for the overall students, but always keeping in mind the requisites given to the subject.

The general architecture of Agent Based Distributed ITS (Figure 4) is formed by the four components that characterize an ITS –

- The Student Model,
- The Domain Model, and
- The Pedagogic Module.
- Also, in the ITS an Tutor Module has been added, which provides the functionality that the teacher of the system needs.

Student Model

In the Student Model the knowledge the system has about the student (profile and interaction with the system) is represented. The model is composed of three knowledge databases (KDBs).

1. The Personal Information KDB stores the necessary personal information of the student to control his access to the system.
2. The Profiles KDB stores the level as well as the presentation styles of the students. The students are assigned different levels depending on their learning rhythm.
3. The Performance KDB stores parameters such as the exercises and tests proposed so far to the students, the time spent on answering the questionnaires and the exercises, the pages of theory visited and the scrolls performed on those pages, or the reinforcement material prepared by the Pedagogic Module.

Domain Model

In the Domain Model the knowledge about the contents to be taught is stored. This model consists of four KDBs:

1. The Theory KDB incorporates the pages of theory that have been prepared for teaching on the matter,

2. The Tests Questionnaire KDB stores the battery of test questions related to the matter,
3. The Exercises KDB stores the battery of exercises on the matter, and,
4. The Remedy KDB contains the information used by the Pedagogic Module to prepare the material to be shown when a student needs to be reinforced.

Pedagogic Module

The Pedagogic Module provides the necessary mechanisms to efficiently present the matter to the student. This module is in charge of carrying out three tasks: (1) to provide the learning guidelines for the student (including any necessary remedial by the system), (2) to update statistics in the Domain Model of the exercises and tests presented, (3) to store into the Evaluation KDB important data as the material prepared to reinforce the student who needs it, the responses given by the student to the exercises and tests proposed, as well as the punctuation that the student has gotten and the time that he has spent in reaching the aims.

Tutor Module

Lastly, the Tutor Module provides the functionality that the teacher of the system needs. Across this module the teacher changes his preferences, gives reinforcement to the students, obtains statistics and consults the matter. This module is in fact devoted to help the teacher to change the contents of the matter on the basis of the information obtained from the Student Model and the Domain Model.

STRATEGY OF THE PEDAGOGIC MODULE

Figure 5(next page diagram) shows the steps followed by the student when studying each topic of the course ("Matter learning").

Figure 4. Architecture of the agent based distributed ITS

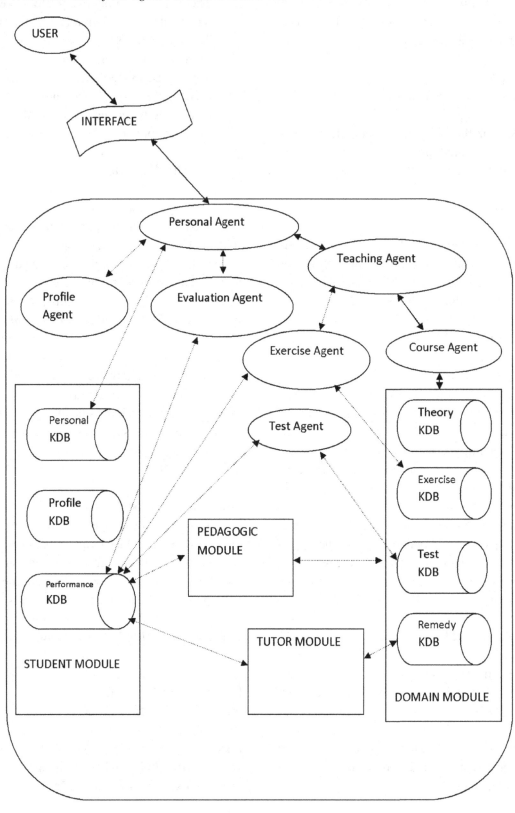

Figure 5. Flow chart of matter learning

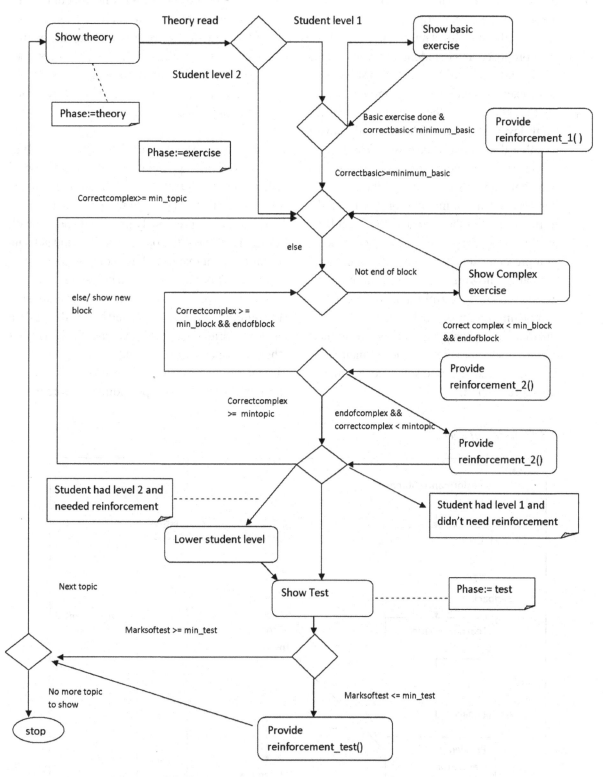

1. Firstly, the student has to read the whole theory for the current topic.

2. Afterwards, the student has to solve the exercises proposed. If the student is a level-1 (low level) student, firstly he/she has to solve the basic exercises and then the complex ones. On the other side, if the student is a level-2 (high level) student, he/she will only have to solve the complex exercises. The basic exercises are all shown in a sequential way, and then the ITS evaluates if the student has reached a minimum score associated to the topic. On the contrary, the complex exercises are shown in blocks (composed of a pre-determined quantity of exercises), and, after showing each block, there is an evaluation to ask for a minimum mark before composing the next block. After correctly fulfilling a number of complex exercises, the system goes on to the test questionnaires.

3. Lastly, the student has to solve the test questionnaire offered.

4. If there are more topics in the course, the system goes back to step (1). Otherwise, the student has finished studying the matter. During steps (2) and (3), if the student does not obtain the minimum scores fixed for the topic, he gets reinforcement in order to reach the objectives for the course.

In activity "Provide reinforcement_1" of Figure 3, you may appreciate the process followed when the student require reinforcement in the basic exercises. The system selects one of the basic exercises previously proposed and not well solved from the set of basic exercises and gets the reinforcement material (based on previous topics studied). This way the system helps the student to correctly solve the basic exercise. After proposing the reinforcement material, and before the student has to solve again the basic exercise, the ITS shows the bad response that the student gave previously. When the student passes the minimum score, the system does not go on providing reinforcement.

Figure 3. Working of agent

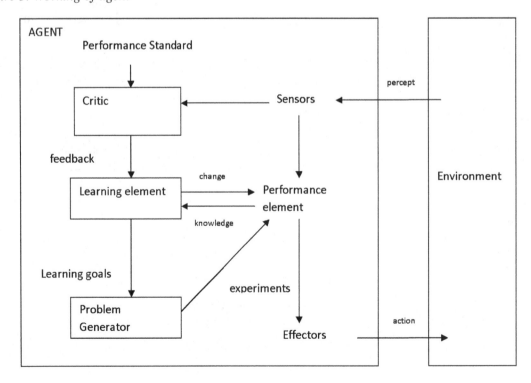

But, and this is the worst situation, if the system has provided reinforcement to all badly answered basic exercises, and even so the student has not been able to solve them, the ITS tells the student to consult the tutor personally. After having his/her meeting with the teacher, the student is permitted to advance in the study of the course. Now, in activity "Provide reinforcement_2" the alumni are reinforced during their phase of solving complex exercises.

The strategy for providing reinforcement to the student in complex exercises is very similar to the strategy followed to give reinforcement in basic exercises. The only difference is that the ITS firstly tries to reinforce with material of the current topic; and, if the student is still not able to solve the complex exercise, he is reinforced by material from previous topics of the course. if he/she already has been offered all the complex exercises blocks, he/she will be reinforced for all complex exercises incorrectly solved and not yet reinforced previously.

Finally, activity "Provide reinforcement_test" show what happens if the student does not get a minimum mark in the test questionnaire proposed for the current topic. The ITS builds a new test questionnaire, offers it to the student, and, if the student does not perform well, the professor personally must reinforce in order to proceed with the learning activity.

Description of the Agents

The Profile Agent

The Profile Agent supervises the style of presentation that the user likes. It perceives the interaction of the student with the user interface and acts when he changes his tastes. The profile agent is continually running to know the student's preferences at any time. When the student decides to change preferences the Profile Agent shows him/her a form with the preferences that he/she has selected in this moment. This way the user can perform the changes that he/she considers to be opportune. After having completed the form, the new elected preferences are updated and an example page is shown to the student with all the features of the new elected style of presentation. If the student does not like the page, he/she may continue changing his preferences again.

The Evaluation Agent

The Evaluation Agent perceives the interaction between the student and the user interface when the student accesses a page of theory. Concretely, the agent is in charge of watching the scroll that the student realizes on a page of theory as well as the time that he/she has remained in that page. When the student leaves studying a page of theory, the Evaluation Agent stores all parameters gathered on a page of theory (scroll and time of permanence) in the learning database.

The Exercises Agent

The Exercises Agent takes charge of choosing the exercises that will be proposed to the student in the topic that he/she is studying. The Exercises Agent is autonomous as it controls its proper actions in some degree. The agent by its own means (proactive) selects the set of exercises to be proposed in the subject studied by the student and adds to each exercise the links to the theory pages that explain the concepts related to the exercise. The Exercises agent stores the chosen exercises in the Performance KDB. When the student has just visited for the first time, the page index of the topic for which he/she is studying the Exercises Agent it realizes the selection of exercises that will be proposed to the student in the above mentioned topic. If the student has level of that time 1 first selects the basic exercises (state to prepare basic exercises) and later the complex exercises (state prepare complex exercises). If the student has level of that time 2 alone selects complex exercises. Once it has selected the exercises it will remain inactive (Idle state) while the student I did not go on to the following topic.

The Tests Agent

The Tests Agent takes charge choosing the questions test that will compose the test that will be proposed to the student in the topic that he/she is studying. The agent by its own means (pro-active) goes on designing a set of tests for the subject the student is engaged in. These tests will be shown to the student in form of a questionnaire. The Tests Agent performs the selection of questions test at the same time that the Exercises Agent realizes the selection of exercises. Once it has selected the questions test it will remain inactive (Idle state) while the student I did not go on to the following topic.

STUDENT MODELING IN AGENT BASED DISTRIBUTED ITS USING CASE BASED REASONING

The Student Model is the main component within the Intelligent Tutoring System and, contains information about the student knowledge. It obtains the information by dynamically observing and recording the student's behavior, answers, problem-solving strategies, and analyzing them in order to deduct their level of understanding about the domain. This information is processed and used to individually adapt the system to each student. Intelligent agents have been quite successful at observing student's behavior and, therefore, they have been widely used in learning environments in order to capture the characteristics of the student and perform student modeling tasks .

Building a student model involves defining; the "who", is modeled; the "what", or the goals, plans, attitudes, capabilities, knowledge, and beliefs of the student; the "how" the model is to be acquired and maintained; and the "why", including

student's information to give assistance, to provide feedback, or to interpret the student behavior. The need for simplicity and ease of understanding in Student Models is very high. It derives from the fact that web based education is addressed to students who vary greatly in their educational background. Due to the lack of physical tutor-student contact, sometimes the distance student has the feeling that the teacher is unreachable when needed. This is the reason why Student Models should provide bi-directional benefit to both instructors and students, by enabling students to monitor their own progress and utilize the feedback provided by the model on a continuous basis. There are many techniques for generating student models; however most of these techniques are computationally complex and time consuming for example: Bayesian Networks, Fuzzy student modeling approach, the Dempster-Shafer theory. Other techniques can only record what a student knows and not the students' behavior and features. Examples are: overlay model, stereotype and combination model. This study shows that CBR is the best and easiest approach for constructing a student modeling.

We propose a multi-agent approach to student modeling in which each student model has a corresponding Personal Agent (PA). This agent uses the CBR paradigm to generate the student profile. The CBR paradigm is simple and do not require complex inference algorithms, moreover offers well-founded methodologies and experiences with respect to both mathematic and algorithmic aspects. In our approach, we included a Teaching Agent to customize the learning considering the psychological characteristics of the student.

In our approach the student model is improved because: it is easy to handle and to maintain beneficiating to both the tutor and the student; to promote student reflection because reporting the student's misconceptions and the reasons why they have happened; and to facilitate the supervision of the students by enabling the tutor to have a solid and continuous view of the student performance.

Student Modeling Process

In order to construct the Student Model, information about student should be acquired.

Content of the Student Model (SM)

A comprehensive student model should contain information about the previous student's knowledge, the student's progress, preferences, interests, goals, personal information and any other information related to the student. Based on the dependence upon the subject domain, the content held in student models consists of two parts: domain specific information and domain independent information.

- **Domain Specific Information (DSI):** It is also named student knowledge model (SKM) which represents a reflection of the student's state and level of knowledge in term of a particular subject domain.
- **Domain Independent Information (DII):** It is slightly different from system to system. The domain-independent information about a student may include learning goals, cognitive aptitudes, measures for motivation state, preferences about the presentation method, factual and historic data, etc.

We propose a student model that includes individual and cognitive characteristics grouped in a component named Knowledge Component. This component contains information related to the (1) knowledge level of the student, (2) personal information, (3) learning preferences, and (4) psychological characteristics.

Constructing the Student Model by Case-Based Reasoning

The student modeling has been recognized as a complex and difficult but important task by researchers. The method of student modeling includes a representation of the knowledge and reasoning of the student, and the way how the student acquires new knowledge in order to perform intelligent learning.

Case-Based Reasoning (CBR) is a problem-solving paradigm that is able to utilize the specific knowledge gained from previous experiences in similar situations (cases) to solve a new problem. Instead of relying on exact reasoning in a well ordered world, CBR focuses on inexact reasoning by a similarity measurement among objects. The process involved in CBR has been described as a cyclic process that integrates four phases (Figure 6) Retrieve, Reuse, Revise and Retain.

An initial description of a problem (Figure 6) defines a new case. This new case is used to RETRIEVE a case from the collection of previous cases. The retrieved case is combined with the new case - through REUSE - into a solved case, i.e. a proposed solution to the initial problem. Through the REVISE process this solution is tested for success, e.g. by being applied to the real world environment or evaluated by a teacher, and repaired if failed. During RETAIN, useful experience is retained for future reuse, and the case base is updated by a new learned case, or by modification of some existing cases.

Student Model Initialization

The initialization of the Student Model is a task of great importance to makes initial estimations of the new knowledge level of the student. When a student starts a new learning session, the system has no previous knowledge about his learning skill.

In our research study, the information about the students is regarded as cases. When the student starts learning, the information about the students is extracted from the student model and is converted into a new case. When there is a new student, he/she is asked to take some tests, then the system analyses his/her tests results to gather information and initialize the student model.

Figure 6. CBR cycle

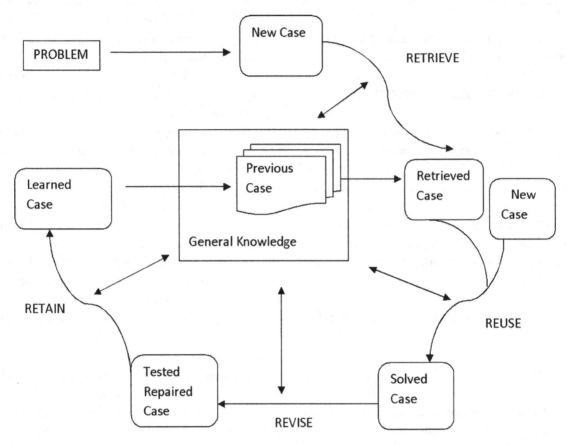

The student model presented here is structured as a multi-agent system integrated by: (1) Personal Agent (PA), (2) Teaching Agent (TA) and (3) Course Agent (CA).

Personal Agent (PA)

It is a CBR-Agent. It is responsible for retrieve the information about the student and identifies his profile. In the retrieval process, the PA agent evaluates cases and uses the k-nearest algorithm to determine the matching grade. After the evaluation, the most similar cases are selected (if there is more than one case, the case with the highest rank is selected and prepared for adaptation). After the process is completed, the PA agent storages the new case in the case base. Additionally, this agent keeps communication with the Teaching Agent and updates the student model.

Teaching Agent (TA)

It selects a specific teaching strategy for the different student's profiles, personalizing the learning process. It interacts with the PA to get information about the students and to produce changes in the teaching paradigm.

Course Agent (CA)

It organizes the learning resources according to the teaching strategy implemented by the TA. It takes into account the student profile to present the contents and information, making a customized learning.

Student Modeling Algorithm

Let us illustrate a modeling algorithm (Figure 7). Below we explain the process referencing every line in the pseudo-code.

Line 3: Initialize the student model. When the student interacts with the system for the first time, the information is acquired.

Line 8: The ProcedureStudenProfile generates the student profile: First the PAAgent evaluates and filters the cases. This agent combines searching and matching techniques. In line 37, the new case is analyzed, and evaluated (e.g. cases with the same goals than the current case).

Line 48: The ProcedureMatching is implemented to check the corresponding features in the cases stored using the k-nearest neighbour algorithm. Based on the result of the matches, PA identify those that best address the requirements of the new situation, ranking the cases from highest to lowest, getting the student profile.

Line 10: The PAAgent sends a request to the TAAgent with the student profile. Then the TAAgent selects the teaching strategy in line 11.

Line 12: The TAAgent sends a request to CAAgent in order to organize the learning resources according to the student preferences. This information is returned to the students through the PAAgent in line 14.

Line 16 and 17: The PAAgent monitorizes the students' tasks and evaluates the students' answers.

Line 18: If the students' answers corresponding to misconceptions or fails, the Procedure-Misconceptions will be called. If the fail is related with an inadequate teaching strategy, the PAAgent sends a request to the TAAgent in order to modify the teaching strategy in line 23. If the fail is due to personality problems the ProcedureEmotionalGuide is called in line 26.

Figure 7. Pseudo-code for the student modeling process

```
1.   Procedure StudentModel()
2.   Begin
3.   Initialize stuentmodel;
4.   do
5.      if (student= newstudent) then
6.         realizeTest();
7.      else
8.         ProcedureStudentProfile();
9.      endif
10.  agentPASendRequestTA(studentProfile);
11.  agentTASelectTeachingStrategy;
12.  agentTASendRequestCA(StudentPrefernce);
13.  agentCAOrganizeLearningResources;
14.  agentCASendInformationTA;
15.  agentTAProvideStudyMaterialPA;
16.  agentEAMonitoring(StudentTask);
17.  agentEAevaluation(StudentPrformance);
18.  if(studentanswer=Error)then
19.     procedure ManageentMisconception(Error);
20.     Begin
21.     If(error=notAdequateTeachingStrategy) then
22.        agentPASendRequestTA(error);
23.        agentTAModifyTeachingStrategy;
24.     Elseif (error=personalityProbem) then
25.        agentPASendRequestAP(error);
26.        procedureEmotionalGuideAP(StudentInformation);
27.        agentPAUpdatedStudentModel();
28.     Endif
29.     Endif
30.  End
31.  Else
32.     endSession();
33.  Endif
34.  Enddo
35.  End
36.
37.  ProcedureStudentProfile(attribute:feature);
38.  Begin
39.     If(retrieveCase)then
40.        Search(attribute=tempatt);
41.        Evaluation(attributes:features);
42.        ProcedureMatching(features);
43.        Adaptation();
44.        Indexing();
45.     Endif
46.  End
47.
48.  ProcedureMatching(features);
49.  Begin
50.     reviseFeatureCaseBase();
51.     computeDegreesimilarity();
52.     computeDegreeMAtch();
53.     rankingCases();
54.  end
```

Line 32: If the students' answers are correct, the session finished and the PAAgent updates the student model in line 27.

WORKING OF AGENT BASED DISTRIBUTED ITS USING CBR

In the ABDITS system architecture (Figure 8), there are three global indices: Student Index, Case Index, and Course Index. The Student Index maintains the record of system log file (IP addresses of the entire network) and student log file (User ID) registered in the entire network managed by the personal profiler or personal agent.

Any student can register as a user at any node over the entire network. The student can select any subject for learning. This can be done through navigation of subject provided by the ITS. The topics in a subject are required. However, before allowing for selection of a topic, the personal agent of the system checks whether a new user or registered. If it is already registered, checks the authenticity of user and the past record of the performance of the student to present the right content, thus the system is adaptable. If a new user, then he would be registered first and personal agent stores all the information in personal database.

The Personal agent maintains the students' profile master, students' learning profile, and usage profile. In profile master user ID, registered node, user personal profile, course ID, and preliminary or past performance, level of student (poor, average, excellent), category of the student(slow learner, normal learner, fast learner) are stored. Similarly, learning profile maintains the record of subject ID, topic ID and topic name, pre-leaning performance, and post learning performance, performance of individual topic and subject, type of errors performed by the student. The usage profile keeps the record of system ID, time in, time out, topic name, number of attempts, questionnaire etc. In this task, two more different agent helps to Personal Agent, 1) Profile Agent and 2) Evalua-

tion Agent. The Profile Agent supervises the user preferred style of presentation (type and size of letter, colors, margins, and so on). When the user changes his style of presentation the Profile Agent creates a personalized sheet of styles for the user and updates the user's interface in accordance with his new pleasures. The information that this agent gathers is stored in the Profiles KDB. The Evaluation Agent observes the student interaction with the interface when the student accesses a page of theory. When the student changes to another page of theory, the Evaluation Agent stores in the Performance KDB some valuable information (the name of the visited page, the time that the student has spent on it and the scrolls performed on it).

The Case Index maintains the record of cases managed by the teaching agent. In Case Index, case type, content of each case, case adaptation condition, case indexing strategy, case retrieval method, case recall method, case updating (addition, deletion, modification) methods, error rate, teaching strategy, location of the case where it is stored, and the remedial strategy used by the system, are stored and maintained. The Teaching agent decides the teaching strategy by using learning profile of the student

and there after presents the right content to the student with the help of course agent using Case Index. The Course Index managed by the Course agent maintains the record of available course content like ordering or sequencing of course material, set of related examples, assignments, questionnaires, a set of exercise problems to access the student's understanding of the topic and remedial content.

Here, the Exercises Agent takes charge of choosing the exercises that will be proposed to the student in the topic that he is currently studying. This agent stores the chosen exercises in the Evaluated KDB as well. In the same way, the Tests Agent is in charge of choosing the test questions that will compose a test questionnaire proposed to the student in the topic that he is studying at this moment. The test questions selected are also

Figure 8. Nodal architecture of agent based distributed ITS using CBR(ABDITS)

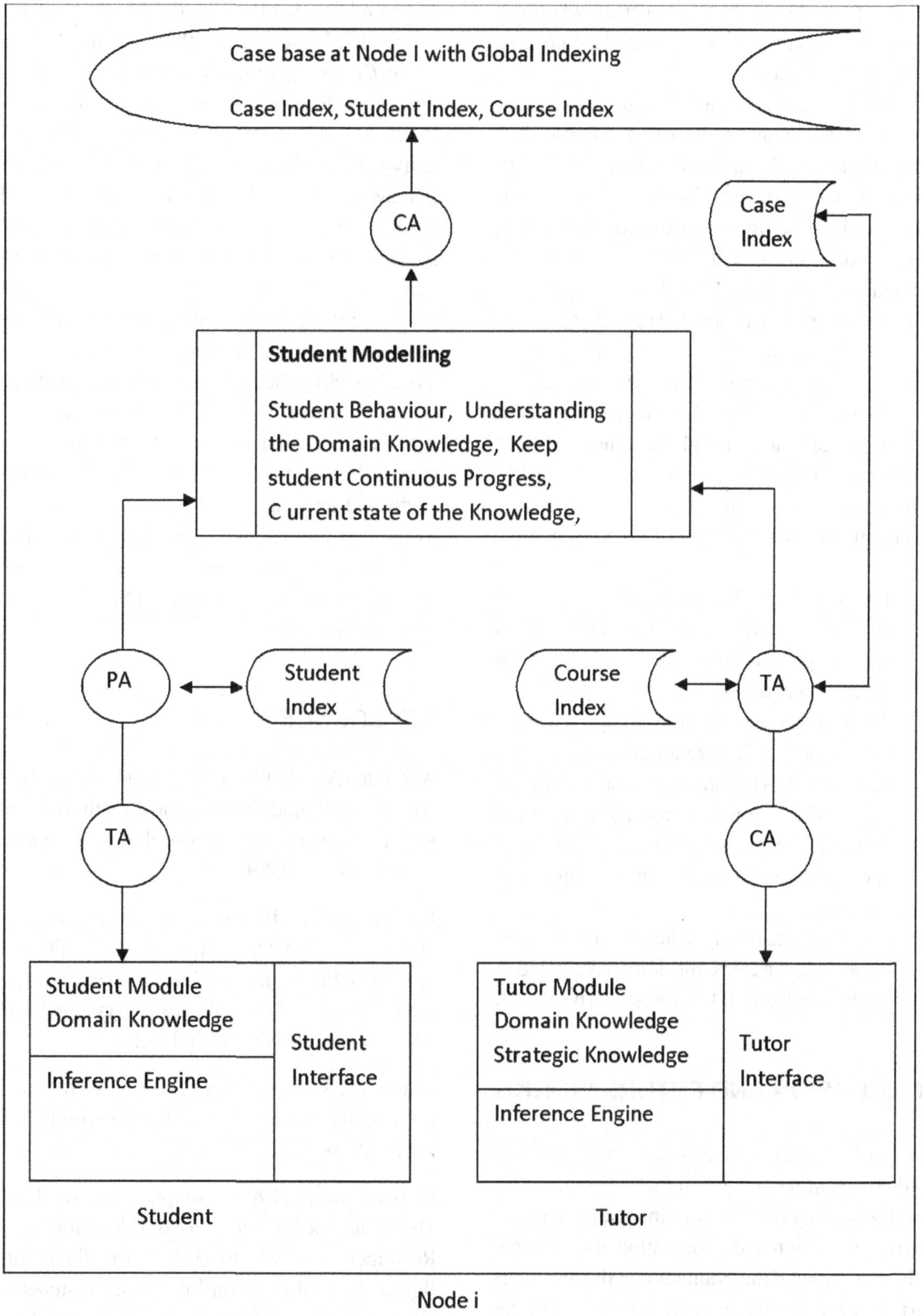

stored in the Evaluated KDB. The Exercises Agent and the Tests Agent do the selection when the student finishes the first visit to the first page of theory of every topic.

We may highlight that the Exercises Agent and the Tests Agent are proactive because they carry out their tasks in parallel with the activity that the student performs. For the purpose of fault tolerance all storage in the distributed environment are maintained in duplicate. It means if a new case is diagnosed and stored at node i, a copy of it is also stored on node j, j being the next nearest node available. Later, one can research on optimum redundancy parameters. Thus with the help of these three agents; personal agent, teaching agent and course agent, and three global indices; student index, case index and course index the complete learning process is managed.

The major characteristics of the System are:

1. The system is fully distributed (not bounded with any network topology) i.e. domain knowledge and strategic knowledge both are distributed.
2. Reduces the need of large storage spaces at the user's site, to store all the cases.
3. Redundancy is maintained for fault tolerance. Load balancing of the cases is achieved at each node by the storage management. Later one can research on optimum redundancy parameter.
4. Case indexing is fully redundant on all nodes.
5. If the node is a LAN, the domain knowledge can be localized and case base can be global.

CONCLUSION AND FUTURE WORKS

The implementation of this study will have as result an agent based system for distributed case based reasoning for ITS with innovative characteristics in relation to the adaptation of the course to the students and the evaluation of the teaching/learning process, that are still not present in the actually developed environments.

In our system, we have a Student Model, a Domain Model, a Pedagogical Model, and a Tutor Model. It uses mainly three agents- *Personal agent, Course agent, and Teaching agent.* All three agents timely interact with the system and manage the student's personal profile along with learning activities, tutoring activities, and course content management. To help this four more agents – the *Profile Agent*, the *Evaluation Agent*, the *Exercises Agent* and the *Tests Agent* - have been added. Also it uses three indexes i.e. student index, course index and case index, which are fully distributed, to keep the record of every student, course content and stored cases by the system within entire network.

To conclude, the proposed agent based ITS gets all needed data, obtained fruit of the interaction of the students with the system, to adapt the rhythm of introducing the contents of the matter to the learning rhythm of each student. On the other hand, the Tutor Module obtains measures that permit to get recommendations to teacher to enhance the course.

REFERENCES

Aamodt, A., & Plaza, E. (1994). Case-based reasoning: Foundational issues, methodological variations, and system approaches. *AI Communications*, *7*(1), 39–59.

Badjonski, M., Ivanovic, M., & Budimac, Z. (1997). Intelligent tutoring system as multi-agent system. In *Proceedings of IEEE international conference on intelligent processing systems (ICIPS '97)*, (vol. 1, pp. 871-875). IEEE.

Braun, A., & Harrer, A. G. (2001). A Framework for Internet-Based Distributed Learning. Academic Press.

Brusilovski, P. (1999). Adaptive and Intelligent Technologies for Web-based Education. In C. Rollinger & C. Peylo (Eds.), Kustliche Intelligenz, Special Issue on Intelligent Systems and Teleteaching, (vol. 4, pp. 19–25). Academic Press.

Brusilovsky, P., Schwarz, E., & Weber, G. (1996). ELM-ART: An Intelligent Tutoring System on World Wide Web. In *Proc. of 3rd International Conference on Intelligent Tutoring Systems, ITS-96*. Springer Verlag.

Burger, C., & Rotherme, K. (2001). *A Framework to Support Teaching in Distributed Systems*. University of Stuttgart.

Burns, H. L., & Capps, C. G. (1988). Foundations of intelligent tutoring systems: an introduction. In M. C. Polson, & J. J. Richardson (Eds.), *Foundations of Intelligent Tutoring Systems*. Hillsdale, NJ: Lawrence Frlbaum.

Chappell, A. R., & Mitchell, C. M. (1997). The Case Based Intelligent Tutoring System: An Architecture for Developing and Maintaining Operator Expertise. In *Proceedings of the 1997 IEEE International Conference on Systems, Man, and Cybernetics*. Orlando, FL: IEEE.

Corbett, K. (2005). *Anderson*. Intelligent Tutoring System.

Cristea, A., & Okamoto, T. (2002). Student model-based, agent-managed, adaptive Distance Learning Environment for Academic English Teaching. In Proceedings of IWALT 2000, (pp. 159-162). IWALT.

Fabiano, A. D., Carlos, R. L., & Marcia, A. F. (2003). A Multi agent architecture for Distance Education Systems. In *Proceedings of the 3rd IEEE International Conference on Advanced Learning Technologies*. IEEE.

Fuhua, O. L. (2005). Designing Distributed Learning Environments with Intelligent Software Agents. *Journal of Educational Technology & Society*, 8(1), 132–133.

Holt, P., Dubs, S., Jones, M., & Greer, J. (1991). The state of Student Modeling. In *Student Modelling: The Key to Individualizes Knowledge-Based Instruction, NATO ASI Series*, (pp. 3–35). London, UK: Springer verlag.

Jose, M. G., & Antonio, F.-C. (2005). *An Agent-based Intelligent Tutoring System for Enhancing E-Learning / E-Teaching*. Academic Press.

Kolodner, J. L. (1993). *Case-Based Reasoning*. San Mateo, CA: Morgan Kaufmann.

McCalla, G.I. & Greer, J.E. (1991). Granularity-Based Reasoning and Belief Revision in Student Models. In *The Key to Individualised Knowledge-Based Instruction, NATO ASI Series*. NATO.

Riesbeck, C., & Schank, R. (1989). *Inside Case-Based Reasoning*. Hillsdale, NJ: Lawrence Erlbaum.

Rishi, O. P., Govil, R., & Sinha, M. (2007). Agent Based student Modeling in Distributed CBR based Intelligent Tutoring System. In *Proceedings of the World Congress on Engineering and Computer Science*. Academic Press.

Self, J. A. (1991). Formal Approaches to Student Modelling. In Proceedings of GREE91, (pp. 295-352). Academic Press.

Shang, Y. I., Shi, H., & Chen, S.-S. (2001). An Intelligent Distributed Environment for Active Learning. University of Missouri-Columbia.

Turgay, S. (2005). *A Multi Agent system Approach for Distance Learning Architecture*. TOJET.

Van Lehn, K. (1988). Student Modeling. Foundations of Intelligent Tutoring Systems. Academic Press.

Weiss, G. (Ed.). (1999). Multiagent Systems: A Modern Approach to Distributed Artificial Intelligence. MIT Press.

Wenger, E. (1987). *Artificial Intelligence & Tutoring System*. Los Altos, CA: Morgen Kaufman. doi:10.1016/B978-0-934613-26-2.50013-X

Yazdani, M. (1987). Intelligent Tutoring Systems: An Overview. In R. Lawler (Ed.), *Artificial Intelligence and Education* (pp. 183–201). Ablex Publishing Corp.

ADDITIONAL READING

Aamodt, A. (2005). *Knowledge Intesive Case-based reasoning and Intelligent tutoring system.*

Allouche, M., Boisser, O., & Sayettat, C. (2000). Temporal social reasoning in dynamic multi-agent systems, *in Proceedings of the Fourth International Conference on Multi-Agent Systems (IC-MAS-2000).* IEEE Computer Society, pp. 23-28.

Beck, J. E., & Woolf, B. P. (1998). Using a learning agent with a student model., *Intelligence Tutoring System (Proc. 4th Int'l Conf. ITS'98),* pages 6-15, Springer.

Brusilovsky, P. (1996). Methods and techniques of adaptive hypermedia. [Kluwer academic publishers.]. *User Modeling and User-Adapted Interaction, 6*(2-3), 87–129. doi:10.1007/BF00143964

Brusilovsky, P. (1998). Adaptative educational systems on the world-wide-web: A review of available technologies. *In Proceedings of Workshop WWW-Based Tutoring at Fourth International Conference on ITS (ITS'98).* San Antonio, TX: Mit Press.

Capuano, N., et al. (2000). ABITS: An Agent Based Intelligent Tutoring System for Distance Learning, *in Proceedings of the International Workshop on Adaptive and Intelligent Web-based Educational Systems,* Montreal, Canada, 2000.

Chalupsky, H. et al. (2002). Electric elves: Agent technology for supporting human organizations. *AI Magazine,* (Summer): 2002.

Chen, W., & Mizoguchi, R. (1999). Communication ontology for learner model agent in multi-agent architecture. *In Proceedings of the International Conference on Artificial Intelligence in Education (AI-EDg9).*

Decker, K., Sycara, K., & Zeng, D. (1996). Designing a multi-agent portfolio management system, *in Proceedings of the AAAI Workshop on Internet Information Systems.*

Dent, L., Boticario, J. G., McDermott, J., Mitchell, T. M., & Zabowski, D. T. (1992). A personal learning apprentice. *In Proceedings of the Tenth National Conference on Artificial Intelligence,* 96-103. San Jose, CA: MIT Press.

Finin, T., Fritzson, R., & McEntire, R. (1994). KQML as an agent communication language, *in Proceedings of the 3rd International Conference on Information and Knowledge Management,* November.

Genesereth, M., & Fikes, R. (1992). Knowledge interchange format, version 3.0 reference manual. Technical Report KSL-92-86, Knowledge Systems Laboratory, 1992.

Jennings, N. R., & Wooldridge, M. J. (1998). *Agent technology: Foundations, Applications, and Markets.* Berlin: Springer. doi:10.1007/978-3-662-03678-5

Julian, V., & Botti, V. (2002). Developing real-time multi-agent systems, in Fourth Iberoamerican Workshop on Multi-Agent Systems, *the VIII Iberoamerican Conference on Artificial Intelligence.*

Kurose, J. F., & Ross, K. W. (2000). *Computer Networking: A Top-Down Approach Featuring the Internet. Addison-Wesley.* TCP Congestion Control.

Leen-kiat Soh, (2005). Incorporating Intelligent tutoring system in to CS1, *SIGCSE06.*

Nagle, " J. (1984). Congestion control in IP/TCP inter networks, Network Information Center, SRI International, Menlo Park, CA, RFC 896.

Pinto, B. Q., Lopes, C. R., Dorça, F. A., & Fernandes, M. A. (2002). Intelligent Multiagent System for Distance Education Techinical Report, Department of Computing/Federal University of Uberlândia, Uberlândia, Brazil, 01/2002. (In Portuguese)

Pinto, B. Q., Lopes, C. R., & Fernandes, M. A. (2003). *Using the IEEE LTSC LOM Standard in Instructional Planning, Learning Technology* publication of IEEE Computer Society, Volume 5 Issue 1, ISSN 1438-0625.

Queiroz, B., Lopes, C. R., & Fernandes, M. A. (2002). Automatic Curriculum Generation for a Web-Based Educational System, *International Conference on Computers in Education (ICCE 2002)*, Auckland. Supplementary Proceedings. Palmerston: Massey University, pp. 26-28.

Shang, Y., Sapp, C., & Shi, H. (2000). An intelligent web representative. *Information*, *3*(2), 253–262.

Shang Y., & Shi, H. (1999). A web-based multi-agent system for interpreting medical images. World Wide Web, 2(4):209{218}.

Shehory, O., Sukthankar, G., & Sycara, K. (1999). Agent aided aircraft maintenance, *in Proceedings of Autonomous Agents '99*, pp. 306-312.

Shi, H., Shang, Y., Joshi, A., & Jurczyk, M. (2000). Laboratory-oriented teaching in web and distributed computing. *In Proc. ASEE Annual Conference & Exposition*, St. Louis, June 2000.

Shiri, M. E., Aimeur, A. E., & Frasson, C. (1998). Lecture Notes in Computer Science: Vol. 1452. *Student modelling by Case Based Reasoning.*

Sinha, M., & Govil, R. (1995). PRABODH: A Distributed online Hindi Grammar Teaching Learning System. IJMS vol 11, No.3.

Stern, M. K., & Woolf, B. P. (1998). Curriculum sequencing in a Web-based tutor. In B. P. Goettl, H. M. Hal, C.L.Redeld, and V. J. Shute, editors, *Intelligence Tutoring System (Proc. 4th Int'l Conf. ITS'98)*, pages 584-593. Springer.

Sycara, K., Decker, K., Pannu, A., Williamson, M., & Zeng, D. (1996). Distributed intelligent agents. *IEEE Expert*, *11*(6), 36–46. doi:10.1109/64.546581

Sycara, K., Paolucci, M., van Velsen, M., & Giampapa, J. (2003). The RETSINA MAS infrastructure," special joint issue of Autonomous Agents and MAS, vol. 7, no. 1 and 2.

Wang, J., Lewis, M., & Gennari, J. (2003). USAR: A game based simulation for teleoperation, *in Proceedings of the 47th Annual Meeting of the Human Factors and Ergonomics Society*, Denver, CO.

Weber, G., & Specht, M. (1997). User modeling and adaptive navigation support in www-based tutoring systems. *In Proceedings of the Sixth International Conference on User Modeling*, 289-300.

Weiss, G. (1999). *Multiagent Systems: A Modern Approach to Distributed Artificial Intelligence.* Cambridge, MA: The MIT Press.

Yang, A., Kemp, R., & Kinshuk. (2001). *Web based intelligent tutoring system.*

Zlotkin, G., & Rosenschein, J. (1989). Negotiation and task sharing among autonomous agents in cooperative domains, in Proceedings of the Eleventh International Joint Conference on Artificial Intelligence, pp. 912–917.

KEY TERMS AND DEFINITIONS

ABDITS: Agent based Distributed ITS is a Web-based, distributed, multi-agent learning system. The system ties the Web clients (for students) and the underlying information servers (for courseware and student profiles) together with the multi-agent resource management. The information and agents are supported by a distributed system consisting of workstations and storage devices connected via high-bandwidth networks. ABDITS is implemented using the prevalent technologies of the Internet, WWW and software agents.

CBR: Case-based reasoning is a problem-solving paradigm that in many respects is fundamentally different from other major AI approaches.

Instead of relying solely on general knowledge of a problem domain, or making associations along generalized relationships between problem descriptors and conclusions, CBR is able to utilize the specific knowledge of previously experienced, concrete problem situations (cases). A new problem is solved by finding a similar past case, and reusing it in the new problem situation. A second important difference is that CBR also is an approach to incremental, sustained learning, since a new experience is retained each time a problem has been solved, making it immediately available for future problems.

Intelligent Agent: An Intelligent agent is considered as a computing system that substitutes a person or process to carry out an activity or to fulfill a requirement. The substitute entity offers capacities to take similar decisions those described by the human intentions. An Intelligent Agent can operate between the boundaries of a general necessity or accurately represented among the limits of a given information space.

Intelligent System: A system, which is based on approach(es), method(s) or technique(s) of the Artificial Intelligence field to perform more accurate and effective operations for solving the related problems.

ITS: Intelligent Tutoring Systems (ITSs) are computer-based instructional systems with models of instructional content that specify what to teach, and teaching strategies that specify how to instruct the student in an intelligent way.

Pedagogical Model: It provides the necessary mechanism to efficiently present the matter to the students.

Student Model: The student model dynamically maintains some representation of the student's emerging knowledge. The function of the student model is to capture a student's understanding and not the knowledge about domain.

Chapter 14
Evaluation of Clustering Methods for Adaptive Learning Systems

Wilhelmiina Hämäläinen
University of Eastern Finland, Finland

Ville Kumpulainen
University of Eastern Finland, Finland

Maxim Mozgovoy
University of Aizu, Japan

ABSTRACT

Clustering student data is a central task in the educational data mining and design of intelligent learning tools. The problem is that there are thousands of clustering algorithms but no general guidelines about which method to choose. The optimal choice is of course problem- and data-dependent and can seldom be found without trying several methods. Still, the purposes of clustering students and the typical features of educational data make certain clustering methods more suitable or attractive. In this chapter, the authors evaluate the main clustering methods from this perspective. Based on the analysis, the authors suggest the most promising clustering methods for different situations.

INTRODUCTION

Clustering student data is a central task in the educational data mining and design of intelligent learning tools. Dividing data into natural groups gives a good summary how students are learning and helps to target teaching and tutoring. This is especially topical in the domain of online adaptive learning systems due to larger amount of students and their greater diversity. Clustering can also facilitate the design of predictive models, which are the heart of intelligent tutoring systems.

Indeed, a number of scholars report successful examples of clustering (for various purposes) in actual educational environments. However, the problem of selecting the most appropriate clustering method for student data is rarely addressed. There is a plenty of mainstream clustering methods and literally thousands of specialized clustering algorithms available (Jain, 2010), and choosing the right method for the given task is not easy. In practice, researchers often just pick up the most popular k-means method without a second thought whether its underlying assumptions suit the data.

DOI: 10.4018/978-1-4666-6276-6.ch014

In practice, this means that one may end up with an artificial partition of data instead of finding natural clusters.

The aim of the present work is to evaluate a variety of clustering methods from the perspective of clustering student data. We analyze the main approaches to clustering and see how useful models they produce and how well their underlying assumptions fit typical student data. We do not try to list as many algorithms as possible, but instead our emphasis is to describe the underlying clustering principles and evaluate their properties. Our main goal is to cover those clustering methods which are generally available in the existing data mining and statistical analysis tools, but we introduce also some promising "future methods". Based on this analysis, we suggest the most promising clustering methods for different situations.

The rest of the chapter is organized as follows: First, we give the basic definitions, analyze domain-specific requirements for clustering methods, and survey related research. Then, we introduce the main approaches for clustering and evaluate their suitability for typical student data. Finally, we discuss future research directions and draw the final conclusions. The basic notations used in this chapter are introduced in Table 1.

BACKGROUND

In this section, we define the basic concepts related to clustering, discuss the goals and special requirements of clustering educational data, and survey related research.

Basic Definitions

The main problem of clustering is how to define a cluster. There is no universally accepted precise definition of clustering. Intuitively, clustering means a grouping of data points, where points in one group are similar or close to each other but

Table 1. Basic notations

Notation	Meaning
m	Number of dimensions (variables)
n	Number of data points
k	Number of clusters
$p_i = (p_{i1}, ..., p_{im})$	Data point in m-dimensional data space
$D = \{p_1, ..., p_n\}$	Data set of n points
C_i	Cluster
c_i	Cluster centroid (representative point of cluster C_i)
$d(p_i, p_j)$	Distance between points p_i and p_j
$D(C_i, C_j)$	Distance between clusters C_i and C_j; inter-cluster distance
$|C_i|$	Size of cluster C_i; number of points belonging to C_i

different or distant from points in the other groups. One may also describe clusters as denser regions of the data space separated by sparser regions or as homogeneous subgroups in a heterogeneous population. Here, we give only a very generic definition of clustering and then describe its different aspects.

Definition 1 (Clustering): Let $D = \{\mathbf{p}_1, ..., \mathbf{p}_n\}$ be a data set of n points, $C = \{C_1, ..., C_k\}$ a set of k clusters, and M some clustering criterion. A *hard clustering* assigns each point $\mathbf{p}_j$ into exactly one cluster C_i according to M. A *soft clustering* defines for each point-cluster pair $(\mathbf{p}_j, C_i)$ a degree of membership according to M.

The above definition emphasizes one important aspect of clustering methods, their "hardness" or "softness". Hard methods produce always separate clusters, even if cluster boundaries were not clear, while soft methods allow overlapping clusters. Usually, the degree of membership is defined as the probability of point $\mathbf{p}_j$ to belong into cluster C_i, but fuzzy membership values are also used.

A related issue is how the clusters are represented. One approach is to define only cluster *centroids* (representative points, typically mean vectors) and use the distance from centroids to assign other points into clusters. If cluster probabilities are required, then other parameters like variance are needed to define cluster density functions. Alternatively, clusters can be represented by their boundaries or simply by listing their members. In *conceptual clustering* clusters are described by logical statements, like $(X \leq 5) \wedge (Y = 1)$.

Another aspect of cluster representation is whether the clustering is *flat* ("partitional" by Jain and Dubes (1988, Ch.3)) or *hierarchical*. A flat clustering is a single partition of data points, while a hierarchical clustering represents a sequence of nested clusterings (partition of larger clusters into subclusters).

The most important aspect of clustering methods is the clustering criterion (the *inductive principle* by Estivill-Castro (2002)). While the representational aspects describe *what kind of clustering models are possible*, the clustering criterion defines *which model fits the data best*. Usually, the clustering criterion is defined in the terms of a *similarity measure*, which tells how close or similar two points are. Given a similarity measure, one can also define inter-cluster similarity and express a clustering criterion that tries to maximize intra-cluster similarity and/or minimize inter-cluster similarity. If the clustering criterion is expressed explicitly, as a mathematical optimization problem (like a goodness function to be maximized), then the clustering problem can be tackled with different search algorithms. However, often the clustering criterion is expressed only implicitly, like rules for merging or splitting clusters based on similarity. In this case, the clustering criterion is usually bound to a certain search algorithm, which complicates an analytic comparison of clustering methods.

In the following, we discuss only the most commonly used similarity measures. For a comprehensive overview of different measures we refer to (Gan et al., 2007).

For numeric data, the most common choice for the similarity measure is the L_p metric or *Minkowski distance*:

$$L_p\left(\mathbf{p_i}, \mathbf{p_j}\right) = \left(\sum_{l=1}^{m} \left(p_{il} - p_{jl}\right)^p\right)^{1/p},$$

where $p \in \mathbb{R}^+$ is a user-given parameter and $\mathbf{p_i} = (p_{i1}, ..., p_{im})$ and $\mathbf{p_j} = (p_{j1}, ..., p_{jm})$ are two (m-dimensional) data points. The best known Minkowski measures are *Euclidean distance* L_2 and *Manhattan distance* L_1. For high dimensional data (at least when $m \geq 20$), L_1 and fractional L_p metrics ($p < 1$) are recommended, because they offer better contrast between distances (Aggarwal et al., 2001). They are also more robust measures for data containing several outliers (Agrawal et al., 1998). The reason is that with small p the distance distribution becomes more homogeneous and clusters can be better separated.

Generally, L_p metrics work well, if the clusters are compact and well-separated, but they fail, if the variables are in different scales. This is often the case with educational data, where variables can measure very different things like age, exercise points, or average studying time per week. As a solution, the data should be standardized to one norm or some variables should be weighed. If the variables are strongly correlated, then one should first remove correlations (by principal component analysis) or use *Mahalanobis metric*, which takes the dependencies into account (Jain et al., 1999). Detecting and removing irrelevant variables is also important, because they can dominate the distance measure and distort the results.

For categorical data, alternative similarity measures have been proposed (see e.g. Kantardzic (2011, Ch.9.2)). Two common choices are the *overlap metric* that is simply the number of common variable values which two data points share and *mutual neighbourhood distance* (*MND*), which reflects how close neighbours two points are to each other.

String values are a special case of categorical data and several distance measures have been developed for measuring distance or similarity between two strings. *Hamming distance* is a special case of the overlap metric, which calculates the number of character positions, where the two strings differ. Another popular measure is *minimum edit distance* that defines the minimum number of edit operations (e.g., insertion, deletion, substitution) needed to transform one string to another.

Mixed data, containing both numerical and categorical variables, is very tricky for clustering, because different types of variables are not comparable. Often, the easiest solution is to discretize numerical variables and use similarity measures for categorical data. Similarity measures for mixed data have also been developed (e.g., (Wilson and Martinez, 1997; Cheng et al., 2004; Ichino and Yaguchi, 1994)), but they are seldom available in general clustering tools.

Domain-Specific Requirements for Clustering Methods

Our main objective is to evaluate different clustering methods in the educational context, especially in distance learning. For this purpose, we should know the special requirements of the domain. These are imposed by two factors: the goals of clustering students and the characteristics of typical data.

According to our literature survey, there are two main reasons to cluster student data. The first reason is purely descriptive: to understand the data, to see if the students fall into subgroups with different characteristics and how this affects learning. This information can reveal successful learning patterns (Käser et al., 2013) or effective ways of using learning tools (Perera et al., 2009), but it can also be used for allocating students into different teaching groups (Huikkola et al., 2008) or targetting tutoring (Schmitt et al., 2007). In this context, outliers which do not belong to any cluster, are also interesting. They represent somehow exceptional students who may need extra concern, like individualized teaching or more challenges.

The second reason is to facilitate construction of predictive models for intelligent tutoring systems or other adaptive learning tools. In the intelligent tools, the main problem is usually classification — the tool should first classify the student and/or the current situation before it can select an optimal action (Hämäläinen and Vinni, 2010). Clustering is often a useful preprocessing step for the classifier construction. It can be used to select representative features which separate classes well (such that clusters have homogeneous class distributions), to select natural classes, or even as an initialization for a K-nearest neighbour style classifiers (Lopez et al., 2012; Käser et al., 2013). Cluster-based linear regression models are also possible (Trivedi et al., 2011a).

Common to these goals is that clustering is used to find a natural grouping of data, irrespective of cluster sizes or shapes. This is in contrast to many applications, where clustering is actually used for segmentation, i.e., partitioning the data in some convenient way (Hand et al., 2002, Ch.9.3). In segmentation, partitioning into balanced hyperspherical clusters may well be convenient, even if it would not capture the real clusters. For this reason, methods which work well in other domains (when used for segmentation) may fail in educational data mining.

In student data, the clusters are often unclear, arbitrary-shaped, or overlapping. Therefore, the clustering method should also be flexible. For overlapping clusters, a soft clustering would be the most natural. It could also help to select optimal actions similarly to probabilistic classifiers (see e.g. (Hämäläinen and Vinni, 2010)).

Characteristics of typical data have a strong impact on the selection of clustering method. In this chapter, our main focus is clustering student data (demographic and performance data). The following characterization of typical student data (available in distance learning and adaptive learning systems) is based on a meta-analysis in the previous research (Hämäläinen and Vinni, 2010) and confirmed by our own and other researchers' experiences (Perera et al., 2009). We list six characteristics and the requirements they impose on the clustering methods.

First, the typical data sets are quite small, usually only 100-300 rows or even less. The reason is that data sets are usually from one course during one semester and thus restricted by the number of students. Sometimes, it is possible to pool data from several years, if the recorded variables (like exercise tasks and their assessment) have remained unchanged. Still, it is unlikely that the data size would exceed 1000 rows. In practice, this means that one can select computationally demanding (and often better quality) methods for clustering.

Second, the data usually consists of both categorical and numerical variables. Numerical variables are typically discrete, like task scores, which can obtain only a few possible values. Continuous numerical variables are rarer. One reason is that physical devices, which are the main source of continuous variables, are seldom used to gather data for educational systems. Binary variables, like gender, whether the student has certain preliminary knowledge or skills, is working aside studies, etc. are relatively common. Answers to multiple choice queries are often recorded as nominal or binary variables (correct or incorrect), but sometimes they can also be ordinal (like a selfassessment of programming skills into excellent, good, satisfactory, or poor). Ideally, the clustering method should be able to handle mixed data, but, in practice, one may have to transform all variables to categorical or cluster only numerical variables.

Third, the number of variables can be very large in proportion to the number of rows (even > 50 variables), if it contains all available demographic features and comprehensive questionnaire data, including scores, error types, habits, preferences, and measures for student activity. However, it is hard to give reliable estimates based on previous research articles, because most of them report only a handful (5-10) variables which they have used for final modelling. Anyway, it seems that the original data can be quite sparse, and some feature selection or combining is required before clustering.

Fourth, the numeric variables are seldom normally distributed. In fact, the distribution may be even valley-shaped instead of hill-shaped. This means that one should be cautious when using methods which assume normality or other fixed distribution families.

Fifth, student data contains often a relatively large number of outliers (exceptional students). Therefore, the clustering method should be robust to outliers and preferably help to detect them.

Sixth, the variables tend to be mutually dependent. This means that the data is not uniformly distributed and we are likely to find clusters. However, some methods (or similarity measures, like L_p metrics) do not allow correlations. If one wants to use such methods, then the correlations (or dependencies, in general) should be removed before clustering.

Related Research

There are many good survey papers which have evaluated and compared different clustering methods and algorithms. Jain et al. (1999) give a very comprehensive survey of the whole clustering process, including similarity measures, clustering methods, applications, and even practical tips. Different clustering criteria and methods are well evaluated in the papers by Berkhin (2006) and Halkidi et al. (2001), although the latter concentrates more on validation. Ghosh (2004) gives an overview of different clustering approaches. The paper by Estivill-Castro (2002) discusses different aspects of clustering methods (models, clustering criteria, and algorithms) and compares some wellknown clustering criteria. All these papers compare only the traditional clustering methods. The survey by Xu and Wunsch (2005) covers also newer methods, like neural network- and kernel-based methods. It gives a comprehensive overview of the most important algorithms, but it can be hard to see which algorithms actually implement the same clustering criteria. In addition, there are survey papers on certain specific topics, like subspace clustering (Parsons et al., 2004) or text clustering (Aggarwal and Zhai, 2012).

In addition, there are domain-specific papers which have either compared different clustering methods empirically or evaluated their suitability for the typical data and problems of the domain. This kind of papers are especially popular in bioinformatics (e.g., (Yona et al., 2009; Andreopoulos et al., 2009)). However, they are of little use in the educational domain, where the clustering purposes and data sets are very different.

In the educational domain, we have not been able to find any evaluations or comparisons between different clustering methods. Still, many interesting use cases and applications have been reported. In most of them, the researchers have just picked up one clustering method (typically the k-means algorithm). In this sense, the work by Lopez et al. (2012) is exceptional, because several algorithms were actually compared. In addition, the researchers constructed a successful cluster-based classifier for predicting course outcomes. Trivedi et al. (2011a) went even further and developed a new prediction method (combining several cluster-based linear regression models) for predicting course grades. Pardos et al. (2012) applied the same model for knowledge tracing. Nugent et al. (2010) modified the k-means clustering algorithm for clustering students according to their skill profiles. The work by Huikkola et al. (2008) is a good example of careful feature extraction and selection when clustering large-

dimensional questionnaire data. There is also an excellent overview on spectral clustering with some discussion how it could be applied in educational data mining (Trivedi et al., 2011b).

EVALUATION OF THE MAIN CLUSTERING METHODS

In this section, we introduce the main approaches for clustering and evaluate their suitability for typical educational (student) data. The number of different clustering methods is so enormous that it is impossible to cover all of them. Therefore, we have grouped the methods into four categories according to what kind of clustering models they produce: Representative-based and hierarchical methods, mixture model clustering, and density-based methods. The goal is to cover clustering methods that are usually available in data mining and statistical analysis tools.

Representative-Based Methods

In *representative-based clustering methods*, each cluster C_i is represented by its centroid c_i. In the case of numerical data, centroid is usually the mean vector of cluster points, although it may be also the median vector or a data point closest to the median, called a *medoid*. Each data point p_j is assigned to the cluster whose centroid c_i is closest, i.e. which minimizes distance $d(p_j, c_i)$ with the given distance measure d. The clustering problem is to select centroids $c_1, ..., c_k$ such that some score function measuring the clustering quality is optimized. The most common criterion is to minimize the total *sum of squared errors*

$$SSE = \sum_{i=1}^{k} \sum_{p_j \in C_i} d^2\left(p_j, c_i\right),$$

where distance measure d is typically Euclidean distance, L_2. In the following, we call this as the *k-means criterion*. This should not be confused with the *k-means algorithm* which is only one way to optimize the *k*-means criterion. Many properties associated to the *k*-means algorithm are actually due to the underlying clustering criterion and thus shared by the alternative search methods.

The *k*-means criterion works well, if the clusters are hyperspherical, compact and well-separated, but otherwise it can produce misleading results. It also tends to produce equal-sized clusters which is desirable in segmentation but seldom makes justice to natural clusters. The main problem of the *k*-means criterion is its sensitivity to outliers. The reason is that a couple of extreme points can have a strong impact on the mean. It is also clear from the definition that the *k*-means criterion can be used only for a strict clustering of numerical data. In addition, the SSE score function does not offer means to determine the optimal number of clusters, *k*. (Jain et al., 1999; Estivill-Castro, 2002; Jain and Dubes, 1988, Ch.3.3; Hand et al., 2002, Ch.9.4).

Some of these problems can be alleviated by modifying the *k*-means criterion. When the Euclidean distance is replaced by the Mahalanobis distance, it is possible to detect also hyperellipsoidal clusters (Jain et al., 2000). The *k-medians* criterion uses medians instead of means as cluster centroids. The criterion is more robust to outliers because medians are less affected by extreme points than means (Estivill-Castro, 2002). However, determining medians is computationally much more costly. As a compromise, it is required that the centroids are data points closest to the medians, known as the *k-medoids* criterion. The criterion allows also ordinal categorical variables, if a suitable distance measure has been defined. For categorical data, one can use modes (the most common values) to define centroids, with an appropriate distance measure (the *k-modes algorithm* (Huang, 1998)). There are even attempts to extend the idea for mixed data (the *k-prototypes algorithm* (Huang, 1998)).

A fuzzy version of the k-means criterion, known as *fuzzy k-means*, defines a soft clustering, where each point can belong to several clusters with different degrees. The minimized score function is

$$FSSE = \sum_{i=1}^{k}\sum_{j=1}^{n} mem_i^b\left(\mathbf{p_j}\right) d\left(\mathbf{p_j}, \mathbf{c_i}\right),$$

where $mem_i(\mathbf{p_j})$ is the grade of membership with which $\mathbf{p_j}$ belongs to the cluster C_i, $= 1$, and parameter $b \geq 1$ regulates the degree of fuzziness.

Soft clustering is quite appealing in the educational context, because the clusters are seldom well-separated and one would not like to force data points into artificial clusters. Fuzzy membership values do also offer extra information, but their interpretation can be difficult, because they are not probabilities. The biggest problem in fuzzy clustering is how to define the membership functions which have a crucial effect on results. Some solutions are discussed e.g. in (Jain and Dubes, 1988, Ch.3.3.8).

Clustering methods based on statistical mixture models could also be considered as soft representative-based methods. However, they are actually more general, and the *k*-means criterion can be considered as a special case of the mixture model clustering, as we will see later.

So far, we have discussed only the clustering criteria of representative-based clustering. These criteria determine what kind of clustering models we could find, if we had a globally optimal search algorithm. However, the optimization problem is intractable even for small data sets, and in practice one has to use heuristic search algorithms. These algorithms have their own bias which can affect the results.

The most popular clustering algorithm for the *k*-means criterion and its variants is the iterative search (*k*-means, *k*-medoids, and fuzzy *c*-means algorithms). The basic *k*-means algorithm begins from some initial set of centroids and assigns all points to their nearest clusters. Then it iteratively calculates new cluster means (centroids) and assigns points to their nearest clusters, until some stopping criterion (e.g. convergence) is met. The *k*-means algorithm is easy to implement and quite efficient even with large data sets. In practice, it can produce surprisingly good results, if the clusters are compact, hyperspherical, and well-separated (Jain et al., 2000). However, it is very sensitive to the selection of the initial partition (centroids) and can easily converge to a local minimum, if the initial partition is far from the final solution (Jain et al., 1999). It is also very sensitive to noise and outliers, which is mostly due to the clustering criterion. An interesting dilemma is that while the k-means criterion itself tends to favour equal-sized clusters (Hand et al., 2002, Ch. 9.4), the k-means algorithm can produce very different sized clusters, even empty ones (Berkhin, 2006).

In common implementations, the user should define the number of clusters in advance, but more sophisticated algorithms (like x-means (Pelleg and Moore, 2000)) can select the number automatically according to some goodness criterion. The fuzzy c-means algorithm (Bezdek, 1981) shares the same drawbacks as k-means, but is has been said to be less prone to converge into a local minimum (Jain et al., 1999).

More advanced search algorithms can produce better results, but at the cost of computational cost. In addition, these algorithms usually require several user-specified parameters, which affect the results.

The most straight-forward solution is to optimize the k-means clustering criterion or its fuzzy variant with the classical optimization methods, like simulated annealing, tabu search, genetic algorithms, or other evolutionary methods. In empirical comparisons, all these have performed better than the basic k-means, but none of them has been consistently superior to others. It seems that problem-specific evolutionary methods are potentially very good at discovering the global optimum, if the data set is small-dimensional and small-sized (less than 1000 rows) (Jain et al., 1999).

Another approach is to search for an optimal clustering using neural networks. Several architectures and algorithms have been suggested for both the k-means and the fuzzy k-means criteria (for an overview see e.g. (Xu and Wunsch, 2008, Ch.5). Common to these methods is that they suit only

to numerical data, the results depend on several parameters, and the clustering can be unstable (Jain et al., 1999). In this group, we should also mention *self-organizing maps* (SOMs) (Kohonen, 1982) that perform a k-means style clustering with extra constraints, but also produce a visual 2-dimensional representation of the clusters and their topological relations. This representation is potentially very informative, but it should be interpreted with caution, because it does not always represent the space density correctly (Xu and Wunsch, 2005). Like most neural network methods, SOMs are also sensitive to initial parameters and can produce unstable results (Jain et al., 1999).

Kernel-based clustering methods, like kernel k-means (Schölkopf et al., 1998), are potentially very robust methods for numerical data. The basic idea of kernel-based methods is to map the original data implicitly (with the kernel trick) into a higher-dimensional space, where clusters become linearly separable. This is useful especially when the clusters are linearly inseparable in the original space and, thus, cannot be separated with the common k-means. The kernel-methods can detect arbitrary-shaped clusters and they are robust to noise and outliers. However, they are too inefficient for large data sets and deciding the parameters can be difficult (Xu and Wunsch, 2005).

In this connection, we should also mention *spectral clustering methods*, because they are closely related to kernel-based methods, in spite of their different looking algorithms. It has been shown that the underlying clustering criteria (optimized objective functions) of the spectral clustering and a particular form of the *weighed kernel k-means* clustering are equivalent (Dhillon et al., 2004). The main idea of spectral clustering methods is the following: First, a similarity matrix, based on point-wise distances between nearest neighbours, is constructed and the corresponding Laplacian matrix is computed. The k first eigenvectors of this matrix are selected as new variables. Then, the data is clustered with the k-means (or any other method) in this new smaller-dimensional space. The spectral methods can detect arbitrary-shaped clusters, which could not be detected in the original data space. In addition, they suit to any data type, because they require only point-wise distances. The results can be very good, if the original similarity matrix was well chosen, but choosing a good similarity matrix is not a trivial task. In addition, the methods do not scale up to large data sets. This can be partially alleviated by considering only the nearest neighbours (i.e., using a sparse similarity matrix), but this can have a strong impact on the clustering results. (Luxburg, 2007; Dhillon et al., 2007). A more promising solution is to solve the spectral clustering problem with a faster weighed kernel k-means method (Dhillon et al., 2007).

For the educational data, the representative-based methods, like the k-means clustering and its neural equivalents, are seldom the optimal choice, even if the data were numerical. The clusters are often unclear or arbitrary-shaped and there are typically several outliers. In this sense, the kernel-based methods sound the most promising, especially when the data sets tend to be small. For categorical and mixed data, the spectral clustering and its solutions with the weighed kernel k-means offer a good alternative. Unfortunately, these new clustering methods are not yet available in common data mining tools.

Hierarchical Methods

Hierarchical clustering methods do not produce just a single partition of data, but a sequence of partitions. The result is a hierarchy of clusters which can be represented visually as a *dendrogram*. The dendrogram is a binary tree structure, whose root corresponds a single large cluster containing all data points and leaves correspond to n small clusters, each containing just one data point. Children of a node show how a cluster is divided into subclusters. An example is shown in Figure 1. In practice, the dendrogram can be constructed

until the desired number of clusters is left or one can select the best clustering afterwards, after analyzing the dendrogram.

Hierarchical clustering methods can be divided into two main approaches, *agglomerative* and *divisive* methods. Agglomerative methods proceed in a bottom-up manner, beginning from clusters of single data points and merging neighbouring clusters until only one cluster is left. Divisive methods work in the opposite way, in a top-down manner, by dividing superclusters into neighbouring subclusters until all points are in their own clusters. In practice, agglomerative methods are more popular, because they are computationally cheaper and easier to implement.

The neighbouring clusters to be merged or split are defined by some score function D, which measures the similarity of clusters. This inter-cluster distance is often called a *linkage metric*. It is calculated from the distances between some or all points in two clusters. The choice of the linkage metric has a strong impact on the clustering results, because it defines the shape, size, and density of clusters which can be found. Most metrics tend to produce hyperspherical (isotropic) clusters. In Table 2, we have listed the most common inter-cluster measures and types of clusters they tend to produce.

The *single-link* metric is flexible in the sense that it can find non-isotropic clusters (with unsymmetrical shapes) and the clusters can be even concentric. On the other hand, it has tendency to produce elongated and straggly clusters. This is called the "chaining effect": the measure combines clusters through other external points and the clusters become chain-like. As a result, the single-link metric works best for well-separated, non-spherical clusters. One advantage of the single-link metric compared to other linkage metrics is that it is independent from the data order and the resulting clustering is always unique. The single-link metric is also quite efficient to compute. In empirical comparisons, the single-link metric has usually performed poorly, although it may some-

Figure 1. An example dendrogram

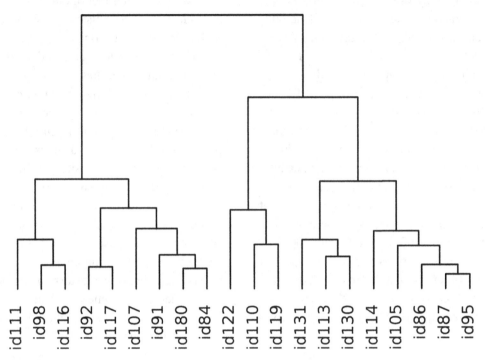

times surprise with good results (Jain and Dubes, 1988, Ch.3.5.2). This is also our own experience, although we have found that the single-link metric is very good at detecting outliers.

The *complete-link* metric works usually better than the single-link metric, but it is slower to calculate and does not suit for large data sets. It tends to produces small, compact, equal-sized clusters, but it cannot separate concentric clusters. The main disadvantage of the complete-link metric is its dependency on the data order. In empirical comparisons, the complete-link metric has usually performed well (Jain and Dubes, 1988, Ch.3.5.2). Our experiences with the complete-link metric have also been quite good, although it has not been able to detect even obvious outliers.

The *average-link* metric produces clusters which are between the single-link and the complete-link metrics in their compactness. It produces dense clusters, letting larger clusters to be sparser than the smaller ones. Its main disadvantage is the dependency on the data order. In addition, the metric is quite inefficient to compute, which may

be a burden for really large data sets. In empirical comparisons, the average-link metric has usually performed quite well (Jain and Dubes, 1988, Ch.3.5.2). In our own experience, the average metric has produced good and stable results, although it has not been able to detect outliers. One possible explanation for the stability is that the metric is based on all points in measured clusters and is thus less affected by outliers and noise than metrics based on single points.

The *minimum variance* metric is famous and it is used e.g. in the classical *Ward's method* (Ward, 1963). It minimizes the variance in the clusters through the *SSE* score function. The resulting clusters are hyperspherical and quite compact, but it is not possible to find elongated clusters. The metric is computationally efficient, because it depends only on the centroids and sizes of C_1 and C_2 (Jain and Dubes, 1988, Ch.3.2.7). Like the previous two metrics, the minimum variance metric is also dependent on the data order. In empirical comparisons, the metric has generally performed well, especially if clusters are of equal

Table 2. Common measures for the inter-cluster distance D, given the distance between points d. Cluster type describes what kinds of clusters the measure tends to produce

Metric	$D(C_1, C_2)$	Cluster type
Single-link	$\min\limits_{\mathbf{p}_1 \in C_1, \mathbf{p}_2 \in C_2} \left\{ d\left(\mathbf{p}_1, \mathbf{p}_2\right) \right\}$	Elongated, straggly, also concentric clusters
Complete-link	$\max\limits_{\mathbf{p}_1 \in C_1, \mathbf{p}_2 \in C_2} \left\{ d\left(\mathbf{p}_1, \mathbf{p}_2\right) \right\}$	Small, compact, hyperspherical, equal-sized
Average-link	$\dfrac{\sum\limits_{\mathbf{p}_1 \in C_1, \mathbf{p}_2 \in C_2} d\left(\mathbf{p}_1, \mathbf{p}_2\right)}{\left\lvert C_2 \right\rvert \left\lvert C_2 \right\rvert}$	Quite compact clusters; allows different sizes and densities
Minimum variance (Ward)	$SSE\left(C_1 \cup C_2\right) - SSE\left(C_1\right) - SSE\left(C_2\right)$	Compact, quite well-separated, hyperspherical; cannot find elongated clusters or clusters of very different sizes
Distance of centroids	$d\left(\mathbf{c}_1, \ \mathbf{c}_2\right)$	Hyperspherical, equal-sized clusters; cannot detect elongated clusters

size (Jain and Dubes, 1988, Ch.3.5.2). Our own experiences have been mixed. In some data sets, the metric has produced very good results, while in others it has produced strange results or showed instability (strong dependence on the data order).

The *distance of centroids* is sometimes used to approximate the minimum variance metric. The metric is really efficient to calculate, but results can be quite poor. It works well (like most methods) if clusters are hyperspherical and well-separated, but if they are arbitrary-shaped, like elongated, the results can be quite insensible (Guha et al., 1998). In empirical comparisons, its performance has not been impressive (Jain and Dubes, 1988, Ch.3.5.2). According to our experiences, this metric has worked relatively well. The results have been quite similar to the average-link metric, although not always as good. In addition, we have observed that the metric seems to be less sensitive to the data order than the minimum variance metric.

In addition to these classical linkage metrics, some algorithms use their own metrics. For example, CURE (Guha et al., 1998) selects several representative points to capture the shape and extent of a cluster, moves them towards the cluster center, and determines the cluster distances by these new points. The metric has many advantages: it can detect nonspherical (like elongated) clusters of different sizes and is robust to outliers (Guha et al., 1998). Another example is CHAMELEON (Karypis et al., 1999), which combines graph-partitioning and agglomerative hierarchical clustering. In the first phase, the algorithm constructs a nearest-neighbour graph, whose edge weights reflect how close neighbours the points are to each other. The graph is partitioned into a large number of small clusters. In the second phase, the algorithm performs an agglomerative hierarchical clustering and merges clusters using a special metric. The metric is actually a combination of two metrics, which measure the *relative inter-connectivity* between two clusters and their *relative closeness*. The resulting clustering criterion is quite flexible and CHAMELEON can detect arbitrary-shaped clusters of different sizes and densities. In practice, CHAMELEON has also performed very well (Han and Kamber, 2006, Ch.7.5.4). However, both CURE and CHAMELEON require user-specified parameters which can be difficult to select.

Another interesting option is to base the metric on the probability of data given the clustering, like in the statistical mixture model methods. These metrics try to evaluate how much the log likelihood of data changes when two clusters are combined. Different variations of this metric and their relations to classical linkage metrics have been described in (Zhong and Ghosh, 2003).

In general, hierarchical methods have several attractive features and suit well to educational data. They can be applied to numerical, categorical, and even mixed data, if the point-wise distances have been defined. The dendrogram contains useful information on the hierarchy and relationships of clusters. In addition, there are several similarity measures to try with different shapes of clusters.

However, there are also drawbacks which should be kept in mind. We have already noted that most hierarchical methods are dependent on the data order and can produce different clusterings with different data orders. In practice, it is always advisable to test the stability of results with different data orders. Deciding the number of clusters or the final level of the dendrogram can also be difficult. Even for a moderate size of data (more than a couple of hundred rows), dendrograms can be too messy to inspect visually. As a solution, one can use methods, like BIRCH (Zhang et al., 1997), which first precluster the data into a large number of small clusters, and then construct the hierarchy. However, these methods may sometimes produce unnatural clusterings (Halkidi et al., 2001).

Other problems are related to the search algorithms and not to the hierarchical methods per se. The main disadvantage of the classical greedy algorithms is the static nature of cluster allocations. When a point has once been assigned to a cluster, it cannot be moved elsewhere. Therefore, the algorithm is not able to correct its earlier misassignments (Xu and Wunsch, 2005). This restriction has been solved in the more sophisticated implementations. For example, when hierarchical clustering is implemented by neural networks,

the points can be moved from a cluster to another during clustering (Khan and Luo, 2005). In addition, hierarchical algorithms are not as efficient as the k-means algorithm for large data sets (a large number of rows or dimensions), although this is seldom a problem with the educational data.

Mixture Model Clustering

Mixture model clustering refers to methods which perform clustering by fitting a statistical mixture model into data. They have also been called "clustering by mixture decomposition" (Jain and Dubes, 1988), "probabilistic model-based clustering" (Hand et al., 2002), or simply "probabilistic clustering" (Berkhin, 2006).

Mixture model clustering methods differ from the previous methods in one fundamental aspect: they do not try cluster the existing data points into crisp clusters, but instead they try to learn a statistical density model for the whole data space. From this model, one can then derive for each data point $\mathbf{p}_j$ the probabilities $P(C_i \mid \mathbf{p}_j)$ by which it belongs to clusters C_i, $i = 1, \ldots, k$. In addition, the model enables us to predict clusters for new data points and update the model when new data points are added or removed. In the 2-dimensional case, the model can be represented visually, by density contours (see Figure 2). The underlying assumption is that the data has been generated by a mixture of probabilistic models (multivariate distributions). Each cluster has a prior probability and its own probability distribution. The whole model is typically represented as a multivariate mixture model.

Definition 2 (Multivariate Mixture Model): Let
S be a numeric data space and k the number of clusters. Let $f_i(\mathbf{p}, \Theta_i)$ be be the density function of cluster C_i with parameters Θ_i and π_i the prior probability of cluster C_i. Then the multivariate mixture model is defined by density function $f: S \rightarrow [0, 1]$ such that for all $\mathbf{p} \in S$

Figure 2. An example contour map that describes data densities

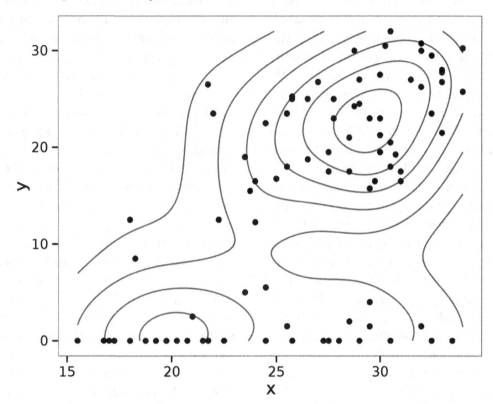

$$f\left(\mathbf{p}\right) = \sum_{i=1}^{k} \eth_i f_i \left(\mathbf{p}, \dot{E}_i\right).$$

Here $f_i(\mathbf{p}, \Theta_i)$ defines the probability that data point p belongs to cluster C_i and $f(\mathbf{p})$ describes the posterior probability of data point $\mathbf{p}$ given the whole model. If $f(\mathbf{p})$ is very low, the point does not fit the model, and it can be interpreted as an outlier.

The density function f_i describes the data distribution in cluster C_i. In principle, we can define a different type of distribution for each cluster. This is useful, when the data is very skewed. However, in practice, it is very difficult to define the appropriate distributional form without any prior knowledge. That is why it is usually assumed that the density in all clusters has the same distributional form, and only the distribution parameters are different. A common choice is to assume the normal distribution.

The whole clustering process consists of four steps:

1. Determine the number of clusters k (optional).
2. Choose the density functions f_i for all clusters C_i.
3. Determine the cluster probabilities π_i and parameters Θ_i (and potentially k) such that the probability of the data given the model is maximized (according to some principle).
4. Assign each point $\mathbf{p}$ to the most probable cluster, i.e. select such C_i that $P(C_i \mid \mathbf{p})$ is maximal.

Usually, the parameters are selected either by the *Maximum likelihood* (ML) principle, which maximizes the data (log-)likelihood given the model, or the *Maximum a posteriori probability* (MAP) principle, which maximizes the posterior probability of the model, given data. If the prior probabilities of clusters are equal, then these two principles coincide (Fraley and Raftery, 2000). The simplest and most effcient way to approximate the parameters is the *Expectation Maximization* (EM) algorithm, which performs an iterative *k*-means style search. In Bayesian approaches, *Markov Chain Monte-Carlo methods* (MCMC) have also been used, but they are computationally much more demanding (Fraley and Raftery, 2000).

The best number of clusters is usually selected automatically, according to some score function like *Minimum Description Length* (MDL) or *Bayesian Information Criterion* (BIC) (Fraley and Raftery, 2000). Both of them maximize the log-likelihood of data with some penalty terms for large *k*. Techniques based on cross-validation have also been applied successfully (Smyth, 2000). According to Stanford and Raftery (2000), both BIC and cross-validation methods converge to the global optimum, when the sample size grows, but BIC is faster to compute.

The mixture model clustering has several advantages. The clustering is not strict, but each data point can belong to several clusters with different probabilities. This means that the clusters can be overlapping, which is often the case with educational data. In addition, the probabilities themselves are useful extra information which can be utilized in adaptive learning systems (e.g., when selecting an optimal action). In the two-dimensional case, the densities have a nice visual representation as contour maps, and outliers are easily recognized.

The mixture models are very flexible and can describe even complex structures. For example, every cluster can have different size and density, even different type of distribution. In addition, it has been observed that several other clustering methods are special cases of mixture model clustering (Fraley and Raftery, 2000; Kamvar et al., 2002). For example, the *k*-means criterion is equivalent to the mixture model, where density functions are Gaussian, all variables are assumed

to be mutually independent, and all variables in all components have the same variance (Fraley and Raftery, 2000). Mixture model clustering can also be applied to categorical data, using e.g. multinomial distributions, but mixed data is problematic.

The flexibility of the mixture model clustering has also a drawback: the resulting clustering depends strongly on the selected form of the distribution which can be hard to define without any prior knowledge. Assuming a wrong parametric model can lead to poor or misleading results. In the worst case, wrong model assumptions can impose a structure into data, instead of finding one. (Duda et al., 2000, Ch.10.6) In principle, unknown distributions can be approximated with a sufficiently large number of Gaussian components (Fraley and Raftery, 2000), but such models do not reveal the real clusters directly. In addition, the most adaptive models are also the most complex and can require a lot of parameters. These can be impossible to determine accurately, if the data is sparse (Fraley and Raftery, 2000). Therefore, many implementations allow only the normal distribution with the assumption of variable independence and uniform variances. This is usually unrealistic with educational data. The normal distribution makes the method also sensitive to outliers, because extreme data points have a strong effect on variance.

There are also problems which are related to the search algorithm. The optimization problem is computationally demanding and even the simple iterative EM algorithm does not scale to large data sets. Fortunately, this is seldom a problem with educational data sets. The EM algorithm is also very sensitive to the initial parameters and can get stuck at a local optimum. As a solution, the data can be first clustered with another method, which defines the initial cluster means and variances. For example, initialization by hierarchical clustering has produced good results and at the same time the ideal number of clusters could be determined (Dasgupta and Raftery, 1998; Fraley and Raftery,

1998). Another alternative is to implement the entire probabilistic clustering in a hierarchical way (Murtagh and Raftery, 1984; Banfield and Raftery, 1993).

In practice, mixture model clustering with the EM algorithm has produced varying results. Usually the results have been good, but the algorithm can fail if some clusters contain only a few data points or there are redundant variables (Fraley and Raftery, 2000). Our own experiences are restricted to clustering numerical data using Gaussian mixture models, with the unrealistic assumption of variable independence. This kind of a model was clearly unsuitable for our student data and could not detect the natural clusters. Still, the composed density function could describe the data well, if the number of clusters was sufficiently large. We have also tested how well the method suits to outlier detection, i.e., whether the most improbable points capture real outliers. The results have been diverse. It seems that if the model is sufficiently simple (only a few clusters), the most improbable points correspond well the real outliers. However, if the model is very complex (many clusters), then all points are relatively probable and no outliers can be detected by their probability. These observations hint that if one wants to get a strict clustering and detect outliers, then a small number of clusters is preferable, but if one prefers an accurate description of the data by densities, then a more complex model with several clusters should be used.

According to this evaluation, the mixture model clustering has a great potential for clustering educational data, but there are still many practical problems to be solved.

Density-Based Methods

Density-based methods regard clusters as dense regions in the data space separated by sparser regions. Some of these methods approximate the overall density function, like mixture model methods, while others use only local density in-

formation to construct clusters. In this sense, the mixture model methods could also be classified as (parametric) density-based methods, although the term usually refers to non-parametric methods, which are discussed here. The advantage of the non-parametric density-based methods is that one does not have to know the number or distributional form of the subpopulations (clusters).

In the following, we introduce three famous algorithms which represent different approaches to density-based clustering. Many of the other density-based algorithms are only improved (better-scalable) variants of these algorithms. In addition, there are hybrid methods (like previously mentioned CHAMELEON and BIRCH) which use density-based techniques only in some phase of the algorithm, like preclustering.

Most density-based algorithms proceed in a two-phase manner: First, they detect the cluster cores in the densest areas and then they expand the clusters, as long as the density remains sufficiently high. DBSCAN (Ester et al., 1996) can be considered as a prototype of this type of algorithms. DBSCAN defines cluster cores as points whose surroundings (inside a certain radius, *Eps*) contain sufficiently many (at least *MinPts*) other points. Then the clusters are expanded, by adding all sufficiently close points, which may lead to merging of clusters. Points which are too far from any cluster cores remain as outliers. The main advantages of DBSCAN are its ability to detect arbitrary-shaped clusters and robustness to outliers. In addition, it can be applied to categorical or even mixed data, given a suitable measure for point-wise distances. However, it is very sensitive to the input parameters. Wrong parameter values can lead to a similar chaining effect as seen with the single-link metric. Another problem is how to detect clusters of different densities, because they would require different parameter values. In addition, DBSCAN does not suit to large-dimensional or large data sets (Halkidi et al., 2001; Guha et al., 1998; Wang and Hamilton, 2003).

DENCLUE (Hinneburg et al., 1998) represents another approach of density-based methods, because it approximates the overall density function to perform the clustering. The main idea is the following: For each data point, the algorithm determines an *influence function* which describes its impact in the neighbourhood. The overall density function is calculated from these influence functions. The local maxima of the density function are defined as *density attractors*, which form the cluster cores. The attractors can be used as cluster centroids like in representative-based methods or one can construct arbitrary-shaped clusters by combining several attractors. All other points are assigned to the same cluster as their attractors, if their density function value is sufficiently high. Otherwise, they are considered as outliers. The DENCLUE algorithm has several advantages: it can detect arbitrary-shaped clusters and give them a compact mathematical representation, it is very robust to noise and outliers and quite efficient (compared to other density-based methods). The main problem is that the results depend on several input parameters (including the influence function), which can be difficult to select. In addition, it can handle only numerical data (Berkhin, 2006; Halkidi et al., 2001; Han and Kamber, 2006, Ch.7.6.3).

Wavecluster (Sheikholeslami et al., 1998) is an interesting clustering algorithm which is sometimes classified as a grid-based method. The basic idea is to divide the data space into small hyper-rectangular cells, map this compressed data with a wavelet transformation, and then search for dense areas in the transformed space. The underlying idea is that in the transformed space even arbitrary-shaped clusters become better distinguishable. Wavecluster has several attractive features. It can detect clusters of different shapes and sizes, it is robust to noise and outliers, produces good quality results, and is quite efficient. However, the user has to define several parameters, including the wavelet type. These parameters affect, among other things, how many and how well-separated clusters are found. In addition, Wavecluster can handle only numerical data (Halkidi et al., 2001; Han and Kamber, 2006, Ch.7.7.2).

For educational data, density-based methods are quite promising, at least for small-dimensional data. They can detect arbitrary-shaped clusters and are robust to outliers. Some methods (like DBSCAN and its successors) can handle also categorical and mixed data. One drawback is that the nonparametric density-based methods do not offer any easily interpretable representation for the clusters like mixture models. Generally, density-based methods are not recommended to high-dimensional data, because all data tends to become sparse in high dimensions (Jain, 2010). In addition, most empirical comparisons of density-based methods have been made with 2- or 3-dimensional data, and it is not known whether they produce equally good results with higher dimensional data.

Which Method to Choose?

As we have seen, all clustering methods have their strengths and weaknesses. There is no universally superior clustering method, but the best choice depends always on the context. Even for typical educational data, we cannot give any unique recommendation. However, we can give some suggestions based on our evaluation.

If the data is purely categorical or contains both numerical and categorical variables, the easiest choice is to use methods, which require only pair-wise distances among data points. These include hierarchical methods, DBSCAN-style density-based methods, and spectral clustering. Among hierarchical methods, CHAMELEON has been especially recommended (Han and Kamber, 2006). The classical hierarchical methods have several weaknesses (especially, the stability problem) and we would not recommend them as a primary choice. All above mentioned methods, CHAMELEON, DBSCAN, and spectral clustering, can detect arbitrary-shaped clusters. At least DBSCAN is said to be robust to outliers. In addition, it has an extra advantage that it does not require the number of clusters as a parameter but it may have problems with clusters of different densities. Spectral clustering is potentially a very powerful technique, but one should be ready to experiment with different similarity matrices.

For numerical data, there are more good choices. For arbitrary-shaped clusters, the best candidates are the kernel k-means, density-based methods like DENCLUE and Wavecluster, previously mentioned CHAMELEON and spectral clustering, and maybe mixture model methods with certain assumptions. The kernel k-means, spectral clustering, and Wavecluster all use the same trick and map the data into a new feature space to detect linearly non-separable clusters. In addition, at least the kernel k-means, DENCLUE, and Wavecluster are said to be robust to outliers. Mixture model methods are especially attractive for the educational data because they allow overlapping clusters and produce extra information in the form of probabilities. However, there are some practical difficulties which can restrict their use. The assumption of Gaussian distributions with variable independence is usually unrealistic, but more flexible mixture models cannot be estimated accurately, unless there is sufficiently data with respect to the data dimensionality. Because educational data sets tend to be quite small, the more complex mixture models can be used only for small-dimensional data.

Finally, we recall that the clustering method alone does not guarantee good or even meaningful results. Feature extraction and selection can have a crucial impact on the results. Irrelevant features or just too many features can easily hide the real clusters. On the other hand, good features may be able to represent the clusters so clearly that even poorer methods can find them. For this reason, it is advisable to try different feature extraction and selection schemes and cluster even the same set of features with different methods and parameter settings. Clustering is anyway exploratory by its nature and one cannot know beforehand, where the most useful clusters hide. One should also remember the possibility that there are no clusters at all in the data, even if the clustering algorithm always tries to return some solution.

FUTURE RESEARCH DIRECTIONS

In distance learning, adaptive and intelligent learning systems play a central role. Therefore, a relevant question is what clustering can offer to these tools. We see at least three different ways how clustering could be used to implement the "intelligence" of a learning system.

First, the clustering process could be automated to give regular reports to teachers on students' performance as the course proceeds. As we have seen, this kind of information can be very important for detecting possible problems or special needs in time. For this purpose, one should first analyze an example data set and select appropriate features, clustering methods, and their parameters. After that, the same clustering procedure could be executed automatically. A related research challenge is how clustering could be done dynamically, by updating the previous clustering, when new feature values are recorded.

Second, clustering methods can facilitate or even be a part of predictive models, which are the heart of intelligent systems. Usually, the predictive models are classifiers, which classify the user or situation, so that the system can select an optimal action. Sometimes, the predictive models can also be regression models, which predict a numerical score. For classifier construction, clustering methods are especially useful. Cluster analysis reveals what kind of classes can be separated with the given features and, thus, clustering can be used to select suitable features or class labels. If the clustering produced sufficiently homogeneous clusters (with respect to class labels), it can be later used as a K-nearest neighbour classifier. Similarly, cluster analysis can reveal reasoning rules for predicting scores or even selecting optimal actions.

Third, clustering can be used to recommend tasks or pieces of learning material. If a student has proved to need more practice in certain kind of tasks or topics, similar items can be selected from the same cluster. On the other hand, if the student already masters one cluster, then the system should recommend material from other clusters.

In addition, clustering can be used to allocate students into homogeneous (intra-cluster) or heterogeneous (inter-cluster) groups. This problem is related to one of the current clustering trends, semi-supervised clustering (Jain, 2010). In semi-supervised clustering, background knowledge is integrated into clustering in the form of constraints. For example, if two students have already collaborated together, one can impose a constraint which either forces them to the same cluster or to different clusters.

Another current trend is research on clustering heterogeneous data, which cannot be represented naturally by a fixed set of variables (Jain, 2010). One interesting problem is how to partition a large graph into cohesive subgraphs, when the nodes and edges are associated by attributes. The problem is actually equivalent to clustering relational data. In the educational domain, this kind of graph partitioning could be used to summarize concept maps (allowing edge labels or different edge types) or to study students' collaboration and communication networks. Another problem is how to cluster a set of graphs, like concept maps. Text clustering is also an important research trend. One tricky problem is how to cluster short pieces of text, which may be only a couple sentences long. A good technique to cluster students' free-formed answers, preferably together with other variables, would help in the analysis of questionnaires.

There are also general research challenges, which are relevant to educational data. One important problem is how to construct a mixture model for mixed data, containing both numerical and categorical variables. Further research on similarity measures for mixed data (like empirical comparisons) would also be welcome. Another

important but often neglected problem concerns the validation of clustering results. A lot of different validation indices have been proposed (see e.g. (Gan et al., 2007, Ch.17)), but without any significance testing, they can be used merely for comparing clusterings. Statistical significance testing would require laboursome randomization tests which are very seldom done. In addition, one should select the validity index according to the clustering criterion which is not always obvious. In this area, we would need more efficient algorithms for significance testing, implementations of indices in data mining tools, and guidelines for matching indices and (often implicit) clustering criteria. A related but easier problem is to test the stability of clustering results (i.e. the effect of small perturbations in the data), but implementations are still missing from data mining tools.

CONCLUSION

In this chapter, we have considered the problem of clustering student data. First, we specified the main purposes of clustering students and the characteristics of typical student data. After that, we described the most important clustering methods and evaluated their suitability to clustering student data.

Based on our evaluation, there is no superior clustering method, which would fulfil all desirable properties. In principle, the mixture model methods could often produce the most informative and attractive clustering models, but there are still practical problems which limit their use. Among strict clustering methods, density-based methods, spectral clustering, kernel k-means, and the hierarchical CHAMELEON algorithm look the most promising.

An interesting dilemma is why the k-means clustering has been so popular in the educational data mining, even if it is among the least suitable methods for typical educational data. In other fields, its popularity is more understandable, due to its efficiency and, perhaps, more easily detectable clusters. However, in our field, the efficiency is seldom a bottleneck and we encourage to try more developed methods.

REFERENCES

Aggarwal, C., Hinneburg, A., & Kleim, D. (2001). On the surprising behavior of distance metrics in high dimensional space. In *Proceedings of the 8th International Conference on Database Theory (ICDT 2001)*, (LNCS) (vol. 1973, pp. 420-434). Berlin: Springer-Verlag.

Aggarwal, C., & Zhai, C. (2012). *A Survey of Text Clustering Algorithms*. Boston: Kluwer Academic Publishers.

Agrawal, R., Gehrke, J., Gunopulos, D., & Raghavan, P. (1998). Automatic subspace clustering of high dimensional data for data mining applications. In *Proceedings of the 1998 ACM SIGMOD International Conference on Management of Data (SIGMOD'98)*, (pp. 94-105). New York, NY: ACM Press.

Andreopoulos, B., An, A., Wang, X., & Schroeder, M. (2009). *A roadmap of clustering algorithms: finding a match for a biomedical application*. Academic Press.

Banfield, J., & Raftery, A. (1993). Model-based Gaussian and non-Gaussian clustering. *Biometrics*, *49*(3), 803–821. doi:10.2307/2532201

Berkhin, P. (2006). Survey of clustering data mining techniques. In J. Kogan, C. Nicholas, & M. Teboulleeds (Eds.), *Grouping Multidimensional Data: Recent Advances in Clustering* (pp. 25–71). Springer. doi:10.1007/3-540-28349-8_2

Bezdek, J. (1981). *Pattern Recognition with Fuzzy Objective Function Algorithms*. Norwell, MA: Kluwer Academic Publishers. doi:10.1007/978-1-4757-0450-1

Cheng, V., Li, C., Kwok, J., & Li, C.-K. (2004). Dissimilarity learning for nominal data. *Pattern Recognition*, *37*(7), 1471–1477. doi:10.1016/j.patcog.2003.12.015

Dasgupta, A., & Raftery, A. (1998). Detecting features in spatial point processes with clutter via model-based clustering. *Journal of the American Statistical Association*, *93*(441), 294–302. doi:10.1080/01621459.1998.10474110

Dhillon, I., Guan, Y., & Kulis, B. (2004). Kernel k-means: spectral clustering and normalized cuts. In *Proceedings of the Tenth ACM SIGKDD International Conference on Knowledge Discovery and Data Mining*, (pp. 551-556). New York, NY: ACM.

Dhillon, I., Guan, Y., & Kulis, B. (2007). Weighted graph cuts without eigenvectors a multilevel approach. *IEEE Transactions on Pattern Analysis and Machine Intelligence*, *29*(11), 1944–1957. doi:10.1109/TPAMI.2007.1115 PMID:17848776

Duda, R., Hart, P., & Stork, D. (2000). *Pattern Classification* (2nd ed.). New York: Wiley Interscience Publication.

Ester, M., Kriegel, H., Sander, J., & Xu, X. (1996). A density-based algorithm for discovering clusters in large spatial databases with noise. In *Proceedings of the Second International Conference on Knowledge Discovery and Data Mining*, (pp. 226-231). Academic Press.

Estivill-Castro, V. (2002). Why so many clustering algorithms? A position paper. *SIGKKD Explorations*, *4*(1), 65–75. doi:10.1145/568574.568575

Fraley, C., & Raftery, A. (1998). How many clusters? Which clustering method? Answers via model-based cluster analysis. *The Computer Journal*, *41*(8), 578–588. doi:10.1093/comjnl/41.8.578

Fraley, C., & Raftery, A. (2000). Model-based clustering, discriminant analysis, and density estimation. *Journal of the American Statistical Association*, *97*(458), 611–631. doi:10.1198/016214502760047131

Gan, G., Ma, C., & Wu, J. (2007). *Data Clustering: Theory, Algorithms, and Applications.* SIAM.

Ghosh, J. (2004). Scalable clustering methods for data mining. In N. Ye (Ed.), *Hand Book of Data Mining.* Lawrence Erlbaum Associates.

Guha, S., Rastogi, R., & Shim, K. (1998). Cure: an efficient clustering algorithm for large databases. In *Proceedings of the 1998 ACM SIGMOD International Conference on Management of Data, SIGMOD '98,* (pp. 73-84). New York: ACM.

Halkidi, M., Batistakis, Y., & Vazirgiannis, M. (2001). On clustering validation techniques. *Journal of Intelligent Information Systems, 17*(2/3), 107–145. doi:10.1023/A:1012801612483

Hämäläinen, W., & Vinni, M. (2010). Classifying educational data: special problems and guidelines. CRC Press.

Han, J., & Kamber, M. (2006). *Data Mining: Concepts and Techniques* (2nd ed.). Elsevier/Morgan Kaufmann.

Hand, D., Mannila, H., & Smyth, P. (2002). *Principles of Data Mining.* Cambridge, MA: MIT Press.

Hinneburg, A., Hinneburg, E., & Keim, D. (1998). An efficient approach to clustering in large multimedia databases with noise. In *Proceedings of the 4th International Conference in Knowledge Discovery and Data Mining (KDD 98),* (pp. 58-65). AAAI Press.

Huang, Z. (1998). Extensions to the k-means algorithm for clustering large data sets with categorical values. *Data Mining and Knowledge Discovery, 2*(3), 283–304. doi:10.1023/A:1009769707641

Huikkola, M., Silius, K., & Pohjolainen, S. (2008). Clustering and achievement of engineering students based on their attitudes, orientations, motivations and intentions. *WSEAS Transactions on Advances in Engineering Education, 5*(1), 342–354.

Ichino, M., & Yaguchi, H. (1994). Generalized Minkowski metrics for mixed feature-type data analysis. *IEEE Transactions on Systems, Man, and Cybernetics, 24*(4), 698–708. doi:10.1109/21.286391

Jain, A. (2010). Data clustering: 50 years beyond k-means. *Pattern Recognition Letters, 31*(8), 651–666. doi:10.1016/j.patrec.2009.09.011

Jain, A., & Dubes, R. (1988). *Algorithms for Clustering Data.* Englewood Cliffs, NJ: Prentice Hall.

Jain, A., Duin, P., & Mao, J. (2000). Statistical pattern recognition: A review. *IEEE Transactions on Pattern Analysis and Machine Intelligence, 22*(1), 4–37. doi:10.1109/34.824819

Jain, A., Murty, M., & Flynn, P. (1999). Data clustering: A review. *ACM Computing Surveys, 31*(3), 264–323. doi:10.1145/331499.331504

Kamvar, S., Klein, D., & Manning, C. (2002). Interpreting and extending classical agglomerative clustering algorithms using a model-based approach. In *Proceedings of 19th International Conference on Machine Learning (ICML-2002),* (pp. 283-290). ICML.

Kantardzic, M. (2011). *Data Mining: Concepts, Models, Methods, and Algorithms* (2nd ed.). John Wiley & Sons, IEEE Press. doi:10.1002/9781118029145

Karypis, G., Han, E.-H., & Kumar, V. (1999). Chameleon: Hierarchical clustering using dynamic modeling. *Computer, 32*(8), 68–75. doi:10.1109/2.781637

Käser, T., Busetto, A., Solenthaler, B., Kohn, J., von Aster, M., & Gross, M. (2013). Cluster-based prediction of mathematical learning patterns. In *Proceedings of the 16th international conference on Articial Intelligence in Education,* (LNCS) (vol. 7926, pp. 389-399). Berlin: Springer.

Khan, L., & Luo, F. (2005). Hierarchical clustering for complex data. *International Journal of Artificial Intelligence Tools*, *14*(5), 791–809. doi:10.1142/S0218213005002399

Kohonen, T. (1982). Self-organized formation of topologically correct feature maps. *Biological Cybernetics*, *43*(1), 59–69. doi:10.1007/BF00337288

Lopez, M., Luna, J., Romero, C., & Ventura, S. (2012). Classification via clustering for predicting final marks based on student participation in forums. In *Proceedings of the 5th International Conference on the Educational Data Mining*, (pp. 148-151). Retrieved from http://www.educationaldatamining.org/

Luxburg, U. (2007). A tutorial on spectral clustering. *Statistics and Computing*, *17*(4), 395–416. doi:10.1007/s11222-007-9033-z

Murtagh, F., & Raftery, A. (1984). Fitting straight lines to point patterns. *Pattern Recognition*, *17*(5), 479–483. doi:10.1016/0031-3203(84)90045-1

Nugent, R., Dean, N., & Ayers, E. (2010). Skill set profile clustering: The empty k-means algorithm with automatic specification of starting cluster centers. In *Proceedings of the 3rd International Conference on Educational Data Mining*, (pp. 151-160). Retrieved from http://www.educationaldatamining.org/

Pardos, Z. A., Trivedi, S., Heffernan, N. T., & Srkzy, G. N. (2012). Clustered knowledge tracing. In *Proceedings of the 11th international conference on Intelligent Tutoring Systems* (LNCS) (vol. 7315, pp. 405-410). Berlin: Springer.

Parsons, L., Haque, E., & Liu, H. (2004). Subspace clustering for high dimensional data: A review. *ACM SIGKDD Explorations Newsletter*, *6*(1), 90-105.

Pelleg, D., & Moore, A. (2000). X-means: Extending k-means with efficient estimation of the number of clusters. In *Proceedings of the Seventeenth International Conference on Machine Learning*, (pp. 727-734). San Francisco: Morgan Kaufmann.

Perera, D., Kay, J., Koprinska, I., Yacef, K., & Zaiane, O. R. (2009). Clustering and sequential pattern mining of online collaborative learning data. *IEEE Transactions on Knowledge and Data Engineering*, *21*(6), 759–772. doi:10.1109/TKDE.2008.138

Schmitt, N., Oswald, F., Kim, B., Imus, A., Merritt, S., Friede, A., & Shivpuri, S. (2007). The use of background and ability profiles to predict college student outcomes. *The Journal of Applied Psychology*, *92*(1), 165–179. doi:10.1037/0021-9010.92.1.165 PMID:17227158

Schölkopf, B., Smola, A., & Müller, K.-R. (1998). Nonlinear component analysis as a kernel eigenvalue problem. *Neural Computation*, *10*(5), 1299–1319. doi:10.1162/089976698300017467

Sheikholeslami, G., Chatterjee, S., & Zhang, A. (1998). Wavecluster: A multi-resolution clustering approach for very large spatial databases. In *Proceedings of the 24rd International Conference on Very Large Data Bases (VLDB'98)*, (pp. 428-439). Morgan Kaufmann.

Smyth, P. (2000). Model selection for probabilistic clustering using crossvalidated likelihood. *Statistics and Computing*, *10*(1), 63–72. doi:10.1023/A:1008940618127

Stanford, D., & Raftery, A. (2000). Principal curve clustering with noise. *IEEE Transactions on Pattern Analysis and Machine Intelligence*, *22*(6), 601–609. doi:10.1109/34.862198

Trivedi, S., Pardos, Z., & Heffernan, N. (2011a). Clustering students to generate an ensemble to improve standard test score predictions. In *Proceedings of the 15th international conference on Artificial Intelligence in Education,* (LNCS), (vol. 6738, pp. 377-384). Berlin: Springer.

Trivedi, S., Pardos, Z., Sarkozy, G., & Heffernan, N. (2011b). Spectral clustering in educational data mining. In *Proceedings of the 4th International Conference on Educational Data Mining*, (pp. 129-138). Retrieved from http://www.education-aldatamining.org/

Wang, X., & Hamilton, H. (2003). DBRS: A density-based spatial clustering method with random sampling. In *Advances in Knowledge Discovery and Data Mining, Proceedings of the 7th Pacific-Asia Conference PAKDD 2003,* (LNCS) (vol. 2637, pp. 563-575). Berlin: Springer.

Ward, J. Jr. (1963). Hierarchical grouping to optimize an objective function. *Journal of the American Statistical Association*, *58*(301), 236–244. doi:10.1080/01621459.1963.10500845

Wilson, D., & Martinez, T. (1997). Improved heterogeneous distance functions. *Journal of Artificial Intelligence Research*, *6*, 1–34.

Xu, R., & Wunsch, D. II. (2005). Survey of clustering algorithms. *IEEE Transactions on Neural Networks*, *16*(3), 645–678. doi:10.1109/TNN.2005.845141 PMID:15940994

Xu, R., & Wunsch, D. (2008). *Clustering*. John Wiley/IEEE Press. doi:10.1002/9780470382776

Yona, G., Dirks, W., & Rahman, S. (2009). Comparing algorithms for clustering of expression data: How to assess gene clusters. *Methods in Molecular Biology (Clifton, N.J.)*, *541*, 479–509. doi:10.1007/978-1-59745-243-4_21 PMID:19381534

Zhang, T., Ramakrishnan, R., & Livny, M. (1997). BIRCH: A new data clustering algorithm and its applications. *Data Mining and Knowledge Discovery*, *1*(2), 141–182. doi:10.1023/A:1009783824328

Zhong, S., & Ghosh, J. (2003). A unified framework for model-based clustering. *Journal of Machine Learning Research*, *4*, 1001–1037.

ADDITIONAL READING

Aggarwal, C., & Reddy, C. (2013). *Data Clustering: Algorithms and Applications. Chapman & Hall/CRC Data Mining and Knowledge Discovery Series*. Boca Raton: Chapman & Hall/CRC.

Aggarwal, C., & Zhai, C. (2012). A survey of text clustering algorithms. In C. Aggarwal, & C. Zhai (Eds.), *Mining Text Data* (pp. 77–128). Boston: Kluwer Academic Publishers. doi:10.1007/978-1-4614-3223-4_4

Berkhin, P. (2006). Survey of clustering data mining techniques. In J. Kogan, C. Nicholas, & M. Teboulleeds (Eds.), *Grouping Multidimensional Data: Recent Advances in Clustering* (pp. 25–71). Springer. doi:10.1007/3-540-28349-8_2

Duda, R., Hart, P., & Stork, D. (2000). *Pattern Classification* (2nd ed.). New York: Wiley-Interscience Publication.

Estivill-Castro, V. (2002). Why so many clustering algorithms? A position paper. *SIGKKD Explorations*, *4*(1), 65–75. doi:10.1145/568574.568575

Everitt, B. (2011). *Cluster Analysis. Wiley Series in Probability and Statistics* (5th ed.). John Wiley & Sons Ltd.

Fraley, C., & Raftery, A. (2000). Model-based clustering, discriminant analysis, and density estimation. *Journal of the American Statistical Association*, *97*(458), 611–631. doi:10.1198/016214502760047131

Gan, G., Ma, C., & Wu, J. (2007). *Data Clustering: Theory, Algorithms, and Applications. ASA-SIAM Series on Statistics and Applied Probability.* SIAM.

Ghosh, J. (2004). Scalable clustering methods for data mining. In N. Ye (Ed.), *Hand Book of Data Mining.* Lawrence Erlbaum Associates.

Halkidi, M., Batistakis, Y., & Vazirgiannis, M. (2001). On clustering validation techniques. *Journal of Intelligent Information Systems, 17*(2/3), 107–145. doi:10.1023/A:1012801612483

Han, J., & Kamber, M. (2006). *Data Mining: Concepts and Techniques* (2nd ed.). Elsevier/ Morgan Kaufmann.

Hand, D., Mannila, H., & Smyth, P. (2002). Principles of Data Mining. MIT Press, Cambridge, Massachussetts, USA.

Hastie, T., Tibshirani, R., & Friedman, J. (2009). *The Elements of Statistical Learning: Data Mining, Inference, and Prediction. Springer Series in Statistics* (2nd ed.). Springer-Verlag. doi:10.1007/978-0-387-84858-7

Huikkola, M., Silius, K., & Pohjolainen, S. (2008). Clustering and achievement of engineering students based on their attitudes, orientations, motivations and intentions. *WSEAS Transactions on Advances in Engineering Education, 5*(1), 342–354.

Jain, A. (2010). Data clustering: 50 years beyond k-means. *Pattern Recognition Letters, 31*(8), 651–666. doi:10.1016/j.patrec.2009.09.011

Jain, A., & Dubes, R. (1988). *Algorithms for Clustering Data.* Englewood Cliffs, NJ, USA: Prentice Hall.

Jain, A., Murty, M., & Flynn, P. (1999). Data clustering: A review. *ACM Computing Surveys, 31*(3), 264–323. doi:10.1145/331499.331504

Kantardzic, M. (2011). *Data Mining: Concepts, Models, Methods, and Algorithms* (2nd ed.). New Jersey: John Wiley & Sons, IEEE Press. doi:10.1002/9781118029145

Kaufman, L., & Rousseeuw, P. (1990). *Finding Groups in Data: An Introduction to Cluster Analysis. Wiley Series in Probability and Statistics.* Wiley-Interscience. doi:10.1002/9780470316801

Kolatch, E. (2001). *Clustering algorithms for spatial databases: A survey. Technical report.* University of Maryland, Department of Computer Science.

Lopez, M., Luna, J., Romero, C., & Ventura, S. (2012). Classification via clustering for predicting final marks based on student participation in forums. In Yacef, K., Zaiane, O., Hershkovitz, H., Yudelson, M., and Stamper, J. (Ed.), *Proceedings of the 5th International Conference on the Educational Data Mining*, pages 148-151. http:// www.educationaldatamining.org/

Luxburg, U. (2007). A tutorial on spectral clustering. *Statistics and Computing, 17*(4), 395–416. doi:10.1007/s11222-007-9033-z

Mirkin, B. (2012). *Clustering: A Data Recovery Approach. Chapman & Hall/CRC Computer Science and Data Analysis Series* (2nd ed.). Boca Raton: Chapman and Hall. doi:10.1201/b13101

Nugent, R., Dean, N., & Ayers, E. (2010). Skill set profile clustering: The empty k-means algorithm with automatic specification of starting cluster centers. In R.S.J.d Baker, A. Merceron, R. B. and Pavlik, P. J. (Eds.), *Proceedings of the 3rd International Conference on Educational Data Mining*, pages 151-160. http://www.education-aldatamining.org/

Parsons, L., Haque, E., and Liu, H. (2004). Subspace clustering for high dimensional data: a review. *ACM SIGKDD Explorations Newsletter - Special issue on learning from imbalanced datasets, 6*(1):90-105.

Trivedi, S., Pardos, Z., & Heffernan, N. (2011a). Clustering students to generate an ensemble to improve standard test score predictions. In Biswas, G., Bull, S., Kay, J., and Mitrovic, A. (Eds.), *Proceedings of the 15th international conference on Artificial Intelligence in Education, volume 6738 of Lecture Notes in Computer Science*, pages 377-384, Berlin, Heidelberg. Springer.

Trivedi, S., Pardos, Z., Srkzy, G., & Heffernan, N. (2011b). Spectral clustering in educational data mining. In Pechenizkiy, M., Calders, T., Conati, C., Ventura, S., Romero, C., and Stamper, J. (Eds.), *Proceedings of the 4th International Conference on Educational Data Mining*, pages 129-138. www.educationaldatamining.org

Xu, R., & Wunsch, D. II. (2005). Survey of clustering algorithms. *IEEE Transactions on Neural Networks, 16*(3), 645–678. doi:10.1109/TNN.2005.845141 PMID:15940994

Xu, R., & Wunsch, D. (2008). *Clustering. IEEE Press Series on Computational Intelligence.* John Wiley/IEEE Press.

Zhong, S., & Ghosh, J. (2003). A unified framework for model-based clustering. *Journal of Machine Learning Research, 4*, 1001–1037.

KEY TERMS AND DEFINITIONS

Centroid: A representative point of a cluster in its center.

Clustering: A grouping of data points, where points in one group are similar or close to each other but different or distant from points in the other groups.

Dendrogram: A tree diagram for representing a hierarchy of clusters.

Density Function: A function that specifies a continuous probability distribution.

Kernel: A function that returns an inner product between the images of data points in some space.

Mixture Model: A probabilistic model which is a combination of simpler models.

Outlier: A data point which does not belong to any cluster.

Chapter 15
Evolutionary Approach for Automatic and Dynamic Modeling of Students' Learning Styles

Fabiano Azevedo Dorça
Federal University of Uberlandia, Brazil

ABSTRACT

Most of the distance educational systems consider only little, or no, adaptivity. Personalization according to specific requirements of an individual student is one of the most important features in adaptive educational systems. Considering learning and how to improve a student's performance, these systems must know the way in which an individual student learns best. In this context, this chapter depicts an application of evolutionary algorithms to discover students' learning styles. The approach is mainly based on the non-deterministic and non-stationary aspects of learning styles, which may change during the learning process in an unexpected and unpredictable way. Because of the stochastic and dynamic aspects enclosed in learning process, it is important to gradually and constantly update the student model. In this way, the student model stochastically evolves towards the real student's learning style, considering its fine-tuned strengths. This approach has been tested through computer simulation of students, and promising results have been obtained. Some of them are presented in this chapter.

INTRODUCTION

Most of the distance education systems don't take into account the individual student's characteristics. As a consequence, the same learning objects, pedagogical strategies and learning resources are commonly used for everybody. However, adaptivity (Brusilovsky, 2001) has been introduced

in these systems during the last years in order to provide individual learning experience (Graf and Kinshuk, 2009). In this way, the main student's characteristics considered in the personalization of a course are: learning goals (Chang and Chung, 2010), cognitive level (Chang and Chung, 2010), interests (Brusilovsky, 2001), stereotypes (Zakaria and Brailsford, 2002) and learning styles (LS)

DOI: 10.4018/978-1-4666-6276-6.ch015

(Felder and Silverman, 1988). The use of LS in adaptive educational systems (AES) is motivated by educational and psychological theories, which argue that learners have different ways in which they prefer to learn (Graf and Kinshuk, 2009).

Learning Styles and their effects on learning processes are carefully exposed by Coffield et al. (2009). Instructional strategies have been massively studied in the new learning space introduced by the Internet, where many researchers point out that linking LS to appropriate learning resources is an important stimulus for the learning process. Some researches reveal that a student's performance improves if the learning environment supports his/her specific LS. On the other hand, learners whose LS are not supported by the learning environment may have more difficulties during the learning process (Haider et al., 2010; Graf et al., 2008; Kinshuk et al., 2009; Alfonseca et al., 2006; Graf et al., 2009; Felder and Silverman, 1988).

In order to provide adaptivity, the student's characteristics have to be known first. However, the traditional approaches for detection of LS in AES are inefficient. Price (2004) analyzes the uncertainty aspect of ILSQ (Index of Learning Styles Questionnaire) by identifying inconsistencies between its results and students behaviors. Besides Price, Roberts and Erdos (1993) analyzes this kind of instrument and the problems related to it. Therefore, many approaches for automatic detection of LS have been proposed. However, in general they present problems which make them either inefficient or difficult to implement, implant and use, as pointed out in section 2.

In this context, we present in this chapter an evolutionary approach to discover students LS which uses a probabilistic student model and a genetic algorithm. This approach is based on the non-deterministic and non-stationary aspects of LS, which may change during the learning process in an unexpected and unpredictable way (Graf and Kinshuk, 2009).

Our approach is based on the Felder and Silverman's Learning Styles Model (FSLSM) (Felder and Silverman, 1988). According to Graf and Kinshuk (2009, 2010a), the FSLSM uses the concept of dimensions, and therefore describes LS in much detail. A very important characteristic of FSLSM to our work is that it uses scales to classify students instead of defined types. In this way, the strength of each LS is finely measured (Felder and Silverman, 1988). Therefore, our approach aims to gradually fine tune LS stored in the student model along the learning process, using a genetic algorithm (Chipperfield et al., 1994) to efficiently optimize students LS. Another important aspect of FSLSM is that it considers preferences as tendencies and therefore, it takes into account that the student may act differently in specific situations, in a non-deterministic way, as pointed out by Kinshuk et al. (2009); Graf and Kinshuk (2009).

Therefore, we consider a student's preferences as probabilities in the four-dimensional FSLSM model, as depicted in section 4. As a result, our approach gradually, constantly and stochastically modifies students LS using a set of rules in order to detect which LS should be adjusted at a specific moment. As a consequence, student model effectively converges towards real student's LS, as shown in section 5. Finally, section 6 presents conclusions and future work.

RELATED WORKS

A diversity of approaches for automatic detection of LS have been proposed, such as (Graf and Liu, 2008; Graf and Kinshuk, 2010b; Castillo et al., 2005). In general, these traditional approaches use deterministic inference systems for detecting students LS through predefined behavioral patterns. These systems infer LS based on students actions. A problem with these systems is the difficulty in the development of rules able to infer LS effectively through students' actions, and to treat students' behavior as evidence and not as possibility. More complex approaches are depicted at (Kelly and Tangney, 2005; García et al., 2007; Carmona and Castillo, 2008; Cabada et al., 2009; Zatarain-Cabada et al., 2009; Zatarain et al., 2010; Carmona et al., 2007). These approaches use learning machine techniques, such as Bayesian and Neural Networks. A problem with these approaches is their high complex implementations and high computation cost, which is a serious concern when we have a high number of simultaneous students using the system. Besides, in general, these approaches are highly coupled either to the system they were designed for or to the whole process aimed at selecting suitable learning resources, making them harder to re-use in other systems. In some of these approaches, once acquired, students LS remain the same throughout the entire learning process (Castillo et al., 2005).

Another well-known problem with learning machine approaches is the complication generated by concept drift and concept shift (Castillo et al., 2005). They occur either because the acquired LS information needs to be adjusted or because the student simply changes his/her preferences. In this scenario, adaptive decision models, which are able to better fit students' preferences, are desirable.

In this scenario, adaptive decision models, which are able to better adapt to students' LS, are desirable. In this context, we believe that our approach brings advantages due to the following specific features:

- It considers that not only LS but also many factors exert some influence on students' performance, making it harder to infer students' LS based only on fixed behavioral pattern rules, because students' behavior and performance may be influenced by other factors besides LS. Some of these factors are pointed out by Haider et al. (2010); Graf et al. (2008); Kinshuk et al.

(2009); Alfonseca et al. (2006); Graf et al. (2009); Messick (1976);

- It considers that the influence of each LS on students' behavior is unknown (Botsios, S. and Georgiou, D. and Safouris, N., 2008);

- It considers that LS can change over time in an unpredictable way. These changes may be associated with other factors, such as knowledge domain, as analyzed by Jones et al. (2003);

- It considers that it is impossible to know the precision of the results obtained from self-assessment questionnaires (which may have inconsistencies) (Price, 2004; Roberts and Erdos, 1993; Castillo et al., 2005);

- It eliminates the necessity to discover students' behavioral patterns, considering that it is hard or impossible to obtain such patterns, considering that students with the same learning styles preferences may, sometimes, act differently, taking into account the concept of tendencies, which means that even a learner with, e.g., a strong active LS can act sometimes in a reflective way (Graf and Kinshuk, 2009);

- It is uncoupled from any Learning Management System (LMS), being independent from any specific students' actions in a specific system, as it always occurs in traditional approaches (García et al., 2007; Graf and Liu, 2008);

- It takes into account the dynamic nature of LS, which may change when the knowledge domain changes (Kelly and Tangney, 2005) or naturally evolve over time (Messick, 1976);

- It eliminates the necessity of using complex machine learning techniques, which are difficult to implement and may bring problems such as the complications related to concept drift and concept shift, as exposed by Castillo et al. (2005);

- It eliminates the necessity of using drift-detection methods and dealing with concept drift and concept shift, which are automatically handled by the approach described in this paper.

The next section presents important aspects of evolutionary algorithms.

EVOLUTIONARY ALGORITHMS

Evolutionary algorithms are adaptive search techniques based on Darwin's theory of evolution, which are characterized by an iterative process, and work in parallel on a number of potential solutions for a problem. In this context, the fitness value is a numerical value which expresses the performance of an individual (a possible solution) for solving a problem. The notion of fitness is fundamental to the application of evolutionary algorithms, and the degree of success in their application may depend critically on the definition of a fitness function that must ensure that individuals can be differentiated according to their capacity for solving the problem. Individuals evolve through an iterative process (Eiben and Smith, 2003).

This process leads to the evolution of a population of individuals, which are better fitted to their environment than the individuals that they were created from, just as in natural adaptation. Evolutionary algorithms often perform well approximating solutions to all types of problems because they ideally do not make any assumption about the underlying problem domain (Eiben and Smith, 2003).

As stated in (Eiben and Smith, 2003), the general scheme of an evolutionary algorithm (EA) is given in Figure 1.

As it can be seen, evolutionary algorithms possess features that may help to position them within in the family of generate-and-test methods (Eiben and Smith, 2003):

- EAs are population based, i.e., they process a whole collection of candidate solutions simultaneously;

Figure 1. General scheme of an evolutionary algorithm

```
INITIALIZE population with random candidate solutions;
EVALUATE each candidate;
while not TERMINATION CONDITION is satisfied do
    SELECT parents;
    RECOMBINE pairs of parents;
    MUTATE the resulting offspring;
    EVALUATE new candidates;
    SELECT individuals for the next generation;
end while
```

- EAs most use recombination to mix information of more candidate solutions into a new one;
- EAs are stochastic.

As pointed out in (Eiben and Smith, 2003), the most important components in EAs are:

- Representation (definition of individuals);
- Evaluation function (or fitness function);
- Population;
- Parent selection mechanism;
- Variation operators (recombination and mutation);
- Survivor selection mechanism (replacement).

Our approach is mainly based on Genetic Algorithms (GA). GAs operate on a population of potential solutions applying the principle of survival of the fittest to produce better and better approximations to a solution (Chipperfield et al., 1994). Individuals, or current approximations, are encoded as strings, chromosomes, composed over some alphabet. The most commonly used representation in GAs is the binary alphabet 0, 1 although other representations can be used, e.g. ternary, integer, real-valued etc (Chipperfield et al., 1994).

Genetic operators are used in genetic algorithms to generate diversity and to combine existing solutions into others. Genetic variation is a necessity for the process of evolution. Genetic operators used in genetic algorithms are analogous to those in the natural world: survival of the fittest (selection), reproduction (crossover or recombination) and mutation (Goldberg, 1989). The next section depicts our approach.

AUTOMATICALLY DETECTING LEARNING STYLES

In this chapter we present in detail an approach for automatic students' LS modeling which uses probabilistic learning styles combinations and a genetic algorithm. This approach uses information from students' performances for frequently updating the student model (SM) while he/she uses the system for learning. In this way, information about students LS is dynamically and constantly revised when learning difficulties are detected, leading to fine-tuned SM and subsequently to more accurate adaptivity. Taking into consideration the entire students' performance brings a global aspect to the student modeling, once it considers all aspects of students' behavior.

Many aspects can be considered in student performance evaluations, e.g., acquired knowledge, time of reply, time spent on a page, scroll bar movement, access to chat and forum, and others (Dorça et al., 2009). A conclusion can be drawn that our approach takes into account the development of an advanced student modeling approach which combines automatic, dynamic, and global student modeling aspects, as pointed out in (Graf and Kinshuk, 2009).

This section is divided in three subsections. Firstly, we present the student model, which can be used to provide adapted interactions with students. Secondly, we present an evolutionary approach for automatically and dynamically discover students LS. Finally, we present a simulation model, which takes into consideration some aspects related to the impact of LS in students performances. This model was used to test and validate our approach. It allowed us to view how students LS were discovered throughout the learning process.

Student Modeling

The approach which is depicted in this chapter is based on the Felder and Silverman's Learning Styles Model (FSLSM) (Felder and Silverman, 1988), as stated before. In this approach, students LS are stored as probability distributions in the SM, indicating the probability of preference for each LS within each of the four dimensions of the FSLSM, here called probabilistic LS (LS_p). Thus, we propose a probabilistic SM in which LS are processed by the system as probabilities, and not as certainties. Hence, students probable LS are stored in the SM as values in the interval [0,1]. Those values represent probabilities of preference in each one of the four FSLSM dimensions, according to the definition below:

Probabilistic Learning Styles (LSp)

$$LS = \{(PrA = x; PrR = 1 - x),(PrS = y; PrI = 1 - y),(PrVi = z; PrVe = 1 - z),(PrSeq = w; PrG = 1 - w)\},$$

where:

PrA is the probability of the student's preference for the Active LS;

PrR is the probability of the student's preference for the Reflective LS;

PrS is the probability of the student's preference for the Sensitive LS;

PrI is the probability of the student's preference for the Intuitive LS;

$PrVi$ is the probability of the student's preference for the Visual LS;

$PrVe$ is the probability of the student's preference for the Verbal LS;

$PrSeq$ is the probability of the student's preference for the Sequential LS;

PrG is the probability of the student's preference for the Global LS.

Using this approach, a student's preferences are represented according to Table 1.

Table 1. Student model

Learning Styles							
Processing		Perception		Input		Understanding	
A.	R.	S.	I.	Vi.	Ve.	Seq.	G.
0.35	0.65	0.17	0.83	0.89	0.11	0.84	0.16

In Table 1 we can consider that the student probably is Reflective, Intuitive, Visual and Sequential. Initially, if the system doesn't have any assumption about a student's LS, the SM is set with balanced preferences, which means that the probabilities of preference for each LS in a dimension are equal (there are no established preferences), considering that, initially, the SM doesn't have any information about how the student probably learns best:

LSp={(A=0.50, R=0.50); (S=0.50, I=0.50); (Vi$_{=0}$.50, Ve=0.50); (Seq=0.50, G=0.50)},

If a psychometric instrument – like the Index of Learning Styles Questionnaire (ILSQ) Van Zwanenberg et al. (2000) – is used to initialize the SM, the system calculates the proportion of answers to each LS. This calculation is done by (1), which divides by 11 the number of answers to a LS (Ai), considering that the ILSQ has 11 questions for each FSLSM dimension, totaling 44 questions. In (1), i represents a LS in a FSLSM dimension, and Ai represents the number of answers to a LS. Pri is the probability of preference for a LS by the student in a dimension, according to the definition made.

$$\Pr i = \frac{Ai}{11} \tag{1}$$

An example would be if a student answers 3 questions to the Active LS and 8 questions to the Reflective LS, we have:

$$\Pr A = \frac{3}{11} = 0.28; \quad \Pr R = \frac{8}{11} = 0.72$$

Discovering Students LS through an Evolutionary Approach

Our approach is based on probabilistic learning styles combinations (Franzoni and Assar, 2009). A learning style combination is a 4-tuple composed by one LS from each FSLSM dimension, as stated by the definition below:
Learning Styles Combination (LSC):

$LSC = \{(a, b, c, d)/a \in D1, b \in D2, c \in D3, d \in D4\}$

where:
$D1 = \{A(A), Reflective(R)\}$
$D2 = \{Sens(S), Intuitive(I)\}$
$D3 = \{V(Vi), Verbal(Ve)\}$
$D4 = \{Sequen(Seq), Global(G)\}$

Considering this model, there are 16 possible learning styles combinations (LSC), such that LSC={(A,S,Vi,Seq), (A,S,Vi,G), (R,S,Vi,Seq), (R,S,Vi,G), (A,S,Ve,Seq), (A,S,Ve,G), (R,S,Ve,Seq),(R,S,Ve,G),(A,I,Vi,Seq),(A,I,Vi,G), (R,I,Vi,Seq),(R,I,Vi,G),(A,I,Ve,Seq),(A,I,Ve,G), (R,I,Ve,Seq), (R,I,Ve,G)}.

As pointed out in section 3, an EA has some important components. We define these components as follows:

- **Representation:** Definition of individuals LSC, as stated by the last definition above.
- **Evaluation Function:** Fitness function (LSC) that calculates a LSC probabilistic preference, as expounded above.
- **Population:** Binary representations of LSC, where preferences A, S, Vi, Seq are represented by 0 and preferences R, I, Ve,

Figure 2. Evolutionary algorithm to discover students LS

```
initPopulation(POPSIZE)
while not reachedLearningGoal(StudentID) do
    ConceptID ← getConceptID(StudentID)
    CL ← getStudentCL(StudentID, ConceptID)
    evaluatePopulation(StudentID)
    LSC ← selectLSC()
    LO[] ← selectLO(CL, LSC, ConceptID)
    showLO(LO[])
    Pe ← evaluateStudent(StudentID, ConceptID)
    CLnew ← updateCL(Pe, StudentID)
    LSnew ← updateLS(LS, Pe, LSC)
    recombination(Px)
    mutation(Pm)
    updateSM(StudentID, ConceptID, CLnew, LSnew)
end while
```

G are represented by 1. Therefore, we have the following population: POP={(0,0,0,0), (0,0,0,1), (1,0,0,0), (1,0,0,1), (0,1,0,0), (0,1,0,1), (1,1,0,0), (1,1,0,1),(0,0,1,0), (0,0,1,1), (1,0,1,0), (1,0,1,1), (0,1,1,0), (0,1,1,1), (1,1,1,0), (1,1,1,1)}.

- **Parent Selection Mechanism:** Roulette Wheel Selection (Goldberg, 1989).
- **Variation Operators:** Recombination and mutation, as depicted below.
- **Survivor Selection Mechanism:** Not applied, as explained below.

The role of survivor selection is to deterministically choose which individuals will be allowed in the next generation. This decision is based on their fitness values, favoring those with higher quality. But, we have to consider that if a student's LS are inconsistent, the best fitted LSC should not be the preferred by the student. Therefore, we do not use any survivor selection mechanism in this approach (Figure 2).

The function initPopulation initializes the first generation population with a size equal to POPSIZE, using binary representation. The first 16 individuals are copied from LSCs (see last definition). The rest of the individuals are randomly generated. Therefore, we guarantee that each LSC in LSCs pertains to the initial population (with at least 16 individuals). This mechanism ensures genetic diversity to the first generation.

The function reachedLearningGoal verifies if the student's learning goals (Bloom and Krathwohl, 1956) have been reached. If not, a new learning section begins. The function getConceptID returns the id of the next concept to be learned, according to the student's curriculum sequencing (Limongelli et al., 2009; Lopes and Fernandes, 2009). The function getStudentCL returns the student's cognitive level (CL) in the concept identified by ConceptID. *The function evaluatePopulation uses the fitness function (2) in order to evaluate the individuals fitness according to the student's LS.*

$$(a, b, c, d) = Pra \times Prb \times Prc \times Prd$$

Thus, the probability of selecting the LSC $(A,, i, Seq)$ is given by $P(A, S, V i, Se_q) = 0.28 \times 0.09 \times_0.45 \times 0_.82$. The selected LSC defines the pedagogical strategy to be adopted for the presentation of course content during a learning session.

In this way, an advantage of our approach is to stochastically consider all LSCs according to the stored *LSp*, which may be inconsistent, and therefore it may not represent the student's real preferences. This feature allows to efficiently diagnosis students LS. Consequently, this approach is naturally able to deal with uncertainties in the process of LS modeling. Uncertainties in this process appear due to the diversity of factors which may exert some influence over the learning process and students performances, as stated by Haider et al. (2010); Graf et al. (2008); Kinshuk et al. (2009); Alfonseca et al. (2006); Graf et al. (2009); Messick (1976).

Taking into consideration that LS are probabilities, a learning styles combination can be probably selected during a learning section according to the probability distribution shown in Table 2, considering the SM depicted in Table 1.

Table 2. LSC probability distribution

LSC	Probabilities
P(A,S,Vi,Seq)	$0,35 \times 0,17 \times 0,89 \times 0,84 = 0,045$
P(A,S,Vi,G)	$0,35 \times 0,17 \times 0,89 \times 0,16 = 0,008$
P(R,S,Vi,Seq)	$0,65 \times 0,17 \times 0,89 \times 0,84 = 0,083$
P(R,S,Vi,G)	$0,65 \times 0,17 \times 0,89 \times 0,16 = 0,016$
P(A,S,Ve,Seq)	$0,35 \times 0,17 \times 0,11 \times 0,84 = 0,005$
P(A,S,Ve,G)	$0,35 \times 0,17 \times 0,11 \times 0,16 = 0,002$
P(R,S,Ve,Seq)	$0,65 \times 0,17 \times 0,11 \times 0,84 = 0,010$
P(R,S,Ve,G)	$0,65 \times 0,17 \times 0,11 \times 0,16 = 0,003$
P(A,I,Vi,Seq)	$0,35 \times 0,83 \times 0,89 \times 0,84 = 0,217$
P(A,I,Vi,G)	$0,35 \times 0,83 \times 0,89 \times 0,16 = 0,043$
P(R,I,Vi,Seq)	$0,65 \times 0,83 \times 0,89 \times 0,84 = 0,403$
P(R,I,Vi,G)	$0,65 \times 0,83 \times 0,89 \times 0,16 = 0,076$
P(A,I,Ve,Seq)	$0,35 \times 0,83 \times 0,11 \times 0,84 = 0,026$
P(A,I,Ve,G)	$0,35 \times 0,83 \times 0,11 \times 0,16 = 0,005$
P(R,I,Ve,Seq)	$0,65 \times 0,83 \times 0,11 \times 0,84 = 0,049$
P(R,I,Ve,G)	$0,65 \times 0,83 \times 0,11 \times 0,16 = 0,009$
Sum of probabilities of all LSC	1.000

We propose that during each learning session the student should interact with a set of learning objects (LO) (IEEE, 2010) that satisfy a specific LSC, stochastically selected according to the student's LS preferences stored in the SM. Which means that, in our approach, a LSC is a specific combination of four random variables (Papoulis et al., 2002). Therefore, in our approach, the student's LS describes the probability of random variables a, b, c and d, considering the last definition.

The fitness value of a specific LSC is given by (2). Once each LSC in population has a fitness value, they can be chosen from the population with probability given by their relative fitness. The function selectLSC selects a LSC to be applied during a learning section.

The selection of a LSC is done through a stochastic selection method (Goldberg, 1989). There are a variety of stochastic selection methods, for example Roulette Wheel Selection, Stochastic Universal Sampling, Simple Tournament and Stochastic Tournament (Goldberg, 1989). The

function selectLSC implements the Roulette Wheel Selection method, due to its adequacy to our approach. In this method, individual candidates have a fitness, which measures how adapted they are to the environment (Goldberg, 1989). It gives them a proportional slice in the roulette.

The individual's probability of selection is given by the proportion between its fitness and the entire population's fitness, as shown in (3). The sum of probabilities of all individuals must equal 1.

$$\Pr i = \frac{fitness_i}{\sum_{x=1}^{n} fitness_x} \qquad (3)$$

So, we calculate the accumulated probability for each individual as shown in (4).

$$q0 = 0; q1 = q0 + Pr1; q2 = q1 + Pr2; \ldots ; qn = qn-1 + Prn = 1$$

Finally, we generate a random number in the interval [0,1] representing the roulette spin. If the generated number is in the interval [q0, q1], the individual 1 is selected. If the number is in the interval [q1, q2], the individual 2 is selected, and so on, as shown in (5).

$$qi-1 < Pri \leq qi$$

In our approach, we consider a LSC's probability of selection as its probability of preference by the student, as shown in Table 2. Applying (4) we have the following accumulated probabilities related to LSC:

$$q0 = 0$$

$$q1 = 0 + ((A,, i, Seq) = 0.045$$

$$q2 = 0.045 + (A,, i, G) = 0.053$$

$$q3 = 0.053 + (R,, i, Seq) = 0.136$$

$q4 = 0.136 + (R_{,,} i,G) = 0.152$

$q5 = 0.152 + (A_{,,} e,Seq) = 0.157$

$q6 = 0.157 + (A_{,,} e,G) = 0.159$

$q7 = 0.159 + (R_{,,} e,Seq) = 0.169$

$q8 = 0.169 + (R_{,,} e,G) = 0.172$

$q9 = 0.172 + (A_{,,} i,Seq) = 0.389$

$q10 = 0.389 + (A_{,,} i,G) = 0.432$

$q11 = 0.432 + (R_{,,} i,Seq) = 0.835$

$q12 = 0.835 + (R_{,,} i,G) = 0.911$

$q13 = 0.911 + (A_{,,} e,Seq) = 0.937$

$q14 = 0.937 + (A_{,,} e,G) = 0.942$

$q15 = 0.942 + (R_{,,} e,Seq) = 0.991$

$q16 = 0.991 + (R_{,,} e,G) = 1.000$

Applying (5) we have:

$q0 \leq (A_{,,} i,Seq) \leq q1 \rightarrow 0 < Pr(A,S,Vi,Seq) \leq 0.045$

$q1 < (A_{,,} i,G) \leq q2 \rightarrow 0.045 < Pr(A,S,Vi,G) \leq 0.053$

$q2 < (R_{,,} i,Seq) \leq q3 \rightarrow 0.053 < Pr(R,S,Vi,Seq) \leq 0.136$

$q3 < (R_{,,} i,G) \leq q4 \rightarrow 0.136 < Pr(R,S,Vi,G) \leq 0.152$

$q4 < PrA_{,,} e,Seq) \leq q5 \rightarrow 0.152 < Pr(A,S,Ve,Seq) \leq 0.157$

$q5 < (A_{,,} e,G) \leq q6 \rightarrow 0.157 < Pr(A,S,Ve,G) \leq 0.159$

$q6 < (R_{,,} e,Seq) \leq q7 \rightarrow 0.159 < Pr(R,S,Ve,Seq) \leq 0.169$

$q7 < (R_{,,} e,G) \leq q8 \rightarrow 0.169 < Pr(R,S,Ve,G) \leq 0.172$

$q8 < (A_{,,} i,Seq) \leq q9 \rightarrow 0.172 < Pr(A,I,Vi,Seq) \leq 0.389$

$q9 < (A_{,,} i,G) \leq q10 \rightarrow 0.389 < Pr(A,I,Vi,G) \leq 0.432$

$q10 < (R_{,,} i,Seq) \leq q11 \rightarrow 0.432 < Pr(R,I,Vi,Seq) \leq 0.835$

$q11 < (R_{,,} i,G) \leq q12 \rightarrow 0.835 < Pr(R,I,Vi,G) \leq 0.911$

$q12 < (A_{,,} e,Seq) \leq q13 \rightarrow 0.911 < Pr(A,I,Ve,Seq) \leq 0.937$

$q13 < (A_{,,} e,G) \leq q14 \rightarrow 0.937 < Pr(A,I,Ve,G) \leq 0.942$

$q14 < (R_{,,} e,Seq) \leq q15 \rightarrow 0.942 < Pr(R,I,Ve,Seq) \leq 0.991$

$q15 < (R_{,,} e,G) \leq q16 \rightarrow 0.991 < Pr(R,I,Ve,G) \leq 1.000$

Figure 3 graphically shows the roulette generated by the exposed above. Each individual (LSC) has an area in the roulette, which is proportional to its supposed adequacy to the student, according to the probabilities stored in SM.

The function selectLO selects learning objects (LO) which should be used in the current learning session, considering the selected LSC, the concept to be learned (ConceptID) and student's cognitive level in the concept. In order to select appropriate LO, this function should take into account LO's metadata stored in a well-known and widespread format, like Learning Object Metadata from IEEE Learning Technology Standards Committee (IEEE, 2010). This function should take into

Figure 3. Roulette wheel selection

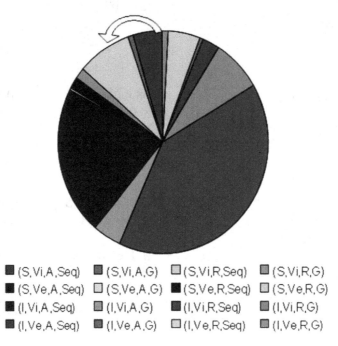

- ■ (S,Vi,A,Seq)
- ■ (S,Vi,A,G)
- □ (S,Vi,R,Seq)
- ■ (S,Vi,R,G)
- ■ (S,Ve,A,Seq)
- □ (S,Ve,A,G)
- ■ (S,Ve,R,Seq)
- □ (S,Ve,R,G)
- ■ (I,Vi,A,Seq)
- ■ (I,Vi,A,G)
- ■ (I,Vi,R,Seq)
- ■ (I,Vi,R,G)
- ■ (I,Ve,A,Seq)
- ■ (I,Ve,A,G)
- □ (I,Ve,R,Seq)
- ■ (I,Ve,R,G)

consideration that sensitive students prefer concrete and factual learning objects, while intuitive students prefer abstract and conceptual material. Visual students prefer pictures, diagrams, films and demonstrations while verbal students prefer lectures, readings and discussions. Active students prefer to process information actively by doing something and working in group, while reflective students prefer to think about the material and work alone. Sequential students prefer to learn through small orderly steps, while global students learn through big leaps (Felder and Silverman, 1988).

The function showLO provides access to the selected LO. In order to provide a welladapted learning section, this function should take into account adaptive educational hypermedia techniques (Brusilovsky, 2001).

The function evaluateStudent evaluates the student's acquired knowledge and behavior during the learning session and infers the student's performance. In order to evaluate students consistently, this function implements appropriate fuzzy logic rules, as depicted in (Dorça et al., 2009).

The function updateCL infers the new student's cognitive level, the CLnew. The student's CL in a concept may increase, decrease or stuck after a learning session, as depicted in (Lopes and Fernandes, 2009). The function updateLS infers the new student's LS, LSnew, as depicted below. Then, updateSM stores CLnew and LSnew in SM.

The function recombination recombines LSC's in population, in order to produce the next generation. The basic operator for producing new chromosomes is crossover. Like its counterpart in nature, crossover produces new individuals that have some parts of both parent's genetic material. The parents are stochastically selected through the function selectLSC, expounded above. The function of parent selection is to distinguish among individuals, based on their quality, in order to allow the better individuals to become parents of the next generation. We are using here the single-point crossover (Chipperfield et al., 1994). This crossover operation is not necessarily performed on all strings in the population. Instead, it is applied with a probability *Px* when the pairs are chosen for breeding.

The function mutation is then applied to the new chromosomes with a probability Pm (mutation rate). Mutation causes the individual genetic representation to be changed according to some probabilistic rule. In the binary string representation, mutation will cause a single bit to flip, 0 to 1 or 1 to 0. The bit to be flipped is randomly chosen. For example, the individual (R,I,Vi,Seq) may be changed through mutation to (A,I,Vi,Seq).

In this way, we propose that in each learning session, students must interact with a set of LO, satisfying a specific LSC. As the learning process evolves, *LSp* in SM are updated as follows. When a student shows a learning problem (unsatisfactory performance) during a learning session – performance value less than *m*, such that *m* is the threshold between good and bad performance – the LS stored in the SM that appear in current selected LSC are decremented, considering a probable inconsistency in these preferences. Students' preferences which do not appear in current selected LSC are incremented (reinforced), making them stronger, considering that the learning difficulties appeared because they were not present in the selected LSC. This process is based on reinforcement learning (RL) techniques Dorça et al. (2013).

In Dorça et al. (2013) we present a comparative analysis between three different strategies for updating *LSp*. It was clearly demonstrated that this is the best one. Following, we present the rules which implement this strategy:

$$(PFM < m) AND (LSC[i] = A) \rightarrow$$
$$LSp[i]A := LSp[i]A - \alpha \times R,$$
$$LSp[i]B := LSp[i]B + \alpha \times R.$$

$$(PFM < m) AND (LSC[i] = B) \rightarrow$$
$$LSp[i]A := LSp[i]A + \alpha \times R,$$
$$LSp[i]B := LSp[i]B - \alpha \times R.$$

such that:

- PFM is the performance value obtained by the student in the current learning session.
- m is the threshold between good and bad performances.
- $LSC[i]$ is the LS that appears in the LSC, considering the dimension i, with i = 1..4.
- $LSp[i]_A$ is the probability of preference for the LS A stored in the SM, in dimension i, with i = 1..4.
- $LSp[i]_B$ is the probability of preference for the LS B stored in the SM, in dimension i, with i = 1..4.
- $0 < \alpha < 1$ is the learning rate, which indicates how fast the system learns.
- R is the reinforcement to be applied to LSp

The reinforcement is calculated according to the performance value (PFM) obtained by the student during a learning session, according to (6).

$$R = \frac{1}{PFM \times DLS} \tag{6}$$

The reinforcement is inversely proportional to performance, since, probably, the lower the performance, the greater the difficulty of learning, which can probably be caused by strong inconsistency in LSp, which should be eliminated as soon as possible, requiring greater reinforcement.

By the other side, it is desirable that the greater the distance between LS (DLS) in a dimension, the lower the reinforcement, so that we can avoid abrupt increases on a considerably strong LSp, and allowing a greater increase when DLS value approximates to 0 (undefined preference). The PFM value is considered in the interval [0,100] and the DLS value is considered in the interval [0,1]. A variable *Rmax* limits the value of *R*, in order of preventing too large reinforcements when DLS or PFM tends to 0.

Simulating Students Performance

In order to test and validate our approach, isolating all the complexity related to students performances evaluation (Virvou et al., 2003; Chiu et al., 2007; Lopes et al., 2008a; Dorça et al., 2009; Lopes et al., 2008b; Zhang et al., 2010), we used a simulated process, taking into consideration some aspects related to the impact of LS in the learning process (Kinshuk et al., 2009; Haider et al., 2010; Graf et al., 2008; Graf and Kinshuk, 2009; Graf and Liu, 2008; Coffield et al., 2009; Alfonseca et al., 2006; Graf and Lin, 2007; Graf and Kinshuk, 2007; Bajraktarevic et al., 2003; Sangineto et al., 2008; Terry et al., 1995; Friedel and Rudd, 2006; Vasilyeva et al., 2006).

In this context, using simulation is essential in order to correct problems and improve new approaches, as it allows immediate evaluations, adjustments and correction of problems since the very beginning of the development process, while running a single test using real students should take months. Simulation is a widespread and widely used technique for testing educational approaches and may bring advantages, as stated by Abdullah and Cooley (2002); Vanlehn et al. (1994); Vizcaino and du Boulay (2002); Virvou et al. (2003); Bravo and Ortigosa (2006); Mertz (1997); Meyn et al. (1996). The computational model that we used to simulate students performances in order to test our approach is presented in details below.

The main aspect of this model is that when a student's real LS (*LSr*) are met by the currently selected LSC, learning becomes easier and the probability of success (*PFM* $\geq m$) is increased. As pointed out by Graf et al. (2008), Strong preferences produce stronger negative effects on students' performances when they are unmet by the teaching process, and this fact is considered by our students' performance simulation process (SPSP). The impact of LS strengths on students' performances is analysed by Kinshuk et al. (2009);

Felder and Silverman (1988); Haider et al. (2010); Graf et al. (2008); Kinshuk et al. (2009).

Results have shown that learners with strong preferences on a specific LS have more difficulties to learn than learners with mild LS preferences. According to Kinshuk et al. (2009), this finding shows that learners with strong LS preferences can especially benefit from adaptivity. According to Kinshuk et al. (2009), in mismatched courses, these students scored significantly low on the final exam than students who did not have preferences as pronounced. This result confirms Felder's argument about the importance of adaptivity with respect to LS, especially for students who have strong preferences Felder and Silverman (1988). In the same way, unmet moderate preferences tend to cause greater negative impact than unmet balanced preferences, since in this type of preference the student tends to have dexterity in both LS, as stated by Kinshuk et al. (2009). These factors were taken into account by SPSP, as shown below.

The SPSP considers an increase of difficulty when student's *LSr* are unmet by the currently selected LSC during the learning session. In this way, the SPSP can infer the degree of difficulty to be faced by the student during a learning session. Increasing the probability of failure also increases the level of difficulty. Therefore, considering the learning process as a non-deterministic process, which is influenced by many factors besides LS, the SPSP considers that the occurrence of inadequately adapted content may contribute to students' failure, but, cannot determine it. Some of these factors are pointed out in (Al-Dujaily and Ryu, 2006; Lim et al., 2007; Zhang et al., 2010; Mosakhani and Jamporazmey, 2010).

In this context, SPSP calculates the amount of unmet LS (*LSu*) between *LSr* and the currently selected LSC, and considers it in the calculation of students performances (PFM), which is given by (7).

$$PFM = M - (D \times K \times \alpha); \qquad (7)$$

such that:

- M is the maximum PFM value.
- D is a difficulty factor in the range [0,5], and it is given by (8)
- K is a constant value, which allows PFM being equal 0 if D and α assumes their maximum value, i.e., considering $M = 100$, then $K = 20$.
- α is a multiplier, valued as a random number in the range [0,1].

It is important to mention that α represents a random difficulty factor multiplier which considers that not only LS but also many factors exert some influence on students' performances, making it harder to infer students' LS based only on fixed behavioural pattern rules, because students' behaviour and performance may be influenced by other factors besides LS, as stated before.

$$D = LSu + \beta + \gamma$$

such that:

LSu is the amount of unmet LS between LSr and the currently selected LSC, and it is in the range [0,4].

β increases the difficulty factor D, and it is valued as a random number in the range [0,1] if there is at least one unmet strong preference in the selected LSC; else β is valued as 0.

γ increases the difficulty factor D, and it is valued as a random number in the range [0, $1-\beta$] if there is at least one unmet moderate preference in the selected LSC; else γ is valued as 0.

Therefore, β and γ allows SPSP to consider that strong preferences may exert stronger impact in students performances than moderate preferences, which may exert stronger impact than balanced preferences, as stated by Felder and Silverman (1988), Haider et al. (2010), Graf et al. (2008), Kinshuk et al. (2009). Furthermore,

D is increased as LSu is increased, which means that unmet preferences increase the difficulty of learning process, and probably decrease students performances. But, how D will affect students performances is determined by α, considering that not only LS but also many factors exert some influence on students' performances.

Because of this, if $LSu = 0$, D is set to a random number in the range [0,1], representing an unknown and non-deterministic probability of difficult, which means that even if all student's LS preferences are met by the educational system, the student may show some degree of difficulty related to other factors, which may be unknown and non-deterministic.

Thus, as $0 \leq LSu \leq 5$ and $K = 20$, we have $0 \leq PFM \leq 100$. We are aware that the probability values considered by SPSP may be specific for each student. But, considering the cited investigations on how LS may exert influence on students' performance, we believe that these values are reasonable. Therefore, SPSP allowed the experimentation of our approach, whose behavior we needed to know before testing it with real students.

According to Wojtusiak et al. (2012), modeling complex systems often requires using simulation techniques that approximate real-world systems behavior. Stochastic simulation is frequently used to model systems whose operation cannot be captured directly by deterministic rules, and thus need to be approximated probabilistically, as it occurred in this work. Important considerations on stochastic modeling and simulation have been presented by Geiss (2009).

The next section presents some experiments and discusses the results.

TESTING AND VALIDATING THE PROPOSED APPROACH

The approach depicted in this chapter has been tested through a set of experiments. Some of them are expounded in this section and their results are discussed. The experiments expounded in this section were executed considering the following parameters:

- POPSIZE = 100
- $Px = 0.2$
- $Pm = 0.1$

This configuration has shown good results. Other configurations have been tested. Each experiment was repeated 20 times. Therefore we could observe the algorithm working under different circumstances but under identical conditions. It was possible to notice that the resulting sequences during an experiment were different, but the final results were very similar. So, the non-determinism and convergence aspects intrinsic to the learning and student modeling processes were very clear.

In each experiment we considered different initial assumptions about students LS. In addition, we set the real students LS, used by SPSP. Four experiments and their results are shown in this section. The execution of an experiment finishes when the student achieves all learning goals. We considered 30 concepts to be learned by students and 6 cumulative cognitive levels to be achieved in each concept, based on the Bloom's Taxonomy for Knowledge Bloom and Krathwohl (1956). Therefore, the simulated learning process, in these experiments, should have, at least, 180 learning sessions (or iterations) in order to achieve all learning goals (30 X 6 = 180).

When students have good performances during a learning session, their cognitive level in a concept evolves, until they reach the maximum cognitive level to the concept. When students fail, their cognitive level in the concept does not evolve. Therefore, the easier the learning process, the fewer iterations necessary to achieve all learning goals. And, the better adapted the content is, the easier the learning process is, as pointed out in Section 1.

For each experiment, we show, graphically, how student's probable LS, stored in SM, are updated during the learning process. In each graph, the x-axis shows the numbers of the iterations of the learning process and the y-axis shows the updating of the LSp throughout the learning process. The main goal was to observe how LSp are gradually updated and tuned along the iterations of the learning process.

In order to validate the approaches, we considered two variables:

- **Consistency:** The LSp effectively converged to the during the learning process?
- **Efficiency:** The converged to the LSr in reasonable time?, i.e., the LSp became consistent in the beginning of the learning process?

The results obtained through experiments show that, considering these variables, both approaches are valid. We could observe different levels of consistency and efficiency when comparing the approaches, as it is depicted hereafter.

Experiment 1

First, we considered a student with the following LSr: {reflective (strong), sensitive (strong), visual (moderate), global (weak) } The students LSr in SM are initially defined as {(70.0,30.0), (35.0,65.0), (60.0,40.0), (45.0,55.0)} As it can be seen, LS are initially inconsistent and doesn't express the students preferences correctly, specifically in dimensions active/reflective and sensitive/intuitive. Figure 4 presents one execution of this experiment and shows how student's LS changes along the learning process. All executions of this experiment produced a consistent SM through a different path, due to the non-deterministic aspect of the student modeling process.

As it can be seen in Figure 4, approximately 460 iterations were necessary to finish the learning process, which is a high number when compared to the next experiments. It shows considerable learning difficulties by the student, considering that two strong preferences were initially inconsistent in SM.

Figure 4. Results from experiment 1

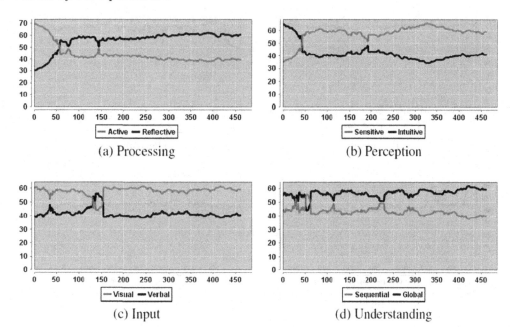

(a) Processing

(b) Perception

(c) Input

(d) Understanding

Experiment 2

In the following experiment, we consider the case in which there are no initial information available about the student. Therefore, LSp was initially {(50.0,50.0), (50.0,50.0), (50.0,50.0), (50.0,50.0)}. The student's LSr was set to { reflective (weak), intuitive (strong), visual (moderate), sequential (weak) }.

Figure 5 presents the results obtained from an execution of this experiment. Figure 5 shows that less iterations were necessary to complete the learning process. This occurred because inconsistencies in SM seemed to be worse than the lack of information. When the system doesn't have any initial information available about student's LS, it can discover them faster and provide accurate adaptivity earlier. All repetitions of this experiment produced consistent LSp.

Experiment 3

This experiment presents a case in which we re-use a consistent SM obtained from experiment 2. The goal is to show how LS are fine-tuned by

the system during the learning process. The student's initial LSp was {(39.0,61.0), (45.0,55.0), (68.0,32.0), (61.0,39.0)}. The student's LSr was the same as in Experiment 2. Figure 6 shows the results obtained from an execution of this experiment. As it can be seen, we had a considerable reduction of iterations in the learning process, due to the initial consistency of the student's LSp.

It is possible to notice that the student's LSp were fine-tuned. Figure 6 clearly shows the differences between LS strengths. All repetitions of this experiment produced consistent LS.

Experiment 4

This experiment considers the case in which the student's LS are initially inconsistent in the four dimensions, where LSp was set to {(70.0,30.0), (70.0,30.0), (70.0,30.0), (70.0,30.0)} and LSr was set to {reflective (weak), intuitive (strong), verbal (moderate), global (weak)}.

As it can be seen in Figure 7, the student's LSp were efficiently detected. All repetitions of this experiment produced consistent results. The number of iterations was smaller than in Experiment 1, due

Figure 5. Results from experiment 2

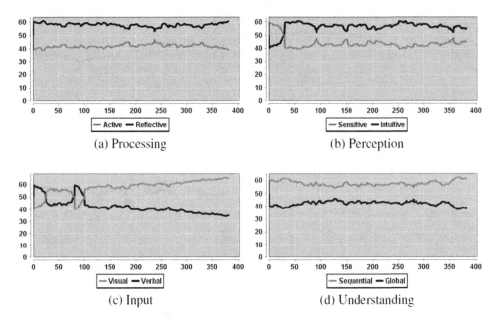

(a) Processing

(b) Perception

(c) Input

(d) Understanding

Figure 6. Results from experiment 3

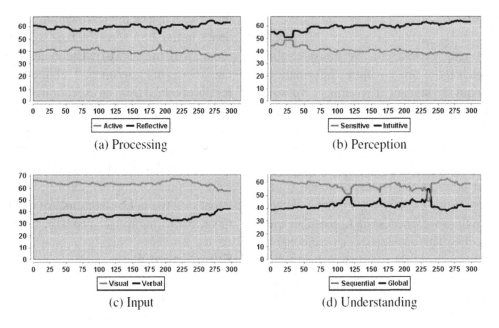

(a) Processing

(b) Perception

(c) Input

(d) Understanding

to the fact that in this experiment only one strong preference was inconsistent. As pointed out by Graf et al. (2008), strong preferences produce stronger negative effects on students' performances when they are not supported by the system.

Finally, we believe that the results obtained from these experiments validate the proposed approach, which can be easily implemented in an existing LMS, like Moodle (Moodle, 2010) or SIMEduc (Dorça et al., 2003), and used with real students. Simulating the learning process was a

Figure 7. Results from experiment 4

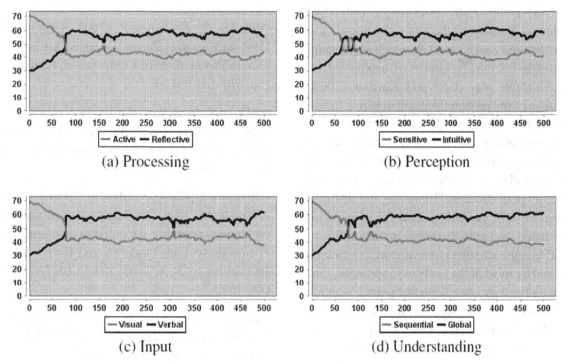

(a) Processing

(b) Perception

(c) Input

(d) Understanding

very important part of our work, which allowed us to test, adjust and correct our approaches since the very beginning, optimizing the development process. In both approaches, a huge number of tests, adjustments and corrections were done in order to achieve these results.

Therefore, without using simulation, it should be impossible to come up with this approach within reasonable time, due to the large amount of time necessary to do experiments with real students and real learning processes. Performing experiments with real students demands long-term data logs, as it can be seen in (Goguadze et al., 2011; Shein and Chiou, 2011). Moreover, without using simulation, it would be very difficult to validate the proposed approach, due to the impossibility to know real students preferences with certainty. Consequently, it would be impossible to compare students' *LSr* with *LSp*, and, as a result, it would be impossible to measure the consistency and efficiency of our approach. Therefore, we con-

sider that it is very important to initially test new approaches in simulated environments, and only after an initial study, test it in real environments.

CONCLUSION AND FUTURE WORKS

Adaptive educational systems have been considered a promising approach to increase the efficiency in computer-aided learning. A necessary characteristic in these systems is the precise, dynamic and continuous identification of students L_S in order to provide well-adapted learning experiences. In this context, one challenge is the development of systems able to efficiently acquire students LS. The information about students LS acquired by psychometric instruments encloses some degree of uncertainty (Price, 2004; Roberts and Erdos, 1993). Furthermore, in most of the existing approaches, the assumptions about students LS, once acquired, are no longer updated.

In this context, this work presents a new approach to automatically detect and precisely adjust students LS based on the non-deterministic and non-stationary aspects of LS, which may change during the learning process in an unexpected and unpredictable way (Graf and Kinshuk, 2009). Because of the probabilistic and dynamic factors enclosed on automatic detection of LS, our approach gradually and constantly modifies the SM using a set of rules that detect which LS should be adjusted at a specific moment, considering students performances. Therefore, the SM converges towards the real students LS, considering fine-tuned strengths, as shown in section 5.

This approach solves some important problems ignored by most of the analyzed approaches, and brings advantages due to specific points, as shown in section 2. The validation of this approach was done through simulation, which took into account some important aspects on how LS exert influence on students performances, as described by some researches, e.g., (Haider et al., 2010; Graf et al., 2008; Kinshuk et al., 2009; Alfonseca et al., 2006; Graf et al., 2009). The evaluation of new approaches is a difficult task, as pointed out by Bravo and Ortigosa (2006). Therefore, the validation of this approach through simulation was vital, due to the time and human resources needed to test real students. Finally, this approach can be easily implemented in any educational system, due to its independence from any specific aspect, as knowledge domain, user interaction features, tools, and so on. This independence is a natural characteristic of genetic algorithms, which are meta-heuristics, of general use. As a future work, this approach will be implemented in SIMEduc, an intelligent and multi-agent web-based educational system, which is depicted in (Dorça et al., 2003).

REFERENCES

Abdullah, S., & Cooley, R. (2002). Using simulated students to evaluate an adaptive testing system. In Proceedings of Computers in Education, (pp. 614–618). IEEE.

Al-Dujaily, A., & Ryu, H. (2006). A relationship between e-learning performance and personality. In Proceedings of Advanced Learning Technologies, (pp. 84–86). IEEE.

Alfonseca, E., Carro, R., Martín, E., Ortigosa, A., & Paredes, P. (2006). The impact of learning styles on student grouping for collaborative learning: A case study. User Modeling and User-Adapted Interaction, 16(3), 377–401. doi:10.1007/s11257-006-9012-7

Bajraktarevic, N., Hall, W., & Fullick, P. (2003). Incor*porating learning styles in hypermedia* environment: Empirical evaluation. In Proceedings of the workshop on adaptive hypermedia and adaptive web-based systems, *(pp. 41–52). Academic Press.*

Bloom, B., & Krathwohl, D. (1956). Taxonomy of educational objectives: The classification of educational goals. In Handbook I: Cognitive domain. Longmans.

Botsios, S., Georgiou, D., & Safouris, N. *(2008). Contributions to adaptive educatio*nal hypermedia systems via on-line learning style estimation. Journal of Educational Technology & Society, 12(4), 322–339.

Bravo, J., & Ortigosa, A. (2006). Validating the evalua*tion of adaptive systems by user profile simulation. In Proceedings of Workshop h*eld at the Fourth International Conference on Adaptive Hypermedia *and Adaptive Web-Based Systems (AH2006), (pp. 479–483). AH.*

Brusilovsky, P. (2001). *Adaptive educational* hypermedia. In Proceedings of International PEG Conference, (pp. 8–12). Citeseer.

Cabada, R., Estrada, M., & Garcia, C. (2009). A Fuzzy-Neural Network for *Classifying Learning Styles in a Web 2.0 an*d *Mo*bile Learning Environment. In Proceedings of Web Congress, (pp. 177–182). IEEE.

Carmona, C., & Castillo, G. (2008). Designi*ng a Dynamic Bayesian Network for Modeling Students Learning Styles. In Proceedings of Eighth IEEE International Conference on Ad*vanced Learning Technologies, (pp. 346–350). IEEE.

Carmona, C., Castillo, G., *& Millán, E. (2007). Discovering Student P*references in E-Learning. In Proceedings of the International Workshop on Applying Data Mining in e-Learning. Academic Press.

Castillo, G., Gama, J., & Breda, A. (2005). An *Adaptive Predictive Model f*or Student Modeling. In Advances in Web-based education: Personalized learning environments, (pp. 70–92). Academic Press.

Chang, W., & *Chung, M. (2010). Automatic applying Bloom's taxonomy to classify and analysis the c*ognition level of English question items. In Proceedings of Pervasive Computing (JCPC), (pp. 727–734). IEEE.

Chipperfi*eld, A., Fleming, P., Pohlheim, H., & Fonseca, C. (1994). Genetic algorithm too*lbox for use with matlab. Citeseer.

Chiu, H., Sheng, C., & Chen, A. (2007). Designing a Dynamic E-learning Project Performance Evaluation Framework. In Proceedings of Advanced Learning Technologies, (pp. 381–385). IEEE.

Coffield, F., Moseley, D., Hall, E., & Ecclestone, K. (2009). Learning styles and pedagogy in post-16 learning: A systematic and *critical review. NCVER.*

Dorça, *F., Lopes*, C., & Fernandes, M. (2003). A multiagent architecture for distance education systems. I*n Proceedings of Advanced Learning Technolog*ies, (pp. 368–369). IEEE.

Dorça, F. A., Lima, L. V., Fernandes, M. A., & Lopes, C. R. (2013). Comparing strategies for modelin*g students learning styles through reinforcem*ent learning in adaptive and intelligent educational systems: An experimental analysi*s. Expert Systems with Applications. doi: doi:10.1016/j.eswa.2012.10.014*

Dorça, *F*. A., Lopes, C. R., Fernandes, M. A., and Lopes, R. S. (2009). Adaptativity Supported by Neural Networks inWeb-bas*ed Educational Systems. Journal of Education,* Informatics and Cybernetics, 1.

Eiben, A., & Smith, J. (2003). Introduction to evolutionary computing. Springer Verlag. doi:10.1007/978-3-662-05094-1

Felder, R., & Silverman, L. (1988). Learning and teaching styles in engineering education. Journal *of Engineering education, 78(7),* 674–681.

Franzoni, A. L., & Assar, S. (2009). Student learning styles adaptation method based on teaching strategies and electronic media. Journal of Educational Technology & Socie*ty, 12(4), 15–29.*

Friedel, *C., & Rudd, R. (2006).* Creative thinking and learning s*tyles in undergraduate agriculture stu*dents. Journal of Agricultural Education, 47(4), 102–111. doi:10.5032/jae.2006.04102

García, P., Amandi, A., Schiaffino, S., & Campo, M. *(2007). Evaluating Bayesian networks*' precision for detecting students' learning styles. Computers & Education, 49(3), 794–808. doi:10.1016/j.compedu.2005.11.017

Geiss, C. (2009*). Stochastic Modeling. Retrieved from user*s.jyu.fi/geiss/scripts/stochastic-models.pdf

Goguadze, G., Sosnovsky, S., Isotani, S., & McLaren, B. (2011). Evaluating a *bayesian student model of decimal* misconceptions. In Proceedings of the 4th International Conference on Educational Data Mining. Academic Press.

Goldberg, D. (1989). Genetic algorithms in search, optimization, and ma*chine learning. Addis*on-Wesley.

Graf, S., & Kinshuk, C. (2009). Advanced Adaptivity in L*earning Management* Systems by Considering Learning Styles. In Proceedings of the 2009 IEEE/WIC/ACM International Joint Conference on Web Intelligence and Intelligent Agent Technology (vol. 3, pp. 235–238). IEEE Comp*uter Society.*

Graf, S., & Kinshuk, C. (2010a). A Flexible Mechanism for Providing Adaptivity Based on Learning *Styles in Learning Management Systems. In Proceedings of 10th I*EEE International Conference on Advanced Learning Technologies, (pp. 30–34). IEEE.

Graf, S., & Kinshuk, K. (2007). Providing Adaptive *Courses in Learning Management Systems with Respect to Learning Styles. In Proceedings of World Conference on E-Learning* in Corporate, Government, Healthcare, and Higher Education 2007, (pp. 2576–2583). Academic Press.

Graf, S., & Kinshuk, K. (2010b). Using Cognitive Traits for Improving the Detection *of Learning Styles. In Proceedings of Database and Expert Systems Applications (DEXA),* (pp. 74–78). IEEE.

Graf, S., Lan, C., Liu, T., et al. (2009). Investigations about the Effects and Effectiveness of Adaptivity for Students *with Different Learning Styles. In Proceedings of 2009 Ninth IEEE International Conference on Advanced Learn*ing Technologies, (pp. 415–419). IEEE.

Graf, S., & Lin, T. (2007). Analysing the Relationship between Learning Styles and Cognitive Traits. *In Proceedings of Advanced Learning Technologies, (pp. 235–239).* IEEE.

Graf, S., & Liu, T. (2008). Identifying Learning Styles in Learning Management Systems by Using Indications from Students' Behaviour. In Proceedings of Advanced Le*arning Technologies, (pp. 482–486). IEEE.*

Graf, S., Liu, T.-C., & Kinshuk, C. (2008). Interactions Between Students Learning Styles, Achievement and Behaviour in Mismatched Courses. In Proceedings of the Internatio*nal Conference on Cognition and Exploratory Le*arning in Digital Age (CELDA 2008), (pp. 223–230). IADIS.

Haider, M., Sinha, A., & Chaudhary, B. (2010). An Investigation of relationship between learning *styles and performance of learners. Internation*al Journal of Engineering Science and Technology, 2(7), 2813–2819.

IEEE. (2010). LOM (Learning Object Metadata). IEEE Learning Technology Standards Committee. Ret*rieved from http://ltsc.ieee.org/wg12/ index.html*

*Jones, C., Reichard, C., & Mokhtari, K. (2003). Are Stude*nts Learning Styles Discipline Specific? Community College Journal of Research and Practice, 27(5), 363–375. doi:10.1080/713838162

Kelly, D., & Tangney, B. *(2005). First Aid for You: Getting to know your learning* style using machine learning. In *Proceedings of Advanced Learni*ng Technologies. IEEE.

Kinshuk, L., Liu, T.-C., & Graf, S. (2009). Coping with Mismatched Courses: Students' behaviour and performance in courses mismatched to their learning styles. Educational *Technology Research and Development, 57(6), 739–752. d*oi:10.1007/s11423-009-9116-y

Lim, H., Lee, S., & Nam, K. (2007). Validating e-learning factors affecting training effectiveness. International Journal of Information Management, 27(1), 22–35. doi:10.1016/j.ijinfomgt.2006.08.002

Limongelli, C., Sciarrone, F., Temperini, M., & Vaste, G. (2009). Adaptive learning with the LS-plan system: a field evaluation. IEEE Transactions on Learning Technologies, 203-215.

Lopes, R. S., Dorça, F. A., Fernandes, M. A., & Lopes, C. R. (2008a). Um sistema de avaliação em ead baseado em lógica fuzzy. In Proceedings of XIX Simpósio Brasileiro de Informática na Educação. Fortaleza, Brazil: Academic Press.

Lopes, R. S., Dorça, F. A., Fernandes, M. A., & Lopes, C. R. (2008b). Um sistema de avaliação em EAD baseado em lógica Fuzzy. In Simpósio Brasileiro de Informática na Educação (pp. 30–34). SBC.

Lopes, R. S., & Fernandes, M. A. (2009). Adaptative Instructional Planning UsingWorkflow and Genetic Algorithms. In Proceedings of Computer and Information Science, (pp. 87–92). IEEE.

Mertz, J. (1997). Using a simulated student for instructional design. International Journal of Artificial Intelligence in Education, 8, 116–141.

Messick, S. (1976). Personal styles and educational options. In Individuality in learning, (pp. 327–368). Academic Press.

Meyn, S., Tweedie, R., & Glynn, P. (1996). Markov chains and stochastic stability. Springer London.

Moodle. (2010). Retrieved from http://www.moodle.org/

Mosakhani, M., & Jamporazmey, M. (2010). Introduce critical success factors (CSFs) of elearning for evaluating e-learning implementation success. In Proceedings of Educational and Information Technology (ICEIT), (vol. 1). IEEE.

Papoulis, A., Pillai, S., & Unnikrishna, S. (2002). Probability, random variables, and stochastic processes (Vol. 73660116). McGraw-Hill.

Price, L. (2004). Individual differences in learning: Cognitive control, cognitive style, and learning style. Educational Psychology, 24(5), 681–698. doi:10.1080/0144341042000262971

Roberts, M., & Erdos, G. (1993). Strategy selection and metacognition. Educational Psychology, 13(3), 259–266. doi:10.1080/0144341930130304

Sangineto, E., Capuano, N., Gaeta, M., & Micarelli, A. (2008). Adaptive course generation through learning styles representation. Universal Access in the Information Society, 7(1), 1–23. doi:10.1007/s10209-007-0101-0

Shein, P., & Chiou, W. (2011). Teachers as role models for students' learning styles. Social Behavior and Personality, 39(8), 1097–1104. doi:10.2224/sbp.2011.39.8.1097

Terry, R. E., Harb, J. N., Hurt, P., & Williamson, K. (1995). Teaching through the cycle: application of learning style theory to engineering education at Brigham Young University. Brigham Young University Press.

Van Zwanenberg, N., Wilkinson, L., & Anderson, A. (2000). Felder and silverman's index of learning styles and honey and mumford's learning styles questionnaire: How do they compare and do they predict academic performance? Educational Psychology, 20(3), 365–380. doi:10.1080/713663743

Vanlehn, K., Ohlsson, S., & Nason, R. (1994). Applications of simulated students: An exploration. Journal of Artificial Intelligence in Education, 5, 135–135.

Vasilyeva, E., Pechenizkiy, M., & Puuronen, S. (2006). The Challenge of Feedback Personalization to Learning Styles in a Web-Based Learning System. In Proceedings of Advanced Learning Technologies, (pp. 1143–1144). IEEE.

Virvou, M., Manos, K., & Katsionis, G. (2003). An evaluation agent that simulates students' behaviour in intelligent tutoring systems. In Proceedings of IEEE International Conference on Systems, Man and Cybernetics, (vol. 5, pp. 4872–4877). IEEE.

Vizcaino, A., & du Boulay, B. (2002). Using a simulated student to repair difficulties in collaborative learning. In Proceedings of the International Conference on Computers in Education. ACM.

Wojtusiak, J., Warden, T., & Herzog, O. (2012). Machine learning in agent-based stochastic simulation: Inferential theory and evaluation in transportation logistics. Computers & Mathematics with Applications (Oxford, England), 64(12), 3658–3665. doi:10.1016/j.camwa.2012.01.079

Zakaria, M. R., & Brailsford, T. J. (2002). User Modeling and Adaptive Educational Hypermedia Frameworks for Education. New Review of Hypermedia and Multimedia, 1(8), 83–97. doi:10.1080/13614560208914737

Zatarain, R., Barrón-Estrada, L., Reyes-García, C., & Reyes-Galaviz, O. (2010). Applying Intelligent Systems for Modeling Students' Learning Styles Used for Mobile and Web-Based Systems. Soft Computing for Intelligent Control and Mobile Robotics.

Zatarain-Cabada, R., Barrón-Estrada, M., Zepeda-Sánchez, L., Sandoval, G., Osorio-Velazquez, J., & Urias-Barrientos, J. (2009). A Kohonen Network for Modeling Students' Learning Styles in Web 2.0 Collaborative Learning Systems. MICAI 2009. Advances in Artificial Intelligence, 512–520.

Zhang, L., Zhang, X., Duan, Y., Fu, Z., & Wang, Y. (2010). Evaluation of Learning Performance of E-Learning in China: A Methodology Based on Change of Internal Mental Model of Learners. Turkish Online Journal of Educational Technology, 9(1), 13.

ADDITIONAL READING

Babu, S. R., Kulkarni, K. G., & Sekaran, K. C. (2014, January). A Generic Agent Based Cloud Computing Architecture for E-Learning. In ICT and Critical Infrastructure: Proceedings of the 48th Annual Convention of Computer Society of India-Vol I (pp. 523-533). Springer International Publishing.

Bäck, T. (1996). Evolutionary algorithms in theory and practice: evolution strategies, evolutionary programming, genetic algorithms. Oxford university press.

Bäck, T., Fogel, D. B., & Michalewicz, Z. (1997). Handbook of evolutionary computation. IOP Publishing Ltd. doi:10.1887/0750308958

Bäck, T., Fogel, D. B., & Michalewicz, Z. (Eds.). (2000). Evolutionary computation 1: Basic algorithms and operators (Vol. 1). CRC Press. doi:10.1887/0750306645

Brusilovsky, P. (1998, August). Adaptive educational systems on the world-wide-web: A review of available technologies. In Proceedings of Workshop" WWW-Based Tutoring" at 4th International Conference on Intelligent Tutoring Systems (ITS'98), San Antonio, TX.

Brusilovsky, P. (2001). Adaptive hypermedia. User Modeling and User-Adapted Interaction, 11(1-2), 87–110. doi:10.1023/A:1011143116306

Brusilovsky, P., & Peylo, C. (2003). Adaptive and intelligent web-based educational systems. International Journal of Artificial Intelligence in Education, 13(2), 159–172.

Carmona, C., Castillo, G., & Millán, E. (2008, July). Designing a *dynamic bayesian network for modeling students'* learning styles. In Advanced Learning Technologies, 2008. ICALT'08. Eighth IEEE International Conference on (pp. 346-350). IEEE.

Charniak, E., Riesbeck, C. K., McDermott, D. V., & Meehan, J. R. (2014). Artificial intelligence programming. Psychology Press.

Chen, S. Y., & Liu, X. (2008). An integrated approach for modeling learning patterns *of students in Web-based instruction: A cognitive style perspective. [TOCHI]. ACM Tran*sactions on Computer-Human Interaction, 15(1), 1–28. doi:10.1145/1352782.1352783

Deb, K. (2001). *Multi-objective optimization u*sing evolutionary algorithms (Vol. 2012). Chichester: John Wiley & Sons.

Dias, S. B., Diniz, J. A., & Hadjileontiadis, L. J. (2014). On Modeling Users' Quality of Interaction with *LMS Using Fuzzy Logic. In Towards an Intellige*nt Learning Management System Under Blended Learning (pp. 1*51-168). Springer Inter*national Publishing.

Du Boulay, B., & Luckin, R. (2001). Modelling human teaching tactics and strategies for tutoring systems. International Journal of Artificial Intelligence in Education, 12(3), 235–256.

García, P., Amandi, A., Schiaffino, S., & Campo, M. (2007). Evaluating Bayesian networks' precision for detecting students' learning styles. Computers & Education, 49(3), 794–808. doi:10.1016/j.compedu.2005.11.017

Goldberg, D. *E. (1994). Genetic and evolutionary algorithms come of age. Com*munications of the ACM, 37(3), 113–119. doi:10.1145/175247.175259

Hsu, C. C., Chen, H. C., Huang, K. H., Huang, K. K., & Huang, Y. M. (2014). The developm*ent of an adaptive group* composition system on Facebook for collaborative learning using an artificial bee colony algorithm. Applications of Mathe*matics, 8(1L), 157–164.*

Kelly, D., & Tangney, B. (2006). Adapting to intelligence profile in an adaptive educational system. Interacting with Computers, 18(3), 385–409. doi:10.1016/j.intcom.2005.11.009

Khan, A. A., & Naseer, O. (2014). Fuzzy Logic Based Multi User Adaptive Te*st System. arXiv preprint a*rXiv:1401.6348.

Klašnja-Milićević, A., Vesin, B., Ivanović, M., & Budimac, Z. (2011). E-Learning personalization bas*ed on hybrid recommendatio*n strategy and learning style identification. Computers & Education, 56(3), 885–899. doi:10.1016/j.compedu.2010.11.001

Magoulas, G. D., *Papanikolaou, Y., & Grigori*adou, M. (2003). Adaptive web-based learning: Accommodating individual differences through system's adaptation. British Journal of Educational Technology, 34(4), 511–527. doi:*10.1111/1467-8535.00347*

Nijhavan, H., & Brusilovsky, P. (2002). A framework for adaptive e-learning based on distributed re-usable learning activities. In World Conference on E-Learning in Corporate, Government, Healthcare, a*nd Higher Education (Vol. 2002, No. 1, pp. 154*-161).

Popescu, E. (2008). An artificial intelligence course used to investigate students' learning style. In Advances in Web Based Learning-ICWL 2008 (pp. 122–131). Spri*nger Berlin Heidelberg. doi:10.1007/978-3-540-85033-5_13*

Popescu, E., Trigano, P., & Badica, C. (2007, July). Towards a unified learning style model in adaptive educational systems. In Advanced Learning Technologies, 2007. *ICALT 2007. Seventh IEEE International* Conference on (pp. 804-808). IEEE.

Russell, S. J., Norvig, P., Canny, J. F., Malik, J. M., & Edwards, D. D. (1995). Artificial intelligence: a modern approach (Vol. 2). Englewood Cliffs: Prentice hall.

Tian, F., Gao, P., Li, L., Zhang, W., Liang, H., Qian, Y., & Zhao, R. (2014). Recognizing and regulating e-learners' emotions based on interactive Chinese texts in e-learning systems. Knowledge-Based Systems, 55, 148–164. doi:10.1016/j.knosys.2013.10.019

Triantafillou, E., Pomportsis, A., & Demetriadis, S. (2003). The design and the formative evaluation of an adaptive educational system based on cognitive styles. Computers & Education, 41(1), 87–103. doi:10.1016/S0360-1315(03)00031-9

Vaessen, B. E., Prins, F. J., & Jeuring, J. (2014). University students' achievement goals and help-seeking strategies in an intelligent tutoring system. Computers & Education, 72, 196–208. doi:10.1016/j.compedu.2013.11.001

Whitley, D. (1994). A genetic algorithm tutorial. Statistics and Computing, 4(2), 65–85. doi:10.1007/BF00175354

Wolf, C. (2002). iWeaver: Towards an interactive web-based adaptive learning environment to address individual learning styles. European Journal of Open and Distance Learning.

Zhang, X. (2014, January). Research of Modern Physical Education Technology Based on Artificial Intelligence. In Proceedings of the 2012 International Conference on Cybernetics and Informatics (pp. 435-442). Springer New York.

Zhao, M., Ni, W., Zhang, H., Lin, Z., & Yang, Y. (2014). A Knowledge-Based Teaching Resources Recommend Model for Primary and Secondary School Oriented Distance-Education Teaching Platform. In Frontier and Future Development of Information Technology in Medicine and Education (pp. 511–521). Springer Netherlands. doi:10.1007/978-94-007-7618-0_50

KEY TERMS AND DEFINITIONS

Adaptive Educational System: Educational software - program which employs some kind of intelligent approaches that enable it to change some features or functions for any changes within the educational environment.

Artificial Intelligence: The name of the scientific area, in which research works for designing intelligent systems simulating the human intelligence are performed.

Evolution: A process explaining the change which occurs among inherited characteristics of biological organisms along successive generations.

Evolutionary: Associated with the evolution and its components explaining the whole evolution oriented concept.

Evolutionary Algorithms: The type of algorithms, which are built on algorithmic approaches derived from essential mechanisms of Darwin's evolution theory.

Genetic Algorithm: An Artificial Intelligence oriented algorithm, which is based on principles of natural selection and draws inspiration from these principles to employ some algorithmic approaches for solving certain problems.

Chapter 16
Ideas on the Future of Intelligent Web-Based E-Learning

Utku Kose
Usak University, Turkey

ABSTRACT

With the outstanding improvements in technology, the number of e-learning applications has increased greatly. This increment is associated with awareness levels of educational institutions on the related improvements and the power of communication and computer technologies to ensure effective and efficient teaching and learning experiences for teachers and students. Consequently, there is a technological flow that changes the standards of e-learning processes and provides better ways to obtain desired educational objectives. When we consider today's widely used technological factors, Web-based e-learning approaches have a special role in directing the educational standards. Improvements among m-learning applications and the popularity of the Artificial Intelligence usage for educational works have given great momentum to this orientation. In this sense, this chapter provides some ideas on the future of intelligent Web-based e-learning applications by thinking on the current status of the literature. As it is known, current trends in developing Artificial Intelligence-supported e-learning tools continue to shape the future of e-learning. Therefore, it is an important approach to focus on the future. The author thinks that the chapter will be a brief but effective enough reference for similar works, which focus on the future of Artificial Intelligence-supported distance education and e-learning.

INTRODUCTION

Technological developments and improvements have a remarkable effect on almost all fields of the life. At this point, our daily activities are also affected rapidly, as a result of affects from the changes – improvements in the technology. One of the most important fields that are very sensitive

to technological changes is education. In time, standards of the education field have changed again and again, especially because of some specific technologies like computer and communication. Today, individuals have chance to experience educational processes via advanced, high technologies, which improve the ways of receiving information, transforming it into a owned knowl-

DOI: 10.4018/978-1-4666-6276-6.ch016

edge, and also keeping a stable system including activities of receiving and sharing information, which points a typical concept of teaching and learning generally.

When we examine today's technological aspects to perform educational activities, we can see that especially E-learning has a great impact on the related processes. Additionally, improving popularity of mobile device usage also causes a continuing power on E-learning solutions. Certainly, revolutionary changes on the Web platform of the Internet technology have a remarkable role on all the changes in today's educational approaches, methods, and techniques.

With the outstanding improvements in the technology, number of E-learning applications is increased greatly. This increment is associated with awareness levels of educational institutions on the related improvements, and power of communication and computer technologies to ensure effective and efficient teaching and learning experiences teachers and students. Consequently, there is a technological flow that changes standards of E-learning processes and provide better ways to obtain desired educational objectives. When we consider today's widely used technological factors, especially Web-based E-learning approaches have a special role on directing the educational standards. Improvements among M-learning applications and the popularity of the Artificial Intelligence usage for educational works have given a great momentum to this orientation.

Considering the related explanations, objective of this chapter is to provide some ideas on the future of intelligent Web-based E-learning applications, by thinking on current status of the literature. As it is known, current trends on developing Artificial Intelligence supported E-learning tools continue to shape the future of E-learning. So, it is an important approach to focus on the future. The author thinks that the chapter will be a brief but effective enough reference for similar works, which focus on the future of Artificial Intelligence supported Distance Education and E-learning.

According to the subject of the chapter, remaining content is organized as follows: Next section is devoted to some brief explanations on Web-based learning, new – future generations of Web platform, and M-learning (Mobile learning). After this section, some brief ideas on the future of intelligent We-based E-learning applications – solutions are explained under the third section and conclusions regarding to the subject are provided in the context of the last section.

FOUNDATIONS

Because the objective of the chapter is based on expressing ideas on the future of Web-based E-learning, some explanations regarding to this subject should be provided in order to enable readers to have idea about it. Additionally, changing functions and features of the Web platform also affects the applications over it; so, new – future generations of the Web should also be taken into consideration. Finally, because the future highly depends on using mobile devices, we should also focus on the learning aspect of mobile based activities by explaining M-learning.

Web-Based E-Learning

Today, there are many different types of E-learning activities, and these activities determine the general name of some certain E-learning related application ways. One of them is called as the "Web-based E-learning" and this application way is based on directly usage of the Web platform provided by the Internet technology.

Briefly, we can define the Web as the application side – platform of the Internet. Over the Web, users can perform any online activities that they can perform via provided tools – applications. Web is something like an "abstract, logical view" of the Internet communication all over the world. If we think about the online activities that are performed over the Web platform only, we directly understand the function of the Web-based E-learning in the sense of general E-learning technique.

Web-based E-learning can be defined as the E-learning, which is performed over the Web platform, via a typical Web-browser, and Web applications that are viewed on it. Because the activities over the Web already employ electronic role, the term Web-based E-learning can be called as also "Web-based learning". In the literature, there are also some more definitions regarding to this term. Tsai *et al.* (2002) defines it as a learning associated with "learning materials delivered in a Web browser, including when the materials are packaged on CD-ROM or other media." On the other hand, Wasim *et al.*, (2014) provide a definition as "an online learning or E-learning because it includes online course content." A typical Web-based E-learning can be provided over some Web applications like learning management systems (LMS) or any other special applications that have been developed via different Web programming languages. In this sense, Khalife *et al.* (2002) indicates the time and location advantage of Web-based E-learning (because of online communication – Web browser usage) while Boisvert *et al.* (2000) see Web-based E-learning as a tool for performing educational activities. As general, some applications that may be provided in the context of Web-based E-learning activities can be listed as follows:

- Dynamic or static text-based course contents (over LMS or just Web),
- Animation based, dynamic or static course contents (over LMS or just Web),
- Different types of evaluation platforms like tests, quizzes...etc.,
- Specially designed tools, which are based on different educational approaches or methods (like game-based learning oriented systems, tutoring related systems... etc.),

- Self-evaluation tools, which can be used by students to evaluate their performances along the E-learning processes,
- Intelligent online E-learning tools, which employ Artificial Intelligence oriented approaches,

Especially the last application indicates the latest status of today's E-learning studies. In this sense, Artificial Intelligence approaches, methods, and techniques are widely used to improve classical E-learning tools – software systems or design and develop newer, and more advanced ones. This application trend is one of the most important factors that forming the future steps of education field and the related research studies in this field.

It is also an important thing that also the form of the Web platform has changed in time. According to the changes in society's needs (as a result of the modern knowledge society), and developments in some technologies like communication and software (computer), features and functions of the Web platform has also change in order to fit to the developments. Currently, the form of Web 2.0, which provides interactive, user-oriented, dynamic and knowledge sharing based, is in running; but some aspects of new – future generations of Web (like Web 3.0 and Web 4.0) have also appeared already.

New: Future Generations of Web

Influence of the Artificial Intelligence field in many fields result to technological improvements that are especially associated with knowledge oriented activities – works. In this sense, future of the Web will be affected too much by the Artificial Intelligence. At this point, new – future generations of the Web platform: Web 3.0 and Web 4.0 are already defined as some kind of intelligent systems to make it possible for users to experience highly flexible, dynamic, and intelligent Web contents.

Nowadays, there are examples of both Web 3.0 and Web 4.0 based applications currently run in the context of Internet. However, these are just the beginning of the new generations and the future will be shaped, thanks to continuing improvements in the context of them.

At this point, one of the most important supportive technologies taking active role on changes over the Web platform is Cloud Computing. Cloud Computing is an effective approach to divide (computing – operation) power of hardware related sources via software related methods; in order to share them with many users. In a more comprehensive definition, it is defined as "the next stage in the Internet's evolution, providing the means through which everything (from computing power to computing infrastructure, applications, business processes to personal collaboration) can be delivered to you as a service wherever and whenever you need" (Hurwitz *et al.*, 2009). As a result of running with the Internet technology, the Cloud Computing has enabled users to create "virtual sources" that can be accessed over the Web; by changing the nature of the current Web platform. There is a remarkable change that in the future users will need no additional hardware except from a keyboard, mouse or monitor, for running a computer system from wherever they want. Also, as a result of high support from the Artificial Intelligence, the form of applications will be more and more advanced and intelligent.

In order to have more idea about the explained changes in the last paragraph, it is better to express some about Web 3.0 and Web 4.0 as follows:

Web 3.0: The third generation of the Web: Web 3.0 can be defined as an evolving extension of the World Wide Web, in which the semantics of information and services on the Web is defined, making it possible for the Web to understand and satisfy the requests of users and machines to use the web contents (Berners-Lee *et al.*, 2001; Herman, 2008). The term "Semantic Web" is also used to define Web 3.0. It is the third generation of the

Web, which requires more using of Artificial Intelligence techniques. In more detail, typical Web 3.0 technologies comprise a set of design principles, collaborative working groups, and a variety of enabling technologies. Some aspects of Web 3.0 are expressed as prospective future possibilities that are yet to be realized. Other elements are expressed in formal specifications (Herman, 2008). Web 3.0 is based on applications and services, which understand what the Web content actually means. As a result of that Web sites can understand the content coming from other Web sources, the "understanding function" of Web 3.0 allows for real data-portability and interoperability. Users can take their web content with them when they go to another web site. Briefly, Web 3.0 related systems can understand the meaning of the content and they can work according to users' needs. At this point, Cloud Computing has a critical role to spread such applications fast and in a secure way, and not wasting too much source; to the users.

Figure 1 presents a brief schema expressing main features of the Web 3.0.

Web 4.0: Web 4.0 is a generation of the Web platform, which is highly based on some important approaches like Artificial Intelligence and Cloud Computing and it seems that it will change all living standards on the world. In the literature, Web 4.0 is called as also "symbiotic" Web (Flat World Business, 2011). At this point, almost all features and functions of Web 4.0 are expressed as prospective future possibilities and can be expressed as follows:

With the Web 4.0, the physical world will be "totally" connected to a virtual world. Users will use online operating systems and applications supported with Artificial Intelligence techniques and more advanced algorithms. Designed and developed applications will have ability to find and correct errors caused on their systems. More effective and advanced devices will be provided to users to control the whole digital world that they are authenticated to access. From a more general

Figure 1. Web 3.0

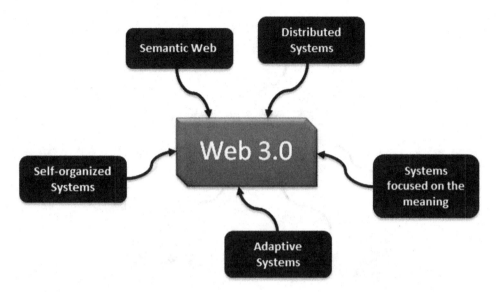

perspective; it can be said that the physical world will be controlled from remote devices and technologies by using Web 4.0 technologies. People will be able to control a TV, washing machine or refrigerator via remote, virtual interfaces. All physical elements in the world will be tagged and controlled. Smart versions of traditional tools will be designed and developed to be controlled via Web 4.0 oriented technologies. In this sense, it is remarkable that Web 4.0 will also be systems employing more and more advanced semantic features and functions. In this sense, Web 4.0 will enable users to communicate with the applications – software systems like they are talking with their friends (PCWorld, 2008). Figure 2 presents a brief schema expressing main features of the Web 3.0.

As an another important factor, nowadays' rapidly influenced technology: mobile technology has a critical role in the future on employing Web 3.0 and Web 4.0 based applications. Maybe, it can be expressed with newer names but the mechanism to ensure mobile communication will continue, thanks to mobile technologies. In this sense, it is also a good idea to explain some about M-learning in order to complete the scope of the subject.

M-Learning (Mobile Learning)

M-learning briefly explains the E-learning activities performed through mobile technologies. This E-learning way includes the usage of all devices like handheld computers, mobile phones, smart phones, tablets in order to make learning experience portable, personal and spontaneous (Kukulska-Hulme,& Traxler, 2007). In time, usage of M-learning is growing by taking students' interest to perform their self-learning and enabling educational institutions to adjust their educational plans to include M-learning based activities (Ally, 2009; Chen *et al.*, 2014; Winters, 2007; Sharples *et al.*, 2010). In the related literature, M-learning is considered as an essential learning approach in the future (Yin *et al.*, 2009).

Certainly, the rapidly grow of mobile device usage has a big impact on the popularity of educational activities, which can be performed over mobile platforms. In addition to active roles of mobile technologies, need on reaching to the wanted information on anytime has enabled researchers to develop mobile applications – software systems that enable both teachers and students to experience M-learning related educational activities. In this sense, today's M-learning applications – soft-

Figure 2. Web 4.0

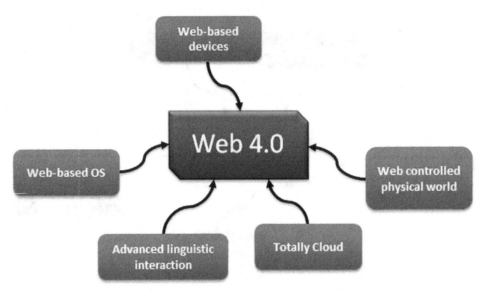

ware systems are also supported with "intelligent" features and / or functions, which are based on Artificial Intelligence oriented approaches, methods or techniques. We can express that the future of education will mostly depend on self-learning that is highly supported with usage of practical, portable, and fast devices, which are in the scope of mobile technologies and employ intelligent applications – software systems.

IDEAS ON THE FUTURE OF INTELLIGENT WEB-BASED E-LEARNING

If we consider today's conditions on Web-based E-learning activities, it is possible to have idea about the future status of the related application area and research works that can be examined in the associated literature. In time, research works and experiences obtained via performed research works will give more clear ideas for us to see the future better. But now, we can also express some brief ideas by thinking about some aspects of current technologies or any other supportive factors play active role on E-learning. The related ideas are provided as follows:

Mobile Standards for Intelligent Web-Based E-Learning: "The More for Every Time – Everywhere Education"

In the future, usage of mobile technologies for educational aims will be something common. There will be more advanced and powerful mobile devices that allows running advanced M-learning oriented applications and probably such mobile devices will include tablets including more multimedia features, and even smart watches that people can use in order to reach to the educational activities. At this point, every people will have at least one mobile device and including the educational activities, such mobile devices will have more connections with the systems that people mostly use to perform their daily activities or works. As we have indicated under the previous section; the role of new generation Web platforms will enable mobile usage to be more common; resulting more and more "every time – everywhere" education in the life.

Because usage of mobile technologies for educational aims will be something common, which points out more "every time – everywhere" education, some standards to ensure desired M-learning related activities will also be determined by educational authorities. These standards will include everything from infrastructure of software and hardware based technologies to educational procedures and plans that should be applied by educational institutions. Certainly, some revolutionary adjustments on educational systems will also be done because of the impact of newer technologies on educational activities. These will enable people to be freer on deciding their own educational processes and having more control on self-learning plans.

In the sense of provided intelligent Web-based E-learning approaches, mobile applications – software systems that will be used by people will include intelligent mechanisms that communicate always with the related communication systems to decide if it is an appropriate time to take mobile education, or decide which E-learning (M-learning) will be most appropriate to be provided over the related mobile device. The applications – software systems will be highly sensible to different environmental factors to make accurate decisions on currently performed M-learning activities or the ones, which are near to be started. Certainly, the sensibility to environmental factors will be very high according to today's systems, because many devices in the life will probably be supported with the Web, in order to ensure the intelligent system that has been explained briefly before within new generations of the Web platform.

Personal Intelligent Web-Based E-Learning Systems

In the future, improving importance of self-learning approach will probably result to design and develop personal Web-based E-learning systems, which are supported with Artificial Intelligence. Such personal systems will be hired or bought by students or any individual, who wants to receive some educational processes in the context of life-long learning. It is also remarkable that the improving importance of life-long learning will also be affected highly from the status of self-learning approach.

Personal Web-based E-learning Systems will include learning contents and applications – software systems, which have been designed and developed via advanced technologies; for special course experiences. All of these contents and applications – software systems will be compatible with any mobile platform – device, so it will be possible for people to carry their own – personal Web-based E-learning systems along them.

Artificial Intelligence supported functions and / or functions of the related Web-based E-learning systems will include intelligent tutoring, teaching applications – software systems, which are more and more advanced than the ones currently widely used in E-learning processes. For example, such systems will employ more intelligent, knowledge-based infrastructure to support individuals via accurate feedback mechanisms, and adaptive functions to change environments of E-learning systems according to an individual's educational evolution. In the future, more advanced algorithmic mechanisms or development platforms to code flexible, intelligent computer programs – applications – software systems will be developed and usage of such approaches will be common; so it will be easier to highly semantic, adaptive systems to support individuals like these systems are real teachers – lecturers. It is still not clear and seems very difficult to develop a system that can totally simulate a human, but we can express that improvements in Artificial Intelligence field will allow researchers to design and develop more "intelligent, virtual educators" according to the systems that are used today.

Intelligent Mechanism to Record Learning Data Along the Life

It seems that the importance of education will be extremely high in the future. Because there will be more need to improve ourselves for high speed flow of new information and more rapid improvements in the technology. People will need more knowledge to keep themselves according to the changing nature and structure of the new world.

As we have also indicated under the previous sub-section, importance of both self-learning and life-long learning will result to appear of some technologies that take the educational processes closer to us.

In the sense of the related explanations, one remarkable idea is that individuals' learning data will be recorded along their life, via some materials employing intelligent programs. Such materials will probably be portable, small things like a credit card or watch, which will be carried by the individual easily. Such materials will be designed in a common communication protocol that can act intelligent and interact with the Web to record all learning related activities performed by the individual. Sometimes, it will also be possible for us to record our own learning status to this material. Along our life, these materials will keep different types of data related to earned knowledge, education level, results for some examinations, or any other information that are important for us or any other authorities that may control our educational status during employment or in the work life.

Intelligent mechanism of recording the related data will include recommendations given to the individual, informing him / her whenever the individual have a chance to experience new learning processes, or control his / her learning flow after graduating from some educational institutions, or just analyzing and transforming the received data to more linguistic forms (to make them clear for the individual) when the system interacts with another device in the sense of educational activities.

Highly Improved Intelligent Multimedia Features

Rapid developments and improvements among multimedia related technologies will also affect the future status of intelligent Web-based E-learning systems. In this sense, some remarkable technologies like advanced sound systems, highly interactive videos, or holograms will appear and they will be widely used along daily life. We can say that usage of such technologies will be a common thing for us. Certainly, developments of these technologies will be associated with also changes within some general technologies like communication and computer; as we have often expressed in this chapter.

Artificial Intelligent mechanisms that will be run in the related highly improved multimedia systems will be depended on usage of advanced algorithms, which will be introduced by researchers in the future. It is important that such algorithms may also enable people to run highly improved intelligent multimedia systems easily by just turning on their mobile devices, which are run thanks to the Web environment of the future.

Special Artificial Intelligence Systems for Only Web-Based E-Learning

We can predict that the future may improve the current Artificial Intelligence field to have specialized sub-fields, which are focused on only certain fields. At this point, because the knowledge will be more and more important in the future, especially scientists and researchers from the education field will take active role on designing special Artificial Intelligence systems, which can be used for only educational activities over the Web platform.

In more detail, such Artificial Intelligence systems will include advanced algorithms, or advanced hybrid systems formed via already introduced methods or techniques and consequently, all of these improvements will make the Web-based E-learning a more specialized and dynamic field in the context of education.

It is also a remarkable idea that Web based programming languages will be improved as a result of using Artificial Intelligence related approaches over the Web platform. It can be expressed that programming languages will also have a revolutionary change and almost all programming languages will be Web-based in the future.

Furthermore, such programming languages will have special coding approaches, which make them Artificial Intelligence oriented to write intelligent applications – software systems easily.

Specialized Jobs Based on Artificial Intelligence and Intelligent Web-Based E-Learning

In the future, there will also be more specialized job types because of improvements in the sense of Artificial Intelligence, computer science, and any other scientific fields connected with the related application concept. Specialized jobs will be extremely important needs of future technologies to run intelligent systems, Web platform, and the related applications – software systems that will be run along the intelligent future of daily life.

Some specialized jobs in the sense of Artificial Intelligence and intelligent Web-based E-learning can be listed as follows:

- Artificial Intelligence expert and/or engineer,
- Intelligent system engineer,
- (Intelligent) Web engineer,
- (Intelligent Web-based) E-learning engineer,
- Intelligent algorithm engineer,
- Multiplatform Artificial Intelligence designer,
- Artificial Intelligence theorist,
- Artificial Intelligence / intelligent system technician.

CONCLUSION

This chapter has been a remarkable reference to bear a torch to the future of Artificial Intelligence and its usage in Web-based E-learning systems. As it is also indicated under the related sections, the future will probably be based on intelligent Web platforms, which enable people to control many devices and live in a world of Artificial Intelligence supported system. As being parallel, the education field of the future will also be affected by the developments in the intersection of communication and computer technologies. In more detail, the E-learning technique will be the most important educational way to keep individuals educated against the rapidly changing future and life conditions.

As it can be understood, there will be many other things to express about the future of education, and also intelligent solutions to ensure effective and efficient approaches for people, who should be adapted to the new world. In this chapter, the author has expressed some brief ideas, which are typical predictions that can be derived from today's conditions in the sense of different scientific fields, and also technologies. With the changes and improvements appeared in time, there will be many similar research works or theoretical papers, which focus on the future of intelligent E-learning.

REFERENCES

Ally, M. (Ed.). (2009). *Mobile learning: Transforming the delivery of education and training*. Athabasca University Press.

Berners-Lee, T., Hendler, J., & Lassila, O. (2001). The semantic web. *Scientific American*. Retrieved from http://www.scientificamerican.com/article.cfm?id=the-semantic-web

Boisvert, L. (2000). Web-based learning. *Information Systems Management*, *17*(1), 35–41. doi:10.1201/1078/43190.17.1.20000101/31212.5

Chen, H., Chen, L., Chen, J., & Xu, J. (2014). Research on Mobile Learning Games in Engineering Graphics Education. In *Frontier and Future Development of Information Technology in Medicine and Education* (pp. 2981–2986). Springer Netherlands. doi:10.1007/978-94-007-7618-0_379

Flat World Business. (2011). *Web 1.0 vs Web 2.0 vs Web 3.0 vs Web 4.0 – A bird's eye on the evolution and definition*. Retrieved from http://flatworldbusiness.wordpress.com/flat-education/previously/web-1-0-vs-web-2-0-vs-web-3-0-a-bird-eye-on-the-definition/

Herman, I. (2008). Semantic web activity statement. *W3C Semantic Web*. Retrieved from http://www.w3.org/2001/sw/Activity.html

Hurwitz, J., Bloor, R., Kaufman, M., & Halper, F. (2009). *Cloud computing for dummies* (Vol. 1). John Wiley & Sons.

Khalifa, M., & Lam, R. (2002). Web-based learning: effects on learning process and outcome. *IEEE Transactions on* Education, *45*(4), 350–356.

Kukulska-Hulme, A., & Traxler, J. (Eds.). (2007). *Mobile learning: A handbook for educators and trainers*. Routledge.

PCWorld. (2008). *Web 4.0 era is upon us*. Retrieved from http://www.pcworld.com/article/143110/article.html

Sharples, M., Taylor, J., & Vavoula, G. (2010). A theory of learning for the mobile age. In *Medienbildung in neuen Kulturräumen* (pp. 87–99). VS Verlag für Sozialwissenschaften. doi:10.1007/978-3-531-92133-4_6

Tsai, S., & Machado, P. (2002). E-Learning basics: Essay. *Elearn Magazine*, (7), 3.

Wasim, J., Sharma, S. K., Khan, I. A., & Siddiqui, J. (n.d.). *Web Based Learning*. Academic Press.

Winters, N. (2007). What is mobile learning. *Big Issues in Mobile Learning*, 7-11.

Yin, C., David, B., & Chalon, R. (2009, August). Use your mobile computing devices to learn-Contextual mobile learning system design and case studies. In *Proceedings of Computer Science and Information Technology*, (pp. 440-444). IEEE.

ADDITIONAL READING

Agarwal, R., Deo, A., & Das, S. (2004). Intelligent agents in E-learning. *Software Engineering Notes, 29*(2), 1–1. doi:10.1145/979743.979755

Aghaei, S., Nematbakhsh, M. A., & Farsani, H. K. (2012). Evolution of the World Wide Web: From Web 1.0 to Web 4.0. *International Journal of Web & Semantic Technology, 3*(1), 1–10. doi:10.5121/ijwest.2012.3101

Ahmad, A. R., Basir, O. A., & Hassanein, K. (2004, December). Adaptive User Interfaces for Intelligent E-Learning: Issues and Trends. In ICEB (pp. 925-934).

Alepis, E., & Virvou, M. (2014). *Object-Oriented User Interfaces for Personalized Mobile Learning*. Springer Berlin. doi:10.1007/978-3-642-53851-3

Ally, M., & Tsinakos, A. (2014). Perspectives on Open and Distance Learning: Increasing Access through Mobile Learning.

Attewell, J. (2005). Mobile technologies and learning. London: Learning and Skills Development Agency, 2(4).

Babu, S. R., Kulkarni, K. G., & Sekaran, K. C. (2014, January). A Generic Agent Based Cloud Computing Architecture for E-Learning. In *ICT and Critical Infrastructure: Proceedings of the 48th Annual Convention of Computer Society of India-Vol I* (pp. 523-533). Springer International Publishing.

Bates, A. T. (2004). *Technology, e-learning and distance education*. Routledge.

Chen, C. M., Hsu, S. H., Li, Y. L., & Peng, C. J. (2006, October). Personalized intelligent m-learning system for supporting effective English learning. In *Systems, Man and Cybernetics, 2006. SMC'06. IEEE International Conference on* (Vol. 6, pp. 4898-4903). IEEE.

Dlamini, B. I. (2014). Web-based learning activities to enhance blended learning for HRM students.

Downes, S. (2005). Feature: E-learning 2.0. *Elearn magazine, 2005*(10), 1.

Evans, M. (2007). *The Evolution of the Web-From Web 1.0 to Web 4.0*. Reading: University of Reading.

Gladun, A., Rogushina, J., Martínez-Béjar, R., & Fernández-Breis, J. T. (2009). An application of intelligent techniques and semantic web technologies in e-learning environments. *Expert Systems with Applications*, *36*(2), 1922–1931. doi:10.1016/j.eswa.2007.12.019

Hannafin, M. J., Hill, J. R., Land, S. M., & Lee, E. (2014). Student-Centered, Open Learning Environments: Research, Theory, and Practice. In Handbook of Research on Educational Communications and Technology (pp. 641-651). Springer New York.

Hendler, J. (2009). Web 3.0 Emerging. *Computer*, *42*(1), 111–113. doi:10.1109/MC.2009.30

Huang, W., Webster, D., Wood, D., & Ishaya, T. (2006). An intelligent semantic e-learning framework using context-aware Semantic Web technologies. *British Journal of Educational Technology*, *37*(3), 351–373. doi:10.1111/j.1467-8535.2006.00610.x

Hyman, J. A., Moser, M. T., & Segala, L. N. (2014). Electronic reading and digital library technologies: understanding learner expectation and usage intent for mobile learning. *Educational Technology Research and Development*, 1–18.

Jones, P., & Skinner, H. (2014). E-learning Globalization-The impact of E-learning: what difference has it made?. *Education+ Training*, *56*(2/3), 1-1.

Kang, D., Sohn, J., Kwon, K., Joo, B. G., & Chung, I. J. (2014). An Intelligent Dynamic Context-Aware System Using Fuzzy Semantic Language. In Mobile, Ubiquitous, and Intelligent Computing (pp. 143-149). Springer Berlin Heidelberg.

Karadimce, A., & Davcev, D. (2014). Adaptive Multimedia Delivery in M-Learning Systems Using Profiling. In *ICT Innovations 2013* (pp. 57–65). Springer International Publishing. doi:10.1007/978-3-319-01466-1_5

Kurilovas, E., Kubilinskiene, S., & Dagiene, V. (2014). Web 3.0–Based personalisation of learning objects in virtual learning environments. *Computers in Human Behavior*, *30*, 654–662. doi:10.1016/j.chb.2013.07.039

Kwanya, T., Stilwell, C., & Underwood, P. (2014). Library 3.0: Intelligent libraries and apomediation.

Lassila, O., & Hendler, J. (2007). Embracing" Web 3.0. *IEEE Internet Computing*, *11*(3), 90–93. doi:10.1109/MIC.2007.52

Lin, Y. T., Wen, M. L., Jou, M., & Wu, D. W. (2014). A cloud-based learning environment for developing student reflection abilities. *Computers in Human Behavior*, *32*, 244–252. doi:10.1016/j.chb.2013.12.014

Ma, N., Yuan, M., & Cao, G. (2014, January). Integration of Digital Campus Resources Based on Cloud Computing. In *Proceedings of the 2012 International Conference on Cybernetics and Informatics* (pp. 1957-1963). Springer New York.

Ma, Z. (Ed.). (2006). *Web-based intelligent e-learning systems*. IGI Global.

Ma, Z., Zhang, F., Yan, L., & Cheng, J. (2014). Fuzzy Semantic Web Ontology Mapping. In *Fuzzy Knowledge Management for the Semantic Web* (pp. 157–180). Springer Berlin Heidelberg. doi:10.1007/978-3-642-39283-2_6

Ma, Z., Zhang, F., Yan, L., & Cheng, J. (2014). Knowledge Representation and Reasoning in the Semantic Web. In *Fuzzy Knowledge Management for the Semantic Web* (pp. 1–17). Springer Berlin Heidelberg. doi:10.1007/978-3-642-39283-2_1

Medjahed, B., Malik, Z., & Benbernou, S. (2014). On the Composability of Semantic Web Services. In Web Services Foundations (pp. 137-160). Springer New York.

Morris, R. D. (2011). Web 3.0: Implications for online learning. *TechTrends*, *55*(1), 42–46. doi:10.1007/s11528-011-0469-9

Motiwalla, L. F. (2007). Mobile learning: A framework and evaluation. *Computers & Education*, *49*(3), 581–596. doi:10.1016/j.compedu.2005.10.011

Rosenberg, M. J. (2001). *E-learning: Strategies for delivering knowledge in the digital age* (Vol. 3). New York: McGraw-Hill.

Sadiku, M., Musa, S., & Momoh, O. (2014). Cloud Computing: Opportunities and Challenges. *Potentials, IEEE*, *33*(1), 34–36. doi:10.1109/MPOT.2013.2279684

Shih, T. K., Lin, N. H., & Chang, H. P. (2003, March). An intelligent e-learning system with authoring and assessment mechanism. In *Advanced Information Networking and Applications, 2003. AINA 2003. 17th International Conference on* (pp. 782-787). IEEE.

Sivaraman, K. (2014). Effective Web Based E-Learning. *Middle-East Journal of Scientific Research*, *19*(8), 1024–1027.

Specht, M. (2014). Design of Contextualised Mobile Learning Applications. *Increasing Access*, 61.

Stankov, S., Žitko, B., & Grubišić, A. (2005, July). Ontology as a foundation for knowledge evaluation in intelligent e-learning systems. In *International workshop on applications of semantic web technologies for e-learning (SW-EL'05) in conjunction with 12th international conference on artificial intelligence in education (AI-ED 2005)* (pp. 81-84).

Stead, G. (2014). Open Formats for Mobile Learning. *Increasing Access*, 99.

Syvanen, A., Beale, R., Sharples, M., Ahonen, M., & Lonsdale, P. (2005, November). Supporting pervasive learning environments: adaptability and context awareness in mobile learning. In *Wireless and Mobile Technologies in Education, 2005. WMTE 2005. IEEE International Workshop on* (pp. 3-pp). IEEE.

Tan, Q. (2014). Location-Based Learning Management System for Adaptive Mobile Learning.

Van Eck, R. (2007). Building artificially intelligent learning games. *Games and simulations in online learning: Research and development frameworks*, 271-307.

Velte, T., Velte, A., & Elsenpeter, R. (2009). *Cloud computing, a practical approach*. McGraw-Hill, Inc.

Vouk, M. (2008). Cloud computing–issues, research and implementations. *CIT. Journal of Computing and Information Technology*, *16*(4), 235–246.

Wagner, E. D. (2005). Enabling mobile learning. *EDUCAUSE Review*, *40*(3), 41–42.

Welsh, E. T., Wanberg, C. R., Brown, K. G., & Simmering, M. J. (2003). E-learning: Emerging uses, empirical results and future directions. *International Journal of Training and Development*, *7*(4), 245–258. doi:10.1046/j.1360-3736.2003.00184.x

Woolf, B. P. (2010). *Building intelligent interactive tutors: Student-centered strategies for revolutionizing e-learning*. Morgan Kaufmann.

KEY TERMS AND DEFINITIONS

E-Learning: Learning activities, which are supported and performed via electronic media – sources, by enabling individuals to experience educational processes on anytime and anywhere.

M-Learning: E-learning, which is performed through mobile technologies.

Semantic: A term, which is used for defining the things focusing and working on meanings of words and sentences.

Symbiotic: A term, which is used to express two objects – organisms, which are too close and have a long term interaction – relations (mutual benefit).

Web: (1) Application side – platform of the Internet. (2) Abstract, logical view of the Internet communication all over the world.

Web-Based E-Learning: E-learning, which is performed over the Web platform, via a typical Web-browser, and Web applications that are viewed on it.

Web 3.0: The third generation of the Web. Web 3.0 includes more intelligent web services and applications that understand users' needs and work according to them. Some features of Web 3.0 are expressed as prospective future possibilities.

Web 4.0: The fourth generation of the Web. Web 4.0 allows users to control the physical world by using more advanced Web technologies. Almost all features and functions of Web 4.0 are expressed as prospective future possibilities.

Compilation of References

Aamodt, A., & Plaza, E. (1994). Case-based reasoning: Foundational issues, methodological variations, and system approaches. *AI Communications, 7*(1), 39–59.

Abdullah, S., & Cooley, R. (2002). Using simulated students to evaluate an adaptive testing system. In *Proceedings of Computers in Education,* (pp. 614–618). IEEE.

ACM CR. (2007). *ACM Curricula Recommendations.* Retrieved from http://www.acm.org/education/curricula-recommendations

AERA. (1999). *Standards for educational and psychological testing.* Amer Educational Research Assn.

Aggarwal, C., Hinneburg, A., & Kleim, D. (2001). On the surprising behavior of distance metrics in high dimensional space. In *Proceedings of the 8th International Conference on Database Theory (ICDT 2001),* (LNCS) (vol. 1973, pp. 420-434). Berlin: Springer-Verlag.

Aggarwal, C., & Zhai, C. (2012). *A Survey of Text Clustering Algorithms.* Boston: Kluwer Academic Publishers.

Agrawal, R., Gehrke, J., Gunopulos, D., & Raghavan, P. (1998). Automatic subspace clustering of high dimensional data for data mining applications. In *Proceedings of the 1998 ACM SIGMOD International Conference on Management of Data (SIGMOD'98),* (pp. 94-105). New York, NY: ACM Press.

Aguilar, R., Mu~noz, V., González, E.J., Noda, M., Bruno, A., & Moreno, L. (2011). *Fuzzy and Multiagent Instructional Planner for an Intelligent Tutorial System.* Paper presented at Appl. Soft Comput. New York, NY.

Akkoyunlu, B. (1995). Bilgisayarların Eğitimde Kullanılması ve Bilgisayar Okuryazarlığı. *Eğitim ve Bilim, 19*(96), 23-30, 33-35.

Alavi, M., & Leidner, D. E. (2001). Review: knowledge management and knowledge management systems. *Management Information Systems Quarterly, 25*(1), 107–136. doi:10.2307/3250961

Al-Dujaily, A., & Ryu, H. (2006). A relationship between e-learning performance and personality. In *Proceedings of Advanced Learning Technologies,* (pp. 84–86). IEEE.

Alexander, S. (2001). E-learning developments and experiences. *Education + Training, 43*(4-5), 240-248.

Alfonseca, E., Carro, R., Martín, E., Ortigosa, A., & Paredes, P. (2006). The impact of learning styles on student grouping for collaborative learning: A case study. *User Modeling and User-Adapted Interaction, 16*(3), 377–401. doi:10.1007/s11257-006-9012-7

Alkan, C. (1995). *Eğitim Teknolojisi.* Ankara: Atilla Publishing. (In Turkish)

Alkan, C., Deryakulu, D., & Şimşek, N. (1995). *Eğitim Teknolojisine Giriş: Disiplin, Süreç, Ürün.* Ankara: Onder Publishing. (In Turkish)

Ally, M. (Ed.). (2009). *Mobile learning: Transforming the delivery of education and training.* Athabasca University Press.

Almaris. (2007). *Financial Accounting Tutor 9.0, Almaris.* Retrieved from http://www.almaris.com/fact/fact-overview.htm

Altın, B. (2006). *İlköğretim 2. Sınıf Öğrencilerinin Matematik Dersindeki Öğrenme Yaşantılarının Bilgisayarda Hazırlanan Zeki Öğretim Sistemlerine Göre İncelenmesi.* (Unpublished master dissertation). Dokuz Eylül University, İzmir, Turkey.

Amandi, A., Campo, M., Armentano, M., & Berdún, L. (2003). Intelligent Agents for Distance Learning. *Journal of Informatics in Education, 2*(2), 161–180.

Anastasi, A. (1997). Psychological Testing. Upper Saddle River, NJ: Prentice Hall

Andreopoulos, B., An, A., Wang, X., & Schroeder, M. (2009). *A roadmap of clustering algorithms: finding a match for a biomedical application.* Academic Press.

Anohina, A. (2007). *Advances in Intelligent Tutoring Systems: Problem-solving Modes and Model of Hints.* Retrieved from http://www.riverland.edu/academics/AcademicPrograms.cfm

Aparicio, F., De Buenaga, M., Rubio, M., & Hernando, A. (2012). An intelligent information access system assisting a case based learning methodology evaluated in higher education with medical students. *Computers & Education, 58*, 1282–1295. doi:10.1016/j.compedu.2011.12.021

Apostol, C. (2000). *Instruirea asistată de calculator a managerilor în domeniul tehnologiei informaţiei.* Raport de cercetare la Contractul nr. 1253, 198/1996, Editura ASE, Bucureşti. Retrieved from http://www.biblioteca.ase.ro/catalog/rezultate.php?c=2&q=&st=s&tp1=1&tp2=1&tp3=1&tp4=1&tp5=1&tp6=1

Arafa, Y., Charlton, P., & Mamdani, A. (1997). *Modelling Personal Service Assistants with Personality: From Metaphor to Implementation.* Imperial College of Science, Technology & Medicine. Retrieved from http://citeseer.nj.nec.com/cs

Arici, N. (2001). *Tarımsal İstatistik Analizlerinde Uzman Sistemlerin Kullanımı* [Usage of Expert Systems in Agricultural Statistical Analyzes]. (PhD Thesis). Ankara University, Institute of Natural Sciences, Ankara, Turkey.

Awad, W. (1996). *Building Expert Systems: Principles, Procedures, and Applications.* St. Paul, MN: West.

Ayoola, O. L., & Phelan, E. M. (2010). Crafting a Personalised Agent-Oriented Mobile E-Learning Platform for Adaptive Third Level Education. In M. Beer, M. Fasli, & D. Richards (Eds.), *Multi-Agent Systems for Education and Interactive Entertainment: Design, Use and Experience. Hershey, PA: IGI Global.* doi:10.4018/978-1-60960-080-8.ch012

Babalik, A. (2000). *Uzman Sistemlerin Teşhis Amaçlı Kullanımı* [Usage of Expert Systems for Diagnosis]. (Master's Thesis). Gazi University, Institute of Natural Sciences, Ankara, Turkey.

Bach, J. (2002). Enhancing Perception and Planning of Software Agents with Emotion and Acquired Hierarchical Categories. In *Proceedings of MASHO 02, German Conference on AI.* Karlsruhe, Germany: Academic Press.

Badaracco, M., & Martinez, L. (2013). A fuzzy linguistic algorithm for adaptive test in Intelligent Tutoring System based on competences. *Expert Systems with Applications, 40*, 3073–3086. doi:10.1016/j.eswa.2012.12.023

Badjonski, M., Ivanovic, M., & Budimac, Z. (1997). Intelligent tutoring system as multi-agent system. In *Proceedings of IEEE international conference on intelligent processing systems (ICIPS '97),* (vol. 1, pp. 871-875). IEEE.

Bahçeci, F. & Gürol, M. (2010). A Model Proposal On Applications Of Intelligent Tutoring Systems In The Edecation. *e-Journal of New World Sciences Academy, 5*(2).

Bajraktarevic, N., Hall, W., & Fullick, P. (2003). Incorporating learning styles in hypermedia environment: Empirical evaluation. In *Proceedings of the workshop on adaptive hypermedia and adaptive web-based systems,* (pp. 41–52). Academic Press.

Banfield, J., & Raftery, A. (1993). Model-based Gaussian and non-Gaussian clustering. *Biometrics, 49*(3), 803–821. doi:10.2307/2532201

Barry, J. (2007). *Advantages and Disadvantages of Online Courses.* Education Training Info. Retrieved from http://www.educationtraininginfo.com/articles/e001-advantages-and-disadvantages-of-online-courses.htm

Bartneck, C. (2003). *Integrating the OCC Model of Emotions in Embodied Characters.* University of Endhoven. Retrieved from http://citeseer.nj.nec.com/cs

Bartol, K. M., & Srivastava, A. (2002). Encouraging knowledge sharing: the role of organizational reward systems. *Journal of Leadership & Organizational Studies, 9*(1), 64–76. doi:10.1177/107179190200900105

Bates, J., Loyall, A. B., & Reilly, W. S. (1992). An Architecture for Action, Emotion, and Social Behavior. In *Proceedings of the Fourth Eurepean Workshop on Modeling Autonomous Agents in Multi-Agent World*. Academic Press.

Bates, J. (1994). *The Role of Emotion in Believable Agents. Communications of the ACM*.

Baykal, N., & Beyan, T. (2004). *Bulanık Mantık Uzman Sistemler ve Denetleyiciler*. Ankara: Bıçaklar Kitabevi.

Beck, J. E. (2007). Does Learner Control Affect Learning?. In *Proceedings of the 13th International Conference on Artificial Intelligence in Education* (pp. 135-142). Los Angeles, CA: IOS Press.

Bector, C., & Chandra, S. (2004). Fuzzy Mathematical Programming and Fuzzy Matrix Games. Springer.

Beldarrin, Y. (2006). Distance education trends: Integrating new technologies to foster student interaction and collaboration. *Distance Education*, 139–153. doi:10.1080/01587910600789498

Bell, B., & Federman, J. E. (2013). *E-Learning Works--Exactly How Well Depends on Its Unique Features and Barriers: CAHRS ResearchLink No. 1*. Center for Advanced Human Resource Studies, Cornell University.

Bell, J. T., & Fogler, H. S. (2004). *The application of virtual reality to (chemical engineering) education*. IEEE. doi:10.1109/VR.2004.1310077

Berkan, R. C. S. L. (2000). Fuzzy Systems Design Principles. New Delhi: Standard Publishers Distributors.

Berkeley, I. S. N. (1997). *What is artificial intelligence?*. Retrieved from http://www.ucs.louisiana.edu/~isb9112/dept/phil341/wisai/WhatisAI.html

Berkhin, P. (2006). Survey of clustering data mining techniques. In J. Kogan, C. Nicholas, & M. Teboulleeds (Eds.), *Grouping Multidimensional Data: Recent Advances in Clustering* (pp. 25–71). Springer. doi:10.1007/3-540-28349-8_2

Berners-Lee, T., Hendler, J., & Lassila, O. (2001). The semantic web. *Scientific American*. Retrieved from http://www.scientificamerican.com/article.cfm?id=the-semantic-web

Beyadar, H., & Gardali, K. (2011, October). *Knowledge management in organizations*. Paper presented at the 5th international conference on application of information and communication technologies. Baku, Azerbaijan. Retrieved from www.aict.info/2011/

Bezdek, J. (1981). *Pattern Recognition with Fuzzy Objective Function Algorithms*. Norwell, MA: Kluwer Academic Publishers. doi:10.1007/978-1-4757-0450-1

Bhatt, M. I. (2010). Harnessing technology for providing knowledge for development: New role for libraries. In T. Ashraf (Ed.), Developing sustainable digital libraries: Socio-technical perspectives. New York: IGI-Global (Information Science References).

Biondo, S. J. (1990). *Fundamentals of Expert Systems Technology: Principles and Concept*. Intellect Books.

Black, P., D. W. (1998). Assessment and classroom learning. *Assessment in Education*, 7–74. doi:10.1080/0969595980050102

Blaine, L., & Smith, R. L. (1977). Intelligent CAI: The Role of the Curriculum in Suggesting Computational Models of Reasoning. In *Proceedings of the 1977 AC Annual Conference*, (pp. 241-246). Seattle, WA: AC.

Bloom, B., & Krathwohl, D. (1956). *Taxonomy of educational objectives: The classification of educational goals. In Handbook I: Cognitive domain*. Longmans.

Boisvert, L. (2000). Web-based learning. *Information Systems Management*, *17*(1), 35–41. doi:10.1201/1078/43190.17.1.20000101/31212.5

Bonnet, A. (1988). *Expert Systems: Principles and Practise*. New York: Prentice Hall.

Botelho, L. M., & Coelho, H. (n.d.). *Adaptive Agents: Emotion Learning*. University of Lisbon. Retrieved from http://citeseer.nj.nec.com/cs

Botsios, S., Georgiou, D., & Safouris, N. (2008). Contributions to adaptive educational hypermedia systems via on-line learning style estimation. *Journal of Educational Technology & Society*, *12*(4), 322–339.

Bou-Llusar, J. C., & Segarra-Cipres, M. (2006). Strategic knowledge transfer and its implications for competitive advantage: an integrative conceptual framework. *Journal of Knowledge Management, 10*(4), 100–112. doi:10.1108/13673270610679390

Bourne, J. R., Brodersen, A. J., Ccampbell, J. O., Dawant, M. M., & Shiavi, R. G. (1996). A Model for On-Line Learning Networks in Engineering Education. *The Journal of Engineering Education, 85*(3), 253–262. doi:10.1002/j.2168-9830.1996.tb00241.x

Bransford, J., Brown, A., & Cocking, R. (2000). *How People Learn, Brain, Mind, and Experience & School.* Washington, DC: National Academy Press.

Braun, A., & Harrer, A. G. (2001). A Framework for Internet-Based Distributed Learning. Academic Press.

Bravo, J., & Ortigosa, A. (2006). Validating the evaluation of adaptive systems by user profile simulation. In *Proceedings of Workshop held at the Fourth International Conference on Adaptive Hypermedia and Adaptive Web-Based Systems (AH2006)*, (pp. 479–483). AH.

Broadbent, M. (1998). The phenomenon of knowledge management: what does it mean to the information profession? *Information Outlook, 2*(5), 23–34.

Brown, G. (1997). *Assessing student learning in higher education.* London: Routledge.

Brown, J. S., Burton, R. R., & Bell, A. G. (1975). SOPHIE: A step toward creating a reactive Learning environment. *International Journal of Man-Machine Studies, 7,* 675–696. doi:10.1016/S0020-7373(75)80026-5

Brusilovski, P. (1999). Adaptive and Intelligent Technologies for Web-based Education. In C. Rollinger & C. Peylo (Eds.), Kustliche Intelligenz, Special Issue on Intelligent Systems and Teleteaching, (vol. 4, pp. 19–25). Academic Press.

Brusilovsky, P. (2001). Adaptive educational hypermedia. In *Proceedings of International PEG Conference*, (pp. 8–12). Citeseer.

Brusilovsky, P., Schwarz, E., & Weber, G. (1996). ELM-ART: An Intelligent Tutoring System on World Wide Web. In *Proc. of 3rd International Conference on Intelligent Tutoring Systems, ITS-96.* Springer Verlag.

Burger, C., & Rotherme, K. (2001). *A Framework to Support Teaching in Distributed Systems.* University of Stuttgart.

Burns, H. L., & Capps, C. G. (1988). Foundations of intelligent tutoring systems: an introduction. In M. C. Polson, & J. J. Richardson (Eds.), *Foundations of Intelligent Tutoring Systems.* Hillsdale, NJ: Lawrence Frlbaum.

Burton, R., & Brown, J. S. (1976). A tutoring and student modelling paragigm for gaming environments. *Computer Science Education, 8*(19), 236–246.

Busch, P. (2008). *Tacit knowledge in organizational learning.* Hershey, PA: IGI Publishing. doi:10.4018/978-1-59904-501-6

Cabada, R., Estrada, M., & Garcia, C. (2009). A Fuzzy-Neural Network for Classifying Learning Styles in a Web 2.0 and Mobile Learning Environment. In *Proceedings of Web Congress,* (pp. 177–182). IEEE.

Capece, G., & Campisi, D. (2013). User satisfaction affecting the acceptance of an e-learning platform as a mean for the development of the human capital. *Behaviour & Information Technology, 32*(4), 335–343. doi:10.1080/0144929X.2011.630417

Carmona, C., & Castillo, G. (2008). Designing a Dynamic Bayesian Network for Modeling Students Learning Styles. In *Proceedings of Eighth IEEE International Conference on Advanced Learning Technologies,* (pp. 346–350). IEEE.

Carmona, C., Castillo, G., & Millán, E. (2007). Discovering Student Preferences in E-Learning. In *Proceedings of the International Workshop on Applying Data Mining in e-Learning.* Academic Press.

Carnobell, J. R. (1970). AI in CAI: An Artificial Intelligence approach to Computer assisted Instruction. *IEEE Transactions on Man-Machine Systems, MMS11*(4).

Cârstea, M. (n.d.). *Instruirea Asistată de Calculator în Şcoala Românească.* Revista PC Report.

Castillo, G., Gama, J., & Breda, A. (2005). An Adaptive Predictive Model for Student Modeling. In Advances in Web-based education: Personalized learning environments, (pp. 70–92). Academic Press.

Castro, F., Vellido, A., Nebot, A., & Mugica, F. (2007). Applying Data Mining Techniques to e-Learning. *Studies in Computational Intelligence*, 183-221.

Cavus, N. (2010) Investigating mobile devices and LMS integration in higher education: Student perspectives. In *Proceedings of World Conference on Information Technology*, (pp. 1469-1474). Academic Press.

Cavus, N., & Al-Momani, M. M. (2010). Mobile system for flexible education. In Proceedings of World Conference on Information Technology. Academic Press.

Cavus, N. (2010). The evaluation of Learning Management Systems using an artificial intelligence fuzzy logic algorithm. *Advances in Engineering Software*, *41*(2), 248–254. doi:10.1016/j.advengsoft.2009.07.009

Çetin, A., Işık, A. H., & Güler, İ. (2010). Learning Management System Selection with Analytic Hierarchy Process. In *Proceedings of 13th International Conference on Interactive Computer Aided Learning*, (pp. 921-926). Academic Press.

Cetin, A. (2010). 3D Web Based Learning of Medical Equipments Employed in Intensive Care Units. *Journal of Medical Systems*, *36*(1), 167–174. doi:10.1007/s10916-010-9456-5 PMID:20703738

Chang, W., & Chung, M. (2010). Automatic applying Bloom's taxonomy to classify and analysis the cognition level of English question items. In *Proceedings of Pervasive Computing (JCPC)*, (pp. 727–734). IEEE.

Chappell, A. R., & Mitchell, C. M. (1997). The Case Based Intelligent Tutoring System: An Architecture for Developing and Maintaining Operator Expertise. In *Proceedings of the 1997 IEEE International Conference on Systems, Man, and Cybernetics*. Orlando, FL: IEEE.

Chatpakkarattana, T., & Khlaisang, J. (2012). The Learner Support System for Distance Education. *Creative Education*, *3*(Supplement), 47–51. doi:10.4236/ce.2012.38B011

Chen, H. (1999). *High-performance digital library classification systems: from information retrieval to knowledge management*. Retrieved October 13, 2010, from http://citeseer.ist.psu.edu/cache/papers/cs/18268/http:zSzzSzwww.dli2.nsf.govzSzprojectszSzchen.pdf/high-performance-digitallibrary.Pdf

Chen, J., Lu, H., Mo, W., & Wang, Z. (2010). The research and design of intelligence wireless Mobile Learning platform based on 3G. In *Proceedings of International Conference on e-Business and Information System Security (EBISS)*, (pp. 1 – 4). EBISS.

Chen, G., & Ueta, T. (1999). Yet another chaotic attractor. *International Journal of Bifurcation and Chaos in Applied Sciences and Engineering*, *9*, 1465–1466. doi:10.1142/S0218127499001024

Cheng, S.-Y., Lin, C.-S., Chen, H.-H., & Heh, J.-S. (2005). Learning and diagnosis of individual and class conceptual perspectives: an intelligent systems approach using clustering techniques. *Computers & Education*, 257–283. doi:10.1016/j.compedu.2004.02.005

Cheng, V., Li, C., Kwok, J., & Li, C.-K. (2004). Dissimilarity learning for nominal data. *Pattern Recognition*, *37*(7), 1471–1477. doi:10.1016/j.patcog.2003.12.015

Chen, H., Chen, L., Chen, J., & Xu, J. (2014). Research on Mobile Learning Games in Engineering Graphics Education. In *Frontier and Future Development of Information Technology in Medicine and Education* (pp. 2981–2986). Springer Netherlands. doi:10.1007/978-94-007-7618-0_379

Chen, J. N., Huang, Y. M., & Chu, W. C. (2005). Applying dynamic fuzzy petri net to web learning system. *Interactive Learning Environments*, 13.

Chen, Y., & Weng, C. (2009). Mining fuzzy association rules from questionnaire data. *Knowledge-Based Systems Journal*, *22*, 46–56. doi:10.1016/j.knosys.2008.06.003

Cheung, B., Hui, L., Zhang, J., & Yiu, S. (2003). Smart Tutor: an intelligent tutoring system in web-based adult education. *Journal of Systems and Software*, *68*, 11–68. doi:10.1016/S0164-1212(02)00133-4

Chia-I Chang, F. (2002). Intelligent assessment of distance learning. *International Journal of information Sciences— Informatics and Computer Science*, *140*(1), 105 – 125.

Chipperfield, A., Fleming, P., Pohlheim, H., & Fonseca, C. (1994). *Genetic algorithm toolbox for use with matlab*. Citeseer.

Chisanu, J., Sumalee, C., Issara, K., & Charuni, S. (2012). Design and develop of constructivist learning environment on learning management system. In Proceedings of WCES 2012, (pp. 3426 – 3430). WCES.

Chiu, H., Sheng, C., & Chen, A. (2007). Designing a Dynamic E-learning Project Performance Evaluation Framework. In *Proceedings of Advanced Learning Technologies,* (pp. 381–385). IEEE.

Coffield, F., Moseley, D., Hall, E., & Ecclestone, K. (2009). *Learning styles and pedagogy in post-16 learning: A systematic and critical review.* NCVER.

Conejo, R., Guzmán, E., Millán, E., Trella, M., De-La-Cruz, J., & Ríos, A. (2004). SIETTE: A Web–Based Tool for Adaptive Testing. *International Journal of Artificial Intelligence in Education, 14,* 1–33.

Conole, G., & Dyke, M. (2004). What are the affordances of information and communication technologies? *Association for Learning Technology Journal, 12*(2), 113–124. doi:10.1080/0968776042000216183

Corbett, A. T., Anderson, J. R., & O'Brien, A. T. (1995). In P. Nichols, S. Chipman, & B. Brennan (Eds.), *Student modeling in the ACT programming tutor* (pp. 19–41). Erlbaum.

Corbett, K. (2005). *Anderson.* Intelligent Tutoring System.

Cortes, C., & Vapnik, V. (1995). Support-vector network. *Machine Learning, 20,* 1–25. doi:10.1007/BF00994018

Crisp, V., & Ward, C. (2008). The development of a formative scenario-based computer assisted assessment tool in psychology for teachers. *Computers & Education, 50,* 1509–1526. doi:10.1016/j.compedu.2007.02.004

Cristea, A., & Okamoto, T. (2002). Student model-based, agent-managed, adaptive Distance Learning Environment for Academic English Teaching. In Proceedings of IWALT 2000, (pp. 159-162). IWALT.

Cuéllar, M. P., Delgado, M., & Pegalajar, M. C. (2011). Improving learning management through semantic web and social networks in e-learning environments. *Expert Systems with Applications, 38*(4), 4181–4189. doi:10.1016/j.eswa.2010.09.080

Dadone, P. (2011). *Design Optimization of Fuzzy Logic Systems.* (Doctoral Dissertation Thesis). Virginia Polytechnic Institute and State University, Electrical Engineering.

Das, A. K., Sen, B. K., & Dutta, C. (2010). Collaborative digital library development in India: A network analysis. In T. Ashraf (Ed.), Developing sustainable digital libraries: Socio-technical perspectives. New York: IGI-Global (Information Science References).

Dasgupta, A., & Raftery, A. (1998). Detecting features in spatial point processes with clutter via model-based clustering. *Journal of the American Statistical Association, 93*(441), 294–302. doi:10.1080/01621459.1998.10474110

Davenport, T. H., & Prusak, L. (1998). *Working knowledge: how organizations manage what they know.* Boston, MA: Harvard Business School Press.

Del Bimbo, A., Gradmann, S., & Ioannidis, Y. (Eds.). (2004, July). *Future research directions.* Retrieved from www.delos.info/files/pdf/events/2004_Jul_8_10/D8.pdf

Demirer, V., & Sahin, I. (2013). Effect of blended learning environment on transfer of learning: An experimental study. *Journal of Computer Assisted Learning, 29*(6), 518–529. doi:10.1111/jcal.12009

Deperlioglu, O., & Kose, U. (2010). An Educational Virtual Laboratory System for Fuzzy Logic. In *Proceedings of 1st International Symposium on Computing in Science* (pp. 1335-1342). Kuşadası, Türkiye: Academic Press.

Deperlioglu, O., & Arslan, Y. (2010). Design principles of web-based distance education system and sample application in Afyon Kocatepe University. *IET Software, 50,* 283–293. doi:10.1049/iet-sen.2009.0061

Depradine, C. (2003). Expert system for extracting syntactic information from Java code. *Expert Systems with Applications, 25,* 187–198. doi:10.1016/S0957-4174(03)00046-0

Dhillon, I., Guan, Y., & Kulis, B. (2004). Kernel k-means: spectral clustering and normalized cuts. *In Proceedings of the Tenth ACM SIGKDD International Conference on Knowledge Discovery and Data Mining,* (pp. 551-556). New York, NY: ACM.

Dhillon, I., Guan, Y., & Kulis, B. (2007). Weighted graph cuts without eigenvectors a multilevel approach. *IEEE Transactions on Pattern Analysis and Machine Intelligence*, *29*(11), 1944–1957. doi:10.1109/TPAMI.2007.1115 PMID:17848776

Doğan, B., & Çamurcu, A. (2008). Association Rule Mining from an Intelligent Tutor. *Journal of Educational Technology Systems*, *36*, 433–447. doi:10.2190/ET.36.4.f

Dorça, F. A., Lopes, C. R., Fernandes, M. A., and Lopes, R. S. (2009). Adaptativity Supported by Neural Networks in Web-based Educational Systems. *Journal of Education, Informatics and Cybernetics, 1*.

Dorça, F., Lopes, C., & Fernandes, M. (2003). A multiagent architecture for distance education systems. In *Proceedings of Advanced Learning Technologies*, (pp. 368–369). IEEE.

Dorça, F. A., Lima, L. V., Fernandes, M. A., & Lopes, C. R. (2013). Comparing strategies for modeling students learning styles through reinforcement learning in adaptive and intelligent educational systems: An experimental analysis. *Expert Systems with Applications*. doi:doi:10.1016/j.eswa.2012.10.014

Drucker, P. (1999). *Management Challenges for the 21st Century*. New York, NY: Harper Business.

Duda, R., Hart, P., & Stork, D. (2000). *Pattern Classification* (2nd ed.). New York: Wiley Interscience Publication.

Dunning, D., Johnson, K., Ehrlinger, J., & Kruger, J. (2003). Why people fail to recognize their own incompetence. *Current Directions in Psychological Science*, *12*, 83–87. doi:10.1111/1467-8721.01235

Eiben, A., & Smith, J. (2003). *Introduction to evolutionary computing*. Springer Verlag. doi:10.1007/978-3-662-05094-1

Elango, R., Gudep, V., & Selvam, M. (2008). Quality of e-learning: an analysis based on e-learners perception of e-learning. *Electronic Journal of e-Learning, 6*, 1-44.

El-Khoury, S., Richard, P. R., Aimeur, E., & Fortuny, J. M. (2005). Development of an Intelligent Tutorial System to Enhance Students' Mathematical Competence in Problem Solving. In G. Richards (Ed.), *Proceedings of World Conference on E-Learning in Corporate, Government, Healthcare, and Higher Education 2005* (pp. 2042-2049). Chesapeake, VA: AACE.

Elmas, Ç. (2003). *Artificial neural network – theory, architecture, training, implementation <> Yapay sinir ağları – teori, mimari, eğitim, uygulama*. Ankara, Turkey: Seçkin Press. (In Turkish)

Erkoç, M. F. (2008). Yapay Zeka Perspektifinde Eğitime Yönelik Uzman Sistem Modellemesi [Expert System Modeling For Education By The Artifical Intelligence Perspective]. (Unpublished master's thesis). Marmara University, İstanbul, Turkey.

Ester, M., Kriegel, H., Sander, J., & Xu, X. (1996). A density-based algorithm for discovering clusters in large spatial databases with noise. In *Proceedings of the Second International Conference on Knowledge Discovery and Data Mining*, (pp. 226-231). Academic Press.

Estivill-Castro, V. (2002). Why so many clustering algorithms? A position paper. *SIGKKD Explorations*, *4*(1), 65–75. doi:10.1145/568574.568575

Fabiano, A. D., Carlos, R. L., & Marcia, A. F. (2003). A Multi agent architecture for Distance Education Systems. In *Proceedings of the 3rd IEEE International Conference on Advanced Learning Technologies*. IEEE.

Farooq, T., Guergachi, A., & Krishnan, S. (2007). Chaotic time series prediction using knowledge based Green's kernel and least-squares support vector machines. In *Proceedings of the IEEE International Conference on Systems, Man and Cybernetics* (pp. 2669–2674). IEEE.

Felder, R., & Silverman, L. (1988). Learning and teaching styles in engineering education. *Journal of Engineering education, 78*(7), 674–681.

Ferrera, J. M., Prater, M. A., & Baer, R. (1987). Using an expert system for complex conceptual training. *Educational Technology*, *27*(5), 43–49.

Finn, A., & Bucceri, M. (2004). *A case study approach to blended learning*. Los Angeles, CA: Centra Software.

Flat World Business. (2011). *Web 1.0 vs Web 2.0 vs Web 3.0 vs Web 4.0 – A bird's eye on the evolution and definition*. Retrieved from http://flatworldbusiness.wordpress.com/flat-education/previously/web-1-0-vs-web-2-0-vs-web-3-0-a-bird-eye-on-the-definition/

Fox, E. A., & Urs, S. R. (2002). Digital libraries. *Annual Review of Information Science & Technology*, *36*, 503–589.

Fraley, C., & Raftery, A. (1998). How many clusters? Which clustering method? Answers via model-based cluster analysis. *The Computer Journal, 41*(8), 578–588. doi:10.1093/comjnl/41.8.578

Fraley, C., & Raftery, A. (2000). Model-based clustering, discriminant analysis, and density estimation. *Journal of the American Statistical Association, 97*(458), 611–631. doi:10.1198/016214502760047131

Franklin, S., & Graesser, A. (1998). It is an Agent, or just a Program? A Taxonomy for Autonomous Agents. In *Proceedings of Third International Workshop on Agent Theories, Architectures and Languages*. Springer-Verlag.

Franzoni, A. L., & Assar, S. (2009). Student learning styles adaptation method based on teaching strategies and electronic media. *Journal of Educational Technology & Society, 12*(4), 15–29.

Frenzel, J. F. (1987). *Understanding Expert Systems.* Howard W. Sams & Company.

Friedel, C., & Rudd, R. (2006). Creative thinking and learning styles in undergraduate agriculture students. *Journal of Agricultural Education, 47*(4), 102–111. doi:10.5032/jae.2006.04102

Fuhua, O. L. (2005). Designing Distributed Learning Environments with Intelligent Software Agents. *Journal of Educational Technology & Society, 8*(1), 132–133.

Gan, G., Ma, C., & Wu, J. (2007). *Data Clustering: Theory, Algorithms, and Applications.* SIAM.

Gan, M., Peng, H., Peng, X., Chen, X., & Inoussa, G. (2010). A locally linear RBF network-based state-dependent AR model for nonlinear time series modeling. *Information Sciences, 180,* 4370–4383. doi:10.1016/j.ins.2010.07.012

Garcia-Crespo, A. et al. (2011). Digital libraries and Web 3.0. The Callimachus DL approach. *Computers in Human Behavior, 27,* 1424–1430. doi:10.1016/j.chb.2010.07.046

García, P., Amandi, A., Schiaffino, S., & Campo, M. (2007). Evaluating Bayesian networks' precision for detecting students' learning styles. *Computers & Education, 49*(3), 794–808. doi:10.1016/j.compedu.2005.11.017

Gartner. (2002). *Knowledge management attracts Powerhouse vendors.* Retrieved November 8, 2009, from www.gartner.com

Geiss, C. (2009). *Stochastic Modeling.* Retrieved from users.jyu.fi/geiss/scripts/stochastic-models.pdf

Georgiev, T., Georgieva, E., & Smrikarov, A. (2004, June). M-learning-a New Stage of E-Learning. In *Proceedings of International Conference on Computer Systems and Technologies-CompSysTech.* Academic Press.

Ghosh, J. (2004). Scalable clustering methods for data mining. In N. Ye (Ed.), *Hand Book of Data Mining.* Lawrence Erlbaum Associates.

Ghosh, M., & Jambekar, A. (2003). Networks, digital libraries and knowledge management: trends & development. *DESIDOC Bulletin of Information Technology, 23*(5), 3–11.

Glogger, I., Holzäpfel, L., Kappich, J., Schwonke, R., & Nückles, M. (2013). *Development and Evaluation of a Computer-Based Learning Environment for Teachers: "Assessment of Learning Strategies in Learning Journals".* International Telecommunication Union (ITU).

Goguadze, G., Sosnovsky, S., Isotani, S., & McLaren, B. (2011). Evaluating a bayesian student model of decimal misconceptions. In *Proceedings of the 4th International Conference on Educational Data Mining.* Academic Press.

Goh, S. C. (2002). Managing effective knowledge transfer: an integrative framework and some practice implications. *Journal of Knowledge Management, 6*(1), 23–30. doi:10.1108/13673270210417664

Goldberg, D. (1989). *Genetic algorithms in search, optimization, and machine learning.* Addison-Wesley.

Graf, S., & Kinshuk, C. (2009). Advanced Adaptivity in Learning Management Systems by Considering Learning Styles. In *Proceedings of the 2009 IEEE/WIC/ACM International Joint Conference on Web Intelligence and Intelligent Agent Technology* (vol. 3, pp. 235–238). IEEE Computer Society.

Graf, S., & Kinshuk, C. (2010a). A Flexible Mechanism for Providing Adaptivity Based on Learning Styles in Learning Management Systems. In *Proceedings of 10th IEEE International Conference on Advanced Learning Technologies,* (pp. 30–34). IEEE.

Graf, S., & Kinshuk, K. (2007). Providing Adaptive Courses in Learning Management Systems with Respect to Learning Styles. In *Proceedings of World Conference on E-Learning in Corporate, Government, Healthcare, and Higher Education 2007*, (pp. 2576–2583). Academic Press.

Graf, S., & Kinshuk, K. (2010b). Using Cognitive Traits for Improving the Detection of Learning Styles. In *Proceedings of Database and Expert Systems Applications (DEXA)*, (pp. 74–78). IEEE.

Graf, S., & Lin, T. (2007). Analysing the Relationship between Learning Styles and Cognitive Traits. In *Proceedings of Advanced Learning Technologies*, (pp. 235–239). IEEE.

Graf, S., & List, B. (2005). An Evaluation of Open Source E-Learning Platforms Stressing Adaptation Issues. In *Proceedings of Fifth IEEE International Conference on Advanced Learning Technologies*, (pp. 163-165). IEEE.

Graf, S., & Liu, T. (2008). Identifying Learning Styles in Learning Management Systems by Using Indications from Students' Behaviour. In *Proceedings of Advanced Learning Technologies*, (pp. 482–486). IEEE.

Graf, S., Lan, C., Liu, T., et al. (2009). Investigations about the Effects and Effectiveness of Adaptivity for Students with Different Learning Styles. In *Proceedings of 2009 Ninth IEEE International Conference on Advanced Learning Technologies*, (pp. 415–419). IEEE.

Graf, S., Liu, T.-C., & Kinshuk, C. (2008). Interactions Between Students Learning Styles, Achievement and Behaviour in Mismatched Courses. In *Proceedings of the International Conference on Cognition and Exploratory Learning in Digital Age (CELDA 2008)*, (pp. 223–230). IADIS.

Greenberg, G. (1998). Distance education technologies: Best practices for K-12 settings. *IEEE Technology and Society Magazine*, *17*(4), 36–40. doi:10.1109/44.735862

Gromov, G. A., & Shulga, A. N. (2012). Chaotic time series prediction with employment of ant colony optimization. *Expert Systems with Applications*, *39*, 8474–8478. doi:10.1016/j.eswa.2012.01.171

Guha, S., Rastogi, R., & Shim, K. (1998). Cure: an efficient clustering algorithm for large databases. In *Proceedings of the 1998 ACM SIGMOD International Conference on Management of Data, SIGMOD '98*, (pp. 73-84). New York: ACM.

Günel, K. (2010). *Zeki Öğretim Sistemlerinde Öğrenci Değerlendirme Modelleri Üzerine*. (Unpublished master dissertation). Ege University, İzmir, Turkey.

Günel, K., & Aşlıyan, R. (2010). Extracting Learning Concepts from Educational Texts in Intelligent Tutoring Systems Automatically. *Expert Systems with Applications*, *37*(7), 5017–5022. doi:10.1016/j.eswa.2009.12.011

Hadjerrouit, S. (2008). Towards a blended learning model for teaching and learning computer programming: A case study. *Informatics in Education-An International Journal*, *7*(2), 181-210.

Haider, M., Sinha, A., & Chaudhary, B. (2010). An Investigation of relationship between learning styles and performance of learners. *International Journal of Engineering Science and Technology*, *2*(7), 2813–2819.

Halkidi, M., Batistakis, Y., & Vazirgiannis, M. (2001). On clustering validation techniques. *Journal of Intelligent Information Systems*, *17*(2/3), 107–145. doi:10.1023/A:1012801612483

Hämäläinen, W., & Vinni, M. (2010). Classifying educational data: special problems and guidelines. CRC Press.

Hand, D., Mannila, H., & Smyth, P. (2002). *Principles of Data Mining. Cambridge*, MA: MIT Press.

Han, J., & Kamber, M. (2006). *Data Mining: Concepts and Techniques* (2nd ed.). Elsevier/Morgan Kaufmann.

Harmon, P., & King, D. (1985). *Artificial Intelligence in Business: Expert Systems*. New York: Wiley.

Harter, S.P. (1997). Scholarly communication and the digital library: problems and issues. *Journal of Digital Information*, *1*(1). Retrieved April 12, 2009 from http://journals.tdl.org/jodi/article/view/jodi-3/4

Hartschuh, W. (1990). Expert Systems in Education. Educational Resources Information Center (ERIC), ED329224.

Hawkins, B. (2000). Libraries, knowledge management, and higher education in an electronic environment. *ALIA 2000 Proceedings*. Retrieved June 25, 2005, from www.alia.org.au/conferences/alia2000/proceedings/brian.Hawkins.html

Haynes, J. A., Pilato, V., & Malouf, D. B. (1987). Expert system for educational decision-making. *Educational Technology, 27*(5), 37–42.

Hedayati, M., Kamali, S. H., & Shakerian, R. (2012). Comparison and Evaluation of Intelligence Methods for Distance Education Platform. *International Journal of Modern Education and Computer Science, 4*(3), 21–27. doi:10.5815/ijmecs.2012.04.03

Herman, I. (2008). Semantic web activity statement. *W3C Semantic Web*. Retrieved from http://www.w3.org/2001/sw/Activity.html

Hicks, D., & Tochtermann, K. (2001). Personal digital libraries and knowledge management. *Journal of Universal Computer Science, 7*(7), 550–565.

Higgins, M., Grant, F., Thompson, P., & Montarzino, A. (2010). *Effective and efficient methods of formative assessment*. Cardiff, UK: Centre for Education in the Built Environment.

Hill, J. R., Wiley, D., Nelson, L. M., & Han, S. (2004). Exploring research on Internet-based learning: From infrastructure to interactions. In Handbook of research on educational communications and technology, (vol. 2, pp. 433-460). Academic Press.

Hinneburg, A., Hinneburg, E., & Keim, D. (1998). An efficient approach to clustering in large multimedia databases with noise. In *Proceedings of the 4th International Conference in Knowledge Discovery and Data Mining (KDD 98)*, (pp. 58-65). AAAI Press.

Holt, P., Dubs, S., Jones, M., & Greer, J. (1991). The state of Student Modeling. In *Student Modelling: The Key to Individualizes Knowledge-Based Instruction, NATO ASI Series,* (pp. 3–35). London, UK: Springer verlag.

Hong, W. C. (2010). Application of chaotic ant swarm optimization in electric load forecasting. *Energy Policy, 38*, 5830–5839. doi:10.1016/j.enpol.2010.05.033

Hopper, S. (1992). Cooperative learning and computer-based instruction. *Educational Technology Research and Development, 21*–38. doi:10.1007/BF02296840

Hu, Y. X., & Zhang, H. T. (2012). Prediction of the chaotic time series based on chaotic simulated annealing and support vector machine. In *Proceedings of the International Conference on Solid State Devices and Materials Science* (pp. 506–512). Macao, China: Academic Press.

Huang, Y., Chen, J., Huang, T., Jeng, Y., & Kuo, Y. (2008). Standardized course generation process using dynamic fuzzy petri nets. *Expert Systems with Applications, 34*, 72–86. doi:10.1016/j.eswa.2006.08.030

Huang, Z. (1998). Extensions to the k-means algorithm for clustering large data sets with categorical values. *Data Mining and Knowledge Discovery, 2*(3), 283–304. doi:10.1023/A:1009769707641

Huikkola, M., Silius, K., & Pohjolainen, S. (2008). Clustering and achievement of engineering students based on their attitudes, orientations, motivations and intentions. *WSEAS Transactions on Advances in Engineering Education, 5*(1), 342–354.

Hurwitz, J., Bloor, R., Kaufman, M., & Halper, F. (2009). *Cloud computing for dummies* (Vol. 1). John Wiley & Sons.

Hwang, G. J., Chen, C. Y., Tsai, P. S., & Tsai, C. C. (2011). An Expert System for Improving Web-Based Problem-Solving Ability of Students. *Expert Systems with Applications, 38*, 8664–8672. doi:10.1016/j.eswa.2011.01.072

Ichino, M., & Yaguchi, H. (1994). Generalized Minkowski metrics for mixed feature-type data analysis. *IEEE Transactions on Systems, Man, and Cybernetics, 24*(4), 698–708. doi:10.1109/21.286391

IEEE. (2010). *LOM (Learning Object Metadata)*. IEEE Learning Technology Standards Committee. Retrieved from http://ltsc.ieee.org/wg12/index.html

Jadhav, K. A. (2011). Digital library: Today's need- A review. *International Multidisciplinary Research Journal, 1*(11), 17–19.

Jain, A. (2010). Data clustering: 50 years beyond k-means. *Pattern Recognition Letters, 31*(8), 651–666. doi:10.1016/j.patrec.2009.09.011

Jain, A., & Dubes, R. (1988). *Algorithms for Clustering Data*. Englewood Cliffs, NJ: Prentice Hall.

Jain, A., Duin, P., & Mao, J. (2000). Statistical pattern recognition: A review. *IEEE Transactions on Pattern Analysis and Machine Intelligence*, 22(1), 4–37. doi:10.1109/34.824819

Jain, A., Murty, M., & Flynn, P. (1999). Data clustering: A review. *ACM Computing Surveys*, 31(3), 264–323. doi:10.1145/331499.331504

Jang, J. S. R., Sun, C. T., & Mizutani, E. (1997). *Neuro-fuzzy and Soft Computing, A Computational Approach to Learning and Machine Intelligence*. Upper Saddle River, NJ: Pearson Education.

Jaques, P., Andrade, A., Jung, J., Bordini, R., & Vicari, R. (2001). *Using Pedagogical Agents to Support Collaborative Distance Learning*. Retrieved from http://citeseer.nj.nec.com/cs

Jaques, P. A., Seffrin, H., Rubi, G., Morais, F., Ghilardi, C., Bittencourt, I. I., & Isotani, S. (2013). Rule-based expert systems to support step-by-step guidance in algebraic problem solving: The case of the tutor PAT2Math. *Expert Systems with Applications*, 40, 5456–5465. doi:10.1016/j.eswa.2013.04.004

Jondahl, S., & Mørch, A. (2000). *Simulating Pedagogical Agents in a Virtual Learning Environment*. University of Bergen, University of Oslo. Retrieved from http://citeseer.nj.nec.com/cs

Jones, G. (1998). Genetic and Evolutionary Algorithms. In Encyclopedia of Computational Chemistry, (pp. 1-10). Academic Press.

Jones, C., Reichard, C., & Mokhtari, K. (2003). Are Students Learning Styles Discipline Specific? *Community College Journal of Research and Practice*, 27(5), 363–375. doi:10.1080/713838162

Jones, T. M. (2008). *Artificial Intelligence: A Systems Approach*. Infinity Science Press LLC.

Jose, M. G., & Antonio, F.-C. (2005). *An Agent-based Intelligent Tutoring System for Enhancing E-Learning / E-Teaching*. Academic Press.

Jun, L., Renhou, L., & Qinhua, Z. (2004). Study on the Personality Mining Method for Learners in Network Learning. *Journal of Xian Jiaotong University*, 575-576.

Ju, Y. (2006). Leveraging levels of information services and developing knowledge services: The trend of information services in libraries. *Library Management*, 27(6/7). doi:10.1108/01435120610702341

Kalles, D., & Pierrakeas, C. (2006). *Using Genetic Algorithms and Decision Trees for a posteriori Analysis and Evaluation of Tutoring Practices based on Student Failure Models*. Springer.

Kamvar, S., Klein, D., & Manning, C. (2002). Interpreting and extending classical agglomerative clustering algorithms using a model-based approach. In *Proceedings of 19th International Conference on Machine Learning (ICML-2002)*, (pp. 283-290). ICML.

Kantardzic, M. (2011). *Data Mining: Concepts, Models, Methods, and Algorithms* (2nd ed.). John Wiley & Sons, IEEE Press. doi:10.1002/9781118029145

Kartalopoulos, S. (2000). *Understanding Neural Networks and Fuzzy Logic, Basic Concepts and Applications*. New Delhi: Prentice-Hall of India Pvt. Ltd.

Karypis, G., Han, E.-H., & Kumar, V. (1999). Chameleon: Hierarchical clustering using dynamic modeling. *Computer*, 32(8), 68–75. doi:10.1109/2.781637

Käser, T., Busetto, A., Solenthaler, B., Kohn, J., von Aster, M., & Gross, M. (2013). Cluster-based prediction of mathematical learning patterns. In *Proceedings of the 16th international conference on Articial Intelligence in Education*, (LNCS) (vol. 7926, pp. 389-399). Berlin: Springer.

Kaya, Z. (2002). *Distance Education*. Ankara: PegemA.

Ke, H., & Hwang, M. (2000). The development of digital libraries in Taiwan. *The Electronic Library*, 18(5), Retrieved May 20, 2012, from http://www.emeraldinsight.com/10.1108/02640470010354590

Kearsley, G. (1985). The CBT advisor: An expert system program for making decisions about CBT. *Performance and Education*, 24(9), 15–17.

Keegan, D. (2004). *Foundations of Distance Education*. New York: Routledge.

Keleş, A., Ocak, R., Keleş, A., & Gülcü, A. (2009). ZOSMAT: Web-based intelligent tutoring system for teaching–learning process. Expert Systems with Applications 36(2), 1229–1239.

Kelly, D., & Tangney, B. (2005). First Aid for You: Getting to know your learning style using machine learning. In *Proceedings of Advanced Learning Technologies*. IEEE.

Kennedy, J., & Eberhart, R. C. (1997). A discrete binary version of the particle swarm algorithm. In *Proceedings of the World Multi-Conference on Systems, Cybernetics and Informatics* (pp. 4104–4109). Piscataway, NJ: Academic Press.

Kerka, S., & Wonacott, M. (2000). *Assessing learners online, Practitioner file*. Retrieved from ERIC database, ED 448285.

Kesdee. (2007). *E-Learning Course - Financial Accounting*. KESDEE Inc. Retrieved from http://www.researchandmarkets.com/reports/310117

Keskin, N. Ö. (2010). Mobil Öğrenme Teknolojileri ve Araçları. *Akademik Bilişim, 10*, 490.

Khalifa, M., & Lam, R. (2002). Web-based learning: effects on learning process and outcome. *IEEE Transactions on Education, 45*(4), 350–356.

Khan, A. I., Shaik, M. S., Ali, A. M., & Bebi, C. V. (2012). Study of Blended Learning Process in Education Context. *International Journal of Modern Education and Computer Science, 4*(9), 23–29. doi:10.5815/ijmecs.2012.09.03

Khan, L., & Luo, F. (2005). Hierarchical clustering for complex data. *International Journal of Artificial Intelligence Tools, 14*(5), 791–809. doi:10.1142/S0218213005002399

Kimblea, C., & Bourdonb, I. (2008). Some success factors for the communal management of knowledge. *International Journal of Information Management, 28*(6), 461–467. doi:10.1016/j.ijinfomgt.2008.08.007

Kim, N., & Maeng, Y. (2008). Online Student Performance Assessment: The Essentials. *Distance Education Report, 12*, 4–8.

Kim, S., & Ju, B. (2008). An analysis of faculty perceptions: Attitudes toward knowledge sharing and collaboration in an academic institution. *Library & Information Science Research, 30*, 282–290. doi:10.1016/j.lisr.2008.04.003

Kim, Y., Smith, M., & Maeng, K. (2000). *Assessment in Online Distance Education: A Comparison of Three Online Programs at a University. Online Journal of Distance*.

Kinshuk, L., Liu, T.-C., & Graf, S. (2009). Coping with Mismatched Courses: Students' behaviour and performance in courses mismatched to their learning styles. *Educational Technology Research and Development, 57*(6), 739–752. doi:10.1007/s11423-009-9116-y

Klir, G., & Yuan, B. (2000). *Fuzzy sets and Fuzzy logic: Theory and Applications*. New Delhi: Prentice-Hall of India Pvt. Ltd.

Kocak, Y., Usluel, S., & Mazman, G. (2009). Adoption of Web 2.0 tools in distance education. *International Journal of Human Sciences, 6*.

Kohonen, T. (1982). Self-organized formation of topologically correct feature maps. *Biological Cybernetics, 43*(1), 59–69. doi:10.1007/BF00337288

Kolodner, J. L. (1993). *Case-Based Reasoning*. San Mateo, CA: Morgan Kaufmann.

Korucu, A. T., & Alkan, A. (2011). Differences between m-learning (mobile learning) and e-learning, basic terminology and usage of m-learning in education. In *Proceedings of World Conference on Educational Sciences*, (pp. 1925–1930). Academic Press.

Köse, U., & Deperlioğlu, Ö. (2010). An educational, virtual laboratory system for fuzzy logic. In *Proceedings of International Symposium on Computing in Science and Engineering 2010* (pp. 1335-1342). Aydın, Turkey: Gediz University.

Köse, U., & Deperlioğlu, O. (2012). Intelligent learning environments within blended learning for ensuring effective c programming course. *International Journal of Artificial Intelligence and Applications, 3*(1), 105–124. doi:10.5121/ijaia.2012.3109

Krishnamurthy, A., & O'Connor, R. V. (2013). An analysis of the software development processes of open source e-learning systems. *Systems, Software and Services Process Improvement – Communications in Computer and Information Science, 364*, 60-71.

Kukulska-Hulme, A., & Traxler, J. (Eds.). (2007). *Mobile learning: A handbook for educators and trainers*. Routledge.

Kumar, B. (2010). Digital library and repositories: An Indian initiative. In T. Ashraf (Ed.), Developing sustainable Digital Libraries: socio-technical perspectives. New York: IGI-Global (Information Science References).

Kutuva, S., Reddy, N., Xiao, Y., Gao, X., Hariharan, S., & Kulkarni, S. (2006). A novel and fast virtual surgical system using fuzzy logic. In *Proceedings of the IADIS Virtual Multi Conference on Computer Science and Information Systems*. IADIS.

LaBay, D. G., & Comm, C. L. (2003). A Case Study Using Gap Analysis to Assess Distance Learning Versus Traditional Course Delivery. *International Journal of Educational Management*, *17*(6/7), 312–317. doi:10.1108/09513540310501003

Lăcurezeanu, R. (2000). *Instruirea asistata de calculator în contabilitate si informatica*. (PhD thesis). Bucharest: ASE.

Latham, A., Crockett, K., McLean, D., & Edmonds, B. (2012). A conversational intelligent tutoring system to automatically predict learning styles. *Computers & Education*, *59*, 95–109. doi:10.1016/j.compedu.2011.11.001

Lee King, D. (2009). Building the Digital Branch: Guidelines for Transforming Your Library Website. *Library Technology Reports*, *45*(6), 5–9.

Lee, C. (1990). Fuzzy logic in control systems:Fuzzy logic controller-Part I/Part II. *IEEE Transactions on Systems, Man, and Cybernetics*, 404–435. doi:10.1109/21.52551

Lee, J. N. (2001). The impact of knowledge sharing, organizational capability and partnership quality on is outsourcing success. *Information Management Journal*, *38*(5), 323–335. doi:10.1016/S0378-7206(00)00074-4

Lee, K. C., & Kim, H. S. (1998). A Fuzzy Cognitive Map-based Bidirectional Inference Mechanism: An Application to Stock Investment Analysis. *Intelligent Systems in Accounting Finance & Management*, *6*(1), 41–57. doi:10.1002/(SICI)1099-1174(199703)6:1<41::AID-ISAF119>3.0.CO;2-J

Lewis Johnson, W. (n.d.). *Pedagogical Agents in Virtual Learning Environments*. Retrieved from http://www.isi.edu/isd/johnson.html

Lewis, M. W., Milson, R., & Anderson, J. (1987). The teacher's apprentice: Designing an Intelligent Authoring System for High School Mathematics. In *Artificial Intelligence & Instruction Applications and Methods* (pp. 269-301). Addison-Wesley Publishing Company.

Li, H. T., & Zhang, X. F. (2009). Precipitation time series predicting of the chaotic characters using support vector machines. In *Proceedings of the International Conference on Information Management, Innovation Management and Industrial Engineering* (pp. 407–410). Xian, China: Academic Press.

Liarokapis, F., Mourkoussis, N., White, M., Darcy, J., Sifniotis, M., & Petridis, P. et al. (2004). Web3D and augmented reality to support engineering education. *World Transactions on Engineering and Technology Education*, *3*(1), 11–14.

Lim, H., Lee, S.-G., & Nam, K. (2007). Validating e-learning factors affecting training effectiveness. *International Journal of Information Management*, *27*(1), 22–35. doi:10.1016/j.ijinfomgt.2006.08.002

Limongelli, C., Sciarrone, F., Temperini, M., & Vaste, G. (2009). Adaptive learning with the LS-plan system: a field evaluation. IEEE Transactions on Learning Technologies, 203-215.

Lin, C. B., Young, S. S. C., Chan, T. W., & Chen, Y. H. (2005). Teacher-Oriented Adaptive Web-Based Environment for Supporting Practical Teaching Models: A Case Study of "School for All". *Computers & Education*, *44*, 155–172. doi:10.1016/j.compedu.2003.11.003

Liu, P., & Yao, J. A. (2009). Application of least square support vector machine based on particle swarm optimization to chaotic time series prediction. In *Proceedings of the IEEE International Conference on Intelligent Computing and Intelligent Systems* (pp. 458–462). Shanghai, China: IEEE.

Lohani, M., & Jeevan, V. K. J. (2007). Intelligent software agents for library applications.[from www.emeraldinsight.com..]. *Library Management*, *28*(3), 139–151. Retrieved November 5, 2011 doi:10.1108/01435120710727983

Lo, J., Wang, H., & Yeh, S. (2004). Effects of confidence scores and remedial instruction on prepositions learning in adaptive hypermedia. *Computers & Education*, *20*, 45–63. doi:10.1016/S0360-1315(03)00064-2

Lopes, R. S., & Fernandes, M. A. (2009). Adaptative Instructional Planning UsingWorkflow and Genetic Algorithms. In *Proceedings of Computer and Information Science,* (pp. 87–92). IEEE.

Lopes, R. S., Dorça, F. A., Fernandes, M. A., & Lopes, C. R. (2008a). Um sistema de avaliação em ead baseado em lógica fuzzy. In *Proceedings of XIX Simpósio Brasileiro de Informática na Educação*. Fortaleza, Brazil: Academic Press.

Lopes, R. S., Dorça, F. A., Fernandes, M. A., & Lopes, C. R. (2008b). Um sistema de avaliação em EAD baseado em lógica Fuzzy. In *Simpósio Brasileiro de Informática na Educação* (pp. 30–34). SBC.

Lopez, M., Luna, J., Romero, C., & Ventura, S. (2012). Classification via clustering for predicting final marks based on student participation in forums. In *Proceedings of the 5th International Conference on the Educational Data Mining*, (pp. 148-151). Retrieved from http://www.educationaldatamining.org/

Lorenz, E. N. (1963). Deterministic non-periodic flows. *Journal of the Atmospheric Sciences*, *20*, 130–141. doi:10.1175/1520-0469(1963)020<0130:DNF>2.0.CO;2

Lotrecchiano, G. R., McDonald, P. L., Lyons, L., Long, T., & Zajicek-Farber, M. (2013). Blended Learning: Strengths, Challenges, and Lessons Learned in an Interprofessional Training Program. *Maternal and Child Health Journal*, 1–10. PMID:23291875

Luconi, F. L., Malone, T. W., & Scott Morton, M. S. (1986, Summer). Expert Systems: The Next Challenge for Managers. *Sloan Management Review*, 3–14.

Luxburg, U. (2007). A tutorial on spectral clustering. *Statistics and Computing*, *17*(4), 395–416. doi:10.1007/s11222-007-9033-z

Magoulas, G. D., Papanikolaou, K. A., & Grigoriadou, M. (2001). Neuro-fuzzy synergism for planning the content in a web-based course. *Informatica*, *25*, 39–48.

Mahonen, P., & Frantti, T. (2000). Fuzzy Classifier for Star-Galaxy Separation. *The Astrophysical Journal*, 261–263. doi:10.1086/309424

Majumdar, A., & Ghosh, A. (2008). Yarn strength modeling using fuzzy expert system. *Journal of Engineered Fibers and Fabrics*, *3*, 61–68.

Mantiuk, R., Aydin, T., & Myszkowski, K. (2008). Dynamic range independent image quality assessment. *ACM Transactions on Graphics*.

Mark, M. A., & Greer, J. E. (1993). Evaluation Methods for Intelligent Tutoring Systems. *Journal of Artificial Intelligence in Education*, *4*, 129–153.

Martin, A. et al. (2012). A framework for development of integrated intelligent knowledge for management of telecommunication networks. *Expert Systems with Applications*, *39*, 9264–9274. doi:10.1016/j.eswa.2012.02.078

Martins, L., & Kellermanns, F. (2004). A model of business school students' acceptance of a web-based course management system. *Academy of Management Learning & Education*, *3*, 7–26. doi:10.5465/AMLE.2004.12436815

Mavrikis, M. (2007). Towards Predictive Modeling of Student Affect from Web-Based Interactions. In R. Luckin, K. R. Koedinger, & J. Greer (Eds.), *Artificial Intelligence In Education* (pp. 169–176). Amsterdam: IOS Press.

McCalla, G.I. & Greer, J.E. (1991). Granularity-Based Reasoning and Belief Revision in Student Models. In *The Key to Individualised Knowledge-Based Instruction, NATO ASI Series*. NATO.

McCarthy, J. (2007). *What is artificial intelligence*. Retrieved from http://www-formal.stanford.edu/jmc/whatisai.html

McDuffie, R. S., & Smith, M. (2006). Impact of an Audit Reporting Expert System on Learning Performance: A Teaching Note. *Accounting Education (UK)*, *15*(1), 89–101. doi:10.1080/06939280600551585

McGill, T. J., & Klobas, J. E. (2009). A task–technology fit view of learning management system impact. *Computers & Education*, *52*(2), 496–508. doi:10.1016/j.compedu.2008.10.002

McInerney, C. (2002). Knowledge management and the dynamic nature of knowledge. *Journal of the American Society for Information Science and Technology*, *53*(12), 1009–1018. doi:10.1002/asi.10109

McQuiggan, S. W., & Lester, C. L. (2006). Diagnosing Self-efficacy in Intelligent Tutoring Systems: An Empirical Study. *Lecture Notes in Computer Science*, *4053*, 565-574.

Mehlenbacher, B., Miller, C. R., Covington, D., & Larsen, J. S. (2000). Active and Interactive Learning Online: A Comparison of Web-Based and Conventional Writing Classes. *IEEE Transactions on Professional Communication*, *43*(2), 166–184. doi:10.1109/47.843644

Mertz, J. (1997). Using a simulated student for instructional design. *International Journal of Artificial Intelligence in Education*, *8*, 116–141.

Messick, S. (1976). Personal styles and educational options. In Individuality in learning, (pp. 327–368). Academic Press.

Messick, S. (1995). Validity of psychological assessment: Validation of inferences from persons' responses and performances as scientific inquiry into score meaning. *The American Psychologist*, *50*, 741–749. doi:10.1037/0003-066X.50.9.741

Meyn, S., Tweedie, R., & Glynn, P. (1996). *Markov chains and stochastic stability*. Springer London.

Middleton, S., De Roure, D., & Shadbolt, N. (n.d.). *Capturing Knowledge of User Preferences: Ontologies in Recommender Systems*. University of Southampton, Marea Britanie. Retrieved from http://citeseer.nj.nec.com/cs

Miller, D., Linn, R., & Gronlund, N. (2009). *Measurement and Assessment in Teaching*. Pearson.

Miller, S. (2001). How Near and Yet How Far? Theorizing Distance Teaching. *Computers and Composition*, *18*, 321–328. doi:10.1016/S8755-4615(01)00065-2

Mirzaee, H. (2009). Linear combination rule in genetic algorithm for optimization of finite impulse response neural network to predict natural chaotic time series. *Chaos, Solitons, and Fractals*, *41*, 2681–2689. doi:10.1016/j.chaos.2008.09.057

Mitrovic, A., Ohlsson, S., & Barrow, D. K. (2013). The effect of positive feedback in a constraint-based intelligent tutoring system. *Computers & Education*, *60*, 264–272. doi:10.1016/j.compedu.2012.07.002

Moodle. (2010). Retrieved from http://www.moodle.org/

Moore, D. A., & Healy, P. J. (2008). The trouble with overconfidence. *Psychological Review*, *115*, 502–517. doi:10.1037/0033-295X.115.2.502 PMID:18426301

Moreno, K., Person, N., Adcock, A., & Van Eck, R. A. O. (2002). *Etiquette and Efficacy in Animated Pedagogical Agents: Rge Role of Stereotypes*. Retrieved from http://citeseer.nj.nec.com/cs

Mosakhani, M., & Jamporazmey, M. (2010). Introduce critical success factors (CSFs) of elearning for evaluating e-learning implementation success. In *Proceedings of Educational and Information Technology (ICEIT)*, (vol. 1). IEEE.

Motiwalla, L. F. (2007). Mobile learning: A framework and evaluation. *Computers & Education*, *49*(3), 581–596. doi:10.1016/j.compedu.2005.10.011

Muñoz-Merino, P. J., Molina, M. F., Muñoz-Organero, M., & Kloos, C. D. (2012). An adaptive and innovative question-driven competition-based intelligent tutoring system for learning. *Expert Systems with Applications*, *39*, 6932–6948. doi:10.1016/j.eswa.2012.01.020

Murray, T. (1998). Authoring Knowledge Based Tutors: Tools for Content, Instructional Strategy, Student Module and Interface Design. *Journal of the Learning Sciences*, *7*(1), 5–64. doi:10.1207/s15327809jls0701_2

Murtagh, F., & Raftery, A. (1984). Fitting straight lines to point patterns. *Pattern Recognition*, *17*(5), 479–483. doi:10.1016/0031-3203(84)90045-1

Mutlu Bayraktar, D. (2012). *Intelligent System Preparing Study Program For Students*. Paper presented at the 6th International Technology, Education and Development Conference. Valencia, Spain.

MYOB. (2007). *Mind Your Own Business*. Retrieved from http://www.myob.com

Nabiyev, V. V. (2005). *Yapay Zeka: Problemler-Yöntemler-Algoritma* [Artificial Intelligence: Problems-Methodologies-Algorithm]. Ankara: Seçkin Yayıncılık.

Nagy, A. (2005). The Impact of E-Learning. In E-Content: Technologies and Perspectives for the European Market. Berlin: Springer-Verlag.

Nemati-Anaraki, L., & Heidari, A. (2011, October). *Knowledge management process in digital age: proposing a model for implementing E-learning through digital libraries*. Paper presented at 5th international conference on application of information and communication technologies. Baku, Azerbaijan. Retrieved November 6, 2011, from www.aict.info/2011/

Nichol, J. (1985). Classroom-based curriculum development, artificial intelligence and history teaching. *Journal of Curriculum Studies*, *17*(2), 211–214. doi:10.1080/0022027850170210

Niu, D., Wang, Y., & Wu, D. D. (2010). Power load forecasting using support vector machine and ant colony optimization. *Expert Systems with Applications*, *37*, 2531–2539. doi:10.1016/j.eswa.2009.08.019

Nonaka, I. (1991). The knowledge creating company. *Harvard Business Review*, *69*(6), 96–104.

Nonaka, I., & Takeuchi, H. (1995). *The knowledge creating company: how Japanese companies create the dynamics of innovation*. New York, NY: Oxford University Press.

Nugent, R., Dean, N., & Ayers, E. (2010). Skill set profile clustering: The empty k-means algorithm with automatic specification of starting cluster centers. In *Proceedings of the 3rd International Conference on Educational Data Mining*, (pp. 151-160). Retrieved from http://www.educationaldatamining.org/

O'Connor, D. (2009). *How to grade for Learning, K-12*. Corwin Press.

Ohio University. (2007). *E-Learning: Accounting & Finance*. Retrieved from http://www.ohiou.edu/noncredit/Elearning/accounting.htm

Ohlsson, S. (1994). Constraint-based student modeling. In J. E. Greer, & G. I. McCalla (Eds.), *Student Modeling: The Key to Individualized Knowledge-based Instruction* (pp. 167–189). Berlin: Springer-Verlag.

Ohlsson, S., & Rees, E. (1991). The function of conceptual understanding in the learning of arithmetic procedures. *Cognition and Instruction*, *8*(2), 103–179. doi:10.1207/s1532690xci0802_1

Okonkwo, C. (2001). *Affective Pedagogical Agents and User Persuasion*. Department of CS, University of Saskatchewan, Canada. Retrieved from http://citeseer.nj.nec.com/cs

Okutsu, M., DeLaurentis, D., Brophy, S., & Lambert, J. (2013). Teaching an aerospace engineering design course via virtual worlds: A comparative assessment of learning outcomes. *Computers & Education*, *60*(1), 288–298. doi:10.1016/j.compedu.2012.07.012

Önder, H. H. (2001). *Yapay Zeka Programlama Teknikleri Ve Bilgisayar Destekli Eğitim* [Artificial Intelligence Programming Techniques and Computer Supported Education]. Paper presented at the International Educational Technologies Symposium. Sakarya, Turkey.

Önder, H. H. (2002). *Uzaktan Eğitimde ICAI ve Yapay Zeka Programlama Teknikleri* [ICAI In Distance Education and Artificial Intelligence Programming Techniques]. Paper presented at the Open and Distance Education Symposium. Eskişehir, Turkey.

Önder, H. H. (2003). Uzaktan Eğitimde Bilgisayar Kullanımı ve Uzman Sistemler[Computer Usage and Expert Systems In Distance Education]. *The Turkish Online Journal of Educational Technology*, *2*(3), 142–146.

Ong, C.-S., Lai, J.-Y., & Wang, Y.-S. (2004). Factors affecting engineers' acceptance of asynchronous e-learning systems in high-tech companies. *Information & Management*, *41*(6), 795–804. doi:10.1016/j.im.2003.08.012

Oppermann, R., & Kinshuk, R. R. (1997). *Adaptability and adaptivity in learning systems*. London: Knowledge Transfer.

Oprea, M. (2010). Artificial Intelligence Applied in Computer-Assisted Students Evaluation. In *Proceedings of International Conference on Virtual Learning*, (pp. 361-366). Academic Press.

Ortony, A., Clore, G. L., & Collins, A. (1988). *The cognitive structure of emotions*. Cambridge, UK: Cambridge University Press. doi:10.1017/CBO9780511571299

Ozdemir, B., & Alpaslan, F. N. (2000). Web-Tabanlı Derslerde Öğrenciye Kılavuzluk Eden Akıllı Bir Ajan [An Intelligent Agent Guiding Students in Web-Based Courses]. In *Proceedings of Conference on Education in the Light of Informatics Technology*, (pp. 71-81). Ankara, Turkey: Academic Press.

Ozvoldova, M., Cernansky, P., Schuer, F., & Lustig, F. (2006). Internet remote physics experiments in a student laboratory. In Proceedings of iNEER, (pp. 297–304). iNEER.

Ozyurt, O., Ozyurt, H., & Baki, A. (2013). Design and development of an innovative individualized adaptive and intelligent e-learning system for teaching–learning of probability unit Details of UZWEBMAT. *Expert Systems with Applications*, *40*, 2914–2940. doi:10.1016/j.eswa.2012.12.008

Ozyurt, O., Ozyurt, H., Baki, A., & Guven, B. (2012). Integrating computerized adaptive testing into UZWEBMAT Implementation of individualized assessment module in an e-learning system. *Expert Systems with Applications*, *39*, 9837–9847. doi:10.1016/j.eswa.2012.02.168

Ozyurt, O., Ozyurt, H., Baki, A., & Guven, B. (2013). Integration into mathematics classrooms of an adaptive and intelligent individualized e-learning environment Implementation and evaluation of UZWEBMAT. *Computers in Human Behavior*, *29*, 726–738. doi:10.1016/j.chb.2012.11.013

Pandian, M. P., & Karisiddappa, C. R. (2007). *Emerging technologies for knowledge resource management*. Oxford, UK: Chandos Publishing.

Panjaburee, P., Hwang, G. J., Triampo, W., & Shih, B. Y. (2010). A multi-expert approach for developing testing and diagnostic systems based on the concept-effect model. *Computers & Education*, *55*, 527–540. doi:10.1016/j.compedu.2010.02.015

Papoulis, A., Pillai, S., & Unnikrishna, S. (2002). *Probability, random variables, and stochastic processes* (Vol. 73660116). McGraw-Hill.

Pardos, Z. A., Trivedi, S., Heffernan, N. T., & Srkzy, G. N. (2012). Clustered knowledge tracing. In *Proceedings of the 11th international conference on Intelligent Tutoring Systems* (LNCS) (vol. 7315, pp. 405-410). Berlin: Springer.

Parsons, L., Haque, E., & Liu, H. (2004). Subspace clustering for high dimensional data: A review. *ACM SIGKDD Explorations Newsletter*, *6*(1), 90-105.

Passerini, K., & Granger, M. J. (2000). A developmental model for distance learning using the internet. *Computers & Education*, *34*(1), 1–15. doi:10.1016/S0360-1315(99)00024-X

Pătruţ, B. (2004a). Agents for Learning Accounting Bases. In *Proceedings of CEECBIS04 (The Central and East European Conference in Business Information Systems)*. Academic Press.

Pătruţ, B. (2004b). Architecture for Intelligent Agents with Temperament. In *Proceedings of the International Conference on Computers and Communications*. Academic Press.

Pătruţ, B. (2010). *Interractive Education in Accounting: A Multi-agent Solution*. Saarbrücken, Germany: LAP Lambert Academic Publishing.

Pătruţ, B. (2013a). Competences versus Competencies in Romanian Accounting Education. *International Journal of Academic Research in Business and Social Sciences*, *3*(1).

Pătruţ, B. (2013b). E-Teaching and E-Asessment in Accounting using Intelligent Pedagogical Agents. In *Proceedings of "Elearning and Software for Education"* (eLSE, Bucharest, 2013), (pp. 499-508). Retrieved from www.ceeol.com

Pătruţ, B. (2003). *Tehnologia Microsoft Agent pentru învăţarea regulilor de funcţionare a conturilor. Informatica Economica*, *4(28)*.

PCWorld. (2008). *Web 4.0 era is upon us*. Retrieved from http://www.pcworld.com/article/143110/article.html

Pea, R. D. (1990). Augmenting the discourse of learning with computer-based learning environments. In *Proceedings of the NATO Advanced Research Workshop on Computer-Based Learning Environments and Problem Solving* (pp. 313-343). NATO.

Peixoto, C. S. A., Boarati, S. S., & Forte, C. E. (2012). Heuristics for User Interface Design in the Context of Cognitive Styles of Learning and Attention Deficit Disorder. In P. Vizureanu (Ed.), *Advances In Expert Systems* (pp. 85–100). Rijeka: InTech. doi:10.5772/51455

Pelleg, D., & Moore, A. (2000). X-means: Extending k-means with efficient estimation of the number of clusters. In *Proceedings of the Seventeenth International Conference on Machine Learning*, (pp. 727-734). San Francisco: Morgan Kaufmann.

Peredo, R., Canales, A., Menchaca, A., & Peredo, I. (2011). Intelligent Web-based education system for adaptive learning. *Expert Systems with Applications*, *38*, 14690–14702. doi:10.1016/j.eswa.2011.05.013

Peredo, R., Leandro, V., Ocan, B., & Sheremetov, L. B. (2005). Development of intelligent reusable learning objects for web-based education systems. *Expert Systems with Applications*, *28*(2), 273–283. doi:10.1016/j.eswa.2004.09.003

Perera, D., Kay, J., Koprinska, I., Yacef, K., & Zaiane, O. R. (2009). Clustering and sequential pattern mining of online collaborative learning data. *IEEE Transactions on Knowledge and Data Engineering*, *21*(6), 759–772. doi:10.1109/TKDE.2008.138

Perez, J. F., Barea, R., Boquete, L., Hidalgo, M. A., & Dapena, M. (2008). Cataract surgery simulator for medical education & finite element/3D human eye model. In *Proceedings of 3ª Conferencia Ibérica de Sistemas y Tecnologias de Información*, (pp. 90–98). Academic Press.

Perez-Nordtvedt, L. P., Kedia, B. L., Datta, D. K., & Rasheed, A. A. (2008). Effectiveness and efficiency of cross-border knowledge transfer: an empirical examination. *Journal of Management Studies*, *45*(4), 714–744. doi:10.1111/j.1467-6486.2008.00767.x

Peters, K. (2009). m-Learning: Positioning educators for a mobile, connected future. *Mobile Learning*, *113*.

Petit dit Dariel, O.J., Raby, T., Ravaut, F., & Rothan-Tondeuret, M. (2013). Developing the Serious Games potential in nursing education. *Nurse Education Today*. doi: doi:10.1016/j.nedt.2012.12.014

Petras, I. (2011). *Fractional-order nonlinear systems: Modeling, analysis and simulation*. Berlin, Germany: Springer. doi:10.1007/978-3-642-18101-6

Pfeifer, R. (1988). Artificial intelligence models of emotion. In *Proceedings of the NATO Advanced Research Workshop*. Dordrecht, The Netherlands: Kluwer.

Pituch, K., & Lee, Y. (2006). The Influence of System Characteristics on E-learning use. *Computers & Education*, *47*, 222–244. doi:10.1016/j.compedu.2004.10.007

Polanyi, M. (1966). *The tacit dimension*. London: Routledge & Kegan Paul.

Post, G. V., & Whisenand, T. G. (2005). An Expert System Helps Students Learn Database Design. *Decision Sciences Journal of Innovative Education*, *3*(2), 273–293. doi:10.1111/j.1540-4609.2005.00070.x

Price, L. (2004). Individual differences in learning: Cognitive control, cognitive style, and learning style. *Educational Psychology*, *24*(5), 681–698. doi:10.1080/0144341042000262971

Quian, J. S., Cheng, J., & Guo, Y. N. (2006). A novel multiple support vector machines architecture for chaotic time series prediction. *Lecture Notes in Computer Science*, *4221*, 147–156. doi:10.1007/11881070_25

Quinlan, J. R. (1993). *C4.5: Programs for Machine Learning*. Morgan Kaufmann Publishers.

Ranier, R. K., & Cegielski, C. G. (2013). *Introduction to Information Systems* (4th ed.). Singapore: John Wiley & Sons Singapore Pte Ltd.

Rao, A. S., & Georgeff, M. P. (1991). Modeling Rational Agents within a BDI-Architecture. In *Proceedings of the 2nd International Conference on Principles of Knowledge Representation and Reasoning (KR'91)*. Retrieved from http://citeseer.ist.psu.edu/rao91modeling.html

Rey-López, M., Díaz-Redondo, R. P., & Fernández-Vilas, A., Pazos-Arias, J. J., García-Duque, J., Gil-Solla, A., & Ramos-Cabrer, M. (2009). An extension to the ADL SCORM standard to support adaptivity: The t-learning case-study. *Computer Standards & Interfaces Journal*, *31*(2), 309–318. doi:10.1016/j.csi.2008.02.006

Riesbeck, C., & Schank, R. (1989). *Inside Case-Based Reasoning*. Hillsdale, NJ: Lawrence Erlbaum.

Rishi, O. P., Govil, R., & Sinha, M. (2007). Agent Based student Modeling in Distributed CBR based Intelligent Tutoring System. In *Proceedings of the World Congress on Engineering and Computer Science*. Academic Press.

Roberts, F. C., & Park, O. (1983). Intelligent computer-assisted instruction: An explanation and overview. *Educational Technology*, *23*(12), 7–11.

Roberts, M., & Erdos, G. (1993). Strategy selection and metacognition. *Educational Psychology*, *13*(3), 259–266. doi:10.1080/0144341930130304

Roknuzzaman, M., Kanai, H., & Umemoto, K. (2009). Integration of knowledge management process into digital library system: a theoretical perspective. *Library Review*, *58*(5), 372-386. Retrieved July 26, 2011, from www.emeraldinsight.com/0024-2535.htm

Romero, C., Zafra, A., Luna, J. M., & Ventura, S. (2012). Association rule mining using genetic programming to provide feedback to instructors from multiple-choice quiz data. *Expert Systems: International Journal of Knowledge Engineering and Neural Networks*. doi: doi:10.1111/j.1468-0394.2012.00627

Roşca, G., Apostol, C.-G., Zamfir, G., & Bodea, C.-N. (2002). Informatica instruirii. Bucharest: Editura Economică.

Rosenblatt, F. (1962). *Principles of Neurodynamics*. Washington, DC: Spartan Books.

Rössler, O. E. (1976). An equation for continuous chaos. *Physics Letters [Part A]*, *57*, 397–398. doi:10.1016/0375-9601(76)90101-8

Russell, S. J., & Norvig, P. (2010). Artificial Intelligence - A Modern Approach (3rd ed.). Prentice Hall.

Russel, S., & Norvig, P. (2002). *Artificial Intelligence - A Modern Approach (2nd ed.)*. Prentice Hall.

Rydberg-Cox, J., et al. (2000). Knowledge management in the Perseus digital library. *Ariadne*, *25*. Retrieved March 13, 2012, from www.ariadne.ac.uk/issue25/rydberg-cox/intro.html

Safigianni, A. S., & Pournaras, S. K. (2008) Virtual laboratory arrangement for measuring characteristic power system quantities. In Proceedings of iNEER, (pp. 379–391). iNEER.

Sampaio, A. Z., Ferreira, M. M., Rosário, D. P., & Martins, O. P. (2010). 3D and VR models in Civil Engineering education: Construction, rehabilitation and maintenance. *Automation in Construction, 19*, 819–828.

Sangineto, E., Capuano, N., Gaeta, M., & Micarelli, A. (2008). Adaptive course generation through learning styles representation. *Universal Access in the Information Society, 7*(1), 1–23. doi:10.1007/s10209-007-0101-0

Sasikumar, M., Ramani, S., Raman, S. M., Anjaneyulu, K. S. R., & Chandrasekar, R. (2007). *A Practical Introduction to Rule Based Expert Systems*. New Delhi: Narosa Publishing House.

Schmitt, N., Oswald, F., Kim, B., Imus, A., Merritt, S., Friede, A., & Shivpuri, S. (2007). The use of background and ability profiles to predict college student outcomes. *The Journal of Applied Psychology, 92*(1), 165–179. doi:10.1037/0021-9010.92.1.165 PMID:17227158

Schölkopf, B., Smola, A., & Müller, K.-R. (1998). Nonlinear component analysis as a kernel eigenvalue problem. *Neural Computation, 10*(5), 1299–1319. doi:10.1162/089976698300017467

Self, J. A. (1991). Formal Approaches to Student Modelling. In Proceedings of GREE91, (pp. 295-352). Academic Press.

Selim, H. M. (2007). Critical success factors for e-learning acceptance: Confirmatory factor models. *Computers & Education, 49*(2), 396–413. doi:10.1016/j.compedu.2005.09.004

Seng, T., Parsons, R., Hinson, S., & Sardo-Brown, D. (2003). *Educational psychology, A practitioner–researcher approach*. Singapore: Thomson Learning Cengage Learning Asia.

Seridi, H., Sari, T., Khadir, T., & Sellami, M. (2006). Adaptive Instructional Planning in Intelligent Learning Systems. In *Proceedings of IEEE International Conference on Advanced Learning Technologies*, (pp. 133-135). IEEE.

Seridi, H., Sari, T., & Sellami, M. (2006). Adaptive Instructional Planning Using Neural. Networks in Intelligent Learning Systems. *The International Arab Journal of Information Technology, 3*(3), 183–192.

Setiarso, B. (2009). *Knowledge management and knowledge sharing in Indonesia Institute of Sciences: facing lot of changes to disseminate scientific knowledge for the society*. Paper presented at the Asia-Pacific Conference on Library & Information Education & Practice. New York, NY.

Shah-Hosseini, H. (2007). Problem solving by intelligent water drops. In *Proceedings of the 2007 IEEE Congress on Evolutionary Computation* (pp. 3226-3231). Singapore: IEEE.

Shah-Hosseini, H. (2008). Intelligent water drops algorithm: A new optimization method for solving the multiple knapsack problem. *International Journal of Intelligent Computing and Cybernetics*, *1*, 193–212. doi:10.1108/17563780810874717

Shah-Hosseini, H. (2009). The intelligent water drops algorithm: A nature-inspired swarm-based optimization algorithm. *International Journal of Bio-Inspired Computation*, *1*, 71–79. doi:10.1504/IJBIC.2009.022775

Shang, Y. I., Shi, H., & Chen, S.-S. (2001). An Intelligent Distributed Environment for Active Learning. University of Missouri-Columbia.

Sharples, M., Taylor, J., & Vavoula, G. (2010). A theory of learning for the mobile age. In *Medienbildung in neuen Kulturräumen* (pp. 87–99). VS Verlag für Sozialwissenschaften. doi:10.1007/978-3-531-92133-4_6

Sheikholeslami, G., Chatterjee, S., & Zhang, A. (1998). Wavecluster: A multi-resolution clustering approach for very large spatial databases. In *Proceedings of the 24rd International Conference on Very Large Data Bases (VLDB'98)*, (pp. 428-439). Morgan Kaufmann.

Shein, P., & Chiou, W. (2011). Teachers as role models for students' learning styles. *Social Behavior and Personality*, *39*(8), 1097–1104. doi:10.2224/sbp.2011.39.8.1097

Shen, R., Tang, Y., & Zhang, T. (2001). The intelligent assessment system in Web-based distance learning education. In *Proceedings of IEEE Annual Frontiers in Education Conference*, (pp TF 7-11). IEEE.

Shi, H., Liu, H., Shang, Y., & Chen, S. (2005). Student Modeling in E-Learning Environments. *International Journal of Education and Information Technologies*, *2*, 1–20.

Shi, Z. W., & Han, M. (2007). Support vector echo-state machine for chaotic time-series prediction. *IEEE Transactions on Neural Networks*, *18*, 359–372. doi:10.1109/TNN.2006.885113 PMID:17385625

Shuchun, P (2002). *Digital libraries and knowledge management: Basis for agricultural scitech innovation*. Retrieved January 1, 2010, from http://zoushoku.narc.affrc.go.jp/ADR/AFITA/afita/afita-conf/2002/part7/p507.pdf

Shuhuai, R. et al. (2009). From information commons to knowledge commons: Building a collaborative knowledge sharing environment for innovative communities. *The Electronic Library*, *27*(2), 247–257. doi:10.1108/02640470910947593

Siler, W., & Buckley, J. J. (2005). *Fuzzy Expert Systems And Fuzzy Reasoning*. John Wiley & Sons, Inc.

Simkova, M., Tomaskova, H., & Nemcova, Z. (2012). Mobile education in tools. In *Proceedings of International Conference on Educational Research*, (pp. 10 – 13). Academic Press.

Singh, H. (2003). Building effective blended learning programs. *Educational Technology*, *43*(6), 51–54.

Sitchawat, S. (2005). E-learning for Accounting Education in Thailand. In *Proceedings of World Conference on Educational Multimedia, Hypermedia and Telecommunications 2005* (pp. 110-115). Chesapeake, VA: AACE.

Skyrme, D. J. (2000). *Knowledge networking: creating the collaborative enterprise*. Read Educational and Professional Publishing Ltd.

Smolin, D. (2011). Testing with the Computer: State of the Art, Needs and Perspective. In *Advances in Psychology Research*, (pp. 71–76). New York: Nova Science Publishers.

Smoline, D. (2008). Some problems of computer-aided testing and interview-like tests. *Computers & Education*, *51*(2), 743–756. doi:10.1016/j.compedu.2007.07.008

Smyth, P. (2000). Model selection for probabilistic clustering using crossvalidated likelihood. *Statistics and Computing*, *10*(1), 63–72. doi:10.1023/A:1008940618127

Song, G., & Salvendy, G. (2003). A Framework for Reuse of User Experience in Web Browsing. *Behaviour & Information Technology*, *22*(2), 79–90. doi:10.1080/0144929031000092231

Song, S. (2001). An internet knowledge sharing system. *Journal of Computer Information Systems*, *42*(3), 25–30.

Sreenivasulu, V. (2000). The role of digital librarian in the management of digital information systems (DIS). *The Electronic Library*, *18*(1), 12–20. doi:10.1108/02640470010320380

Srinivasan, B., & Parthasarathi, R. (2013). An intelligent task analysis approach for special education based on MIRA. *Journal of Applied Logic*, *11*(1), 137–145. doi:10.1016/j.jal.2012.12.001

Stanford, D., & Raftery, A. (2000). Principal curve clustering with noise. *IEEE Transactions on Pattern Analysis and Machine Intelligence*, *22*(6), 601–609. doi:10.1109/34.862198

Stathacopoulou, R., Magoulas, G. D., & Grigoriadou, M. (1999). Neural Network-based Fuzzy Modeling of the Student in Intelligent Tutoring Systems. In *Proceedings of International Joint Conference on Neural Networks*, (pp. 3517 – 3521). Academic Press.

Stevens, A. L., Collins, A., & Coldin, S. E. (1982). *Misconceptions in Student's Understanding*. New York: Intelligent Tutoring Systems.

Su, J., Hu, J., & Ciou, Y. (2006). Low-cost simulated control experimentation conducted in Electrical Engineering Department of National Yulin University of Science and Technology. In Proceedings of iNEER, (pp. 397–408). iNEER.

Sun, J., & Yuan, B.-Z. (2012). Development and characteristic of digital library as a library branch. In *Proceedings of International Conference on Future Computer Supported Education*. Elsevier.

Sun, P.-C., Tsai, R. J., Finger, G., Chen, Y.-Y., & Yeh, D. (2008). What drives a successful e-Learning? An empirical investigation of the critical factors influencing learner satisfaction. *Computers & Education*, *50*(4), 1183–1202. doi:10.1016/j.compedu.2006.11.007

Support Vector Machine. (2013). In *Wikipedia*. Retrieved from http://en.wikipedia.org/wiki/Support_vector_machine

Şuşnea, E. (2013). Improving Decision Making Process in Universities: A Conceptual Model of Intelligent Decision Support System. *Procedia - Social and Behavioral Sciences*, *76*, 795-800.

Tang, C., Lau, R., Li, Q., Yin, H., Li, T., & Kilis, D. (2000). Personalized Courseware Construction Based on Web Data Mining. In *Proceedings of the First international Conf. on Web information Systems Engineering*, (pp. 204-211). Washington, DC: IEEE.

Technopedia. (2014). *Artificial Intelligence (AI)*. Retrieved from http://www.techopedia.com/definition/190/artificial-intelligence-ai

Terry, R. E., Harb, J. N., Hurt, P., & Williamson, K. (1995). *Teaching through the cycle: application of learning style theory to engineering education at Brigham Young University*. Brigham Young University Press.

Thiry, M., Khator, S., Barcia, R. M., & Martins, A. (2000). *Intelligent Agent-Based Approach for Distance Learning*. Retrieved from http://citeseer.nj.nec.com/cs

Thissen, D., & Mislevy, R. J. (2000). Testing Algorithms. In H. Wainer (Ed.), *Computerized Adaptive Testing: A Primer*. Mahwah, NJ: Lawrence Erlbaum Associates.

Thorkildsen, R. J., Lubke, M. M., Myette, B. M., Beverly, M., & Parry, J. D. (1985-1986). Artificial intelligence: Applications in education. *Educational Research Quarterly*, *10*(1), 2–9.

Torkul, O., Sezer, C., Över, T., & Över, A. G. T. (2002). İnternet destekli öğretim sistemlerinde bilişim gereksinimlerinin belirlenmesi. *Turkish Online*, *122*.

Torrisi-Steele, G., & Drew, S. (2013). The literature landscape of blended learning in higher education: the need for better understanding of academic blended practice. In *Proceedings of International Journal for Academic Development*. Academic Press.

Toskari, M. D. (2009). Estimating the net electricity energy generation and demand using the ant colony optimization approach. *Energy Policy*, *37*, 1181–1187. doi:10.1016/j.enpol.2008.11.017

Traub, R. (1997). Educational Measurement: Issues and Practice. *Classical Test Theory in Historical Perspective*, *16*(4), 8–14.

Trivedi, S., Pardos, Z., & Heffernan, N. (2011a). Clustering students to generate an ensemble to improve standard test score predictions. In *Proceedings of the 15th international conference on Artificial Intelligence in Education*, (LNCS), (vol. 6738, pp. 377-384). Berlin: Springer.

Trivedi, S., Pardos, Z., Sarkozy, G., & Heffernan, N. (2011b). Spectral clustering in educational data mining. In *Proceedings of the 4th International Conference on Educational Data Mining*, (pp. 129-138). Retrieved from http://www.educationaldatamining.org/

Tsaganou, G., Grigoriadou, M., Cavoura, T., & Koutra, D. (2003). Evaluating an intelligent diagnosis system of historical text comprehension. *Expert Systems with Applications*, 493–502. doi:10.1016/S0957-4174(03)00090-3

Tsai, S., & Machado, P. (2002). E-Learning basics: Essay. *Elearn Magazine*, (7), 3.

Tsolis, D., Stamoub, S., Christiaa, P., Kampanaa, S., Rapakouliaa, T., Skoutaa, M., & Tsakalidisa, A. (2010). An adaptive and personalized open source e-learning platform. In *Proceedings of World Conference on Learning, Teaching and Administration,* (pp. 38–43). Academic Press.

Tufekci, A., & Kose, U. (2013). Development of an artificial intelligence based software system on teaching computer programming and evaluation of the system. *Hacettepe Üniversitesi Eğitim Fakültesi Dergisi*, *28*(2), 469–481.

Turan, F. (2007). *Stereotip Öğrenci Modeli Kullanılarak Zeki Öğretim Sistemi Tasarımı*. (Unpublished master dissertation). Marmara University, İstanbul, Turkey.

Turban, E. (1992). *Artificial Intelligence*. California State University at Long Beach.

Turban, E., Aronson, J. E., Liang, T., & Sharda, R. (2007). *Decision Support and Business Intelligence Systems* (8th ed.). Pearson Education.

Turgay, S. (2005). *A Multi Agent system Approach for Distance Learning Architecture*. TOJET.

Uğur, A., & Kınacı, A. C. (2006). *Classification of web pages by using artificial intelligence techniques and artificial neural networks <> Yapay zeka teknikleri ve yapay sinir ağlari kullanilarak web sayfalarinin siniflandirilmasi*. Ankara, Turkey: Inet-TR. (In Turkish)

Ünler, A. (2008). Improvement of energy demand forecasts using swarm intelligence: The case of Turkey with projections to 2025. *Energy Policy*, *36*, 1937–1944. doi:10.1016/j.enpol.2008.02.018

Upadhyay, P. K., & Moni, M. (2010). Digital library and E-governance: Moving towards sustainable rural livelihood. In T. Ashraf (Ed.), Developing sustainable Digital Libraries: Socio-technical perspectives. New York: IGI-Global (Information Science References).

Van Aerle, E. J. M., & Van den Bercken, J. H. L. (1999). The Development of A Knowledge-Based System Supporting the Diagnosis of Reading and Spelling Problems (II). *Computers in Human Behavior*, *15*, 693–712. doi:10.1016/S0747-5632(99)00041-2

Van Lehn, K. (1988). Student Modeling. Foundations of Intelligent Tutoring Systems. Academic Press.

van Raaij, E., & Schepers, J. (2008). The acceptance and use of a virtual learning environment in China. *Computers & Education*, *50*, 838–852. doi:10.1016/j.compedu.2006.09.001

Van Zwanenberg, N., Wilkinson, L., & Anderson, A. (2000). Felder and silverman's index of learning styles and honey and mumford's learning styles questionnaire: How do they compare and do they predict academic performance? *Educational Psychology*, *20*(3), 365–380. doi:10.1080/713663743

Vanlehn, K., Ohlsson, S., & Nason, R. (1994). Applications of simulated students: An exploration. *Journal of Artificial Intelligence in Education*, *5*, 135–135.

Vapnik, V. (1998). *Statistical learning theory*. New York: John Wiley and Sons, Inc.

Vasilyeva, E., Pechenizkiy, M., & Puuronen, S. (2006). The Challenge of Feedback Personalization to Learning Styles in a Web-Based Learning System. In *Proceedings of Advanced Learning Technologies,* (pp. 1143–1144). IEEE.

Vassileva, J. (1997). *Goal-Based Pedagogical Agents*. Federal Armed Forces University. Retrieved from http://citeseer.nj.nec.com/cs

Vasupongayya, S. et al. (2011). Open source library management system software: a review. *World Academy of Science Engineering and Technology*, *77*, 973–978.

Virvou, M., Manos, K., & Katsionis, G. (2003). An evaluation agent that simulates students' behaviour in intelligent tutoring systems. In *Proceedings of IEEE International Conference on Systems, Man and Cybernetics,* (vol. 5, pp. 4872–4877). IEEE.

Vizcaino, A., & du Boulay, B. (2002). Using a simulated student to repair difficulties in collaborative learning. In *Proceedings of the International Conference on Computers in Education*. ACM.

Waalkens, M., Aleven, V., & Taatgen, N. (2013). Does supporting multiple student strategies lead to greater learning and motivation? Investigating a source of complexity in the architecture of intelligent tutoring systems. *Computers & Education*, *60*, 159–171. doi:10.1016/j.compedu.2012.07.016

Wachter, R. M., & Gupta, J. N. D. (1997). Distance Education and The Use of Computers as Instructional Tools for Systems Development Projects: A Case Study of The Construction of Expert Systems. *Computers & Education*, *29*(1), 13–23. doi:10.1016/S0360-1315(97)00027-4

Wang, X., & Hamilton, H. (2003). DBRS: A density-based spatial clustering method with random sampling. In *Advances in Knowledge Discovery and Data Mining, Proceedings of the 7th Pacific-Asia Conference PAKDD 2003,* (LNCS) (vol. 2637, pp. 563-575). Berlin: Springer.

Wang, T., Wang, K., & Huang, Y. (2008). Using a style-based ant colony system for adaptive learning. *Expert Systems with Applications*, *34*, 2449–2464. doi:10.1016/j.eswa.2007.04.014

Ward, J. Jr. (1963). Hierarchical grouping to optimize an objective function. *Journal of the American Statistical Association*, *58*(301), 236–244. doi:10.1080/01621459.1963.10500845

Warr, H., & Hangsing, P. (2009, March). Open source digital library software: A literature review. In T. M. Devi & C. I. Singh (Eds.), *National Seminar on Preservation and Conservation of Information Resources in Knowledge Society: Issues, Challenges and Trends* (pp. 238-258). Canchipur: Manipur University.

Wasim, J., Sharma, S. K., Khan, I. A., & Siddiqui, J. (n.d.). *Web Based Learning*. Academic Press.

Weiss, G. (Ed.). (1999). Multiagent Systems: A Modern Approach to Distributed Artificial Intelligence. MIT Press.

Weiss, G. (2000). *Multiagent Systems: A Modern Approach to Distributed Artificial Intelligence*. Cambridge, MA: MIT Press.

Weiss, G. (Ed.). (2000). *Multiagent Systems - A Modern Approach to Distributed Artificial Intelligence*. Cambridge, MA: The MIT Press.

Wen, S. (2005, March). *Implementing knowledge management in academic libraries: A pragmatic approach*. Paper presented at the third China-US Library Conference. Shanghai, China.

Wenger, E. (1987). *Artificial Intelligence & Tutoring System*. Los Altos, CA: Morgen Kaufman. doi:10.1016/B978-0-934613-26-2.50013-X

Weng, S. S., & Liu, Y. H. (2006). Mining time series data for segmentation by using ant colony optimization. *European Journal of Operational Research*, *173*, 921–937. doi:10.1016/j.ejor.2005.09.001

Wertheimer, R. (1990). The geometry proof tutor: An "intelligent" computer-based tutor in the classroom. *Mathematics Teacher*, *84*(4), 308–317.

Wiesner, P. (2000). Distance Education: Rebottling or A New Brew? *Proceedings of the IEEE*, *88*(7), 1124–1130. doi:10.1109/5.871313

Wilson, D., & Martinez, T. (1997). Improved heterogeneous distance functions. *Journal of Artificial Intelligence Research*, *6*, 1–34.

Winters, N. (2007). What is mobile learning. *Big Issues in Mobile Learning*, 7-11.

Witten, I. (2011). *Data Mining Practical Machine Learning Tools and Techniques*. Morgan Kaufmann.

Wojtusiak, J., Warden, T., & Herzog, O. (2012). Machine learning in agent-based stochastic simulation: Inferential theory and evaluation in transportation logistics. *Computers & Mathematics with Applications (Oxford, England)*, *64*(12), 3658–3665. doi:10.1016/j.camwa.2012.01.079

Wong, W. K., Xia, M., & Chu, W. C. (2010). Adaptive neural network model for time-series forecasting. *European Journal of Operational Research*, *207*, 807–816. doi:10.1016/j.ejor.2010.05.022

Wooldridge, M. (2002). *Introduction to MultiAgent Systems*. Wiley & Sons.

Xu, R., & Wunsch, D. (2008). *Clustering*. John Wiley/IEEE Press. doi:10.1002/9780470382776

Xu, R., & Wunsch, D. II. (2005). Survey of clustering algorithms. *IEEE Transactions on Neural Networks, 16*(3), 645–678. doi:10.1109/TNN.2005.845141 PMID:15940994

Yadav, R. N., Kalra, P. K., & John, J. (2007). Time series prediction with single multiplicative neuron model. *Applied Soft Computing, 7,* 1157–1163. doi:10.1016/j.asoc.2006.01.003

Yaghmaie, M., & Bahreininejad, A. (2011). A context-aware adaptive learning system using agents. *Expert Systems with Applications, 38*(4), 3280–3286. doi:10.1016/j.eswa.2010.08.113

Yalcin, N., & Köse, U. (2009). *A Web Based Education System for Teaching and Learning Fuzzy Logic. ICITS'09 III* (pp. 378–385). Trabzon, Turkey: Uluslararası Bilgisayar ve Öğretim Teknolojileri Eğitimi Sempozyumu.

Yamamoto, G. T., & Karaman, F. (2011). Education 2.0. *On the Horizon, 19*(2), 109–117.

Yang, Z. H. O., Wang, Y. S., Li, D. D., & Wang, C. J. (2009). Predict the time series of the parameter-varying chaotic system based on reduced recursive lease square support vector machine. In *Proceedings of the IEEE International Conference on Artificial Intelligence and Computational Intelligence* (pp. 29–34). Shanghai, China: IEEE.

Yang, C.-S. (2011). *Nature-inspired metaheuristic algorithms.* Frome, UK: Luniver Press.

Yang, S., & Chang, Y. (2011). An active and intelligent network management system with ontology-based and multi-agent techniques. *Expert Systems with Applications, 38*(8), 10320–10342. doi:10.1016/j.eswa.2011.02.115

Yapicioglu, N. (1991). *Uzman Sistemler ve Uygulamaları* [Expert Systems and Their Applications]. (Master's Thesis). Istanbul Technical University, Institute of Natural Sciences, Istanbul, Turkey.

Yavuzer, Y. (1996). *Uzman Sistemler ve Yapay Zeka.* Istanbul: War Academy Publishing. (In Turkish)

Yazdani, M. (1987). Intelligent Tutoring Systems: An Overview. In R. Lawler (Ed.), *Artificial Intelligence and Education* (pp. 183–201). Ablex Publishing Corp.

Yeung, E. N., Bogacz, R., Holroyd, C. B., Nieuwenhuis, S., & Cohen, J. D. (2006). *Generation of simulated EEG data.* Retrieved from http://www.cs.bris.ac.uk/~rafal/phasereset/

Yin, C., David, B., & Chalon, R. (2009, August). Use your mobile computing devices to learn-Contextual mobile learning system design and case studies. In *Proceedings of Computer Science and Information Technology,* (pp. 440-444). IEEE.

Yona, G., Dirks, W., & Rahman, S. (2009). Comparing algorithms for clustering of expression data: How to assess gene clusters. *Methods in Molecular Biology (Clifton, N.J.), 541,* 479–509. doi:10.1007/978-1-59745-243-4_21 PMID:19381534

Zadeh, L. A. (1965). Fuzzy sets. *Information and Control, 8*(3), 338–353. doi:10.1016/S0019-9958(65)90241-X

Zahra, S. A., Neubaum, D. O., & Larraneta, B. (2007). Knowledge sharing and technological capabilities: the moderating role of family involvement. *Journal of Business Research, 60*(10), 1070–1079. doi:10.1016/j.jbusres.2006.12.014

Zakaria, M. R., & Brailsford, T. J. (2002). User Modeling and Adaptive Educational Hypermedia Frameworks for Education. *New Review of Hypermedia and Multimedia, 1*(8), 83–97. doi:10.1080/13614560208914737

Zamfir, G. (2000). Instruirea asistata de calculator in domeniul economic. Bucharest: Inforec. Retrieved from http://www.biblioteca.ase.ro/catalog/rezultate.php?c=2&q=&st=s&tp1=1&tp2=1&tp3=1&tp4=1&tp5=1&tp6=1

Zatarain-Cabada, R., Barrón-Estrada, M., Zepeda-Sánchez, L., Sandoval, G., Osorio-Velazquez, J., & Urias-Barrientos, J. (2009). A Kohonen Network for Modeling Students' Learning Styles in Web 2.0 Collaborative Learning Systems. *MICAI 2009. Advances in Artificial Intelligence,* 512–520.

Zatarain, R., Barrón-Estrada, L., Reyes-García, C., & Reyes-Galaviz, O. (2010). *Applying Intelligent Systems for Modeling Students' Learning Styles Used for Mobile and Web-Based Systems.* Soft Computing for Intelligent Control and Mobile Robotics.

Zhang, J., Cheung, B., & Hui, L. (2001). An intelligent tutoring system, Smart Tutor. In *Proceedings of 2001 world conference on educational multimedia, hypermedia and telecommunications* (pp. 2130–2131). Academic Press.

Zhang, D., & Nunamaker, J. F. (2003). Powering e-learning in the new millennium: An overview of e-learning and enabling technology. *Information Systems Frontiers, 5*(2), 207–218. doi:10.1023/A:1022609809036

Zhang, J. S., Dang, J. L., & Li, H. C. (2007). Local support vector machine prediction of spatiotemporal chaotic time series. *Acta Physica Sinica, 56*, 67–77.

Zhang, L., Zhang, X., Duan, Y., Fu, Z., & Wang, Y. (2010). Evaluation of Learning Performance of E-Learning in China: A Methodology Based on Change of Internal Mental Model of Learners. *Turkish Online Journal of Educational Technology, 9*(1), 13.

Zhang, T., Ramakrishnan, R., & Livny, M. (1997). BIRCH: A new data clustering algorithm and its applications. *Data Mining and Knowledge Discovery, 1*(2), 141–182. doi:10.1023/A:1009783824328

Zhao, L., & Yang, Y. (2009). PSO-based single multiplicative neuron model for time series prediction. *Expert Systems with Applications, 36*, 2805–2812. doi:10.1016/j.eswa.2008.01.061

Zhong, S., & Ghosh, J. (2003). A unified framework for model-based clustering. *Journal of Machine Learning Research, 4*, 1001–1037.

Zhou, Q. (2005). The development of digital libraries in China and the shaping of digital librarians. *The Electronic Library, 23*(4). doi:10.1108/02640470510611490

Zimmerman, H. (1996). *Fuzzy Set Theory and Its Applications* (2nd ed.). New Delhi: Allied Publishers Limited. doi:10.1007/978-94-015-8702-0

About the Contributors

Utku Kose received a BS degree in 2008 in computer education from Gazi University, Turkey as a faculty valedictorian. He received an MS degree in 2010 from Afyon Kocatepe University, Turkey and now, he pursuing a DS / PhD at Selcuk University, Turkey in the field of computer engineering. Between 2009 and 2011, he worked as a Research Assistant in Afyon Kocatepe University. Following, he also worked as a Lecturer at a Vocational School and Vice Director at Afyon Kocatepe University between 2011 and 2012. Currently, he is a Lecturer in Usak University, Turkey. His research interests include artificial intelligence, chaos theory, distance education, e-learning, computer education, and computer science.

Durmus Koc received a BS degree in 2008 in computer and instruction technologies education from Samsun 19 May University, Turkey. He is pursuing a MS degree at Suleyman Demirel University, Turkey in the field of educational technologies. Currently, he is also a Lecturer at Usak University, Turkey. His research interests include educational technologies, computer education, distance education, and e-learning.

* * *

Ahmet Arslan received a BS degree in 1984 in electrical – electronic engineering from Firat University, Turkey. He received an MS degree in 1987, in the same field from Firat University, Turkey and completed a DS / PhD at Bilkent University, Turkey in the field of computer engineering. Between 1992 and 1999, he has worked as an Assistant Professor in Firat University. Following, he has also worked as Associated Professor at the Firat University, until 2005. Currently, he is a Professor in Selcuk University, Turkey. His research interests include data mining, machine learning, computer learning, and computer assisted designing.

Göksel Aslan was born in Ankara, Turkey, in 1966. He received his BS degree in Computer Science from Hacettepe University, Ankara, Turkey, in 1988. He received his MS and PhD degrees from the University of Southern California (USC), Los Angeles, U.S.A, in 1991 and in 1998 respectively. He worked as a Senior Software Engineer for Adventive Technologies Inc. in Santa Monica, California, U.S.A., which was a company focusing on "Enterprise Application Integration" domain. He also worked as a Manager of Application Engineering for the company "Warner Bros. Online / Advanced Digital Services" in Burbank, California, U.S.A., which is a Time Warner company. His current research interests include database interoperability, database design, data warehousing, distributed computing and semantic web.

Sergey Butakov graduated from the Altai State Technical University, Russia in 1996 with an MS in CS. He received a PhD in CS in 2000 from Altai State University. For a number of years, he worked as a professor of IT at the Altay Academy of Economics and Law and served as a chief information officer in the same institution. Since 2004, he is an associate professor at the American University of Nigeria. In 2008-2012, he worked for universities in South Korea. In present, he is a program coordinator at Concordia University College of Alberta, Canada. His research interests include information security, artificial intelligence, networking and curriculum development.

Ibrahim Arda Cankaya received his BS degree in 2012 from Suleyman Demirel University in the Computer Engineering Department in Turkey. He pursuing his MS in education at Suleyman Demirel University in Computer Engineering Department in Turkey. He is in the thesis stage. His masters thesis involved the designing and implementation of an indoor navigation system with augmented reality on the IOS mobile platform. Future directions of study will likely include Big Data and Big Data Management. He has been working as a Research Assistant at Suleyman Demirel University in the Computer Engineering Department since 2012.He has an instructor cerfiticate from Oracle / PLSQL programming. His research interests include Algorithm and Programming, Database Management, Mobile Programming, and PLSQL programming.

Esad Esgin received a BS degree in 2007 from Computer Education and Instructional Technologies program at Boğaziçi University, Turkey. Then he received an MS degree in 2010 from same program at Marmara University, Turkey and now, he is pursuing a PhD at Marmara University in the same program. After working as an ICT Teacher between 2007 and 2008, he has been working as a Research Assistant at Marmara University since 2008. Following, he has also been working as an IT Coordinator at Marmara University Rectorate since 2011. His research interest includes human-computer interaction, usability, cognitive psychology, digital game based learning, design of e-learning environments, and software quality.

Wilhelmiina Hämäläinen received a MTh degree in 1998 and a MSc degree in 2002, both from the University of Helsinki, Finland. He received a PhLic. degree in 2006 from the University of Joensuu, Finland, and a PhD degree (Computer Science) in 2010 from the University of Helsinki, Finland. She has worked as a lecturer, an assistant professor, and a researcher of Computer Science in several Finnish universities. Currently she is working as a researcher at the Academy of Finland, in the School of Computing in the University of Eastern Finland. Her main interests include statistically sound data mining, machine learning, algorithmics, and mathematics. In addition, she is interested in applied data mining and machine learning in the fields of biology and education.

Azadeh Heidari received a BS degree in 2003 from the Medical Library of Information Science at the Iran University of Medical Science, Tehran, Iran. She received an MS degree in 2007 from the Library of Information Science at the Islamic Azad University, North Branch, Tehran, Iran. Now, she is a PhD graduate in the field of library and information science from the Islamic Azad University, science and research branch, Tehran, Iran. Following, she has also worked as a lecturer in librarianship and information science. Her research interests include digital library, knowledge management and knowledge sharing, digital divide, e-learning, learning organizations, and popularization of science. She has published several papers in Persian and English.

Ali Hakan Isik was born in Burdur, Turkey, in 1980. He received a BS and MSc degree in electrical-electronics engineering from Gazi University, Ankara, Turkey. He received a PhD degree in the field of Electronics from the Computer Education department at Gazi University, in 2012. He worked for Turk Telekom Corporation which is an incumbent telecommunication operator in Turkey, and it has 17 million subscribers. He also worked as a system administrator at Gazi University Distance Education system in the Institute of Informatics. He is currently the Assist. Prof. Dr. in the department of Computer Engineering in Mehmet Akif Ersoy University. His current research interests include experts systems, distance education, telemedicine, signal processing, computer education, and computer science.

Arif Koyun received a BS degree in Mechanical Engineering and Computer Engineering from Akdeniz University, Turkey in 1995 and 1988 respectively. He received his MS degree in 1991 from Akdeniz University, Turkey and a PhD in 2006 from Suleyman Demirel University, Turkey. Between 2001 and 2007, he had worked as a Lecturer at Suleyman Demirel University. Currently, he is an Assist. Prof.Dr. in Suleyman Demirel University, Turkey. He teaches Database Management, Algorithms and Programming, and Client Server Systems courses. His research interests include artificial intelligence, data mining, database management systems, distance education, e-learning, computer education, client server systems, and computer science.

Ville Kumpulainen is currently a student of computer science in the School of Computing at the University of Eastern Finland. He has work experience in software development. In addition, he has been involved in projects in the area of data mining. His research interests include artificial intelligence, machine vision, data mining, mathematics, and algorithmics.

Maxim Mozgovoy received a PhD degree in Applied Mathematics (2006) from St Petersburg State University (Russia) and a PhD degree in Computer Science (2007) from the University of Joensuu (Finland). Currently, he is employed as an associate professor at the University of Aizu (Japan). He studies practical game-oriented observation-based AI systems. The main purpose of his research is to demonstrate the advantages of machine learning and case-based reasoning over traditional approaches to game AI development that often require enormous handwork. His other research interests are focused around natural language processing technologies. In particular, he is currently working on a "virtual language lab" that will combine natural language processing algorithms with a computer-assisted language learning environment. Maxim Mozgovoy is also an author of several books on programming and computer science.

Duygu Mutlu-Bayraktar received a BS degree in 2007 from the Computer Education and Instructional Technology Department at Cukurova University, Turkey. She received an MS degree in 2009 from the Computer Education and Instructional Technology Department at Hacettepe University, Turkey and now, she received a PhD degree in 2014 from Marmara University, Turkey in the field of Eye Tracking Method about Multimedia Learning. She has worked as a Research Assistant in Istanbul University since 2008. Her research interests include multimedia learning, instructional design, eye tracking, human computer interaction and artificial intelligence. She is currently working towards a PhD on the eye tracking about multimedia learning environment.

Leila Nemati-Anaraki has a PhD in Library and Information Science from the Islamic Azad University, Science and Research Branch, Tehran, Iran and a member of Young Researchers and Elites Club at the Islamic Azad University. She has a BSc in Medical Library and Information Science from the Iran University of Medical Science and a MA in Library and Information Science from the Islamic Azad University, North Branch, Tehran, Iran. She Worked as a cataloger and process administrator in the National Library of Iran from 2006-2007. She also has worked as a reference librarian and an expert on information services at Iran University of Medical Science since 2007 till now. She teaches in Different Universities. Her research interests include IT and Research Strategies, E-learning, Education, Digital Divide and new Technologies, and interaction of end Users with web-based search tools, Sientometrics, Knowledge Management, and Knowledge Sharing in Organizations and Educational Institutions.

Bogdan Pătruţ is an associate professor in computer science at Vasile Alecsandri University of Bacău, Romania. He holds a PhD in computer science from Babeş-Bolyai University of Cluj-Napoca, Romania, and a PhD in accounting from Alexandru Ioan Cuza University of Iaşi, Romania. His domains of interest/research are multi-agent systems applied in accounting education and computer science applied in social and political sciences. He published or edited more than 25 books on programming, algorithms, artificial intelligence, interactive education, and social media, including *Social Media and the New Academic Environment* and *Social Media in Higher Education*, books published by IGI Global.

Denis Smolin obtained an MS in CS in 1996 from the Altai State Technical University, Russia. He received a PhD in CS in 2000 from Novosibirsk State University, Siberia. In 1998-2003, he worked as a professor of IT at ASTU and in 2003 switched to industry. In 2003-2009, he served as a chief of IT in Altay Kray Adminstration. IT infrastructure of this territory covers about 500.000 km^2 and a 2.4 million population. In 2009, he joined the bright team of the American University of Nigeria where he was CS program coordinator. In 2012, he was in Bosnia at the American University of BiH. In 2013, he was promoted to the dean. His research interests include artificial intelligence, e-learning and testing and programming.

Guray Sonugur was born on May 3rd 1973 in Balıkesir, Turkey. In 1994, he graduated from the Electrical and Electronic Engineering Department in Anadolu University. In 2012, he graduated with a masters degree from the Afyon Kocatepe University in Computer Technologies. Since July 2012, he has been pursuing a PhD in Mechanical Engineering at the Afyon KocatepeUniversity, Turkey. He worked as a field engineer in the Gurmas Machinery Industry Co, Afyonkarahisar, Turkey, from 1995 to 1997, and as the director of the IT department at the Turkish Telecommunication Company, Afyonkarahisar, Turkey, from 1997 to 2010. Currently, he works as an engineer at Afyon Kocatepe University IT Department, Afyonkarahisar, Turkey. His research interests include image processing, artificial intelligence, distance education, and e-learning.

Kadir Suzme received a BS degree in 2010 from the computer engineering deperment of Eastern Mediterranean University, in Cyprus. He received a MS degree in 2013 from Afyon Kocatepe University, Turkey .He is currently studying Afyon Kocatepe University, in Turkey. His research interests include computer-based control systems, fuzzy logic control, neuro-fuzzy control.

Aslihan Tufekci received a BS degree in 1994 in computer education from Gazi University, Turkey. She received an MS degree in 1997 from Gazi University, Turkey and completed a DS / PhD in 2002, at the same university, in the field of electronic and computer education. She has worked at Gazi University as a Research Assistant between 1994 and 2002, and as a Lecturer between 2002 and 2006. Currently, she is an Assistant Professor in Gazi University, and she also works on spreading the international certifications in Turkey for increasing business quality and bringing the country to a desired situation. Her research interests include educational technology, computer assisted instruction and distance education, human computer interaction, artificial intelligence, policies for using ICT in education, and international certifications.

Tuncay Yigit received his MS and PhD degrees in Electrical Engineering from the Institute of Natural and Applied Sciences of Gazi University, in 2000 and 2005, respectively. He worked as a lecturer at the Computer Education University at Gazi University until 2007. He is currently an Associate Professor of Computer Engineering at the Faculty of Engineering in Suleyman Demirel University. He has extensive experience in teaching, object-oriented programming, software engineering, and Artificial intelligence and e-learning. His research interests include object-oriented software development with the UML, computer science and software engineering education development of e-learning, and Web-based learning systems. He has published over 20 papers in international journals and conference proceedings.

Asim Sinan Yuksel received his BS degree in 2006 from Ege University in the Computer Engineering Department, Turkey. He worked as a Software Developer at the Social Security Institution between 2006 and 2007 in Ankara. He received his MS degree at the Indiana University School of Informatics and Computer, USA in 2010 and he is pursuing his PhD education at Istanbul University Computer Engineering Department, Turkey. He has been working as a Research Assistant in Suleyman Demirel University in the Computer Engineering Department since 2012. His research interests include privacy and security of social networks, mobile security and privacy, human computer interaction, object oriented programming, and design.

Index